THE LIBRARY
ST. MARY'S COLLEGE OF MARYLAND
ST. MARY'S CITY, MARYLAND 20686

THE CHEROKEE GHOST DANCE

THE CHEROKEE GHOST DANCE

Essays on the
Southeastern Indians
1789-1861

by
WILLIAM G. McLOUGHLIN
with
Walter H. Conser, Jr.
and
Virginia Duffy McLoughlin

MERCER

ISBN 0-86554-128-0

The Cherokee Ghost Dance
Copyright ©1984
Mercer University Press
All rights reserved
Printed in the United States of America

All books published by Mercer University Press are produced
on acid-free paper that exceeds the minimum standards set by the
National Historical Publications and Records Commission.

Library of Congress Cataloging in Publication Data
McLoughlin, William Gerald.
The Cherokee ghost dance.
Includes bibliographical references and index.
1. Indians of North America—Southern States—Social conditions—Addresses, essays, lectures. 2. Cherokee Indians—Social conditions—Addresses, essays, lectures. 3. Indians of North America—Southern States—Missions—Addresses, essays, lectures. 4. Indians of North America—Southern States—Slaves, Ownership of—Addresses, essays, lectures. I. Conser, Walter H. II. McLoughlin, Virginia Duffy. III. Title.
E78.S65M37   1984   975.00497   84-14880
ISBN 0-86554-128-0

CONTENTS

P A R T III: *Missionaries*

DEDICATION

This book is affectionately dedicated to
David and Faith Duffy,
Douglas and Betty Duffy,
Betty and Lester Hawkins,
Alice Rinehart and the memory of Bob Rinehart,
and all of their wonderful children.

LISTS OF ABBREVIATIONS

SHORT TITLE LIST FOR "JAMES VANN" FOOTNOTES

BIA (see also OSW below)—The prefix referring to Record Group 75 of the microfilm series published by the Bureau of Indian Affairs. RG 75 consists of many different sets of papers. The following are cited in this essay:
M-15, Letters Sent by the Secretary of War Relating to Indian Affairs, 1800-1824
M-208, Records of the Cherokee Indian Agency, Tennessee, 1801-1835.

de Baillou—Clemens de Baillou, "The Chief Vann House at Spring Place, Georgia," in *Early Georgia* 2 (Spring 1957): 3-12.

Fries—Adelaide L. Fries, ed., "Records of the Moravians in North Carolina," published in various volumes of the *Publications of the North Carolina Historical Commission*, Raleigh, North Carolina, 1943-1955.

Georgia Archives—"Cherokee Indian Letters, Talks and Treaties, 1786-1838," compiled under the direction of Mrs. E. J. Hays, and divided into three typescript volumes; WPA Project No. 4341, 1939, Atlanta, Georgia.

Payne Papers—The John Howard Payne Papers, Newberry Library, Chicago. Volume numbers refer to the typescript volumes.

MAS—Moravian Archives, Winston-Salem, North Carolina.

Mauleshagen—translation of the Moravian Springplace Diary by Carl C. Mauleshagen; the typescript is on file in the Department of Natural Resources, Atlanta, Georgia. (Scholars should be aware that Mauleshagen sometimes transcribed rather loosely and inaccurately, and quotations should be checked against the originals in the Moravian Archives, Winston-Salem, North Carolina.)

OSW—The prefix referring to Record Group 107. Records of the Office of the Secretary of War, published in various microfilm series of which the following are cited in this essay:
M-221, Letters Received by the Secretary of War, Main Series, 1801-1870.
M-222, Letters Received by the Secretary of War (unregistered), 1789-1861.

A LIST OF ABBREVIATIONS
FOR NATIONAL ARCHIVES MICROFILM

A. For Record Group 75, Records of the Bureau of Indian Affairs:

  ★M-15: Letters Sent by the Secretary of War Relating to
  Indian Affairs, 1800-1824.

  ★M-21: Letters Sent by the Office of Indian Affairs, 1824-1882.

  ★★M-208: Records of the Cherokee Indian Agency in Tennessee,
  1801-1835.

  M-234: Letters Received by the Office of Indian Affairs,
  1824-1880.

  M-271: Letters Received by the Secretary of War Relating to
  Indian Affairs, 1800-1823.

B. For Record Group 107, Records of the Office of the Secretary of War:

  M-221: Letters Received by the Secretary of War: Main Series,
  1801-1870.

[N.B. Frame numbers, where available, appear as #0037, #1421,
and so forth.]

★The letters in M-15 and M-21 are in letterbooks and I
  have cited them by page number.

★★The papers in M-208 have no frame numbers but appear in
  chronological order on each roll.

INTRODUCTION

*The
Cherokee
Ghost Dance*

INTRODUCTION

*For God hath made of one
blood all nations.*

*E pluribus unum.
One nation under God.*

BETWEEN 1789 AND 1861 white Americans wrestled mightily with what they called "the Indian question" without recognizing that it was really the question, "Who is an American?" They should have seen that "the Indian question" was integral to all the other vital questions of our national life, questions such as the balance between federal power and states' rights, the spread of slavery and the abolition of slavery, the need for religious freedom and the desire for religious unity, the faith in self-reliance and the demands of social conformity, the belief in a classless society and the growing disparities of wealth, the faith that God had made all men equal and the scientific claim that there was an ineradicable hierarchy of races. The Indian question kept pressing into each of these areas of national concern until finally the Indians themselves were forced to chose between fighting on the side of the Confederate States of America or on the side of the Union. Of course, the Indians, like the white men, ended up fighting on both sides.

The essays in this collection are concerned with specific episodes in the efforts of red and white Americans to answer the Indian question as it provoked other questions vital to the development of the United States as a nation. Was federal treaty power supreme over the states' rights to Indian land? Were Indians "Americans" or capable of becoming integrated into America? Must Indians be segregated on reservations to save them from disappearing before the advancing tide of white expansion? Were Indians more like white men or black men—people of color? Could the United States be a multiracial country or was it a white man's country? Must the Indians' paganism be replaced by the white man's Christianity? Were Indian tribes "nations" or anomalous empires within the empire? Should Indians own black slaves?

Of the 125,000 Indians in more than eighty-five tribes who lived east of the Mississippi River in 1820, blocking the way to white settlement of the Mississippi Valley, the five Southeastern Indian tribes contained 70,000. Some people by 1820 called these "the five civilized tribes" because they had taken the greatest steps toward acculturation—adopting codes of written laws, centralizing their government under elected chiefs, establishing a regular police force, and most important, adopting the farming and plantation life practiced by the whites who surrounded them. Indian women had moved out of the fields and into hewn-log cabins; the men had left the fur trade to work behind a plow or herd cattle. Missionaries brought them schools and churches. They dressed like whites, adopted the white man's dress and much of his diet, and they learned to cope with the white man in trade and politics. The Southeastern tribes had also adopted the practice of buying black slaves to perform much of their menial labor, to tend their livestock, to cultivate their corn and cotton, to hew their wood and draw their water. Whites in the South considered this a signal mark of their "civilization," although many missionaries from the Northern states considered slavery a sin.

While most white Americans agreed with Andrew Jackson on the necessity of "removing" the Indians west of the Mississippi after 1830, the Indian question did not disappear. The missionaries followed the Southeastern tribes into what is now Oklahoma and continued to try to Christianize and civilize them. The white frontier advanced across the Mississippi and the same problems that had troubled Indian-white relations in the East arose in the West. The political side of this struggle has been told many times. This book does not focus on that part of the story. It is a study of cultural clash and cultural persistence told, so far as possible, from within the Indian nations themselves. It relies heavily on missionary records because the missionaries were in a unique position to see more closely into the lives and thoughts of the Indians than the distant government agencies in Washington. Furthermore, by their vocation, the missionaries saw themselves as neutral in the political battles. Their purpose was to help, to uplift, to educate, to befriend the Indian, not to take his land or belittle his arguments for sovereignty. They came to the Indians with the noblest of motives—friendship and the desire to help. They thought of themselves as impartial, nonpartisan servants of God.

Yet to the Indians, who welcomed the missionaries for their friendship, they were also at times opposed to the deepest cultural needs and aspirations of those they sought to help. In many respects the missionaries were acting as government agents; they received much of their financial support from the federal government. By their very ethnocentricity, they were opposed to much that the Indian held dearest. As Christians, they were intent on destroying the religious world view and spiritual beliefs of the Indian. As white men, they tended to make white behavior, morals, and laws the norms by which to measure Indian progress. The missionaries were committed to denouncing the sinfulness of having more than one wife, of tolerating abortion, of performing dances to the manifold spirits of the Indian pantheon, of practicing Indian medical magic, of seeking out and killing witches. As they came face to face with Indian culture, the missionaries therefore took more careful note (though with a decided bias) of the fundamental aspects of the cultural clash that lay behind the Indian question. They did not defend or sympathize much with the Indian's way of life, but they recorded its persistence. They became friendly enemies or inimical friends. More than one missionary came to deplore the injustices of his own government and people toward the Indians; a few rose up to defend some aspects of Indian rights against white oppression. It deeply shocked many missionaries in 1832 that the federal government would do nothing to prevent the state of Georgia from harassing and jailing missionaries whose sole aim was to preach the word of God to the heathen.

Facing the impossible demands that they abandon all of their own beliefs and habits and wholly adopt those of the whites who invaded and conquered them, the Indians struggled for some form of accommodation. Their problem was how much of their own identity and self-respect they might retain. Most of their leaders favored a policy of acculturation to the economic necessities of an agrarian order and to the benefits of education in the white man's language, but hoped for considerable tribal self-government in exchange for sustaining good relations with the federal government. Most of the Indian people wanted to take as little as possible from the white man. Cherokee priests and medicine men felt particularly strong about the retention of their own rituals and religious system. Despite the principles of religious freedom and separation of church and state, which were written into the white man's basic law, these rights did not seem to include the right of the pagan to keep his paganism. As a result, Indian prophets and priests countered the missionary claim that all men and women descended from the same father and mother with their own creation myth: the Great Spirit had originally created not one but three men out of clay—one red, one white, and one black. He had placed them on different continents, separated them by huge bodies of water, and given them different ways of life. The purpose of this polygenetic view of creation was to place the white man in the wrong for having left his appointed sphere, stolen black men from Africa, and invaded the red man's appointed land. Someday the Great Spirit would take vengeance upon the whites for destroying the proper order of things. Apocalyptic visions circulated among the traditionalists of all tribes describing the destruction the Great Spirit would wreak upon the whites in order to rescue his favorite red children and return their land to them as it was before the white man came. When the Indian had such visions, it was called "a Ghost Dance movement"; when the white man talked of God's catastrophic vengeance upon injustice, it was called "eschatology."

Yet Christian theology offered a bridge over the dilemmas posed by the Indian question. If God was a just and righteous God, whether he was called Jehovah or the Giver of Breath, his role was to protect the weak, to help the oppressed, to bring order and justice to a world of oppression and misery. Once the Indian convert learned to transpose Christian symbols into his own language, he was able to appropriate its message to his own needs and hopes, just as the displaced African did in "the invisible church" of the slave quarters.

It has become fashionable since Reinhold Niebuhr coined the phrase to speak of "the irony of American history." I confess to writing many of the essays in this collection in ironic terms. But I write neither from the cynical sense of irony as hypocrisy nor from the Christian sense of *felix culpa* or of overrighteousness. My stance is that of the humanist who is concerned with man's frail but constant striving somehow to make his ideals square with his needs—the irony of the human condition in which man is a little lower than the angels and sometimes scarcely above the beasts.

I have another goal in this anthology: to rescue individuals from stereotypes. As the study of Native American history continues to discover new materials and to dig deeper into the internal life of each tribe, we are able to move away from trite images and to see the Indians and missionaries as individuals. There is no such person as "the" Indian, "the" missionary, "the" federal agent, or "the" frontiersman. Nor is there such a person as "*the* progressive" Indian or "*the* backward" Indian. As any historian will tell you, the figures of fiction pale in comparison to the figures of history. There are no characters in our novels more dramatically alive, more gripping in their actions, more poignant in their feelings than our ancestors. As William Faulkner put it to a reporter who complained that he was always writing about the dead past: "The past isn't dead; hell, it isn't even past." The past is part of us and we are part of it. The people portrayed in history books faced the same questions about loyalty to friends and to ideals that we face and, relatively speaking, they are as closely related to us as most of our living relatives.

In addition to making some of the more colorful figures in Southeastern Indian history come to life, I am trying here to give shape to the evolving story of the Native American's attempt to find his place in "American" culture between 1789 and 1861. If America is not a melting pot but a nation of nations, and if we believe in a pluralistic society, as we like to think these days, we have to understand better what binds us together as "one nation under God." The whole is more than the sum of its parts. Most Native American peoples learned about nationality and nationalism after they were conquered by the Euro-American. Nationhood was thrust upon them as the Euro-American tried to form his own sense of national identity. Prior to 1789 no one had to ask what it meant to be a Cherokee, Choctaw, Chickasaw, Creek, or Seminole. Soon thereafter, every Southeastern tribe had to ask what it was that gave integrity to its people: was it a common language, a common religious system, a common code of behavior, a special relationship to a particular territory, or was it simply kinship? Under attack at all levels by white traders, white frontiersmen, government agents, and missionaries, each tribe had to ask what was most important to defend. Which aspects of life were absolutely essential? What could be modified and what could not without losing a sense of who they were?

These essays try to demonstrate in concrete, personal terms, how various people within various Southeastern tribes faced the combined attack on their cultural identity and what they did to preserve what they considered most important. We know that "the Indian" did not disappear as so many whites sadly but self-servingly predicted. We know that Indian cultures persisted despite all the assaults upon them. Yet we also know that all cultures, white, red, and black, change over time. I write of the persistence of culture, not of its demise. I have tried to place the abstract concept of tribal identity (or national identity) into specific contexts.

Few of the figures in this book are heroic. Most were only half-right, like the rest of us. Nor have I tried to find villains. Each worked in his own way for what he thought was best in his own culture. Each felt that he was working for something beyond his own self-respect. If the white men sought to assimilate the red, the red tried to preserve their status by enslaving the black. If the missionaries sacrificed much to "uplift" their red brethren, they also exalted their own superiority. If mixed-blood chiefs worked tirelessly to defend their people's tribal rights, their policies often created terrible divisions among their people. History is not a study of right and wrong, winners and losers, good guys and bad guys. It is the study of mixed motives, mixed victories, mixed defeats. In the realm of immediate day-to-day struggles at the grass-roots level, where these essays are focused, most of the issues remain unresolved. If, as Faulkner said, the past is with us still, then we are looking at ourselves in action when we read history.

Native American history is full of ferment today, but I have not tried here to take sides in the many scholarly controversies that mark this field. I do not believe that what happened was inevitable because I am not a determinist. Choices were made; other options were available. I do not believe that the missionaries were sinners for trying to acculturate the Indians, nor were the Southeastern Indians sinners to enslave Afro-Americans. There is a saying that "history shall judge," but fortunately judgmental history is currently out of fashion. True, some of our ancestors were more obtuse, more self-serving, more hypocritical than others; others were more honest, perceptive, and generous. I have not masked my sympathies. The white man was the oppressor; the missionary was ethnocentric; the frontier whites were racists; the mixed-blood leaders were too smug; the full bloods were too careless. Or so I judge.

This collection of essays is divided into three categories, although they are all cut from the same cloth. The first section of the book focuses upon critical turning points in the rise of Cherokee nationalism between 1789 and 1835. The second focuses upon important racial complications and confrontations among red, white, and black Americans in the Southeast between 1789 and 1861. The third section focuses upon the difficult decisions that various missionaries to the Southeastern Indians (as well as their mission boards and denominations) had to make in choosing which aspects of Christianization and civilization belonged to Caesar and which to God.

The essays are cut from the same cloth not just because they are all written by the same person (with coauthorship in two of the essays), and not just because they all deal with the Southeastern Indians. They are united by the common methodological approach of social and intellectual (or cultural) history, and because they all are concerned with the issues of race and religion in the United States. During the years 1789-1861 this nation shifted dramatically from the Jeffersonian view that "all men are created equal" and all have "inalienable natural rights" to the Jacksonian view that this was a white, Anglo-Saxon, Protestant country. The hope of a multiracial America suffered calamitously from that shift. The desire for national conformity resulted in civil war.

Because I am assaying to understand American culture, I would argue that this book is about the cultural history of the United States and not about the history of Native Americans. After 1789, for better or worse, the Native American became part of the broad cultural evolution of the United States; his intense efforts to assimilate or to retain something of his own ethnic identity occurred within the framework of the dominant culture. As recent studies in multiracial history have demonstrated, the development of American culture was not a one-way street. It cannot be adequately told in terms of the white man's actions and the black or red man's responses (any more that it can be told in terms of men's actions and women's responses). Each took from, each gave to, each changed the other's cultural perspective and behavior: it is the interaction that concerns me here.

While each essay in this volume was written to stand alone, anyone who reads the volume straight through will see that certain themes unite it. One theme is the white man's varied efforts to dominate and manipulate the Native American; another theme concerns how the Native American retained his own agenda and developed his own means of ethnic survival and independence. The themes of racial interaction are pervasive as red, white, and black struggled to define their mutual relationship. The themes of civilization and Christianization are portrayed in terms of what the various missionaries learned from the Southeastern Indians and not simply vice versa.

Cultural historians tend to focus upon the religious life of a people because religion gets to the heart of any community's beliefs, values, and behavior. Missionaries may have believed that they were simply bringing individual souls into personal harmony with God, but in achieving that spiritual goal, they also inculcated specific moral and behavioral norms. Thus spiritual commitment to Christianity brought converts into many social conflicts with their friends and relatives. I am interested in the choices that were made as a result of these conflicts.

Primary emphasis is placed in this volume upon the Cherokee. The choice is dictated in part by the greater richness of documentary evidence available to the historian of that group of Native Americans. The Cherokee were articulate in expressing their positions and able in defining them. No historian, of course, will ever obtain sufficient documentation with respect to the non-English speaking (and the most traditionalist) people in any tribe; this means that the views of the majority are less available to us. Yet there were many ways in which the traditionalists expressed their stands—notably in their refusal to accept assimilation, their persistent adherence to their own ways, their unwillingness to follow leaders who made too many concessions to the dominant white culture and its economic and political demands. The Cherokee developed strong leaders and also strong factions. The leaders ignored the majority at their peril, and most leaders consciously tried to seek maximum support for their actions. Hence the force of both the traditionalist and the full blood made itself felt. I have tried to stress the generally neglected attitudes and actions of the full-blood traditionalists wherever possible.

The Cherokee were served by five different missionary bodies, each of which kept records that are available to the historian. The missionary records frequently are at variance with the official records of the federal authorities. No one would say that the Cherokee, or any one Indian nation, is typical. The Cherokee were in many respects quite exceptional. Yet because they faced essentially the same kinds of problems and then articulated their views so clearly and fully, their very exceptionalism provides justification for the focus upon them. Nonetheless, I make no claim for the primacy of Cherokee cultural history as the key to Native American history. I only claim that there is no necessary weakness in giving them particular emphasis in light of the questions raised in this volume.

The basic purpose of writing history is to make the reader understand more about himself or herself through the power of the past, which is within us all. It dictates more of our action than most of us care to admit. We are what we were and we will be what we are. And yet, we are always changing. If that is hard to believe, so is history.

ACKNOWLEDGMENTS

I wish to acknowledge with thanks the permission of the following journals and publishers to reprint the articles that appear in this book:

American Baptist Quarterly (formerly *Foundations*) for permission to reprint "The Cherokee Baptist Preacher and the Great Schism of 1844-1845," which appeared in *Foundations* 24:2 (April-June 1981).

American Indian Quarterly for permission to reprint "New Angles of Vision on the Cherokee Ghost Dance Movement of 1811-1812," 5:4 (November 1979).

American Quarterly for permission to reprint "Red Indians, Black Slavery and White Racism," 26 (Fall 1974) and "Experiment in Cherokee Citizenship," 33:1 (Spring 1981); copyrights 1974 and 1981, Trustees of the University of Pennsylvania.

Church History for permission to reprint "Indian Slaveholders and Presbyterian Missionaries, 1837-1861," 42 (December 1973) and "Cherokees and Methodists, 1824-1834," 50 (March 1981).

Ethnohistory for permission to reprint "Cherokee Anti-Mission Sentiment, 1824-1828," 21:4 (Fall 1974).

The Historian for permission to reprint "Cherokee Slaveholders and Baptist Missionaries, 1845-1860," 45:2 (February 1983).

Journal of American Folklore for permission to reprint "A Note on African Sources of American Indian Racial Myths," 89 (June-September 1976); not for further reproduction.

Journal of American History for permission to reprint "The Cherokees in Transition: A Statistical Analysis of the Federal Cherokee Census of 1835," 64 (December 1977).

Journal of Presbyterian History for permission to reprint "Civil Disobedience and Evangelism among the Missionaries to the Cherokee," 51:2 (Summer 1973) and "Parson Blackburn's Whiskey," 67:4 (Winter 1979).

Journal of the West for permission to reprint "The Choctaw Slave Burning: A Crisis in Missionary Work among the Indians," 13 (January 1974).

Little, Brown Publishers for permission to reprint "Cherokee Anomie," which originally appeared in Richard Bushman and Stephan Thernstrom, eds., *Uprooted Americans: Essays in Honor of Oscar Handlin*, 1979.

Prologue: The Journal of the National Archives for permission to reprint "The Cherokees' Right to Lay Internal Taxes," 14 (Summer 1982).

William and Mary Quarterly for permission to reprint "Thomas Jefferson and the Beginning of Cherokee Nationalism, 1806-1809," 3d series, 32:4 (October 1975).

I wish also to thank Douglas Wilms of the Department of Geography of East Carolina University for permission to reprint his map of the "District Boundaries of the Cherokee Nation, 1820."

PART I

Cherokee Nationalism

CHEROKEE ANOMIE, 1794-1810:
NEW ROLES FOR RED MEN,
RED WOMEN, AND BLACK SLAVES

Many histories of the Cherokee Indians paint such a glowing picture of the rapid acculturation of this people after 1789 that it is easy to forget how difficult their revitalization was. The Upper Towns had been decimated in the brief warfare of 1776-1777; the Lower Towns (often dragging the Upper Towns into their conflict) were decimated by border warfare that went on sporadically until 1794. The Cherokees did not realize that their old way of life was doomed, that they could no longer support themselves by the fur trade. Thus, after the fighting stopped, a cultural conflict took place within the nation over whether to adopt farming, as the white conqueror urged, or to persist in their mixed hunting-farming economy as the majority of the Cherokees preferred.

The essay that follows is an effort to demonstrate how difficult those years of confusion from 1794 to 1810 were to the Cherokees, and accordingly, to make us reassess the high level of achievement that in the end brought about Cherokee revitalization. Emil Durkheim's use of the term "anomie" may not be wholly applicable to this shift in Cherokee culture. It may be more appropriate to see this period as one in which a gradual redefinition of the Cherokee social order was taking place, led at first by intermarried white men and those of mixed ancestry but ultimately adopted from necessity by the great bulk of the Cherokees. Few tribes were able to come through this period of confusion so rapidly and, on the whole, so successfully, as the Cherokees. Some have attributed this to the leadership of the whites and mixed bloods and others to the efforts of the federal government and its agents. To me, it seems more likely that other factors were much more important, such as the size and variety of the Cherokees' land (which enabled them to move more gradually from the hunting to the farming economy), the sparseness of white settlements around them (and the fact that the Cherokee Nation was bound on the south by other Native Americans), the ability of their hunters to move out to new hunting grounds (sometimes even crossing the Mis-

sissippi), and the willingness of Cherokee women to undertake the growing, spinning, and weaving of cotton to make up for the lack of income from hunting.

*As we begin to come to grips with the details of these early years of Native American adjustment, I hope scholars will provide us with more extensive and detailed studies of the years 1789 to 1810, because they were critical in every Native American tribe. A. F. C. Wallace has provided us with a fine study of how this transition took place among the Senecas (*The Death and Rebirth of the Seneca*). The rebirth or revitalization of the Cherokees, as this and the succeeding essays in this section demonstrate, was very different from the process that took place among the Senecas. The Senecas present a model of spiritual revitalization under a visionary prophet; the Cherokees present a model of secular revitalization under a succession of chiefs and conflicting factions. Where the Senecas received an answer to their problems from on high, the Cherokees worked out their problems pragmatically from hard, mundane experience.*

> Anomie—a dissociation between
> culturally prescribed aspirations
> and socially structured avenues for
> realizing these aspirations.
>
> Robert K. Merton

THE RISE OF THE CHEROKEE REPUBLIC in the eastern part of the United States between 1794 and 1828 has generally been written as a success story with an unhappy ending: the Cherokees lifted themselves by their own bootstraps after their defeat in the American Revolution to become "the most civilized tribe" in America, only to be forcibly ejected from their homeland in 1838. Standard histories of the Cherokees explain their rapid acculturation in terms of the benevolence of the federal government's civilization program, the dedicated zeal of evangelical missionaries, the able leadership of chiefs like Charles Renatus Hicks and John Ross, the brilliant invention by Sequoyah of a written Cherokee language, and the high percentage of Cherokees of mixed Indian-white ancestry who led the march to success.[1] A closer look at the record, how-

---

[1]The standard histories of the Cherokee Nation are Henry T. Malone, *Cherokees of the Old South: A People in Transition* (Athens: University of Georgia Press, 1956); Charles C. Royce, "The Cherokee Nation of Indians: A Narrative of Their Official Relations with the Colonial and Federal Governments," U.S. Bureau of American Ethnology, *Fifth Annual Report* (Washington DC, 1887); James Mooney, "Myths of the Cherokee," U.S. Bureau of American Ethnology, *Nineteenth Annual Report*, pt. 1 (Washington DC, 1900); Grace S. Woodward, *The Cherokees* (Norman: University of Oklahoma Press, 1963); Marion L. Starkey, *The Cherokee Nation* (New York: Knopf, 1946).

ever, indicates that their rise was not so simple an upward-curving arc. In fact, the true measure of Cherokee accomplishment can be appreciated only if we understand how totally disoriented their culture became between 1794 and 1810. They had to sink even lower than military defeat. Before their revitalization process began, they had first to drink the dregs of anomie.

They had taken a more fatal step than they realized by remaining loyal to the British in 1776. Joining hands with Southern Tories in the summer of 1776, they initiated a concerted series of destructive raids upon the white settlements from the Ohio River to the Carolinas. But the king and the Tories were unable to give them sufficient supplies or military assistance to sustain the attack. White frontiersmen quickly mobilized a massive counterattack which, by August 1777, so devastated the Cherokee villages and overwhelmed their warriors that the chiefs sued for peace. To gain that peace the tribe was forced to yield more than half of its 100,000 square miles of territory, forcing thousands of Cherokees to resettle within the shrunken nation. In addition, this defeat divided the tribe against itself.

Many younger chiefs, angry at the price the victors exacted, withdrew to the westernmost edge of their territory and took their families with them. Aligning themselves with the Creeks, on whose borders they settled, these dissidents founded a series of new towns along the lower Tennessee River Valley from Chickamauga to Muscle Shoals. Known as "the Lower Towns" or "Chickamaugans," this Cherokee faction continued to raid the white settlements in a guerrilla war that flared sporadically from 1780 to 1794. Refusing to honor treaties made with the new American government by the Upper Town chiefs in 1785, 1791, and 1792, the Lower Towns continued fighting long after the British had made peace. Time after time the white frontiersmen sent invading armies to burn the Lower Towns, destroy their crops, slaughter their livestock, burn their granaries. But the Chickamaugans always melted into the forest before them, returning later to rebuild the towns, reconstruct their homes and farms, continue their raiding parties. Enraged frontier settlers refused to distinguish between the friendly Upper Towns and the guerrillas in the Lower Towns. Invading peaceful Cherokee villages, they provoked many of them to join the guerrillas. Eventually almost every Cherokee village, of which there were close to sixty, was ravaged, often more than once. The population of the tribe was cut from an estimated 22,000 in 1770 to perhaps 14,000 in 1794. In 1809 there were only 12,395. Almost one thousand Cherokees left the East in these years to find peace in Spanish Territory across the Mississippi.

This devastating war back and forth across their land was only the military culmination of the gradual destruction of the Cherokee way of life. The Cherokees had first seen the white European in 1540 and since 1640 had been in continual contact with the English colonists. This contact slowly destroyed the old patterns of life and rapidly disrupted the equilibrium that had existed among the various tribes in the Southeast. The original Cherokee economic system was only marginally subsistent, based upon a combination of hunting, fishing, food gathering, and agriculture.[2] Except for overpopulation (usually kept in environmental balance by famine, war, disease, and infanticide), they had managed, like most Indians, to live off the land without depleting its resources and without excessive effort. The soil was rich, the climate generally mild, the fish and game plentiful. The territorial imperatives necessitated by a similar economic system among the neighboring tribes made for constant warfare, but at the beginning of the eighteenth century a generally harmonious relationship among the Indians existed throughout the South. In that era tribal war served primarily socioeconomic purposes; it was a highly traditionalized system for maintaining vague hunting boundaries and a cultural process by which young braves established their status. But the European method of massive warfare, the political competition of empires to control the New World, and the economic restructuring brought by the fur trade radically altered Indian life. Moreover, the rapid influx of British settlers after 1640 and their expanding settlements forced the Indians into bitter wars in which the Europeans frequently manipulated the Cherokees to assist in the extermination of smaller Eastern tribes.

The European concepts of permanent alliances, trade treaties, total war, and enforced land cessions compelled the Cherokees to create "kings" or "emperors" who were, at least in European logic, held re-

---

[2]See Leonard Bloom, "The Acculturation of the Eastern Cherokees," *North Carolina Historical Review* 19:4 (October 1942): 323-58; Fred Gearing, *Priests and Warriors: Social Structures of Cherokee Politics in the Eighteenth Century*, American Anthropological Association, Memoir no. 93 (Menasha WI, 1962); William H. Gilbert, Jr., "The Eastern Cherokees," Bureau of American Ethnology, *Bulletin 133*, Anthropological Paper no. 23 (1943) 169-413; John Philip Reid, *A Law of Blood: The Primitive Law of the Cherokee Nation* (New York: New York University Press, 1970).

sponsible for the behavior of the whole tribe. This began a long process of limiting the local self-government of individual towns, the power of local chiefs, and the general concept of noncoercive, consensus government, which had formerly constituted what little governance there was. In addition, the trade alliances made the Cherokees partners in exploiting the game that had formerly been hunted only for food or clothing. It also made them increasingly dependent upon the manufactured goods of the Europeans—guns, traps, powder, lead, knives, axes, kettles, cloth, and blankets. Their own native skills in pottery and weaving deteriorated and, for some, spirituous liquor became a major necessity. As exploited employees of European trading companies, the Indians destroyed their own supply of game and found themselves thrown into the vagaries of European market fluctuations over which they had no control. Gradually new life-styles were introduced among them by English and Scottish traders who settled in their villages, married Cherokee wives, introduced European agricultural methods (including the use of black slaves), and taught them the uses of horses, cattle, pigs, and chickens. Prior to 1776 the acculturation process was essentially voluntary. The Cherokees took from the Europeans what seemed useful to them, while the major aspects of their daily life and culture remained the same. Despite periodic epidemics of European diseases, the Cherokees managed to grow and thrive as a people. It was the warfare between 1776 and 1794 that destroyed them.

By 1800 their hunting grounds in Kentucky and Tennessee were wholly occupied by white Americans, and their role in the fur-trade economy was gone. Even by extended hunting expeditions across the Mississippi, it was impossible to obtain enough furs and hides to pay for the manufactured goods that had now become necessities. The only way to avoid starvation was to accept the white man's way of cultivation and animal husbandry. But the problems of such a social reorientation were almost overwhelming. Daily contact with white settlers who now surrounded them on three sides (leaving only their southwestern borders contiguous to other Indians) made the transition even more difficult. Charles Royce, writing of the Cherokees in these years, said that "they were, as a nation, being slowly but surely compressed within the contracting coils of the giant anaconda of civilization; yet they held to the vain hope that a spirit of justice and mercy would finally prevail in their favor. Their traditions furnished them no guide by which to judge the results certain to follow. . . ."[3]

The surrounding settlers, bristling with greed, contempt, and animosity, darted in and out of the tribal area, carrying on illicit trade, cheating, robbing, frequently assaulting the now-defenseless Cherokees.[4] Ostensibly the treaties had left the political infrastructure of the tribe intact. Their chiefs and councils were still free to govern internal affairs. However, with white men continually in their midst and encroaching upon their borders, with the critical control over crimes between whites and Indians fixed by treaty in the hands of white troops and courts, it was almost impossible for the local town chiefs to retain order under the old, unwritten patterns of noncoercive authority and clan revenge. The efforts of tribal chiefs with broader authority to sustain order were thwarted by continuing animosity between the Upper Towns and the Lower.[5] They were harried from without and divided within.

Furthermore, the frequent cessions of land forced upon the Cherokees after 1777 (in the treaties of 1798, 1804, 1805, and 1807) cut the heart out of the original Cherokee homeland along the western borders of South Carolina, the eastern valleys of the Great Smokies, the upper valleys of the Tennessee River and its tributaries in northeastern Tennessee.[6] In these years their oldest settlements fell into white hands and thousands of Cherokees made homeless by these cessions had to reestablish themselves in what remained of their land to the west and south. By 1800 more than forty of their towns had disappeared in the advancing

---

[3]Royce, "Cherokee Nation," 218.

[4]For the inability, and often the unwillingness, of the federal government to uphold its treaty guarantees against white intruders in these years, see ch. 7 in Francis P. Prucha, *American Indian Policy in the Formative Years* (Cambridge: Harvard University Press, 1962) 139-87.

[5]For the political factionalism within the Cherokee Nation in these years, see John P. Brown, *Old Frontiers: The Story of the Cherokee Indians from Earliest Times to the Date of Their Removal to the West, 1838* (Kingsport TN: Southern Publishers, 1938) 148-453; and Mooney, "Myths of the Cherokees," 82-87. For clan revenge, or "the blood law," see Reid, *Law of Blood.* According to this custom, the closest male relative of a murdered man was personally responsible for avenging his death by taking the life of the murderer or a close relative of the murderer.

[6]Royce, "Cherokee Nation," provides detailed descriptions and maps of these cessions.

white tide. More than two-thirds of their families were uprooted and forced to move—some two or three times. Resettling into already over-crowded and disorganized towns, they placed a severe strain upon lim-ited resources, depleting precious supplies of grain and livestock. Before they could start new fields and harvest a crop, these displaced families often reduced whole communities to virtual starvation.[7] To this great de-mographic disruption must be added the psychological and spiritual shock of leaving behind so many of their graves and sacred places; in an animistic or zootheistic religious culture, every spring, waterfall, moun-tain, cave, or lake had special supernatural significance. When villages were forced to abandon these sacred sites to white desecration, they lost basic spiritual landmarks as well as the territory itself. In addition, much of the Cherokee medicine, as well as many religious potions, was based upon the gathering and concocting of certain kinds of herbs and flowers not always or so easily available in their new homes.

Cutting even deeper than economic hardships into cultural vitality was the breakdown of traditional patterns of enculturation such as child-rearing. It struck the Southern Indians with particular pain to learn that they were no longer allowed to raise their sons and nephews to be war-riors. In 1802 a Creek chief, speaking to the resident federal agent, in-formed him that he hoped the government would not see fit to prevent the customary small-scale warfare between the Cherokees, Creeks, Choctaws, and Chickasaws. How else, he asked, were their young men to learn the skills to attain manhood and respect? "Brother, if we red men fall out, dispute and quarrel, you must look upon it as two children quarreling and you, our white friends and brothers, must remain neu-tral. There is among us four Nations old customs, one of which is war. If the young, having grown to manhood, wish to practice the ways of the old people, let them try themselves at war, and when they have tried, let the chiefs interpose and stop it. We want you to let us alone."[8] There was

---

[7] In 1804 and 1807 the tribe faced general starvation, which only timely gifts of food from the federal agent alleviated. However, in both cases he exacted a price in land ces-sions for his generosity.

[8] Walter Lowrie, ed., *American State Papers: Indian Affairs* (Washington, 1832) 1:631; hereafter cited as ASP (IA). As late as 1821 young Cherokees still were torn by the urge to establish themselves as warriors. One such youth left a missionary school that year: "He said he wished to leave his country and go [west] to war against the Osage." Papers of the American Board of Commissioners for Foreign Missions, Houghton Li-brary, Harvard University, 18.3.1, 2, Brainerd Journal, 15 November 1821; hereafter cited as ABCFM Papers.

in Cherokee culture an achievement orientation, which encouraged young and old warriors to measure their status by exploits of daring in war and hunting—through the number of their scalps or captives, the quantity of their furs and hides. These exploits were then celebrated in songs and dances for the edification and glory of all. More than self-achievement, they were measures of a man's importance to his family, clan, and tribe, and signs of his harmony with the spirits that controlled life.

What for the Cherokee was basic training, education, and testing was to the American government, after 1794, merely a source of troublesome "savagery." According to the treaties, the Indians were to give up hunting and war for farming and book learning. The Cherokee treaty of 1791 stipulated that in order for "the Cherokee nation [to] be led to a greater degree of civilization and to become herdsmen and cultivators, instead of remaining in a state of hunters, the United States will, from time to time, furnish, gratuitously, the said nation with useful implements of husbandry."[9] Henceforth Cherokee boys were to prove their mettle by the sweat of their brows. Plowing a straight furrow, not shooting a straight arrow, was to be the test of a man. But this was not a skill their fathers, uncles, and chiefs could teach them.

What role, then, were the old to play and what respect could they sustain? Not only had they nothing worth teaching the young, but they were held responsible for the failure of the old system. Power, skill, prestige, and hence legitimate social authority now rested with "the white fathers" who found the warfare of the old chiefs merely a childish game. With the breakdown of the tribal elders, authority, the disintegration of self-regulating custom, and the imposition of external force (the soldiers patrolling the borders, the government factor regulating trade, the federal agent enforcing their treaty obligations, the state constables and courts arresting and trying criminals), the internal political structure of the nation fell apart. It had no function to perform. Before the Cherokees could reestablish legitimate authority over their people, the chiefs and councils had to learn new roles, deal with new political and economic realities, accept the responsibility for inculcating new social values and sustaining new behavior patterns.

---

[9]Richard Peters, *The Case of the Cherokee Nation Against the State of Georgia* (Philadelphia, 1831) 253.

Even religious rituals and festive ceremonies had to be recon-
structed. The old songs, rites, and dances associated with war (like the
Eagle Dance) fell into disuse. The decline of hunting made the Bear and
Buffalo dances obsolete. The communal ceremonies of the new year and
the relighting of the clan fires lost their meaning. The spiritual leaders
of the community—priests or shamans—lost their authority as well.
Cleansing and purification rites made sense only if one knew what values
were being reaffirmed and what was pure and what impure. Of all the
Cherokee ceremonies, only the Green Corn Dance and the Ball Plays retained any vitality in these years. But even these became increasingly
secularized. The Green Corn Dance, originally a harvest ritual, became
a plaything of the federal agents, who worked with the chiefs to have it
scheduled at times and places convenient to the government, either when
annuities were to be distributed or when a treaty was about to be made.
The government contributed provisions and whiskey for these occasions
on the grounds that they put the Indians in a good mood for bargaining.

The Ball Plays, instead of communal festivals with religious overtones, became spectacles for white visitors and scenes of wild orgies of
gambling, drunkenness, and brawling. Instead of replacing hunting and
war as they might have done to enable young men to exhibit skill,
strength, endurance, and daring, they became a kind of professionalized
gambling, a quick way to make money (or to lose it)—a symptom of despair, not of vitality. In better days, and in the more conservative parts
of the nation, the Ball Plays were hallowed by sacred prayers, dances,
and rituals; players abstained from sexual intercourse prior to playing in
order to retain their strength; to be chosen as a player marked one as a
person of high integrity and honor. But during the Cherokee nadir, all
this was forgotten. In 1792 Governor William Blount reported two Ball
Plays on two successive days in the Lower Towns where Chief Eskaqua
(or Bloody Fellow) "was on the losing side and having staked much bore
it not quite well" the first day. "His getting drunk on Monday night was
supposed to be a maneuver to get some of the best players of the adverse
party in the same situation, which he effected. He did not play himself
and none of his players drank to excess," so the next day Eskaqua's team
recouped his losses because of the hangovers of the opposing team.[10]

---

[10]ASP (IA), 1:267.

Bloody Fellow had previously been a mighty war leader; now he seemed concerned only to enrich himself.

The distribution of the federal annuity itself became a great national holiday, though it had no religious significance to the Cherokees. Its only purpose was the selfish one of getting all the liquor and booty one could for oneself. These occasions attracted hordes of disreputable white men—traders, gamblers, whiskey dealers—eager to extort some of these treaty funds from the Cherokees. The secretary of war instructed the agent to discourage the whole business in 1802, but it did not come to an end until the council regained its authority and asserted tribal control over the annuities in the form of a national treasury in 1817.

Recognizing the importance of national holidays in establishing national pride, the Cherokee agent appointed by the government in 1801, Colonel Return J. Meigs, tried to encourage new ones more in keeping with the new status of the Indians as wards of the Republic. A native of Connecticut and a loyal Jeffersonian, Meigs sought like a true *philosophe* to construct a new civil religion for his charges. Why not have "festival days [on] 4th July and New Year's Day, dividing the year equally," he wrote. "On those occasions political and moral sentiments will be diffused while the mind is alive and awakened by agreeable impressions made on such occasions not easily effaced."[11] No doubt he expected orations on the rising glory of America and the role of the Indian in that destiny, but nothing appears to have come of his suggestion. The Cherokees were not exactly moving in that direction.

For reasons not necessarily associated with Christianization, the Cherokees and other Southern tribes appear to have adopted the festival of the Twelve Days of Christmas. The first New England missionaries noted this with surprise in 1818: "Christmas is a great day among the whites and half breeds in this country. It has been kept in such a manner that the Cherokees have given it the name which signifies shooting-day. Almost all the slaves have their time from Christmas to the end of the

---

[11]Microfilm Records of the Cherokee Indian Agency in Tennessee, 1801-1835 (M-208), Roll 6, Records of the Bureau of Indian Affairs (RG 75), National Archives, [December?] 1814. These records consist mostly of letters from the federal agent in the Cherokee Nation to the secretary of war. The microfilm has no frame numbers, nor are the records paginated. The documents are given in chronological order. This undated document is placed between documents dated November 1814 and January 1815. Hereafter documents from this archive will be cited as M-208 with date.

year and generally spend it in frolicking and drinking."[12] Few Cherokees were Christians at this time, however, and as the description implies, it was more a secular than a holy day. Trying to capitalize on the day's popularity, some of the missionaries held a religious service on Christmas, but only the blacks attended. The obvious inference is that the more prosperous Cherokees adopted it from their slaves and not out of any respect for the founder of Christianity. Christmas had long been a slave holiday in the white South. It was probably brought into the tribe by white traders and Tory refugees, if not by the slaves themselves.

The first missionaries to ask to establish a mission station and school among the Cherokees were Moravians from North Carolina. Their first request to do this in 1799 was rejected, but approval came in 1801 when the Cherokees were convinced that it would be useful for their children to learn to read and write English. The Moravians did not accept their first pupils in Spring Place, Georgia, until 1804, and taught only a handful of children prior to 1810. A more successful missionary school was started near the federal agency in eastern Tennessee in 1804 by the Presbyterians, but it collapsed in 1810 for want of denominational support. By and large the missionaries provided little help to the Cherokees in these trying times; but by the same token, neither can they be blamed as a major source of the Cherokees' cultural disorientations.[13]

In 1800 the possibility that the Cherokees would ever recover their old tribal integrity and self-respect as a people must have seemed nonexistent. Nor did the alternative way of total assimilation offered by the American government appear feasible. Quite apart from the fact that few Cherokees possessed at that time the skill, the tools, or the capital to become successful farmers, almost everything about this new system ran counter to their traditions and beliefs. "Exclusive property"—the idea of private ownership of the land—ran counter to the staunch belief in tribal ownership of the land; private profit ran counter to communal sharing and the hospitality ethic; aggressive personal ambition ran counter to

---

[12]ABCFM Papers, Brainerd Journal, 25 December 1818.

[13]For the Moravian missionaries, see Edmund Schwarze, *History of the Moravian Missions among the Southern Indian Tribes of the United States* (Bethlehem PA: Times Publishing Co., 1923); for the first Presbyterian schools, see Dorothy C. Bass, "Gideon Blackburn's Mission to the Cherokees," *Journal of Presbyterian History* 52 (Fall 1973): 203-26.

the high value placed upon self-effacement and affability. To leave the village, stake out a clearing in the woods, and start farming for oneself and family alone meant to repudiate neighborliness. Perhaps most important of all, it meant the establishment of a nuclear family system, patrilineal inheritance, the end of the clan relationships, and a reversal of roles for both men and women. Anomie at bottom meant for the Cherokees not only a loss of sovereignty and land, but with the breakdown of the cultural order, it also meant a loss of identity. What exactly did it mean after 1794 to be a Cherokee?

The changing role of Indian women in the years 1794 to 1810 was directly related, not only to the changing role of Indian men, but to the changing status of black men in the Cherokee Nation and in the white South. Where there were only whites and blacks in a community, the role of each was clearly defined. But among the Cherokees, there were red, white, and black men (not to mention mixed bloods). Since the red was told that his future lay in adapting himself to white beliefs and behavior, the status of the black became even more problematic. In the eighteenth century the first blacks to enter the Indian nations, usually as runaways, were treated with lenience and familiarity. They provided useful skills and manpower and served as interpreters. There is evidence of black intermarriage and adoption; moreover, a number of freed slaves had an independent status. In the Revolutionary fervor for natural rights, the Indian was considered by philosophers like Jefferson to be virtually equal to the white, even if there were doubts about the black man. But as this fervor faded, as the white South moved toward the cotton kingdom, and as the Indian was forced to defend his own status as a "man of color" in the face of white frontier prejudice, the multiracial aspect of Cherokee society posed bitter problems for black and red.

Similarly, the new role of yeoman farmer or planter compelled a new relationship between Indian men and women. The Indian male, though he had in former days labored occasionally in the field with the women, never had his dignity as a warrior or hunter questioned for this any more than did the poor white who sometimes labored beside his slave. The respective status lines in both cases were established beyond doubt. But as the Cherokee woman went into the farmhouse to spin, sew, cook, after 1794 she lost some of her former dignity and decision-making power in the tribal councils. At the same time, the Cherokee man, shorn of his primary status as a hunter-warrior and told to work steadily with ax and hoe, had to worry about how he could henceforth distinguish himself from black field hands.

Working in the fields was as hot and burdensome to the Cherokee as to the white Southerner. He did not share Jefferson's view of the nobility of that occupation. At first the Cherokee man considered it ignoble to be only and always working in the fields. Many years later, after the Cherokees had completed their transformation and could look back with less embarrassment on this problem, the editor of the *Cherokee Phoenix* wrote of the Cherokees at the turn of the century, "From the soil they derived a scanty supply of corn, barely enough to furnish them with gah-no-ha-nah [a corn dish] and this was obtained by the labor of women and grey headed men, for custom would have it that it was disgraceful for a young man to be seen with a hoe in his hand except on particular occasions."[14] Like his white Southern counterpart, an acculturated Cherokee farmer hoped someday to own slaves to do his work. His model of American farming and capitalism was inevitably that of the Southern cotton plantation, not the Northern diversified subsistence farm that the federal government and Eastern philanthropists held up to him. Hence to sustain his new role as a Cherokee man, and his wife's as a Cherokee woman, he would have to reduce the blacks to a servile laboring caste and transform his women into genteel mistresses of the hearth and home.

Eighteenth-century observations regarding the status of Cherokee women varied widely. James Adair argued in 1762 that their status was virtually equal to that of Cherokee men. Jefferson in 1783 believed they were little more than slaves: "The women are submitted to unjust drudgery. This, I believe, is the case with every barbarous people. With such, force is law. The stronger sex imposes on the weaker. It is civilization alone which teaches us to subdue the selfish passions and to respect those rights in others which we value in ourselves. Were we in equal barbarism, our females would be equal drudges."[15] A Tennessee

---

[14]*Cherokee Phoenix*, 21 January 1829. I have used the microfilm at the American Antiquarian Society, Worcester MA.

[15]Thomas Jefferson, *Notes on Virginia*, in Adrienne Koch and William Peden, eds., *The Life and Selected Writings of Thomas Jefferson* (New York: Modern Library, 1944) 211.

historian of the Cherokees, drawing upon a wide variety of early sources, came closer to Adair's conclusion:

> The Cherokees [in 1760] were just emerging, as were all Iroquoian people, from the matriarchal stage. "They have been a considerable while under petticoat government," Adair comments. Extraordinary respect was paid to womankind. When a Cherokee married, he took residence with the clan of his wife. His children were the property of the mother, and were classed as members of her clan. The wigwam and its contents belong to the woman. She had a voice in the daily council and the deciding vote for chieftainships.
>
> The women of each clan selected a leader. These leaders constituted the Women's Councils, which did not hesitate to override the authority of the chiefs when it was thought that the welfare of the tribe demanded it. The head of the Women's Council was the Beloved Woman of the tribe, whose voice was considered that of the Great Spirit speaking though her. . . . The white pioneer mother, with her large family, was far more of a drudge than her red sister.[16]

While the evidence is scanty and contradictory on details, there seems general agreement that prior to 1794 Cherokee women did have a participatory role of some kind in tribal decisions, a major interest in household property and care of the children, and the largest share of work in cultivating the fields. Thereafter, their role in tribal affairs became almost negligible. Part of the difficulty in "civilizing" the Indian was that it bothered nineteenth-century white Americans intensely to see women working in the fields. The government considered it a primary object of its civilization program to get the Indian women out of the field and into the kitchen. It was considered a marked step forward when Indian women began to take up spinning and weaving while the men grudgingly and of necessity took to the plow. In August 1802 the federal agent to the Cherokees reported the following items of husbandry and domestic manufacture, which he had so far distributed among the Cherokees as part of the government's economic aid program: 58 plows, 13 mattocks, 44 hoes, 215 spinning wheels, 4 looms, 204 pairs of cotton cards, 53 sheep, 28 reels. He reported with mixed feelings that "the raising and manufacturing of Cotton is all done by the Indian Women; they find their condition so much bettered by this improvement that they apply for wheels, cards, etc, with great earnestness" and were disappointed that the government could not give them more. "The Indian

---

[16]Brown, *Old Frontiers*, 18-19. See also Reid, *Law of Blood*, 37-47, 67-70, 114-16, 119-21, 128-29, 187-88.

men," however, "attend to the raising of Cattle and Swine—this costs them no labour, a thing they will avoid as long as possible."[17]

In 1805 Colonel Meigs reported that what seemed like progress to most white Americans was not so viewed by most Cherokee males. "Raising cotton, spinning and weaving is carried on the domestic way in almost every part of the nation, but this is totally done by the females who are not held in any degree of reputable estimation by the real Indian and therefore neither them [women] nor their occupation have any charms to tame the savage."[18] To the Cherokee man, whether the women made clothes by preparing skins and furs or by spinning cotton, it was all the same. The great difficulty now was that she, not he, was providing the clothing for the family while he could contribute almost nothing. Only by growing a good crop could he sustain his prestige as a provider. Being unable to maintain his old role as hunter-provider was frustrating in the extreme.

By 1802 Cherokee hunters who did not make the long trek across the Mississippi to hunt were bringing to the trading posts only the skins of small animals—"raccoons, foxes, and wild cats"—for which they received twenty-five cents each.[19] American Indian agents, observing the reluctance of the Indian men to undertake the onerous task of farming, concluded that they were inveterately lazy and shiftless: "Labour is painfull and the idea to the most of them dishonorable; the love of ease is their predominant passion," wrote the Cherokee agent, Return J. Meigs, in 1808.[20] It never occurred to him that the Cherokee did not oppose all labor, but only that degrading to his status and lacking in the sort of self-respect that came from the exercise of traditional skills.

Since working all day behind a plow, hoeing a cornfield, or feeding hogs was considered honorable and rewarding by a Connecticut Yankee, Return J. Meigs could not see why it had so little appeal to the Cherokees. What he saw as feckless Cherokee "roaming" in worn-out hunting grounds week after week was not a desire to avoid work but in part an urge to cling to an older way of life and in part a need to hide an igno-

---

[17]M-208, Return J. Meigs's "Journal of Occurrences," August 1802.

[18]Ibid., 13 February 1805.

[19]ASP (IA), 1:676.

[20]M-208, 3 January 1808.

rance of husbandry. It also was necessitated by lack of capital and tools to become a farmer. Despite its good intentions the government seldom provided more than a few hundred dollars' worth of agricultural tools per year; a Congress interested in keeping taxes low found it easy to cut the budget for nonvoting Indians. Consequently the Cherokees did not have in these years enough plows, hoes, or mattocks, and the few the government did supply were not evenly distributed.[21] Nor could the Indians keep the implements they did get in repair without a blacksmith, and these were always in short supply. Cherokees in mountainous regions or among the sandhills had little chance of making a living from farming. Even white frontiersmen who had grown up on farms in the East, who had some experience and capital and were able to pay for the services of blacksmiths, wheelwrights, or coopers, often had a difficult time starting out in the wilderness. Yet the Protestant ethic of hard work, self-discipline, and delayed gratification was assumed to be the divinely ordained system of values for all men. God had ordered Adam to support himself by the sweat of his brow and to cultivate the fields, and the sooner the Indian adopted this way of life the happier and more prosperous he would presumably be. The economic whip was there, but not the religious, social, or cultural incentive.

Those Cherokees, however, who were the sons and grandsons of white traders, Tory refugees, army deserters, and those white men who had married into the nation and cast in their lot with it made the most of the government's economic aid and got the lion's share of it. They also used their superior experience to take up the best farming land in the Cherokee Nation. And, most important of all, they had the capital to invest in slaves. By 1809 there were 583 black slaves in the Cherokee Nation, but they were owned by comparatively few of the 2,000 families. Not only did some have ten, fifteen, or twenty of them, but geographically the great bulk of them were in northern Georgia and Alabama where the rich black soil was fit for cotton plantations. Among that third of the Cherokees who lived in "the Valley Towns" of the Unicoi and Great Smokey mountains where there was the least intermixture of white an-

---

[21]For the uneven distribution of government technical assistance and the complaints of the Upper and Lower Towns, see Mooney, "Myths of the Cherokee," 82-83.

cestry and intermarriage, there were only five black slaves.[22] The Valley Towns long remained a center of traditionalist friction within the nation.

Eventually there were those who argued that the progress the Cherokees made toward civilization was primarily "owing to the prevalence of slavery" among them.[23] Others argued that their progress resulted from the high proportion of white blood in their veins: "When every effort to introduce among them the ideal of separate property as well in things real as personal shall fail, let intermarriages between them and the whites be encouraged by the Government. This cannot fail to preserve the race, with the modifications necessary to the enjoyment of civil liberty and social happiness."[24] The problems of mingling red, white, and black in the Southeastern United States led the Indians logically to wonder whether the white man was sincere in suggesting, as Jefferson and others did, the hope that the Indian could ultimately attain full and equal citizenship within white America.

Seeking to discover their new role within the American system now that they had agreed to give up the right of arms to sustain their sovereignty, the Cherokees received three conflicting answers. In official documents of the federal governments, they were "wards" or "younger brothers" with a potential for full citizenship when they became fully "civilized" and "Christianized." To many American scientists they were "a dying race" more to be pitied than censured, but nevertheless incapable of meeting the challenge required to become part of that Anglo-Saxon people who stood at the forefront of human progress. To the neighboring frontiersmen, they were irredeemable "savages," defeated enemies who had lost all right to their land and whose existence, on mere sufferance, was an irritating impediment to the westward march of white civilization. The only reason most frontier people tolerated them was that they wished the federal government would bear the expense of re-

---

[22]According to a census taken by Meigs in 1808-1809, the Valley Towns contained 3,648 out of 12,395 Cherokees, 5 out of 583 black slaves, 72 out of 341 whites in the nation as a whole. M-208, 17 October 1808. By 1828 the Cherokees had developed a black code within their nation in order to protect their own status. See W. G. McLoughlin, "Red Indians, Black Slavery and White Racism: America's Slaveholding Indians," *American Quarterly* 26 (October 1974): 367-85.

[23]Secretary of War Lewis Cass quoted in the *Cherokee Phoenix*, 14 January 1832.

[24]Secretary of War William H. Crawford, ASP (IA), 2:28.

moving them. The federal government took pains to treat the tribes as quasi-independent states partly because it wanted them as a buffer zone or potential allies should France, Spain, or England press their claims to the Mississippi Valley and partly because it could not decide whether to "civilize" them where they were or remove them westward. (Prior to the Louisiana Purchase in 1803, there was no place to which they could be removed, but one of Jefferson's reasons for acquiring the Louisiana Territory was to facilitate such a relocation.)

The ambivalence of the white American's attitude toward the Native American is clearly revealed in an early missionary letter. The missionary who wrote it was a New England Federalist and philanthropist. Arriving in Tennessee, he was shocked to find that "the sentiment very generally prevails among the white people near the southern tribes (and perhaps with some farther to the north) that the Indian is by nature radically different from all other men and that this difference presents an insurmountable barrier to his civilization."[25] The missionary, however, believed that "Indians are men and their children, education alone excepted, [are] like the children of other men." This same ambivalence prevailed among the Cherokees in different form. Colonel Meigs reported in 1805 that most Cherokees were not ready to accept white men as their equals: "Many of the Cherokees think that they are not derived from the same stock as the whites, that they are favorites of the great spirit and that he never intended they should live the laborious lives of the whites; these ideas, if allowed to have a practical effect, would finally operate [to] their destruction."[26]

Despite this theory of racial polygenesis—the belief that God had, in effect, created the races biologically different—there were Cherokees ready to take up the white man's ways and work toward the goal of ultimate citizenship. These civilizationists were generally Cherokees of mixed white and Cherokee ancestry, the so-called mixed bloods, but not always. The chief whom James Mooney considered the leader of the "progressive" faction among the Cherokees after 1794 was a full blood called Doublehead. Colonel Meigs commented upon this theme in 1805: ". . . where the blood [of the Cherokees] is mixed with the whites, in

---

[25]ABCFM Papers, Brainerd Journal, 24 January 1818.

[26]M-208, 13 February 1805.

every grade of it, there is an apparent disposition leaning toward civilization and this disposition is in proportion to its distance from the original stock. But it is evident at the same time that this does not arise from any augmentation of their intellectual power, for it is a fact that in this nation several of the Chiefs who are from unadulterated Indian [stock] have strong minds and more acute discernment than any of the Half Breeds."[27]

Meigs fully sympathized with the federal government's plan to civilize and ultimately "incorporate" the Indians into the nation as citizens, but he recognized that it would take time. It might appear, he wrote to his subagent, Major William S. Lovely, in 1802, that "the civilization of a whole people of Savages seems sometimes a hopeless piece of business, but patience and perseverance will overcome great difficulties." It was the job of the federal agents to push this effort with vigor. The method, however, was ruthless in its disregard for their traditional way of life. "If it was within my power," said Meigs, "I would do away [with] every [Cherokee] custom inconsistent with civilized life." He noted with regret that "the Cherokees are extremely jealous of their Customs, Customs which have descended down to them from their Ancestors from time immemorial, many of which it is to be wished were done away [with]. . . ."[28]

Meigs viewed his task as that of a latter-day, enlightened Pygmalion, hewing away with vigor at the marble block of savagism within which the civilized man was held captive by the encrusted prejudices and superstitions of his forefathers. Government agents, he said, were to hammer away at the stone of culture until every vestige of the old ways was chipped away: "They, like that Statuary [sculptor], believe that the Statue is in the Block and that by the repeated strokes of the means, the desired effect will be produced."[29]

However, an irresistible urge to attribute white supremacy to hereditary or biological superiority provided Meigs with a convenient explanation for the apparent reluctance of many of the full bloods—"the real

---

[27]Ibid., 18 February 1805.

[28]Ibid., undated, but filed between 25 December 1801 and 1 January 1802; ibid., 6 June 1806.

[29]Ibid.

Indians"—to adapt to the white man's ways: "The number of the real Indians and those of Mixed Blood are nearly equal.[30] The last are almost without exception in favor of improvements and have very much thrown off the savage manner and habits: But those of the real Indians still hug the manners and habits of their ancesters [sic] and are unwilling to give [up] the pleasures of the shade and idleness. . . ."[31]

Almost all the attention focused by historians on families of inter-married whites and Cherokees has been given to that small but usually respectable element of resident traders and government officials (and later a few missionaries) who established themselves for life, married with serious intentions (and increasingly in Christian ceremonies), and accepted a certain responsibility to act for the best interests of the nation that had adopted them and bestowed full tribal rights upon them. It is the names of these families that have come down through the years as mixed-blood chiefs and influentials: Adair, McDonald, Ross, Lowery, McIntosh, Chisholm, Rogers, Riley, Baldridge, Vann, Foreman, Walker, McCoy, Pettit, Brown, Martin, Hicks. In later years, when the Cherokees became very conscious of their ancestry, it was fashionable to trace it back to the first respectable white trader or agent to intermarry, and for many of these families we can ascertain precise dates and places of entry into the nation. The children of such marriages tended to inter-marry among the same group, creating what some considered a mixed-blood elite. Despite animosities between this group and the full bloods, their contributions to Cherokee life were considerable. They provided skills in trade, farming, domestic manufactures, technology, record keeping, and diplomacy, which they put at the disposal of the Cherokees. They helped not only by their activities but by their example. More in-directly, but not less important, they inculcated historical perspective and memory; they stressed the importance of long-range planning, the need to see Cherokee affairs in the broader perspective of the wider world around them.

---

[30]This estimate is far too high and probably indicates that Meigs associated primarily with a special group of Cherokees and seldom ventured into the more remote regions of the nation. See *Cherokee Phoenix*, 1 January 1831, for an estimate that "less than one-fourth" of the Cherokees were of mixed ancestry. An analysis of the federal census of the Cherokees in 1835 reveals that the figure was less than twenty-three percent.

[31]M-208, 27 July 1805.

These contributions, however, were sometimes offset by their disdain for those Cherokees who did not zealously push toward acculturation and progress. They made few concessions to tribal custom, and insisted upon raising their children by white standards. These families caused serious internal problems after the 1790s by their disruption of clan kinship patterns and their desire to alter customs regarding private property and inheritance. Furthermore, because of their obvious advantages in dealing with whites, they began to assume important positions of leadership. Their children—normally called "half-breeds" by whites—grew up in the most difficult position of all, between two worlds. Their white fathers wanted them to live, act, and think like white men; their peers and Indian relatives wanted them to assert their Indian loyalty. The most popular, and yet typical, story illustrating this dilemma is the one told by Chief John Ross of his own childhood. His father, Daniel Ross, a Scottish trader from Baltimore, entered the Cherokee Nation in the 1780s on a trading trip, married the daughter of "Tory" John McDonald, who was then living at Chickamauga, and settled down to raise his family among the Cherokees. In 1797 young John Ross, then about seven years old, attended the festival of the Green Corn Dance. His mother

> on this occasion had dressed him in his first suit of nankeen, brand new, made after the white man's style, and he sauntered out to meet his playmates with all the self-consciousness of one wearing, for the first time, his new spring suit. . . . Shouts of derision and taunts of "Unaka" [white boy] greeted him on all sides; even his most intimate friends held aloof. . . . While being dressed by his [Cherokee] grandmother the next morning, he burst into tears and after much coaxing told her of his humiliation the day before. She comforted him as grandmothers are wont to do . . . the nankeen suit came off, the hunting shirt, leggins, and moccasins went on, and the small boy ran shouting to his play, happy and "at home" again, as he termed it. . . .[32]

Ross's father, however, took care to hire white tutors to teach his son English and arithmetic so that he could learn his father's business, and Ross grew up to be a wealthy trader. His first marriage was to a Cherokee full blood; his second, after he had become principal chief, was to a well-to-do white Quaker who lived in Baltimore. Ross never overcame his

---

[32]Rachel Eaton, *John Ross and the Cherokee Indians* (Muscogee OK: Star Printery, Inc., 1921) 3.

"twoness." From the profits of trade, he bought a large number of slaves to till his plantation fields and lived according to the style of a Southern gentleman, while defending to the last ditch the right of the Cherokees to remain on their homeland in the East. He was so unsure of his command of Cherokee language that as a chief he always spoke and wrote in English.

In regard to racial equality as well as in regard to adopting the white man's ways, the Cherokee was left with an impossible dilemma: either he adopted a theory of polygenesis and racial separatism (that God had created the different races and they must not be mixed)—thereby throwing his weight on the side of reactionary bigots along the frontier—or he accepted the "enlightened" view of liberal philanthropists and accepted amalgamation, assimilation, and disappearance. Either route led to his extinction. I have found only one explicit statement by a Cherokee of what may have been a more general view, a faith that heredity and complexion were not the real issues. This occurred during a conversation that Meigs had early in the century with the Lower Town chief named Eskaqua, or Bloody Fellow. Meigs had tried to persuade him that it might be best if he led his people to the West since he appeared reluctant to adopt total acculturation. "Bloody Fellow replied that he had no inclination to leave the country of his birth. Even should the habits & customs of the Cherokees give place to the habits & customs of the whites, or even should they themselves become white by intermarriage, not a drop of Indian blood would be lost; it would be spread more widely, but not lost. He was for preserving them together as a people regardless of complexion."[33] It was this fundamental racial pride and confidence attached, let it be noted, to the critical notion of roots in their homeland, which sustained the Cherokees in their struggle for survival as a distinct people in the years ahead.

Although the Cherokees probably learned of the importance whites attached to racial differences primarily from daily experience with them, they also experienced their legal implications in various courtroom situations. Sometimes they found that there were advantages to be gained, as in the case of the Cherokee who was placed on trial for murdering, in a fit of drunken anger, a black slave owned by a white man. A white jury in Tennessee found him guilty of manslaughter, a crime punishable by

---

[33]John Howard Payne Papers, Newberry Library (Chicago), 2:23.

branding. But when the judge examined the statute, he discovered that it applied only to the killing of white men. Nevertheless, the attorney for the state demanded that the Indian be branded. The judge refused and the Cherokee was released. He had, however, learned an important lesson about the nice legal distinctions involved in interracial criminal justice. Meigs wrote that the Cherokees were pleased at the fairness of the trial and its outcome; but it was a fairness they seldom found in trials involving Indians charged with crimes against white men.[34]

While Southern state courts may have shown partiality toward Indians who murdered black slaves, they were not prepared to deal in the same way with Indians accused of crimes against whites. Meigs discussed this matter with the secretary of war in 1812 when Governor Tatnall of Georgia demanded the arrest of two Cherokees accused of murdering two white Georgians. He said the Cherokees were "afraid of a trial" by a white jury. They had reminded Meigs that in a recent trial involving a white man accused of murdering a Cherokee, the case was dismissed for want of evidence because only Cherokees had witnessed the murder. The Cherokees, Meigs told Tatnall, had also informed him that there were at least eight recent cases where state courts refused to bring charges against white murderers. "This I have no doubt is true," Meigs told the governor. The reason the white murderers had not been tried was that there was "no proof but that of Indians" available as evidence. In such cases, he said, "the murderers could not be convicted and never will." He went on to remind the governor that "the state of Indians is a deplorable one in this respect. We arraign them as moral agents, charge them with crimes that cannot be committed without including an idea that they are more like ourselves, at the same time we exclude them from all the advantages of beings capable of moral or religious conceptions; their testimony on oath is not admissable."[35]

Meigs fought consistently against this double standard of American justice. Like a true Jeffersonian, he deplored the effort to read the Chris-

---

[34]M-208, 10 March, 1 May 1807. Meigs noted of this crime, "It was an act perpetrated in a barbarous manner not in defence of life but in a rage of passion excited by the pride of the Indian to be opposed by a Negro, which even Indians effect to look down on with contempt." Ibid., 22 February, 20 April 1810. Meigs's phrase, "even Indians," speaks volumes on this issue.

[35]Ibid., 19 March 1812.

tian religion into the common law. Indians were denied the right to give legal testimony on the ground that they were heathens. Heathens did not believe in a God who administered rewards and punishments after death. Presumably, therefore, they would have no compunction about lying. Meigs was always eager to demonstrate that the Indians did indeed believe in a God and an afterlife. "I have been informed," he wrote to a lawyer in Tennessee who was trying to help an Indian named Stone (or Stone Carrier) on trial for horse stealing, "that the Moors have been admitted to give Evidence at Gibralter in Capital cases. The religion of the Cherokees is as good as that of Mahomet." Though not Christians, "the Indians believe in the being of a God and in the immortality of the soul; it is an instinctive idea with them."[36] He and Silas Dinsmoor, agent to the Choctaws, searched through Blackstone's *Commentaries* until they found support for their position. Dinsmoor wrote to Meigs about it in 1803: "In 3d Blackstone, Lib. 3, cap. 23, p. 369, it is said, 'All witnesses of whatever religion or country that have the use of their reason are to be examined except such as are infamous or such as are interested in the event of the cause. All others are competent witnesses though the jury from other circumstances will judge of their credibility.' This being the law, the Indians are and of right ought to be admissible as witnesses."[37]

Dinsmoor argued that it was not "absolutely necessary that an Indian should take an oath to make his testimony valid" because, as in the case of Quakers, "an affirmation might be sufficient." But even admitting that an oath was necessary and that an Indian had no idea of the being of a God nor of future existence, "should these considerations bar an Indian from being admitted to oath and testimony? Which would be the most dubious testimony, the honest Indian who has never heard of or known a God or the Atheist or Deist who has convinced *himself* that there is none, or if there be, that he suffers the actions of men to pass unheeded and unnoted? Yet no one pretends to bar a whiteman on account of his religious opinions."[38] Despite Dinsmoor's arguments, he could not make the courts of the Mississippi Territory admit Indian wit-

---

[36]Ibid., 10 June 1802.

[37]Ibid., 26 July 1803.

[38]Ibid.

nesses any more than Meigs could in Tennessee or Georgia.[39] Even where Indians' cases were taken to court, Meigs frankly acknowledged, "it is a fact that they cannot have justice done to them in the courts of law." The judges, he said, were "just and liberal in their Sentiments and look on the human race with equal eye as far as related to distributive justice," but "a jury impaneled in the frontier Counties dare not bring in a Verdict to take the life of a Citizen for killing an Indian." The result was that Indians were regularly "accused, tried, and condemned and executed on the testimony of any white citizen of common character and understanding when at the same time a white man can kill an Indian in the presence of 100 Indians and the testimony of these hundred Indians to the fact amounts to nothing and the man will be acquitted."[40] The impact of this upon the dignity and self-respect of the Indian was devastating. Richard Brown, one of the leading Cherokee chiefs, wrote to Meigs in 1811 about the feelings aroused in the Indians by their not being allowed to testify against white horse thieves: "We have found a horse belonging to an Indian near Dittoes landing or near Huntsville [in Mississippi Territory, now part of Alabama]. We cannot recover him without aid. The oath of the Indians is not known by your laws. Decide in some way to give us our right. Are we considered as negroes who cannot support our claims?"[41]

The Indians were always described as a proud people. They considered themselves the equal not only of white men but of the upper class of white men in the South. In 1760 Henry Timberlake noted that the Cherokees "are extremely proud, despising the lower class of Europeans; and in some athletick diversions I once was present at, they refused to match or hold conference with any but officers."[42] But after 1794 frontier whites became contemptuous of the rights of Indians, knowing that no white jury would ever convict them for anything they did to an Indian. In 1813 Meigs described four separate cases of Indian murders in which "prosecutions were instituted and all failed of producing punish-

---

[39]Ibid., 7 April 1801.

[40]Ibid., 6 April 1812.

[41]Ibid., 21 July 1811.

[42]Henry Timberlake, *Memoirs*, ed. Samuel C. Williams (Marietta GA: Continental Book Company, 1948) 79.

ment." It seriously undermined Meigs's faith in the Republic: "Let us not advocate a system of Ethics that only subjects the weak and simple honest man to become the prey of the Bold villain who laughs at the restraints which bind the multitude."[43] The only means by which Meigs and the secretary of war could make a pretense of justice was to offer the family of a murdered Indian a cash compensation. In 1802 Secretary of War Henry Dearborn wrote to Silas Dinsmoor, the Choctaw agent: "You will endeavor to settle the disputes and if necessary engage to satisfy the Chickasaws for the loss of their friend by a pecuniary compensation not exceeding two or three hundred dollars to the family or friends of the deceased."[44] In this case the Chickasaw appears to have been murdered by a Delaware Indian, but the same "satisfaction" was offered for murders attributed to whites. In 1803 Dearborn authorized Meigs to provide "such pecuniary satisfaction as in your Judgement may be acceptable and proper" to the families of murdered Cherokees. He suggested a figure of "from one hundred to two hundred dollars for each man or woman actually murdered by white citizens since our last Treaty." Of course, the Cherokees were to be told that "the compensation is not intended to opperate [*sic*] as an acquittal of the murderers."[45] In effect, though, such payments ended the agent's and the government's concern with the case.

The use of murder-compensation payments continued until 1820 when John C. Calhoun, as secretary of war, decided to put a stop to it. "I have received your letter of the 14th November last," he wrote to Meigs, "submitting the claim of the Headmen of the Cherokees for the Indians killed by Americans." Grudgingly he acknowledged the precedents for the practice and said "you will accordingly pay the sum of $100 to the widow of the deceased." But he added, "You will inform the chiefs that the practice will not be continued in future as it is repugnant to those principles by which we govern ourselves in such case."[46] Calhoun either had forgotten or did not realize that the practice had arisen in the

---

[43]M-208, 11 February 1813.

[44]Microfilm, Letters Sent by the Secretary of War Relating to Indian Affairs, 1800-1824 (M-15), Records of the Bureau of Indian Affairs (RG 75), National Archives, 18 May 1802; hereafter cited as M-15.

[45]M-15, 30 May 1803; 7 January 1804.

[46]Ibid., 6 July 1820.

first place because the principles by which the "Americans" governed themselves did not seem to be available to Indians. Nor did he take notice that the cost of an Indian's life had declined in twenty years from three hundred to one hundred dollars.

The failure of American jurisprudence in regard to white murderers was equally glaring in the much more frequent cases of fraud and theft perpetrated by white men upon the Indians: their horses, their furs, their traps, their guns—virtually anything they owned of any value was fair game for marauding whites. The federal agent, faced with trying to evaluate and adjudicate these claims, was compelled to establish his own investigatory and judicial system: "The nature of these kinds of claims cannot be equitably determined by strictly adhering to the law of evidence. The Indians cannot give legal testimony and by means of this disability the whites have an advantage; but by attending carefully to all the circumstances and to the character of the parties, justice can be done to the claimant, for altho' the claims may be just, the parties, especially the Indians, cannot support their rights and some characters of each party cannot be credited; but by care here we can, with few exceptions, make equitable decisions."[47] In short, Meigs heard the evidence and made the decisions himself; they were forwarded to the Department of War, and the Department more or less had to accept his word in compensating the Indian or the white involved. Consequently, much depended upon the honesty and ability of the agent; and not a little on how much money the War Department felt it could afford for this sort of thing.

Meigs was an honest and conscientious agent; many agents were neither. Trying to explain to a friend why, after all the Americans had tried to do for them, the Cherokees still had certain "prejudices" against the white man, Meigs said, "It does not arise from pride, as ours does; it arises in the Indian from his humble conception of himself and of his race from the discovery he makes that we look down on him as an inferior being [which] has a tendency to make him despise himself as the offspring of an inferior race of beings."[48] Lack of respect by others led to loss of respect for himself. This self-rejecting rage, frustration, and despair often led Indians to drink themselves into oblivion, but at other

[47]M-208, 22 February 1810.

[48]Ibid., 3 August 1817.

times they found more objective vents for their anger. There were other ways to avenge themselves on their persecutors. Although some took vengeance into their own hands, as traditional tribal custom formerly prescribed, this was usually self-defeating. A more subtle and satisfying way to get even with the white man was to steal his horses. For several reasons horse stealing became a way of life for many Cherokees in these years of anomie.

According to all early accounts of the Cherokee people, they were notable for their honesty. Not only had they no locks on their own houses, barns, and stables, but a visitor might leave his horse, gun, or goods with any of them for months at a time and find it unharmed when he called for it. In a culture committed to sharing even the last piece of food with strangers as well as neighbors, neither avarice nor acquisitiveness was a virtue. Not placing a high value on personal property and seldom needing much, the Cherokees had no written laws governing theft, only social disdain for the thief. Robbery was not a crime included in clan revenge, no matter what the object stolen. Not even the extensive use of western manufactures (guns, axes, kettles, and blankets) after 1700 seems to have produced any problem in this regard. So long as the cultural values were intact and healthy, the Cherokees maintained their standards of honesty. But as the cultural system broke down, so did its values. By the last decade of the eighteenth century, the problem of horse stealing and its allied vices had risen to monumental proportions.

In times of war, horse stealing had always been an understandable and acceptable source of plunder. In times of peace it became a source of revenge, of excitement, of courageous achievement for those denied other means of self-esteem and success. Horse stealing had become a major problem during the guerrilla warfare of 1780-1794, and the treaty ending that war prescribed that "in the future, to prevent the practice of stealing horses, attended with the most pernicious consequences to the lives and peace of both parties," the Cherokees were to "agree that for every horse which shall be stolen from the white inhabitants by any Cherokee Indians and not returned within three months, that the sum of fifty dollars shall be deducted" from the annuity the government paid to the tribe annually for the land the Cherokees had sold to the government.[49] In addition, the congressional acts regulating trade and inter-

---

[49]Treaty of 26 June 1794, cited in Richard Peters, *The Case of the Cherokee Indians* (Philadelphia, 1831) 254.

course with the Indians passed in 1796, 1799, and 1802 all contained clauses designed to prevent this illicit traffic.

Horse stealing, of course, was not merely a symptom of the breakdown of Indian culture; it was so endemic upon the American frontier that it obviously represents also the breakdown of European culture on its outer fringes. Horse stealing provided one of the few areas of frontier life in which Indians and whites worked harmoniously together (sometimes in trying to catch the thieves who stole from both groups with equal disregard, sometimes in belonging to the "pony clubs" constituted to do the stealing). Slave stealing, while closely allied, was more dangerous as well as more profitable.[50] Cattle rustling was less profitable in the eastern woodlands because cattle were slow-moving, noisy, and difficult to conceal. When out to steal, thieves might take whatever came first and most easily to hand, but only in regard to horse stealing was the traffic so common as to become a profession. The members of the pony clubs were thieves by vocation.

Horse stealing was directly related to the depletion of game in the old hunting grounds and the loss of status faced by Indian men who could not use their old skills to provide for their families. Return J. Meigs explained this (from the white man's viewpoint) in a letter to Benjamin Hawkins, the Creek agent, in 1805. He was justifying the government's effort to persuade the Indians to cede "the mountainous land lying between East and West Tennessee. . . . That land is of no use to them; there is not a single family [living] on it, and the hunting is very poor. Yet those of an idle disposition spend much time in ramblin' there and often return with a stolen horse which they have afterwards to pay for [from the annuity]. In fact, it is only a nursery of savage habits and opperates [*sic*] against civilization which is much impeded by their holding such immense tracts of wilderness."[51] The "savage habit" of stealing horses from an enemy was an old one, but too many otherwise honest Indians felt jus-

---

[50]For an example of illicit slave trading among the Cherokees, see ABCFM Papers, Brainerd Journal, 10 October 1819. A white man was purchasing Osage and other captive Indian children within the Cherokee Nation and claiming they were "Mulattos"; he sold them as black slaves to whites outside the nation. "This man," said the missionaries, "had endeavored to persuade another to join him in this business, stating that there were a number of [Indian] captives in the Cherokee Nation which he thought he could obtain at a low price."

[51]M-208, 13 February 1805.

tified in resorting to it when their best efforts to support their families by hunting failed—largely because the whites had killed or chased away the game. How could a man return empty-handed from an extended hunting trip without feeling disgraced? While horse stealing had its roots in tribal warfare, in which booty taken from an enemy was always a sign of prowess and bravery, it also stemmed from the fact that Cherokees owned their land in common. Since no man could buy or sell land as a means of enriching himself, this prime source of frontier enterprise was closed to them. (The fact that Indians had to measure private wealth in terms of personal property—horses or slaves—and not, as whites did, in terms of real estate, was of course part of the argument used by those who demanded that the Cherokees adopt the practice of owning their land "in severalty.") Hence movable or personal property became more important to them than to a white man as a means of investment or growing wealth once they were told to become capitalists. Moreover, horse stealing utilized many of the old-fashioned skills of the warrior and hunter: it was exciting; it tested a man's daring; it required quick wits and courage for, make no mistake about it, human life was at stake in these encounters. The respectable among the older generation frowned upon this practice and did not find it a valid substitute for war and hunting; but the elders had lost their right to command. Many young Indians preferred the risk of sudden death to the plodding routine of grubbing and hoeing in the fields day after day. Moreover, the profits from horse stealing were not only quicker but much larger than any Cherokee farmer could earn. Some less respectable chiefs managed to profit by it, if not to justify it.

Horse stealing, like slave stealing, was more than simply a way to vent one's anger at the white man or prove oneself a hell of a daring fellow. It also fulfilled an economic need on the frontier. The slave dealer had provided cheap labor for a system desperately in need of it. The horse dealer provided a substitute for specie in an economy desperately short of cash. The dishonest vendors in stolen goods were simply providing more cheaply in the black market what there was a high demand for from the public. In this sense it was not strictly a white-Indian problem but a source of economic livelihood for those willing to take chances—the poor, the desperate, the angry, the alienated.[52]

---

[52]My analysis here owes something to the chapter entitled "Crime As a Way of Life" in Daniel Bell, *The End of Ideology* (New York: Free Press, 1961).

Meigs readily recognized this aspect of the profession: "A considerable part of the land purchased in this country is paid for in horses; they serve as a kind of currency for this purpose all over this western country and hence arises the facility with which they are stolen by Indians and others."[53] Governor William Blount of Tennessee (the superintendent of Indian affairs for the Southern District of the United States—south of the Ohio) noted this same bartering aspect when he asked James Carey, the official Cherokee interpreter, in 1793, "In what manner do the Indians dispose of stolen horses?" Carey answered, "Generally they sell them to the traders for a trifle, who run them out of the nation in a different direction to that from whence they came and barter them off for negroes or articles of merchandise."[54]

A detailed study of horse stealing on the frontier would reveal a great deal about its economic development and difficulties. For example, it seems evident that in the 1790s the Cherokees stole horses in the West and bartered them for goods in the East where the market was better, while in the early nineteenth century the need for specie on the frontier made it more profitable to steal horses in the East and trade them in the West. "This business is carried on by white people and Indians in combination," wrote Blount in 1792, "and as soon as a horse is stolen he is conveyed through the Indian nation to North or South Carolina or Georgia and in a short time to the principal towns on the seaboard for sale so as to effectually prevent recovery."[55] But fifteen years later Meigs reported, "The number of horses carried thro' and into this [Cherokee] country is almost incredible—from Georgia, both the Carolinas and Kentucky."[56]

The Indian nations were ideally situated for the business. Being centrally located between East and West, among various settlements scattered throughout the frontier, and being largely wilderness without roads, the various Indian territories became common channels for shuttling stolen horses. "Considerable numbers of horses are stolen by citizens and by Indians," wrote Meigs, "that never will or can be detected

---

[53]M-208, 19 December 1807.

[54]ASP (IA), 1:438.

[55]Ibid., 265 (5 May 1792).

[56]M-208, 19 December 1807.

on account of the Wilderness country, so that detection is easily avoided."[57] Not only was it difficult for victims to interrogate friendly Indians who might have been willing to help them trace the thieves, but the Indians themselves possessed no system of internal police to keep track of their own people and recapture their own horses. Since the traffic was interstate and through federal territory, the policing of it was the job of the federal government.

With only one agent or two in the thousands of square miles of wilderness that constituted each Indian nation, it was impossible for the federal government to provide adequate policing. Even the licensing system under the trade and intercourse acts produced no convictions. "Horse stealing is a subject of complaint (almost continual) to me," wrote Governor Blount in 1792, "without my being able to give any redress. The only thing I can do is to give passports to the sufferers to go into the nation in search of their horses and letters to the chiefs, which, as yet, has never been attended with recovery."[58] The chiefs, even if they knew who the thieves were, were hardly likely to turn them over to frontier justice. Consequently, horse stealing became of the most constant causes of friction between Indians and whites on the frontier—each tending to lay the blame primarily on the other. "Horse stealing," Blount continued in this letter, "is the grand source of hostility between the white and red people in this district, and I fear will actually produce it if not desisted from. It is a subject on which the whites are very sore and with difficulty restrain themselves from taking what they call satisfaction, that is from killing some of the Indians."

While the Indians usually acted as the employees of white traders, who paid them a trifle for the dangerous work and then shuttled the horses off to profitable sales in distant communities, more than once Indians bought stolen horses from each other—sometimes knowingly, sometimes not. On one occasion a white man forcibly took from a Cherokee a mare he said had been stolen from him by the Creeks. The Cherokee complained that the white man should pay him what he had paid the Creek for it. The white man refused, and the case was taken to Blount by a Cherokee chief. Blount told the chief that the white settler

---

[57] Ibid.

[58] Cited in Prucha, *American Indian Policy*, 204.

who "took possession of her brought her to me and proved her before a justice of the peace, by the oath of several disinterested evidences, to be his property; and by the law of the white people, he is entitled to keep her without paying anything. The [Cherokee] man when he bought her from a Creek must have known she had been raised by the white people [white people's horses were said to be rounder in the belly] and was stolen. Does not all your nation agree in informing me that the Creeks are daily stealing horses from the white people? Then why do they purchase horses from them?"[59]

There was, of course, no honor among thieves. They stole from each other and sold to each other, and when questioned by white authorities, blamed each other. Since there was no effective way to enforce the laws, both sides took the law into their own hands. Vigilantism prevailed and real or suspected horse thieves were frequently whipped, beaten, or shot by angry owners not too concerned about trying to differentiate one Indian from another. It was generally the Indians who suffered the most from vigilantes since they dared not assault any white man openly; yet because their oath was unacceptable before a justice of the peace, it was impossible for them to "prove" legal ownership without written evidence or white witnesses. Even when Meigs accepted Indian evidence in his extrajudicial proceedings regarding depredation claims, they had no assurance of success. Meigs might trust their word, but the government auditors frequently demanded more concrete evidence before they would authorize payment.

> I forward a number of claims of Citizens and Indians for damages stated by them to have been sustained, principally for Horse stealing, in which the citizens as well as the Cherokees have a share. It is very difficult to ascertain facts in these cases. The difficulty arises from the inaccuracy or want of testimony; the want of testimony arises from the impossibility of obtaining it in the places where the stealing is perpetrated [it] being nearly all done in a wide wilderness principally in the Indian country. This lays the white people under great distress to make legal proof of their losses. And the Indians suffer from the same cause, and in addition to that their testimony is not allowed to be valid in a legal sense.[60]

The shortcomings of horse stealing as a way of life were obvious, and it was never respectable. Still, what was respectable anymore? What op-

---

[59]ASP (IA), 1:281 (13 September 1792).

[60]M-208, 19 December 1807.

tions for a viable life-style with a hopeful future were there? Having lost faith in their own prowess, the Cherokess saw little they could depend upon in the white man's program. It might be said that the Cherokees had nowhere to go but up at the turn of the century. In fact, the miracle is that they did not, as did so many other Indian nations, disintegrate entirely. To their own surprise, as well as to that of many of their closest observers, they discovered resources within themselves and their culture they had not realized were there.

The crisis that finally enabled them to regain a sense of their own dignity and self-respect was the effort made in the years 1806 to 1809 to persuade them to move west of the Mississippi. Their internal frictions reached a peak in 1807 when Doublehead, the "progressive" leader of the Lower Towns, was assassinated. The fact that he had been caught accepting bribes from the federal government, hidden in secret clauses of the treaties of 1805 and 1806, was only partly to blame. The deeper issue was lack of consideration for the feelings of a large proportion of the tribe, particularly the conservative elements in the Valley Towns, who wished to find a middle ground between total assimilation and the old ways. In the press of the emergency that arose when Meigs, disillusioned by the murder of his favorite chief, tried to coerce the tribe into total removal to the West, a new group of leaders emerged.

Their first task was to reunite the various regions of the tribe in a concerted effort to hold on to what remained of their ancestral land. Their second task was to create a new instrument of political control— an elected executive body empowered to act on the nation's behalf when the council of chiefs was not in session. Although about one thousand Cherokees departed for Arkansas in 1810 in the wake of the crisis, the remaining 12,000 Cherokees acquired a new sense of solidarity and purpose. Henceforth the Cherokees knew that to be a Cherokee meant to live in the land of their forefathers, to put the unity and prosperity of the "nation" before the aggrandizement of individual sections or chiefs. With the new confidence gained from their successful resistance to disunion and removal, the Cherokees were ready to begin the more difficult task of restructuring their social order. This political revitalization culminated between 1817 and 1828 in a new form of government and a firm conviction that they must retain their own distinct ethnic identity. By their own effort, the Cherokees evolved a policy that avoided both of the white man's unpalatable alternatives. They would not assimilate, and neither would they be moved. They would remain an independent, quasisovereign nation. By acting on these fundamental principles the Cherokee people were reborn, like the phoenix, from the ashes of defeat and confusion.[61]

---

[61]For a discussion of the first removal crisis of 1806-1809 and the revitalization that emerged from it, see W. G. McLoughlin, "Thomas Jefferson and the Beginning of Cherokee Nationalism, 1806-1809," *William and Mary Quarterly*, 3rd ser., 32 (6 October 1975): 547-80.

JAMES VANN:
INTEMPERATE PATRIOT,
1768-1809

Every Native American people has its heroes either among those who fought most bravely to try to hold back the European invaders or among those who most enabled them, after the conquest, to sustain their tribal identity and self-respect. Among the Cherokees, the most notable heroes have been Sequoyah and John Ross. But their accomplishments came after 1820 when their tribe had already come through a generation of trial and tribulation. Historians have noted that there were other Cherokee leaders in the first decade of the nineteenth century, but they have been shadowy figures. They left little in the way of written record, and the heat of the controversies within the nation in these years did not permit any single figure to achieve permanent fame. Nonetheless, most histories of the Cherokees single out Doublehead (the leader of the Cherokee Lower Towns) and James Vann (by 1806 the leader of the Cherokee Upper Towns) as the principal antagonists in the early phase of Cherokee revitalization. However, neither has fared well under scrutiny, and the violent death of both has led historians to conclude that neither was a successful leader.

The point of this essay is to stake out a claim for James Vann as an early, if ambiguous, hero among the Cherokees. I have tried to piece together all of the known facts and to get beneath the many hearsay and contradictory stories about Vann that survive. I am not wholly satisfied that I have adequately portrayed this intemperate patriot in all his many dimensions. He will probably never merit a book-length biography, for there is too little to flesh out such a volume. Vann himself did all he could to obscure his own political actions, in part because he feared that they might cost him his life. It is my hope that this brief biographical sketch will spur others to dig more deeply into his career as well as into that of his archrival, Doublehead. Cherokee history will become real for most readers only when we are able to delineate such leaders as complete personalities. Certainly they both merit the closest possible scrutiny; be-

tween them they shaped the destiny of their people in the critical period of transition from the old way of life to the new.

EVEN IN HIS OWN DAY James Vann was an awesome, inexplicable, and turbulent figure among the Cherokees. After his death, the legends about him grew rapidly. Although he played a leading role in Cherokee affairs from 1795-1809, historians disagree in their estimate of his contributions. One historian calls him "a peculiar combination of benevolent leader and rip-snorting hoodlum."[1] Another calls him "one of the most intemperate characters in the nation"—"captious," "irresponsible," "homicidal," "a thoroughly godless man," who "when drunk . . . became as deadly as a water moccasin."[2] Contemporaries described him as "a desperado," "a villain," "an assassin." Thirty years after Vann's death, John Howard Payne spoke to Cherokees who remembered Vann as "aristocratic, impetuous, and full of chivalric daring," but "with all his errors, he was a patriot."[3] The Moravian missionaries called him "the wildest of men" and "a long-standing enemy of Christ." When he died, they spoke of him as "this wretched, pitiable man"—"this well-known man, loved by few, hated by many, feared by almost the whole Cherokee Nation."[4] Few at the time, or since, have fully understood his complex personality or the critical part he played in the development of Cherokee nationalism.

There is considerable confusion about Vann's parentage, his marriages, his children, and even the date of his birth, but about the date and manner of his death there is no doubt. He was murdered while

---

[1]Henry T. Malone, *Cherokees of the Old South: A People in Transition* (Athens: University of Georgia, 1956) 60.

[2]Thurman Wilkins, *Cherokee Tragedy* (New York: Macmillan, 1970) 34. Edmund Schwarze, *History of the Moravian Missionaries among the Southern Indian Tribes of the United States* (Bethlehem PA: Times Publishing Co., 1923) 55-56. Schwarze describes him as "very dissipated and drunken, yet kind and hospitable."

[3]Payne Papers, 2:43. Numerous evaluations of Vann can be found in the files of the government Indian agency among the Cherokees. (See BIA, M-208.)

[4]Gambold to Benzien, 23 February 1809, MAS. The Moravian Archives in Winston-Salem contain the most important material on Vann's private life but little on his public life.

standing in a tavern with a bottle of whiskey in one hand and a half-filled glass in the other. No one knew at the time who murdered him or even why he was murdered.

Vann was a man of action, not of words. He left almost no private letters and his extensive business papers have disappeared. Born of a white trader and a full-blood Cherokee, Vann was, by 1800, the richest man in the Cherokee Nation. He owned more than fifty black slaves, operated three separate trading posts, managed two ferries, and ran two farms of several hundred acres. His two-story, balconied, brick mansion is today a tourist attraction near Chatsworth, Georgia; his restored tavern on the old Georgia turnpike to Nashville has been moved to the Cherokee historical site at New Echota, Georgia. His gristmill and distillery have disappeared along with his gravesite. From the early 1790s, Vann and his various business partners (most of them white men) drove large herds of 200 to 300 cattle, horses, and hogs to market outside the Cherokee Nation; several times a year he loaded 30 to 40 packhorses with furs and deerskins and drove them to Augusta, Knoxville, Baltimore, or Charleston. Here he exchanged the hides for manufactured goods to trade in his stores in the Cherokee and Creek Nations. He kept as much as $3500 in hard cash (a small fortune in those days) in a trunk under his bed. He was a fine horseman, a superb shot (with pistol or rifle) and he could drink more rum, brandy, or whiskey than anyone in the nation.

When drunk, however (as he often was—he said he needed to get drunk to sleep), this shrewd, calculating man became a roaring demon. His normally generous and courteous nature was transformed; he vented his pent-up rage and frustration on whoever happened to cross him. Under these transformations, he would beat his wives, slash out with his dirk at guests (white or Indian), cruelly whip his slaves, and several times he wounded white acquaintances with his pistols. When recovered from these drunken fits, he would be exceedingly solicitous toward the friends he had abused, express profound regret, and do all he could to make amends. (He did not apologize to his slaves, who feared and hated him. They frequently tried to run away, but he always caught them.)

Apparently Vann believed that both red and white people despised him and tried to impose on him. He desperately wanted to be admired and respected, but only on his own terms. Caught between the irreconcilable worlds of red and white, he was consumed by a profound impulse toward self-destruction, which many took to be brash courage.

Chief John Lowery, who knew him well, said in 1808, "His life is a misery to him and he wishes every body to be the same way."[5] His deep sense of injured pride led him to conceal his most constructive actions; it also led him to fits of sadistic violence toward those he thought guilty of crimes against him. This vindictive streak ultimately was his undoing. His whole life was framed as a dare to anyone to challenge his haughty integrity; yet those who knew him well said that he tried desperately to make people like him and could not bear to be without constant companionship (made convivial by his freely dispensed kegs of whiskey). He even shared his kegs with his slaves. Like Mr. Kurtz in Conrad's *Heart of Darkness*, Vann caroused and frolicked with his blacks, teetering always on the edge of murdering them for taking too many liberties. Vann, said one contemporary, liked to "act the savage." At his death, his slaves broke loose in riotous exultation.[6] Everyone said that Vann was his own worst enemy. Nevertheless, his contribution toward the revitalization of his people was immense.

In addition, James Vann's short and troubled career as a Cherokee chief reflects the ambivalence of American Indian policy. He was at first admired and courted by officials of the War Department, who saw him as a force for law, order, and acculturation. But when he concluded that the federal government was not going to deal fairly with the Indians, he turned his remarkable energy toward uniting the Cherokees to stand up for their treaty rights; then the War Department decided that he was a malevolent force that must be curbed at any cost. Secretary of War Henry Dearborn and President Thomas Jefferson tried for years to curry favor with Vann, then decided in 1808 to arrest and imprison him: "James Vann is a dangerous man," wrote the resident federal agent of the Cherokees to Dearborn in 1808; his conviction in the white courts of Tennessee for his insolent behavior, the agent said, "would have a good effect and would strengthen the hands of the friends of Government."[7] Secretary Dearborn concurred: "If Van [*sic*] is properly brot to Justice, it will have a very good effect, will silence his partizans—negotiations

---

[5]John Lowery to R. J. Meigs, 3 October 1808, OSW, M-222, roll 3, #1311.

[6]Fries, 7:3074. R. J. Meigs to Henry Dearborn, 11 June 1808, BIA, M-208.

[7]R. J. Meigs to Henry Dearborn, 4 September and 30 September 1808, BIA, M-208.

[for land cessions] will be conducted with ease."[8] Dearborn's order was carried out. Dangerous to himself, Vann turned his self-destructive drive to constructive ends; he became a danger to those who would destroy his nation. It was a game worthy of his ability, and he played it well.

James Vann was probably born in 1768. His father is said to have been a Scottish trader from Charleston, North Carolina, named Clement Vann (1747-1829), although the missionaries who knew Clement Vann spoke of him as James Vann's "step-father." Vann's mother was a Cherokee full blood named Waw-li.[9] His father at first established a trading post near the Chattahoochee River and later moved further into the Cherokee Nation near the Connesauga River where the Vann mansion now stands. In 1809 this area was known as "Vannsville" or "Vann's Town," but when Vann wrote letters, he gave his address as "Diamond Hill." Vann's father was moderately successful, but the Revolution brought difficult times for the Cherokees. The Cherokees sided with the king in 1776, and they were overwhelmed the following year when invading white armies of American militiamen destroyed many of their towns and people. The Upper Town Cherokees (in Georgia, North Carolina, and eastern Tennessee) made peace with the United States in 1777; but the western part of the nation, known as the Lower Towns or Chickamauga Towns (built along the lower Tennessee from Chickamauga to Muscle Shoals, Alabama) continued to wage guerrilla warfare with the white frontiersmen until 1794.[10]

When peace finally came to the nation, James Vann was a young man of twenty-six. He was rapidly expanding his father's trading activities and doing his best to cooperate with the Indian policy that George Washington had adopted for the transformation of the Indians from fur-trading hunters into citizen-farmers. Vann's role in this acculturation

---

[8]Henry Dearborn to R. J. Meigs, 23 October 1808, BIA, M-208.

[9]Some sources spell her name Wa-wii and some Faw-li. Some sources say Vann was born in 1765 and some say 1770. The Moravians said he was forty-one at his death. See de Baillou, 3-8. De Baillou's article also contains illustrations of Vann's home and tavern.

[10]The best historical discussions about the Cherokee in this period are in Malone, *Cherokees of the Old South*; Wilkins, *Cherokee Tragedy*; James Mooney, *Myths of the Cherokees* (Chicago: Aldine Publishing Co., 1975); and Grace Woodward, *The Cherokees* (Norman: University of Oklahoma Press, 1963).

process was to provide his people with the plows, spinning wheels, hoes, harnesses, looms, and other implements of agricultural and domestic industry. Though he had considerable competition from white traders who entered the nation from the trading post established by the War Department, he had the advantages of being bilingual and of being trusted by those with whom he traded. No one ever accused him of dishonesty as a trader. In exchange for their furs and hides, or their cattle, hogs, and corn, he gave the struggling Cherokees credit at his stores and provided them with the seed and tools they needed to provide food and clothing for their families. Shrewd, hardworking and equally conversant with the ways of Indians and whites, he rapidly rose to affluence. He traded with the Creek Nation as well, and ingratiated himself with the federal authorities by keeping them informed of the machinations of the French, Spanish, and British, who still hoped to win control of the Mississippi Valley (which, of course, is why the secretary of war was responsible for Indian affairs). One of the first extant letters from Vann, written in 1792, informs Colonel Henry Karr of the Georgia militia that he has seen "a spanish officer in the Lower Towns of the Creeks [near Florida]; you may put the People on their guard."[11]

Vann was already a solitary and secretive man, distrustful of others and cautious in his relations with government officials. He had gone through a particularly cruel experience as a youth, which left a deep mark upon him. By Cherokee custom, the members of each of the seven exogamous, matrilineal clans that bound the nation together were obliged to take vengeance (called "clan retaliation" or "the law of blood revenge") upon anyone who killed a member of their clan.[12] This obligation fell upon the nearest male relatives, and the person upon whom they took vengeance had to be either the murderer or one of his close kin. (Vann's mother was a member of the Blind Savannah clan and hence he was too.) One of Vann's clan relatives, Chief Sour Mush, who was an old and respected chief, got a bit drunk one night and made insulting remarks about a member of the Paint clan named McPherson. McPherson fell upon Sour Mush and beat him badly with his fists. After the fight

---

[11]James Vann to Henry Karr, Georgia Archives, 1:7.

[12]For discussions of clan revenge and its importance, see John P. Reid, *A Law of Blood* (New York: New York University Press, 1970) and Rennard Strickland, *Fire and Spirits* (Norman: University of Oklahoma Press, 1975).

Sour Mush noted bitterly that his clan members, some of whom were present, should have defended him. This complaint was taken seriously by Vann's uncle, Charles Hughes.[13] Hughes gathered some sturdy members of the Blind Savannah clan and, at the next opportunity, gave McPherson such a savage beating that he died shortly after. McPherson's death obligated the Paint clan to seek retaliation upon his murderer, but Hughes got together with other members of the Blind Savannah clan and persuaded them that he was more valuable to them than the young and headstrong James Vann: "James Vann was a boy, ungovernable and unpromising," according to the version of this event that a close relation of Vann told John Howard Payne many years later. "He had never yet done anything for the good of this country and could be spared without regret."

The Paint clan agreed to accept the suggestion of Hughes and to take revenge upon young Vann instead of upon his uncle. Vann heard of this arrangement but refused to run away. In fact, he rode boldly into an ambush that he knew the Paint clan had laid for him, and though wounded by one of the four shots fired at him, spurred on his horse and escaped. The Paint clan was not stopped by this. A few months later the avengers of McPherson tried again. This time Vann was on foot and standing near his uncle when McPherson's clan surrounded him. Refusing to be sacrificed for his uncle's mistake, "He deliberately walked up to his uncle and shot him dead" with his pistol. This, according to Payne's informant, "quieted the claim," but it was highly unusual. The bizarre act astounded the Cherokees and can only be seen as a further example of the anomie that pervaded their society in these years. By it, Vann cleverly and boldly escaped the ritual murder his uncle had callously planned for him. Apparently Vann felt justified in his action and thought he had demonstrated his courage by riding into the ambush. But it does not appear that the rest of the Cherokees shared his view. While shooting his uncle did not make him an outlaw, it marked him as a strange and perverse Cherokee. To have attained respect, he should have accepted his death stoically, in which case Hughes might have suffered some loss of respect.

---

[13]If Hughes was his uncle, as Payne asserts, he must have been a maternal uncle married to a sister of Waw-li. This story is told in Payne Papers, 2:43-46. Payne obtained it from Major George Walters, a close relative of Vann.

Vann married his first wife, Jenny Foster, sometime in the late 1780s and had several children by her.[14] Jenny found him difficult to live with and left him (a practice fully sanctioned by Cherokee tradition). She also had the right to take her children with her, but whether she took them all is not clear. Vann then married Elizabeth Thornton who, like his first wife, was the daughter of a white man and a full blood. Elizabeth was the mother of Delilah or Lily. Elizabeth left him, and then he married two daughters of a Scottish trader named Wallace (or Walter) Scott. According to Cherokee custom, polygamy was perfectly acceptable. There is a rumor that Vann may have married the two Scott women before Elizabeth left him. Margaret (Peggy) Scott Vann bore him his favorite son, Joseph, in 1798.[15] In 1809 six of his children were living: Mary, Robert, Lily, Sally, Jenny, and Joseph.[16] Peggy and Polly Scott did not have a happy time with Vann, and Polly eventually left him. Peggy, who loved him despite his ill-treatment of her, remained faithful until his death, though she was always frightened of him.

Vann's first important act as a town chief (or "headman") of the Upper Towns was his decision to take the Moravian missionaries under his protection. After 1799 the Cherokees, though ostensibly united under Chief Little Turkey, remained regionally and politically divided. The Upper Towns met together in council at the town of Ustanali, sixteen miles from Vann's town, to manage their affairs; the Lower Towns, located west of Lookout Mountain, met at Willstown to manage their affairs. Because the Lower Towns had won the admiration of the nation's warriors for their long guerrilla fight against whites and because the federal government feared that the Cherokee might yet ally themselves with the Spanish, French, or British, the Lower Town chiefs became the dominant faction in the national councils when the two regions united to consider overall tribal affairs. The leaders of the Lower Towns after 1794 were Little Turkey, Black Fox, Pathkiller, Doublehead, Dick Justice, The Glass, Toochelar (or Toochalee), Tolluntuskee, The Seed, The

---

[14]Penelope Johnson Allen has published a genealogy of Vann's immediate family, but it does not always square with contemporary documents. See de Baillou, 8.

[15]Ibid. It is not known which of Vann's children were born to which of his wives, but it seems fairly certain that Joseph was Peggy's child.

[16]The decision of the Cherokee Council invalidating Vann's will is cited in de Baillou, 8.

Flute, John Lowery, Terrapin, Sleeping Rabbit, and John D. Chisholm. The leaders of the Upper Towns were Chulioa, Sour Mush, Katahee, The Bark, Warrior's Nephew, Thomas Pettit, George Parris (or Pearis), and Rising Fawn. James Vann was at this time one of the young or minor chiefs. He had devoted more of his time and effort to his business than to the civil affairs of the nation. Still, he kept a close eye on tribal business and when a group of Moravian missionaries (the United Brethren) came to the council in 1800 from Salem, North Carolina, to ask permission to start the first permanent mission station among the Cherokees, Vann and his friend, Charles Hicks, decided to support their request.

Little Turkey, the principal chief, and Doublehead, the speaker of the council, had no interest in missionaries and neither did most of the chiefs. Vann himself was not concerned with the Christianization of the nation (as the missionaries soon learned), but he was interested in having a school where he and other Cherokees could send their children to learn to read and write and understand basic arithmetic so that they could deal adequately with white men in business affairs. Furthermore, the Moravians agreed to include vocational training at their mission station: they would teach Cherokee boys the essentials of farming and Cherokee girls how to spin, weave, sew, make butter and cheese, and perform the other tasks of farmers' wives.[17]

Largely through Vann's efforts, the national council voted that the Moravians could occupy a small plot of land if they opened a school with free room, board, and tuition within two years. Many Cherokees were suspicious of any white man who came to them asking for a piece of their land to farm. Had not Vann offered the Moravians his protection, and thus assumed responsibility for their good behavior, they probably would not not have been admitted to the nation; they were grateful to him. As Vann left the council in October, 1800, to conduct the missionaries to his town, he made a revealing self-deprecatory remark: "You may get offended in what you see in me," he said, referring to his habitual carousing and profane way of life.[18]

---

[17]For the history of the Moravian mission in the Cherokee Nation, see Schwarze, *Moravians*, and the Moravian Archives in Winston-Salem, North Carolina.

[18]This remark was noted in the journal kept by Thomas de Schweinitz and Abraham Steiner of their journey to the Cherokee Nation in September-November 1800; the original is at MAS. A translation is also in Mauleshagen, unpaginated.

When they reached Vannsville, he assisted the missionaries in purchasing some old buildings and cleared land from Robert Brown about
two and one-half miles south of his home at a spot they called Spring
Place. For a time before Brown moved, the missionaries lived with
Vann. Then in July, 1801, they moved into Brown's old cabin; they re-
paired it and began to build other cabins for their farm and mission.
This proved a long and arduous task. These German pietists built solidly
and carefully. Vann was very helpful to them. He sent his slaves to assist
in raising their barn, clearing their fields, planting and hoeing, erecting
their stable. Later the missionaries paid Vann's slaves fifty cents a day
(on Sundays, their free day) to split rails for them. Vann loaned them two
milk cows and later purchased a slave woman for them in Augusta for
$350 to help with the cooking, washing, and housework. The diaries,
letters, and mission journals of the Moravians provide an intimate account of their awkward relationship with Vann over the next eight
years.[19]

The Moravians never knew quite what to make of him. They found
him kind and generous in his formal dealings with them. He would allow
no one to mock or disturb them. He attended some of their early religious services with his family and, because the Moravians never learned
to speak Cherokee, he served as interpreter of their sermons when he was
present (which was not often). He regularly brought back supplies for
them on his trips to Augusta and Charleston and gave them credit to buy
whatever they needed at his store. When passing Indians stole things
from the mission, Vann made every effort—as headman of the area—to
apprehend the thieves and return the stolen goods. When the Cherokee
council became angry with the missionaries in 1803 and ordered them
to leave the nation because they had not yet opened their boarding
school, Vann withstood heavy criticism for asking that the missionaries
be given more time.[20] When their school opened, he sent his children
Mary and Joseph, and his nephew George to attend it.

Vann had no interest in learning about Christianity and bluntly told
the missionaries that he did not believe their biblical stories. Once, when
he was very ill, the missionaries came to his sickroom to beg him to seek

---

[19]See MAS correspondence of the missionaries and also the journal kept at the Spring
Place Mission for the years 1801-1809. MAS.

[20]See W. S. Lovely to R. J. Meigs, 13 June 1803, BIA, M-208.

Christ before he died. Vann told them "he did not believe there was a Jesus Christ." When the missionaries persisted in saying he would go to hell for his sinful ways, Vann "jumped from his bed, seized a bottle and drank as much as he could in one gulp and said in anger,that it was [his] house and he could drink as much as he pleased, dance, fornicate and what not and that it was none of our business."[21] The shocked missionaries hurriedly departed.

Not only were the missionaries shocked at his violent behavior when drunk and his frequent abuse of his wife, employees, and white visitors, but they were horrified when he lured their male students (aged ten to twelve) to his home, encouraged them to indulge in pagan Ball Play (a form of lacrosse) and gave them so much brandy that they all returned intoxicated and were sick for days afterwards.[22] Frequently they lamented to their mission board in Salem that they should never have located in that area of constant savagery and debauchery. In the end, the Moravians established a polite but distant relationship with Vann, thankful for his assistance but fearful of his unpredictable temper. Eventually they found themselves caught up in his rebellion against federal policies toward the Cherokees and were told that by occasionally helping Vann to write letters to President Jefferson and others attacking the federal agent, they themselves were implicated in his antigovernment activities. He was a dangerous man to know even distantly.[23]

As a headman in his town, Vann did his best to help those of his people who ran afoul of the white man's law. In 1803, for example, the records of the federal agency show that Vann made prodigious efforts to assist a Cherokee who was arrested by white law officers for stealing a horse and carried off to jail in Georgia. Vann urged the agent to obtain a lawyer for the Cherokee because by Georgia law no Indian was allowed to testify in court, even in his own defense.[24]

---

[21]Mauleshagen, 45 (6 June and 20 June 1805).

[22]John Gambold to Reichel, 20 July 1808, MAS, and Mauleshagen, 71 (30 April 1808).

[23]Fries, 7:3092. John Gambold to Benzien, 9 April 1809, MAS.

[24]James Vann to R. J. Meigs, 29 December 1801, and 5 February 1802; R. J. Meigs to Henry Dearborn, 2 April 1802, BIA, M-208.

At the same time that he was helping the Moravians to establish their mission, Vann became increasingly involved in the government's effort to obtain a right-of-way to build a federal turnpike through the Cherokee Nation in order to connect Athens, Georgia, and Nashville, Tennessee. Closely related to these negotiations was Vann's effort to make the government remove a group of white intruders who had settled (they said, inadvertently) within the boundaries of the Cherokee Nation. They were building cabins and starting farms as though they owned the land and intended to remain permanently on it. Vann proved to be one of the most active supporters of the effort to build the Georgia turnpike, for it would be of great help to his trading activities. But he also proved to be vehement in his demands that the government remove the white intruders from the Cherokee land. In the interest of efficiency, President Jefferson and Secretary of War Dearborn instructed the negotiators whom they sent in 1801 to try to settle both these problems at once.

The government's way of settling the intruder problem was to ask the Cherokees to sell the land on which the squatters were illegally living. The Cherokee council responded by saying that it would not enter into any discussions about a federal turnpike until the government first removed the squatters. Because these squatters were in Vann's area of the nation (between Currahee Mountain and the Oconee River), he led the fight for their eviction. So strong were the objections to selling any land to these whites that Jefferson was finally obliged to tell his negotiators to drop the matter and concentrate upon obtaining the right-of-way for the turnpike. Jefferson considered the road of major importance both to link Georgia to the frontier and to provide an effective military route to the Mississippi Valley in case of war with the British, French, or Spanish. Vann's decision to help the government to obtain the right-of-way may in part have been motivated by his expectancy that in return, the government would oblige the Cherokees by removing the squatters. His efforts proved invaluable in the prolonged negotiations about the road from 1801 to 1803.[25] The federal agent to the Cherokees, Colonel Return J. Meigs, told Dearborn that Vann was becoming one of the most influential leaders in the "progressive" or "forward-looking" wing of the na-

---

[25]The long controversy over the Georgia Road and Wafford's intruders is told in great detail in the files of the BIA, M-208. It is also summarized in Charles C. Royce, *The Cherokee Nation of Indians* (Chicago: Aldine Publishing Co., 1975) 55-61.

tion. Dearborn replied that "if Van and one or two others could be induced to encourage and advocate the measure [of a right-of-way], there would be very little difficulty in obtaining a general consent. Perhaps it may be proper to offer an inducement to Van."[26] "Inducement" was the government's fancy name for a bribe.

The Lower Town chiefs, led by Little Turkey and Doublehead, were at first reluctant to allow the road, but by 1802 they had decided to accept various "inducements" that Dearborn offered to curry their support. However, the great mass of Cherokees could not be persuaded to accept the proposal. Because the Cherokee council did not like to act until a general consensus of chiefs and warriors was reached, Jefferson had to wait three years until the "forward-looking" leaders could persuade the Cherokee people to grant the right-of-way. When it was finally granted, in October 1803, Meigs wrote to Dearborn, "Mr. Vann has done much in bringing the minds of the Indians to the measure of agreeing to the opening of the road, and yet they do not know it, and he wishes it to remain so."[27] Vann was duly rewarded by having the road surveyed so as to pass directly through his town near his trading post and tavern. He also obtained certain ferry rights where the road crossed unbridgeable rivers, and he even received part of the franchise for providing horses, forage, food, and lodging for the federal mail service along the turnpike. With the profits that accrued to him after this, he commenced building his great brick mansion—the showplace of the Cherokee Nation. He also built the first gristmill in the region and started a distillery so that he would no longer be dependent upon whites for whiskey. For all these endeavors he hired white artisans and with his white slave overseer, white storekeeper, white carpenters, white millwright, white blacksmith, and white business partners, he was a major source of employment for nearby whites.

To Vann's great annoyance, however, he discovered that while the government was willing to reward him when he worked to advance its goals, it was not willing to oblige him when he opposed its wishes. For example, the War Department was not willing to remove the squatters who had crossed over the Cherokee border with Georgia. No sooner did

---

[26]Henry Dearborn to R. J. Meigs, 30 May 1803, BIA, M-208.

[27]R. J. Meigs to Henry Dearborn, 25 October 1803, BIA, M-208.

Jefferson obtain the right-of-way for the turnpike than he sent negotiators to obtain a land cession for these squatters. This squatter problem arose because the government had delayed so long in surveying the border established by the Cherokee treaty of 1785, that by the time it was completely marked, over one hundred families, led by Colonel James Wafford, were settled on farms inside the line. Governor Josiah Tatnall of Georgia pleaded with Jefferson to allow these citizens to remain on their farms. The Cherokees, he believed, had more than enough land for their own people.[28]

Despite the fact that by treaty the government had obliged itself to remove all white intruders into the Cherokee Nation (or to allow the Cherokees to remove them), Jefferson preferred to oblige the voters of Georgia. Vann was furious, but in the end, the chiefs gave in and sold what was then known as "Wafford's Tract" for $5,000 in October 1804. Vann had fought bitterly against the cession, and so influential was he that Dearborn again urged Meigs to offer any reasonable inducement to him to change his mind. He had given $3,000 to the chief negotiator, General Daniel Smith, Dearborn said, and told him "to use any means he may possess to induce Van [*sic*] to favor the views of Government; if by two or three hundred dollars in Money or goods, Van can be induced to use his influence in favor of the cession," the government would gladly pay it, as it was paying other chiefs for their help. Meigs replied that to Vann such a paltry sum would be laughable. Vann "is so independent of mind and circumstances that the ordinary motives for some persons would not succeed with him."[29] The only kind of inducement that might influence Vann, Meigs said, would be some form of government honor and respect, but this was not forthcoming.

After the treaty was concluded, Vann became suspicious that the white men who had been selected to survey the boundaries of Wafford's Tract would not run it fairly. He therefore saw to it that he and his friend, Chief Kattahee, should serve as the guides to the surveyors to point out the correct lines. Dearborn had appointed General Buckner Harris of Georgia to head the survey, and Harris deliberately misconstrued the

---

[28]For Governor Josiah Tatnall's request to Jefferson, see BIA, M-208, 20 July 1802. For the survey of the Cherokee-Georgia border, see Royce, *The Cherokee Nation*, 55-61.

[29]Henry Dearborn to R. J. Meigs, 23 April 1804, BIA, M-15, and R. J. Meigs to Henry Dearborn, 28 June 1804, BIA, M-208.

wording of the treaty in order to try to include a much larger area for the cession than the Cherokee council had approved. Vann told him that he would not allow this and blocked the completion of the survey. Harris accused Vann and Katahee of malicious interference in official government business. In the end, the matter was compromised through the efforts of Captain James Blair of Georgia, a friend and sometime partner of Vann. But Harris thereafter carried on a bitter vendetta against Vann and did his best to turn the government against him.[30]

In 1804 Vann turned his attention to another problem—the establishment of an efficient Cherokee police force. (Perhaps violence-prone men are often sticklers for law and order because they feel their own need for limits.) The Cherokees were at this time in the midst of a very difficult transition from a hunting to a farming economy. Most of them wished to continue to be hunters, a profession they knew, and performed well. But since 1794 they had obtained fewer and fewer pelts and hides each season from their old hunting grounds in central Tennessee and northern Alabama (north of the Tennessee River). Unable to support their families by hunting, most were forced to turn to farming, accepting the plows, hoes, axes, and other government assistance proferred by the federal agent as part of the government's "civilization program." However, few Cherokees were competent to farm in the white man's way. Moreover, in order to adopt this new vocation, they had to overcome a long tradition, which held that farming was women's work; war, hunting, ballplays, and religious ceremonies were men's allotted sphere. The task of plowing and hoeing all day in the field was thus not only arduous and dull but embarrassing and demeaning to a Cherokee warrior and hunter. As a result, a growing number of men chose another alternative. They became cattle rustlers and horse thieves. This was a quicker and easier road to wealth, and it had the added attraction of being an exciting surrogate for war. Most of the stealing of livestock was done from whites on the Cherokee borders, but occasionally some thieves stole from wealthy Cherokees as well. Vann was a frequent victim of their work.

---

[30]Buckner Harris's correspondence about Vann is in BIA, M-208, 28 August 1805. See also James Blair to R. J. Meigs, 19 March 1805; James Vann to Meigs, 23 March 1805; R. J. Meigs to Henry Dearborn, 11 October 1808, BIA, M-208; and Buckner Harris to Meigs, 29 July 1808, OSW, M-221, roll 23, #7342. For Harris's attempt to distort the treaty line, see also Royce, *The Cherokee Nation*, 55-61. The trouble over intruders in this region continued long after the treaty of 1804.

By treaty, the council had to reimburse whites out of its own treasury for every stolen horse; and by 1804 the problem had become so acute that the council voted (over the objection of most of the Lower Town chiefs and many of the older chiefs) to permit the creation of lighthorse patrols (or mounted police) in order to check the crime wave. Vann was influential in obtaining the passage of this law. The lighthorse patrols were to be organized and directed by the local chiefs, not by the council itself. This allowed the Lower Towns and more conservative chiefs to ignore the law while those (like Vann) who were eager for it were allowed to institute it in their own localities.[31] Opposition to the establishment of the lighthorse patrol came in part because the Cherokees had traditionally operated without any coercive central authority and in part because they were traditionally opposed to corporal punishment. In the absence of courts and jails, the men of the lighthorse patrol became judges, juries, and executioners, much in the manner of white frontier posses or vigilantes. (Because of the law of clan revenge, there could be no death penalty for horse thieves or cattle rustlers, but severe whippings were permitted.) Vann and other "forward-looking" young chiefs accused the Lower Town chiefs of opposing the lighthorse because they were themselves sharing in the profits or winking at the actions of those warriors who were more resistant to acculturation. Vann wanted the Cherokees to become farmers and to learn to respect the rights of private property.

As with so many other aspects of his activities, Vann's practice in leading the lighthorse was extreme. He used his power to express his own inner anger. His pursuit of thieves was tenacious and his punishments vindictive. Thieves were often whipped 100 to 130 lashes with a stout stick, and when a thief refused to surrender quickly to such punishment, Vann did not hesitate to take him by violence.[32] This was dangerous business because if a thief were accidently killed, that death had to be avenged by members of his clan. Any member of the lighthorse could be held responsible, and probably the leader of the patrol would

---

[31]The lighthorse patrol had first been instituted in 1797 when the federal government had paid half of the cost for it, but after 1801 Jefferson's administration declined to continue the payments and the lighthorse ceased to function again until 1804. W. S. Lovely to Upper Town chiefs, June [no date], 1804, BIA, M-208.

[32]R. J. Meigs to Henry Dearborn, 25 July 1804, BIA, M-208. Mauleshagen, 27; Schwarze, *Moravians*, 81.

be the logical choice for revenge. Vann therefore spoke of his patrol activities as being taken at the risk of his life. The work certainly won him few friends. He once explained to Colonel Meigs that while he (Vann) was trying to show the white man that Cherokees were law-abiding, the government was allowing the whites on their borders to go unpunished in their lawlessness. In a conversation with Vann in July 1804, Meigs reported that Vann had said "with some degree of warmth, that instead of the Intruders on their lands in the Georgia Frontier going off, the number was increasing, while at the same time, he was, at the risque of his safety, punishing the Cherokees for Stealing Horses and other bad conduct towards the white people."[33] If whites were to go unpunished for stealing Cherokee land, why should Cherokee chiefs punish their people for stealing white men's horses?

Just how vindictive Vann could be when he believed people took advantage of him was revealed in the late summer of 1805 when he was robbed of $3,500, which he kept in a chest under his bed. He was away when the robbery occurred. When he returned, he tortured a white woman who lived with him (but who was not married to him) and discovered that the thieves had been three of his own slaves. He then went out and captured them. By torturing them, he discovered that they had been put up to the theft by two white men (one a former slave overseer of Vann). These white men had given one slave a rifle to kill Vann and promised to help all three slaves escape to freedom if they succeeded. Vann took out his vengeance on the three slaves by burning one alive, shooting another, and hanging the third in order to strike terror into the rest of his slaves. Then he went out and caught the two white men. They too were tortured until they agreed to sign a written confession of their actions.[34] When they had done this, a council of the Upper Town chiefs was called and they voted to support Vann's request for the death penalty. Vann was just about to hang them when he received an order from

---

[33]R. J. Meigs to Henry Dearborn, 25 July 1804, BIA, M-208.

[34]There are many accounts of the theft from Vann and his punishment of the thieves. See Payne Papers, 2:45; Mauleshagen, 47-49 (13-26 September 1805); John Gambold to Benzien, 20 April 1806, MAS; R. J. Meigs to Henry Dearborn, 28 August 1805; and James Vann to R. J. Meigs, 27 September 1805, BIA, M-208. In an undated letter filed at the end of the agency correspondence for 1805, there is a letter from Mrs. Jacob Wohlfahrt to R. J. Meigs describing how Vann tortured the white girl who lived with him by hanging her first by her thumbs and then by her big toes.

Colonel Meigs saying that he must turn the two white men over to him to be tried for their crime in white courts. Vann reluctantly did so, but he told Meigs, "wee are all dissatisfied that wee shall not punish a white-man when he steals and makes Plotes with Negroes to Kill any man that has property in the nation."[35] Vann was convinced that no white jury would convict a white man for robbing an Indian, especially when no Indian would be allowed to testify against him.

But this did not end the matter. John Falling, son of a white farmer and an Indian, had married Vann's sister, Nancy, over Vann's strong objection. Falling disliked Vann because he believed Vann had cheated Nancy out of some slaves her father had given her. Some months after the theft from Vann, Falling confessed while drunk that although Vann had recovered most of the stolen $3,500, he (Falling) still had $800 of it. When this was reported to the Upper Town Council, the council demanded that Falling return the money. Falling then claimed he had said no such thing and did not have Vann's money. Perhaps to cover his own guilt, Falling challenged Vann to a duel in December 1805. Vann refused to accept the challenge at first, but Falling kept insisting and probably accused him of cowardice.[36]

Finally Vann agreed, and the duel took place early in May 1806, in a wooded area near Vann's home. The two men (each with seconds) advanced toward each other on horseback with loaded rifles. Falling fired first; his shot went through Vann's sleeve without wounding him. Vann fired an instant later and his shot killed Falling instantly. Falling's brother-in-law, who was his second, then threatened to shoot Vann himself (perhaps on the basis of clan revenge), but when Vann faced him, he lost his nerve and fled. Nonetheless, Vann was certain that Falling's clan would appoint someone to avenge the death, if not upon him, then upon his beloved young son, Joseph. The next day he left for the Creek Nation. He was at this time about to open a trading store among the Creek at the town of Ocmulgee. The Moravians heard that he might live among

---

[35] James Vann to R. J. Meigs, 27 September 1805, BIA, M-208.

[36] There are various accounts of this duel, and they differ in details. See Payne Papers, 2:45 and John Gambold to Benzien, 20 April 1806, John Gambold to Reichel, 30 May 1806, John Gambold to Benzien, 28 June 1806, MAS; Mauleshagen, 53-56 (7 May 1806). According to one account, Falling's second fired at Vann after Falling fell, but he missed, and Vann simply rode off.

the Creeks. However, the whole matter was brought before the Upper Town Council in October 1806, and Vann's friends managed to get the council to declare that the duel had been Falling's fault. The council not only voted that Falling's clan had no right to exercise the law of blood revenge against Vann, but it also voted to raise Vann from the rank of local headman to senior counselor or chief.[37] When Vann heard this, he decided to continue to live in the Cherokee Nation, but he always felt that he was living on borrowed time. The tradition of clan revenge was not easily overruled, even by a vote of the council.

Vann was promoted to the rank of a senior chief because of the important part he had played in the treaty negotiations of 1805 and 1806. These treaties were initiated by the federal government at the request of the state of Tennessee.[38] Their purpose was to persuade the Cherokees to sell their old hunting ground (ten million acres of woodland north of the Tennessee River), most of which was in Tennessee. The government argued that the hunting was no longer profitable there and that most Cherokees should be turning to agriculture for their livelihood. Furthermore, the hunting ground was uninhabited and the money the government would pay for the land would provide a major source of capital for further Cherokee acculturation. It could be used to buy plows, to build mills, to purchase cotton gins, to subsidize schools for their children and otherwise advance their progress toward civilization. (Once fully civilized, government policy called for their "incorporation" or assimilation as individual citizens of the United States and detribalization.)

Because Meigs had always insisted that the Lower Town chiefs were the true chiefs of the nation, he dealt primarily with them in making arrangements for this large cession. The cession was complicated, however, by the fact that the Chickasaw Nation, which bordered the Cherokees to the west, claimed that part of the hunting ground—west of Muscle Shoals—belonged to them. Vann had no objection to the sale of the hunting ground, but he was determined that the Chickasaws should not profit by selling land that he and the other chiefs firmly believed be-

---

[37]John Gambold to Benzien, 20 April 1806; John Gambold to Reichel, 30 May 1806; John Gambold to Benzien, 28 June 1806; John Gambold to Benzien, 7 December 1806, MAS.

[38]These treaties are described in Royce, *The Cherokee Nation*, 61-69.

longed to the Cherokees. Meigs told Dearborn in May 1805, Vann "has no objection" to the cession and "Vann's influence is more than all the rest of the Chiefs, and yet he never comes openly forward, his life is in danger perhaps."[39]

However, many Cherokees were not willing to give up their hunting ground. Even though they knew it could never again yield enough pelts to support the nation solely by the fur trade, still there were enough bear, deer, beaver, mink, and raccoons to help a poor man make a little extra money during the winter months when he could not farm. The chiefs who favored the sale had to work hard to convince the ordinary Cherokees that more could be done for national survival by the money to be obtained from the sale than by hanging on to the hunting ground, risking the anger of the federal government, and facing the inevitable intrusion of white squatters into the area whom the government would never remove.

Vann worked with Meigs and the Lower Town chiefs to bring about the sale, and he traveled to the Chickasaw Nation to try to resolve the problem of ownership of the southwestern portion of that area. He was angry that the Chickasaws were determined not to yield their claim, and refused to make any compromise.[40] In order to solve the dilemma regarding this conflicting claim, the Cherokee chiefs decided to sell the hunting ground in two large parcels rather than in one piece. They told Meigs it would be necessary for a delegation of chiefs to go to Washington to discuss with President Jefferson the superior claim of the Cherokees to the southwestern portion.

The upper part of the hunting ground, consisting of 5.4 million acres, was ceded by a treaty in October 1805. Unknown to Vann and most of the Upper Town chiefs, this treaty included a secret clause granting a large tract of land in the hunting ground to Doublehead and his friends.

In December 1805, the national council appointed a delegation of sixteen chiefs to go to Washington to discuss the sale of the other 4.2 mil-

---

[39]R. J. Meigs to Dearborn, 21 May 1805, BIA, M-208.

[40]Meigs's correspondence to Dearborn on this is in BIA, M-208 for 21 May 1805, 27 July 1805, 4 August 1805, and 22 September 1805.

lion acres (including the part claimed by the Chickasaws).[41] Doublehead and Vann were both members of this delegation. During the course of the discussions in Washington, Vann and other chiefs learned for the first time about the secret clause in the treaty of 1805 granting Doublehead and his friends a tract three miles square, which they were to be allowed to sell to whites as a land speculation and pocket the profits. Furthermore, as the negotiations for the second part of the hunting ground proceeded, Doublehead persuaded Dearborn to grant him and his friends another tract, this one of 100 square miles north of Muscle Shoals. This tract was to become their private territory under no control by the tribe. Doublehead planned to lease some of it to whites and use the rest for farms for himself and his friends. He justified these grants (and several smaller tracts or "reserves" to various other friends of his in the Lower Towns) on the grounds that they were located on land being ceded to the whites in the treaties. It did not hurt the Cherokee Nation, he argued, if some of that ceded area north of the Tennessee River went to their own chiefs for profit. Colonel Meigs justified the grants on the grounds that Doublehead was instrumental in persuading the Cherokee rank and file to accept the cession and that the 100-mile area, under Doublehead's leadership, would become a model community of Indian acculturation.[42]

Vann and most of the Upper Town chiefs were astonished and shocked by these private grants to Cherokee citizens. They believed that any land not sold to the whites belonged to the tribe and could not be given by the government to individual Cherokees either for their own speculative purposes or for model communities. They saw the reserves simply as bribes to enrich influential chiefs at tribal expense. One night during their stay in Washington, Vann walked into Doublehead's hotel room and flatly accused him of being a traitor to the nation. Doublehead drew a knife and Vann drew his, but before they could attack each other, the other chiefs pulled them apart and calmed them down.[43] Doublehead

---

[41]These sales did not include all of the hunting ground. Doublehead kept back 1.5 million acres, which he tried to sell later. See below.

[42]For these private reserves, see Royce, *The Cherokee Nation*, 64-65; and for Meigs's correspondence with the Cherokee Council, see BIA, M-208, 2 April 1806. See also R. J. Meigs to Doublehead, 7 February 1807, BIA, M-208.

[43]Payne Papers, 2:26-27; Wilkins, *Cherokee Tragedy*, 36.

believed that he was just as disinterested and patriotic a chief as Vann, but henceforth the two men became bitter enemies. When they quarreled, the nation, already divided, began to edge toward civil war. In the course of the next twelve months; Vann became the head of what Meigs called "the rebellious faction" of the Cherokee Nation.

The treaty was concluded on 8 January 1806. President Jefferson made a speech lauding Doublehead's far-sighted leadership and made him a personal gift of $1,000 from the government; he also included in the treaty the gifts of a gristmill and cotton gin to be erected among Doublehead's people.[44] Vann and his friends had not been able to prevent Doublehead and his cohorts from obtaining their private reserves, including the 100 square miles north of Muscle Shoals known thereafter as "Doublehead's Tract." Perhaps to solace Vann, the delegates voted that out of $10,000 the Cherokee Nation received for this sale, $8,000 should be used to pay off the debts that various Cherokees owed to traders in the nation. (The other $2,000 went to pay bills of the delegation in Washington.)[45] Since Vann was one of the principal traders and many owed him a great deal, he undoubtedly received a large part of this $8,000. But in his eyes, this was a just payment of honest debts and would relieve the burden upon those Cherokee farmers to whom he had extended credit to assist them toward a new way of life. He refused to accept any reserves of land, however, for he considered these unjustifiable expropriations of land belonging to the tribe.

Throughout the year 1806 controversies raged throughout the nation over the sale of the last of their hunting ground. Many Cherokees were upset that their chiefs would do such a thing, especially that they would do so in Washington, far away from the eyes of the people at large. Others were shocked at the secret clauses granting reserves to Doublehead and his friends. Many objected to the use of $8,000 from the second sale to pay off the trading debts of individuals rather than having that sum deposited in the treasury for the benefit of the whole nation. At least six

---

[44]Thomas Jefferson to Cherokee Delegation, 10 January 1806; Henry Dearborn to R. J. Meigs, 8 January 1806; Henry Dearborn to R. J. Meigs, 7 January 1806, BIA, M-15.

[45]Cherokee Delegation to R. J. Meigs, 4 January 1806, BIA, M-208. Also under the terms of this treaty, Black Fox, the principal chief, was to receive an annual stipend of $100 for life. Royce, *The Cherokee Nation*, 66.

different councils were held in different parts of the nation that year to debate these matters, and from them gradually emerged two distinct factions: one led by Doublehead and his friends, the other led by Vann and his friends.[46] Roughly the two factions represented the old split between the Upper and Lower Towns. However, some chiefs and warriors in the Lower Towns were becoming disillusioned with Doublehead's leadership and sympathized with Vann's effort to dislodge him from power.

The rivalry between Vann and Doublehead is not easy to explain. Both were wealthy traders and both had learned how to manipulate the federal Indian policy to their own advantage. Moreover, both were convinced that it was in the best interest of the Cherokee people to become farmers and accept the white man's way of life. Neither had any interest in Christianity nor any particular commitment to the religious traditions of the Cherokee. They did not respectively lead pagans against Christians, acculturationists against traditionalists, full bloods against mixed bloods, rich against poor. Return J. Meigs considered Doublehead and Vann to be the most important figures in the nation and did his best to court the cooperation of both. Doublehead's trading interests were the same as Vann's except that Doublehead traded with the whites and Indians to the west of the nation and Vann traded with those to the east. Doublehead owned a keelboat (perhaps two or three), which he took down the Mississippi to New Orleans loaded with hides, cotton, livestock, corn, and salt pork. There he bought trade goods, which he took up the Arkansas River to sell to what he called "the wild Indians" west of the Mississippi.[47] The two men had their own spheres of interest and were not in conflict on that score. Both were shrewd, strong-willed, self-reliant, and fearless; both drank too much and could be cruel and vindictive. Doublehead so abused his pregnant wife that she died from his beatings. She was a sister of Vann's wife and that caused hard-feeling between them.

The heart of their rivalry, though, appears to have come from the ambition of each to be the dominant force in the nation coupled with their differences over the best policies for their nation. Both were eager for the

---

[46]The various councils and their resolves are cited in the files of BIA, M-208 throughout this year.

[47]See Malone, *Cherokees of the Old South*, 145.

respect and friendship of government officials. Vann suffered from being a younger chief and hailing from the weaker of the two tribal regions, politically speaking. On the other hand, the Lower Towns were, on the whole, less acculturated and less interested (apart from Doublehead's circle) in acculturation. Lower Town warriors often crossed the Mississippi in the hunting season and continued to bring back good catches for the fur trade. Meigs may have been right in saying that Vann was simply "envious" of Doublehead. Still, it seems just as likely that Vann was quicker to realize how Meigs was manipulating the nation. He certainly saw more clearly than Doublehead that the nation was rapidly losing its power to compel the United States to live up to its treaty obligations (particularly in terms of removing intruders). He also seems to have realized the importance of achieving tribal unity so that the government could not continue to play off one faction or region against another in order to obtain land. After 1806 Vann steadily worked to achieve tribal unity in order to strengthen its resistance to federal efforts to obtain more of the Cherokee land. Doublehead remained oblivious to this question, continued to offer more land for sale, and readily cooperated with all of Meigs's plans. Vann's change of perspective in Washington led him to consider Doublehead's leadership a grave threat to Cherokee national interests.

At one of the councils in 1806, when Doublehead was too ill to attend, the faction led by Vann actually gained temporary control. It passed a series of resolves attacking a whole variety of actions taken by Doublehead and the Lower Towns. It also passed a resolution that henceforth no treaty would be binding unless it was ratified by a full national council; this would prevent small delegations, hand-picked by Meigs or Doublehead, from negotiating treaties in the name of the whole nation. The council, held at Willstown in September 1806, also appointed a small committee of chiefs (mostly Vann's friends), which was delegated as the group to whom the federal agent should pay the tribal annuity from the federal government.[48] The chiefs who controlled the annuity would clearly run the nation.

The actions of this council were repudiated by Black Fox (who had become principal chief after Little Turkey's death in 1801). Doublehead and other Lower Town chiefs also wrote to Meigs telling him to ignore

---

[48]Resolves of the Willstown Council, 19 September 1806, BIA, M-208.

the actions of this council. Meigs agreed to do so. Vann had not been present at Willstown, but his influence had been felt. "Mr. Van [*sic*] and Mr. Macdannal . . . were not there but they give their orders to thies men" wrote Doublehead's friend, John Lowery, to Meigs.[49]

In June 1807, Doublehead and his friends began negotiating with Meigs for the sale of another tract of 1.5 million acres of tribal land north of the Tennessee River.[50] Doublehead insisted that all the money from this cession should go to the Lower Towns. He also told Meigs that he should get rid of one of his official interpreters, Charles Hicks, because Hicks had now joined Vann's faction and acted as its spy in the government agency. Meigs did fire Hicks, who became one of Vann's most important allies.[51] A month later, Vann called a secret meeting of the leaders of his faction. Among those present were John Rogers, The Ridge, Charles Hicks, George and Alexander Sanders. These men agreed that Doublehead had lost the confidence of the nation, that he had betrayed the Cherokee people, and that because Meigs could never be convinced to stop making private arrangements through him, the only course for those who did represent the popular will was to execute Doublehead for treason. Four men were chosen to undertake this: James Vann, The Ridge, Alexander Sanders, and John Rogers. They planned to execute Doublehead at the great ballplay at Tellico in August. On their way to that rendezvous, Vann became ill and was excused from the undertaking.[52] The other chiefs carried out their bloody deed on 8 August, to the utter consternation of the federal agent and the War Department. The leading members of Doublehead's faction feared that they too might

---

[49]John Lowery to R. J. Meigs, 23 October 1806, BIA, M-208. See also Doublehead and Black Fox's criticisms of the Willstown Council—Doublehead to R. J. Meigs, 3 October 1806, and Black Fox to R. J. Meigs, 23 October 1806, BIA, M-208.

[50]R. J. Meigs to Henry Dearborn, 1 May 1807, BIA, M-208; R. J. Meigs to Henry Dearborn, 20 June 1807, OSW, M-221, roll 10, #3134.

[51]Doublehead to R. J. Meigs, cited in Henry Dearborn to R. J. Meigs, 20 June 1807, OSW, M-221, roll 10, #3134.

[52]There are many versions of the execution/assassination of Doublehead. See Wilkins, *Cherokee Tragedy*, 36-38; Payne Papers, 2:28; J. P. Brown, *Old Frontiers* (Kingsport TN: Southern Publishers, 1938) 451-53; R. J. Meigs to Henry Dearborn, 30 August 1807, OSW, M-221, roll 10, #3137; A. B. Armistead to R. J. Meigs, 9 August 1807; Sam C. Hall to A. B. Armistead, 12 August 1807; and Joseph Phillips to R. J. Meigs, 15 August 1807, BIA, M-208.

be slated for execution. It was said that the assassins had also planned to murder Doublehead's close associate and business partner, a white man named John D. Chisholm, but Chisholm was not at the ballplay.[53] Meigs told Dearborn in his report of the murder, "It is supposed that Vann is at the head of all these discords."[54]

As most historians have pointed out, the fact that no vengeance was ever taken by any of Doublehead's relatives or friends against the assassins seems to indicate that the nation as a whole took Doublehead's death to be a quasi-official and justifiable execution and not a murder under the law of blood. Meigs, though outraged, was unable to do anything because it was strictly an internal matter for the council to resolve, and the council took no action. Nevertheless, Meigs refused to yield to such pressure. He continued to deal with Doublehead's friends (led by The Glass, Black Fox, Tolluntuskee, Toochelar, and Dick Justice) as though they still represented the majority will. He believed that Vann and his faction were a small group of insurgents ("no more than one in ten of the chiefs") who must somehow be put down if the Cherokees were to pursue peacefully the benevolent program of acculturation that the government thought best for them.

Vann and his friends were frustrated in this effort to assume control of Cherokee affairs. They became even more upset when, in December 1807, Meigs concluded a new treaty with a handful of chiefs from the Lower Towns. This treaty granted a tract of six miles square in the heart of the nation to Colonel Elias W. Earle, a trader and entrepreneur from Greenville, South Carolina. Earle wished to establish a foundry on the site of some iron-ore deposits he had found near the mouth of the Chickamauga River. Dearborn had supported this on the assumption that Earle's iron foundry would become a major arsenal for the manufacture of war materiel in the west. In fact, Earle appears to have been acting as an agent of the government; ostensibly the treaty ceded the land to the War Department, although all the rights and profits from the cession

---

[53]R. J. Meigs to Henry Dearborn, 15 August 1807, BIA, M-208.

[54]R. J. Meigs to Henry Dearborn, 30 August 1807, OSW, M-221, roll 10, #3197. The Presbyterian missionary to the Cherokees, the Reverend Gideon Blackburn, told Dearborn, "Doublehead entered more into the real interest of the Nation than any Indian in it, and it was because [of] his plans with the selfish designs of Van[n] and his party that he was murdered." (7 November 1807, OSW, M-221, roll 4, #1144).

and from the iron foundry were to accrue to Earle himself. Writing to Dearborn the day after the treaty was signed, Meigs said, "Col. Earle will inform you of the difficulty in obtaining the cession, . . . principally thro' the opposition of Vann. Yet he has the art to keep himself out of the way and put the unfortunate task of opposition on others." Meigs believed Vann had somehow threatened the lives of those who favored the cession: "This threatening the friends of good order is intolerable and requires some strong measures of an exemplary kind on the part of the United States to deter such hardy villains."[55]

Vann and his friends considered Earle's treaty the height of treason and believed that Meigs had grossly overstepped his bounds as federal agent in allowing twenty-three out of more than 100 chiefs to conclude it with no review at a full meeting of the national council. They drafted long letters to Jefferson and Vice-President George Clinton in January and February 1808 (which the Moravians copied out for Vann), explaining the illegality of this "sham treaty" and urging that the Senate (over which Clinton presided) refuse to ratify a treaty that only a handful of chiefs had signed. Jefferson realized the letter to be from "Van's [*sic*] party" and made no answer to it.[56]

Earle meanwhile hired one hundred workers and their families in South Carolina to move onto his tract and commence clearing the ground, planting crops, digging for ore, and building the refinery. Vann and his friends were determined to prevent this entourage from passing through their part of the nation—by force if necessary. Earle and his wagon train had to pass over the Georgia turnpike to get to Chicka-

---

[55]R. J. Meigs to Henry Dearborn, 3 December 1807, OSW, M-222, roll 2, #0883, and 30 December 1808, OSW, M-222, roll 3, #1313. Also for Earle's treaty, see Royce, *The Cherokee Nation*, 71-72, and R. J. Meigs to Henry Dearborn, 4 December 1807, OSW, M-221, roll 10, #3246; R. J. Meigs to Henry Dearborn, 4 April 1807, OSW, M-221, roll 10, #3108; R. J. Meigs to Henry Dearborn, 20 June 1807, OSW, roll 10, #3134; R. J. Meigs to Henry Dearborn, 4 December 1807, OSW, M-221, roll 10, #3246; R. J. Meigs to Henry Dearborn, 9 December 1807, OSW, M-221, roll 10, #3249.

[56]Pathkiller and Vann's letter to Jefferson can be found in a variety of sources (and they wrote more than one): 4 June 1808, OSW, M-222, roll 3, #1343. Charles Hicks et al. to George Clinton, 24 January 1808, OSW, M-222, roll 3, #1152; Cherokee Chiefs to George Clinton, 18 February 1808, OSW, M-222, roll 3, #1154. See also John Gambold to Benzien, 30 January 1808, and John Gambold to Benzien, 17 October 1808, MAS. Jefferson passed this letter of Vann on to Congress, where it was read in the Senate, 15 February 1808.

mauga. The chiefs of the Upper Towns sent a message to Earle in Tou-galoo, South Carolina, where his workers were meeting in January 1808, prior to their departure. The message, signed by Chulioa and Sour Mush, told them that the treaty was unacceptable to the Upper Town chiefs and the Upper Town Cherokees had resolved not to allow Earle to pass through their region to begin the foundry.[57] The Upper Town chiefs believed they could persuade the United States Senate not to ratify the treaty. Earle scoffed at this message, but many of his employees were frightened and refused to enter the Cherokee Nation without an army es-cort. Earle therefore sent forward a smaller contingent of several wagons containing his overseer, William Brown, along with some carpenters and slaves to demonstrate that the Cherokee threat was an empty bluff.

It was no bluff, however. William Brown and his wagons left Tou-galoo late in January and were two miles from the turnpike gate at the entry of the Cherokee Nation when they were met by a band of armed Cherokees, led by George Sanders and Will Crittenden (or Crittington). These Cherokees threatened Brown's people with guns and tomahawks and refused to let them pass. Brown stopped the wagons, and wrote a letter to Vann asking whether, as the most influential chief in that area, he supported this illegal action. While awaiting Vann's answer, Brown rode to the home of his sister, Nancy Falling (now Widow Falling): "She informed me," Brown later wrote in his affidavit on February 15, "that I and my whole party was in danger of Being Killed and that I had better return if possible, that James Vann, her brother, had plenty of armed In-dians waylaying the Federal Road and that it would be dangerous for us to fall into their hands." When Brown left her house, he was accosted by a band of Cherokees led by The Ridge, who took his gun while another Cherokee brandished a tomahawk in his face. Brown was told he could not proceed. He decided to take that advice, turned his wagons around, sold all of the equipment he had brought with him at the nearest trading post, and returned to South Carolina.[58]

---

[57]Chulioa et al. protest against Earle's treaty, [undated] 1808, OSW, M-221, roll 55, #9458; Elias Earle to Henry Dearborn, 31 October 1808, OSW, M-222.

[58]Kattahee to R. J. Meigs, 15 February 1808, BIA, M-208; Elias Earle to Henry Dearborn, 31 October 1808, OSW, roll 3, #1194; William Brown and Elias Earle to R. J. Meigs, 15 February 1808, BIA, M-208. Ironically, it turned out that the land ceded to Earle was not located in Georgia, as Meigs had thought, but in Tennessee. Tennessee refused to permit the grant, claiming that the area was under Revolutionary Bounty War-rants. Congress refused to ratify Earle's treaty until he located land within Georgia. See Royce, The Cherokee Nation, 71-72.

When Meigs learned of this, he was certain that "the party under the influence of Vann" (whom he now called "desperadoes") was plotting some kind of rebellion under the influence of the British; "it is not impossible," he wrote to Dearborn, "that some of these people may have been tampered with by the English. Vann and others trade at Charleston where it might be done with Security." By this time, Meigs had become convinced that there would never be any end to factionalism within the Cherokee Nation and that the whole plan of "civilizing" the Cherokees in their present location was impossible. He therefore suggested to Dearborn that the government try instead to persuade the Cherokees to emigrate to the west of the Mississippi where they could be given an equal amount of land in Arkansas Territory for the land they now had in the East. He asked for, and obtained, Dearborn's permission early in 1808 to begin negotiations for such a removal and exchange of land.[59] For this plan he found a ready ear among the Lower Town chiefs, who feared that their days as leaders of the nation were numbered.

Vann and his friends were, in fact, gaining influence daily. Not only had the tribe done nothing to avenge Doublehead's execution, it was delighted with Vann's boldness at stopping Earle's wagons and apparently agreed with him that the treaty with Earle was illegal. In fact, most probably agreed with the statement signed by forty-six chiefs and sent to Jefferson in January 1808 that claimed the treaty of 1806 was also illegal.[60] John Lowery, Doublehead's friend, thought that Vann had become a deluded fanatic; he suggested that Meigs arrest Vann because "he has turned boney part" and would soon embroil the nation in civil war.[61]

Vann seems to have become increasingly tense and nervous about his problems of leadership. Most of the planning and execution seems to have fallen upon him, and while he received staunch assistance from other chiefs like Charles Hicks, The Ridge, John Rogers, and Kattahee, they let him take the lead. As usual when he was under strain, he drank

---

[59]R. J. Meigs to Henry Dearborn, 9 February 1808; and R. J. Meigs to Henry Dearborn, 24 March 1808, BIA, M-208.

[60]Charles Hicks et al. to the United States Senate, 24 January 1808, OSW, M-222, roll 3, #1152; Cherokee Chiefs to George Clinton, 24 January 1808, OSW, M-222, roll 3, #1154.

[61]John Lowery to R. J. Meigs, 8 February 1808, BIA, M-208, and John Lowery to R. J. Meigs, 8 February 1808, OSW, M-222, roll 3, #1311.

too much and on two occasions in 1808 this led him to serious attacks upon white men. The first occurred in January 1808, when he shot and seriously wounded Leonard Rice of Georgia during a wild party at Diamond Hill. The second took place in April when he stabbed a Tennessee wagoner named Samuel Moore at his ferry on the Chattahoochee.[62] On the day after he shot Leonard Rice and when it appeared that Rice might die from the wound, Vann was overheard to say, "Damn me if I care, for if the young man dies, I must die for it, and if he does, I will mount my horses and kill all my enemies and then blow my brains out."[63] Rice did not die, nor did Moore. Vann not only provided all the funds for their medical care, he also paid them large sums in damages. In addition, he wisely obtained statements from them saying that because of these payments they would not prosecute him for assault.

In October 1808, one of Vann's chief lieutenants, Charles Hicks, engaged in an equally ill-advised action. He tried (unsuccessfully) to arrest Meigs's interpreter, a white man named Samuel Riley, to take him to a council investigation involving the ownership of a slave; when Riley refused to go with Hicks, Hicks threatened him with a butcher knife.[64] Riley believed that Hicks's real intent was to search his dispatch case in which, at the time, he was carrying secret messages from Meigs to Lower Town chiefs about the removal of the Cherokee Nation to Arkansas. But Hicks knew nothing about this. Meigs was now convinced that the Vann-Hicks-Rogers-Ridge faction was totally out of hand. He demanded that the Cherokee Council arrest Hicks and Vann and turn them over to him for prosecution in white courts. Hicks he would punish for stopping and threatening a government official—Riley—in the performance of his duty; Vann he would prosecute for his assaults upon Rice and Moore. Fearful that these arrests might stir the "insurgents" to open violence, Meigs wrote to Governor Sevier of Tennessee and told him to alert the militia. Sevier promised any aid necessary. When the council

---

[62]There are many papers relating to these two incidents in BIA, M-208 (for example, see 25 March 1808; 20 April 1808; 4 June 1808; 11 June 1808; 11 September 1808). See also Gambold to Benzien, 30 January 1808 (Rice was shot 15 January), MAS; Malone, *Cherokees of the Old South*, 60; Georgia Archives, 1:88-90, 94.

[63]Affidavit of Sheldon Thompson, 8 February 1808, OSW, M-22, roll 3, #1311, and R. J. Meigs to Henry Dearborn, 14 July 1808, OSW, M-221, roll 26, # 8667.

[64]Samuel Riley to R. J. Meigs, 3 September 1808; R. J. Meigs to Samuel Riley, 4 September 1808; and R. J. Meigs to Henry Dearborn, 30 September 1808, BIA, M-208.

refused to arrest Vann (the confusion over the Hicks matter had been cleared up), Meigs sent a squad from the United States army barracks to arrest him on 22 October.[65] Vann went peacefully to Nashville where he was arraigned, but within six days he was freed by the court because neither Moore nor Rice would prosecute charges against him.[66]

This did not stop Meigs, but rather encouraged him to speed up the plan for removal and exchange of the Cherokee land. He persuaded the Lower Town chiefs to accept the plan and in November 1808, he set off for Washington with a delegation of six chiefs—three from the Upper Towns, three from the Lower Towns. The three from the Upper Towns thought they were simply going to have a general discussion with Jefferson about their nation's problems. The three from the Lower Towns expected to work out with Jefferson a plan of removal and exchange. Shortly after the delegation had departed from the nation, James Vann and his friends discovered that Meigs planned to work out a treaty between the government and Lower Towns for their removal (in the hope that once the Lower Towns emigrated to Arkansas, the Upper Towns would be obliged to follow them). Vann hastily called a council at Hiwassee Town where most of those in attendance angrily repudiated the notion that half the nation could secede, giving its land to the government, without the consent of the other half. They voted to depose Black Fox as principal chief because he had secretly supported the plan. They installed Pathkiller (the second principal chief) in his place because he strongly opposed it. At Vann's suggestion, this council also deposed three other Lower Town chiefs who had worked with Meigs to advance the plan: John Chisholm, Tolluntuskee, and The Glass. Then the council appointed two delegates (picked by Vann) to mount fast horses and catch up with the six delegates who were still on the road to Washington. These two new delegates were instructed to reveal the removal plot of the Lower Town delegates and then to vote with the three Upper Town delegates to prevent any agreement for removal and exchange from taking place in Washington.[67]

---

[65]Affidavit of A. L. Campbell, 23 September 1808, BIA, M-208.

[66]R. J. Meigs to Henry Dearborn, 30 September, 30 October, and 28 October 1808, BIA, M-208.

[67]See W. G. McLoughlin, "Thomas Jefferson and the Rise of Cherokee Nationalism," *William and Mary Quarterly* 32 (October 1975): 547-80. This article discusses in detail the whole incident and the removal crisis that followed.

The two extra delegates caught up with Meigs in Alexandria, Virginia, but Meigs refused to accredit them. He said that the council that appointed them was not a legal council but merely a group of Vann's insurgents. He also refused to accept Pathkiller as their new principal chief. Nevertheless, these two extra delegates continued to Washington where they kept in close contact with the others. Through their efforts, Jefferson and Dearborn became fully aware of the sharp division in the nation over Meigs's removal plan. They therefore wisely refused to make an explicit agreement with the Lower Towns about this. However, Meigs persuaded Jefferson to make a statement to the delegates in January 1809, in which he said that if any Cherokees wanted to go across the Mississippi River to live, the government would provide them with land in Arkansas. Jefferson also said that any such decision should be based on an agreement in which the whole nation concurred. The Upper Towns took his words to mean that their approval would be necessary before the Lower Towns could effect a removal and exchange of any part of the nation. The Lower Towns, with the full encouragement of Meigs, chose to assume that Jefferson had encouraged them to emigrate to Arkansas and would assist them regardless of the wishes of the Upper Towns.

Throughout the year 1809 Meigs worked feverishly to encourage the Lower Town chiefs to emigrate, and a number of them agreed to do so; several town chiefs promised that with them all of the people in their towns would emigrate. Meigs wrote to Dearborn that he expected thousands to emigrate and that once the tide of emigration started, he was convinced it would only end with the removal of the whole tribe. His hopes exceeded reality: the nation as a whole recoiled at the idea of giving up its homeland and moving to Arkansas. Vann and his "rebellious party" had at last succeeded in awakening the Cherokee people to the dangerous position into which Doublehead and his friends had led them. Instead of the national exodus that Meigs expected, only about 1,100 Cherokees chose to emigrate. What was worse for Meigs, Jefferson's successor, James Madison, declined to support the removal project. The government instructed Meigs to desist from his efforts, and it failed to provide any grant of land in Arkansas in exchange for the land that the 1,100 emigrants had left behind in the East.

More important, the Cherokees faced this removal crisis with a groundswell of nationalist patriotism and unity. In September 1809, a national council met and voted to end forever the old division between the Upper and Lower Towns. Instead they inaugurated a new form of joint leadership under chiefs from both regions. Black Fox, moving with the tide, renounced the removal plan and was restored as principal chief while Pathkiller again became second principal chief. Vann's friends assumed the major role in the new leadership of the council and even many of those formerly in Doublehead's inner circle (such as The Glass and Toochelar) decided to remain and support the new patriotic coalition. Meigs was forced to admit the defeat of his proposal and to accept the new leadership that Vann had done so much to create. The Cherokees now embarked upon a new era of national revitalization that supported both acculturation and the maintenance of their national homeland, vowing never again to sell any of their land. The emigrants to Arkansas were repudiated as expatriates who had betrayed and deserted their people.

Vann did not live to see this successful conclusion to his efforts. He was murdered on 19 February 1809. He had already alienated many of those who had formerly supported him. His wild and irresponsible private behavior was harmful to his cause. Probably most of his friends felt that his death saved them from much future embarrassment.

Vann died in the midst of one of his more violent efforts to round up horse thieves. During the course of this tour with the lighthorse in February, he had caught and severely whipped several thieves and had even shot to death one who refused to surrender. The Moravians heard that the members of his patrol rebelled against his cruelty and against his opening them to the dangers of clan revenge.[68] Vann was said to have sarcastically ridiculed one of his oldest and most loyal friends in the patrol, Alexander Sanders, perhaps calling him a coward for not being willing to take the same risks Vann took. In any case, the patrol apparently decided to kill Vann before he got them into more trouble. They may have drawn straws for the deed or (as the Moravians thought) Sanders may have volunteered to do it. As Vann was raising a drink in Thomas Buffington's tavern to celebrate the day's activities, the door of the tavern

---

[68]There are many accounts of Vann's death. See John Gambold to Benzien, 23 February 1809, MAS; Fries, 7:3074; Payne Papers, 2:46; Wilkins, *Cherokee Tragedy*, 48; Springplace Diary, 21 February 1807, MAS; Mauleshagen, 77-78 (21 February 1809). While a law passed by the Council in September 1808 ostensibly freed the lighthorse from clan retaliation in any death that occurred in the line of duty, there was no certainty that the clans would always observe this, and there are many cases when they did not.

silently opened just a crack, a rifle barrel appeared in the opening, and a single shot killed him instantly. No one saw the killer, and he was never caught. The patrol dispersed the next morning and Buffington barely managed to persuade two of them to dig a shallow grave for Vann's body. Vann's eleven-year-old son, Joe, who was with him, fled the tavern with a trusted slave. Legend has it that someone wrote on a wooden slab erected at the gravesite:

> *Here lies the body of James Vann.*
> *He killed many a white man.*
> *At last by a rifle ball he fell,*
> *And devils dragged him off to hell.*[69]

Even after his death Vann continued to be a figure of controversy. In his will he left his loving but mistreated wife, Peggy, all his household furniture. But he left all his remaining possessions to his son, Joseph. The Council voted on 17 April 1809, to invalidate his will because it was contrary to a law passed in September 1808 requiring that a man's property be divided among all of his children and that a fair share should be given to his widow.[70] A year later his wife Peggy became the first convert to Christianity at the Moravian mission.[71]

James Vann had few mourners, and he has received a mixed judgment from historians. Nonetheless, he was a Cherokee patriot who risked much to defend his nation's rights.

---

[69]Quoted in Woodward, *The Cherokees*, 5.

[70]The will and the action of the Council nullifying it are published in de Baillou, 6-8. Nevertheless, Joseph Vann inherited most of his father's estate and he too became the richest man in the Cherokee Nation. He was known as "Rich Joe" Vann.

[71]Schwarze, *Moravian Missionaries*, 103; Mauleshagen, 86-87 (10-11 June 1810); John Gambold to Benzien, 15 August 1810, MAS.

THOMAS JEFFERSON
AND THE BEGINNING
OF CHEROKEE NATIONALISM,
1806-1809

The Cherokee removal crisis did not begin with the election of Andrew Jackson in 1828, but with the second administration of Thomas Jefferson. The Cherokees had twice fought off determined efforts by the federal government to move them across the Mississippi before Jackson took office. (The second time was under James Monroe in the years 1817-1819, although Jackson's hand was behind that.) In fact, it might be said that from the moment the Cherokees gave up warring against white Americans in 1794, their history became essentially an effort to resist removal.

In this first effort to resist removal, the Cherokees were forced to forge a new sense of what it meant to be a Cherokee. If they were not a people whose identity was attached to a specific homeland, which sustained them in all kinds of experiential, historical, and spiritual relationships, then they would live up to the white man's stereotype of the Indians as nomadic hunters who would follow the game to the West and leave their "worn out" hunting grounds to white farmers who knew how to make better use of it. "Wasteland" was the term that Jeffersonian administrators used when they told the Cherokees to sell their homeland because now that it had so few fur-bearing animals, it was of no use to them. By defining it as "wasteland," the War Department justified the ridiculously low price it was prepared to pay for that land—some of it the most valuable black cotton-belt soil in the South.

Thomas Jefferson's role in this first removal crisis was ambiguous. The notion of promoting removal and exchange of Cherokee land was initiated by the Cherokee agent, Colonel Return J. Meigs, because he was unable to resolve the many problems forced upon him in his unenviable job. The result of his effort was ironic, for in his attempt to persuade the Cherokees that they had nothing to gain by remaining in the East, he helped instead to persuade them that they had everything to lose by leaving. Contrary to his wishes, Meigs's removal effort led not to further fragmentation of the nation but to its first real sense of national unity. On the other hand, the sense of na-

tional identity that the Cherokees developed owed more to the European concept of nationality than to the Native Americans' concept of "a people." In this respect, the first removal crisis was a watershed in Cherokee acculturation and revitalization.

TO MANY GEORGIANS and other worried Southern frontiersmen, the thirteen thousand Cherokee people on their borders appeared by 1827 to have established an *imperium in imperio* of such internal strength and stability as to pose a threat that could be countered only by their forced removal. While ethnohistorians disagree about the nature and extent of nationalism, acculturation, and deculturation among the various Indian tribes of North America, they generally concur that in the early nineteenth century the Cherokees achieved the closest approximation to nationhood of any tribe east of the Mississippi.[1] One of the largest and wealthiest tribes, they adopted a written constitution in 1827 (modeled closely upon the United States Constitution), published a national newspaper in their own language (utilizing the unique Sequoyan syllabary), and developed such a sophisticated legislative, judicial, and educational system that their social order was more advanced than that of many of the rude white settlements around them. Many Americans in the North, particularly in New England, thought the Cherokee deserved serious consideration as a potential Indian state within the Union.

Most accounts date the beginning of Cherokee nationhood from 1817 when a law of the council established "a republic" with a "national bicameral legislature."[2] In important respects, though, the impulse to-

---

[1]See the excellent survey of ethnohistorical research on these issues, with particular reference to the Cherokees, by Robert F. Berkhofer, Jr., "The Political Context of a New Indian History," *Pacific Historical Review* 40 (1971): 357-82. Tribal nationalism, as discussed here, of course differs radically from pan-Indian nationalism. Important articles on acculturation and nationalism can be found in William N. Fenton and John Gulick, eds., *Symposium on Cherokee and Iroquois Culture*, U.S. Bureau of American Ethnology, Bulletin 180 (Washington DC, 1961); Edward H. Spicer, ed., *Perspectives in American Indian Culture Change* (Chicago, 1961); and Stuart Levine and Nancy Oestreich Lurie, eds., *The American Indian Today* (Deland FL, 1968).

[2]Henry Thompson Malone, *Cherokees of the Old South: A People in Transition* (Athens GA, 1956) 77-78. The basic histories of the Cherokees have been compiled by Charles C. Royce, "The Cherokee Nation of Indians: A Narrative of Their Official Relations with the Colonial and Federal Government," U.S. Bureau of American Ethnology, *Fifth Annual Report* (Washington DC, 1887) 121-378; and James Mooney, "Myths of the Cherokee," ibid., *Nineteenth Annual Report*, part 1 (Washington DC, 1900) 3-548.

ward Cherokee nationalism began much earlier. Administratively it started with the reunification of the tribe in 1794 under a national council with a principal and second principal chief. Institutionally significant was the development of the Cherokee mounted police. Supported in part by the American government from 1797 to 1801,[3] and reinstituted by the Upper Town area in 1804,[4] this police force achieved permanence by statute in 1808 with the establishment of the lighthorse guard paid for and supervised entirely by the national council.[5] Two years later a major cultural shift took place with the legal abolition of clan revenge for murder.[6] These Cherokee statutes of 1808 and 1810 not only created new administrative precedents for coercive central control over all Cherokees but also instituted new patterns of inheritance for widows and orphans.[7]

Still, laws and administrative institutions are not in themselves the basis of nationhood. Nationalism involves the manifest spirit and will of a people engaged in a concerted drive toward unity and self-government. The Cherokee people clearly displayed these nationalistic qualities during the removal crisis of 1817-1819, and their will to survive as an autonomous people produced the brilliant burst of political development that culminated in the constitution of 1827. This sense of national identity originated, however, at least as early as the first decade of the nineteenth century, during the first removal crisis of 1806-1809. It was in that crisis that the Cherokees first faced the real possibility of dissolution, schism, and separatism that forced a profound reassessment of their identity. The emergence of this cohesive and dynamic national spirit was marked by the creation of the national executive committee in 1809, uniting the dis-

---

[3]Report of a conference with a Cherokee delegation headed by The Glass in Washington DC, dated 30 June 1801, found in Letters Sent by the Secretary of War Relating to Indian Affairs, 1800-1824, M-15, roll 1:72, Records of the Bureau of Indian Affairs (RG 75), National Archives. Hereinafter cited as M-15.

[4]See W. S. Lovely, Address to the Cherokee Chiefs in Council, June [?] 1804, Records of the Cherokee Indian Agency in Tennessee, 1801-1835, M-208, roll 2, Records of the Bureau of Indian Affairs (RG 75), National Archives. Hereinafter cited as M-208. In this letter Lovely praises the Cherokee chiefs for their new "regulating laws."

[5]*The Constitution and Laws of the Cherokee Nation: Passed at Tahlequah, Cherokee Nation, 1839-51* (Tahlequah, Cherokee Nation, 1852) 3-4.

[6]Ibid., 4.

[7]For example, the law of 1810 clearly leaned toward a new patrilineal inheritance system.

parate factions and regions of the tribe, and by the declaration of the national council that any Cherokees who accepted President Thomas Jefferson's offer to emigrate west of the Mississippi would be considered expatriates—Cherokees without a country. The famous "bicameral law" of 1817 did little more than reaffirm and codify these earlier actions.[8]

A key feature of the rise of Cherokee nationalism was the redefinition of membership in "the Cherokee nation"—an old but ambiguous term related more to cultural identity and treaty-making powers than to any precise definition of residence or citizenship.[9] After 1809 membership in the Cherokee Nation, and the rights and privileges associated with it, required residence within the boundaries of the ancestral homeland in the Southeastern part of the United States. In effect, between 1806 and 1809 the Cherokees became consciously aware of the quintessential importance of a fatherland, with all the religious and emotional connotations of the phrase "love of country."[10] Not all of them welcomed this new definition of what it meant to be a "Cherokee," but given the political exi-

---

[8]Ibid., 4-5. In addition to specifying the duties and tenure of "the Standing Committee," this law reasserted, in the face of a new federal effort to force migration westward, that "the authority and claim of our common property [in the land, annuities, and so forth] shall cease with the person or persons who shall think proper to remove themselves without the limits of the Cherokee Nation."

[9]For the eighteenth-century phase of Cherokee nationhood, see Fred A. Gearing, "Priests and Warriors," *American Anthropological Association Memoir 93* (1962), and David H. Corkran, *The Cherokee Frontier: Conflict and Survival, 1740-62* (Norman OK, 1962). Unfortunately, the sources do not provide a precise, step-by-step account of changing Cherokee opinion between 1806 and 1809. There are letters from various Cherokee individuals and groups presenting their grievances or fears to the agent, to Jefferson, or to other officials; we have formal proclamations by councils; but we have virtually no correspondence by Cherokees speaking freely and frankly to each other. Most unfortunate of all, there are no written records of the debates in the several councils that slowly evolved into the new consensus. Nevertheless, the issues are plainly stated, and the actions of the Cherokees speak with sufficient clarity to substantiate the thesis educed here.

[10]Some suggestive articles on the relationship of acculturation to national identity are Edward H. Spicer, "Types of Contact and Processes of Change," in Spicer, *Perspectives*, 517-43; Fred A. Gearing, "The Rise of the Cherokee State as an Instance in a Class: The 'Mesopotamian' Career to Statehood," in Fenton and Gulick, *Symposium*, 125-34; Anthony F. C. Wallace, "Cultural Composition of the Handsome Lake Religion," ibid., 143-51; and John Witthoft, "Eastern Woodlands Community Typology and Acculturation," ibid., 69-76. See also D'Arcy McNickle, *The Indian Tribes of the United States: Ethnic and Cultural Survival* (London, 1962), and Anthony F. C. Wallace, *The Death and Rebirth of the Seneca* (New York, 1969).

gencies of their situation, the overwhelming majority acquiesced in it and were willing to accept the sacrifices necessary to sustain it.[11]

Underlying the legal, administrative, and political institutions of emerging Cherokee nationalism was a set of interlocking policies agreed upon after extensive formal and informal participatory debate. The most important of these consensual decisions were (1) the refusal to grant any further land cessions that might deplete the fatherland; (2) the rejection (by a preponderate majority) of Jefferson's option, first offered in 1808, of removal to the West; (3) the exclusion from membership in the Cherokee Nation of "stragglers" who did remove; (4) the union of all geographical regions of the tribe under one national council whose policies were to be carried out between council meetings by a national executive committee made up of representatives from all factions and regions; (5) the insistence that the federal government live up to its treaty guarantees of Cherokee borders against frontier and state intrusions; (6) the commitment to acculturation and deculturation at a rate slow enough to accommodate all groups while still permitting enforcement of national regulations for the good of the whole (such as the use of Cherokee lighthorse to punish horse thieves and the substitution of tribal or American judicial processes for clan revenge); (7) the rejection of Jefferson's offer—the alternative to removal—to integrate Cherokees into the surrounding American states as fee-simple farmer-citizens of the United States.

While the implementation of these and other decisions had yet to be worked out in detail, by 1809 most of the Cherokees had become convinced that the integrity, identity, and survival of their nation were integrally related not only to residence in the ancestral homeland but also to maintenance of communal ownership of that land and perpetuation of tribal self-government. These decisions remained unchanged until Andrew Jackson broke the supreme law of the land in 1832 and thereby de-

---

[11]Needless to say, the federal government did not accept this new definition of the Cherokee Nation nor did the national spirit prevent the voluntary withdrawal of individuals and groups from the East to join friends and relatives in the West. The problem of whether the Cherokees east and west constituted one or two nations was not solved until what was tantamount to a Cherokee civil war in the years 1839-1846. For the story of the earlier Cherokee migrations to the West in the 1780s and 1790s, see Mooney, "Myths," 99-101; for the story of the final resolution of the division, see Morris L. Wardell, *A Political History of the Cherokee Nation, 1838-1907* (Norman OK, 1938).

stroyed the assumptions upon which they rested. To the extent that
Cherokee nationalism required new legal and political procedures, it
constituted an acceleration of acculturation (or biculturalism) traceable
in the Cherokees' developing adoption of and adaptation to American
political and economic practices; but to the extent that it protected geographical integrity, participatory self-government, and the ethic of consensus, it also preserved basic aspects of Cherokee values, beliefs, and
practices.[12] In that sense the rise of Cherokee nationalism constitutes one
of the most important revitalization movements in nineteenth-century
Indian history.

In addition to the immediate removal or separatist crisis precipitated
by the options Jefferson offered to the quarreling Cherokee factions,
there were other less direct but equally important causes for the drastic
reassessment and restructuring that began at this time. Ever since their
final military defeat in 1794, the Cherokees had fallen into increasing
confusion and disunity. Factional division, plummeting morale, economic hardship, social dislocation, and cultural disorientation almost
overwhelmed them. Only the closely knit family structure and hospitality ethic seemed to keep them together. In 1806 the Cherokees inhabited
a territory of fifteen million acres (twenty thousand square miles) where
the states of North Carolina, Georgia, Alabama, and Tennessee adjoin.
The tribe had been divided into two regions, known as the Upper and
Lower Towns, since 1777 when a large group of young chiefs, led by
Dragging Canoe (Tsiyugunini), had refused to accept the peace treaty
and land cessions granted by the older chiefs to terminate Cherokee participation with the British in the Revolution. Withdrawing down the
Tennessee River Valley to the area between Chickamauga and Muscle
Shoals, these dissident warriors waged guerilla warfare with frontier
whites until 1794.[13] When the decimation of the Lower Towns finally

---

[12]For excellent studies of the harmony ethic and the noncoercive consensus governmental system of the Cherokees, see Gearing, "Priests and Warriors"; Gearing, "Rise of
the Cherokee State," in Fenton and Gulick, *Symposium*; and John Phillip Reid, *A Law
of Blood: The Primitive Law of the Cherokee Nation* (New York, 1970).

[13]Detailed accounts of the withdrawal of the Lower Town dissidents and their guerrilla warfare can be found in John P. Brown, *Old Frontiers: The Story of the Cherokee Indians from Earliest Times to the Date of Their Removal to the West, 1838* (Kingsport TN,
1938); John Haywood, *Civil and Political History of the State of Tennessee . . .* (Nashville
TN, 1821); and R. S. Cotterill, *The Southern Indians: The Story of the Civilized Tribes
before Removal* (Norman OK, 1954).

forced them to make peace, they returned to an uneasy alliance with the Upper Towns (themselves divided into an upper and lower division) and accepted the nominal leadership of Little Turkey (Gunadiga) as principal chief of the two sections. When Little Turkey died in 1802, he was succeeded as principal chief by his brother, Black Fox (Enolee, Inali). While general councils met for tribal business, each of the two regions continued to hold its own sectional council that asserted control over its area. In the general breakdown of traditional authority, the popularly chosen town chiefs asserted what little power there was locally. These internal divisions left the Cherokees highly vulnerable both to federal pressures for land and road concessions and to the lawless frontiersmen who surrounded them.

Internal confusion led to factionalism, government bribery, angry clashes over land cessions, and bitter quarrels over the distribution of government technical assistance, payments for land, and annuities.[14] Local government disintegrated as families moved out to distant farms to try to make an independent living. Frustrated and angry younger men, denied self-fulfillment through war or hunting, turned to horse stealing as a way of finding adventure and displaying courage. Tribal religion fell away, drunkenness increased, children and old people were ill cared for, and the old patterns of communal responsibility, ritual, and unity were severely disrupted as rival chiefs plotted to secure the rewards that the white agents and frontier commerce offered.[15] Some Cherokee chiefs and traders became rich, while the vast majority of the people often hovered on the border of starvation.

---

[14]Since 1792 government policy had included the regular distribution of plows, axes, hoes, looms, spinning wheels, and other implements of "husbandry and domestic manufacture" to the Cherokees as part of the government's "civilization" policy. In addition, the government provided gristmills, sawmills, and "cotton machines" as well as white blacksmiths and artisans to train the Cherokees in these skills. The federal agent naturally used this economic aid to gain the support of those local chiefs whom he found most pliant, cooperative, or, in his words, "well-disposed to government and to progress." See Francis P. Prucha, *American Indian Policy in the Formative Years* (Cambridge, 1962), and Bernard W. Sheehan, *Seeds of Extinction: Jeffersonian Philanthropy and the American Indian* (Chapel Hill NC, 1973).

[15]The taverns, mail stands, and ferries on federal highways were lucrative sources of revenue for which chiefs competed, usually in partnership with enterprising whites who then leased these concessions from the chiefs. Saltpeter caves were another lucrative internal franchise.

In this situation the old ethic of harmony was temporarily lost; the more aggressive and domineering chiefs strove to aid their own relatives, towns, and friends. Warrior chiefs, to whom the Cherokees in the past had granted authority only in time of war, now maintained leadership in time of peace because relations with the surrounding whites constituted a continual state of siege—a battle of wits, strength, and cunning in which neither tribal nor American law provided any real restraint.[16] Some chiefs not only refused to punish horse thieves from their towns but actually abetted them.[17] Individual retaliation for murder, especially when whites were involved, led to indiscriminate bloodshed and to vigilantism. As stated, the first important laws expressing the new spirit of revitalization sought to establish internal control over theft and violence by a national police force and national protection of property inheritance for widows and orphans. Assertion of coercive national authority was not simply a reaction to federal removal policies. Internal needs and external pressures came together in a crisis that only national unity could overcome.

The dominant figures in the Lower Town region between 1794 and 1809 were Doublehead, The Glass (Tauqueto), Tolluntuskee, Toochalee (Toochelar or The Flute), Dick Justice, John D. Chisholm, John Lowery, Turtle at Home, Skiuka, The Seed, The Gourd, Kategiskee, and John Riley. It should be noted that Black Fox, although ostensibly chief of all the Cherokees, tended to align himself with the Lower Town faction. As the nephew of Dragging Canoe, he was intimately associated with these towns in the guerilla warfare of 1781-1794, but he does not appear to have become as interested in acculturation as Doublehead and the other Lower Town chiefs. Belonging to an older generation, he

---

[16]See Gearing's very suggestive analysis of the personality types associated with the red and white Cherokee infrastructure in "Priests and Warriors." For a discussion of the complexities of Indian factionalism, see James A. Clifton, "Factional Conflict and the Indian Community: The Prairie Potawatomi Case," in Levine and Lurie, *American Indian Today*, 115-31.

[17]Subagent Lovely, praising the "regulating law" of 1804, noted that horse thieves "will now find that they can't impose upon their head men as formerly by saying that their great men were as bad as themselves in sharing the proffits arrising from stolen horses." Lovely, Address to the Cherokee Chiefs, June [?] 1804, Cherokee Agency, TN, M-208, roll 2. These and other aspects of internal disorganization are amply documented in the federal Indian records for these years.

looked backward rather than forward; unable to solve the mounting crisis of his people or overcome the sectional divisions, he let Doublehead speak and act on his behalf in dealing with the hard-driving whites. Although he took his full share of "presents" from the government for cooperating in treaties, he seems to have allowed himself to be too easily led or misled by his old warrior friends.

Doublehead (Taltsuske or Chequlaloga) owed his ascendance in the Lower Towns to his status as a great war chief, to his native shrewdness and forcefulness, and to his ability to manipulate government largesse so as to obtain the lion's share of presents and annuities for himself and his people—this in exchange for his support of government requests for road and land cessions. By 1802 he had become a wealthy trader, land speculator, farmer, and slaveowner The federal agent, Colonel Return J. Meigs, held him in great respect as a force for law, order, progress, and cooperation. Jefferson was so impressed by Doublehead's progressivism that he presented him with a gift of one thousand dollars in January 1806 and an official commendation "in consideration of his active influence in forwarding the views of Government, in the introduction of the arts of civilization among the Cherokee Nation of Indians, and for his friendly disposition towards the United States and for the purpose of enabling him to extend his useful example among the Red People."[18]

Although a full blood, Doublehead appears to have had little interest in trying to sustain Cherokee culture. Having been defeated in 1794 by the superior manpower and technology of the white frontiersmen, he seems to have concluded that the best course for the Indians was to adopt the way of life of their conquerors, and the sooner the better. Because he was successful in this pursuit, he had little patience with those Cherokees who held back—"people who have hardly any holes in their heads" to let in the light of new ideas, he told the federal agent.[19] Although chosen "Speaker of the Council" for his ability, Doublehead was never hon-

---

[18]Henry Dearborn to R. J. Meigs, 8 January 1806, Letters Sent, Sec. War, M-15, roll 2:153. Some measure of Doublehead's commercial success may be seen in the letter he sent to Meigs, 20 November 1802, requesting him to build a keelboat for Doublehead's private trade with New Orleans and "the western wild Indians" up the Arkansas and White Rivers. Quoted in Malone, *Cherokees of the Old South*, 145.

[19]Lovely quotes this remark of Doublehead in a letter to Meigs, 13 June 1803, Cherokee Agency, TN, M-208, roll 2.

ored as "a beloved man," and Meigs was specifically rebuked after 1806 by some of Doublehead's opponents for applying this title to him.[20] Egocentric, self-reliant, and aggressive, as a war chief should be, Doublehead nevertheless sincerely believed that he was acting in the best interests of his people. It can be argued that the wealth acquired by the nation from annuities, land cessions, turnpike franchises, and technical assistance, although not evenly distributed under Doublehead's leadership, was a vital factor in Cherokee survival up to 1806.

Doublehead's power was never supreme. He had always to win the cooperation of enough chiefs in the Upper Towns to gain a majority in the national council. Until 1806 there were plenty of Upper Town chiefs who shared his views and ambitions; most of them lived in the contiguous "lower part of the Upper Towns." The "upper division" of the Upper Towns, located predominantly in the Great Smoky Mountains of western North Carolina and eastern Tennessee, was generally known as "The Valley Towns" or "The Hill Towns." By all accounts, the people of The Valley Towns remained the most traditional or, in Meigs's terms, "backward," largely because they were more isolated and poor.[21] Their land was not especially coveted by whites, and they managed in the

---

[20]Chulio signed a communication from the Cherokee council at Oostenaleh to Meigs, 25 April 1806, in which the council directed him to point out that "you know that Double Head is not a beloved man but only a speaker, which you was informed of that two years agoe in this council." Ibid., roll 3. Gearing argues that "beloved men" were older chiefs with priestly functions, skilled in the art of leadership by consensus because of their patience, restraint, affection, and sensitivity to unspoken feelings. Gearing, "Rise of the Cherokee State," in Fenton and Gulick, *Symposium*, 128-32; Gearing, "Priests and Warriors." I find that between 1806-1809 it was younger chiefs like Hicks, The Ridge, and Ross who demonstrated these qualities. Hicks, after his conversion to Christianity in 1813, added some priestly qualities to his role. All three of these leaders, by their active participation in the Creek War, also added some of the warrior qualities to their status. The new nationalistic leaders seem to have embodied the syncretic features of the new Cherokee state in their own personalities. Probably Pathkiller, who was born in 1745, provided the important link between the older, traditional leadership of "beloved men" and the new, mixed-blood, bicultural leadership.

[21]When Meigs sent George B. Davis to make a census of the Valley Towns in 1808, Davis wrote back, "I had not an Idea of seeing such Indians as there is over the hills and in the Valies; they are at least twenty years behind the lower town Indians." Of 583 black slaves in the Cherokee Nation in 1808, the Valley Towns owned only 5; of 500 plows in the nation, they possessed only 40; of 1,600 spinning wheels, they had only 271; of 467 looms, only 70. Yet their population totaled 3,648 out of 16,395 Cherokees, or almost one-fourth. Davis to Meigs, 17 October 1808, Cherokee Agency, TN, M-208, roll 2.

mountains to sustain a hunting-farming economy very similar to that which had preceded the fur-trading economy. They had the highest proportion of full bloods in any region in the nation, the lowest proportion of black slaves, and the smallest proportion of those who could read or write English. They were also the most profoundly attached to their land—perhaps because their traditionally animistic religious beliefs and medical practices were more intact and were intimately related to the mountains, streams, rocks, trees, waterfalls, springs, caves, herbs, and flowers of the region. The Valley Towns were far from unsullied by contact with white men, however, and they too were eager to obtain government assistance in the form of plows, axes, hoes, looms, spinning wheels, and mills in order to improve their meager subsistence economy.

Whites who argued that the more "backward" Cherokees should be those most eager to move West in order to maintain their old hunting ways never understood that the people of the Valley Towns were the most culturally conservative of the Cherokees and therefore the most unwilling to move West. Less directly involved in national affairs, their names appear infrequently in extant documents, but among their identifiable leaders in this period were The Big Bear, Stone Carrier, Woman Holder, James Davis, Nepheu, Kalawiska, Chatloe, The Moose, Juliat, and Wilosey. While they left few records of their sentiments, it is clear from their actions that they remained fiercely loyal to the new concept of the territorial integrity of the Cherokee Nation.[22] After 1808 they staunchly supported those nationalistic chiefs who utilized the legalistic arguments of treaty guarantees to oppose removal and to sustain self-government, although at one moment during the crisis their rancor against the more "progressive" regions of the nation almost led them into a schism. Their seeming inconsistency in asking Jefferson in 1808 to grant their region independence so that they might become fee-simple farmer-citizens resulted from their failure at first to understand the full implications of this request—as Jefferson seemed to realize. Their primary purpose was to guarantee their rights against further frontier aggression and their integ-

---

[22]If there has been such a thing as a "peasant" caste among American Indians, the Valley Town Cherokees represented that intense attachment to the soil and customs of their ancestors that is associated with peasant people. See Robert Redfield, *Peasant Society and Culture: An Anthropological Approach to Civilization* (Chicago, 1956). It also appears that the conservative Valley Town people were shocked at the lawless individualism and violence of the Lower Towns and favored stringent policing against horse thieves.

rity as a regional group whose interests they felt were misrepresented and undermined by the chiefs of both the Lower Towns and the lower division of the Upper Towns.

In the opening years of the century, Doublehead's counterpart in the Upper Towns was James Vann, whose influence, according to Meigs in 1805, was "more than all the rest of the Chiefs and yet he never comes openly forward; his life is in danger [from rivals], perhaps, but he can opperate [*sic*] on some of the best men in the nation and I think [he] has no objection to the cession [of land] we ask for."[23] Vann was neither a warrior chief nor a "beloved man." Like Doublehead, he was an aggressive, shrewd spokesman for those Cherokees who were ready to try to cope with the whites on the whites' own terms of ambitious entrepreneurship, commercial speculation, and pragmatic bargaining. The son of a Scotch trader and a Cherokee woman, Vann was, by 1806, the richest man in the Cherokee Nation, richer even than his sometime ally and later archrival, Doublehead. He owned a large farm and cattle herds at Diamond Hill (Springplace), Georgia; he possessed a score or more of black slaves and managed two large trading posts (one in Alabama); he had a grist mill and a ferry near his home and, like Doublehead, had made considerable profit from favors given for his part in obtaining treaty concessions.

From 1801 to 1806 Meigs regarded Vann as the chief friend of the government in the Upper Towns; thereafter he was considered its most dangerous enemy. Meigs always believed that Vann initially clashed with Doublehead "thro' envy" and personal rivalry for power. Yet after 1806 Vann gradually moved toward the new concept of national unity that Doublehead rejected. He also became a vehement opponent of removal to the West and of granting franchises within the nation to whites, and a strong supporter of the laws against horse thieves and other criminals. The owner of an imposing two-story brick mansion where he entertained lavishly, Vann may be seen as the first exemplar of a rising red bourgeoisie, the bicultural mixed bloods, who dressed, thought, acted, and lived like the nouveaux-riches white cotton planters but who identified themselves as Cherokees. He was, however, so headstrong, irascible, and

---

[23]Meigs to General Daniel Smith, 21 May 1805, Cherokee Agency, TN, M-208, roll 3.

unstable that he gradually alienated most of the new nationalist leaders who, like true "beloved men," were willing to be patient, tactful, and sensitive to the feelings of all groups for the sake of tribal unity.

Another prominent figure in the opposition to Doublehead was Charles Hicks, who by 1806 was beginning to emerge as a leader of a coalition of Upper and Lower Town nationalists. Hicks, like Vann, was of mixed white and Indian ancestry, but he was neither as rich nor as commercially ambitious. Born in 1767, he was appointed an official interpreter for the federal agency in 1801 and so knew intimately the machinations of the government. His opposition to further land cessions after 1806 earned him the enmity of both Doublehead and Meigs. Hicks's rise to leadership can only be surmised from his increasing participation in documented protest meetings after 1806. By 1808 one of the government interpreters described the anti-Doublehead faction to Meigs as "the insurgon party of the Cherokees, the Backers of Charles Hicks." A few weeks after receiving this information, Meigs wrote to Washington that "Charles Hicks had joined the party against Double Head." Later that year Meigs fired Hicks as an interpreter for being "insolent." A diplomat rather than a warrior, Hicks chose to work for harmony within the nation; he acted in concert with his fellow rebels, not as their leader. At first he let Vann take the dominant role in the coalition against Doublehead; but as Vann's impetuous, drunken, and violent behavior revealed his instability, Hicks and other Upper Town chiefs gradually isolated him from their councils. Later, when the rebels deposed Black Fox and installed Pathkiller as principal chief, Hicks played virtually the same role for him that Doublehead had played for Black Fox—that of power behind the throne.

An important aspect of the Cherokees' acculturation difficulties was that elderly, traditionalist chiefs, while important for purposes of tribal unity, lacked necessary skills to deal with the whites. Their role came to be that of holding the less acculturated members of the tribe together by representing their views in councils (of which we unfortunately have no records). The articulate mixed bloods, like Hicks, or the acculturated full bloods, like Doublehead, did the official talking and correspondence with the whites as speaker or secretary or second principal chief. Significantly, Hicks is identified in official correspondence in 1809 as "Secretary of the Upper Town Council" and in February 1810 as "Secretary of the National Committee."[24]

The crisis began for the Cherokees in January 1806, when the second of two important treaties was completed by a tribal delegation in Washington, D.C.[25] By this treaty and its predecessor of October 1805, the Cherokees ceded to the United States 8.6 million acres of their old hunting ground in Tennessee at less than two cents per acre. The sixteen chiefs who made the treaty, including Doublehead and Vann, stipulated that the government would not only pay off eight thousand dollars in private debts owed by them and other chiefs to private white traders (an indication of how "progressive" in commerce and trade some chiefs had become), but also liberally reward a number of these chiefs with tracts of land and monetary gifts. Some of these presents were hidden in secret clauses of the treaty of 1806 and not discovered until later by the rest of the Cherokee Nation. Vann did not profit as much as Doublehead and the Lower Town chiefs, and he appears to have been at the center of the opposition that gathered force in a series of councils and countercouncils that spring and summer. In addition to expressing dissatisfaction with the treaty negotiations, these debates raised a host of other issues that had been troubling the nation. Objections were leveled in particular against the presence within the nation's boundaries of increasing numbers of whites; some of these whites were intruders whom the government neglected to expel; but others were there as the partners or employees of wealthy chiefs to exploit the land, resources, and trade of the nation. This opposition culminated in a bitter conference at Willstown in September 1806 that so offended the friends of Doublehead—

---

[24]Letter from the Cherokee Council at Fortville to the Creek Nation, 27 May 1809, ibid., roll 4; letter from the Cherokee Council at Oustennalligh to Meigs, 11 April 1810, Letters Received by the Secretary of War, Main Series, 1801-1870, M-221, roll 38, frame 5238, Records of the War Department: Records of the Office of the Secretary of War (RG 107), National Archives.

[25]The details of all Cherokee treaties, including references to the secret clauses, are in Charles C. Royce, comp., *Indian Land Cessions in the United States*, U.S. Bureau of American Ethnology, *Eighteenth Annual Report* (Washington DC, 1899). Because much of this ceded area was also claimed by the Chickasaw, the bargain to sell it may have been a good one; but the manner in which it was done and the subsequent efforts to enlarge the cession without consulting the council precipitated the crisis.

notably The Glass and Dick Justice—that they stalked out in anger.[26] Meigs tried to soothe the animosities and defend the treaties, but the criticism continued to mount.

Doublehead defended himself angrily in letters to Meigs and other chiefs, calling his opponents "half Breeds," hypocrites, "Desin[in]g and foolish persons that are Enemies to all Improvement, Enemies to all those that wish to improve."[27] John Lowery, a chief allied with Double-head at that time, described the opposition as "yong chiefs and indede some of them no chiefes atole," who were trying to upset lawful treaties: "What is our cuntry cum to if the yong, simple, drunken idel people is to breake laws that all the Chiefes and king [principal chief] makes . . . my feelings was much Hurte to think these young people was holding their Ta[l]ke [council] to think that we old chiefs and King shold be made as if Thay was Nothing."[28] Black Fox, the principal chief, was tech-nically leader of both the Upper and Lower Towns, but he lived in the Lower Town area and sided steadily with Doublehead's faction. Hence when opposition arose, it appeared to Meigs as a rebellion against duly constituted authority. Its leadership contained not only "half breeds," as Doublehead said, but many full-blood chiefs, especially those from the Valley Towns, and even a few white men married into the nation, like John Rogers. Although designating themselves at first only as spokes-men for the Upper Towns, the opposition leaders found as time passed that many in the Lower Towns shared their views. While Doublehead and Meigs described them as "backward," "indolent," and "enemies to progress," their later course of action indicates the contrary.[29]

Those chiefs who repudiated the treaties of 1806 at Willstown iden-tified themselves in their letter to Meigs as Hicks, John Walker, John Ross, Will Shorey, Young John Watts, Young Wolf, George Fields, Dick

---

[26]For the grievances of this council, see Willstown Council to Meigs, 19 September 1806, Cherokee Agency, TN, M-208, roll 3. The council also protested franchises given by Doublehead and his friends to "white men without the smallest privilege [rent or roy-alty]" to the nation. Nationalism was obviously spurred by growing awareness of national profits to be made from national assets.

[27]Doublehead to Meigs, 3 October 1806; 14 January 1807, ibid.

[28]John Lowery to Meigs, 23 October 1806, ibid.

[29]Pathkiller et al. to Meigs, 19 September 1806, ibid. These chiefs came from both divisions of the Upper Towns.

Fields, James Brown, Colaqueskee, John Spears, and Naw-the-Whits.[30] From the evidence of later activities, the names of The Ridge, Pathkiller, Chulioa, Stone Carrier, Woman Holder, George and Alex Sanders, John Doherty, John Beamer, Sharp Arrow, Sour Mush, Dreadful Water(s), Kelachula, Katahee, Tuskegatahee, Cabbin Smith, Thomas Wilson, Nawayontaeh, and John McIntosh (Quotiqueskee) can be added. Some of the Valley Town chiefs, such as Stone Carrier and Woman Holder, at first opposed not only Doublehead but Vann. Many seem to have shifted from one side to another between 1806 and 1809, depending on the specific issue or strategy under consideration. After 1810 even such ardent former supporters of Doublehead as The Glass, Black Fox, Lowery, and Toochalee swung over to support the new leadership and its policies. For the sake of simplicity, the anti-Doublehead faction (Meigs called it "the anti-government faction" or "the insurgents") will be designated the Hicks-Ridge-Pathkiller faction, for these were the men who maintained leadership for the next generation and, together with Ross, became the pillars of the rising nationalist program.[31]

The rise to power of the Hicks-Ridge-Pathkiller leadership was assisted by the deaths of Doublehead in February 1807 and Vann in 1809. Doublehead's authority had been undermined by the rewards he reaped from the treaty of 1805 and by his agreement to the secret clauses in the treaty of 1806 that surrendered tribal land and enriched him and his friends. The assassination of Doublehead was plotted by Upper Town chiefs who privately agreed that he had betrayed the nation. It appears from later events that these chiefs saw themselves as official agents of

---

[30]Lowery to Meigs, 23 October 1806, ibid.

[31]The absence of genealogical data makes it difficult to say which faction contained more Cherokees of mixed ancestry, but obviously neither can be defined in these terms. Pathkiller (1745-1827) and perhaps The Ridge (1771-1839) were full bloods; Hicks (1767-1827) was the son of a white father and a Cherokee mother; Ross (1790-1866) was seven-eighths white; John Rogers was a white married to a Cherokee. However, as noted above, the staunchest support for the new nationalism came from the Valley Towns where there had been comparatively little intermarriage with whites. Nor was there any such thing as a Christian or a pagan party; missionary activity had barely started in the nation. The following details indicate the continuity of the new leadership that arose in 1806: Pathkiller was principal chief from 1811 to 1827; Hicks was second principal chief from 1819 to 1827 and succeeded Pathkiller for a short time in 1827; Ross was principal chief from 1828 to 1866; The Ridge was probably the second most important leader from 1827 to 1839.

tribal justice and that their action was accepted as just by the majority of the tribe. Vann, who participated in the plot, was himself killed two years later, but he had already been pushed aside by the new Upper Town leaders.[32] Although the violence that destroyed Vann and Doublehead accents the intensity of the passions aroused in this critical period, when one considers the stresses involved in the transfer of authority to new leadership under new policies, the transition appears remarkable for its lack of bloodshed. The successful attempt in November 1808 to depose Black Fox as principal chief and replace him with Pathkiller confirms the view of Meigs that what took place was an internal revolution. However, the peaceful reinstatement of Black Fox as principal chief in 1810, after the crisis had passed, indicates that fundamental policies, not personal animosities or the desire of ambitious individuals for power, were at the heart of the matter.

Jefferson's role in the crisis was ambiguous. His wisdom lay in recognizing the complexity of the situation and in refusing to interfere in the Cherokees' internal affairs. He preferred rather to create options than to choose sides. His mistake lay in failing to control the subordinates who took advantage of his ambivalent options to push their own program. Moreover, because Meigs and Secretary of War Henry Dearborn wanted total removal of the Cherokees and total exchange of their land, it became possible eight years later for General Andrew Jackson, Secretary of War John C. Calhoun, and Governor Joseph McMinn of Tennessee to construe Jefferson's words of 1809 as supporting their plan for removal.[33] Jefferson, by suggesting removal and exchange to the Cherokees in 1809; Meigs and Dearborn by pushing it; Doublehead's

---

[32]Doublehead's assassination is described in ibid., 9 August 1807, and in Brown, *Old Frontiers*, 452; for Vann's death, see Malone, *Cherokees*, 60. For a different version of Doublehead's murder, indicating elements of clan revenge, see the John Howard Payne Papers, typescript 2:26-30, 43-46, Newberry Library, Chicago.

[33]See the opening paragraph of the treaty of 8 July 1817, printed in Richard Peters, *The Case of the Cherokee Nation Against the State of Georgia* . . . (Philadelphia, 1831) 265. Just as logically, Elias Boudinot, the Cherokee editor of the *Cherokee Phoenix* (New Echota GA), could quote Jefferson in the first issue—21 February 1828—to demonstrate that the Cherokee constitution was instituted in accord with Jefferson's advice in 1809. For Jefferson's early interest in encouraging, but not forcing Indian removal in 1803 and 1805, see Annie H. Abel, *The History of the Events Resulting in Indian Consolidation West of the Mississippi* (Washington DC, 1906). He did not broach it to the Cherokees, however, until 1806.

faction (led then by Tolluntuskee and The Glass) by claiming to represent a majority in favor of it; and Meigs, by carrying out the first stage of the program, in effect converted Jefferson's option into "an agreement." During the second removal crisis of 1817-1819 the Hicks-Ridge-Pathkiller faction would argue that Jefferson had made no such agreement, but Meigs and Jackson insisted that he had and that they were obliged to carry it through as an official commitment to the Lower Town faction.[34]

In 1808 and 1809 Cherokee delegations traveled to Washington to meet with Jefferson. Not only is the precise wording of the president's talks to the Indians important, but so are the circumstances in which he spoke, particularly the circumstances among the Cherokees before and after their delegates presented their diverse positions to him. Jefferson's name had been brought into the controversy as early as September 1806, when Rogers, a leader of the Hicks-Ridge-Pathkiller faction and a year later one of the appointed assassins of Doublehead (together with The Ridge and Alex Sanders), accused the president of using unfair tactics to force the Cherokee Nation to sell its land to the government. This was reported to Meigs by Samuel Riley, a government interpreter, who said that Rogers claimed to have his information from John W. Hooker, the government factor at the Cherokee trading post. Hooker reportedly told Rogers "that in conversation with Mr. Jefferson, he [Jefferson] asked him if he could get the Cherokees to run in debt to the amount of ten or twelve thousand dollars in the public store. Mr. Hooker told him for answer, fifty thousand. Well, says he, that is the way I entend to get there cuntry, for to get them to run in debt to the public store and they will have to give there land for payment."[35] Rumors were spread and believed (amid mounting tribal paranoia) that Doublehead's faction and other chiefs might run up such heavy debts so that more, perhaps all, of the Cherokee lands would have to be sold to cancel them. Nevertheless, even after Doublehead's assassination, Meigs continued to deal primarily with

---

[34]This second crisis is discussed in Cotterill, *Southern Indians*, 203-10.

[35]Samuel Riley to Meigs, 29 November 1806, Cherokee Agency, TN, M-208, roll 3. Meigs heard the same story from David Fields, who had heard it from Pathkiller. Fields to Meigs, 18 November 1807, ibid. See also Sheehan, *Seeds of Extinction*, 171; Prucha, *American Indian Policy*, 88; and Cotterill, *Southern Indians*, 139-40.

Doublehead's friends as the spokesmen for the nation; in view of Black Fox's support, Meigs had some justification for this.

On 11 September 1807, Meigs bribed Black Fox, The Glass, and several other Lower Town chiefs to alter and extend the cession line of 1806 during surveying operations.[36] Then in December 1807, over strong objections from Vann, he negotiated a treaty signed by only twenty-three chiefs, most of them from Doublehead's faction, for a cession of six square miles of Cherokee land in the heart of the nation near Chickamauga Creek. The cession was made to Colonel Elias Earle, an entrepreneur from South Carolina, who had convinced Jefferson and Dearborn that there was valuable iron ore in that area that he could mine and manufacture for the benefit of himself, the Cherokees, and the government.[37] The Hicks-Ridge-Pathkiller faction immediately wrote to Jefferson, Dearborn, and George Clinton, president of the Senate, which was then considering ratification, denouncing the "sham treaty" that they said had been forced upon a few chiefs by intimidation.[38] Another letter from the same group went to Black Fox declaring that "the upper towns had never sanctioned the treaty" and that they regarded it as invalid.[39]

Earle nevertheless collected one hundred white families in South Carolina, plus a wagon train of supplies with a superintendent and some slaves, and started them off to his newly acquired property. Hearing that the Cherokees were angry, most of the white families turned back, but Earle ordered his superintendent, slaves, and several white employees to proceed. No sooner had their wagon train entered Cherokee territory in Georgia than it was surrounded by armed Cherokees whom Vann had

---

[36]In addition to personal gifts to the chiefs who agreed to the alteration, Meigs agreed to cancel "a debt to the United States of 1,803 dollars." Meigs to Dearborn, 28 September 1807, Cherokee Agency, TN, M-208, roll 2.

[37]See Meigs to Dearborn, 3 December 1807, Letters Received by the Secretary of War, Unregistered Series, 1789-1861, M-222, roll 2, frame 0883, Records of the War Department: Records of the Office of the Secretary of War (RG 107), National Archives. Hereinafter cited as M-222. The Glass was the chief proponent of this treaty with Earle.

[38]Pathkiller et al. to Thomas Jefferson, 24 January 1808, ibid., roll 3, frames 1152-1153; Pathkiller et al. to George Clinton, 24 January 1808, ibid., frames 1154-1155.

[39]Charles Hicks to Black Fox, 15 February 1808, Cherokee Agency, TN, M-208, roll 4.

equipped and directed. After threatening and harassing the superintendent and other white employees, the Indians forced them to turn back to South Carolina. Meigs, living two hundred miles west in Tennessee, did not learn of this "warlike" event until it was over. Doublehead's faction, now led by The Glass, Tolluntuskee, Black Fox, and John D. Chisholm—a white man married into the tribe and the executor of Doublehead's estate—denounced Vann as "a boney part" for his high-handed action and suggested that Meigs arrest him.[40] Vann told William Brown, Earle's superintendent, that "the chiefs had given orders for Mr. Earle's waggon[s] to be stoped."[41] Lowery, writing to Meigs on 8 February 1808, said with stark understatement, "It appears that there is a part of our Nation in grate confusion."[42]

In March 1808 a group of Upper Town chiefs, who were no friends of Vann but were also angry at the Lower Town chiefs, set out for Washington to see Jefferson. They carried a letter from Gov. John Sevier of Tennessee vouching for them as "friendly" to the United States, but they obviously distrusted Meigs for they neither sought his permission nor told him of their departure.[43] Led by Stone Carrier and Woman Holder, they were from "the vicinity of Blount County and Tellico Blockhouse" and apparently represented the upper division of the Upper Towns. In an interview with Dearborn in April, they complained that Meigs was giving to the Lower Towns an unfair proportion of the government's technical aid and annuities; that the chiefs who had signed the treaty of 1806 had no right to use the payment for tribal land or the money from the annuities to discharge their personal debts to white traders since the land belonged to the whole nation; and that they were tired of being dominated by the chiefs of the Lower Towns. The delegation asked the

---

[40]Lowery to Meigs, 8 February 1808, Letters Received, Unregistered Series, M-222, roll 3, frame 1311.

[41]Affidavit signed by William Brown, 15 February 1808, Cherokee Agency, TN, M-208, roll 4.

[42]Lowery to Meigs, 8 February 1808, ibid.

[43]Sevier's letter, dated 9 February 1808, is in the Daniel Parker Papers, Box 2, Historical Society of Pennsylvania, Philadelphia. He lists some of the chiefs in this delegation: The Stone Toater (or Stone Carrier), John of Chilhowa, The Crawling Boy, Chilcochatah, and The Deer Biter. They appear to have been from the upper part of the Upper Towns. I am indebted to Julian P. Boyd for calling the Parker Papers to my attention and for suggestions made after reading an early draft of this paper.

government to erect a gristmill in its area and to send them more plows, spinning wheels, looms, and hoes.[44]

These chiefs also offered a plan of their own to solve the nation's problems. We have no record of it in their own words, but Jefferson paraphrased it in a talk to the delegation on its departure from Washington on 4 May 1808: "You propose, my children, that your nation shall be divided into two, and that your part, the upper Cherokees, shall be separated from the lower by a fixed boundary, shall be placed under the government of the United States, become citizens thereof, and be ruled by our laws; in fine, to be our brothers instead of our children." Apparently these chiefs, seeing that their rights were not well represented by the Lower Town chiefs and that their lives and property were not respected by the white frontiersmen who intruded upon them, sought the protection of citizenship. But Jefferson wondered if they understood the degree of acculturation this would require: "Are you prepared for this?" he asked, outlining the process necessary. "Have you a resolution to leave off hunting for your living, to lay off a farm for each family to itself, to live by industry, the men working that farm with their hands, raising stock or learning trades as we do, and the women spinning and weaving clothes for their husbands and children?" He urged them to "consult with the lower towns" and, if the Lower Town chiefs agreed, to have delegates sent to Washington "with power to arrange with us regulations" by which the Cherokees would be governed as citizens. He would then ask the assistance of "the Congress, whose authority is necessary to give validity to these arrangements." Whether this would entail granting them full citizenship or merely some intermediate status under further federal supervision was not stated.[45]

---

[44]Dearborn, in describing the complaints of this delegation to Meigs, said, "They state that for several years their part of the nation has received scarcely anything from the United States either as annuities or as pay for the lands sold; that the great chiefs generally live in the lower part of the nation and after receiving the annuities, etc. they divide nearly the whole among those of their own neighborhood." He also noted that "they speak of Vann as a turbulent and dangerous man." Dearborn to Meigs, 5 May 1808, Cherokee Agency, TN, M-208, roll 4. For previous complaints of this sort and an earlier threat of secession from the nation (at that time by the Lower Towns), see Mooney, "Myths," 83.

[45]Jefferson to the Cherokee delegation in Washington DC, 4 May 1808, Letters Sent, Sec. War, M-15, roll 2:374.

More important, perhaps, Jefferson suggested that those Indians who opposed this solution might "go, if they choose it, and settle on our lands beyond the Mississippi." Although he said nothing about an exchange of land, he did indicate that the government would establish "a store there among them where they may obtain necessaries" in trade for their hides. But he would agree to nothing until "the principal part of your people determine to adopt this alteration." Since Meigs and Dearborn had been discussing removal and exchange for the preceding three months, it is surprising that nothing specific was said about exchange; the problem may have been that Meigs and Dearborn favored total, not partial, removal of the Cherokees.

Frustrated by increasing factionalism, unable to hold back the white intruders as he was supposed to do, and dubious about the speed with which the Cherokees could be "civilized," Meigs had written to Dearborn in February 1808: "I understand some years ago that the Government had in contemplation an exchange of lands with the Indians South of the Ohio. It is my opinion that if specific propositions were made to the Cherokees, holding out suitable encouragement and protection, that it would in a short time produce a general sentiment amongst them in favor of exchange. Some who are well situated as farmers would probably require reservations of competent tracts for their use, but even these would finally sell out and follow the nation."[46] Dearborn wrote back on 25 March, "If you think it practicable to induce the Cherokees, as a nation generally, to consent to exchange of their present country for a suitable tract of country on the other side of the Mississippi, you will please to embrace every favorable occasion for sounding the Chiefs on the subject; and let the subject be generally talked about [among] the natives until you shall be satisfied of the prevailing opinion."[47] Although we do not know whether Dearborn discussed this plan with Jefferson, it presented such difficulties and expense that it would seem strange for him to have encouraged it without doing so. Yet there is no evidence that Jef-

---

[46]Meigs to Dearborn, 9 February 1808, Cherokee Agency, TN, M-208, roll 4. For the earlier "contemplation" of removal to which Meigs refers, see Lovely to Meigs, 27 October 1803, ibid., roll 2, and Abel, *History of the Events*, 252.

[47]Dearborn to Meigs, 25 March 1808, Cherokee Agency, TN, M-208, roll 4. There were probably about 800 Cherokees who had voluntarily moved across the Mississippi between 1780 and 1808 for various reasons, but no one had paid much attention to them. See Mooney, "Myths," 99-101.

ferson had considered it in May 1808 when he addressed Stone Carrier's delegation.

Meigs, close to the scene and seeing a general emigration as a way of solving most of his problems, at once started talking with "well-disposed" chiefs and working on plans for removal and exchange. While admitting in June 1808 that the Cherokees were at "a crisis in their national existence," Meigs was so confident of cooperation from the Lower Town chiefs on his removal strategy that he planned to take a delegation of them to Washington to discuss its details. On 3 June he wrote to Dearborn that "there is a good number who wish to go over the Mississippi," and that "the general idea of an exchange" of land should be pushed.[48]

Meigs may thus be seen as the architect of Cherokee removal. Yet he promoted it not to destroy but to preserve that nation. When Dearborn wrote that Jefferson had told Stone Carrier's delegation how to prepare for citizenship, Meigs responded that this was a forlorn hope. Furthermore, the granting of plots of land in severalty to Upper Town farmers would undermine the project of total removal and exchange. The Cherokees, he believed, once given individual title to their land, would soon sell it or be defrauded of it by unscrupulous whites. What then would they have to exchange? "Their existence as a distinct people depends on their migration; they must change their ground or their idle habits. . . . Their women . . . are industrious, the greater part of the labor is imposed on them and this trait [male laziness] in the character of their people proves that they are better fitted for migration to a new Country than to remain here surrounded now by white people where something is continually arrising to arouse their reciprocal prejudices into acts of injustice."[49] Consequently, he wrote, "I found it necessary to go a step further than simply mentioning the exchange," as Dearborn had authorized him to do. He had, in fact, given a written statement to certain chiefs saying, "It is proposed to place the Cherokees on good hunting ground" in the West and the "protection and fostering hand of Government will go with you. . . . [T]o enable you to make the removal they will make the necessary advancements and your present annuities will be continued" in

---

[48]Meigs to Dearborn, 8 June 1808, Letters Received, Main Series, M-221, roll 26, frame 8670.

[49]Ibid.

the West.[50] Meigs had no authority to offer such a proposition, but so skeptical had he become of the federal Indian policy of civilization and incorporation *in situs* that for the rest of his career as agent to the Cherokees (until his death in 1823), he bent every effort toward total removal.

Having found more sympathetic ears among the Lower Town chiefs, Meigs next had to convince Dearborn that removal, although expensive, would be well worth the cost: "Suppose the U. States give them land [in the West] equal to one-half by estimation [to that they leave in the East], having some natural boundaries, and buy the other half at one-half cent per acre, say total 105,000 dollars, payable by installments in twenty years. If they move, they will want one or two of these installments to buy arms, powder, lead, and provisions to support them untill their first crops come in." The remaining installments and economic aid would be in the form of trust funds or annuities to give the Indians regular income with which to purchase such items as plows, hoes, gristmills, and cotton gins. While $105,000 seemed a large sum, it would "bring millions into the Treasury" from the sale of the Cherokees' present lands, and the transaction would settle innumerable thorny problems along the Southeastern frontier. In addition, twelve hundred Cherokee warriors in the West "will be a formidable Barrier against savages or people of any other character." Meigs excused his generous promises of aid to the chiefs on the ground that they had to be induced to persuade others: "It must be considered that notwithstanding they are Indians, they have strong local prejudices, and to induce them to migrate they must have strong excitements to leave the place of their nativity and the graves of their fathers." Jefferson's plan to make farmer-citizens of the Indians was deemed totally impracticable by Meigs because "they can no more hold property than a sieve can hold water." Whatever Stone Carrier's delegation may have told Jefferson, Meigs claimed that only "a small part" of the Upper Town Indians really wanted "to put themselves under the laws of the United States and become citizens."[51]

---

[50]Ibid. Division of the annuities between Cherokees east and west posed serious problems, then and afterward, which Meigs glossed over here.

[51]Ibid. Meigs said that there might be "perhaps three hundred families" in the entire nation (mostly mixed bloods) "that might hold land as individuals and make useful citizens."

Three months later, in September 1808 at a council held at Broomstown, Meigs put removal to the chiefs as an either-or proposition. "You
have your choice, to stay here and become industrious, like white people, so that the women and children shall not cry any more for bread, or
go over the Mississippi, where meat is plentiful and where corn may be
raised as well as here." He did not deny that they had made important
strides toward "civilization" but turned his argument into an appeal for
national unity: "The Cherokees have more knowledge as farmers, as
manufactur[er]s and have more knowledge of literature than any nation
of Red men of equal numbers in America. I wish to excite in yourselves
a just pride, that is to have you value yourselves as *Cherokees*; the word
Cherokee or *Cherokees* should always convey an idea of Respectability to
your people and to preserve your nation from being lost, to keep up your
National existence as a distinct people, you must not let your people
straggle one or two at a time or in small parties [to the West] because
small parties cannot support the character of the Nation."[52] It is ironic
that Meigs should have utilized an appeal to the rising nationalism of the
Cherokees on behalf of his program. Far from uniting them behind the
few who wanted to emigrate, it united the majority against removal and
also against a permanent division of the nation into Upper and Lower
sections. If the Cherokees were to be a distinct nation, and if, as Meigs
implied, they had succeeded so well where they were, it seemed to most
of them more logical to continue in the East than to leave it.

The council at Broomstown and a second council a month later at
Highwassee Garrison constituted major turning points in the national
mood. These councils decided to send a joint delegation to Jefferson,
composed of three chiefs from the Lower and three from the Upper
Towns. It appears, however, that the Lower Town delegates, with the
connivance of Meigs, went to Washington under instructions from their
chiefs to discuss removal and exchange of lands, while the Upper Town
delegates went under the assumption that the tribe was now opposed to
removal and exchange. The confused and conspiratorial aspects of these
councils make them difficult to describe. According to the fullest account, written in 1818, "during the session of the Council [at Brooms-
town] a private meeting of the river chiefs was called in the woods, half
a mile or more from the Council house, to vote for emigrating west of the

---

[52]Meigs, Address to the Cherokee Council, 6 September 1808, ibid., roll 27.

Mississippi. Those wishing to emigrate lost the majority of votes," but nevertheless, "after the close of this Council it was said by some of the river chiefs that they would go to the City of Washington to exchange the Country."[53] If this was true, the Lower Town chiefs were not acting, as Jefferson was led to believe, for a majority of their own people, much less for a majority of the nation. According to this account, the council at Broomstown agreed only to meet at Highwassee Garrison a month later to choose six delegates to go to Washington to offer formal thanks to Jefferson for the help he offered during his administration. This was a suggestion made by Meigs.

There is no copy of the instructions, but apparently the delegates, while free to discuss other matters informally, were not empowered to make any official agreements or treaties. However, according to the same account of 1818, the chiefs of the Upper Towns discovered at Highwassee Garrison that the Lower Town chiefs, in concert with Meigs, had issued secret instructions to their three delegates to work out a plan for removal and exchange with Jefferson. In so doing, "considerable difference arose between the parties and three of the river chiefs were broke [deposed] in consequence of it. That is, the Glass, Tahlantuskey, and the Black-fox. After which the council then in session at that place elected John Walker, Quotoquaskee, Toochala, Ridge, Skeaka, and the Seed delegates to see our father, Thomas Jefferson, and to communicate to him that the Cherokees did not wish to exchange any part of their country." Despite this action, the three Lower Town delegates still considered themselves bound to present the views of the Lower Towns and the deposed chiefs. In fact, it appears that neither they nor Meigs accepted the validity of the deposition.

The Upper Town chiefs, according to another account—written in 1817—discovered "a few days before the delegation started to the city of Washington" that the Lower Town delegates planned to follow the orders of the deposed chiefs. They held a council and "appointed two other delegates in addition to those who were first chosen in order to frustrate the designs of that part of the delegation who should attempt to do anything that would be in any wise injurious to the nation in general. But, unfortunately when the delegates arrived at the city of Washington, the two

---

[53]Copy of a letter signed by forty-nine Cherokee chiefs to Joseph McMinn, 30 June 1818, American Board of Commissioners for Foreign Missions Papers, 18.3.1, 2, Houghton Library, Harvard University, Cambridge MA; hereafter cited as ABCFM 18.3.1, 2.

[additional] delegates, in whom the faith and confidence of the nation was placed, were rejected and were not admitted to a hearing."[54] Thus if these accounts are to be believed, Meigs not only abetted a conspiracy to divide the nation, he also saw to it that the additional delegates were denied the right to participate in the discussion with Jefferson.

Since these documents of 1817 and 1818 present the viewpoint of the Hicks-Ridge-Pathkiller faction, it is necessary to check them against what little contemporary evidence is available. One such document is a letter from The Glass to Dearborn dated 2 November 1808, at the time the council at Highwassee Garrison was in session. It corroborates the view that the Lower Town delegates were expected to discuss removal and exchange: "Our people [in the Lower Towns] expects that Exchange of land will take place with the United States."[55] A more important letter, written about the same time by fifteen of the Lower Town chiefs, protested the deposition of The Glass, Tolluntuskee, and Black Fox, and the latter's replacement by Pathkiller. It also confirms that the Lower Town chiefs instructed their delegates to discuss proposals for removal and exchange. Claiming to represent "the sentiment of 13 Towns composing nearly one half of the Cherokee Nation and taking into view our people that are already crossed the Mississippi, we are a majority," these fifteen wrote.

> It is only 4 days since the upper Division of the Nation met in Council and had very contrary talks and very distant from our wishes; they therewith usurped authority, attempted to stop the mouths of four of our old and beloved chiefs and leaders [the fourth was Chisholm]. . . . These men had done nothing that could be laid to their charge except holding fast to our father the President and Governments advise and wishing the true happiness of the Nation and Interest of the United States . . . we wish you to inform us pointedly if you will permit us and protect us in Removing if we should wish to do so. . . . We have also sent 3 of our Chiefs to see you, they will inform you of our minds, viz. Too-cha-lee, The Seed, and Ski-u-ka.[56]

---

[54]*American State Papers. Documents, Legislative and Executive* . . . (Washington DC, 1834), *Indian Affairs*, 2:143. Dated 2 July 1817, this was signed by sixty-seven chiefs, some of whom had been on the opposite side in 1808.

[55]The Glass to Dearborn, 2 November 1808, Letters Received, Unregistered Series, M-222, roll 3, frame 1206. By "our people," The Glass meant the Lower Towns.

[56]Ibid., frame 1156. Addressed to Jefferson from "The Head Men of River Division," it was obviously written before the delegation left the nation on 15 November and was probably presented secretly by the Lower Town delegates.

They closed by praising Meigs and signed their names with marks: The Glass, Dick Justice, Turtle at Home, Toochalee, The Seed, Skiuka, John Boggs, Waskah, Eusononu, The Gourd, Chickasawtahee, Conwaloe, Tickachulaste, Black Bird, and Parch[ed] Cornflour.

What the contemporary documents do not settle is when and by whom the two additional delegates were chosen or even whether the council at Highwassee Garrison was a full national council or only an Upper Town council. A letter from Meigs to Dearborn, dated Kingston, Tennessee, 15 November 1808, indicates that when he and the first six chosen delegates left for Washington, he knew nothing of the appointment of two additional delegates: "I am thus far on my way to the City with my accounts. Five or Six Cherokee Chiefs accompany me to see the President previous to his leaving the Administration and to converse with him on the subject of exchange of Country. If dependence can be placed on my information, more than one half are in favor of going over the Mississippi. A party is already formed to explore the lands on the waters of Arkansas and Red rivers. I have persuaded them to wait 50 days for an answer from me which I promised to send them after my arrival at the City. I was induced to this not knowing on what part of the Country the U.S. would choose to place them."[57] Another letter, dated 23 November 1808, from subagent Major William S. Lovely (Meigs's son-in-law) to Meigs, states that he had just learned of the appointment of two additional delegates by what he called a "nocturnal council" presided over by "the now great Chief, the Path Killer, Damn his brains, that he could not foresee the consequence that would result."[58] Lovely was not at the council but knew that it had been called to oppose removal and exchange.

While such evidence confirms the view that information concerning the actions of the Lower Town chiefs had been kept secret from the chiefs of the Upper Towns, it does not explain why the latter waited until after Meigs's departure to appoint additional delegates—that is, unless they only then discovered that the Lower Towns planned to betray a presumed agreement reached at the last council. It also implies that the "nocturnal council" was not the council at Highwassee Garrison but a

---

[57]Meigs to Dearborn, 15 November 1808, ibid., frame 8971.

[58]Lovely to Meigs, 23 November 1808, ibid., frames 1314-1315.

rump group of Upper Town chiefs. Lovely noted that this council had appointed Rogers and Thomas Wilson (Hicks's nephew) as additional delegates and sent them to catch up with the original six. He blamed Vann as the prime mover of this "deceitful conspiracy." A letter to Jefferson from Highwassee Garrison on 25 November by The Glass, Tolluntuskee, and Turtle at Home indicates no knowledge of the extra delegates, but it denounces the depositions and makes clear that Toochalee, The Seed, and Skiuka (and not the whole delegation) would speak for them. In fact, it specifically attacked The Ridge and cautioned that "we do not wish the [Upper Town] Chiefs to hear this letter read. Our hearts are true to the U. States." Tolluntuskee added a revealing personal postscript: "I have tried to make our people sensible of our own good, but they would not listen. I and my part are determined to cross the river toward the sunset. Our bad brothers may dispute, but with me 12 towns go."[59]

The two additional delegates sent by Pathkiller, together with a chief named Cabbin Smith, caught up with Meigs at Alexandria, Virginia, on 13 December. Meigs refused to acknowledge them as representatives of the nation and advised Dearborn not to recognize them: "After the Council [at Highwassee] had gone home, Vann and Hicks having a jealousy that those that were regularly appointed would not transact the business agreably to their factious views, sent on three person[s] to oppose the others."[60] Despite Meigs's opposition, Rogers, Wilson, and Smith went on to Washington and met regularly with the other delegates. The communications to Jefferson that have survived indicate that the Upper and Lower Town delegates were working against each other throughout their meetings, which lasted from mid-December to 9 January. Without impugning the motives of either faction as to what was best for the nation, and admitting that there were chiefs on both sides who had venal interests of their own, it seems clear that Meigs and the Lower Town chiefs did not represent the majority, their assertions to the contrary notwithstanding.[61] Events would prove that all the efforts of

---

[59]Turtle at Home et al. to Jefferson, 25 November 1808, ibid., frame 1151.

[60]Meigs to Dearborn, 13 December 1808, ibid., frame 1306.

[61]Evidently the definition of a "town" varied considerably, but most estimates state that there were between forty and fifty Cherokee towns at this time.

these chiefs and Meigs could not induce more than one-tenth of the Cherokees to emigrate.

The talks began with the presentation to Jefferson on 21 December of the noncontentious thanks of the nation for "his protection and fostering hand" as president.[62] Yet in the following week the Lower Town delegates evidently met separately with Dearborn and presented the letters from their faction to him and to Jefferson. When the Upper Town delegates discovered this, they wrote an indignant note to Jefferson on 28 December saying, "We did not think that we were bringing the talks of our old chiefs that we have dismissed. We thought that we were bringing the talks of our beloved man, the Path Killer, our present Principal Chief, and the talk of 42 towns that are also of his mind." The "old chiefs" were deposed because "they had already made up their minds to move us out of our houses [and across the Mississippi] before we knew anything of it." Apparently they adopted Meigs's view that removal and exchange applied to the whole nation and not just to one part of it. They then reiterated the complaint about the unfair proportion of annuities and economic aid that had gone to the Lower Towns: "You advise us to learn your ways; it is that we mean to do; we have learned many things. And if it had not been for them [the Lower Towns], we would have learned more."[63]

On 29 December the six delegates presented a letter that apparently represented an agreement that a boundary line should be drawn between the two parts of the nation, although this was not in any way related to removal and exchange. The six chiefs seemed ready to blame the need for a boundary upon "the old chiefs," who had not proceeded rapidly enough to educate the young or to make laws against horse thieves:

> We want to do the best we can for ourselves and our Nation. But the old people of our nation are hard to [find it hard to?] understand what is for the benefit of [the] Nation. You know that learning has been recommended to our people when our children are small. Since that [time] our children have grown up and we do not know of but very few of the old chiefs that has given their children learning. . . . For if we follow the old customs of our people, we will never do well, for now

---

[62]The copy of this document in the Parker Papers, Box 2, differs somewhat from that in Cherokee Agency, TN, M-208, roll 4, 21 December 1808.

[63]Parker Papers, Box 2. The letter was signed by The Ridge, Walker, and McIntosh, but Thomas Wilson's signature was crossed out.

our children are not grown up fit for any business that we wish them to follow.
. . . When a man wants anything he ought to work for it and then he would be
called an honest man. This is our reason that we wish to secure land to persue
honesty and Industry."[64]

To indicate that the establishment of this boundary was not intended to
give the Lower Towns the right to remove or sell their lands by unilateral
action, the delegation's letter concluded: "The proposition that we proposed was for a division line to run from Tennessee River so as to take
in all the waters of Hiwassee to be the boundary between us and your
people. All north of that line to be under the laws of their own forming.
This line would be made for no other purpose than to suppress theft and
to secure our land and keep our chiefs from selling our land (or another
part of the Nation)."[65]

The Lower Town delegates did not interpret this letter as preventing
them from pursuing their own plan for removal and exchange. On 4 January 1809, Toochalee wrote to Jefferson asking him to confirm the removal plan that had been worked out with Meigs: "Father, I am sent by
my peopel, the princeable Chefes of the Lower towns . . . my part of the
Nation, the Lower towns, is deturm[in]ed to move over the massippa if
they like the Cuntry when they exploar it, pervided there father will assist them in their persute. A father knows the wants of there Children
when Going to travel; he fits them out Comferubly; if we should wish to
move we shall Lack Boates to move in and Good Guns to kill meet to Liv
on and to Gard our wimmen and Children."[66]

The last message to Jefferson came from the Upper Town delegates
in response to Toochalee's letter of 4 January. They attacked the Lower
Town chiefs for deceiving them and for turning against the government's
policy of civilization. "They are asking you for assistance to move. They

---

[64]Ibid. The letter also said "our old chiefs will see people with stolen property but
wont try to put a stop to it."

[65]Ibid. Signed by the original six delegates; the signatures of Cabbin Smith and Wilson were crossed out. Jefferson noted on this document, "The Upper are about 10 towns
and about 1200 [warriors? families?]."

[66]Ibid. Jefferson noted on this letter that "12 towns wish to remove across Misipi and
want to be well fitted out." Adding these twelve Lower Towns to the ten Upper Towns
(see n. 65) gives a total of only 22, which seems to leave many unaccounted for (see n.
61).

are asking you for Guns. Your advise has Been to us, Lay by our Guns and Goe to farming. Git hoes, plowes, and axes. The yung peopel holds your talk fast Respecting farming and Industrey. . . . Like wise our wimmin was told for to Set in the house and make Close [clothes] for their family. . . . The wimmin is to be pitted [pitied]. It tis by them that we are all Borne and Raised. They love their Children to be Near them as when they are in the Corne field they Expect to See them at mele times."[67] Apparently the women opposed removal too.

On 9 January 1809, Jefferson delivered his written answers, one to the Upper Town delegates and one to the delegates of both factions. No treaties or agreements were signed. Jefferson knew that treaties could only be made with the consent of councils.[68] To the Upper Towns Jefferson said, "With respect to the line of division between yourselves and the lower towns, it must rest on the joint consent of both parties." The division seemed "reasonable" to him, however, and he would be "willing to recognize these on each side of that line as distinct societies." He went on to advise the Upper Towns on how to establish laws that were "only for the present" and such as "suit your present condition." They should call a council and consult with Meigs about such laws, particularly "a law giving to every head of family a separate parcel of land," which should go to his descendants. "I sincerely wish," he concluded, "you may succeed in your laudable endeavors to save the remains of your nation by adopting industrious occupations and a government of regular law." He did not mention future citizenship, but this was his clearly implied goal.[69] Interpreting this message to Chisholm after returning to the agency, Meigs noted that the Upper Towns had "requested to be divided by a line of division" and that within their bounds "they propose to introduce a regular government but not denationalize themselves. . . . If

----

[67]Ibid.

[68]In April 1808, to prevent Meigs from making treaties only with those well disposed to the government, "a full council" passed a law "that no act of any Chief or Chiefs should be considered binding on the Nation unless they were first appointed in a council and then to be ratified by a full counsel of the Nation before whom these proceedings is to be laid." The Ridge, Pathkiller, and seventeen other chiefs sent a copy of this law to Jefferson, 4 June 1808, Letters Received, Unregistered Series, M-222, roll 3, frame 1343. The law was adopted, however, by a council dominated by the Upper Town chiefs.

[69]Jefferson, Address to the Cherokee Chiefs of the Upper Towns, 9 January 1809, Letters Sent, Sec. War, M-15, roll 2:414.

that be agreed to, that section East of Highwassee will try to organize a regular government by selecting such laws of the United States as may be found adapted to the state of information among them."[70]

Jefferson's message to the whole delegation took note of the distinction between those Cherokees who wished "to remain on their [ancestral] lands and "betake themselves to agriculture" and those who, "retaining their attachment to the hunter life . . . [,] are desirous to remove across the Mississippi." The government wished to satisfy both parties—"those who remain" and "those who wish to remove." Jefferson therefore permitted the Lower Towns to send an exploring party up the Arkansas and White Rivers to find "a tract of country suiting the emigrants and not claimed by other Indians." When such a tract had been found, "We will arrange with them and you the exchange of that for a just portion of the country they leave and to a part of which proportioned to their numbers they have a right. Every aid towards their removal and what will be necessary for them there will then be freely administered to them."[71]

The chiefs appear to have been satisfied with the proposal because each faction had a different interpretation of it. The Upper Towns took Jefferson to mean by "joint consent" and a future arrangement "with them and you" that both sides would have to agree to the terms of removal after the explorations and before any division of their homeland or exchange of land. The Lower Towns took him to mean that they might move as soon as they found a suitable spot in the West. They further presumed that the government would provide them with transportation and the means of support in their journey and settlement, and that only the details of the sale or exchange of lands would need to be worked out by later councils. The latter view was also taken by Meigs, who told the Cherokees upon their return to the nation that "the exchange does not depend on the consent of the nation because emigration cannot be restricted."[72] (It is likely that "exchange" in this context meant simply the right of emigrants to settle in the West.) Tolluntuskee, Meigs reported

---

[70]Meigs to John D. Chisholm, 28 March 1809, Cherokee Agency, TN, M-208, roll 4.

[71]Jefferson, Address, 9 January 1809, Letters Sent, Sec. War, M-15, roll 2:416.

[72]Meigs to Chisholm, 28 March 1809, Cherokee Agency, TN, M-208, roll 4.

in March 1809, did "not want to explore [the West] because he has already the necessary information" and said that he would be ready to leave shortly with his followers. Meigs assumed that they were free to go.

By the middle of August 1809 Tolluntuskee had 1,130 men, women, and children ready to move, and Meigs wrote at once to the secretary of war that "they expect the aid of Government" for their journey. He outlined the aid necessary: one keel boat, 200 rifles, 200 pounds of powder, 1,000 flints, 800 pounds of lead, 200 beaver traps, 100 axes, 100 corn hoes, 50 grubbing hoes, 250 wool and cotton cards, and 50 small ploughs. He expected "some thousands" more to follow this first contingent and noted that they would need similar assistance. The government should be prepared to buy up Cherokee land in the East in proportion to the percentage of Cherokees who had removed. "I estimate the whole number of Cherokees as 12,000, the whole quantity of land at 15,000,000 acres. Admitting this to be correct, . . . each man, woman, and child are entitled to 1,250 acres; at this ratio, 2,000 emigrants settled on those rivers [Arkansas and White] will intitle the United States to 2,500,000 acres [of the eastern Cherokee homeland]. If the United States grant the aid now asked, there will be upward of 2,000 Cherokees on those rivers before spring and probably double that number within two years."[73]

On 24 July, however, The Ridge and fifteen Upper Town chiefs, meeting at Oostenali, had sent Meigs a letter reminding him that "our father [Jefferson] has told us that our whole nation should be present at the sales of our lands, which we think is just."[74] The Upper Towns clearly expected that no emigration would be permitted until the terms of exchange had been worked out jointly. They were disappointed in this

---

[73]Meigs to William Eustis, 17 August 1809, Letters Received, Unregistered Series, M-222, roll 3, frame 1574.

[74]Meigs to The Ridge and the chiefs of fifteen Upper Towns, 2 August 1809, referring to action taken in council on 24 July, Cherokee Agency, TN, M-208, roll 4. The Ridge claims in this letter (sent after the meeting) that this council represented the will of the same forty-two towns that had instructed the delegates to Washington "that the path killer and 42 towns held to their country." In 1818, forty-nine chiefs said, "On the return of the deputation [from Washington] a Council was convened at this place [Oostenali] of 30 towns. They unanimously rejected a division line between the upper and lower towns." ABCFM 18.3.1, 2. If the Upper Towns did cast such a vote in July 1809 (whether by fifteen or thirty towns), it still needed to be ratified at a council of, or including, the Lower Towns. This came at Willstown in September 1809.

hope. Not only did Meigs not believe the Upper Towns had any right to prevent removal and exchange, but on 17 August he described the talks with Jefferson as "a negotiation with the President. The result was an agreement to exchange lands here for lands on the Arkansas and White rivers."[75] It seems highly unlikely that Jefferson and the delegates at that time saw it as a "negotiation" and "agreement," although Tolluntuskee and Meigs later chose to interpret it as such.

Meigs still thought that the current of Cherokee opinion was moving toward mass emigration. He wrote James Robertson on 1 September, asking him to inform Sevier that at the coming general council of the whole nation "it is probable, as has always been the case in such business, some of the Chiefs of the refractory party will try to get resolutions not to sell land," but within a short while "they will cast eyes and thoughts to the Mississippi and a sale or exchange will amount to the same thing eventually."[76] On 21 September he predicted that if Congress would only provide forty or fifty thousand dollars for expenses, there would soon be "a migration over the Mississippi" of "one half at least of the Cherokees."[77] But while Meigs persisted in this hope, the Cherokees were reaching the final stage of a very different consensus. Recognizing that Tolluntuskee and a few others probably could not be stopped, the majority of chiefs, Upper and Lower, concluded that national unity was the only way to prevent another land cession.

Late in September 1809, at a council at Willstown, the Cherokee nation at last overcame its internal divisions and animosities. Uniting behind the leadership of the Hicks-Ridge-Pathkiller party, a new coalition rejected both the proposed division line between the Upper and Lower Towns and Jefferson's suggestion that the Cherokees became fee-simple farmer-citizens. Moreover, they voted to merge the sections of the nation by abandoning entirely their old regional division into Upper and Lower Towns. Doublehead's old faction had finally dissolved. Pathkiller in-

---

[75]Meigs to Eustis, 17 August 1809, Letters Received, Unregistered Series, M-222, roll 3, frame 1574.

[76]Meigs to James Robertson, 1 September 1809, Cherokee Agency, TN, M-208, roll 4. Sevier was hoping to obtain a cession of all the remaining Cherokee land in Tennessee at federally sponsored negotiations later in September.

[77]Meigs to James Trumble, 21 September 1809, Letters Received, Main Series, M-221, roll 34, frame 1752.

formed Meigs of the new situation on 27 September: "It has now been along time that we have been much confused and divided in our opinions, but now we have settled our affair[s] to the satisfaction of both parties and become as one. You will now hear from us not from the lower towns nor the upper towns but from the whole Cherokee nation." This new national union was institutionalized by the creation of a national executive committee empowered to act for the nation when the national council was not in session. "We have this day," wrote Pathkiller, "appointed thirteen men to manage our national affairs, for we found it very troublesome to bring anything to bear where there were as many as we formally [formerly] had in our council."[78] This executive committee, which henceforth played an important role in Cherokee affairs, became the upper house of the bicameral national legislature in 1817. The committee chosen in 1809 consisted of influential chiefs from all three regions of the nation: Charles Hicks, The Ridge, John Walker, John McIntosh, Turtle at Home, John Lowery, Richard Brown, George Lowery, George M. Waters, Thomas Pettit, Doghead, Tuscock, and Sower John.[79]

On behalf of the united nation, the Willstown council also refuted Meigs's interpretation of Jefferson's address: "Concerning the people that want to move over the Mississippi, we have read the president's speech and we understand by it that nothing could be done without a national council and the majority of the nation." Commenting on Meigs's request to the secretary of war for a boat, guns, and other equipment for Tolluntuskee's emigrants, the council said, "we have read the letter" and "you ought not to have wrote so soon on that subject for it never was brought to a national council."[80]

---

[78]Pathkiller and other chiefs to Meigs, 27 September 1809, Cherokee Agency, TN, M-208, roll 4. This was signed by Pathkiller, Chulio, The Glass, Sour Mush, Big Half Breed, Dick Justice, Toochalee, Keuchestenasky, "and the rest of the Chiefs." Black Fox sent a representative who was well received. Unfortunately, details are lacking on this council.

[79]Apparently Hicks, The Ridge, Walker, McIntosh, and Pettit represented the lower division of the Upper Towns; Brown, the Lowerys, and Turtle at Home, the Lower Towns; and the remainder, the Valley Towns. For other actions of this committee and its changing membership, see Cherokee National Committee to Eustis, 13 February 1810; Meigs to Eustis, 14 February 1810; and Cherokee Council at Oostenali to Meigs, 9 April 1810, ibid., roll 5.

[80]Pathkiller and other chiefs to Meigs, 17 September 1809, ibid., roll 4.

Obtaining no response from Washington by the time the first emigrants were ready to leave, Meigs told the secretary of war, "I furnished this party with provisions" from the factory.[81] The first contingent left on 14 January 1810—sixty-three men, women, and children, "all from one town 160 miles above this post." A few days later another party of 100 departed "from two Towns situated about 100 miles below this place on the Tennessee River." On 16 February 1810, "Tolluntuskee left this place with a considerable party." Meigs had feared some opposition from the national committee, which was present at the embarkation, but he said they did not "use any arguments to dissuade the migration."[82] With Tolluntuskee's departure, emigration came to a halt; the nation would not be moved. Part of Meigs's problem was that he had no help from Washington. William Eustis, James Madison's secretary of war, informed Meigs that "the removal of the Cherokees and Choctaws to the Western Side of the Mississippi as contemplated by Mr. Jefferson has been considered by the present President. A gradual migration, until some general arrangements could be made, has been preferred."[83]

The final act in this first removal crisis took place on 11 April 1810, when a council of the newly unified nation recognized that with the recent departure of 1,000 emigrants, there were now almost 2,000 Cherokees living in Arkansas.[84] What relationship did they bear to the nation and what equity did they have in its ancestral land? For their own survival, the Eastern Cherokees concluded that the Western emigrants had forfeited all rights to their national patrimony:

> The country left to us by our ancestors has been diminished by repeated sales to a tract barely sufficient for us to stand on and not more than adequate to the purposes of supporting our posterity. . . . Some of our people have gone across the Mississippi without the consent of the nation although our father, the President [Jefferson] in his speech, required that they should obtain [it] previous to their

---

[81]Meigs to Eustis, 22 January 1810, ibid., roll 5.

[82]Meigs to William Blount, 16 February 1810, ibid.

[83]Eustis to Meigs, 27 March 1811, ibid.; Abel, *History of the Events*, 255, n. 6.

[84]In subsequent years the birthrate among the Eastern Cherokees more than made up for these and later emigrants. By 1825, although there were 3,500 to 4,000 Cherokees in Arkansas (as the result of the second removal crisis), there were 13,583 in the East. In 1835 there were almost 5,000 Cherokees in the West and 16,542 in the East. Mooney, "Myths," 125.

removing. We hope that the advice of our former president in encouraging our people to apply their minds to improvements in agriculture and the arts may be continued that their knowledge in these arts may be extended, and we rest assured that the General Government will not attend to, or be influenced by, any straggling part of the Nation to accede to any arrangement of our country that may be proposed contrary to the will and consent of the main body of the Nation.[85]

Henceforth, to be a Cherokee meant to dwell in the land of the Cherokee forefathers: "stragglers" from that land were now expatriates. (In 1816 the Cherokees suggested that the government compel return of the Western Indians to the fatherland; in 1818 the Westerners were deemed traitors for insisting on fulfillment of the land exchange.) Not surprisingly, in May 1810 Meigs referred to the Hicks-Ridge-Pathkiller coalition as the party "of popularity and blind patriotism."[86] By restoring Black Fox as principal chief later that year, the Cherokees stood united at last by a clear conception of their identity and their destiny.[87] The crisis of 1806-1809, threatening the fragmentation of the tribe, ended in the reunification and revitalization of the Cherokee Nation.

---

[85]Cherokee chiefs at a council in Oostenali to Meigs, 11 April 1810, Cherokee Agency, TN, M-208, roll 5.

[86]Meigs to Eustis, 10 May 1810, Letters Received, Main Series, M-221, roll 38, frame 5198.

[87]When the Cherokees told the treaty commissioners in 1817, "We consider ourselves a free and distinct nation and that the government of the United States have no police over us farther than a friendly intercourse in trade," they were simply reiterating a decision made in 1809. Copy of a letter signed by forty-nine Cherokee chiefs to McMinn, 30 June 1818, ABCFM 18.3.1, 2. Although the government always insisted that the Cherokees east and west constituted a single nation, it was unwilling or unable to provide a permanent home for those who moved West until 1828, when they were finally sent to what is now the northeastern corner of Oklahoma.

THE CHEROKEE
GHOST DANCE MOVEMENT
OF 1811-1813

We shall probably never know much about the Cherokee religious revival of 1811-1813, which James Mooney labeled a "Ghost Dance" movement. Mooney was commissioned to write a definitive study of the Ghost Dance movement among the Oglala Sioux that had led to the tragedy at Wounded Knee in 1890. In the course of that study, he correctly pointed out that similar movements had occurred much earlier in the century among many tribes east of the Mississippi. We know from the studies of "Cargo Cults" in Melanesia and witch-finding cults in Africa that similar movements continue today around the world. Weston La Barre in his controversial study, The Ghost Dance, *described some of the critical turning points in European history as Ghost Dance movements.*

This essay tries to coordinate the few documentary accounts we have about the Cherokee movement and to match them with the models that A. F. C. Wallace, Peter Worsley, and Kenelm Burridge have devised to delineate such movements. The accounts cited here vary greatly both in their details and in the interpretations they place on the movement. Perhaps the most important new source I was able to uncover was the account in the letters and journals of the Moravian missionaries to the Cherokees, which are in the Moravian Archives at Winston-Salem, North Carolina, written in German script. I owe a great debt to Mary Creech and Elizabeth Marx of the Moravian Archives for their assistance in this. When this article was submitted to the American Indian Quarterly, *the editor was forced to cut out six of the seven appendices because of the length of the manuscript. It is good to be able to include them here, and I hope that other accounts may eventually be found that will throw further light on this important event in Cherokee history.*

Although the Cherokee Ghost Dance movement was clearly a traditionalist revival resulting from the grave psychosocial stresses of the years 1789-1810, it can also be seen as a celebration of the Cherokee victory over the efforts to remove them from their homeland in 1808-1810. From this victory they achieved a new sense of unity and national pride. In addition, the rumors of war in the West, natural catastrophes such as earthquakes, and the wondrous sign of the comet of 1811, all contributed to this many-sided movement. Perhaps the most important point to emerge from a study of all the available sources is that this was not a movement inaugurated by the visit of Tecumseh to the Creeks in October 1811. The Cherokee movement preceded his visit, and it constituted a revival of traditional Cherokee dances and ceremonies, not the adoption of the new dances of the Shawnee prophet Tenskwatawa (Tecumseh's brother). The most puzzling point, which still awaits resolution, is whether there was a single Cherokee prophet named Charley (or Tsa-li) who assumed leadership of the movement or whether, as the evidence seems to indicate, there were many different prophets.

THE CHEROKEE GHOST DANCE MOVEMENT OF 1811-1813 got its name from James Mooney in 1891, but it has been known to historians since the first account was published by Thomas L. McKenney in 1838.[1] Recently a number of important studies have generated new insights into Ghost Dance religions, Cargo Cults, millenarian movements, and nativist revivals. They suggest the need to reexamine the Cherokee phenomenon. I have tried to assemble here all the primary accounts and to reassess them in the light of these recent studies, particularly those by A. F. C. Wallace, Peter Worsley, and Kenelm Burridge.

Although the evidence is still fragmentary, it casts serious doubts on the claim that there was a direct link between the Cherokee movement and the Ghost Dance religion of the Creeks. Not only did the Cherokee movement precede that of the Creeks, it remained passivist in tone where the Creek movement was militantly activist.[2] Reexamination of the evidence also makes questionable McKenney's account of a single prophet who inaugurated and directed the movement. By following McKenney and conflating a variety of prophets, prophecies, and events, historians and ethnographers have given the Ghost Dance a coherence and consistency it did not have. Furthermore, previous accounts have, in my opinion, dismissed the movement rather too easily on the basis of

---

[1]See Appendix A for McKenney's account and Appendix B for Mooney's.

[2]See Appendix C for an account of the Ghost Dance religion among the Creek as recorded by Benjamin Hawkins, federal agent to the Creek, in 1814. Mooney was among those who thought the Cherokee movement was directly influenced by the Creek. See Appendix B.

its more extreme manifestations and mistakenly attributed its demise to the failure of some of the more extravagant predictions to materialize.[3] Far from being a trivial incident, the Cherokee Ghost Dance movement marked a critical turning point in Cherokee history.

The standard version of the Cherokee Ghost Dance movement derives essentially from the account given to McKenney by the Cherokee chief, The Ridge, in the 1830s, and the account given to Mooney by the Cherokee, James Wafford, in 1891.[4] It can be summarized as follows: In the troubled years 1811-1812, when war with Britain and the Creek Nation seemed imminent, a prophet named Charley appeared among the Cherokee and described a dream or vision in which the Great Spirit spoke to him. The Great Spirit said he was angry with the Cherokees because they had departed from the customs and religious practices of their ancestors and were adopting the ways of the white man. To regain the favor of the Great Spirit and overcome their troubles, the Cherokees were told by their prophet to give up everything they had acquired from the whites (clothing, cattle, plows, spinning wheels, featherbeds, fiddles, cats, books) and return to the old ways: they must dance their old dances and revive their old festivals. The prophet also said that those who did not heed this message would be punished and some would die. Though Charley met some opposition, he found many ready to accept his revelation, and he went on to say that it had been revealed to him that on a specific date, three months hence, a terrific wind and hailstorm would take place that would annihilate all the white men, all the cattle, and all the works of the white man. The hailstones would be "as large as hominy blocks" and would crush all those who did not retreat to a special, charmed spot high in the Great Smoky Mountains where they would be safe. After the storm, these true believers would be able to return to their towns where they would find all of the deer, elk, buffalo, and other game that had disappeared. Then they would live again as their ancestors did in the golden era before the white man came. Most accounts of the Cherokee Ghost Dance maintain that the failure of the predictions discour-

---

[3]Even the Cherokee trivialized the movement. See Appendix D.

[4]Mooney himself conflated the accounts of Ridge and Wafford in his *Myths of the Cherokee* (Washington, 1900).

aged the followers of the prophet, and his movement came to an end in ridicule.[5]

However, when all of the accounts written at the time or recalled later by observers are assembled, it becomes evident that the movement was much more complex and disjointed than the standard accounts indicate. There was not one prophet (and only McKenney's account gives him a name) but a number of different prophets; some of the visions appeared not to one person but to several witnesses. While some of the prophecies did speak of a catastrophic hailstorm, others predicted a three-day eclipse. While some looked forward to a restoration of an idyllic past, others spoke of the end of the world or of the beginning of "a new earth." Some messages from the Great Spirit appear to have been hostile to all white men, but others made distinctions between good whites and bad. Some called for total rejection of the white man's culture and some for selective rejection. Some of the prophecies show obvious influences of Christian millennialism.

Taken together, the various accounts of the movement indicate that it started slowly in January or February of 1811, and then gained much wider credence after a series of earthquakes shocked the Cherokee Nation in December of that year (a fact that few historians have noted).[6] The movement then faded away in 1812 and was eclipsed by the Cherokees' entry into the Creek War of 1813. The recently translated diary of the Moravian mission at Springplace, Georgia, in the heart of the Cherokee Nation, provides the most striking evidence of the gradual development of the movement and its complex variations. These missionaries recorded six different prophetic messages (including those mentioned by McKenney and Mooney), but they also said there were many others.[7]

---

[5]Only Thurman Wilkins in *Cherokee Tragedy* (New York, 1970) provides a somewhat more complex account based upon excerpts from the Moravian diary (see Appendix E). However, Wilkins simply conflates his new evidence with the older versions. See Appendix G.

[6]Closely related to the famous New Madrid earthquake in Missouri, the first of these quakes was felt in the Cherokee Nation on 16 December 1811, and by 10 April 1812, no less than ten separate tremors had been felt, often accompanied by terrific claps of thunder, strikes of lightning, sinkings in the ground, windstorms, and the shaking of houses off their foundations. See the Moravian mission diary, Appendix E, for some of these reports.

[7]See Appendix G for relevant citations from this diary. These accounts are discussed at greater length below. The translation was made for the author by Elizabeth

Conditions among the Cherokee in 1811-1812 were certainly ripe for a millenarian or apocalyptic movement as we have come to understand the origins of such events. The nation had been through a long period of social disorganization starting with its defeat as British allies in the continuous and bitter warfare from 1776 to 1794. By 1800 the Cherokee had been forced to yield half of their original tribal land in treaties resulting from these defeats, including the loss of their oldest towns and most sacred places. (These losses figure prominently in some of the revelations of 1811-1812). In 1805-1807 new treaties, fraudulently effected, cost them another sixth of their territory. As a result of this shrinkage in their boundaries, whole villages had to be moved within the decreasing tribal area; some families had to move two or three times in twenty years. Nevertheless, white intruders kept crowding into their territory from surrounding frontier settlements and the federal government was reluctant to keep its promises to remove the whites despite the friction they caused.

During the American Revolution the Cherokees divided into two political factions, the Upper and Lower Towns; the former made peace with the Americans in 1777, but the latter, in alliance with the Creeks and Shawnees, waged guerrilla war until 1794. This internal division continued until 1807 when the chief of the Lower or Chickamauga faction was killed in a semiofficial execution by the chiefs of the Upper Town faction. It was by playing upon this factionalism that the state and federal governments managed to obtain so many cessions of Cherokee land. In 1808 some of the chiefs began to negotiate with the government for removal and agreed to exchange land in the East for land west of the Mississippi. Despite the opposition of the vast majority of Cherokees and the deposition of the principal chief, who supported removal, this scheme was vigorously pushed by the government from 1808 to 1811, resulting in the departure for Arkansas Territory of roughly 1,200 out of 12,000 Cherokees. The government failed, however, to complete the "exchange" of lands due to the resistance of those who remained in the East. Nevertheless, the white authorities continued to exacerbate the division by arguing that those in the West deserved a share of the annuities, although those in the East considered the Westerners expatriates if not traitors.[8]

Marx through the courtesy of Mary Creech, archivist of the Moravian Archives, Winston-Salem, North Carolina, and is used here with permission.

[8]For more detailed discussion of the critical period in Cherokee history from 1794 to

Concurrently with these political divisions another type of factionalism developed between those who favored the government's "civilization plan" (to lead the Cherokees into becoming self-subsistent yeoman
farmers on individual plots of land) and those who wished to retain as
much as possible of their traditional mixed economy—hunting, fishing,
gathering, and farming on the basis of communal ownership of the land
and water rights. As the fur trade waned, men were forced to spend their
time cultivating food while women had to become spinners and weavers
of cotton, wool, and flax in order to provide clothing for their children.
Those Cherokees who favored acculturation (often those of mixed Cherokee and white ancestry, who constituted almost one-quarter of the population) were deemed "the progressives" by the government and grew
richer and more influential, while the traditionalists (considered "backward" by the government) grew comparatively poorer and lost influence.
The progressives avoided the drudgery of cultivation by purchasing
black slaves. In addition to the disappearance of game, which had provided the traditionalists with a cash income, their inexperience as farmers, their lack of adequate tools and capital to run a farm, and a series of
droughts, frosts, and pestilences created famine conditions among the
poor on several occasions between 1801 and 1811. Government gifts of
food to the starving were provided in exchange for additional land cessions. The breakdown of traditional values, tribal mores, and internal
authority led to increasing drunkenness, crime, and violence between
1794 and 1810.

Partly to cope with this breakdown but also to adapt to the demands
of the more acculturated, the Cherokee National Council passed in 1808
its first written law (in English) establishing a mounted police force to
suppress horse stealing and other crimes through summary punishment
on the spot.[9] This same law revised the practice of matrilineal descent of

---

1810, see W. G. McLoughlin, "Cherokee Anomie, 1794-1809," in *Uprooted Americans*,
ed. R. L. Bushman et al. (Boston: Little, Brown, 1979) 125-60 and W. G. McLoughlin,
"Thomas Jefferson and the Beginning of Cherokee Nationalism," *William and Mary
Quarterly*, 3rd ser., 32 (October 1975): 547-80.

[9]It is noteworthy that the first version of which we have an account (in February 1811)
specifically expresses opposition to the harsh execution of these laws by the mounted police. See Appendix E.

property, while another law in 1810 put an end to the age-old tradition of clan revenge.

In order to counter the divide-and-conquer policy of the whites, the Cherokees reunited the Lower and Upper Towns in 1810 and established a National Committee of thirteen chiefs to conduct tribal affairs between councils. While this gave the nation necessary unity in facing white aggressions, it also detracted from the local authority of the fifty-odd towns and their chiefs. The traditional democratic and decentralized authority of the nation was being centralized and bureaucratized. In place of their old participatory democracy and local home rule, the Cherokees were being forced to accept a new power structure in which authority emanated from the top down.

Not only did the dominant white culture impose new economic, social, and political practices upon the Cherokees, it also encouraged the introduction of a rival religious ideology. The first Christian missionaries, the Moravians, were allowed to form a mission school and conduct worship at Springplace, Georgia, in 1801. From 1803 to 1810 the Presbyterians conducted mission schools in the Tennessee area of the nation. Other itinerant preachers from the Baptists and Methodists passed through the nation sporadically. Although the Cherokee needed and wanted schools to learn to read and write, to farm and spin, the missionaries also brought a new set of beliefs and values that contrasted sharply with those of their traditional priests and medicine men. The Protestant ethic of hard work as the key to individual success and wealth promoted the capitalist system of cash-crop farming, encouraged the nuclear family, and fostered an intensely competitive, individualistic, materialistic acquisitiveness in contrast to the communal cooperation, mutual sharing, and open hospitality of the Cherokee tradition. Technically the nation maintained the concept of communal ownership of the land, but those who adopted the Protestant ethic and cash-crop farming rapidly attained the best farmland and pasturage, acquired ferry and tavern franchises, built trading posts, grist mills and saw mills, and charged the poorer Cherokee on the marginal lands for the necessities of life. In short, class divisions began to match political divisions. Nevertheless, by white standards, the nation was improving. A census taken by the federal agent in 1809 demonstrated both population and economic growth. At that time the Cherokee possessed 583 black slaves, 13 gristmills, 3 saw mills, 567 plows, 429 looms, 1,572 spinning wheels, 1 powder mill, and hardly any Cherokee family lacked some hogs, chicken, sheep, cattle, or horses.[10]

By 1811 the Cherokee people had clearly reached a critical stage in their history. Thousands who had previously drifted along as best they could between the old ways and the new began to realize that they were reaching—perhaps had already reached—a point of no return so far as their traditional way of life was concerned. The Ghost Dance movement represented the recognition of this fact in symbolic form.

In addition to these long-range aspects of cultural change and dislocation, there were a number of short-range crises that heightened tensions after 1810. At that date the two Presbyterian schools closed, and it was not clear whether the nation should or should not seek missionary help to replace them. In 1811 the revered old principal chief, Black Fox, died and had to be replaced. During the course of 1811 there was a severe famine and the outbreak of a strange disease that killed many horses. In the fall of 1811 a large comet blazed across the sky for weeks. There were increasing rumors of a new war with Britain; Tecumseh began to arouse the Western tribes for a final effort to throw the whites back across the Appalachians; a war between the Cherokees and the Creeks appeared imminent. In December 1811, a horrendous series of earthquakes seemed to portend the collapse of Mother Earth from old age—as if the Cherokee people and Mother Earth were dying together under the strain of acculturation and the confusion it caused.

The studies of A. F. C. Wallace, Kenelm Burridge, and Peter Worsley indicate that it is under precisely such tensions, confusions, frustrations that a community "anticipates the emergence of a hero who will restore their prosperity and prestige," give them a new sense of order and direction, and provide them with authority from "on high" to reveal and sanctify a new code of values.[11] Though a much larger tribe than the

---

[10]It is interesting that the existence of these gristmills, to which the Cherokee brought their corn and had to pay for it to be ground, are also a matter of concern in the vision of February 1811. See Appendix E.

[11]Kenelm Burridge, *New Heaven, New Earth* (New York: Shocken, 1969) 3. Other discussions of cultural breakdown that I have relied upon can be found in Peter Worsley's introduction to *The Trumpet Shall Sound* (New York: Shocken, 1968) and A. F. C. Wallace, "Revitalization Movements," *American Anthropology* 58 (1956): 264-81. All of these writers portray millenarian movements as the religion of the disinherited, the poor, the oppressed. This is true for the Cherokee as a community vis à vis the whites, but within that community, the Ghost Dance movement appealed to all classes, not simply to the traditionalists or the poor.

Seneca and with more resources available to them, the Cherokee nevertheless exhibited many of the same problems of "cultural distortion" or social breakdown that Wallace found underlying the emergence of Handsome Lake's visions and movement among the Seneca in 1799–1803; the stresses included the failure of the structured avenues of advancement, extreme pressures of enforced acculturation, decreasing efficiency of the traditional "stress release system."[12] At this point in a mounting concatenation of public and private strain, the people of any community would become desperate to find alternatives.

Two particular aspects of cultural stress seem most critical according to Worsley and Burridge: competing value systems and competing ideological systems. Burridge stresses the former, noting that it is the tension between competing means of acquiring power (competition between impinging white and waning native norms) within a tribe that creates the confusion, frustration, and anomie out of which new prophets rise:

> . . . in those places where the representatives of the two kinds of social order continually encounter each other and were pushed into competitive roles . . . there we find chiliasms. Where there seemed to be a quite unfair and arbitrary or capricious access to the goods of the environment, there too we find the stirring of messianic or millenarian activities. And common to both situations is the fact that, given the differences inherent in the two social orders, neither issue was susceptible to a qualitative decision acceptable to both parties.[13]

In the Cherokees' case, the competition lay between the materialistic, acquisitive values of the white capitalist system and the old communal sharing of the Cherokee tradition. The ability of the dominant white authorities to grant prestige, wealth, and power to those who went along with the new social order, appeared to the traditionalists unfair and arbitrary. The old social order gave prestige and influence to those who had proven themselves as warriors or hunters, and who were wise in council and adhered to the values of sharing. Now honor went to individuals whom the whites labeled "progressive," often because of their

---

[12] See A. F. C. Wallace, *The Death and Rebirth of the Seneca* (New York: Random House, 1969) 184, 239-40, and Wallace, "Revitalization," 265-67. While Wallace says that revitalization movements spring from the vision "of a single individual" (270), Peter Worsley argues that at the outset of such movements many different prophets and visions may occur and only later, through a very complex process (which he calls "social validation"), does a "movement" begin to develop. Worsley, *Trumpet*, xii-xviii.

[13] Burridge, *New Heaven*, 38.

white ancestry. Because of their willingness to put personal aggrandizement ahead of communal rights, these individuals were given large "presents," taken to the federal capital to meet the president, and hence obtained power over the destiny of the nation. Those who did not accept the new standards were called "backward," "ignorant," "enemies of government," and kept from power.

In such a situation, Burridge notes, "millenarian activities provide the opportunity for becoming someone distinct and worthwhile."[14] By adhering to them, one becomes a member of the chosen few and, through adherence to the prophet and his message, attains special harmony with the divine powers that control the universe. A transcendent sense of order replaces temporal confusion. The disinherited accept the messages of catastrophe and supernatural intervention because they lack in real life the political and economic mechanisms needed to reform their world.[15]

Peter Worsley argues that millenarian movements seem to arise where a competing Christian ideology is present. While it is incorrect, he notes, "to ascribe the spread of millenarianism . . . merely to the activity of fundamentalists sects" in a direct, one-to-one relationship, nevertheless "it was not until the coming of the Whites that such [millenarian or apocalyptic] myths were transformed into expectations of proximate deliverance and turned into burning programmes of action by organized cults" among non-Christian people.[16] The presence of Christians, the consciousness of a competing ideology with millennial doctrines, the belief that there is one Great Spirit over all peoples and that elements in what He has revealed to whites may have been distorted but are true if correctly reinterpreted—all of these factors contribute to the kinds of prophecies and visions that occur in this kind of cultural breakdown. Both "conscious selection" and "unconscious reinterpretation of Christian thought," Worsley notes, take place between the competing ideologies. The Cherokees, in short, may have adapted the Christian apocalypse to their own ends. Whites, however, saw these ends as anti-Christian and antiwhite even though the Cherokee prophets prescribed

---

[14]Ibid., 46.

[15]Worsley, *Trumpet*, 227.

[16]Ibid., 244-46; Burridge, *New Heaven*, 35.

only passive waiting for supernatural action. "All millenarian activities," Burridge states, "must be in some part challenging, rebellious or revolutionary . . . whether or not the activities in question are initially directed against the administration."[17]

Because the account of the Cherokee Ghost Dance movement in the Moravian diary is the most complete, the most detailed, and covers the full chronological span from February 1811 to April 1812, it seems logical to use its entries as the basis for a closer exposition and examination. Although the Moravians did not speak or understand Cherokee, they utilized native interpreters and tried to write down as carefully as possible the words of their informants. Room must be allowed, however, for considerable distortion. The Moravians inevitably translated Cherokee terms into white, Christian terms. The most notable example is their use of the word *God* (*Gott* in German) for what the Cherokees must have understood as the Great Spirit, the Earth Mother, or the Creator of Life and Breath.

The first version appeared in January or early February of 1811 and was related by those who saw it to a council in the town of Oostenali (or Ustanali) on 7 February. It was told to the Moravians on 10 February by Chief Keychzaetel (or Koy, ch, z, o, te, la), known as The Warrior's Nephew.[18] He said it occurred to a man and two women at dusk near a hill called Rocky Mountain while they were on a journey. They heard a loud noise in the air and saw a crowd of Indians coming out of the sky and landing on a nearby hill. They rode black horses and their leader was beating a drum. He told them not to be afraid because they were his brothers, and he had been sent by the Great Spirit with a special message. The Great Spirit was upset that they were allowing so many white people into their country "without any distinction" between good and bad whites. The Great Spirit did not like their planting the white man's variety of corn and wanted them to return to their old Indian corn. Nor did he want them to grind it in the white man's mills but to have their women pound it in mortars "in the manner of your forefathers."

"The Mother of the Nation" had forsaken them and allowed the game to disappear because she did not like the millstones, which "broke her

---

[17]Burridge, 61.

[18]I have paraphrased the Moravian diary here to save space. The full text is given in Appendix E.

bones." However, she would return and help the Cherokee if they would get rid of the bad white people and return to their old way of life. After all, "the white people are entirely different beings from us; we are made from red clay; they, out of white sand."[19] So long as whites stayed outside the nation's boundaries, the Cherokees might "keep good neighborly relations with them," but it was necessary for the whites to return the land on which their "beloved" or sacred towns were built; these had been given to the Cherokee forever. The Mother of the Nation also told them to stop punishing each other so severely and whipping people till the blood came for infractions of the new laws. The Indian drummer on the black horse then pointed to the sky where four white houses appeared in a beautiful light; he said they were to build houses like that in their beloved towns for those white men who were good to them and others "who can be useful to the Nation with writing, etc." This was the message they were to tell not only to their own people but to the federal Cherokee agent, Colonel Return J. Meigs. Furthermore, the spirit drummer had said it would "not be well" with those who refused to believe in the vision and its message.

The Warrior's Nephew also told the Moravians that this spirit message had been very reverently received by the chiefs and warriors at the Oostenali Council except for one chief, The Ridge, who had been "ill treated" for attempting to deny its validity.

No more is known of this vision or its adherents, but in May 1811, The Warrior's Nephew again visited the Moravians and told them that at a recent council the chiefs had asked Colonel Meigs to remove all the whites from the Cherokee Nation (except for those who could be useful, like blacksmiths, school teachers, the Moravian missionaries, and—despite the vision—those who were building mills for them). Meigs had agreed to do this and it is clear from the agency records that regular army troops did go out in the summer of 1811 and force hundreds of whites who had illegally built cabins and started farms on Cherokee land to move back across the boundary. It is also known that as soon as the

---

[19]This statement of different creations of man based upon color is a common theme in Native American thought in this era. It expresses both the fact of ethnic diversity and the need for national self-assertion.

troops were gone, many of these whites returned to the nation and continued to live there.[20]

In the days after the first severe earthquake on 16 December 1811, the Moravians recorded that a great wave of fear and confusion swept across the Cherokee Nation. Many chiefs and ordinary people came to the missionaries to seek an explanation. Some of these suggested that "the earth is probably very old" and would "soon collapse." Others said that a large snake must have crawled under their homes and shaken them. The Ridge, who had had no use for the first vision, and whose children attended the mission school, came to ask the missionaries whether the earthquakes signified "the end of the world." Another prominent chief, Charles Hicks, who was shortly to present himself to the Moravians for baptism, told the missionaries he thought the earthquake foretold "the last day" mentioned in the Bible.[21]

However, not until 17 February 1812, did the Moravians record another vision. Although different in details, it had some striking similarities to the vision recorded a year earlier. A Cherokee named Big Bear said he had heard it from another man whom he did not name. It occurred soon after the first earthquake. A Cherokee father was sitting in front of his fire caring for two sick children. Suddenly a tall man "clothed entirely in the foliage of the trees, with a wreath of the same foliage on his head," appeared in the cabin. He was "carrying a small child in his arm and had a larger child by the hand." The man said that the child in his arm was God and that God might soon destroy the earth. God was displeased that the Cherokee had sold so much land to the whites and especially that they had sold [in 1777] the sacred town of Tugaloo in western South Carolina. Tugaloo was "the first place which God created" and where he had "placed the first fire." Now the whites had desecrated the sacred hill and built a house on it. That house should be destroyed and the hill returned to grass. He was also angry because the

---

[20]White intruders were a perennial and frustrating problem; by treaty, whenever a clash between Cherokees and whites occurred, it had to be settled in white courts. Since Indians were not allowed to testify in these courts, they seldom won such cases. One reason for the separatist tendency in the Ghost Dance movement was to avoid the sense of inferiority and second-class status resulting from this fact.

[21]Hicks presented himself for baptism in July 1812, though he was not actually baptized until February 1813. See Kenneth G. Hamilton, trans., "Minutes of the Mission Conference Held in Springplace," *The Atlanta Historical Bulletin* (Winter 1970): 70.

Cherokee were neglecting their festivals, particularly their feast of the first fruits [the Green Corn Dance?] when they were supposed to express their gratitude to Him. Then he implied that the Indian's children were sick because the Cherokees had forgotten their Indian remedies (or failed to consult their medicine men). The spirit messenger gave the Indian "two small pieces of bark from a certain tree" and said if he brewed a drink from that and gave it to his children, they would become well. He then "told him about other remedies" for illness. Finally he said he would now take God back home and disappeared.

When the Moravians responded that they did not trust in such dreams and instead found in their Bible that God loved all men and would love and help the Indians who honored Him, Big Bear said that was good, but while "the white people know God from the Book . . . we [know] him from other things." However, he expressed nothing but respect for the missionaries, about whom he had never heard "anything bad," though there were many bad white people around.

Throughout February the Moravians learned that "fear and terror" were spreading "through the whole Nation." They heard "much about dreams and false prophets," and on 23 February they recorded the first apocalyptic prophecy about imminent destruction. Only a few details of this prophecy are given in the diary, but the missionaries said that the residents of one Cherokee town had heard a prediction that "hail stones the size of half bushels" would fall "on a certain day," and when that day came they all fled to the nearby hills and hid themselves in caves or under stones.[22] When the hailstorm did not materialize, they returned home but remained "ready and willing to believe every new deceiver."

Perhaps the prophet who made this prediction later revised it or perhaps another prophet had a similar revelation, but in any case the Moravians recorded a somewhat different account obtained a week later from another Cherokee, an elderly woman named Laughing Molly. She had heard that "in the space of three months, the moon would become dark, and thereafter hailstones as large as hominy blocks would fall, all cattle would die and soon thereafter the earth would come to an end." The "sorcerer" who said this claimed that there would be no war until that time but "after that, he did not know." Clearly rumors of war had

---

[22]It should be noted that in Georgia hailstones had been known to fall that were "as large as an infant's head," killing horses and doing great damage to homes.

something to do with this prediction, but Molly was simply worried about being killed by hailstones.[23] She was reassured, however, when the Moravians told her that "God loves people unspeakably" and she should "pray to Him faithfully that He would have mercy on her and save her." "I am no longer afraid," she said, "I will believe your words and no longer listen to liars and sorcerers."

By 1 March 1812, Charles Hicks and other leading chiefs had regained their composure and were ready to use their influence against the prophets who were causing or intensifying the anxiety. When a group of local chiefs from the town of Etowah (in northwestern Georgia) came to Hicks for advice about the prophets, "He told them not to give the liars any hearing at all, but much rather to embarrass them publicly, indeed, to punish them." Like Laughing Molly, Hicks preferred "God's word— the Old Book, as they call the Bible." He told the Etowah chiefs, as the Moravians had told others, that while God sometimes sent earthquakes to warn people of their sinfulness or to discipline them, still He loved them and wanted to forgive them and help them. When the Etowah chiefs said that a statement of disbelief by an Indian named The Duck in their town had resulted in his death, Hicks said all men must die and disbelief in these visions had no bearing on the Duck's death. They said they were convinced by his argument.

Nevertheless, more visions and prophecies occurred and were believed. On 8 March, the Moravians recorded a fifth prophecy. This they heard from Mrs. Clement Vann, the Cherokee widow of a white trader who lived close by the mission. She was told that there was going to be an eclipse that would last for three days, "during which all the white people would be snatched away as well as all Indians who had any clothing or household articles of the white man's kind, together with all their cattle." When this would occur she did not know or say, but the prophet who had the vision told the Cherokee to "put aside everything that is similar to the white people and that which they had learned from them, so that in the darkness God might not mistake them and snatch them away with the former." This was the most sweeping version recorded of the destruction of the whites along with their manners and civilization, yet it has curious overtones resembling the biblical story of the Passover.

---

[23]War with England officially began in July 1812; battle with the Prophet in the fall of 1811.

Mrs. Vann said many Cherokees were selling or "doing away with their household articles and clothing," but since she did not believe the prophecy, "she had offered to buy one item or another from them." The believers told her that she and other nonbelievers would "die at once" together with all their livestock. The Cherokee she had talked to cited the death of The Duck as confirmation of this. The growing amount of overlap in these various prophecies and messages seems to indicate that over the fifteen months a standardized version of the revelations was evolving, though it still lacked consistency.

The Moravians were particularly disturbed by this version from Mrs. Vann because it spoke explicitly of the necessity of rejecting all that the Cherokees had learned from white men. This the Moravians considered a direct attack upon Christianity and their school. The Cherokee priests or "sorcerers," as the missionaries saw it, did not really mean that the Cherokee should put away "the outward garb of the poor heathen" but that they should reject "their change of heart"—their growing sympathy for the Christian religion. This was a "new stratagem of the Devil," said the Moravians, who "wants to warn them against the teaching of the White people of Jesus, the crucified, their only rightful Lord and Master."

On the same date the Moravians also reported another kind of vision: "The false prophets pretend to have seen ugly and terrifying appearances of God," and one pupil at their school, named Johnston, "said that in his neighborhood there was also the talk that a new earth would come into being in the Spring." What the nature of "the new earth" would be, Johnston did not say or they did not record. But this is the last of the prophecies and visions reported by the Moravians or anyone else. The movement either died out or went underground in 1812.

The Moravians unfortunately did not record any rituals connected with the movement. The only account we have describing them was recorded by Colonel Meigs on 19 March 1812.[24] Meigs attributed the movement to the fear created by "the late shocks of the earth," which the Cherokees explained as "the Anger of the Great Spirit." In order to "appease" this anger, "They have revived their religious dances of ancient origin" with much "solemnity." They had also revived the practice of

---

[24]See Appendix F for Meigs's account.

"going to water"; that is, after their dances they went to the nearest river or stream, jumped in, and washed themselves. "These ablutions are intended to show that their sins are washed away and that they are cleansed from all defilements." Like the Moravians, Meigs heard that "some fanatics" had arisen who told them "that the Great Spirit is angry with them for adopting the manners, customs, and habits of the white people who they think are very wicked." Part of the ritual associated with the revival of the ancient dances "was to throw their clothing into the fire" and burn it up. "Some of the females are mutilating fine muslin dresses and are told they must discontinue their dancing reels and country dances which have become very common amongst the young people." Meigs evidently heard nothing of hailstorms, eclipses, or the snatching away of nonbelievers and whites by the Great Spirit. Nor did he record anything about the effort to regain beloved towns. If there was only Meigs's version, we would have to term the movement a nativist or restorationist one and not an apocalyptic or millenarian one.

However, putting together all the accounts we have, it is evident that the Cherokee Ghost Dance movement contained many different elements. It was nativistic in its rejection of alien persons, customs, values, and materials (or technology); it was revivalist or restorationist in its effort to restore old rituals, festivals, values, and customs; it was apocalyptic in predicting a sudden and drastic transformation of the world by supernatural powers (using natural catastrophes as the means); it was messianic in being led by prophets with divine revelations who demanded obedience and total commitment on pain of death; it was millenarian in looking forward to "a new earth" or a return to an idealized golden age. In addition, if a cargo cult is that which seeks to import or incorporate into the existing community some of the customs, values, or beliefs of the dominant or colonial culture, the Cherokee Ghost Dance can bear that definition as well.[25]

Although the Cherokee Ghost Dance movement contained many of the ingredients of such cultural phenomena, it seems necessary to conclude that it was an abortive movement. It did not, in the end, come together into a unified, coherent pattern; it apparently had no single

---

[25]See Wallace, "Revitalization," 265, for these various definitions. As he points out, however, most Ghost Dance or revitalization movements contain more than one of these elements.

prophet or leader so far as contemporary reports show. It did not inaugurate a concerted reform program. Various efforts have been made to classify the stages in such movements. Wallace states that the most successful ones begin with the vision of a single prophet; he then communicates the revealed message to others; the believers or converts are then organized into groups by disciples; then comes the routinization of charisma, the adaptation of the message and program to political realities in order to cope with opposition, and, finally, the emergence of a viable cultural alternative to solve the problems that led to the emergence of the prophet.[26] Peter Worsley describes the development of a cargo-cult movement as beginning with the prophet and his vision; then the prophet finds an audience; next he obtains a following (converts, disciples); then a movement begins, organization takes place, and finally the whole body of doctrines, priests, and believers is institutionalized as a recognized part of the culture.[27] Clearly the Cherokee Ghost Dance did not get far along in this process.

Most ethnographers and historians have attributed this to the fact that the threats of death to nonbelievers and the predictions of the hailstorm did not materialize. Such specific predictions regarding events, places, and dates are, as Worsley notes, likely to make such a movement extremely "vulnerable." By no means did all the prophecies contain such predictions. The general threat of harm to nonbelievers was in fact confirmed for many Cherokees by the death of The Duck in Etowah, and the predictions of catastrophe seem to have been generally vague or subject to postponement.

Nor is it sufficient to blame the failure of the movement upon the lack of charisma among the prophets. As Worsley has made clear, inherent personal charisma is probably never sufficient in itself to make such movements effectual. An audience becomes a following and later an organization only when the followers find the prophet's message relevant to their personal and social needs. Charisma in this sense is social not personal; it requires interaction between the prophet and the hearers. They must, "in a dialectical way," *create* the prophet, the message, and the movement by accepting it as their own. Worsley describes this as the

---

[26]Ibid., 270-75.

[27]Worsley, *Trumpet*, xxvi.

"social validation" of a leader or prophet.[28] Somehow the Cherokees (though they listened earnestly to their prophets and though some of them wanted to believe in their alternatives) could not establish that rapport, that give-and-take with any of them that would have defined and refined their vision into a viable program for a reformation. The prophets expressed general, abstract hopes and fears, but what they said was not "validated by reference to experience," to the Cherokees' own sense of reality—psychological and social. Perhaps also the lack of official efforts to suppress the prophets by the dominant white culture played a part in abating the movement. Most students of such movements have discovered that attempts at suppression tend to provide the best means of consolidating them.

If we examine the content of the visions and messages from the Great Spirit and the varied reactions to them, we find not only a broad variety of meanings but an even more important confusion in interpretations. Not only was it unclear whether the prophets wanted the Cherokees to reject all or only part of the white man's culture, it was also unclear whether the Great Spirit was primarily angry at the whites or with the Cherokee. There appears to have been a sophistication among the Cherokee, an awareness of the ambiguities in their situation, which kept them from accepting simplistic answers to their dilemmas. This in itself was an indication that a watershed had been crossed. Even the prophets acknowledged that there were benefits to be gained from certain aspects of acculturation.

One of the most curious gaps in the records we have of the movement is the absence of any mention of a new code of morality. Wallace, Burridge, and Worsley all stress the critical importance of such codes in these kinds of movements. "All prophets stress moral renewal," Worsley notes; there is a very heavy "emphasis laid in all cults upon a new morality," even if, in fact, the "new" moral code contains large elements from the traditional code.[29] Wallace notes the importance of Handsome Lake's moral code with its emphasis on hard work and restraint from drink. Mooney noted the importance of Wovoka's ethic among the Paiutes: "Do not tell lies"; "Do no harm to anyone"; "Do right always."

---

[28]Ibid., xii-xiv.

[29]Ibid., 251.

The Shawnee Prophet told his people to give up alcohol, have respect for the aged and infirm, give up marriage with whites, be kind to children, and abstain from lying and stealing. Nowhere, though, do we find such a code expressed in any of the Cherokee visions. Implicitly, of course, a return to the golden past would mean a return to the ethic of brotherhood, community, and a life without rum and whiskey. But this was not sufficient. It did not address the particular guilts felt by the Cherokee about their own bad behavior in 1811-1812.

Meigs reported that some of those who attended the revived dances were disappointed that the prophets seemed interested only in destroying clothes, hats, and fiddles. One "young Cherokee woman" told Meigs that when the believers urged her to throw her clothes into the fire, "she told them that was nothing; they ought to become good people and leave off stealing horses and drinking whiskey." Another Cherokee told the dancers, "It is no matter what cloaths I wear while my heart is straight." Obviously there was already a clearly understood moral code available. I suspect, however, that it resembled too closely the Christian ethic, and the prophets had not yet found a way to work out a new code that would mesh with the traditional Cherokee code. Insofar as a return to traditional mores and customs called for at least an implicit rejection of materialism, acquisitiveness, cut-throat competition and individual self-aggrandizement, the prophetic messages were attractive to many. But unlike Handsome Lake, the Cherokee prophets failed to unite the old and the new ethic into a clear moral alternative.

Still, the movement was far from negligible. At its peak it attracted general interest and concern. It attracted the disinherited, the poor, the traditionalist, and it also attracted those who were sufficiently acculturated to wear fine muslin dresses, to own slaves, to have featherbeds. It attracted the old who clung to their ancestral ways, and it also attracted the young who felt uneasy about abandoning those ways. Some of the most noted chiefs as well as the most simple folk felt its appeal.

Those individuals closest to the missionaries were least attracted to the movement. This itself is an important clue to the failure of the movement. The Cherokee were, by 1811-1812, becoming much better acquainted with Christian ideology. For some it had distinct attractions: if the white man's science, technology, and firepower were superior, so must his God be (or his way of obtaining God's power). For others, the missionaries, after a decade among them, had proved the most fair-minded, even-handed, and helpful of all the whites; they had an ethic of brotherhood and sharing and preached that all men were equal under God. They instructed Cherokee children to be industrious, kind, sober, and honest; without charge they provided them with the vocational skills needed to survive in the new circumstances. It was true that missionaries had taken up some of their land, creating large and apparently permanent establishments. Some feared they ultimately had designs on the land rather than on the souls of the Cherokee. But most were more impressed by the missionaries' self-sacrifice than by their acquisitiveness. As The Warrior's Nephew told the Moravians in May 1811, "We do not consider you as white people but as Indians. God has sent you to teach our people. You do not want our land. You are here only out of love for us." Hence the missionaries deserved attention when they questioned the prophecies and suggested other ways to appease God's anger or disappointment with the Cherokee.

In answering inquiries generated by the prophecies and visions, the missionaries were clear and specific. They explained the hard times, the displeasure of God, the meaning of the earthquakes, in terms of the Cherokees' failure to accept the Christian view of God and their failure to lead sober, honest, industrious lives. Patiently the Moravians told them that earthquakes were as much a sign of God's love and concern as of his anger. Explicitly they showed that "the Old Book" had its own version of the Last Judgment and the Millennium in which all God's children, white and red, were to share if they believed. Frankly they admitted that there were bad white men as well as bad red men. The proper response to God's anger, they said, lay in individual commitment to higher ethical values and to the Christian ideology, not in rejecting the advantages offered by technology and farming. Faced with the choice of believing in the immediate, apocalyptic millennialism (Max Weber's "this worldly" millennialism) of their prophets or believing in the ultimate "other-worldly" form espoused by the missionaries, those Cherokees who understood the missionaries' argument found the latter more helpful. It offered both the hope for a better world and a means of comprehending and coping with the present world. As Chief Sour Mush, one of the leading chiefs in the nation, said to the Moravians before the federal agent and the whole National Council in April 1812, he was not so upset by the white people in general as by "the misconduct of his own people." He said to the council, "As the earth moved sometimes a short time ago, you were in great anxiety and feared that you would sink into it, but when you go among the white people to break down their stables and steal their horses, you are not afraid, and there is much greater danger, for if they should catch you in such an act, they would surely shoot you down, and then you would surely be sunk into the earth."[30]

In this respect the Ghost Dance movement may have marked a watershed between Cherokee adherence to the old religious world view of their forefathers and the new Christian ideology of the white man. Not that the missionaries were making or would soon make large numbers of converts. Over the next two decades only a tiny minority of Cherokee sought Christian baptism. But by 1811-1812 the Christian ethic and world view had become, in William James's phrase, "a live option." It was relevant; it had answers; it instilled confidence. It was worth considering.

It may be that for most Cherokees an unconscious choice had already been made before the first prophetic vision occurred. The revelations and the earthquakes revived some latent fears among the doubtful about the path they had embarked upon and forced a conscious assessment of the leaders and policies they had chosen in 1810. But by and large the Cherokee concluded, once they had dealt with the earthquakes, that to accept the new prophets would be self-defeating. It would mean rejecting their secular leaders and adopting a radical change of course. By refusing to change course they acknowledged that a viable revitalization movement was already underway in their community—a secular not a religious one. Both the religious and secular leaders expressed strongly felt nationalistic impulses that the Cherokee needed if they were to sustain their identity as a people vis à vis the dominant white culture. That had been the key to the first vision in February 1811, which spoke of the Cherokee being created from "red clay" and the Euro-American from "white sand."[31] The Ghost Dance prophets preached that this ethnic

---

[30]See Appendix E. This speech of Sour Mush to his people not only shows the practical tendency of Cherokee thought but also some of its sardonic humor. Evidently some of the prophets had claimed that those who didn't believe in their revelation would disappear into sinkholes during subsequent earthquakes.

[31]There is a much larger question at stake in the rise of a polygenetic theory of creation in the nineteenth century and the rise of romantic nationalism. But in the Cherokee situation the prophets were asserting a reality that the secular leaders were loath to admit. Having chosen the path of acculturation, the secular leaders had to sustain, as the missionaries and Jeffersonian scientists did, the theory of monogenesis. That way they

identity and pride could be asserted only in terms of the old social, political, and economic life-style of the distant past; they were separatists. The secular leaders, chosen in 1810 to resist removal and reunite the Upper and Lower Towns, believed that the nation's best chance for renascence lay in beating the white men at their own game. They were activist reformers. The prophets, believing the problems were too great for human solution, left the destiny of the Cherokees in the hands of the Great Spirit.

The political reunion of 1810 had put at the head of the nation a group of dedicated, talented, dynamic, and creative chiefs who were to carry the nation forward with remarkable success in the next twenty years: men like Charles Hicks, The Ridge, George Lowery, and John Ross. These men had already brought the nation through one crisis. They had successfully resisted the demand for an exchange of land to accommodate those who wanted to move across the Mississippi in 1809-1810. These secular leaders had made no cessions of land since 1807 and had sworn to make no more. They continually pressed the federal government to remove intruders, to provide them with the means of self-support, and to live up to its treaty obligations. They managed the tribal funds honestly.

It was true that these new leaders encouraged acculturation, but they did not force it on anyone. Realistically, what choice did the Cherokee have? It was also true that the new leaders advocated written laws, centralization of power, and a vigorous police force; but again, were these not essential to good order, unity, survival? If the Cherokee needed a sense of self-confidence and national pride, what better way was there to gain it than through the efforts of these new secular leaders to assert the treaty guarantees of ethnic self-government?[32] They held out the prom-

---

could appeal to both Christian brotherhood and national rights for social justice and equality before the law (having little but moral suasion to fight with). To have opted for polygenesis would have been to play into the hands of racial bigots who were only too eager to call all "people of color" (red, black, yellow) separate from *and inferior to* whites. In the long run the Ghost Dance prophets foresaw the future more clearly than the "enlightened," progressive secularists.

[32]In effect, Colonel Meigs was right when he said of the Ghost Dances: "This fanaticism will, I think probably, for a short time, have a partial retrograde effect as respects civilization, but will, after the present frenzy has subsided, acellerate improvement." See Appendix F.

ise of a return of Cherokee prosperity, stability, dignity and sovereignty, and as we know, they came close to obtaining it. Kenelm Burridge maintains that millenarian movements are "the symptoms of a dying culture" and "incipient anomie."[33] Such was not the case with the Cherokee. Their period of anomie had passed. Their culture was embarked upon revitalization. Not all Cherokee saw it or were enthusiastic about it. The earthquakes aroused latent fears and doubts about the choices they were making. However, once the Ghost Dance prophets forced them to a conscious choice, the great majority preferred to reaffirm their commitment to acculturation rather than to reject it.

One other important point needs to be made. Most historians have seen a relationship between the Creek War of 1813-1814 and the Cherokee Ghost Dance movement because they have misconstrued the result for the cause. It was not the influx of Creek prophets who started the Cherokee visions and dances in an effort to stampede them into supporting Tecumseh's confederacy. The war became for the Cherokees the chief outlet for the suppressed frustration and heightened tension that their own prophets generated. Although the older chiefs of the Cherokee preferred neutrality, several younger chiefs saw early in 1812 that there was something to be gained by enlisting volunteers to fight with the United States. To join with the United States in war was to put the United States in their debt and ensure better treatment in the future. More important, it provided a means by which ambitious, able, energetic men (who had missed out on promotions to power under the new rules) could gain prestige, booty, and influence according to the traditional rules. Energy that might have gone into the Ghost Dance movement was redirected into no less traditional avenues of success. The Ridge and Charles Hicks were among those most active in promoting this volunteer army in 1813.[34]

The rejection of the Ghost Dance prophets had unforeseen benefits for the Cherokee. It confirmed the view of those whites benevolently disposed toward helping the Indian that the Cherokee were indeed the most progressive and enlightened of Indian tribes. In rejecting the reactionary programs of these prophets (as these whites saw it), the Cherokee

---

[33]Burridge, *New Heaven*, 37.

[34]I do not have evidence that this was a conscious motive for entering the war on the parts of The Ridge, Hicks, or other chiefs; I rather suppose it was unconscious.

had demonstrated their good sense. In the years ahead the Cherokee found many allies among the whites because of this confidence in their sound judgment. What the Cherokees lost, only the traditionalists knew.

Burridge notes that "as an experiment in finding new ways, a millenarian movement never fails entirely."[35] By that he means that the persons involved do establish a new awareness of themselves and even a new-felt pride, prestige, and self-worth by the choices they make. One prophet may fail, but another will appear. For the traditionalist, loyalty to the faith is itself a measure of pride. Open espousal of the new religion may cease, but the religion may continue underground, in personal talks, in the hopes of private thought. Mooney concluded that the believers came home from the mountain top after the failure of the hailstorm and the millennium in 1812 "yet believing in their hearts that the glorious coming was only postponed for a time." Such is the faith of millenarians in all ages. The Messiah is yet to come. For some Cherokees he returned with Sequoyah, a new kind of prophet and genius who gave them the miracles of recording their history and faith in their own language in 1821. For others the prophet was White Path, who led a peaceful rebellion against acculturation from 1823 to 1827. For others the messiah was John Ross, the chief who fought to the bitter end for the homeland, and then led his people into a new era of hope in Oklahoma. In any case, traditionalism did not die with the Ghost Dance movement.

---

[35]Burridge, *New Heaven*, 112.

APPENDIX A

[The Cherokee Ghost Dance as told to Thomas L. McKenney by Major Ridge in the early 1830s. From Thomas L. McKenney and James Hall, *Biographical Sketches and Anecdotes of Ninety-five of 120 Principal Chiefs from the Indian Tribes of North America* (U.S. Department of Interior, Washington DC, 1967) 191-92.]

[About the year 1811] some of the Cherokees dreamed and others received, in various ways, communications from the Great Spirit, all tending to discredit the scheme of civilization. A large collection of these deluded creatures met at Oostenalee town where they held a grand savage feast and celebrated a great medicine dance which was performed exclusively by women, wearing terrapin shells, filled with pebbles, on their limbs, to rattle in concert with their wild, uncouth songs. An old man chanted a song of ancient times. No conversation was allowed during the ceremony; the fierce visage of the Indian was bent in mute attention upon the exciting scene, and the congregated mass of mind was doubtless pervaded by the solemnising conviction that the Great Spirit was among them. At this opportune crisis, a deputation from Coosa Wathla, introduced a half breed Cherokee from the mountains who professed to be the bearer of a message from heaven. His name was Charles. He was received with marked respect and seated close to Ridge, the principal person present, and who, though he deplored the superstition that induced the meeting, had thought proper to attend and ostensibly to join in the ceremonies. The savage missionary did not keep them long in suspense; he rose and announced that the Great Spirit had sent him to deliver a message to his people; he said he had already delivered it to some of the Cherokees in the mountains, but they disbelieved, and had beaten him. But he would not desist; he would declare the will of the Great Spirit at all hazards. The Great Spirit said that the Cherokees were adopting the customs of the white people. They had mills, clothes, feather beds, and tables—worse still, they had books and domestic cats. This was not good—therefore the buffaloe and other game were disappearing. The Great Spirit was angry and had withdrawn his protection. The nation must return to the customs of their fathers. They must kill their cats, cut short their frocks, and dress as became Indians and warriors. They must discard all the fashions of the whites, abandon the use of any communication with each other except by word of mouth, and give up their mills, their houses, and all the arts learned from the white people. He promised that if they believed and obeyed, then would game abound, the white man would disappear, and God would love his people. He urged them to paint themselves, to hold feasts, and to dance—to listen to his words and to the words the Great

Spirit would whisper in their dreams. He concluded by saying, if any one says that he does not believe, the Great Spirit will cut him off from the living.

This speech, artfully framed to suit the prejudices of the Indians and to inflame the latent discontent of such as were not fully enlisted in the work of reform, caused a great excitement among them. They cried out that the talk was good. Major Ridge perceived at once the evil effect that would be produced by such haranges, and, with his usual decision, determined not to tamper with the popular feeling but to oppose and correct it. He rose in his place and addressing the tumultuous assemblage with his wonted energy said, "My friends, the talk you have heard is not good. It would lead us to war with the United States, and we should suffer. It is false; it is not a talk from the Great Spirit. I stand here and defy the threat that he who disbelieves shall die. Let the death come. I offer to test this scheme of impostors!" The people, mad with superstition, rushed upon the orator who dared thus to brave their fury and rebuke their folly and would probably have put him to death had he not defended himself. Being an athletic man, he struck down several of the assailants but was at last thrown to the ground, and his friend, John Harris, stabbed at his side. Jesse Vann and others rallied around him, and beating back the crowd, enabled him to rise; and at length an old chief had sufficient influence over the infuriated savages to quell the tumult. As the tempest of passion subsided, the fanaticism which had caused it died away. The threat of the pretended messenger of heaven had proved false. His challenge had been accepted, and the daring individual who had defied him lived, an evidence of his imposition.

The storm of fanaticism passed on to the Creek nation, among whom dreams were dreamed and prophets arose who professed to have talked with the Great Spirit. The daring and restless Tecumthe, who had traversed the wilderness for several hundred miles for the purpose of stirring the savages to war against the Americans, appeared among the Creeks at this juncture and artfully availed himself of a state of things well suited to his purpose. Besides bringing tidings from the Great Spirit, he brought assurances from the British king and greetings from the Shawanoe nation. The Creeks rose against their chiefs, broke out into war against the United States, and having surprised the frontier post of Fort Mimms, massacred the whole garrison without distinction of age or sex.

APPENDIX B

[The Cherokee Ghost Dance as told to James Mooney by James Wafford in 1891. From James Mooney, *The Ghost-Dance Religion and Wounded Knee* (Dover Publications, New Publications, 1973) 676-77.]

. . . among the Cherokee and probably among the Creek, it was believed that there would be a terrible hailstorm which would overwhelm with destruction both the whites and the unbelievers of the red race, while the elect would be warned in time to save themselves by fleeing to the high mountain tops. The idea of any hostile combination against the white race seems to have been no part of the doctrine. In the north [among the Shawnee], however, there is always a plain discrimination against the Americans. The Great Father, through his prophet, is represented as declaring himself to be the common parent alike of Indians, English, French, and Spaniards; while the Americans, on the contrary, "are not my children, but the children of the evil spirit. They grew from the scum of the great water when it was troubled by an evil spirit and the froth was driven into the woods by a strong east wind. They are numberous, but I hate them. They are unjust; they have taken away your lands which were not made for them."

From the venerable James Wafford of the Cherokee nation, the author in 1891 obtained some interesting details in regard to the excitement among the Cherokee. According to his statement, the doctrine first came to them through the Creek about 1812 or 1813. It was probably given to the Creek by Tecumtha and his party on their visit to that tribe in the fall of 1811, as will be related hereafter. The Creek were taught by their prophets that the old Indian life was soon to return, when "instead of beef and bacon they would have venison, and instead of chickens they would have turkeys." Great sacred dances were inaugurated, and the people were exhorted to be ready for what was to come. From the south the movement spread to the Cherokee, and one of their priests, living in what is now upper Georgia, began to preach that on a day near at hand there would be a terrible storm with a mighty wind and hailstones as large as hominy mortars, which would destroy from the face of the earth all but the true believers who had previously taken refuge on the highest summits of the Great Smoky mountains. Full of this belief, numbers of the tribe in Alabama and Georgia abandoned their bees, their orchards, their slaves, and everything else that might have come to them through the white man, and, in spite of the entreaties and remonstrances of friends who put no faith in the prediction, took up their toilsome march for the mountains of Carolina. Wafford, who was then about 10 years of age, lived with his mother and stepfather on Valley river, and vividly remembers the troops of pilgrims with their packs on their backs, fleeing from the lower country to escape from the wrath to come. Many of them stopped at the house of his stepfather, who, being a white man, was somewhat better prepared than his neighbors to entertain travelers and who took the opportunity to endeavor to persuade them to turn back, telling them that their hopes and fears alike were groundless. Some listened to him and returned to their homes but others went on and climbed the mountain where they waited until the appointed day arrived only to find themselves disappointed. Slowly and sadly then they took up their packs once more and turned their faces homeward, dreading the ridicule they were sure to meet there, but yet believing in their hearts that the glorious coming was only postponed for a time. This excitement among the Cherokee is noted at some length in the *Cherokee Advocate* of November 16, 1844, published at Tahlequah, Cherokee Nation. Among the Creek the excitement, intensified by reports of the struggle now going on in the north and fostered and encouraged by the emissaries of Spain and England, grew and spread until it culminated in the summer of 1813 in the terrible Creek War. . . .

APPENDIX C

[An account of the Ghost Dance religion of the Shawnees and other Great Lakes nations as reported to Colonel Benjamin Hawkins by Creek informants who heard it from Shawnee prophets at Tuckabatchee in the Creek Nation in September 1811. Hawkins wrote this on 16 June 1814. From *American State Papers*, ed. Walter Lowrie and Matthew St. Clair Clarke (Washington DC, 1832) 4: 845.]

. . . What was the actual meaning of this British talk? Your whole nation can answer this question: Kill the old chiefs, friends to peace; kill the cattle, the hogs and fowls; do not work, destroy the wheels and looms, throw away your ploughs and everything used by the Americans. Sing "the song of the Indians of the northern lakes and dance their dance." Shake your own war clubs, shake yourselves; you will frighten the Americans, their arms will drop from their hands, the ground will become a bog and mire them, and you may knock them on the head with your war clubs. I will be with you with my Shawaneese as soon as our friends the British are ready for us. Lift up the war club with your right hand, be strong, and I will come and shew you how to use it. . . .

APPENDIX D

[The Cherokee Ghost Dance as told to the editor of the *Cherokee Advocate* in 1844 by "a friend." From the *Cherokee Advocate* published at Tahlequah, Cherokee Nation, 16 November 1844.]

PARSON MILLER THIRTY YEARS BEHIND THE INDIANS

Parson Miller, it appears from late accounts, perceiving that this "terrestrial ball" continues still to run its wonted rounds, contrary to his *figurative* revelations, has been induced to "calculate" over his former *exercise*, and in so doing, detected some slight errors of addition or subtraction. From his more recent deductions a few more days of sunshine and rain are allowed to illume and make glad this "bright little world of ours," before it shall be "rolled together as a scroll." In speaking of this discovery, a day or two since to a friend, we were not a little surprised to learn that the Catastrophe Preacher and his *enlightened* followers, are treading almost in the very footsteps of some old Cherokee Conjuror and his *benighted* followers, who have gone before them. Some thirty years ago, a declaration spread among the Cherokees and gained creedence of many, that the world would be destroyed on a certain day not then far distant, not however by the raining down of fire and brimstone, but by wind and storm and the falling of hail stones large as the *mortars* in which was pounded the corn for making *hominy*. The destruction was not to be complete; one small spot, of some ten acres square, was to be spared, and to which, all who fled, would find security in the hour of woe and annihilation.

So firmly fixed was this belief—in the minds of many that, deserting their negroes, their orchards, their bees and almost everything about them that came from, or savored of the *pale-faces*; they tore themselves, amid entreaties and tears, from their unbelieving friends and started for the *reservation* located in that part of their country now in western North Carolina. Such however, after proceeding a day or two on their journey, became convinced that the end of all things was not yet at hand, returned to their homes and, unlike the Millerites of the present day, resumed their duties, ashamed of their folly.

APPENDIX E

[The Cherokee Ghost Dance as recorded in the official mission diary of the Moravians at Springplace, Georgia, through various entries from 10 February 1811, to 30 April 1812. I have included only relevant entries, noting elisions. Translated from the German by Elizabeth Marx through the courtesy of Mary Creech, archivist, Moravian Archives, Winston-Salem, North Carolina.]

February 10, 1811: Early in the morning when Bro. and Sister Gambold [the missionaries] were paying a visit at Peggy's [widow of James Vann], the old Chief Keychzaetel [or Koy, ch, z, o, te, li, The Warrior's Nephew] was very much surprised to see them and told them the following among other things: "In order that you might know how things are going in the world today," thus began his narrative, "I want to tell you what happened here in the Nation just the other day. Just three nights ago I was at a Talk [a National Council] in Oostenally. To that place came a man and two women who told that while they were on a journey, they came to an unoccupied house near a hill called Rocky Mountain and entered it in order to spend the night there. Just as it had become dark, they heard a violent noise in the air and wondered whether a storm was brewing. As they went outside because of that to see about it, they saw a whole crowd of Indians arriving on the hill from the sky; they were riding on small black horses and their leader was beating a drum and came very close to them. They were much frightened and for that reason had wanted to go back into the house, whereupon that one [the drummer] called to them: "Don't be afraid; we are your brothers and have been sent by God [*Gott* in the Moravian diary] to speak with you. God is dissatisfied that you are receiving the white people in your land without any distinction. You yourselves see that your hunting is gone—you are planting the corn of the white people—go and sell that back to them and plant Indian corn and pound it in the manner of your forefathers; do away with the mills. The Mother of the Nation has forsaken you because all her bones are being broken through the grinding [of the mills]. She will return to you, however, if you put the white people out of the land and return to your former manner of life. You yourselves can see that the white people are entirely different beings from us; we are made from red clay; they, out of white sand. You may keep good neighborly relations with them, just see to it that you get back from them your old Beloved Towns. Furthermore, your Mother is not pleased that you punish each other so hard; you even whip until [you draw] blood. Now I have told you what God's will is and you are to pass it on. If you don't want to believe my words, however, then look up at the sky." They did that and saw the heaven open and [coming from it] an indescribably beautiful light and in it four white houses.

The leader continued saying, "Such houses you are to build in your Beloved Towns, one for Capt. Blair (a white man in Georgia, who had already rendered many a *raulen* [*sic*] service to the Indians and for that reason is much beloved by many), the rest are to be for other white men who can be useful to the Nation with writing, etc. You are to report everything which you have just heard to Col. Meigs [the federal agent to the Cherokee]. Now when you publish this and there is someone who does not believe it, then know that it will not be well with him."

. . . the old chief was very eager to hear our ideas about this story; he himself believed it precisely and firmly and had himself spoken with the people who had had this vision and at the Council no one had contradicted them except The Ridge, who, however, had been ill-treated by the others because of it. Since we are well aware that the Indians have already considered in many council meetings how to get rid of the many white people who have penetrated [intruded upon their land], have also made various resolutions in that regard but have not carried anything out until the present time, so we could easily think for what purpose this story had been thought up. We sent to tell the good man that we could not express an opinion on the matter as we did not understand such visions; if there is something in the story, it might have been a dream. . . .

May 10, 1811: The old Chief, Koh, ch z, o, te, li (The Warrior's Nephew) visited us with his wife. He said he had come to bring us a report from the Council at which he is the most famous speaker. "It is true," he said, "the white people must all go out of the Nation; however, 4 smiths, some school teachers and those who are building mills for us are to be tolerated, but later they, too, must return to their own country; and no one shall put anything in their way. We do not consider *you* as *white people* but as *Indians*. God has sent you to teach our people. You don't want our land. You are here out of love for us. . . .

December 16, 1811: Early at three o'clock two shocks of an earthquake were felt. The house[s] trembled and everything in them was in movement. The hens fell to the ground from their roosts and set up a pitiful cry. At 8 o'clock another but lighter shock was felt.

December 17, 1811: Chief Bead Eye, his brother The Trunk, and two other Indians came to us to get information about the earthquake. They all seemed to be very much disturbed and said that the earth is probably very old, would it soon collapse? We explained to them what causes earthquakes; but with the addition that Almighty God has made the earth and everything on it and has maintained it until now and He also has the might and power to discipline people who live on it in various ways and for this purpose He has also used concussions of the earth from time to time. The inhabitants of this land have reason to thank Him that He has been so gracious to them this time and should regard it as a warning to do away with the service to sin and listen to his voice. One thing is certain that God has destined one day on which He will judge all people, will reward each one according to his works. At that time the earth will be consumed by fire, etc. They bowed their heads and seemed to be in deep thought.

In the evening during heavy rain, we had the pleasure of seeing coming here to us our former pupil Tommy with his father [Chief Chulioa, Shoeboot] and our friend Chulioa and his wife. They also were in deepest perplexity and fright because of the earthquake. Chulioa brought us a letter from Mr. Charles Hicks [a leading chief closely attached to the Moravians] in which among other things he reported the following: "I am not able to describe the great perplexity [consternation] into which we came last night. Our dwelling house was in the most violent movement so that it seemed to be near to falling in. Just before that there was a strong violent noise heard from the W. N. W. and some saw a streak of lightning having its beginning from the same direction as the noise. This morning between 7 and 8 o'clock we felt two more shocks but not as strong as the former one, and without the slightest noise. But our house was trembling very much and the roof moved. The trees were also all in movement without the slightest wind. Oh," Mr. Hicks added, "that we might glorify merciful God for his protection from day to day and implore Him for future help to improve our life." Mr. Hicks had sent this company as well as the above-mentioned one [letter] for our instruction in this matter. We talked with them in a similar manner as with the former ones and our Tommy [a pupil at the Moravian school] translated our words with the greatest seriousness.

Our Peggy [widow of Chief James Vann, converted to Christianity by them in 1809], who had been on business today with neighboring Indians, could not describe vividly enough the perplexity [terror] in which she found the people everywhere. Some of them attribute the occurrence to the sorcerers; some, to a large snake which must have crawled under their house; some to the weakness of old age of the earth which will now soon cave in [or collapse]. Our sister took advantage of this occasion to proclaim to them emphatically the love and severity of God and to remind them that they should be concerned about the salvation of their souls.

February 6, 1812: An Indian came to us in order to get information about the frequent earthquakes and toward evening another, who is a Chief and is called Dargungi [came] for the same purpose. Both of them looked very troubled. We talked with them in the usual way and they seemed to give assent to our words. . . .

February 9, 1812: . . . we heard today from a traveler that in Taloni, an Indian town 30 miles from here along the road to Georgia, in a field 13 sink holes appeared as a result of the earthquake, the largest of which is 20 feet deep and 120 feet in circumference and is supposed to be full of greenish water.

February 11, 1812: The Ridge [a prominent chief] visited us and asked profoundly [seriously] about the earthquake, and said he had also discussed the matter with Mr. Charles Hicks, who had told him that God lets them come about. Now he would also like to know whether the end of the world were not near? We answered him, as we had others who asked similar questions, that no man knows this, but that it behooves us to be prepared and ready. . . . The Ridge said, "It is true, we are very bad! May God make us better!" . . . As we talked further about the day of Judgment and the eternal blessedness of the believers, he asked the question: whether on that great day God's Son would not treat very angrily those who had spent a large part of their lives in evil [deeds] but had later improved and regretted their former bad life? . . . He sat a long while in deep thought, and finally said, "Oh, we are all too bad. Now I also want to tell a story which took place not far from Tellico a short time ago. The Indians there were killing each other in a very cold-blooded way. A respected Indian—who is well known to us, and in other respects had a good character, invited some Indians to his house for drinking and dancing; a tired old man laid down to sleep at one side of the house; the owner of the house beat him dead with a piece of wood, dragged him to the hearth and on to the fire and let him roast. For another one, without any reason, whatsoever, his skull was split so that the brain ran out!" Then he asked, "What do you think of such things?" We expressed to him our compassion because of the hard slavery in which the Evil Spirit keeps the poor Indians imprisoned. . . .

February 17, 1812: . . . [a chief] The Shoeboot [Chulioa], confessed his perplexity in regard to the unusual earthquakes here in the land and said in a very emphatic way that many Indians believe that the white people were responsible because they had already taken possession of so much of the Indian land and wanted still more. God was angry because of that and He wanted to put an end to it through the earthquakes. This much was believed by all the Indians that God was causing the earthquakes. We then let our understanding be told and asked them to pray very diligently the publican's prayer, "God be merciful to me, a sinner."

In reply, the other one, called Big Bear, said, "I should also like to tell something as I should like to know what you think about it. Soon after the earth had trembled so for the first time [in December 1811], an Indian was sitting in his house in deep thought, and his children were lying sick in front of the fire. At that point a tall man, clothed entirely in the foliage of the trees, with a wreath of the same foliage on his head, who was carrying a small child in his arm and had a larger child by the hand, said to him, 'The small child on his [my] arm is God. I am not able to tell you now whether God will soon destroy the earth or not. But God is not pleased that the Indians have sold so much land to the white people. Tugalo [formerly a Cherokee town in South Carolina], which is now possessed by white people, is the first place which God created. There in a hill he placed the first fire, for all fire comes from God. Now the white people have built a house on that hill. They should abandon the place; on that hill there should be grass growing, only then will there be peace. And the Indians no longer thank God before they enjoy first fruits of the land. They are no longer organizing, as was formerly the custom, dances in his honor before they eat the first pumpkins, etc. Furthermore,' the messenger said to the Indian, 'You are sad because you think your children are ill; they are really not ill, but have only taken in a little dust.' Thereupon he gave him two small pieces of bark from a certain tree, which he also named, and told him to cook them and to give the drink to his children, and from that they became well right then. He then also told him about other remedies for use during illnesses and at the end he said he would now take God back home."

During this silly narration, the Indian looked so solemn as if he were really proclaiming God's will and word. We told him that we are no judges of such visions nor do we get involved in such things. We adhere to God's word and in that his will is clear. It is good to thank God for his gifts, but we wish with all our hearts that the poor Indians might really learn to know Him in his great love and might honor and love Him truly. "That is well said," said Big Bear. "Yes," said Shoeboot, "The white people know God from the Book and we, from other things." He said further, "I love you; I have never heard anything bad about you. But there are also very bad white people." In which we agreed with him.

February 23, 1812: . . . toward evening the wife of Mr. Charles Hicks brought us a very pleasing letter from him in which he wrote among other things: "The present is a very strange point in time. May God in his great mercy prepare us for the life to come. The people in my neighborhood [near Oostenali] are deeply disturbed because of the earthquakes, and I believe that fear and terror have spread through the whole Nation. How else could it be? Do not these belong to the signs which are to come to pass before the [last] great day? . . ."

Mr. [David] McNair [a white man living in Tennessee, married to a Cherokee] came in the evening and spent the night here. Again we heard much about dreams and false prophets. May God have mercy. There is at the present time a real tumult [of feeling] in the Nation and a dark, heavy feeling. . . . It is unbelievable to what kind of foolish fables the blinded heathen will give hearing. During these days the residents of one town fled into the hills and tried to crawl into hiding in the holes of the rocks in order to escape the danger of the hail stones, the size of half bushels, which were to fall on a certain day. As the stated terrible day passed without hail, they came back to their dwelling places, ready and willing to believe every new deceiver.

March 1, 1812: Early an old Indian woman, called Laughing Molly, came to us in great perplexity. She asked us very urgently that we should tell her if the talk of the Indians has any basis, namely that in the space of 3 months the moon would again become dark, and thereafter hail stones as large as hominy blocks would fall, all cattle would die and soon thereafter the earth would come to an end. A sorcerer had said until then there would be peace; how things would be after that he did not know. It was true that she was already old and presumably would not live much longer, but she did not want to spend her remaining days in anxiety.

We expressed comfort to her through Peggy and said that the eclipses of the moon are natural phenomena and occur annually and do not do any harm to the earth: that the tales of the Indians are nothing but lies, that God loves people unspeakably much and would like nothing more than that all should believe in Him and be saved; that He had destined a day in which He will make an end to the world, but when this day would come no man could know. She should pray to Him faithfully that He would have mercy on her and save her, etc. Oh, how happy the poor soul was! She pressed our hand repeatedly and said: "I am no longer afraid! I will believe your words and no longer listen to the liars and sorcerers."

After that Mr. Charles Hicks came to attend our services. We had several deep conversations with this dear man. The Chiefs had sent him an embassy from Hightower [Etowah, in northwestern Georgia] in order to learn his opinion concerning the various fantastic predictions. He told them not to give the liars any hearing at all, but much rather to embarrass them publicly, indeed to punish them, and showed them out of God's word—the Old Book, as they call the Bible—what our dear Lord himself has said about the end of the world. And then they brought out that the Indian called The Duck, because he did not want to believe the visions and the messengers from God to the Indians, had soon after that died; so he said to him, "Was The Duck given the right ahead of other men never to die, [if] had he also believed the lies or pretended to believe? None of them knows how soon he will have to die whether he believes the visions or not." They agreed that he was right and promised to report his words faithfully to the Chiefs [at Etowah].

March 8, 1812: . . . because there was another earthquake shock last night, Mother Vann [mother-in-law of Peggy Vann] talked with us another time about this occurrence; . . . she told us that new lies are being broadcast among the Nation. Namely, that it has been revealed to one Indian by God that there would be an intense darkness [an eclipse] and that it would last three days; during which all the white people would be snatched away as well as all Indians who had any clothing or household articles of the white man's kind, together with all their cattle. Therefore, they should put aside everything that is similar to the white people and that which they had learned from them, so that in the darkness God might not mistake them and snatch them away with the former. He who does not believe this will die at once together with all his stock. This had already happened to one Indian [presumably The Duck]. Mother Vann added that in fact many are already doing away with their household articles and clothing, but *she* had offered to buy one item or another from them just to show them that she did not pay any attention to the lies.

We see only too clearly for what this evil enemy is aiming: this cunning spirit does not mean in any way the outward garb of the poor heathen but their change of heart. He wants to warn them against the teaching of the white people of Jesus, the crucified, their only rightful Lord and Master, in order that he might keep them securely fettered in his chains. We find for that reason much need to plead very urgently to our good Lord that He might destroy very soon this new strategem of the Devil and in general his work in this land.

In addition, the false prophets pretend to have seen ugly and terrifying appearances of God. Johnston [a pupil at the mission school] said that in his neighborhood there was also the talk that a new earth would come into being in the Spring, but he did not pay attention to their absurd talking and was glad that he had heard the truth here and knew now what to believe.

April 30, 1812: . . . Col. Meigs had prevailed upon Bro. [John] Gambold [head of the Moravian mission] to make this journey to the Council [at Oostenally in northwestern Georgia] in order to calm as much as possible the emotions of the Indians which were made very fearful through the oft-mentioned false prophets. They found, however, to their joy, that those present and particularly the Chiefs, were sufficiently convinced of the vanity of these things and instead of being detained by [attracted by] them they undertook useful considerations and decided on several new [tribal] arrangements. All the Indians and especially the older Chiefs showed themselves very friendly towards Bro. Gambold and when the old Chief Sower Mush had once talked [very heatedly] in the Council with much effort, he had a translator say to Bro. Gambold that he was angry neither with him nor with the white people in general, but rather that the misconduct of his own people had brought him to such zeal. In his address he had said among other things to those present: "As the earth moved sometimes a short time ago, you were in great anxiety and feared that you would sink down into it, but when you go among the white people to break down their stables and steal their horses, you are not afraid, and there there is much great danger for if they should catch you in such an act they would surely shoot you down, and then you would surely be sunk into the earth.

APPENDIX F

[The Cherokee Ghost Dance as described by Colonel Return J. Meigs, federal agent to the Cherokee, on 19 March 1812. From his memorandum entitled "Some Reflections on Cherokee concerns, manners, state, etc." in the National Archives microfilms, record group 75, roll M-208, "Records of the Cherokee Indian Agency in Tennessee, 1801-1835," reel 5.]

. . . [The Cherokee] are at this time in a remarkable manner—occasioned by the late shocks of the earth—endeavoring to appease the Anger of the great Spirit, which they conceive is manifest by the late shocks of the earth. They have revived their religious dances of ancient origin with as much apparent solemnity as ever was seen in worship in our churches. They then repair to the water, go in and wash. These ablutions are intended to show that their sins are washed away and that they are cleansed from all defilements.

Amongst them are some fanatics who tell them that the Great Spirit is angry with them for adopting the manners, customs, and habits of the white people who they think are very wicked. In some few instances some have thrown off their clothing into the fire and burned them up; some of the females are mutilating fine muslin dresses and are told they must discontinue their dancing reels and country dances which have become very common amongst the young people, being told by these fanatics that these are amongst the causes of the displeasure of the Great Spirit.

This fanaticism will, I think probably, for a short time have a partial retrograde effect as respects civilization, but will, after the present frenzy has subsided, acellerate improvement. At a late meeting when a man burned his hat as a sacrifice, he called on a young chief present to follow his example. The young chief told him that he would not and, putting his hand to his Breast, said it is no matter what cloaths I wear while my heart is straight. This was sufficient to silence further importunity. A young Cherokee woman told me that she was told that the Cherokees ought to throw away the habits of the white people and return to the ancient manners and that she told them that was nothing, that they ought to become good people and leave off stealing horses and drinking whiskey instead of destroying their clothes. They deserve some pity and compassion because they are looking from the effect to the cause. . . .

APPENDIX G

[The Cherokee Ghost Dance as described by Thurman Wilkins, based in part on a translation of portions of the Moravian Springplace diary by Sophie Wilkins and in part on the accounts of McKenney and Mooney. Wilkins, *Cherokee Tragedy* (New York: Collier-Macmillan, 1970) 57-60.]

Certain backward Cherokees, those who balked at the advancement program, had meanwhile proved responsive to the Creek contagion. "Some of the Cherokees dreamed dreams," McKenney wrote, "and others received, in various ways, communications from the Great Spirit, all tending to discredit the scheme of civilization." Conservatives had arranged a great medicine dance at Oostanaula the year before [1811], and after "a grand savage feast" the women began to dance with tortoise shells fastened to their ankles. Pebbles inside the shells rattled in unison with their movements and with the beat "of their wild uncouth songs." One ancient warrior chanted about the glories of former days; all others were quiet, many doubtless awed by a feeling that the Great Spirit moved among them.

At this psychological moment a delegation from Coosewatie introduced a half-blood prophet called Charley, perhaps the conjurer pictured by John R. Ridge as the "old Cherokee magician, contemporary with Tecumseh, [who] inspired great dread from the fact that two demons attended him in the shape of . . . ferocious black wolves." Hailing from the mountains, Charley insisted that he brought a message from the Great Spirit. The assembly received him with hushed respect, and he was led to a seat not far from the bench occupied by The Ridge, who was one of the principal persons present. The people were eager to hear what Charley had to say; all were silent when he rose. The Great Spirit was displeased, he cried, that the Cherokees had taken up the white men's ways. "They had mills, clothes, feather beds, and tables—worse still, they had books, and domestic cats!" This was not good—therefore the buffaloes and other game were disappearing. The Great Spirit was angry, and had withdrawn his protection.

One evening He had sent His warning to Charley and his friends. In the darkness they had heard a noise in the air and thought a storm was ready to break. They stepped outside the house to look at the clouds, and there in the sky they saw gigantic Indians riding on black horses. The leader of the riders was beating a drum. He approached quite close to Charley and his friends, who wanted to run and hide. Suddenly the leader called:

"Do not be afraid. We are your brothers, and have been sent by the Great Spirit to speak to you. He is displeased with you for accepting the ways of the white people. You can see for yourselves—your hunting is gone and you are planting the corn of the white men. Go and sell the same back to them, and plant Indian corn and gather it according to the ways of our ancestors, and do away with the mills. The Mother of the nation has abandoned you, because the grinding breaks her bones. She wants to come back to you, if you will get the white men out of the country and go back to your former ways."

And then the voice added: "You can see for yourselves that the whites are different from you, for you were made of red clay, and they from white sand. You may live as good neighbors with them, but see to it that you get your old beloved towns back. Nor does your Mother like it that you punish those so hard who break your new laws, even whipping them till the blood comes. Now I have told you the will of the Great Spirit, and you must pass it on. But if you don't believe my words, look up into the sky."

This they did, and they saw the clouds part, and from the sky came a bright light. Within that light they saw white houses—houses which the leader told them they should build for certain men who would help them if they returned to their ancient ways. The leader repeated that they must tell their people all they had seen and all they had heard. And it would go ill with any man who disbelieved.

"The [Cherokees] must return to the customs of their fathers," Charley cried. "They must kill their cats, cut short their frocks, and dress as became Indians and warriors. They must discard all the fashions of the whites, abandon the use of any communication with each other except by word of mouth, and give up their mills, their houses, and all the arts learned from the white people."

The prophet promised his silent audience that the game would then return and the whites would go away. Therefore the Cherokees must believe his words and obey his appeal. Let them paint themselves as in former days, let them hold feasts, let them dance, let them listen to the whispered inspiration of the Great Spirit in their dreams. And then Charley ended with an ominous threat. If anyone denied his message, the Great Spirit would strike him dead.

The harangue produced an awesome effect, especially on those who disliked the new ways. The talk was good, they cried, with great excitement. But The Ridge foresaw what mischief might come of Charley's agitation, and he determined to counter it with all his energy. He rose and shouted to the applauding company: "My friends, the talk you have heard is not good. It would lead us to war with the United States, and we should suffer. It is false; it is not a talk from the Great Spirit. I stand here and defy the threat that he who disbelieves shall die. Let the death come upon me. I offer to test this scheme of imposters!"

At The Ridge's defiance, excited Cherokees rushed upon him, intent on his death; but he was ready for their assault. He struck several down, until their numbers overwhelmed him. They threw him to the ground. They might have killed him; indeed they stabbed a friend, John Harris, who fought at his side. But a friend, Jesse Vann, and others rushed to his aid; together they beat the crowd back, and The Ridge sprang up again to hold his assailants at bay, until an influential old chief exerted enough personal magnetism to stem the violence. The Ridge had won his point; he had defied the prophet. Although battered and bloody, he continued to live.

His stand shook Charley's credibility for many of the aroused Cherokees. Others, more benighted, retained their belief in the prophet. They rallied round him when he set a judgment day for those who spurned his doctrine. On that day, Charley claimed, the Great Spirit would send a storm with hailstones as large as hominy mortars. The ice balls would destroy all but the faithful, provided they collected on the highest peak of the Smoky Mountains. There a consecrated ground of ten acres would remain secure for them, a haven of peace in a fury of ice. In the wake of Charley's prophecy hundreds of Cherokees left their homes. They deserted "their negroes, their orchards, their bees and almost everything about them that came from, or savored of, the *pale-faces*; they tore themselves, amid entraties and tears, from their unbelieving friends and started for the 'reservation,' " on a mountaintop somewhere in the western part of North Carolina. The hailstorm failed to materialize, and Charley was at last disgraced conclusively. From that time on the furor of the prophets waned among the Cherokees, if not among the Creeks.

EXPERIMENT IN
CHEROKEE CITIZENSHIP,
1817-1829

Every scholar in the course of his research for a book comes across masses of doc-uments that he knows he can never include in the final work. Sometimes they are sufficiently well defined that they can stand as a self-contained episode. Such, it seems to me, are the documents in the War Department and state archives relating to the abortive efforts by the federal government in 1817-1819 to grant citizenship to over 300 Cherokees. The experiment was laudable in the sense that it was consistent with George Washington's original Indian policy of civilizing and then incorporating the Indians into the new Republic. However, it was so poorly planned and executed that it became a lamentable failure seriously undermining the whole basis of the Indian policy. It failed because it did not take into account the tremendous hostility of frontier whites to granting full equality to Native Americans, particularly in the South where they were seen as "a people of color" and hence closer to Afro-Americans than to Eu-ropeans. Thomas Jefferson had said, speaking as a scientist, that the Indian was fully the equivalent of the European in his physical and mental capacities. Upon that assumption the policy of civilizing and incorporating the Indians was erected, but it was never shared by the frontiersmen who had fought the Indians and thought they knew them best.

The documents cited here testify also to the inefficiency of the War Department and its failure to provide the Cherokees "reservees" (as they were called) with a clear title to the land or clear instructions on how to protect their rights as citizens in the four states where they were given individual tracts of land. The War Department was even more culpable in failing to work out prior agreements with the governors and leg-islatures of each state (and the Territory of Alabama), considering how important it was that this experiment should succeed. Once the experiment began to flounder, the War Department belatedly came to the assistance of the Cherokees and spent a great deal of money on lawyers' fees to try to sustain the rights of the reservees. John C.

Calhoun, the secretary of war who was responsible for this fiasco, knew that failure of the experiment would seriously undermine the government's credibility with all Indian nations. Surprisingly, despite the abysmal failure of this experiment, the War Department continued to hold out citizenship on individual tracts of land as a viable goal for Cherokees who achieved sufficient progress in civilization. Mary K. Young has written an excellent study of a later experiment in citizenship among the Choctaws in her book, Redskins, Ruffle Shirts and Red Necks. *That too was a failure and for exactly the same reasons. Bureaucrats never seem to learn. Or perhaps the desire to hold out even the flimsiest promises in order to obtain Indian land overcame their common sense and their humanity.*

UNDER THE TERMS OF A TREATY signed 8 July 1817, "upwards of 300 Cherokees (Heads of families) in the honest simplicity of their souls, made an election to become American citizens."[1] This was one of the first efforts to test the federal government's "civilization program" started in 1789 under President Washington.[2] "The [treaty] Commissioners, keeping in mind the benevolent views of the United States to give civilization and refinement to the Indians and to make them citizens, offered the Heads of families who wished to become citizens, 640 acres of land each." By the act of becoming landholders outside the bounds of the Cherokee Nation, these Cherokee were automatically citizens. Their allotments were located in Georgia, North Carolina, Tennessee, and the Territory of Alabama. While the government hoped that some of the acculturated Cherokee (principally those of mixed white and Indian ancestry) would benefit from the plan, it had doubts about the ability of many of these "to prevent artful men from acquiring titles to said lands." In order to protect them from being cheated out of their land, the treaty placed a temporary entail upon it; the 640-acre tracts could not be sold during the lifetime of the persons to whom they were first granted. However, "as life estates," these tracts descended "with a right of Dower to the Widow . . . at the demise of such Heads of families

---

[1]National Archives Microfilm, M-208, Records of the Cherokee Indian Agency in Tennessee, 1801-1835, roll 9, 12 November 1822, Meigs to Roane. A copy of the register of life reserves is in the Georgia State Archives, and I am grateful to Mrs. Pat Bryant for making a copy for me. See appendix at the end of this essay.

[2]Mary E. Young has written an excellent study of the later tests of this plan under the allotment system among the Choctaw, Chickasaw, and Creek nations in the 1830s. *Red Skins, Ruffle Shirts and Red Necks: Indian Allotments in Alabama and Mississippi* (Norman OK, 1961). For her reference to the Cherokee reserves, see 11-12.

. . . in fee simple to their heirs."[3] In all other respects these Cherokee were to be considered fully equal to other citizens. These 311 Cherokee were, in effect, the test cases for a policy started in 1789 by Henry Knox, Washington's secretary of war. Knox predicted that within "fifty years" his plan would bring about the total integration of the Indians east of the Mississippi.[4]

The government wanted this experiment to succeed for several reasons. First of all, it hoped to demonstrate the effectiveness and benevolence of its policies; second, it wished to honor its commitments to the reservees; and third, it hoped to separate the acculturated from the unacculturated. Ultimately the War Department spent thousands of dollars in lawyers' fees to protect the claims of these Cherokee. Some officials feared that if this "liberal" program failed, the government would have future difficulty obtaining consent to further cessions of tribal land from those influential Indian leaders who had become successful farmers and planters. The goal of Knox's "civilization policy" was to extinguish all tribal titles to land, denationalize the tribes, and leave only individual Indian landholders scattered as farmer-citizens among the whites (a program that would place millions of acres of uncultivated Indian land for sale in order to expand white settlements in the West).

Despite all that was at stake, several aspects of this experiment raise serious questions about the care with which the plan was executed. The War Department's ineptitude, its lack of planning and supervision, almost wrecked the experiment at the outset. First, the offer of citizenship in these treaty negotiations appeared to come more as a threat than a reward, which did little to boost the morale of the reservees. The Cherokees were told flatly that if they did not denationalize and become landholding citizens, their only alternative was to move west of the Mississippi en masse.[5] Second, the federal agent to the Cherokee, Colonel

---

[3]M-208, roll 9, 12 November 1822.

[4]*American State Papers: Indian Affairs*, ed. Walter Lowrie and Walter S. Franklin (Washington DC, 1834) 1:13-14, 53-54. Hereinafter cited as ASP.

[5]For the forceful expression of this choice by treaty commissioner Joseph McMinn, see National Archives Microfilm, M-234, Letters Received by the Office of Indian Affairs, 1824-1880, roll 71, #0295, 26 June 1818, "Journal of Negotiations." The purpose of these Cherokee cessions of 1817 and 1819 was to obtain land for those Cherokee who had migrated to Arkansas since 1809. The federal government insisted that land in the East must be ceded by the Cherokee Nation in order to provide land in Arkansas for those who emigrated. See the preamble to the treaty of 1817 in Richard Peters, *The Case of the Cherokee Nation* (Philadelphia, 1831) 268.

Return J. Meigs, stated flatly a few years after the experiment began, that it had been "foreseen" and "anticipated" that very few of the Cherokee would succeed in holding their land, yet little was done to prepare them for the role of taxpaying citizens.[6] Third, the War Department was so slow to survey the reserves that many were sold off to white speculators by the states in which they were located. Had the experiment succeeded, the story of Indian-white relations in the Old Southwest might have been somewhat different. There were persons who worked hard for the experiment; there were others who wanted it to fail.

It could be argued that the failure of the program resulted from forces beyond the government's control and reckoning. Attempts to assess the failure at the time placed most of the blame upon the official opposition of state governments, on the social prejudice of the frontier whites, and on the mistakes made by the Cherokee citizens in carrying out the program. The historian is more apt to perceive an unconscious collusion among the federal officials, the various state politicians, and the frontier settlers, each of whom wished to blame the others, although all three had ample reasons for desiring failure. The land was fertile and in high demand; great profits were to be made from both its sale and its produce. In the contest for power, the Indian had no vote.

There is, however, another possible answer. The Cherokee Nation wanted the experiment to fail. The treaty of 1817 did not succeed in coercing the Cherokee either to move west or to denationalize. To encourage resistance to the government, the Cherokee Council voted in 1819 to deny citizenship in their nation to any who emigrated or accepted a reserve.[7] Strong Cherokee leadership, surprising solidarity, and intransigence among the Cherokee people forced a compromise. In exchange for the cession of 3.8 million acres of their land (parceled out among Georgia, North Carolina, Tennessee, and Alabama), the 12,000 Cherokee who objected to removal obtained a treaty in 1819 that enabled them to maintain communal ownership over ten million acres of their

---

[6]National Archives Microfilm, M-221, Letters Received by the Secretary of War: Main Series, 1801-1870, roll 90, #6758, 8 February 1821, Meigs to Calhoun.

[7]See *Laws of the Cherokee Nation* (Tahlequah, Cherokee Nation, 1852) 9-10, and the statement by Charles Hicks, second principal chief, that Cherokees who took reserves were now considered citizens of the states in which they resided and expatriates of the Cherokee Nation; M-208, roll 8, 20 March 1820, Hicks to Meigs.

ancestral land. They believed this sacrifice would end the effort to move them across the Mississippi, though in the end it bought them only another twenty years in the East. In any case, it put an end to the removal effort of 1817-1819 after less than 3,000 had emigrated to Arkansas. The treaty of 6 July 1819 made the experiment in citizenship less appealing to many Cherokee (while keeping that option open for a time).

If Cherokee nationalism was strong enough and Cherokee leadership firm enough to withstand this intensive effort at removal and denationalization, it appeared that there was a stable future for the tribe. Some of the Cherokee who had opted for citizenship among unfriendly whites began to consider selling their right to the 640 acres and moving back among their friends and relatives. Others hesitated for some years to give up their tracts because they had put a great deal of money and work into building up the farms and plantations on which they lived.[8] They realized they would not get a fair price for their improvement if they chose to sell out. Moreover, starting a new farm within the nation meant finding a good piece of land and facing a great deal of work. There was also a certain loss of personal pride in such a decision, but that might be balanced by a renewed pride in their nation. The choice was not easy, but it was a choice that the federal government had not foreseen.

The experiment began with Article Eight of the treaty of 8 July 1817, which defined the land allotments known as "reserves" or "life estates":

> And to each and every head of any Indian family residing on the east side of the Mississippi river, on the lands that are now, or may hereafter be, surrendered to the United States, who may wish to become citizens of the United States, the United States do agree to give a reservation of six hundred and forty acres of land, in a square, to include their improvements, which are to be as near to the centre thereof as practicable, in which they will have a life estate, with a reversion in fee simple to their children, reserving to the widow her dower. . . . Provided that if any of the heads of families for whom reservations may be made should remove therefrom, then, in that case, the right to revert to the United States.[9]

---

[8]One reason so few Cherokee had registered to become citizens was that the tribal council had exerted such strong pressure against it; but having braved that opprobrium, those who registered consequently found it hard to admit their mistake and return to live in the nation among those who had branded them as expatriates.

[9]Peters, *Case of the Cherokee Nation*, 268. This clause was reiterated in Article 2 of the treaty of 1819; see 270.

In addition to the 311 "life estate reservees" (who registered for 640 acres apiece under this article between 1 July 1817 and 6 December 1819), there were 31 "fee-simple reservees" who received similar tracts under Article 3 of the treaty of 1819. A fee-simple reserve was made available to those heads of Cherokee families "believed to be persons of industry and capable of managing their property with discretion."[10] The difference between the two groups was that the life-estate reservees (sometimes called "life-interest" or "life-entail" reservees) were not permitted to dispose of their tracts during their lifetimes because they were considered wards of the government incapable of managing their property with discretion. As the federal agent put it, they became "legitimate landholders and American citizens and yet for the preservation of these lands [they remained] under the special protection of the law." They were, in effect, treated as "minors" because they lacked mastery of the English language and knowledge about the legal technicalities of landholding; "for the condition of the Indians in the present state of their information [is that they] are in fact minors and under the pupilage of a benevolent Government."[11]

The thirty-one Cherokees who were given fee-simple reserves, on the other hand, were persons of mixed white and Cherokee ancestry (in some cases, white men married to Cherokee, known as "Indian Countrymen" because marriage automatically gave Cherokee citizenship); they spoke and wrote English and fully understood the complexities of Anglo-Saxon law. Unfortunately, they discovered that they met the same obstructions and animosities from white frontiersmen as their less sophisticated countrymen. Little distinction was made between the two kinds of reservees in the surrounding states, and in the following discussion the 342 reservees of both kinds are considered as a single entity, part of the same experiment in citizenship. While the fee-simple reservees were limited to the thirty-one persons named in the codicile of the treaty of 27 February 1819, the federal government allowed Cherokees to continue to register for life estates after that date.[12]

---

[10]A list of the 31 fee-simple reservees follows the treaty as printed in ASP, 2: 189.

[11]M-208, roll 9, 12 November 1822, Meigs to Roane.

[12]Life estates for 154 Cherokee were registered between 27 February 1819 and 1 January 1820. See manuscript-registry list, Georgia State Archives.

In addition to motives of "benevolence," the government obviously had some practical purposes in view. The treaty negotiations of 1817 were designed to extinguish Cherokee title to roughly 14,500,000 acres in Georgia, North Carolina, Tennessee, and the Territory of Alabama. Because the Cherokee were told they must either accept an equivalent tract of land in the Territory of Arkansas or become citizens, the life estates and fee-simple reserves can be seen as an effort to overcome the resistance of those who had made extensive improvements on their farms and were reluctant to leave them to start over again in the West. These grants broke down opposition to the treaty and to removal by satisfying the objections of those unwilling to emigrate. Others who registered for reserves did so out of sentimental attachment to the land of their forefathers or out of fear of the primitive conditions and poor soil they might find in Arkansas. This choice in effect made them expatriates who were separated from their people; but to the more highly acculturated it was preferable to starting over and to the sentimental it was preferable to an exchange of land. Nevertheless, the fact that only 311 chose life estates and 31 chose (or were eligible for) fee-simple reserves—out of about 2,600 Cherokee heads of families—indicates the strong attachment of the Cherokee to their tribal identity.[13]

By the terms of the treaties a life estate or fee-simple reserve was to be granted only on land ceded in the treaties, and the 640-acre tract was to center around a farm or plantation (called "an improvement") on which the head of family resided. But some had registered their farms as life estates prior to 1819 when they thought the whole Cherokee Nation would be ceded. After 1819 these persons had to move out and start new improvements on the ceded land or to give up the chance to become citizens. One of the ambiguities for these late choosers was the date by which they had to register their decision. Secretary of War John C. Calhoun set the deadline at six months following the treaty signing (it was signed 27 February 1819). The attorney general, William Wirt, thought the deadline should extend to 20 January 1820. Some of the states con-

---

[13]While almost all of those given fee-simple reserves were of mixed white and Cherokee ancestry, it is difficult to tell what proportion of the life-estate holders were mixed bloods or full bloods. The names alone are not sufficient evidence. The fact that most allegedly could not speak or write English suggests that even if of mixed ancestry, they were among the less acculturated of the Cherokees.

cerned, however, held that the deadline was the date the treaty was signed.[14]

A more difficult problem for the would-be citizens arose because the states were quicker to sell the ceded land to their own citizens than the federal government was to survey it for the Cherokee reservees. Thus land presumably exempt from state sales was in fact sold, and the buyers had no compunctions about moving off Cherokee reservees who lacked a certified survey. Some states even challenged the validity of those surveys, which had been completed before they sold the land. In some cases, even before the reserve land was sold by the state or surveyed by the federal government, white squatters moved on to it in order to claim pre-emption rights.[15]

All of these difficulties could have been overcome had the states and the frontier whites shown any concern to cooperate with the government for the experiment in Cherokee citizenship. Instead, they showed the utmost hostility toward it and used every possible means to thwart it. The federal government, thinking in terms of the ultimate goal of freeing millions of acres for white settlement, considered the appropriation of a few thousand acres to individual Cherokees a small price to pay for removal. The secretary of war had many other Indian nations to deal with, and if he could use the Cherokee experiment as an example to satisfy opposition to removal in other tribes, it would make the task of total extinction of Indian land titles east of the Mississippi much easier. Yet the states and the individual frontiersmen had a much different perspective. They saw every 640-acre plot reserved to an Indian as so much fertile land taken from deserving white citizens and from land-sale revenues. Moreover, the state governments were resentful that the federal government was granting citizenship to "aliens" within their sovereign boundaries without consulting their wishes. Under the Constitution, each state was free to establish its own qualifications for citizenship. None of the states

---

[14]National Archives Microfilm, M-271, Letters Received by the Secretary of War Relating to Indian Affairs, 1800-1823, roll 3, #0775, 12 August 1820, Wirt to Calhoun.

[15]By federal law, any citizen (or squatter) who settled on unsold public land and made improvements was given the right to purchase the land at the official rate of $2 per acre when it was put on sale. Squatters who forced Cherokee farmers off their reserves of course assumed the right to their improvements.

was prepared to grant total equality to "savages" who had within the past generation slaughtered its early settlers and burned its settlements.[16]

Many, if not most, frontier whites were convinced that the Indian could never be civilized: "Once an Indian, always an Indian" was their axiom. Many believed that Indians were innately inferior to whites. Furthermore, in the Southern states, where the color line was increasingly important, the Indians were "a people of color." The extent of this racial prejudice can be measured by a letter that the governor of Georgia sent to Calhoun during the difficulties over the life-estates experiment. In response to Calhoun's inquiry regarding the state's willingness to integrate civilized and refined Indians into its citizenry as equals, Governor George M. Troup made the color line clear:

> If such a scheme were practical at all [i.e., "their incorporation into and amalgamation with our society"], the utmost of the rights and privileges which public opinion would concede to Indians would be to fix them in a middle station between the negro and the white man; and that as long as they survived this degradation, without the possibility of attaining the elevation of the latter, they would gradually sink to the condition of the former—a point of degeneracy below which they could not fall.[17]

Georgians, for a number of reasons, raised the first and strongest opposition to the experiment. Georgia had been the last of the original thirteen states to yield control of its western lands to the federal government. By its royal charter it claimed land from the Atlantic Coast to the Mississippi. Following the famous Yazoo frauds, however, Georgia reached an agreement with President Jefferson to cede the area west of the state's present boundary in exchange for the government's assuming responsi-

---

[16]The last Cherokee War ended in 1794, but the Creek War ended only in 1814 and the first Seminole War was just beginning in 1819.

[17]ASP, 2: 735, Troup to Calhoun, 23 February 1824. In other words, Troup meant that Cherokee "citizens" would be treated as free blacks; they could not vote, hold office, testify in court, or send their children to public schools. See also the protest of Georgia's congressional delegation, 10 March 1824, stating that it was improper for the federal government to "fix permanently upon them [the people of Georgia] any persons who are not, and whom she will never suffer to *become*, her citizens." M-234, roll 71, #0135, 10 March 1824. It is astonishing that in the face of such frank and open racial animosity toward Indians, officials of the War Department continued to urge the possibility of equal citizenship for Indians in the South throughout the next fifteen years. See, for example, National Archives Microfilm, M-21, Letters Sent by the Office of Indian Affairs, 1824-1835, roll 3, #0130, 27 December 1826, McKenney to Barbour.

bility to pay off the Yazoo claims against the state. In addition, in this famous "Compact of 1802," Jefferson agreed that the federal government would undertake to negotiate with the Indians "and extinguish at its own expense for the use of Georgia" all Indian land title within the boundaries of the state and turn their land over to the state.[18] The compact did not say when this would occur, but it did say that it would be "as early as the same can be peaceably obtained, upon reasonable terms." However, it also said that it would take place only with the voluntary consent of the Indians. Until Jackson's victory in New Orleans, the Georgians were too fearful of Indian attacks (fomented by Spain, Britain, or France) to complain about the failure to carry out the compact. But after 1815 the Georgians became increasingly clamorous for all the Indian land within their borders. The recognition that cotton would be the chief agricultural crop of the South and the fact that the Indian tribes still occupied much of the best cotton-growing soil, naturally increased the demand that these heathen "savages" be removed in order that civilized, Christian men could exploit the land as God intended.

At the session of the Georgia legislature that followed the treaty of 1819 with the Cherokee, a resolution was passed protesting the failure of the War Department to remove them totally to Arkansas. The Georgians took particular exception to the experiment when fee-simple estates and citizenship were included in the treaty. "The grant of reserves in 'fee simple' to Indians is an act which your memorialists view as not only violatary of the compact between the United States and Georgia but an infringement of our rights and an exposure of our citizens." (By "exposure" of its citizens, the legislature meant that Indians were likely to revert to barbarism and would always remain a threat to life, limb, and property.) Moreover, granting fee-simple rights to Cherokee or their heirs permitted the owner to sell the land for his own profit and this was an infringement of the Compact of 1802: "In the event of alienation by the reservee, where is the power of the United States to extinguish 'for the use of Georgia' the title to such reserve?" A profit for a Cherokee was of no use to Georgia. "Shall we be told that all these measures find their justification in policy and their apology in benevolence? Shall this treaty be passed upon us in the imposing form of humanity? . . ." Where was

---

[18]U. B. Phillips, *Georgia and State Rights* (Washington, 1902; Macon GA: Mercer University Press, 1983) 34-50.

the benevolence or humanity in placing the rights of "savages" above those of citizens? If Georgians seemed to place their interest above that of the Union, "excuse may be found in the extended catalogue of Indian aggression and the aggravated series of frontier suffering" by their citizens ever since the first settlements. Benevolence toward Indians was injustice toward whites.[19]

Realizing that these resolutions would have little weight with the War Department, Georgians instructed their congressmen, led by George Gilmer, to persuade Congress to appoint a select committee to investigate the whole issue. Congress obliged and made Gilmer the chairman. The report of Gilmer's committee on 7 January 1822 fully substantiated Georgia's protest. To grant Indian reservees title to Georgia's land was an abridgment of the compact with Jefferson. Furthermore, the executive branch of the federal government had no right to confer citizenship within the boundaries of sovereign states:

> The Committee cannot but view this attempt on the part of the United States to grant lands in fee-simple within the limits of Georgia as a direct violation of the rights of that State. The United States have no jurisdiction over the country or interest in the soil of the lands belonging to the Indians within the limits of Georgia. . . . But it is not the rights of Georgia alone that are violated by this treaty; the rights of Congress are equally disregarded. . . . The committee are [*sic*] not aware of the existence of a power of conferring the rights of citizenship in any other branch of the government than Congress.[20]

Gilmer's committee spoke for all the western states anxious to be rid of the Indians on their lands. Its report went on to accuse Calhoun and Monroe of deliberately trying to break the compact of 1802: "It appears from the last treaty that the United States are endeavoring to fix the Cherokee Indians upon the soil of Georgia" forever. In order to fulfill that compact, "it will be necessary for the United States to relinquish the policy which they seem to have adopted with regard to civilizing the Indians and rendering them permanent upon their [Georgians'] lands." The Gilmer report was the opening gun in the battle for total and enforced Indian removal west of the Mississippi, a reversal of Washington's policy that followed with Jackson's election.

---

[19]M-221, roll 92, #8105, 11 December 1819, Georgia Legislature to Monroe (printed resolution).

[20]ASP, 2: 259-60.

Gilmer's committee recognized that the ratification of the treaties of 1817 and 1819 had made their articles "the supreme law of the land." Georgians had not yet reached the point of nullification, secession, and states' rights; they were to employ these after 1827. The committee offered a simpler solution to the problem. Let the federal government apologize for its error; let it reaffirm its intention to carry out the Compact of 1802 with all deliberate speed, and let it appropriate a fund to be used "for the purpose of holding treaties with the Creek and Cherokee Indians for the extinguishment of their title to lands within the limits of Georgia."[21] Such treaties would include extinguishing the life estates and fee-simple reserves.

While Congress was deliberating over Georgia's complaints, the reservees whose 640-acre tracts were located within the lands ceded to Georgia in 1817 and 1819 were running into serious difficulties. The state surveyed the ceded area, generally ignoring the spots reserved to the new red citizens. Following the lotteries, by which Georgia parceled out the land to its white citizens, those who drew reserved land assumed that their state claim was superior to the treaty claim. Consequently a large number of reservees began to complain to the War Department that they had been forcibly ejected from their farms by Georgians. A typical case was that of Walter S. Adair, a fee-simple reservee. Adair wrote to Congressman Joel Abbot on 11 January 1821, stating that two white men, Reuben Harrison and William Arthur, had driven him from his plantation on the basis of the tract awarded to them in the Georgia lottery in Habersham County. He reported that four other reservees in the area (Ben Cooper, Darky Duncan, Moses McDaniel, and Samuel Ward—all life-estate reservees) had suffered similar ejectments.[22] Abbot was a bit

---

[21]Ibid., 260.

[22]M-221, roll 88, #4970, 11 January 1821, Adair to Abbot. The Cherokee chiefs kept a careful eye upon the treatment of the reservees, although they left full responsibility for their security up to the War Department. Charles Hicks spoke for the nation when he said in 1822, "We are not unapprized of the treatment of our people left on the ceded lands who had been provided for by treaty to take reservations and in number[s] of instances have been turned [out] of their houses without any respects of their certificates as reservees, and other[s] have had their lands run of[f] in quarter sections and made to pay rent to the state of Georgia which must subject the reservees to sue the State or quit-claim all together, for the Indian knows not what it is to goe into and stand suites at law, for he has nothing to support his suite against the State, where he may be sure to be cast in their courts nor does he know anything about the federal court to have his cause tried

nonplussed to find these red men claiming him as their representative, but he sent their complaint on to the secretary of war. In his letter, Abbot was totally honest about the situation: "His land is granted to individuals under the lottery law. These individuals have an overwhelming popular prejudice in their favor against the right to reservations under the Treaty."[23]

John C. Calhoun hired lawyers to take these cases to court and in a notable decision rendered by Judge A. S. Clayton (against tremendous public clamor) succeeded in establishing the superiority of the treaty rights over the lottery law.[24] This caused such an uproar among the Georgians that Congress hastily passed an appropriation to be used "for the purpose of holding treaties with the Creek and Cherokee Indians for their extinguishment of their title to lands within the limits of Georgia."[25] Included in this appropriation was a fund for buying out the Cherokee reservees in Georgia. It was probably fortunate for the government that this expedient put an end to what promised to be endless litigation. Gabriel Moore, the War Department's lawyer in Georgia for the reservees, reported to Calhoun in September 1822, that he was having great difficulty getting his clients reinstated upon their farms. In fact, most of the reservees had become so discouraged that they requested Moore to ask Calhoun whether he could remove the entails on the life-estate reserves so that they could sell out to the whites and move back into their nation.[26]

President Monroe appointed two commissioners from Georgia, Duncan Campbell and James Meriwether, to travel through Georgia and

---

there. And how can he keep his land from vendue, for he neither knows nothing or even has money to support his claim." M-271, roll 4, #0131, 10 January 1822, Hicks to Calhoun.

[23]M-221, roll 88, #4968, 5 February 1821, Abbot to Calhoun.

[24]National Archives Microfilm, M-15, Letters Sent by the Secretary of War Relating to Indian Affairs, 1800-1824, roll 5, #0183, 19 February 1823, Calhoun to Roane; M-221, roll 96, #0813, 20 November 1822, Meigs to Calhoun.

[25]M-21, roll 1, #0018, 25 March 1824, Calhoun to McLane.

[26]M-208, roll 9, 15 September 1822, Moore to Calhoun. Moore opposed the request to remove the entails from the reserves on the grounds that intimidation by whites would force the reservees to sell cheaply or otherwise be defrauded of the true worth of their farms. He suggested having white men appointed as guardians or trustees over the reservees.

buy out the reservees. They were instructed, however, not to pay more than two dollars per acre; the reservees were not to be allowed to make a profit from the government's mistake.[27] The commissioners began this task in the fall of 1822, but found their work full of difficulties. Most Cherokee knew the value of their land and were not eager to sell for two dollars an acre. Others had already sold their rights to speculators (or been cheated out of it) and the commissioners found themselves bargaining with shrewd Georgians rather than simple Indians. (Georgians were not opposed to making a profit from the government's mistakes.) One of the more common methods by which speculators tried to profit from the confusion was to marry a Cherokee woman who was entitled to a reserve (although by Cherokee law a women's property remained her own even after marriage). In February 1823, Campbell and Meriwether wrote to Calhoun for instructions on some of these legal complexities:

> We are instructed to purchase the reserves which have been taken within the limites of Georgia under the treaties of 1817-1819. We have given some attention to the subject and have appointed a time to make a valuation of the improvements. There is no doubt but that impositions have been practiced and that many individuals have taken reserves who, according to a fair construction of the treaties, are not entitled. The provisions of these treaties were dictated by policy and benevolence, but they have been used for purposes of speculation. Whitemen, fugitives from justice, have run into the nation since the treaties and by intermarriages with a native have obtained certificates of being the "head of an Indian family" and obtained reserves. We would inquire the extent of our authority—whether we have any judicial powers or whether we must take the purchase of the reserve and its improvements without reference to the title or the manner in which it was obtained.[28]

They were told to do the best they could but generally to bargain for the cheapest price without trying to adjudicate questions of fraud. It took them more than a year of hard work, but by 24 December 1823, they reported that they had completed the job. They had had to pay on the

---

[27]M-15, roll 6, p. 281, 15 June 1822, Calhoun to Floyd et al., and M-221, roll 97, #1562, 9 June 1823, Campbell to Calhoun. Campbell and Meriwether were also instructed to undertake negotiations with the Cherokees for a cession of all their land in Georgia. The House Ways and Means Committee of Congress estimated in 1823 that there were twenty-seven Cherokee reservees holding 17,280 acres within the borders of Georgia, but this estimate is probably low. ASP, 2: 391-92.

[28]M-221, roll 95, #0237, 28 February 1823, Campbell to Calhoun.

average more than the $1,280 prescribed for each reserve. The average they paid was $1,627, but in some cases the price was as high as $4,000.[29] This land was turned over to the sovereign state of Georgia to sustain it as a white man's country.

The state of Tennessee also had a compact with the federal government, which it used to frustrate the experiment in citizenship, but it lacked the comprehensiveness of the Georgia compact. Tennessee had been part of the western land claimed by North Carolina under its royal charter. When it yielded that land to the federal government in 1783, it had already given out a large number of land warrants or bounties to Revolutionary War veterans, many of them in areas still held by the Cherokee and Chickasaw. The legislature of North Carolina therefore specified that once Indian title was extinguished in Tennessee, the government was to honor the warrants for these tracts (few of which remained in the hands of any veteran or his family by 1819). One of the signal failures of Calhoun in negotiating the treaties of 1817-1819 was to take the Revolutionary veterans' bounties seriously. The Cherokee were wiser than he about this and warned him that unless he surveyed the reserves and negotiated with the state of Tennessee regarding conflicts or overlapping claims, there would be trouble. Calhoun cavalierly insisted that treaties, being the supreme law of the land, took precedence over all such minor claims.

"At the time of making the treaty," wrote James Brown, a fee-simple reservee, to Calhoun in November 1823, "I told you that there were extensive surveys of land claimed under the Grants of the State of North Carolina which might probably interfere with some of the reservations and desired your opinion on the subject whether the reservations within the claims under those grants would be affected by them. Your reply was that the Treaty reservations were the best of titles and consequently you were of the opinion that those grants could not effect [sic] them."[30] Brown now discovered that Calhoun had been wrong. The courts of Tennessee had challenged Brown's claim, and he was in difficulty. Perhaps he had foreseen this, for he had sold his reserve; but the buyer had been

---

[29]M-21, roll 1, p. 7, 25 March 1824. Calhoun to McLane; see also M-221, roll 97, #1679, 24 December 1823, Campbell to Calhoun. In this letter Campbell mentions paying $4,000 for Daniel Davis's fee-simple reserve.

[30]M-221, roll 97, #1550, 27 November 1823, Brown to Calhoun.

given time in which to pay for it. Now that the right to the land was being challenged, the buyer refused to fulfill the bargain, and Brown was caught short: "I sold my reservation on time," he told Calhoun, "and have made other contracts under the anticipation of meeting them as I received payment for my land." However, "Mr. Charles McClung of Knox County, Tennessee, entered a suit against me last Court for the land under claim of a North Carolina grant, the trial of which will take place in October next. In consequence of the suit being instituted, Mr. Smith, the purchaser of my land, has refused making me any payments agreeably to contract, until the suit is determined." This left Brown "in an unpleasant predicament," for he lacked funds to meet his contracts. "If I loose [lose] the suit, I shall be ruined. I depend upon and have confidence in the justice of the Government and hope you will not loose time in giving me necessary aid." Calhoun did his best. He instructed the Cherokee agent to hire a lawyer to defend Brown's claim, but few such cases were won.[31] Brown's situation was not an isolated one. He noted in closing his letter to Calhoun, "There are eight or nine other reservations similarly situated waiting the issue of my suit."

Revolutionary veterans' warrants were not in themselves sufficient to prevent all Cherokee reserves from taking effect within the state of Tennessee. The legislature therefore put its lawyers to the task of reading the fine print in the treaties and devising some other means of invalidating them. The lawyers came up with precisely the kind of technicality needed to bog down the whole process, making adjudication so expensive that the government would find implementation of the experiment very costly. The War Department had allowed Cherokee heads of families to register for life estates from July 1817 to December 1819, but the legislature of Tennessee concluded that, strictly interpreted, no life estates should have been registered after 1 July 1818. Consequently, in the spring of 1820 the legislature passed a law that declared 184 of the 311 life estates invalid.[32] Informed of this law, the War Department's surveyor, Robert Houston, did not bother to survey any of the reserves in Tennessee registered after 1 July 1818. The state proceeded to survey the land ceded by the Cherokee within its borders, ignoring the claims of

---

[31] Brown's case was still dragging through the courts of Tennessee four years later. See M-208, roll 10, 1 May 1826 and 1 March 1827.

[32] M-271, roll 3, #0351, 10 July 1820, Houston to Calhoun.

these reservees. In October 1820, the state's commissioner of land sales placed all the surveyed lands up for public sale. The federal agent (at that time, Colonel Return J. Meigs) rushed to Knoxville to try to prevent the sale. He carried with him an opinion of the attorney general of the United States, William Wirt, asserting that the treaties (as he read them) permitted registration of life estates through 1 January 1820.[33] "But the Commissioners for the sales, having no discretionary powers to deviate from their instructions, the sales were made in conformity to the law." As a result, Meigs reported, "This has embarrassed the Indian who had made his election to become a Citizen of the United States on the stipulations contained in those treaties . . . the purchasers in some instances have by force and arms dispossessed the Indian. They are almost daily asking my aid and advice. My advice has uniformly been, 'Stay on your reservation until legally dissiezed [*sic*] and in no instance make personal violent opposition; behave well and it will strengthen your claim for redress.' "[34]

Suddenly the government was faced with extensive litigation and placed in the awkward situation of having no surveys of its own by which to justify its Indian plaintiffs. "I was surprised," Meigs told Calhoun, "to see a law of Tennessee" opposing the treaty and the attorney general; "I thought respect to the general Government would have induced silence on that point." He simply underestimated the drive for states' rights and the power of land speculation in the West. However, he sought to palliate the problem by undercutting the experiment and placing the blame on the Cherokee:

> The number of just claimants is not great, but the right of each individual is his right; and is his all! and is the hope of his children, including the dower of the widow. The door for entry was open without limitation as to the number. The whole number registered is 311 and more than four fifths of that number voluntarily moved off their reservations, and they reverted to the United States; this state of things was foreseen at the time and anticipated. The small number remaining, it would seem, may with propriety claim the protection of the Government in the enjoyment of their lands and citizenship.[35]

---

[33]For Wirt's opinion, solicited by Calhoun after the passage of the Tennessee law, see M-271, roll 3, #0775, 12 August 1820, Wirt to Calhoun.

[34]M-221, roll 90, #6757, 8 February 1821, Meigs to Calhoun.

[35]Ibid.

The assertion that four-fifths of the life-estate reservees "voluntarily moved off their reservations" is specious. The majority appear to have been forcibly ejected or threatened with violence. The treatment of those who tried to defend their rights provided a warning to discourage others.[36] The most egregious examples of this in Tennessee were the treatment of Eight Killer and Peggy Shorey, both of whom had life estates registered in Marion County. Sometime in 1819 "some white persons came and drove the Indians off" their estates and they complained to the federal agent. Meigs asked the United States Army garrison commander to look into the matter. "When Captain Call went round the frontier to remove Intruders, he dispossessed the [white] persons in possession of Peggy Shorey's reservation" and she reoccupied it. Nevertheless, "shortly after, when she was absent, they returned, carried her furniture out [of her home] and retook possession and have held it ever since." At one point Peggy Shorey was temporarily restored to her farm, but she soon lost it again to a scheming white man named McGowen. Pretending to be her ally against those who had thrown her out and threatened vengeance, McGowen persuaded her to sign a paper that deeded the reserve to him. Once he had the paper, he then dispossessed her and took the reserve for himself.

Captain Call also looked into Eight Killer's claim of dispossession. Those who had taken his home "were taken prisoners" by Call, but unfortunately "Capt. Call came to a compromise" with them when "they gave bonds and security to be off in a given number of days." Call left them in possession, "but when the days were expired, he, the Eight Killer, went with a white man to get possession as Capt. Call told him to do." The intruders not only refused to honor their agreement, but "they beat and abused him very much and drove him off, and he has been afraid ever since to go back."[37] Eight Killer had taken a white man with him because Indians were not allowed to give testimony in court against whites, but evidently this white man was intimidated as well. In 1825 Meigs's successor, Hugh Montgomery, asked the War Department what he should do about these two cases. They were not exceptional, he re-

---

[36]For a description by Meigs of the violence used by whites to drive Cherokees off their reserves, see M-208, roll 9, 17 May 1822, Meigs to Calhoun.

[37]M-234, roll 71, #0611, 2 July 1825, Ross to Montgomery; M-208, roll 10, 1 August 1825, Montgomery to Calhoun.

ported: "There are six or eight others in that neighborhood all of whom have been dispossessed and kept out of their reservations in the same way."[38]

The War Department instructed the federal agent to hire lawyers to try to defend all of the reservees in Tennessee, but the lawyers were expensive and the agents lacked funds to support the litigation. Montgomery complained in 1827 that the lawyers in Tennessee wanted $40 for each case they took to court; the surveyor wanted $8 for each reserve that had to be surveyed; and the claimants needed money to pay for themselves and witnesses who had to travel to the various county courthouses and wait for their cases to come up. When the cases were lost, Montgomery also was asked to pay the costs of court. He did not have such funds available in his agency budget, he said, hence declined making payments except for the lawyers' and surveyors' fees.[39]

Montgomery, like Meigs, blamed many of the Cherokee reservees for the disputes over their land, pointing out that they had failed to reside on the land they had registered or that they were not heads of families.[40] Ultimately he supported those Cherokee who gave up all hope of establishing themselves as citizens in Tennessee and petitioned the War Department to evaluate their improvements. Upon payment, they agreed to yield their claims and return to live in the nation.[41] It did not matter whether the Cherokee reservee was a well-educated, highly acculturated man like James Brown or a poor, uneducated woman like Peggy Shorey or even a white man married to a Cherokee, like Templin Ross; the frontiersmen of Tennessee were not prepared to give up any of their land to Indians.[42]

---

[38]M-208, roll 10, 24 October 1825, Shorey to Montgomery (via John Ross) and M-234, roll 72, #0201, 31 December 1826, Montgomery to Calhoun.

[39]M-234, roll 72, #0402, 20 September 1827, and #0409, 25 September 1827, Montgomery to Calhoun.

[40]M-208, roll 10, 28 April 1826, Montgomery to Calhoun. After describing what he considered "a Doubtfull Case" of a reservee, Montgomery added that there were, in his opinion, "nearly fifty others" like him that did not merit support.

[41]M-208, roll 10, 10 May 1826, Montgomery to Barbour.

[42]Templin W. Ross complained that in June 1819, he left his life-estate reserve on a short trip to take his pregnant wife to stay with her family during her confinement and returned to his house to find that "doors were broken open and possession taken of the premises" by white men "and out of which I am kept to this day." See M-234, roll 72, #0417, 16 February 1827, Ross to McKenney.

The state of North Carolina was equally determined to prevent the success of this experiment in Indian citizenship. As in Tennessee, the issue of Revolutionary veterans' warrants produced conflicts that invalidated some of the grants. But North Carolina found a legal technicality of its own to invalidate many of the others. Judge John Hall of the state's Supreme Court ("thought the best judge in the State" by some attorneys) rendered an opinion in the case of *Euchellah v. Welsh* that invalidated all surveys made for life estates on the grounds that the surveyor had not acted upon a direct commission from the chief executive.[43] Euchellah (or Euchulah, of Cowee Town) had sued a white man for ejecting him from his farm. He offered as proof of ownership the certificate of survey given to him by the federal agent for his reserve. But the certificate was not signed by the president nor by a surveyor commissioned by the president. The president had commissioned Robert Houston of Knoxville, Tennessee, to survey all reserves under the two treaties and Houston, being busy with the surveys in Tennessee, had employed Robert Armstrong to run the surveys in North Carolina. Calhoun considered Hall's opinion absurd, but this did the government's attorneys little good.[44]

The War Department hired William Roane as attorney for the reservees in North Carolina in 1821 and two years later authorized Joseph Wilson to assist him. After six strenuous years, Roane wrote a long letter to the secretary of war trying to sum up the frustrations he had faced and still faced. "I am impelled by humanity to make the following statement," he said in July 1827. By act of the General Assembly of North Carolina in December 1819, "it was made the duty of the governor to appoint a commissioner and surveyor to survey and lay off for sale 'all the land lately acquired by treaty from the Cherokee nation.'" However, "The Commissioner and Surveyor took upon themselves to judge that the reservations made under the aforementioned treaties were none of them well made" except for the fee-simple reserves given to Big Bear and Richard Walker. Therefore, they "paid no attention to the claimants of about 45 or 50 other reservations but actually ran them out [i.e., surveyed them] as unappropriated lands." The state then sold off this land to its

---

[43]M-234, roll 72, #0425, 8 July 1827, Roane to Barbour.

[44]M-15, roll 5, #0183, 19 February 1823, Calhoun to Roane. Calhoun sent Roane a copy of Houston's commission and also a copy of Judge Clayton's decision in Georgia. See also M-21, roll 4, #0051, 7 August 1827, Hamilton to Roane.

citizens and "those who bought them (claiming to hold under the state) drove off the Indians, saying in the language of the barbarous county of Haywood that 'they were heathens and had no business in a christian land.' "[45]

The Cherokee complained of this to Colonel Meigs in 1820 and he, through Roane, brought suit for them on behalf of the War Department. "After long struggles with the tenants of the State," fourteen of these suits were successful. Still, the state refused to accept the decisions as final. In 1823 "an act was passed by the General Assembly authorizing the Governor to appoint two commissioners to treat with the Reservees, examine their titles, ascertain for what price they would each of them sell, report which of their titles they thought good, which bad, and the evidence on which each of them rested." When they had reported, the general assembly authorized the governor "in all cases where the commissioners should report the title bad, to employ some able attorney to appear in behalf of the State in opposition to the Indian claims."

At this point the work of Roane and Wilson became very difficult. "Such is their power ["the parties who are opposed to the Indian claims"] and the [anti-Indian] prejudice of the County, that all Indian suits have to be removed out of the county for a fair trial"; no jury would support an Indian against a white claimant. The suits were therefore tried in the Superior Court of the county of Buncombe. Roane found that most of the reservees were too timid and frightened to try to stand up to the harassment that issued from local whites when the Indians chose to defend their claims. "By the Laws of the United States," Roane continued, "the Indian reservees are made citizens of the United States [so] of course they can hold said land[s] and sue for them in the courts of North Carolina, but in examining our statute book we see so many impediments thrown in the way that the Indians can scarcely obtain Justice. Not the least of these impediments is that an Indian cannot prove by his Indian's neighbour[s] that he lived at his own house on his own reservation." In short, the Indian's testimony on his own behalf was not accepted as evidence. "If he had no white neighbors" who would testify for him, "he is in a bad way."[46]

---

[45]M-234, roll 72, #0425, 8 July 1827, Roane to Barbour.

[46]M-234, roll 72, #0426, 8 July 1827, Roane to Barbour. For an example of the same problem of the inadmissibility of Indian evidence in Georgia, see M-208, roll 9, 1 March 1822, Hicks to Montgomery.

Furthermore, because of Judge Hall's ruling, the reservee's "plat and certificate of survey is no evidence where Indian lines are" concerned. Thus even when a reservee won a case of trespass, he "only recovers by showing that his improvements is intruded in by the Ejector (such being the case he has no land but such as he has cleared and improved)" and no reservees had improved their whole 640 acres. Roane concluded that the only real way to help the Cherokee was to have the president issue new orders to survey the reserves and then to sign the plats himself. He accompanied this letter with a petition from thirteen reservees (including the famous Chief Junaluska) stating, "The State of North Carolina refused to let them hold their own lands . . . they have suffered much by being driven away to live in the woods" and "now would beg that they may again have certificates" validated by the president.[47]

According to Roane, the limited success the Cherokees had attained in North Carolina up to 1827 was due primarily to the heroism of two men. In the cases "in behalf of the Indian Reservees *vs.* State purchasors," the Indians "were backed by but two white men, Gideon F. Morris and William Reid." Both of them were married to Cherokees and held reserves. "Morris, a keen, active Georgian" and "Reid, a simple and slothful Scotchman" were treated as traitors to the white race for taking the side of the Indians. Morris's reservation had been sold by the state to General Thomas Lane, one of the state's leading citizens. Lane was still in possession of it in 1827. "Morris was, and is still poor; Lane, wealthy and powerful." The state bought out Reid's claim in 1825 and "Reid, with those of his kindred who had sold [their reservations], moved off into the [Cherokee] nation, leaving Morris to fight the battle out as well as he could." Under the law, "when an Indian sues the person in possession under the state, no matter how poor and worthless the defendant, the Sovereign Power, the state, is to back the defendant, and the Indian has no friend but poor Gideon F. Morris." Because Morris's courage had inspired the reservees to fight back, "the whites (for so they are called) therefore have been trying every means to break up and drive off Morris, and then the Indians of course must go. Nothing but the un-

---

[47]M-234, roll 72, #0435, 2 April 1825, Junaluska et al. to Barbour. These thirteen, Roane said, "together with 38 reservees have been Driven off of their Improvements." Though dated 1825, this was marked as received in the Indian Office 3 May 1827.

daunted spirit, firmness and pride of Morris would enable him to withstand the wealth and power of the most powerful men in Haywood."

What astonished Roane was that the Cherokee federal Indian agents
since 1820 had done nothing to help the reservees in North Carolina.
When Morris traveled 150 miles across the Appalachians to visit the
Cherokee agency in Tennessee to obtain copies of the surveys, he discovered that the agent (Hugh Montgomery) had lost all touch with the
situation in North Carolina. He told Morris "that the Government of the
United States looked upon it that the Indians [in North Carolina] were
satisfied and gone off," having been paid for their reserves by the state.
Roane's point in writing this detailed account was to let the War Department know that its left hand did not know what its right hand was
doing. He also wished to solicit "pecuniary aid" for Morris and the other
reservees to pursue their claims. For years they had to pay all their court
expenses (except lawyers' fees) and travel expenses themselves.

For a time the War Department continued to press a few of the most
solid reserve cases in the North Carolina courts, but by 1829 the experiment was declared a failure. On 2 March 1829, Congress appropriated
$20,000 to buy out all Cherokee reserves in that state. Thomas L.
McKenney, commissioner of Indian Affairs, appointed the Reverend
Humphrey Posey (a Baptist missionary) and General Romulus M. Saunders, to go around that state "for the purpose of purchasing such Reservations of land as are yet claimed by Indians or Indian Countrymen
within the limits of the State of North Carolina."[48] All of Roane's efforts
and all the fortitude of Gideon F. Morris went for nothing.

Alabama was admitted to statehood in 1819. Its settlers were no more
eager to cooperate with the experiment in Indian citizenship than the
other three states within which the Cherokee owned land. Like Georgia,
it appealed to Congress to appropriate money and appoint commissioners to negotiate for the cession of all Cherokee land within its borders.[49]
As in North Carolina, it insisted that the surveys of the reserves were

---

[48]M-21, roll 5, #0210, 5 June 1829, Eaton to Posey and Saunders. See also *Cherokee
Phoenix*, 10 September 1828. It is worth noting that as early as 1824 Congress had con-
sidered buying out all reserves in North Carolina and Tennessee; M-21, roll 1, p. 7, 25
March 1824.

[49]M-221, roll 96, #0837, 14 February 1823, legislature of Alabama to the secretary
of war.

invalid because they lacked the signature of the president.[50] Like Tennessee, its frontiersmen intimidated, harassed, and defrauded the reservees. "I need not tell you," the federal agent of the Cherokees told the War Department in 1828, in reference to Alabama's opposition to the reserves, "that all the difficulties that the States and State Councilars can possibly throw in the way of Recovery in those Reservations are to be surmounted or no Recovery can be had."[51]

Typical of the dilemma of reservees in Alabama was the case of Sally Lowry. She had registered for a 640-acre plot four to seven miles below the mouth of "Sail Creek" in Jackson County, but the government was slow to survey it. In 1826 the agent found that while this area was "public land unsold," it was "all in occupancy by whitemen who will not let her have possession or survey the land." She requested the government to give her a certificate of survey so that she could take her claim to court. But the agent thought her claim was weak because she had not resided on the land as required by the treaty.[52]

Somewhat less typical was the effort to invalidate three reserves in the same county on the grounds that the reservees were really blacks claiming to be Cherokees. Hiram Ross, the postmaster of Woodville in that county, felt obliged to call this to the attention of the federal authorities because these reserves "are the Valuablest that is in this Countrey" and he did not want the government defrauded. His evidence, however, was second or thirdhand. Joseph Elliott, married to a Cherokee, held a reserve for his wife, one for his brother, Sutton Stephens, and one leased from Andrew Lacy. According to Ross, "There is an old lady in this county by the name of Caty Wilson that was with Elliott's mother probably at his birth and knew his family for years before he was born, who upon oath, I think, would say that the deceased mother of Elliott never saw a Cherokee in her lifetime, besides she was certainly as Black as any

---

[50]M-234, roll 72, #0601, 18 August 1828, Montgomery to Porter. E. P. Hale, attorney for the War Department in Alabama, refused to press claims for any reserves without a survey of the reserve signed by the president; M-234, roll 72, #0603, 29 July 1828, Hale to Montgomery.

[51]M-234, roll 72, #0601, 18 August 1828, Montgomery to Porter.

[52]M-208, roll 10, 25 April 1826, Montgomery to Barbour, and M-234, roll 72, #0338, 24 March 1827, Montgomery to Barbour.

other Negro according to report."[53] Elliott described himself as a "mixed blood," but Ross said it was a mixture of white and black; there was no Indian in it. Likewise his sister was black and she was the wife of Sutton Stephens. Ross requested that his name be kept secret, for he said he feared reprisals; it seems more likely he hoped to acquire the land himself. There is no evidence that the War Department acted on this information. In any case, being married to a Cherokee, Elliott was legally a member of the nation. No one ever questioned this in cases where whites married Cherokee women in order to obtain reserves. Whether the state of Alabama would have recognized Elliott's right to equal citizenship, however, was a different question.

In 1823 and again in 1828 the legislature of Alabama followed the precedent of the other states in which the Cherokee Nation was located. It formally requested the Congress to appropriate funds to buy out all Indian land titles within the boundaries of the state. It also asked the War Department for a list of any reserve claims that the department still considered valid, noting that the ceded lands had been settled by white citizens "and improvements which add value to the land [have been] erected by the citizens with a view to purchasing whenever the land shall be brought into market. Wherefore it is necessary they should know with certainty which of the reservations are valid particularly as the pretended claimants are offering all the valuable part of Jackson County for sale under the reservation titles."[54] By 1828 the Cherokee reservees in Alabama had given up hope of establishing their claims and attaining citizenship.

Two years earlier the federal agent, Hugh Montgomery, had summarized the sad status of the experiment:

> There are on the Register kept in this office 311 entered for life Estate Reservations Exclusive of the [31] Fee simple ones. I should suppose that about 50 had been paid or would take pay for their improvements and Relinquish their Claim to the Reservations. I should suppose also that there were about 50 whose Reservations were not on the Ceded land but in other parts of the nation, and I think it probable that there are 100 that are Illegal and who ought not to hold, either from their not Residing on the ceded Lands or from other causes. The balance, or about that number, I believe to be justly intitled to the land, and it seems

---

[53]M-234, roll 72, #0309, 28 November 1827, H. Ross to George Graham.

[54]M-234, roll 72, #0536, 15 March 1828, Alabama House of Representatives to McKenney.

to me to have some claims of the government to have their rights defended. They have all, or with few exceptions, been driven off their Land. . . . They have no person to apply to . . . and I have been able to give them no incouragement. . . . The Result is that a great number of them are giving to a set of speculators use of the Land to get them Repossessed . . . and many others are selling out for a Song.[55]

Return J. Meigs had reported that as early as 1821 four-fifths, or about 250 of the life-estate reservees had left their reservations.[56] Like Montgomery, he cast much of the blame for the failure upon the Cherokee themselves, though how the government expected them to succeed in this complex effort when "few of them can write or even speak the english Language" is not clear.[57] They had been given title, under ambiguous circumstances, to extremely valuable pieces of land amidst extremely hostile and avaricious and unscrupulous white neighbors who had little respect for them or their rights. Then they had been left to fend for themselves (until dispossessed, often through no fault of their own) apparently with the "anticipated" hope that they would quit. They had acted, as Meigs noted, "on the recommendation of the United States Commissioners" in 1817-1819 and "placed all their hopes and prospects for support of themselves, as many of them have large families," in the promise of citizenship. By so doing, they cut themselves off from their own people: "This property is their only hope, their Sheet Anchor to save the Ship in a storm. . . . By embracing the offer of the Commissioners, they of course relinquished all their rights to and in their native country. If they shall be now deprived of the locations here, they become outcasts and beggars and placed in a Country [the surrounding states] where for the crime of wearing a complexion a shade a little darker than

---

[55]M-208, roll 10, 10 May 1826, Montgomery to Barbour. Montgomery also noted that while many reservees were willing to give up their reserves and return to the nation if the government would simply reimburse them for their houses, barns, and cultivated fields so that they would have some capital to start over, it was now too late to obtain accurate evaluations of Indian improvements: in most cases white men had been living on the reserves for some years and had destroyed much of the Cherokee improvements and added their own.

[56]M-208, roll 9, 12 November 1822, Meigs to Roane. By 1826 Montgomery expressed sympathy for the life-estate reservees, "all of whom were out of possession" of their tracts, "some by process of law, some by force and violence." M-208, roll 10, 28 April 1826, Montgomery to Barbour.

[57]M-208, roll 10, 10 May 1826, Montgomery to Barbour.

our own, our selfish pride and conceit looks down upon them with sentiments devoid of magnanimity." Meigs praised men like William Roane and Joseph Wilson for braving the spite of their white neighbors to defend these dark-skinned people: "Your task by some may be looked on as invidious (perhaps), but men of liberal minds will look upon it as highly honorable to defend the weak against the strong."[58] The Cherokee leaders, it might seem, displayed more liberalism by allowing these expatriate deserters to return to the nation and take up new land after resistance by the majority to the threats of the commissioners from 1817 to 1819 had enabled the nation to hang on to its homeland.

A few Cherokees who returned had managed to make a good deal of money from the affair. These were mixed bloods who sold their reserves quickly, for cash, and at good prices. Records indicate that several obtained $4,000 for their tracts and some others obtained a good deal more. Gideon Morgan, Jr. reported that George Harlin's reserve on rich cotton land in Alabama sold for $5,120. Morgan said that even that price was ridiculously low and that he had paid $30 an acre for land just like it. In 1820 the reserve of Margaret Morgan sold for $6,000 and soon after was resold for $8,000; James Riley sold his reserve for $6,700 and Richard Riley for $6,000.[59] This was the era of the great "black belt" cotton boom. Speculation ran prices sky-high for those shrewd enough or lucky enough to capitalize on the market.

A few reservees managed to hold on to their property, or at least continued to sue for it, in Tennessee and Alabama in the early 1830s; but after Andrew Jackson's election, the whole situation changed drastically for the Indians. Jackson came into office in 1829 with a mandate to alter the federal Indian policy. He did not believe in dealing with Indians by treaties and argued that the federal government should yield to the sovereign states the right to assert control over all the Indian land within their boundaries. Georgia set the stage for the final removal of the Indians when it asserted its authority over all Cherokee and Creek land in its borders in 1829. By acquiescing in this, Jackson and his secretary of war, John Eaton, put an end to all efforts to aid the few remaining reservees. The Cherokee Nation struggled on for ten more years against the

---

[58]M-208, roll 9, 12 November 1822, Meigs to Roane.

[59]M-234, roll 72, #0589, 1 August 1828, Morgan to McKenney, and M-221, roll 96, #1424, 16 September 1822, Morgan to Calhoun.

effort to remove it but finally had to yield to force. Public opinion supported Jackson's belief that the Indians were not yet sufficiently civilized to become citizens. Perhaps after another fifty years in the wilds of "The Great American Desert," they might raise themselves to the point of another trial.

The Cherokee learned a valuable lesson from the experience. Denationalization and integration into the white community ceased to be a viable option. Thenceforth the Cherokee adopted a policy of separatist nationalism with a firm commitment to national ownership of the land. The experiment in citizenship and "exclusive property" demonstrated what the Cherokee leaders already were convinced of in 1817. Euro-Americans were not yet prepared to accept native Americans as equal citizens. Thus the same intensive nationalism that (in terms of "manifest destiny") provided justification for white Americans to override treaty rights and Indian land titles, produced, inadvertently, an equally intensive nationalism among the Indian nations. The experiment in Cherokee citizenship boomeranged, as perhaps it was unconsciously intended to do. All of the Southern states effectively used the argument against *imperium in imperio* as grounds for moving the Indian nations out of their borders.

TABLE 1

DATES	NUMBER OF RESERVATIONS	NAMES	NUMBER IN FAMILY	RESIDENCE	REMARKS
		REGISTER OF PERSONS WHO WISH RESERVATIONS UNDER THE TREATY OF JULY 8, 1817			
July 1817	1	James Lesley in right of his wife....................	5	Coosa River	
	2	White Man Killer...........	3	Coosa River	
	4	Parker Collins in right of his wife....................	5	Waters of Chatahoochee	
	5	Thomas Cordery in right of his wife....................	4	do do	
	6	David Cordery do do	1	do do	
	7	Henry Vickery do do	4	do do	
	10	Thomas Foreman (native)	11	On the road from McNairs to Knoxville	
	11	Bark Foreman..............	2	do do	
	12	Archy Foreman.............	7	do do	
	13	James Bigby	9	do do	
	14	M! McDonald in right of wife....................	1	Lookout Mountain	
	15	Daniel Ross in do do	4	do do	
	16	M!: Coody.................	6	do do	
	17	M!: Nave	4	do do	
	18	Eliza Ross	1	do do	
	19	John Ross	1	do do	
	20	Lewis Ross	2	South fork of High-wassee opposite the Agency	
July 10th	21	Andrew Ross..............	1		
	22	Walter Adair	6	East side of Chatahoochee 100 acres to include a lime Kill & 540 Acres where he lives	
1817	23	M!: T. Guereneau...........	2		
July	24	David McNair	7	Both sides of Connawawga	
10th	25	Edward Odier	2	Connasawga River	
"	26	William Burgess............	5	do do	
"	27	Joseph Phillips in right of wife	6	Tellico Plain	

TABLE 1 [CONTINUED]

	28	Samuel McDaniel in do.......	3	Coyeeta Old Fields	
	29	William Keys in do..........	3	Waters of Mud Creek	
	30	Samuel Keys in do	3	do do	
	31	Isaac Keys in do	3	do do	
	32	John McNary do do.......	3	Between Sawta and Crow Creek to include his Improvements	
	33	William Barnes do do	5	Long Savannah	
	34	Cap! Jnᵒ Woods (native)	1	Boxes Cove	
	35	Nathaniel Peak..............	5	Island of Highwassee	
	36	John Langley................	4	Chestatee Waters	
	37	Daniel Short for wife.........	5	Chatahoochee	
	38	William Backley do do ...	9	Oolstever	
1817	39	Moses Alberty for wife.......	4	Hightower	
	40	Taylor Eldridge do do.....	3	Sweet Water	
	41	Martin Maney do do......	4	do do	
	42	John Maney do do	3	do do	
	43	William Haniger for wife	5	Acooee	
	44	William England do do	5	Near Chatahoochee	
	45	Buffington.................	6	Head of Highwassee	
	46	Isaac Vann.................	2	Sweet Water	
	47	William Many..............	1	do do	
Jan 28 1818	48	David Taylor for Wife	2	On south side of Little Tennessee about 12 miles below Morganton Bugbys old place	
	49	Thomas Starr (native)	2	Connasawga, north brance of Highwassee	
Feb. 7	50	Uriah Hubbard	10	Warhough Creek	
	51	Darcob Duncan.............	3	do do	
	52	Edmund Duncan	6	do do	
	53	John Duncan	3	do do	
	53 [sic]	Charles Gordon Duncan	-	do do	Had been omitted
	54	Drury Jones................	2	Battle Creek	
Mar. 11	55	Daniel Thorn for wife	7	Crow Creek	
"	56	Alexander Brown (native).....	2	Creek path Sour Mush Old place	
"	57	John Brown Junior	7	Late residence of his father Col. Richard Brown	

TABLE 1 [CONTINUED]

,,	58	Thomas Jones in right of wife	7	Where Bill Brown lived formerly on Tennessee River	
,,	59	James Jones	3	do do	
,,	60	William Jones	2	Near do do	
Apr. 9	61	Caleb Starr for wife	8	Long Savannah	
,,	62	Austin Rider do	8	Tellico Plains	
	63	John Bean in right of wife	4	Highwassee	
11	64	John Wilson do do	6	Blue Spring Tennessee River	
19	65	Reuben Tiner do do	6	Highwassee River	(Enrolled for Arkansas)
	66	John Pace	5	Wills Creek	(For do do)
	67	Ahamah	2	do do	
27	68	Samuel Ridley in right of wife	8	South side of Tennessee	
May 1	69	Andrew Taylor do do	2	Selice Old Town	
10	70	Eli M. Hale do do	5	Running Water Town	
	71	Robert B. Vann (A native)	1	Near Creek Path	
14	72	James Dohorty Junʳ	9	Hightower	
	73	Charles Tucker	6	Highwassee River	
	74	David McGloherlin	7	Hightower	
	75	James Dohorty Senʳ	5	do	
	76	John Martin right of wife	2	do	
	77	Nancy Graves	2	do	
17	78	Benjamin Tempson	3	Head of Highwassee River	
	79	Swimmer (A native)	2	Tusquittah	
1818 May 18	80	Alexander McDaniel	11	Nottlee	
	81	Thomas Raper in right of wife	5	Tusquitah	
	82	Jessee Raper do do	3	Coosa Town	
19	83	Skeleskee or Beard	-	Nottlee	
19	84	Chesquah or the Bird	-	Nottlee	
	85	Baltalatee or Fermament	-	ditto	
20	86	B. Robert Rogers for wife	5	Cho as te ee	
,,	88 [sic]	James Ward	7	Mouth of Deep Creek	
,,	89	George Ward	6	do do	
,,	90	Caty Ward (a widow)	3	Chatahoochee	Entered proxy per William England

TABLE 1 [CONTINUED]

"	91	Lucy Briant (a widow)	7	Caumanee	
"	92	Samuel Ward...............	4	Soquee	
	93	Charles Ward...............	2	Deep Creek	
	94	Bryant Ward	2	Chatahoochee	
22	95	Amos Robinson............	3	Little Paint Rock Creek	
	96	Edward Adair	5	Soquee	
	97	Samuel Adair	5	Chestatee	
	98	Benjamin Cooper Right of Wife	4	Waters of Chatahoochee	
23	99	Reuben Daniel do do	2	Hightower River	
	100	Evan Nicholson do do	6	Soquee	
24	101	Andrew Miller do do	8	Toqua	
25	102	Charles Coody (a native)	5	Near southwest point Rock Creek	Enrolled for Arkansas
25	103	Nancy Thornton	9	Near southwest Point	
	104	Wiley Tuton for Child	1	To include the place where he now lives to opposite the Seven Islands	
	105	Polly Brown (a native)	2	Creek Path town on the road leading from Gunters Landing	
	106	Hannah L. Harlin in right of her own children	4	Highwassee River	
	107	David England in right of wife	2	Chatahoochee	
26	108	James Ore do do...........	7	Sawtee Town Tennessee River	
27	109	Sarah West (a native)	8	To Notley Old Town	
	110	Caty Harlin do	1	Turnpike Town to include place where Mr. Bible lives	
27	111	Washing Face (a native)	8	Long Savannah near the Long Creek	
28	112	Uriah Wilkerson	3	Pond Creek	
	113	John Drew.................	5	Creek Path	
29	114	Catharine Lacy	4	On [sic]	
	115	John Thompson.............	9	Thompsons Ferry Tennessee River	
	116	Alexander Thompson	4	North side of Tennessee at a place called Race Paths	
30	117	Nancy Merrell..............	4	Creek Path near Pain Creek	
	118	Catharine Cheeks	7	do do above do	
	119	John Brown Sen!............	4	Creek Path	

TABLE 1 [CONTINUED]

	120	Isaac N. Wade for wife	4	Near Fort Deposit Tennessee River	
June	121	Willis Stephnes do do	2	do do	
	122	John Shoemake in do.	3	Crow Town	
June 1	123	George Harlin (a native)	4	Coosawattee River	
8	124	John Harlin right of wife	4	Little Kiuka Creek west side of Highwassee	Enrolled for Arkansas
	125	Samuel Candy (a native)	6	do do	do
9	126	The Bird . . .do	6	Shooting Town Hiawassee River	
16	127	Jenney Wolf. . . do	4	Big Spring on Georgia Road	
July 11	128	William Wilson right of wife . .	3	On Flint River	
22	129	Alexander Carter	2	Mouse Creek	Enrolled for Arkansas
28	130	John Still	2	Head waters north fork Flint River	
	131	Thomas Wilson	3	Hurricane Fork of do	
	132	Giles McAuntley for wife	2	do do	
28	133	William McDaniel for wife	7	Ooltee wah	Enrolled for Arkansas
Aug. 6	134	Abraham Davis . . . do . . . do	5	About $1^1/_2$ miles south of E. Gunters	
11	135	Moses Elders	3	$^1/_2$ mile from Gunters landing	
28	136	Elijah Sutton right of wife	4	Tus quit ah	
29	137	Kananooleeskee or Chalange . .	2	Flint River	
Sep. 13	138	Jesse Scott right of wife	4	At a spring four miles above John Wilson	
14	139	Betsey Woodard (a native)	2	Ooltewah Creek	
15	140	John Looney (a native)	4	Creek Path to include the place where the black fox lived and died	
23	141	Cooloocha (a widow)	3	Near Jack Thomp- sons Creek Path	
Oct. 6	142	Charles Thompson (a native) . .	3	Paint Rock ferry	
14	143	William Richey for his child . . .	1	Near Tennessee River	
Nov. 2	144	Syastah or Spoiler	4	Long Savannah	
Nov. 3	145	John Hilderbrand for Children	6	At the mouth of the creek where the Pub- lick Mill stands on Highwassee River	
6	146	Edmond Fawlin (a native)	6	On the path from Crow Town to Gunters Landing	

TABLE 1 [CONTINUED]

10	147	John Cochrain for wife	6	South side of Chatahoochee River near the Shallow Ford
14	148	William Ratley	8	On Wills Creek
16	149	George Fields (a native)	8	South side of Thompsons Creek
17	150	Owen Brady for wife	5	Head of Browns Creek
21	151	Silas Shoat in right of do	3	Near the ford on Wills Creek
28	152	Robert Parris (a native)	5	Chatahoochee
Dec. 4	153	Joel Kerby for wife	3	On Yellow Creek Waters of Chestatee
6	154	Elizabeth Walker (a native)	5	Pumpkin Town late residence of A. Miller deceased
10	155	Daniel Thorn for wife	6	Lying between Battle Creek and widow Annatous Creek
	156	Nancy Ward (a native)	1	One mile below John McIntosh on Mouse Creek where the old trace crosses said creek
28	157	John Speers (a native)	7	Near Cherokee Agency
1819 Mar. 21	158	John Miller do	4	Highwassee River
26	159	Charles McIntosh do	6	On the path from Tellico to agency
26	160	Betsey McIntosh	5	On Mouse Creek
31	161	Nancy Goard (a native)	3	On do do
	162	Bold Hunter Jr (a native)	2	On Little Tellico
June 2	163	Augie a widow (native)	-	Near Highwassee Old Town
7	164	James Coody	3	Clinch River
14	165	Path Killer (a native)	5	On Tennessee River
14	166	Toka Will (a native)	6	At Toka where he lives
20	167	The Pigen [sic] (a native)	3	On Battle Creek
23	168	The Eight Killer (a native)		On side of Gizzard Battle Creek
	169	John Langley	-	On north fork Little River
25	170	James McIntosh	-	On Sweet Water Creek

TABLE 1 [CONTINUED]

July 1	171	Arthur Burnes	-	At Sata Cave	
	172	William Jones	-	On small creek between Cowes and Wataga	
	173	John Welsh	-	Adjoining Jones Place	
	174	The Trout.	-	Below Cowee Town	
	175	Edward Weld.	-	On Wataga 4 miles above Cowee Town	
	176	Whipperwill	-	At Cowee on small creek	
	177	Antoweh (a native)	-	Cowee Town on the River	
	178	Ahseenee.	-	do—below on do	
	179	Axe	-	Cowee Town	
1819 June29	180	Allen B. Grubb in right of his children	2	Near Major Walkers Mills	
July 2	181	Sutton Stevens	-	Yellow branch waters of Paint Rock	
	182	Joseph Elliott.	-	At the Double Branch Spring	
7	183	Oosteke ho tee.	-	Cherokee near Tuckabachee	
	184	Tatahlea.	-	do do do	
	185	Quaty a widow	-	do do do	
8	186	Anthony Billegus a Spaniard in right of his Cherokee family . . .		Mill Creek	
10	187	Peggy Short a widow.	-	At Big Field on Battle Creek	
18	188	Tall Otees Kee (a native).	11	Highwassee Creek	
	189	Mouse Pain	7	Adjoining Tall Oteeskee	
	190	Alexander Kell for wife.	-	In Tucaleechee Old Town	
20	191	Sour John (a native)	-	On Chestatee	
21	192	Chocklaw (a native)	3	Goodfield Creek	
21	193	Bill Rattle do.	4	Little Tellico River	
	194	Smoke do do.	6	do adjoining Bill Battle	
	195	Situwakee	9	do 1 mile below Smokes	
	196	Tee las Kaask	3	do below Situwakees	
	197	Rue kee lus Kee.	8	do opposite to Caty Harlins	
	198	Oo wo hooskee	4	do adjoining Ruskeeluskee	

TABLE 1 [CONTINUED]

	199	Bee lee na ha	5	do adjoining Oowohooskee
	200	Oo wah ah	8	do opposite Bill Rattles
	201	Deer in the water	2	At Wests old Mill Place
	202	George Wilson	4	2 miles from Austins Riders
	203	Alexander Drumgold	-	Sweet Water Creek
	204	Gideon Morgan	3	At the mouth of Scetice Creek
	205	Sally Lowry (a native)	-	Battle Creek
22	206	Tak esk teesk	2	Little Tellico River
28	207	John Terrell for his wife	8	Chatahochy 10 miles above Shallow Ford
	208	James Landrum do do	6	On Warhoo Creek 3 miles above Duncans
	209	Delilah Welsh for children	-	Yellow Creek Waters of Chestatee
29	210	Willis Maw	4	Waters Little Tellico
Aug. 3	211	Gideon F. Morris for wife	3	Tennessee River
	212	Ool lah Nottee (a native)	5	Below Governors Island
	213	Yoon negiskah	16	At the Governors Island
	214	Juneluskey	7	Above Sugar Town
	215	Jack	5	On Tesnetee Creek waters of the Tennessee
	216	Ca te hee	8	Above Sugar Town on Tennessee
	217	Roman Nose	7	Near Governors Island
	218	Toolenoostah	6	On Tuckaseedge River
	219	Parch Corn Flour	9	Yeleerkey Creek
	220	Stan es tah	7	On Deep Creek
	221	Thomas	3	On Tusenty Creek
	222	Cul sow wee	7	Adjoining Thomas on Tusenty
	223	John Quchey	7	At Cowee
	224	Jacob	13	On Shoal Creek
	225	Connaughty	9	On Tuckusedge River
	226	Big Tom	10	At Tuckasedge River
	227	Autee hale John	2	Ooconuesufta

TABLE 1 [CONTINUED]

1819					
Aug. 3	228	Bag or Sap Sucker............	10	On Tuckasedge	
	229	Arhalooke	2	On Bighead Creek	
	230	Cooleechee	5	On Tellico Creek	
Aug. 9	231	Weah Skullah or Shell........	-	On Cowee River	
	232	Stanking Turkey	-	do do do	
	233	The Bear Going In	-	On a creek above Cowee	
	234	John......................	-	do do do	
	235	The Wolf..................	-	On Cowee River	
	236	John Walker...............	-	At Scotch Creek	
	237	Testoeskee or Shave Head	-	On ditto ditto	
	238	Kah Rullah or the Thigh......	-	Steecoy Old Fields	
	239	John Ben	-	On Cany Fork of Tuskasedge	
	240	Old Nancy Widow...........	-	Tennessee Old Town on Tuckasedge	
	241	Tegentasey.................	-	On Culloughbee Creek	
	242	Whayakah or Grass Grow.....	-	do do do	
	243	William Reed for wife	-	On Tuckaseedge River	
	244	Andrew Bryson do do	-	Near the War Ford on Tuckaseedge	
	245	Terrell Henson do do	-	At Easterly Head Waters	
	246	Templin W. Ross do do....	-	On Mill Creek 5 miles from Walker	
15	247	Polly Smith (a native)	-	Lick Creek	
16	248	Andrew Lacy for wife........	-	Paint Rock Creek	
17	249	Otter (a native)	-	Sweet Water Creek	
	250	Wally do	-	3 miles above Hilderbrands Mill	
	251	Nelly do...................	-	do do do	
19	252	Thomas Harrison for children	-	Tennessee River	
	253	Colonesskee...............	-	3 miles above Hilderbrands Mill	
25	254	Peter Johnson for wife........	-	Head of Widows Creek	Johnson is a slave for life
28	255	Shedrick Biddy	5	On Ball Play Creek	
Sep. 6	256	Cealey a native (widow)	8	On Sugar Town Creek	
	257	Cate geeskee	9	On Sugar Town Creek	
	258	Wallee...................	11	do do	

TABLE 1 [CONTINUED]

	259	The Bear Going in the Hole ...	5	Near Cowee Town House	
	260	John Colson................	6	On Chatugachee Creek	
	261	Little Deer.................	4	Burning Town Creek	
	262	The Tarrapin	5	Waters of do do	
	263	Jenny (a widow)	4	On Tennasee	
	264	Tom	5	Sugar Town	
	265	Buffalow	2	Mouth of Tesenty	
	266	Skeken....................	4	Tellico Creek	
	267	Dick	6	On Bighead Creek	
	268	Toochostosteh	6	Sugar Town Creek	
	269	The Shale	7	do do do	
	270	Six Killer.................	6	On Tennessee	
	271	Chuallugah	3	Sugar Town	
	272	He ne lah..................	6	On Tennessee	
1819	273	Betsey (a widow)	18	Head waters of Tennessee	
	274	Wallee do	3	Burning Town Creek	
	275	Oo santertake	5	On Tellico Creek	
	276	Suaga	2	do do do	
	277	Ah leah	3	Tennessee	
	278	Jack	3	do do	
	279	Yellow Bear...............	9	Burning Town Creek	
	280	The Cat	4	Near Sugar Town	
	281	The Club..................	2	Sugar Town	
	282	Ne ne tuake	5	Near Cowee	
	283	Sharp Fellow	4	Tennessee	
	284	Teh Nooah	3	do do	
	285	Eunoch or Trout	6	do do	
8	286	Toonangh heale	8	Near Cowee Town	
	287	The Old Mouse	5	below do do	
	288	The Fence	6	Cowee Town	
	289	Euchulah	3	in do do	
	290	Panther	4	do on Tennessee River	
	291	Ammacher.................	5	On Tennessee	
	292	Johnson	4	On Tuckaluchee	
	293	Old Chuneluskey	6	On Deep Creek	
	294	Back Water	6	do do	
	295	John Car a widow	7	Aquanalusta	
	296	Will......................	10	On Tuckasedge River	

TABLE 1 [CONTINUED]

	297	Chiule	6	do do	
	298	Beaver Toter	9	Peach Orchard	
	299	Chunestee tee	8	On Tennessee River	
	300	Big George	4	On the waters of do	
19	301	John Gunter Senr	-	On the north side of Tennessee	
	302	The Musk Rat	-	On Chatugajoy Creek	
	303	Cainla	-	On the waters of do	
	304	Cone Wastah	-	On Chatugajoy Creek	
	305	Weychutta	-	On Chatugajoy Creek	
	306	Richard Dowing	-	At Eastertoy	
	307	Little Betty (a widow)	-	At do	
Nov. 8	308	The Mink	2	In the bounds of Chotee	
12	309	Usquelusquee or Squirrel	5	Mud Creek Cherry Log	
27	310	Moses McDaniel (a native)	2	On Chatahoochee below the mouth of Mud Creek	
Dec. 6	311	Luney Riley (a native)	2	On the south side of Tennessee	
				River opposite south west Point Reserve not in possession of the land.	
	I certify the foregoing to be a correct transcript from the Books of Agent for the Cherokee Indians.				
				William Triplett Secrety to the State Commrs	
		[Reverse] Indian Affairs 1817			

THE RIGHT
TO LAY
INTERNAL TAXES,
1820-1828

The first American Indian policy was as flexible as the American Constitution and as subject to various interpretations and misunderstandings. One point never clarified was the extent of self-government that it allowed to each tribe. By treaty, each tribe was allowed to maintain its own tribal form of government, but no treaty spelled out the limits of self-government. This ambiguity was complicated by the remarkable strides that the Cherokees made in adapting to the white man's way of life—particularly their progress in developing a highly centralized, bureaucratic system and an acquisitive, capitalist economic structure. By 1820, the Cherokees needed additional income to sustain their new governmental order. To them it seemed logical to lay taxes upon their people to provide more revenue. However, the Cherokees tried to do two things at once when they levied a tax upon all traders doing business within their boundaries. They tried not only to obtain revenue but also to equalize the trading advantages between Cherokee and white traders. By levying lower taxes upon Cherokee merchants than upon white merchants, the second principal chief, Charles Hicks, commented that they were hoping to make up for the fact that white wholesalers outside the nation were far more ready to extend credit to white than to Indian traders. The Indian trader was at a disadvantage because he had to sell all his goods and replenish his stock with cash while the white trader could import new items on credit before he had sold all his stock.

While this was the immediate ground for the refusal of certain white traders to pay their tax (thus subjecting them to having their goods seized and sold at auction by Cherokee sheriffs), the Cherokee rightly saw a more important issue at stake—the extent of their sovereignty as a nation. They were able to find white legal authorities who agreed with their interpretation of their basic rights as a nation. The controversy marks a critical confrontation featuring a Native American tribe able and willing to take on the federal government in a clearly defined legal battle within the established rules of Anglo-Saxon jurisprudence and political theory. It also produced an acute wave of concern among frontier whites, who expected all Indians to quietly "disappear" or cede their land and move west. Many frontiersmen no doubt voted for Jackson in order to cut the gordian knot and effectively demonstrate to the various tribes that in no sense were they entitled to conceive of themselves as sovereign nations, no matter how "civilized" or "acculturated" they might become. Having closed out the possibility of United States "citizenship" for Indians, the white man now closed out the possibility of national separatism—at least, upon any place of land that the white man thought usable.

AS THE ANOMALOUS STATUS of the Indian nations within the American political system forced itself upon the national consciousness after 1815, the Cherokee took the lead in demanding recognition of their internal autonomy. With the establishment of an elective, bicameral legislature and a centralized judicial and police system in 1817-1820, the Cherokee finally achieved political stability and steady economic growth. Generally recognized as "the most civilized" of the Indian tribes, the Cherokee were developing a sense of nationalism which resembled that of the thirteen British colonies in the early 1770s or the thirteen sovereign states in the Confederation period. Not surprisingly, the Cherokee began to draw parallels between their own quest for group identity and that of the Anglo-Americans in their formative struggles with the British Empire. While acknowledging the right of the federal government to regulate foreign policy and international trade, the Cherokee insisted upon their right to home rule and control over internal trade.

Despite all that has been written about the Cherokee, little has been said about their effort in the 1820s to develop a system of taxation in order to provide revenue for their government and to regulate their internal trade. That effort produced a legal and constitutional confrontation with the federal government in 1824, which raised in dramatic form the problem that white Americans spoke of critically as *imperium in imperio*. The Cherokee, however, described their effort in terms of government by the consent of the governed and no taxation without representation. While the Georgians complained that the Cherokee were interfering with their sovereign rights, the Cherokee expressed the same view of the Georgians and of the United States.

Ultimately the secretary of war obtained a lengthy and learned opinion from the attorney general, William Wirt, regarding a law passed by the Cherokee Council that laid a tax on white merchants doing business within the Cherokee Nation. When this opinion went against the Cherokee, they appealed to the Congress to protect their rights. When Congress failed to give them liberty and justice, they adopted a constitution of their own in 1827 based on that of the United States, an act many contemporaries described as a bold and dangerous "declaration of independence."[1]

In his opinion against the Cherokee in 1824, Wirt utilized John Marshall's recent decision in *McCullough v. Maryland*, yet he recognized that the Cherokee had become a very different people since 1785 when they signed their first treaty with the United States of America. Ironically, both Wirt and Marshall, eight years later, defended the Cherokees' right to quasi-independence within the American commonwealth. The tax dispute in 1824 deserves attention not only because it reveals the high level of political sophistication Cherokee leaders had attained but also because it marks the start of the final confrontation with American imperial law that ended in the adoption of "King" Andrew's new policy to remove the unruly Indians (an option not available to King George in dealing with his unruly colonies in 1776.)

Because we lack concrete information about the motives of the Cherokee leaders, it is not clear whether the confrontation over internal taxation in 1824 was intentional or accidental. The latter seems more likely, though certain chiefs clearly wanted to strengthen the nation's control over its own destiny and were determined to assert national autonomy. Some undoubtedly saw the taxing power as a means of regulating white mercantile intrusions that siphoned off Cherokee income and competed with the profits of Cherokee merchant traders. By 1820 a growing number of Cherokee were engaged in extensive trading operations within the nation and with whites around its borders. The Cherokee exported large quantities of livestock (cattle, hogs, and horses) to the white frontier communities and an increasing amount of corn and cotton. They imported manufactured goods necessary for cash-crop farming. In addition, there was a growing traffic in black slaves, whom the Cherokee used to cultivate their fields and to provide skilled labor. Ostensibly,

---

[1]Henry T. Malone, *Cherokees of the Old South* (Athens GA, 1956) 88.

however, the law laying an annual tax upon white and Cherokee traders was passed for revenue purposes, to pay the costs of the new centralized governmental system—the legislators, the judges, the marshalls, the mounted police, the rangers, the couriers, paper, ink, postage, and delegations to Washington—needed to manage a nation of 13,000 people on a tract as large as Massachusetts, Connecticut, and Rhode Island.

The Cherokee received an annuity from the government (disgruntled frontier whites described it as a "tribute" to restrain savage depradations) of between six and seven thousand dollars in these years. This money was awarded for the millions of acres the Cherokee had ceded to the United States since 1791. Most of this went into stimulating the new market economy by providing plows, hoes, spinning wheels, looms, and skilled workers—blacksmiths, wheelwrights, weavers, tinsmiths—necessary for their transition to subsistence farming. The annuity was used largely to pay off debts incurred annually to traders who provided manufactured goods. It seemed perfectly fair to tax these traders in order to pay for the stable social order that protected private property and made this economy possible. Yet by limiting permanent stores or trading posts to Cherokee citizens, the Cherokee were clearly seeking to curb the economic hegemony of whites. Passed on 28 October 1819, the law reads:

> All citizens of the Cherokee Nation establishing a store or stores for the purpose of vending merchandize, shall obtain license for that purpose from the Clerk of the National Council, for which each and every person so licensed shall pay a tax of twenty-five dollars per annum and that no other but citizens of the Cherokee Nation shall be allowed to establish a permanent store within the Nation.
>
> And it also decreed that no pedlar or pedlars, nor citizens of the Nation shall be permitted to vend merchandize in the Nation without first obtaining license from the Agent of the United States; and each and every one so licensed shall pay eighty dollars[2] to the treasury of the Cherokee Nation per annum.[3]

The law prescribed a fine of $200 for all violations and further decreed that no one should "bring into the Nation and sell any spirituous liquors"

---

[2]By an amendment in 1822, this fee was reduced to $50. *Cherokee Laws* (Tahlequah, Cherokee Nation, 1852) 30.

[3]Ibid., 6. Many other laws were passed in these years regulating all aspects of Cherokee internal trade. A law of 1820 levied a poll tax upon all adult Indian males under sixty (13). A law of 1819 established official fees for turnpike tolls and ferries (7). Other laws regulated the lease of mineral resources (50) and the creation of turnpike companies (20, 23, 25).

upon pain of confiscation by the lighthorse police (or "Regulators") and a payment of a fine of $100. The final clause of the law provided "that nothing shall be so construed in this decree as to tax any person bringing sugar, coffee, malt, iron and steel into the Cherokee Nation for sale, but no permanent establishment for disposal of such articles can be admitted to any persons not citizens of the Nation."

Recognizing that these and other laws needed to be published before they could be enforced, Charles Hicks, the second principal chief and treasurer of the nation, wrote to the federal agent who resided in the Cherokee Nation, Colonel Return J. Meigs, on 2 November 1819, to say that he was sending him copies of the laws passed over the past two years by the council:

> We would desire likewise that you will please to have the laws published in some of the printers [newspapers] and that the law[s] may be well known among our white brethren that none may plead Ignorance of those [laws] who it may concern of the whiskey pedlars and other pedlars of merchandize . . . and [we request you] to furnish the nation with fifty printed copies of the laws passed here and charge the expense to our Annuity.[4]

Upon receiving the manuscript copies of the laws passed in 1817-1819, Meigs sent them to John C. Calhoun, the secretary of war, expressing his own approval and asking Calhoun's opinion.[5] Calhoun wrote back that "the Cherokee Nation has a right to adopt any rules and regulations it pleases for its own police not inconsistent with the existing treaties and the law regulating intercourse with the Indian tribes."[6] He apparently saw nothing in the Trade and Intercourse Law that was inconsistent with taxing white traders or he would have saved the War Department and the Cherokee a great deal of difficulty by pointing it out. Meigs then printed fifty copies of the laws, advertised them in the local papers, and wrote to Hicks commending the Cherokee legislature on its progress: "I think you have made some good regulations."[7]

---

[4]M-208, roll 8, 2 November 1819, Pathkiller and Hicks to Meigs. The same requests were made with respect to subsequent laws after each legislative council; e.g., M-208, roll 8, 27 November 1820, Hicks to Meigs.

[5]M-271, roll 2, #1401, 15 November 1819, Meigs to Calhoun.

[6]M-15, roll 4, p. 405, 20 April 1820, Calhoun to Meigs.

[7]M-208, roll 9, 20 January 1821, Meigs to Hicks.

Having received the approbation of Meigs and the imprimatur of Calhoun, the Cherokee proceeded to put their tax laws into operation, only to discover that some of the white traders refused to obey them. When the law went into effect, there were fourteen white citizens engaged in trade with the Cherokee Nation, some of them partners.[8] Nine of these agreed to pay the license fee; five refused and took their case to the government. The five refusing were Jacob Scudder (or Scudders), the partnership of Gideon Morgan and Michael Huffacre (or Huffaker), and the partnership of John S. McCarty and John McGhee.[9] When Meigs discovered that these traders were going to appeal, he had second thoughts about the laws: "The indians are now beginning," he wrote to Calhoun, "to exercis[e] a kind of sovereignty in making laws for the Government of their people perhaps inconsistent with their subordinate condition."[10] He took the position of the white traders who held that under the Trade and Intercourse Law, the federal government was to control who might or might not trade with the Indians and under what circumstances. "No American citizen," Meigs now declared, "can recognize their laws as legal, having concurrent jurisdiction, etc. etc. If we suffer them to go on in this way a few years, we may be said tacitly to have admitted their right to assert their independence." He had no objection to their regulating the actions of their own people, but he denied their claim to authority over whites within their nation. By treaty, disputes between Indians and whites were to be settled in white courts. Under the new Cherokee assertion of authority, the white traders were subject to arrest, trial, confiscation of property, and fines by the Cherokee courts. Indians, by Meigs's definition, being "subordinate" to whites, as children are to their guardians, could not possibly assert authority over whites.

The Cherokee decided to seek legal advice on the matter. They selected Judge Hugh L. White of Tennessee, a brother-in-law of Governor Willie Blount and a close friend of General Jackson. White's opinion in May 1823 fully endorsed their right to lay internal taxes: "In my opinion,

---

[8]For a list, see M-234, roll 71, #0363, 31 August 1825.

[9]Apparently some of the Cherokee traders also refused at first to pay this tax. It was later asserted that "Native Traders were compelled to pay their taxes." M-234, roll 71, #0073, 25 February 1824, Cherokee delegation to Calhoun.

[10]M-221, roll 93, #9083, 12 February 1822, Meigs to Calhoun.

the Nation have the right to impose this tax. By treaty, the United States have the power to regulate trade and intercourse with the Cherokee Indians"; indeed, Congress required the federal agents to license traders, for "without such license no individual has a right to go into the Nation for the purpose of merchandizing, with it he has no right to carry on merchandize[ing] in opposition to a local regulation of the Nation. The license is an evidence that the United States think the individual may safely be trusted in the Nation for the purpose expressed in the license but was not intended to take from this Nation the right of judging whether their people should trade with him or not, nor the right of fixing the terms and conditions upon which such trade should be conducted."[11]

When Colonel Meigs died in January 1823, Joseph McMinn, former governor of Tennessee, was appointed to replace him.[12] In July 1823, McMinn wrote to the Cherokee Council that "your Marshall, Mr. Foreman, has presented Mr. McCarty with a claim" for back taxes. But "Mr. McCarty has expressed to me his unwilling[ness] to pay" the taxes levied upon him, as "he conceives it to be levyed without any regard to the Principle of Equality, which is one of the grand constituents in all the revenue laws of the several states."[13] In sum, McCarty and McGhee took the view that the law was illegal because it taxed white traders more than Cherokee traders and because it allowed Cherokee traders to establish permanent stores while white traders could only be itinerant pedlars. "Messrs. McCarty and McGhee," McGinn continued, "have long been Stationary merchants in your nation," and if the Cherokee would consider "placing them on an equal footing with all other merchants within the nation . . . they would pay their tax with great pleasure." McMinn went on to give the Cherokee some gratuitous advice:

I beg leave to propose to you as a friend to both parties, that you suspend the Collection of this debts until you can forward a memorial to [the] next Congress in which I will most cheerfully cooperate with you . . . and let the memorial ex-

---

[11]M-234, roll 71, #0045, 27 May 1823; Judge White's opinion. As noted above (n.2), the council had lowered the tax on white traders from $80 to $50 and upon Cherokee traders from $20 to $12. *Cherokee Laws*, 30.

[12]For the Cherokees' objections to McMinn, whom they considered unfriendly toward their welfare, see M-234, roll 71, #0073, 25 February 1824, Cherokee delegation to Calhoun.

[13]M-208, roll 9, 19 July 1823, McMinn to Hicks.

hibit your true situation (namely) that you have a government to support which cannot be carried on without actual resources, that many of your people are unable to contribute any considerable amount without great embarrassment and hence the necessity of resorting to a tax on merchants, etc., and ask Congress to pass a law vesting the Cherokee Nation with the Power to levy taxes and raise revenue under such limitations as they may prescribe, by which means you would avoid all difficulty that might otherwise accrue from passing laws that might be considered as infringing either upon the Constitution or the Laws of the United States.

It hardly seems likely that McMinn expected Congress to pass such a law, and certainly the Cherokee doubted it. They answered McMinn in very short terms. Hicks told him that the reason white citizens were asked to pay more than Cherokee traders was because they had more money and more credit. The law had been worded, he said, to take account of "the different advantages enjoyed by the partys in their capitals and opportunityes of laying in their goods in the United States, as one has ample resources to lay in fresh goods should his old stock remain on hand at the end of the year and the other are obliged to sell out his old stock before he is enabled to make remittance to his creditors in order to obtain fresh supplies of Goods to enable him to continue his mercantile pursuit."[14] In short, white wholesalers in Knoxville, Nashville, Augusta, and Charleston were willing to extend credit to their white friends but made Cherokee traders pay cash. The law sought to overcome an economic inequity, not to create one.

Hicks went on to assert the nation's long-established right to govern its own internal affairs. McMinn observed that "the nation have exercised the right of legislating and executing your laws for some time," that is, since the new centralized form of Cherokee governance began in 1817. Hicks, however, reminded him that "the nation has enjoyed this right upwards of thirty years to my knowledge of legislating for themselves, and she claims no other right now since the form of Government have been changed." The council had passed this law "from a belief [that] where the treaties and intercourse law does not forbid of the internal regulation of our Government," the Cherokee had the right to do it. A loose construction of the nation's relationship to the general government was assumed. Since this law was derived from just legislative power, Hicks

---

[14]M-208, roll 9, 8 August 1823, Hicks to McMinn.

wrote, "I conceive the licensed traders ought to conform to the regulation." Hicks had read the Trade and Intercourse Law (first passed in 1791 and amended in 1797 and 1802); it "never was intended," he maintained, "to take from the nation the right of judging whether their people should trade" with men like McCarty and McGhee. Nor was it intended to limit "the right of fixing the terms and conditions upon which such trade should be conducted."

Hicks went on to accuse McMinn of breaking the long-standing practice of his predecessor, Meigs, who as agent from 1801 to 1823 had never licensed a white man to operate a public franchise within the nation without first obtaining the consent of the National Council. Recently McMinn had failed to do this "in respect of Mr. Jacob Scudders and Simon White, of whom I am creditably informed of both keeping houses of entertainment for travelers under the privileges of licensed traders, the former on the Hightower Road and the other on the Federal Road." Hicks considered this a violation of Cherokee sovereignty, of administrative precedent, and of federal treaty rights that enabled the Cherokee to govern their internal affairs. "I solemnly protest," Hicks wrote, "against such libertys being taken . . . for with the same propriety the Agency may grant licenses to other citizens to establish houses of entertainment on our roads." From the time that the first road (the Cumberland or Knoxville Road in 1798) had been run through the nation, the Cherokee Council had assumed the power to set the terms for leasing taverns or inns and to approve specific, written contracts with those— Cherokee or white men—who wished to profit from them. Ferry keepers and tollgate keepers had been subject to the same tribal regulation. The object was to give the national treasury a certain percentage of the receipts or a specific rent from these public franchises. McMinn's new practice extracted no contract from the whites and thus defrauded the nation of this income. Such an infringement of long-standing national rights opened the way for collusion and fraud between the agent and those eager to obtain such privileges.

Having obtained the legal opinion of Judge White regarding their right to tax white traders and having expressed their defense of this right to the federal agent, the Cherokee proceeded to put the law into effect. In October 1823, the council ordered Anthony Foreman to carry out the penalty of the law against all traders who refused to pay; "a part of their goods were attached and sold by the Marshall to satisfy the amount of their taxes."[15] The five traders so distrained later claimed that a total of $1,589.25 worth of their goods was seized and sold at vendue to pay their taxes and fines, a claim the Cherokee considered highly inflated.[16] Huffacre and Morgan protested this confiscation and sale of their goods, entering a claim "for Spoilations [*sic*] on our merchandize by the Cherokees when we thought we were protected by a Liscence from and Laws of the United States."[17]

Because Gideon Morgan was married to a Cherokee and hence considered an adopted citizen of the nation, and also because he had been closely involved in Cherokee affairs for over fifteen years, the other merchants gave him their power of attorney to collect their claims. McCarty and McGhee claimed $557; Morgan and Huffacre, $474; Jacob M. Scudders, $507; William Thorp, another white married to a Cherokee, who had been taxed as a Cherokee and paid his tax, now decided to claim it back; he also gave Morgan power to act for him. They expected to be repaid out of the Cherokee annuity. Morgan laid the claim before the council in 1824, but the council denied its validity. The Cherokee Nation, the council asserted, had "the right to tax traders in their nation whether licensed or not" by the federal agent.[18]

The case was appealed to the War Department. John C. Calhoun met with a delegation of Cherokees in Washington late in February 1824 to discuss the matter.[19] The delegation consisting of John Ross, Major

---

[15]M-234, roll 71, #0005, 11 February 1824, and #0024, 25 February 1824, Cherokee delegation to Calhoun.

[16]Idem.

[17]M-234, roll 71, #0179, 12 February 1824, Morgan to Calhoun.

[18]Idem; M-21, roll 1, p. 364, 22 February 1825, McKenney to Cherokee delegation; and M-21, roll 2, p. 41, 10 June 1825, McKenney to Montgomery.

[19]The Cherokee delegation was in Washington on a different matter. It had come to inform Calhoun that "the Cherokee have come to a decisive and unalterable conclusion *never* to *cede away* any more lands" and to suggest that the United States satisfy Georgia's claim to the Cherokees' land by ceding to that state a portion of the territory of Florida. In the course of this discussion, the delegation also asserted that "the States by which they [the Cherokee] are now surrounded have been created out of lands which were once theirs; and that they cannot recognize the sovereignty of any State within the limits of their territory. . . . It rests with the interest, the disposition and the free consent of this nation to remain as a separate community or to enter into a treaty with the United States for admission as citizens under the form of a Territorial or State Government." M-234, roll 75, #0005, 11 February 1824, Cherokee delegation to Calhoun.

Ridge, George Lowery, and Elijah Hicks told Calhoun they believed the law was within "their own right of making municipal regulations" to govern their internal affairs. "The Cherokees have a Government of their own to support," they said, and must find "means to raise a revenue for its support." Calhoun responded that by the treaties of 1785 and 1791, the Cherokee had granted to the United States the right to regulate their trade. The delegates said that it was rather late to bring up this point. They had submitted these laws to Meigs in 1819 and Meigs had submitted them to Calhoun; at that time he had expressed no such opinion of them. As they read the treaties, "We cannot see that the Cherokees conceded their own right of making municipal regulations for themselves. . . . Therefore, we are at a loss to know how you can conceive that our Nation have violated the stipulations of those Treaties by the mere circumstance of imposing a tax on the licensed Traders from the United States as well as on their own citizens." They presented Calhoun with a copy of Judge White's opinion and said they had a full right "to raise a revenue" for their own use. Calhoun persisted, saying they must repeal the law. The delegates remained firm: "We believe it would not be expedient for the Nation to repeal this law and to refund the money[s] which have been levyed under it." To do so would undermine their whole claim to self-government and sovereign rights.[20]

Calhoun then sought advice from the attorney general. William Wirt's long and detailed response on 2 April 1824 stated that in his opinion the Cherokee had acted unconstitutionally, but this was not so much their fault as the fault of Congress for failing to take into consideration the changing nature of their nation as it advanced in civilization, economic success, and political stability. Wirt's effort to assess the boundary between the Cherokees' right of self-government and the right of the general government to assert its federal power over them deserves careful scrutiny. It prefigures John Marshall's later views in the case of *Worcester v. Georgia* in 1832. Men like Meigs, McMinn, and Calhoun held that the Cherokees were, in effect, wards of the United States and subject to its control in all their affairs. Wirt argued that however "savage" or "primitive" their government may have been in 1785, it had progressed to such a high stage of political coherence and legal order by 1824 as to justify an alteration in the relationship between the two nations.

---

[20]M-234, roll 71, #0073, 25 February 1824, Cherokee delegation to Calhoun.

As Wirt saw it, the basic question at issue was the Cherokees' right "to tax persons trading among them under the authority of the United States." He began his opinion obliquely by saying, "If the Cherokee nation is to be considered as an independent nation and this question is to be answered by an appeal to the natural law of nations, there can be no doubt of their right to pass what laws they please." But, of course, this assumption was "fallacious." The treaties governing the relationship with the United States "will not permit us to regard the question as one between equal sovereigns." Furthermore, "Whatsoever philosophy or philanthropy might, in the abstract, dictate upon this subject, we are constrained to look at things as they are and to decide this question on narrower grounds."[21]

Starting then with the Treaty of Hopewell in 1785, Wirt noted, Congress from the outset had the right to regulate trade and intercourse with the Indians, and this was confirmed by clauses in the treaties of 1791, 1798, 1805, and 1817. The Cherokee might deny that in these treaties they ever "conceded their own right to make municipal regulations for themselves," but "it is to be remembered that when those treaties were entered into there were no such things as municipal regulations in the Cherokee Nation." Wirt held a common view about Indian nationhood. Because they had no written law and operated by social and property relationships unclear to Europeans, he assumed that they lived in a kind of anarchy. Being no anthropologist, Wirt thought of law and order in terms of clearly discernible institutions and written codes of law. In his view the Cherokee in 1785 had been "in the first stage of society, the hunter state"; that is, "a state of nature," a state in which "government, laws, and taxes were wholly unknown." Consequently the treaties gave to the United States, after a just war, the power necessary to regulate this disorganized, inchoate, primitive system. "The treaty [of 1785] meant to give" to the United States "the right to prescribe the whole system of regulations *on both sides* under which trade should be carried on." And "neither the Cherokee nor any other nation had the right to touch the subject" of trade.

Next Wirt defined the government's right to regulate interstate commerce according to the latest definition by the United States Supreme Court: "A power to regulate commerce between the several states is an

---

[21]M-234, roll 71, #0441, 2 April 1824, Wirt's opinion to Calhoun.

exclusive power because commerce is a *unit.*" The treaties with the Cherokee stated that the United States shall regulate "their trade," but "the imposition of the tax on the traders is the imposition of a new condition on which alone the Cherokees say that this trade shall be carried on. It is a new *regulation of the trade* instituted by them." Thereby they derogate from the exclusive power and right of the United States to regulate it. John Marshall's decision in *McCullough v. Maryland* was to the point: the power to tax was the power to destroy.

> If they have a right to impose a tax of $50, they have the same right to impose a tax of 500, 5000, or 50,000 dollars. If they may tax for revenue, they may tax for exclusion . . . they may impose such a burthen as to defeat the regulation altogether. In the case of McCullough against the state of Maryland the supreme court of the United States decided that although the state of Maryland was a sovereign and independent state and consequently possessed the general power of taxation, yet they had no right to tax an institution [the Bank of the United States] which the constitution had given to congress the power to create, because a power to tax was a power to destroy.

In the case of the Cherokee Nation, trade was an institution of the federal government. The treaties "place this whole subject exclusively in the hands of congress," hence "the Indians have no power to interfere with these regulations either by addition or subtraction." He concluded, "I am of the opinion that the Indians have no right to impose this tax on traders licensed under the authority of the United States."

Had Wirt's opinion stopped here, it would have offered little of value to the Cherokee, and he might not, eight years later, have been chosen by them to champion their cause before John Marshall against the state of Georgia. But having rendered his legal opinion on the specific constitutional issue, Wirt went on to make some highly important remarks about the advance of the Cherokee since 1785 and the necessity for Congress to take this into consideration in its relationships with them. The whole difficulty had arisen, Wirt said, either from the current Cherokee leaders' "forgetfulness of the political condition of the Cherokees at the period" when they first entered into treaties with the United States, or else, these leaders had falsely assumed that because "a change in the conditions of the parties" had taken place, this was "a very good reason for changing the stipulations" of the contract. Unfortunately treaties and contracts "cannot fluctuate with the changing conditions of the parties."

Still, Congress had the power to take these changes under consideration. He therefore deigned to "hint at" what might be a solution to a dilemma that left the Cherokee without the means of supporting their new government. He asked whether the United States might not wisely and justly "have respect to the altered condition of the Cherokees, to the stage of civilization to which they have been carried by the measures adopted by the United States to produce this very effect, whether Congress will not adopt their further regulations to their altered condition so as to enable that nation to raise a revenue for the support of their government by an equal tax upon our traders as well as their own?" While these were "political considerations" rather than legal ones, he nevertheless concluded that "the time has passed away in which it could be tolerated to treat these people as we please because we are christians and they are heathen."

In this last respect Wirt's opinion was a signal tribute to the political rebirth of the Cherokee. Had more American leaders accepted his view, the subsequent history of white-Indian relations might have been far different. But the rising tide of expansionist feeling in the South and on the frontier maintained that if the Cherokee had got this far, it was better not to let them get any farther: the next step would be to create an empire within an empire, a nation within a nation.

Calhoun forwarded Wirt's opinion to McMinn on 18 June 1824, with instructions to tell the Cherokee Council to repeal its tax law on traders and to refund the money taken from those who had refused to pay it as well as to those who had. McMinn sent this message to the council in October, and once again suggested that if they complied with the order of the secretary of war, he would personally support them in "submitting the matter to Congress, who, I have no doubt, will grant you the power under proper limitations."[22] Huffacre and McCarty appeared at the same council at New Echota expecting to have their money refunded. The council, though, rejected the order and told McMinn that it had already "appealed from the opinion of the attorney General." This had been done by its delegation in Washington last spring, which had sent a memorial to Congress, "and as the subject has not been acted upon and is now pending in Congress, the law imposing taxes still remains in ful[l]

---

[22]M-234, roll 71, #0471, 20 October 1824, McMinn to Cherokee Council.

force."[23] McMinn may not have been aware that Thomas L. McKenney, the federal commissioner of Indian affairs, had passed Wirt's opinion along to the Cherokee delegation on 7 April and with his permission, they had submitted the memorial to Congress asking for a resolution asserting their right to lay internal taxes.[24] Calhoun, of course, did not consider this memorial a sufficient excuse for retaining the law or refusing to reimburse the traders.[25]

Upon receiving the letter from the council refusing compliance with Calhoun's request, McMinn announced that he would withhold their annuity until they agreed to deduct from it the sums needed to repay the traders. John Ross, president of the National Committee (or Upper House of the Cherokee legislature), wrote to protest: "By the Consent of the [War] Department the Delegation [last April] presented a Memorial before the last session of Congress with a view to deciding definitively upon the question of the right of the Cherokee Nation to levie taxes upon the licensed traders of the United States. This question not being as yet disposed of by Congress, we cannot consent to refund the money collected from these traders." Furthermore, he said, the claims being made against the annuity by the traders "demand an investigation" of their "correctness."[26] (Ross said their demands for compensation were highly inflated.) Hugh Montgomery of Georgia, who succeeded McMinn as agent after McMinn's death in November 1824, carried out Calhoun's orders by unilaterally deducting the amount claimed by McCarty and Huffacre from the annuity in 1825, and paid it to them.[27]

When the other traders learned of this, they pressed their claims for reimbursement. Montgomery obligingly deducted their claims as well from the annuity.[28] While the council refused to repeal the law, it did, on 10 November 1825, suspend for two years "the law imposing a tax

---

[23]M-234, roll 71, #0474, 5 November 1824, Cherokee Council to McMinn; M-234, roll 71, #0467, 16 December 1824, J. G. Williams to Calhoun.

[24]M-21, roll 1, p. 27, 7 April 1824, McKenney to Cherokee delegation; M-21, roll 1, p. 52, 25 April 1824, McKenney to Cherokee delegation.

[25]M-21, roll 1, p. 321, 24 January 1825, Calhoun to Houston.

[26]M-234, roll 71, #0497, 28 February 1825, Ross to Calhoun.

[27]M-208, roll 10, 10 June 1825, Calhoun to Montgomery.

[28]M-21, roll 1, p. 364, 22 February 1825, McKenney to Cherokee delegation.

upon citizen merchants of the Cherokee Nation."[29] If the white aliens or noncitizens were not paying the tax, it seemed unfair to make the Cherokee citizen traders pay.

Congress took no action on the Cherokee memorial in 1826, and Montgomery once again asked the Cherokee Council to repeal the law in December of that year. In response to this, Charles Hicks and John Ross wrote a long and detailed letter that constituted the nation's rebuttal to all of Wirt's arguments. Taking a leaf from the rebellious patriots of 1775, they said that since the American Constitution forbade their representation in Congress, they had the right to lay taxes for their own support. They claimed, in fact, that the wording of the Constitution virtually acknowledged their sovereignty as an independent nation. The letter reveals how sophisticated the Cherokee leaders had become in the use of the kind of legalism so popular among American constitutional lawyers of that day.

Because Section 8 of the first article of the Constitution said that Congress had the power to regulate commerce "with foreign nations and among the several states and with the Indian tribes," it appeared to Hicks and Ross that "by this section we are placed precisely on the same footing with Foreign Nations and the several states." This being so, "by this power can Congress prevent Great Britain, France and the several states from adopting municipal regulations affecting Trade within their own sovereign limits? and have not the several states ever exercised the right of taxing merchants, pedlars, etc. without molestation within their respective limits for the purpose of creating a revenue?" The answer being obvious, "in the name of common sense and equal justice, why is the right of the Cherokee Nation in this respect disputed?"[30]

Wirt had pointed to the various treaties made with the Cherokee to show that they had yielded their sovereignty and their right to regulate their own trade. But Hicks and Ross argued that the Treaty of Hopewell in 1785, in which this concession had indeed been made, was no longer "in force and that it is abrogated by the [Cherokee] wars which followed it." The Treaty of Holston in 1791 was the first formal Cherokee treaty, and it stated in Article 6 that "it is agreed on the part of the Cherokees

[29]*Cherokee Laws*, 55-56.

[30]M-234, roll 72, #0042, 11 December 1826, Ross to Montgomery.

that the United States shall have the sole and exclusive right to regulate their trade." However, Hicks and Ross argued, "By the words *sole* and *exclusive* we exclude all other sovereigns [non-American nations] from acting upon the subject"; as to regulating "their trade," these words "fix the subject to be regulated, that is, *their* trade, the trade of the Cherokee *Nation* as a *Nation*, not the trade between A and B within the Nation. In other words, Congress alone is to have the power of regulating the trade of Indian [nations] with all other *sovereigns*," but not within its own sovereign bounds. So it was, Hicks and Ross said, with the original thirteen states of the Union. "Each state was once sovereign; each had the power to regulate its commerce with other sovereigns," but after 1789 this power was vested in Congress. However, like the Indian nations, the thirteen original states under the Constitution had lost only "the power to regulate commerce with foreign nations and among each other, but neither [the states nor the Indian nations] has lost the power to regulate transactions between A and B within its own limits."

This letter went on to note that "the Cherokee Nation, like other nations, require[s] money to support its government." Clearly Congress was not going to "defray this expense." The issue, then, was one of taxation without representation: "The American government, we believe, never has advocated the doctrine that taxes can be imposed by a body where the people taxed are unrepresented." Since the Constitution "prohibits an enumeration of the Indians for the purpose of representation," they cannot be taxed by Congress. All that the treaties had ever done was to state that Congress could regulate international commerce between the Cherokee and France, England, and Spain. They had not—and could not have, under the American Constitution—given power to Congress to regulate the internal trade of the Cherokee because they were "unrepresented in Congress."[31]

The Cherokee had correctly assessed the anomalous position of the Indian nations. When the United States wished to obtain land from them, it treated them as if they were foreign powers. The missionary

---

[31]Historically the views of Hicks and Ross are more accurate than that of Wirt. It was essentially the fear of trade alliances with Britain, Spain, and France that motivated the clauses restricting trade in early treaties. So far as internal trade was concerned, the United States was mainly concerned to protect the Cherokee from unscrupulous white traders.

agencies all placed Indian missions under their *foreign* mission boards. The United States claimed that it did not have any colonies; it was not an empire but a republic. Hence the Indians within its borders were neither citizens nor imperial subjects. The only alternative, as Hicks and Ross saw it, was to recognize them as independent citizens of independent, sovereign states such as the states of the Union were under the Articles of Confederation—or, more precisely, as these states were between the time they declared independence from Britain and the time they gave up their right to regulate their own affairs in exchange for representation in Congress. Some Cherokees talked at this time of the possibility that "in a few years . . . you shall see an aborigine in congress who will act in the capacity of a representative from the Cherokee Nation."[32]

The Hicks-Ross letter also pointed out another inconsistency in American Indian policy: "If the Congress of the United States alone possess the sole right to pass all the laws affecting the internal as well as the external trade of the Cherokees, why did they approbate the *exclusive priveledge* granted by the Cherokee Nation to the Unicoi Turnpike Company to carry on trade on their road over other licensed traders?" The charter for this company had been drawn up by the Cherokee Council and approved by the agent and the War Department in 1813,[33] and ever since the Cherokee had regulated trade on that turnpike. "It is well known that Congress has never passed any law by which such licensed traders could collect their debts in the Cherokee Nation; the only laws resorted to by them has ever been those passed by the Cherokee Nation." It seemed obvious then that "the Cherokee Nation possess[es] the same right of making municipal regulations for their internal government for the purpose of creating a revenue as any other nation." The letter concluded, "Therefore our opinion in regard to our right of taxing licensed traders cannot be changed until Congress or the Supreme Court of the United States have made a final decision on this question and denying to us the right."[34]

---

[32]M-221, roll 95, #0003, 28 February 1823, David Brown to McKenney. However, another Cherokee at this time spoke of the Cherokee as "an infant Nation"; M-234, roll 71, #0157, 20 November 1824, Elijah Hicks to McKenney.

[33]M-221, roll 56, #0762, 10 May 1813, charter of Unicoi Turnpike Company.

[34]M-234, roll 72, #0042, 11 December 1825, Hicks and Ross to Montgomery.

Although their memorials to Congress in 1824 and 1825 had not been acted upon, the Cherokee leaders informed Montgomery that "another memorial was submitted thro' you to the last session of Congress and to which it appears the War Department has replied, and whether the memorial was laid before Congress or not we are not informed, but nothing in relation to it appears in the proceeding of Congress."[35] When the War Department failed to follow through on the memorial, the fault lay with it and not the Cherokee Nation that no progress had been made in clarifying this important question.

Montgomery forwarded the letter to Thomas L. McKenney, who wrote back in February 1827, "I think it is much to be regretted that the idea of *Sovereignty* should have taken such a deep hold of these people. It is not possible for them to erect themselves into a state of such independence and a separate and distinct Government, and the sooner they are enlightened on the subject, I think the better."[36] Evidently the War Department did not want the Cherokee memorial to come before Congress (though both Calhoun, McMinn, and McKenney had earlier said this was the only solution and that they would help the Cherokee with such a memorial). The issue was far too complicated, and once it got before Congress in this form, the growing antipathy between the Southern states and the federal government over Indian removal was bound to be thoroughly embarrassing to John Quincy Adams and his party.

The Cherokee did make one concession, however. On 18 October 1827, the council voted to reduce the tax on noncitizen traders "so as to make it equal to the tax imposed on citizen merchants."[37] This obviated the question of the tax inequity and allowed the more important question of the right of internal taxation to be decided on its merits. The council also voted in 1827 to "prolong" the suspension of the tax on "citizen traders," thereby indicating that in its opinion the matter was still alive. However, Congress never did take action on this question, and it was never resolved. The tax on traders remained on the Cherokee lawbooks, but no further attempts were made to collect it. The nation continued,

---

[35]Idem.

[36]M-21, roll 3, p. 390, 20 February 1827, McKenney to James Barbour.

[37]*Cherokee Laws*, 88-89.

however, to assert its right to lay such taxes and to manage all of its other internal affairs.

The position of the War Department was explained by McKenney as early as March 1825. As far as the department was concerned, the decision of the attorney general was final. "The Secretary of War never considered your memorial to Congress in the light of an appeal" from the opinion of Wirt to a higher authority. At most, Calhoun had believed that "there could be no objection to it." McKenney claimed that the department never agreed to support it. In 1824 Calhoun had graciously waited until the end of the spring session of Congress to see whether it would take any action on the original memorial. When it did nothing, he considered the matter settled. "To have done more by continuing the subject until the Congress should decide upon it (which may never be) would have been an assumption of power—for the laws give him no such authority."[38] This was a very weak answer and it did not comport either with the attitudes expressed earlier by McMinn, Calhoun, or McKenney himself. McKenney concluded by saying he regretted that "you should persist in your erroneous conception" that it was possible to appeal over the head of the secretary of war to the Congress. Yet the power of Congress in such matters was clear, and in the Treaty of Hopewell one article concerning traders stated that the article could not be clarified "until the pleasure of congress be known."[39] In that same treaty it was stated "that the Indians may have full confidence in the justice of the United States respecting their interests, they shall have the right to send a deputy of their choice, whenever they think fit, to congress."[40] Traditionally the secretary of war received such "deputies" and acted for the president and Congress, but obviously the Congress held the decisive power.

---

[38]M-21, roll 1, p. 380, 1 March 1825, McKenney to Cherokee delegation.

[39]Article 10 of the Treaty of Hopewell reads: "Until the pleasure of congress be known respecting the ninth article, all traders, citizens of the United States, shall have liberty to go to any of the tribes or towns of the Cherokees to trade with them, and they shall be protected in their persons and property and kindly treated." Article 9 reads: "For the benefit and comfort of the Indians, and for the prevention of injuries or oppressions on the part of the citizens or Indians, the United States, in congress assembled, shall have the sole and executive right of regulating the trade with the Indians, and managing all their affairs in such manner as they think proper." Richard Peters, *The Case of the Cherokee Nation* (Philadelphia, 1831) 250.

[40]Idem.

When Congress declined to clarify the extent of their autonomy, the Cherokee took matters into their own hands. In 1826 the council called for the election of delegates to a convention to meet on the Fourth of July to draw up a constitution modeled on that of the United States. Through this constitution, adopted in 1827, the Cherokee assumed the right of internal sovereignty. They were convinced that sooner or later Congress or the Supreme Court would uphold their position.

Unfortunately the development of a separatist, states' rights position by the Cherokee Nation conflicted directly with the rising states' rights movement among the states on its borders. Combined with the growth of Jacksonian democracy, Manifest Destiny, and the cotton kingdom, this overwhelmed them. Not even John Marshall, William Wirt, the New England missionaries, and the Whig political strategists were able to save them from removal after 1828. Pride and prejudice, not justice or treaty rights, resolved the dilemma of Indian rights within the republican empire. But no one could say that the Cherokee had not done their utmost to make the case for Indian home rule in terms the Anglo-Americans should have understood—or perhaps understood too well.

THE CHEROKEE CENSUSES
OF 1809, 1825, AND 1835*

coauthor
WALTER H. CONSER, JR.

When Walter Conser and I undertook this article, we planned simply to measure Cherokee growth in population, wealth, and agricultural production in a few simple economic tables. We wanted to compare the three Cherokee censuses of 1809, 1825, and 1835. However, three of our colleagues at Brown, Burr Litchfield, Howard Chudacoff, and Steven Hochstadt, told us that we would reap far greater information from our statistics if we utilized the functions that a computer could provide. The result was indeed a far more sophisticated essay than we had originally envisaged. According to the bylaws of the Journal of American History, *we were not allowed to give thanks to our colleagues for their help when we published this paper and we are happy to rectify that now.*

We felt that we had sufficient data to make three kinds of measurements: first, a simple comparison of growth in population, wealth, skills, and production; second, the emergence of a cleavage between the more and less acculturated parts of the nation; and third, the beginnings of a Cherokee class system that had produced by 1835 a small, wealthy elite, a somewhat larger middle class and an extensive peasant class (or in terms of the American frontier, a class of poor, one-horse, dirt-farmers).

The result is less scientific than it may seem. We did not have all the statistics we needed to make precise comparisons because the three censuses were organized on different principles and did not measure the same things. We were further hampered because none of the censuses provided specific data for Cherokee individuals or Cherokee towns; in fact, it was scarcely possible to identify various regions within the nation, other than the artificial boundaries of the surrounding states in the last census. Some

---

*We wish to give special thanks and acknowledgment to Steven A. Hochstadt, R. Burr Litchfield, and Howard P. Chudacoff for essential help in designing the statistical methodology and the tables for this study.

censuses also failed to measure some of the items we were most interested in, such as the years of schooling, the number of Christian converts, the production of cotton, the specific numbers of mechanics or skilled artisans of various kinds. However, with the aid of the computer we were able to construct comparative groupings that we called "Community Type" and "Family Type," and these yielded valuable comparative data. Although this essay has serious limitations, it does indicate that Native American history can provide statistics for quantitative measurement. We wish also to acknowledge assistance from Douglas Wilms of East Carolina University; he has made important statistical analyses of Cherokee society in the field of geography and land use.

ALTHOUGH SCHOLARS HAVE LONG BEEN AWARE of the detailed, family-by-family census of the Cherokee Nation taken by the federal government in 1835, no one has yet subjected that census to a detailed analysis. In part this was because of certain shortcomings in the census figures and in part because of a lack of comparative data for other tribes or even the Cherokee Nation. These problems still remain, but despite them there are ways to derive valuable information from that census about the Cherokees: some of the data corroborates other historical evidence; some is corrective. This study indicates that Andrew Jackson and many other government officials responsible for the forced removal of the Cherokees were seriously misinformed about several important aspects of Cherokee life. For example, War Department records prior to 1835 indicate that officials persistently underestimated the total number of Cherokees in the East, generally using a figure of 10,000 when in fact the figure was over 16,500 in 1835 and never below 12,000 since the first census was taken in 1808-1809.[1]

Andrew Jackson habitually spoke of the Cherokee Nation (and other Southern Indian nations) as though they consisted of only two classes of people, those he called "the real Indians" and those he called the "half-

---

[1]Governor Joseph McMinn of Tennessee, who became the federal agent to the Cherokees in 1823, said in a letter to the War Department, 23 July 1824, that although the Cherokees had numbered 12,000 in 1809, "many of the stragling class have gone over the Mississippie so that I presume the present strength of the nation does not exceed from 7 to 9 thousand souls." Record of the Bureau of Indian Affairs, National Archives Microcopy M-234, "Letters Received, 1824-1881," roll 71, frame #0302.

breeds."[2] According to Lewis Cass, Jackson's second secretary of war, the "real" Indians were still basically "warriors" and "hunters" who, with advancing white encroachment, were ready—even eager—to move west because the hunting would be better there and they could more easily maintain their old way of life;[3] this highly desirable aim, Cass claimed, was thwarted by the "halfbreeds," a small clique of wealthy Indians intermarried with the whites or descended from such intermarriages. The chief of the Bureau of Indian Affairs, Thomas L. McKenney, claimed that the half-breeds did not want the tribe to move because they had made heavy investments in cultivating the land or acquiring stores, ferries, taverns, or other entrepreneurial activities that they would have to give up.[4] Jackson's first secretary of war, John Eaton, portrayed these "halfbreeds" as the principal stumbling block to the benevolent policy of removal because, he insisted, they controlled tribal affairs and dictated tribal policy. He believed also that they forcibly intimidated those "real Indians" who actively supported removal.[5]

---

[2]Referring to the Cherokees' opposition to land cessions, on 10 June 1816, Jackson said, "In this matter the Indians—I mean the real Indians, the natives of the forest—are little concerned; it is a stratagem only acted on by the designing halfbreeds and renegade white men who have taken refuge in their country." *American State Papers: Indian Affairs*, ed. Walter Lowrie (Washington DC, 1834) 2:110-11.

[3]On 4 March 1830, Hugh Montgomery, as federal agent to the Cherokees, wrote to Jackson's secretary of war, "I must be permitted to divide the Cherokees into two classes—and in the first I would include the descendants of white parentage of those of mixed blood. This class contains a large portion of this nation (I would say nearly one half) . . . the govt. of this nation having latterly devolved upon them or fallen into their hands to the almost entire exclusion of the old Indian chiefs . . . [among] the great mass of the fullblood Indians the improvement, if progressing at all, is so slow that it is scarcely perceptible. . . . " M-234, roll 74, frame #0264-65. Secretary of War Lewis Cass stated in his official report to Congress in 1831 regarding the Cherokees, "War and hunting are his [sic] only occupations." *Executive Documents*, 1st Session, 22nd Congress (Washington, 1831) "Report of the Secretary of War," 1831, document 2, p. 32.

[4]Thomas L. McKenney, chief of the Bureau of Indian Affairs, wrote to the secretary of war on 27 December 1825, that it was "those enlightened half-breeds from whom the opposition to emigration generally comes. . . ." Bureau of Indian Affairs, National Archives Microcopy M-21, "Letters Sent, 1824-1881," roll 3, pp. 273-75.

[5]John Eaton, Jackson's secretary of war, wrote to William Carroll 30 May 1829, appointing him a secret agent to induce emigration among the Cherokees: "There is no doubt however but the masses of these people would be glad to emigrate and there is as little doubt that they are kept from this exercise of their choice by their Chiefs and other interested and influential men amongst them who, tenacious of their authority and their

It must therefore have come as a surprise to such officials that when removal was forcibly carried out by the government, the "real" or full-blood Indians resisted it far more stubbornly than many of the mixed bloods. Indeed, almost 1,000 Cherokees hid in the hills of North Carolina and never were removed.

The government apparently was mistaken about several things. The census of 1835 revealed that there was a consistent overestimation by federal officials regarding the amount of intermarriage with whites among the Cherokees; some estimates ranged as high as fifty percent "mixed bloods," but in fact the figure was less than twenty-three percent in 1835. Analysis of the Cherokee census of 1835 (and such other census data as is available for earlier years) not only helps to correct these erroneous impressions but also to prove that by 1835 Cherokee society was exceedingly complex and varied. Skills and economic status varied greatly, but virtually no Cherokees lived by hunting alone. The figures also demonstrate that the full bloods did not live in isolated pockets in the mountains, as some accounts state, but were scattered throughout the nation. The gradation of economic wealth and acculturation (measured in this census in terms of the acquisition of white skills) seems to indicate that at least a three-tiered class system was emerging: a very wealthy group (consisting of less than fifty out of 2,637 families), a sizable middle class, and a large class of poor families tilling only two or three acres.

Because the census of 1835 contains family data on racial intermarriage, on economic status, and on acquired skills, which is geographically identifiable, this analysis examines variations by region, by family type, and by communities. The result of this investigation, apart from indicating certain fallacies (consciously or unconsciously adopted) among advocates of removal, has been to sustain the claim by many others at this time that the Cherokee people were indeed far advanced in the acquisition of wealth and skills and that those with a high proportion of mixed Cherokee-white ancestry tended to have more skills and more wealth. It also appears that there was a definite trend toward an agrarian capitalist social order; that economic classes were beginning to appear; that communal life, the clan system, and the extended family were fading. The Cherokee were moving steadily (partly by choice but more by

---

power and unwilling to forego their gainful positions, keep them under the ban of their dictation." Ibid., roll 5, p. 456.

circumstance) toward the nuclear-family pattern and the life-style found in surrounding white settlements. However, the statistics also indicate such wide variations within the nation that historians must be wary of making simplistic cultural generalization in any of these categories. Because of the limited data available, this study contains a minimum of cultural analysis. The intent is to utilize the unique data of this census to exhibit the complexity of Cherokee life as of 1835.

I

The War Department, in the census of 1835, gathered information under thirty-six headings for a total of 2,637 Cherokee households or families, listing each item under the name of the head of household. The most significant items for this analysis were males and females (adult and children), black slaves (male and female), intermarriages (with whites, blacks, Spanish, Catawbas), farm size and produce, readers of English and/or Cherokee, acquired skills (spinning, weaving, "mechanics"), and the racial mixing according to the census headings "half-bloods" (Cherokee-white), "quadroon" (1/4 Cherokee-3/4 white), "fullblood," "mixed negroes" (Cherokee-black). Less detailed analysis has been given to items where the census figures lacked definition or were incomplete ("houses," "mills," "ferryboats," acres under cultivation, value of land, bushels of corn and wheat raised, value of produce). One could wish that many other items had been included in this census, such as the amount of cotton grown, number of years of schooling, converts to Christian denominations, free blacks, merchants, trading posts, keelboats, cotton gins, various kinds of livestock owned, sharecroppers (i.e., whites sharecropping for Indians), specific mechanical skills (blacksmiths, wheelwrights, silversmiths), plows, wagons, children attending school, and so forth. Data have been found on some of these items in earlier censuses of the Cherokees taken in 1809 and 1825. It would have added greatly to an understanding of social change and acculturation among the Cherokees had it been possible to make comparisons in detail. As it is, only the aggregate totals for the earlier censuses can be shown and matched against comparable totals for the census of 1835 (see Tables 1-A, 1-B).

Nevertheless, even from this very simplistic comparative data, it is evident that the Cherokees increased steadily in population (despite the Creek War, the intermittent emigration to Arkansas, and deaths due to recurring famine and sickness). The tables also indicate the rapid increase in wealth (measured in livestock, slaves, cultivated land, and other kinds of personal property) and the increasing acquisition of white skills (spinning, weaving, mechanics, trade, manufacture, and undoubtedly the ability to converse in English). Comparative data for the other four "civilized tribes" of the old Southwest is lacking, but it seems unlikely that the Creeks, Seminoles, Choctaws, and Chickasaws were able to match this growth.

In 1897, when the federal government was preparing for the transformation of the Cherokee Nation into the state of Oklahoma in order to end forever the reservation system of the Cherokees, a typescript of this 1835 census was prepared in Washington, D.C., under the direction of Acting Secretary of the Interior J. D. C. Atkins. Because the manuscript is extremely difficult to read (and on microfilm difficult to work with), we Xeroxed a copy of this typescript, which is at the Thomas Gilcrease Institute of American History and Art in Tulsa, Oklahoma. This 265-page typescript, when compared to the microfilm, was found to be generally very accurate, although it omitted some important items (i.e., it did not usually list acres of wheat or corn cultivated, bushels raised or sold, the breakdown of males and females, the breakdown of children and adults). The basic items on the typescript are: total persons in the household, racial breakdown of household, number of slaves owned, basic literacy and skills. Since coding was taken from the typescript rather than the often illegible microfilm of the manuscript, it is useful to offer here some typical entries as they appear in the typescript:

Typical verbatim entries for Tennesssee.

Hamilton County—Lookout Valley

JOHN BROWN   Six Cherokee Half-breeds. 1 intermarriage with the white race. They owned 12 slaves. 1 farm, 2 farmers, 2 mechanics; 3 read English; one weaver and two spinsters (spinners); 1 Reservee and 4 descendants of Reservees.

C. H. STOFFLE   Four Cherokees—1 fullblood and 3 half breeds; a farm and one farmer; 1 reader of English; 2 weavers, 3 spinsters, 1 descendant of reservees.

JOSEPH VANN   Fifteen Cherokee quadroons. Owners of 110 slaves, 55 of each sex. One farm, 1 farmer, one mill, one ferry boat. Five readers of English. Three weavers, 5 spinsters (spinners).

Typical verbatim entries for Alabama:

Lookout Valley

CHARLES McINTOSH Eleven fullblood Cherokees. Two farmers, 1 reader of Cherokee and one of English; 1 weaver, 3 spinsters (spinners).

JOHN PELONE Seven Cherokees, *5 mixed Spaniards*, 1 mechanic, 1 weaver, 1 spinster (spinner).

CHE CHEE Ten Cherokees (9 fullbloods, 1 halfblood). One farmer, 1 reader of English, 1 weaver, 1 spinster (spinner).

Typical verbatim entries for North Carolina:

Stecoe

THE STANDING WOLF Sixteen fullbloods, 2 farms, 4 farmers, 5 readers of Cherokee, 3 weavers, 3 spinsters (spinners).

Tuskega Tenn. River

AHTOWEE Seven Fullbloods, 2 farms, 4 farmers, 2 readers of Cherokee, 3 spinsters (spinners).

Uhelarkey Tenn. River

OOTETIE Eight fullbloods, 2 farms, 1 farmer, 1 reader of Cherokee, 2 spinsters (spinners).

Typical verbatim entries for Georgia:

Ahmacolola River

NANCY Four fullbloods, 2 halfbreeds, no farm or farmer, 1 weaver, 3 spinsters (spinners).

Etower

JAMES LANDRUM Twelve halfbreeds and 3 quarterbloods, 8 slaves. Six farms, 5 farmers, 1 mechanic, 2 readers of Cherokee, 4 weavers, 7 spinsters. One reservee and 7 descendants of reservees. Also one marriage with the white race.

Chatahoochee River

MASTER BRANNON   Eight quarterbloods, owned 14 slaves, and had one
marriage with the white race; 2 farms and 2 farmers;
one ferryboat, 5 readers of English, 3 weavers, and 3
spinsters (spinners).

Because even the manuscript records are incomplete in terms of
acres under cultivation, bushels of wheat and corn raised and sold, and
the like, it was decided to code only the following items from the typescript: head of family (by name), location (by state, county, and local
place-name), racial mixture, white intermarriage, slaves, children by
sex, total family size, the number of farms, farmers, mechanics, weavers, spinners, boats, mills, the number who read English and/or Cherokee, and the reservees. Where the typescript was incomplete or
inaccurate for these items, it was checked against the manuscript census.[6] Undoubtedly the use of the typescript has led to the inclusion of
some errors (either from original manuscript errors or errors in making
the typescript in 1897). These are not statistically significant in any of
the categories discussed.[7] The census takers made serious errors in adding their figures. Scholars who may use the manuscript census should
not accept any of the totals either in single items or in county or state
aggregates without checking the addition.

The manuscript census contains totals for two important economic
categories: land under cultivation (in each of the four states where Cherokees lived) and the size of crops raised. Inasmuch as the manuscript

---

[6]Two families were discovered later in the manuscript census who had been omitted
from the typescript of 1897 and hence were omitted in the coding. One of these families,
headed by Big Bear, contained eleven full bloods in Georgia owning no slaves; the other,
David McNair's family, was made up of eight half bloods owning twenty-one slaves. It was
also discovered after coding that the typescript had omitted to mention that the family of
Major Ridge in Georgia owned fifteen slaves.

[7]This microfilm is available from the National Archives, Record Group 75, T-496,
"Census Roll, 1835, of Cherokee Indians East of the Mississippi." A similar microfilm,
which was not examined, T-275, is a census of the Creek Indians, 1832. It might provide
some useful comparative data.

It is necessary to note here that there are basically two different sets of totals available
for this study: (1) the manuscript census totals on the microfilm, which are often inaccurately added and (2) the totals of the computerized statistics taken here from the typescript of 1897 as corrected against the manuscript. Because the computer totals appeared
basically the most accurate available, this study has relied upon them in all calculations
except where indicated.

census did not consistently record these items for each household, only averages in each of these categories could be obtained. (See Tables 2-A, 2-B).[8] These figures are incomplete and do not include large areas under cultivation for cotton, potatoes, beans, orchards, and other crops (see Tables 4, 6). This information should therefore be seen as presenting minimal figures for the Cherokee farming wealth in terms of corn and wheat production. The market value of the tillable land within the Cherokee Nation as estimated by the census takers is obviously too low. Probably the land values were deliberately set very low in order to cheat the Cherokees and save the government money in reimbursements for improvements after the removal.

The most salient feature of Tables 2-A, 2-B is the eccentric aspect of North Carolina's figures. The smaller size of its farms and the smaller yield of its crops (particularly its low wheat yield) are evidence both of the mountainous area, the poor soil, the lack of money to invest in slaves or plows, and consequently of the general poverty of the Cherokees in this region. Possibly isolation from white settlements, adherence to traditional life-style, and deliberate resistance to change contributed to these differences.

The eccentricity of the North Carolina data, however, provides a working hypothesis and tool for measuring the different rates of acculturation within the nation. Although there is much debate over the meaning of the term acculturation, it is used in this study to mean simply the acquisition of new skills (economic, handicraft, or linguistic). Care has been taken to avoid unwarranted generalization regarding the overall significance of these acquisitions either in terms of voluntary vs. forced acculturation or in terms of laudable adjustment to exigencies vs. laudable resistance to the dominant white culture. Such judgments require far more data than this census can provide.

---

[8]Professor Douglas C. Wilms of East Carolina University (North Carolina) has provided considerable help in this study that is gratefully acknowledged. He has utilized other state and national sources to provide more detailed descriptions of Cherokee land use within the state of Georgia in the years 1800-1838. Wilms's methods, if carried out for Tennessee, Alabama, and North Carolina, would provide the most complete and useful measurement of Cherokee acculturation. See Douglas C. Wilms, "Cherokee Land Use in the State of Georgia, 1800-1838" (Ph.D. thesis, University of Georgia, 1972). See also Wilms's articles and maps in "Cherokee Settlement Patterns in Nineteenth Century Georgia," *Southwestern Geographer* 14:1 (May 1874); "Georgia Land Lottery of 1832," *The Chronicles of Oklahoma* 52:1 (Spring 1974).

From the coded material of the 1897 typescript census, it was possible to measure Cherokee acculturation in two ways as of the year 1835 (apart from the obvious implications of the totals in Tables 2-A, 2-B). Because the Cherokees were a comparatively large tribe (over 16,000 plus 1,600 slaves and 250 intermarried whites, Spaniards, and Catawbas) and because they were spread out over 20,000 square miles (an area larger than Massachusetts, Connecticut, and Rhode Island combined), it is well known that different parts of the nation had acculturated or resisted acculturation at different rates. Historical evidence from contemporary documents is unanimous in stating that the full-blood families were the most resistant to acculturation and that these families (sometimes called "the conservatives" or "traditionalists" and sometimes, pejoratively, "the backward" or "the savage" or "the Pagan" portion of the tribe) tended to be located in certain areas.

By common account, the most traditionalist area, with the highest proportion of full bloods, was the mountainous region of the Great Smokies on the border between North Carolina and Tennessee and extending somewhat into northwestern Georgia and northeastern Alabama. Another area of conservative strength was reported to be in the southern and southwestern part of the Cherokee Nation where its borders touched those of the Creek and Chickasaw nations. Study of the coded data confirms this estimate and also indicates other areas of full-blood concentration. On a map of the Cherokee Nation, the full blood-traditionalist area would include the northeastern section of the nation (all of the North Carolina region, the eastern half of the Tennessee region, and the northeastern Georgia region of the nation) as well as along the whole southern part (from the westernmost tip near Muscle Shoals to the Chattahoochee River in Georgia) where the nation bordered on the Chickasaw and Creek nations (see map). Full bloods were not, of course, limited to these areas; but having particularly strong concentrations there probably enabled them to preserve their traditional life-style in more security than where white settlements impinged or where interstate turnpikes and major waterways produced heavy traffic by whites. These remote areas were also less infiltrated by missionaries. A map showing the locations of the major missionary stations would indicate that they were least heavily concentrated in the northeastern section and along the southern border (the full blood-traditionalist areas).

One of the issues we hoped to resolve by analysis of the census of 1835 was the extent to which the data might correlate resistance to, or lack of resistance to, acculturation either in terms of full-blood families per se or areas of the nation with high proportions of full bloods. A simple approach to this question was provided by the fact that the census was conducted on a state-by-state and county-by-county basis (the four states having assumed by 1835 some local jurisdiction over the Cherokee within their borders). Unfortunately it proved impossible to analyze the census along county lines with any high degree of accuracy because the census takers were not sufficiently specific in indicating for each family the county they lived in.[9] Geographical locations in the census are predominantly given in terms of waterways and valleys because the Cherokee, when they left their communal towns, settled mainly along riverbanks where the soil was best and where water was readily available for religious ceremonies.

However, if one accepts the strong and consistent historical evidence that the mountain area of North Carolina was an especially conservative area with a high proportion of full bloods, then one can utilize the census data for the Cherokee in that state (virtually all of which is in the Great Smokies) as a possible basis for a model of traditionalism. To offer just one of many corroborative accounts as to the nature of this region, we cite a report by George Barber Davis, the man hired by the federal agent, Colonel Return J. Meigs, in 1808, to conduct the census completed in 1809. Writing to Meigs from the North Carolina area (then known as the Overhill or Valley Towns) on 17 October 1808, Davis said, "I had not an Idea of seeing such Indians as there is over the hills and in the Valies; they are at least twenty years behind the lower town Indians."[10] Davis

---

[9]Douglas Wilms, by using surveys undertaken by the state of Georgia to assess Cherokee "improvements" prior to removal, has been able to achieve comparatively accurate locations of Cherokee households within each county in Georgia as well as a precise evaluation of their farms and other possessions. But no one has yet undertaken this for the states of North Carolina, Alabama, and Tennessee. See n. 4 above.

[10]George Barber Davis to Return J. Meigs, 17 October 1808, National Archives Microcopy, Record Group 75, M-208, "Records of the Cherokee Indian Agency in Tennessee," under the date 17 October 1808. The "Lower Towns" was the name given to Cherokee settlements on the Tennessee River in Tennessee and Alabama to the west and south of the Great Smokies. A copy of Meigs's printed census of 1809, entitled *A General Statistical Table for the Cherokee Nation*, was provided by Miss Mary Creech, archivist for the Moravian Missionary Archives in Winston-Salem, North Carolina. Unfortunately it does not contain a geographical breakdown of the data by identifiable geographic regions. See also n. 1 above for a statement similar to that of Davis by Hugh Montgomery.

included in this letter his census of this North Carolina mountain region. It reveals that of 583 black slaves in the Cherokee Nation in 1808, there were only five within the Overhill area; of 567 plows owned in the nation, the families in this region possessed only 40; of 1,572 spinning wheels, they had only 270; of 429 looms, only 70. Yet their population totaled 3,648 out of 12,395 Cherokees—or almost one-third of the entire nation.

Unfortunately the precise geographical boundaries that Davis (or Meigs) included for this Overhill part of the nation are not known; they may have extended beyond the exact boundaries of North Carolina since Davis appears, like later census takers, to have moved from one river or valley to another without particular regard to state boundaries. However, for possible comparison, Table 3 presents four sets of totals that roughly correspond to this particular area of the Cherokee nation. If Davis's Overhill region is an area larger than the North Carolina portion of the Cherokee Nation, the Aquohee District (established for electoral purposes by the Cherokee National Council in 1820) was clearly smaller than the total North Carolina area. Hence not too much can be made of these comparative totals except that proportionate to the percentage of families out of the tribal total, these areas in or around North Carolina consistently show less wealth in every category in 1809, 1825, and 1835. This is significant for the model.

II

Assuming then that in 1835 the mountain region of the Cherokee Nation—which includes all that part of the nation within the boundary of North Carolina (and, as noted, extends southwest into Georgia and slightly west into Tennessee)—remained significantly more conservative and contained the highest proportion of full bloods, the following tables compare this part of the tribe with those parts located in Tennessee, Alabama, Georgia (acknowledging some parts of these state areas are also mountainous and traditionalist, though presumably proportionately much less so). (See Tables 4-A, 4-B.) The Cherokee of North Carolina were distinctly different from the rest of the nation in 1835. Those Cherokees living in the Great Smokies had less racial mixing (i.e., proportionately more full bloods), proportionately fewer white skills, proportionately less wealth, and proportionately fewer readers of English. But they did not have a proportionately larger number of readers of Cherokee than those Cherokees living in Georgia, presumably because of the large number of full-blood families in that state.[11]

III

It would be wrong to attribute these statistics specifically or solely to full bloods since they are based upon geographical locations. Not all Cherokee families in the Great Smokies were full-blood families and Georgia, as noted, had a high percentage of full bloods. However, it seemed feasible to use the North Carolina area of the nation as a model for further measurement. Using as predictive factors the smaller amount of racial mixing, the smaller proportion of white skills, of wealth, and of English readers, the analysis then proceeds to its second stage. This was done in terms of the more and the less full-blooded communities throughout the nation as a whole. To derive this approach to differing rates of acculturation or deculturation, a strategy of analysis was constructed based upon "Community Types." Using the various place-names for Cherokee settlements indicated by the census takers as they moved through the nation, the census yields a total of 128 "communities" (or Cherokee settlements) varying in size from one family with nine persons to 110 families with 830 persons; there was an average of twenty families per community. These 129 communities were divided into two halves: (a) those communities whose populations were composed of 71% or more full bloods and (b) those communities composed of less than 71% full bloods. The 71% figure was used because it is the median of the percentage of full-blood families in the 129 communities. (N.B. In section IV below, this large proportion of full bloods will be discussed in terms of "Family Types.") These two types of communities were then compared in terms of their proportionate acquisition of white skills (spinning, weaving, mechanics), in terms of economic wealth (measured in terms of farms and slaves), and in terms of literacy (measured in terms of the ability to read Cherokee and/or English). (See Tables 6-A, 6-B.)

These figures indicate that the percentage of families owning farms in communities with more than 71% full bloods is roughly equal to this

---

[11]The Cherokee language was reduced to writing in 1821 or 1822 by the Cherokee silversmith and linguist, Sequoyah (or George Guess or Gist). He created eighty-six symbols to represent every syllable in the language. Anyone who could speak Cherokee could learn to write and read it within a few days by learning the syllabary.

percentage in communities where the proportion of full bloods was less than 71%. While the median percentage of families owning farms was 94.2%, the communities with less full bloods owned 93.2% and the communities with more full bloods owned 95.1%. Significantly, however, while farm ownership was relatively equal, slave ownership in the more full-blooded communities amounted to only 2.4% of the families while in the communities with more mixed bloods, the slaveowning families reached 13.5%. Moreover, as Table 5 indicates, while only 7.4% of the tribe as a whole owned slaves, six times as many families in the less full-blooded communities owned 1-4 slaves and three times as many families owned either 5-9 or more than 10 slaves than in the more full-blooded communities.

The meaning of the higher percentage of farms owned by families in the more full-blooded areas is ambiguous. Agriculture provided the basis for the economy of the Cherokee Nation. However, the larger percentage of farms in more highly full-blooded areas may indicate that the farms were smaller (though as we shall see, the average family size was not significantly different). This may mean that the more full-blooded families tended to live on poorer soil (in mountainous regions, sandhills, swamps) and therefore such families might have several plots that they tilled as farms. The small number of slaves owned in heavily full-blooded communities may indicate poverty, lack of capital to invest in this form of labor, or lack of interest in farming by slave labor (and a willingness to maintain a subsistence economy). It may also be a function of the poor soil, which did not make large-scale farming with slaves feasible. Perhaps also these families were less acquisitive or less skilled at farming or had fewer of the implements for farming. The Overhill Towns earlier in the century complained bitterly to the secretary of war that they were not given their fair share of plows (or spinning wheels, looms, and mills) as part of the government's technical aid to the Cherokees: the Lower Town chiefs along the Tennessee River seem to have taken more than their share of these implements, thereby creating a depressed section of the nation. There is no evidence at this time of antislavery sentiment among the full bloods or conservatives, though we do know that in the 1850s missionaries (some of whom preached abolitionist views) reported that the full bloods were sympathetic to antislavery views (perhaps out of antagonism toward the mixed bloods).

In regard to acquired skills within each community type, Table 6-B indicates that the two kinds of areas were similar to each other. The percentage of families with at least one member engaged in skilled work (either as spinner, weaver, or mechanic) was 90.1% in the less full-blooded communities and 87.7% in the more full-blooded communities. The communities of less full bloods had more weavers and spinners and twice as many mechanics as did the areas of more full bloods.

The most distinctive area of difference shown on Table 6-B (apart from slave ownership) is in the area of linguistic acculturation. Percentages of readers of either Cherokee or English were close (64.7% for the less full-blooded and 53.9% for the more full-blooded communities). However, of those who could read only English, the less full-blooded areas contained seven times more English readers than in the more full-blooded areas. Whether this disparity between the two types indicated a lack of interest on the part of individuals in the more full-blooded communities in learning English, a lack of need for this skill (because of their more isolated location), lack of opportunity to learn (for lack of schools and missionaries), or conscious resistance to acculturation (a desire to sustain old ways and culture) cannot be stated with any certainty.

Likewise the meaning of the statistics regarding readers of both Cherokee and English is unclear. As noted, the census of 1835 fails to record commercial trade activity, though we know that such activities were extensive. Clearly the ability to utilize both English and Cherokee would be important in such commercial activities. Thus the overwhelming concentration of individuals with these abilities in the areas of less full bloods suggests the possibility that these areas were the centers of commerce.

Perhaps one of the most unexpected findings of this study has been the fact that apparently only about half of the families in the nation had at least one reader of Cherokee, 1,331 out of 2,637 families or 50.85%. Historians and contemporary observers estimate a much higher proportion who learned to write and read Sequoyah's syllabary. A possible explanation for the low figure is that by 1835 many of those most hostile to acculturation had already moved west of the Mississippi, including Sequoyah himself. Nonetheless, it is significant that of those individuals able to read Cherokee still remaining in the East, 47.7% lived in the more full-blooded communities, while only 33.9% resided in the less full-blooded communities.

Efforts to distinguish between more and less full-blooded communities using the census of 1835 corrects some common misconceptions and confirms some other assertions regarding the amount of racial mixing between Cherokees, whites, blacks, Spanish, and other Indians. No evidence exists, however, as to how the census takers determined racial status. The only official comment in the census that bears on this is an equivocal certification of accuracy, which reads: "I do hereby certify upon honor that the foregoing is a correct census of the Cherokees residing in the limits of [my state] composing the District assigned to me by the Superintendent of Cherokee removals and that the other items of information under their appropriate heads are as correctly stated as practicable without a precise and thorough examination of each subject respectively."

In addition to the 69.5% of Cherokee families composed entirely of full bloods, the analysis of the census shows that there were 12.6% of the families composed of some mixed bloods and some full bloods and another 17.9% of the families that contained no full bloods. These figures vary sharply from contemporary assumptions about the amount of racial mixture among the Cherokees. Statements by the federal agents and missionaries seem to have greatly exaggerated the amount of intermarriage with whites, presumably because these officials came in contact predominantly with families of this kind. Some contemporary estimates state that one-quarter to one-half of the families (or individuals) were of mixed ancestry. Jedidiah Morse, for example, in his famous *Report to the Secretary of War . . . On Indian Affairs* in 1822, stated that in 1809 there were 12,395 Cherokees, "half of whom were of mixed blood."[12] The census of 1835 indicates that 12,776 of the individuals listed or 77.27% were full bloods; 1,391 individuals or 8.4% were half-bloods; 1,468 or 8.87% "quadroons" (one-quarter Cherokee); 897 individuals or 5.55% had no racial status indicated in the census.

While these statistics relating to mixed white and Indian ancestry tend to refute the general belief in 1835 that racial intermarriage was extensive, the census statistics tend to confirm the contemporary view that

---

[12]Jedidiah Morse, *A Report to the Secretary of War . . . on Indian Affairs* (New Haven CT, 1822) 152. Morse does not indicate his source for this statement, but it was commonly made by federal agents and readers in correspondence and many missionaries repeated it in their letters. See a similar statement by Hugh Montgomery cited in n. 2 above.

there was comparatively little intermarriage between Cherokees and blacks (or at least they confirm the failure of such miscegenation to be noted, admitted, or recorded). According to the census figures, there were only sixty "mixed negroes" (Cherokee-black) within the nation or .036% of the total population. Similarly, as Table 4-A reveals, the percentages for mixture with the Catawba ("Catawby") Indians, with Spanish ancestry, and white intermarriage, are extremely small. Unlike the census taken by the Cherokee themselves in 1824-1825, this census does not indicate which of the intermarriages with whites involved white males and which white females. But the proportions were probably about the same in 1824 and 1835, and we may assume that roughly one-third were females and two-third males out of the total of 193 "intermarriages with whites."

IV

Further efforts to explicate the census materials are offered in Tables 7-A, 7-B, and 7-C. In these tables three types of families were compiled: (a) those listing every member of the family in the census as a full blood; (b) those families listing no full bloods; and (c) those families listing one or more full bloods, but which were not wholly full blood. Where the "Community Type" model investigates the issue of acculturation with reference to areas (settlements) of white families with more or less full bloods, this "Family Type" model looks at acculturation simply in terms of the racial composition of the family itself. Contrary to expectations, the results of the Family Type analysis were very similar to those of the Community Type model.

For example, as shown in Table 7-B, while 7.4% of the families in the entire nation owned slaves, only 1% of the all-full-blood families owned slaves, while 10.8% of the mixed families and 30.4% of the no-full-blood families owned slaves. Clearly the families with no full bloods, though they constituted only 17.9% of the families in the nation, owned by far the largest number of slaves.

In the area of linguistic acculturation, only 6.8% of the all-full-blood families had at least one reader of English, while 54.7% of the families with no full bloods had at least one and 22.8% of the mixed families had at least one. The Cherokee Nation as a whole had 17.4% of its families claiming one or more readers of English. In general, the full-blood families were not only proportionately much lower in the number of English readers but probably lower also in the number able to speak or write English. Not surprisingly, families composed entirely of full bloods had the highest percentage of readers of Cherokee (52.7%), followed by mixed-blood families (51.3%) and families with no full bloods (38.8%). Conversely, readers of both English and Cherokee were highest in the no-full-blood families (23.4%) and lowest in the families with all full bloods (5.0%).

Table 7-C correlates these three family types with slave ownership, skills, and literacy. As the Pearson table indicates, the all-full-blood families have a strong positive correlation with Cherokee reading and a strong negative correlation with slaveowning and English reading. Conversely, families with no full bloods correlate positively with slaveowning and English reading and have a strong negative correlation regarding Cherokee reading and acquired skills. Interestingly, this absence of skills and the high positive correlation between no-full-blood families and readers of both English and Cherokee, again suggests the possibility that these were the individuals engaged in commerce and trade. In this regard, families of mixed blood represent something of an intermediate position; they have positive correlations to slave ownership, acquired skills, and the ability to read both Cherokee and English, yet a negative correlation to Cherokee reading.

On the whole, then, these correlations imply that the acquisition of white skills and English reading, along with the ownership of slaves, was a function of acculturation, increasing wealth, and upward mobility, very much as in the surrounding white settlements. The Cherokees, in short, were acquiring by 1835, only a generation after giving up warfare against advancing white expansion, a bourgeois socioeconomic structure. In fact, as will be indicated later, there was not only an expanding Cherokee bourgeoisie but a growing planter or upper-class gentry who lived very much on the same scale and with the same values and life-style as the surrounding white planter class. So much for the Family Type model.

V

At this point it is useful to introduce a discussion of the Cherokee upper class. Table 8 constitutes a detailed description, taken from the manuscript census of 1835, of the forty-two wealthiest families (defined on the basis of their owning ten or more slaves).[13] As might be expected, these figures reveal that these forty-two or more families hold an inordinate share of the wealth in all categories and an inordinate share of the skills (with the notable exception of the reading of Cherokee, though even here their average was above that of most mixed families. One may hazard that as a ruling elite some of these men learned Cherokee for political purposes.)

All of these families were racially mixed and most had a very low proportion of full bloods. Owning more slaves, they cultivated more acres, raised more corn and wheat (and undoubtedly cotton), and obtained more income therefrom. There is also a high correlation regarding the proportion of intermarriage with whites; there is no sign of mixing, in these families, with black, Spanish, or Catawba ancestry. If one seeks a model for the extreme level of Cherokee acculturation, these forty-two families provide that side of the spectrum in contrast to the all-full-blood model. Conversely, however, they are totally unrepresentative of the remaining 2,595 Cherokee households, except for the important fact that they too average six persons (three adults, three children) per family.

One must avoid the easy conclusion that the wealthy, mixed-blood elite was necessarily the ruling body or oligarchy of the Cherokee Nation at this time. This was a claim commonly made by those frontier whites (and officials like Jackson, Cass, Joseph McMinn) who wished to have the Cherokees removed on the grounds that the full bloods were eager to go west to retain their old ("savage") hunting way of life but were intimidated by the powerful mixed bloods who dominated the National Council. As this totally mistaken view had it, the wealthy mixed bloods opposed removal because they had the most property and power to lose by it. Much could be said on this point, and historians have debated it at considerable length. One quotation will suffice to indicate the care that should be taken in this debate. This is a statement made by twelve white missionaries (led by the Reverend Samuel A. Worcester) in a manifesto that appeared in opposition to removal in the *Cherokee Phoenix* for 1 January 1831. These missionaries pointed out that the Cherokee legislature was divided into two houses, the National Committee (or upperhouse) and the National Council (lowerhouse). By tradition and

---

[13]See n. 6 above for two omissions of slaveowning families in the computerized statistics. These omissions have been corrected for part V, the study of the elite.

design, the Cherokee consistently gave the well-to-do a larger role in the upperhouse while retaining popular control of the lowerhouse.

> It may not be amiss to state what proportion of the Indian blood actually bears to the white in the principal departments of the Cherokee Government. The present principal chief, Mr. John Ross, is, we believe, but one-eighth Cherokee. Maj. [George] Lowery, the second principal chief, is one-half Cherokee. The Legislature consists of two branches styled the National Committee and Council, the former number 16 members and the latter 24. The presiding officers of both these branches are full Cherokees. Of the committee, two only, including The President, are full Indians; of the rest seven are half Indian, two more [than half], and five less than half. Of the Council, 16 are supposed to be full Indians, seven half, and one only one-fourth. No measure can be adopted without the concurrence of both houses, and frequently every public measure has the sanction of a body of which two-thirds of the members are of unmixed Indian blood.[14]

In addition to this check on oligarchy, one ought to remember the tradition of the Cherokee whereby all decisions affecting the general welfare of the tribe or nation should be made only after long debate had produced a consensus. In such debates, the numerical weight of the full bloods obviously played a large part. These forty-two families should perhaps be regarded as a social elite in terms of acculturation rather than as a ruling class.

Fourteen of these families resided in Tennessee in 1835, eight in Alabama, twenty in Georgia, and none in North Carolina. (There were two families in North Carolina who owned six slaves but none who owned more.) Since the nation retained communal ownership of its land, financial worth and invested capital could best be demonstrated by slave ownership. These forty-two families owned two-thirds of the black wealth of the nation (1,013 out of 1,592 slaves). Among the largest slaveholders was "Rich Joe" Vann, who owned 110 slaves. Next to him came George Waters with 100, John Martin with sixty-nine, and Lewis Ross with forty-one. But many of these families made as much or more income from trade as from agriculture.

Another way of studying this elite would be to trace the kinship ties. Simply by using the last names and not considering marriages among them (or possible clan ties), it can be seen that three members of the

---

[14]*Cherokee Phoenix*, 1 January 1831, microfilm copy from the American Antiquarian Society, Worcester MA.

Gunter family owned eighty-two slaves between them; three members of the Vann family owned 137; John and Lucy Martin owned eighty-nine between their two households; John and Lewis Ross owned sixty between them; Major Ridge and his son John owned thirty-six. In these terms the upper-class was an even more tightly knit group than this list might imply. Perhaps something like twenty-five or thirty families out of a total of 2,637 in the nation (or roughly one percent) seem to have accumulated the major share of wealth. The detailed genealogies of Cherokee families printed by Emmet Starr in his *History of the Cherokee Indians* (Oklahoma, 1921) confirm the fact that mixed bloods tended to intermarry most frequently with other mixed bloods or with whites. Further information might well reveal that the clan system was retained longer among the full bloods and consequently militated against intermarriage with white or mixed bloods who were obviously outside the clans.

The racial mixtures of these forty-two families is also revealing. Out of 283 persons in forty-two households, only twelve (4.24%) were listed as full bloods. Eighty-six (30.38%) were listed as half bloods; 170 (60.07%) as quarter bloods. None of these families had any members listed as "mixed Negro," though there were sixty such persons listed in the nation. On the other hand, out of 193 whites intermarried into the nation, twenty-one (or over 10%) were among this 1.59% of the families. Since none of these forty-two families had more than one white person intermarried, this means that 50% of them contained either a white man or white woman.[15]

Similarly, as one would expect, there is a high correlation between the number of persons in this group who read (and presumably spoke) English. (There are no statistics on how many Cherokee could write English.) Since 1,070 Cherokee out of 16,542 were listed as able to read English, that means slightly over six percent (6.46%) could read English. But while 18% of the members of the tribe could read Cherokee, less than 10% of the members of these forty-two families (twenty-eight per-

---

[15]It is necessary here to note discrepancies between the computer totals (from the typescript of 1897) and the manuscript census totals of 1835. The manuscript census shows seventy-four "mixed Negroes" (i.e., Cherokee-Negro racial mixture) while the computer figure was only sixty. The manuscript total for whites intermarried with Cherokees was 201; the computer total was 193.

sons) could read Cherokee. Other skills show high percentages among the 283 members of these families: 10.24% of the members of the elite were mechanics, but only 2.03% of the total population; 20.14% of the elite were weavers but only 15.01% of the whole nation; 27.56% of the elites were spinners, but only 18.91% of the nation. Another way of pointing out the disproportionate amount of craft skills among the forty-two elite families is to note that while these families had an average of .5 mechanics per family, 1.3 weavers per family, and 1.9 spinners per family, the rest of the tribe had .02 mechanics per family, .015 weavers per family, and .018 spinners per family.

Finally, it follows logically from the above that these families were able to cultivate sizably larger farms and produce proportionately larger crops. The average Cherokee family had a farm or group of farms of 14.12 acres; the average of these forty-two families cultivated 162.52 acres. The average Cherokee family produced each year an average of 213.87 bushels of corn and sold an average of 44.48 bushels of corn; the average elite family produced 2,407.25 and sold 761.26 bushels. The average Cherokee family made about $20.24 per year from its sales of produce; the average elite family made about $380.23. It should be noted that much of the produce of the elite families probably went toward the care of their slaves.

The average Cherokee family in the nation contained 6.28 members; the average elite family had 6.2 members. Both categories had three males and three females, three adults and three children per family.

VI

The final effort has been to arrive at some mean figure for the average Cherokee family and also to show the range within a single household. These figures are most easily seen in table 9 at the end of this essay. While there were anomalies in the listing of "households" (as indicated by the household in which the census taker noted that four families were living together),[16] it appears from the census that the Cherokee were

---

[16]Because the census takers were evidently instructed to select a single name for "head of household," they often failed to note when more than one family was living together. One entry, however, does state that the household of Big Dan included four separate families ("Big Dan, Doing, and Two Other families living together"). Though listed as a single unit in the census, this household had twenty-eight Cherokees, twenty-seven full bloods, five farms, five farmers, four readers of Cherokee, three weavers, six spinners.

moving toward the prevailing white frontier practice of the nuclear family living on its own subsistence farm. This was certainly what the federal agents and missionaries encouraged, and with the breakdown of the enclosed townships with common gardens after 1800, this practice was becoming a general pattern. One of the leading Cherokees, John Ridge, confirmed this in a letter written to Albert Gallatin in February 1827:

> The above population is dispersed over the face of the County on separate farms; villages or a community having a common enclosure to protect their patches have disappeared long since . . . the inhabitants . . . are gradually [moving] to the woods where they prefer to clear the forest and govern their own individual plantations . . . they are farmers and herdsmen. . . . Their principal dependence for subsistence is on the production of their own farms.[17]

To that extent, even the full-blood families were acculturating, but it was acculturation enforced by the decline of their old economy of hunting, farming, fishing, and gathering.

However, the apparent existence of small families may be misleading—the result of the census format and the white census takers' perceptions. Undoubtedly many families lived in close proximity, and extended kinship patterns made extended visits common among them. Unfortunately we cannot tell from the census figures what the familial relationships were within each household.

CONCLUSIONS

Obviously no comparisons can be drawn with other Indian nations from this one, though one would guess that the contemporary opinion was correct—the Cherokee were the most "civilized" of the large tribes still claiming autonomy in America in 1835; that is, if one means by "civilized" the acquisition of Euro-American skills (like farming, spinning, weaving), literacy (reading English or Cherokee), wealth (slave ownership and acres under cultivation), enterprise (meaning trade, ferryboats, mills, cotton gins, blacksmiths), education (meaning attendance at schools), Christianization (meaning conversions to Christianity and

---

[17]John Ridge to Albert Gallatin in the typescript of the John Howard Payne Papers, The Newberry Library, Chicago, Illinois, 8:103-105.

church membership or nominal adherence),[18] and racial mixture (though smaller tribes farther east or in New England probably exceeded them in intermarriages). This does not mean that the Cherokee were assimilationist or deculturated. In many respects they were strongly resistant to deculturation, as their determined opposition to removal indicated. What was taken by contemporary white observers as "civilization" (out of wishful thinking) was simply the acquisition of sufficient skills for economic survival and for political self-government—part of a conscious strategy to resist removal and maintain autonomy. But this issue lies beyond the scope of this paper.

The steady increase in Cherokee population and wealth seems to indicate a strong, dynamic, coherent cultural organization and a vital, healthy tribal coherence, though increasing centralization was necessary for national unity and consequently destructive of other aspects of traditional life (especially local town government). It should also be stressed that this census ignores the 3,500 to 5,000 Cherokee who had migrated to the West between 1780 and 1835 (the majority of these migrating between 1817 and 1835). Nor do these statistics take into account the intense anxiety and disruption forced upon the nation after 1828 by the combined pressure of the surrounding states (especially Georgia) and the federal government in their effort to implement by fair means or foul Jackson's policy of total removal. Undoubtedly, a census taken in 1832, or even 1828, would indicate a much wealthier society. Many of the wealthiest Cherokees moved West or outside the limits of Georgia after 1828 under the threat of persecution and as a result of violent white intrusions. The discovery of gold in the eastern part of the nation in 1828 led to further disorder. There is no way to measure what the Cherokee Nation might have become had it been permitted to develop its own mineral and timber rights.

The principal concern in this study has been a delineation of the Cherokees in transition; that is, it demonstrates the levels of development among different groups and parts of the nation. This has been undertaken by four means of measurement: (1) geographic (using North

---

[18]According to statistics gleaned from various missionary records, there were in 1835 about 1,320 Christian church members (all Protestants) in the Cherokee Nation. This proportion, about nine percent, was probably not too different from the church membership figures in neighboring white settlements.

Carolina as a traditionalist region); (2) Community Type (through statistical construction of more and less full-blooded communities); (3) Family Type (through statistical construction of all-full-blood, no-full-blood, and mixed families) and (4) by definition of a social elite. From these models significant correlations have been found between what are designated as full-blood-traditionalist regions and families and what are designated as upper-class ("progressive") families. But this analysis raises as many questions as it answers. There is additional data available with which to pursue these questions, particularly in the various claims against the federal government by Cherokee families during and after removal, and in the surveys conducted to assess the payments to be made by the government for "improvements" after the Cherokee were forced to move. These provide a wealth of intimate detail comparable to wills and land records in white communities. Eventually similar sources will provide comparable data for other Southeastern tribes and scholars may begin to make more accurate statements about what the "civilization" of "the Five Civilized Tribes" consisted of. We hope that this essay will stimulate such efforts.

TABLE 1-A

	MEIGS TOTALS OF CENSUS OF 1809	BOUDINOT ADDRESS OF 1826	*PHOENIX* TOTALS OF 1828	MS. CENSUS OF 1835
COMPARATIVE TOTALS FOR CENSUSES OF 1809, 1825 (BOTH BOUDINOT AND PHOENIX), MS. 1835				
Cherokees	12,395	13,963 (& 3,500-4,000 in West)	14,972	16,542
males	6,116			
females	6,279			
Whites intermarried	341	211	205	201
males		147	144	
females		73	61	
Black slaves	583	1,277	1,038	1,592
Black cattle	19,165	22,000	22,405	
Horses	6,519	7,600	7,628	
Swine	19,778	46,000	38,517	
Sheep	1,037	2,500	2,912	
Looms	429	762	769	
Spinning wheels	1,572	2,488	2,428	
Wagons	30	172	130	
Ploughs	567	2,943	2,792	
Grist mills	13	31	20	
Sawmills	3	10	14	
Ferries		18	10	
Silversmiths	49		55	
Blacksmiths		62		
Powder mills	1		6	
Cotton gins		8		
Salt petre works	2		9	
Schools	5	18	19	
Scholars	94		292	

Sources: R. J. Meigs Census, Moravian Archives, Winston-Salem NC; Elias Boudinot, *An Address to the Whites* (Philadelphia, 1826); *The Cherokee Phoenix*, 18 June 1828. Both the figures given by Boudinot and the figures printed in *The Cherokee Phoenix* are based on a census taken by the Cherokee Council in 1825. It is not clear why they differ.

TABLE 1-B

ADDITIONAL INFORMATION FROM THE MEIGS CENSUS (1809) AND THE MANUSCRIPT CENSUS OF 1835

MEIGS CENSUS PROVIDES THE FOLLOWING USEFUL DATA:

6,519 horses @ $30	$195,570
19,165 cattle @ $8	153,320
1,037 sheep @ $2	2,074
19,778 swine @ $2	39,556
13 gristmills @ $260	3,380
3 sawmills @ $500	1,500
30 wagons @ $30	1,200
583 negro slaves @ average $300	174,900
	$571,500

THE MANUSCRIPT CENSUS OF 1835 LISTS THE FOLLOWING ADDITIONAL INFORMATION:

Males under 18	4,237
Males over 18	3,992
Females under 16	3,984
Females over 16	4,338
Houses	8,184
Farmers	2,809
Mechanics	339
Spinners	3,129
Weavers	2,484
Mills	24
Ferryboats	66.5
English readers	1,070
Cherokee readers	3,914
Halfbloods	1,454
Quarterbloods	1,492
Fullbloods	12,463
Mixed Catawbas	71
Mixed Spanish	56
Mixed Negro	74
Reservees	123
Descendents of Reservees	650
Total Reservee claims	773
Farms	3,120
Acres cultivated	44,070
Bushels of wheat raised	2,502
Bushels of corn raised	50,394
Bushels of wheat sold	622
Bushels of corn sold	117,320
For how much	$533.68
Bushels of corn bought	13,547
For how much	$47.12

TABLE 2-A

	TOTAL TILLABLE ACREAGE	ACRES IN CULTIVATION	AVERAGE FARM SIZE IN ACRES	NUMBER OF FARMS
	AVERAGE SIZE OF FARM BY STATE IN MANUSCRIPT CENSUS OF 1835			
Tenn.	251,005	10,692	25.92	412
Ala.	292,480	7,256	28.01	259
N.C.	35,000	6,906	9.67	714
Ga.	614,000	19,216	11.07	1,735
TOTAL [TRUE TOTAL]	1,192,480 [sic] [1,192,885]	44,070	14.12	3,120

Source: Manuscript Census of 1835

TABLE 2-B

	TOTAL BUSHELS OF WHEAT GROWN	AVERAGE BUSHELS PER FARM	TOTAL BUSHELS OF CORN GROWN	AVERAGE BUSHELS PER FARM	ESTIMATED WORTH OF TILLABLE LAND
	AVERAGE SIZE OF GRAIN PRODUCTION AND LAND VALUES BY STATE IN MANUSCRIPT CENSUS OF 1835				
Tenn.	976	2.37	129,179	313.54	(@ $2. per acre) $443,290.00
Ala.	240	.92	88,776	342.76	(@ $2. per acre) $594,640.00
N.C.	65	.09	78,392	109.79	(@ $5 per acre) $175,000.00
Ga.	1,221	.70	267,664	154.26	(@ $2. per acre) $1,228,800.00
TOTALS	2,502	.80	563,991	180.76	$2,441,730.00

Source: Manuscript Census of 1835

TABLE 3

COMPARATIVE TOTALS OF "OVERHILL TOWNS" (1809), AQUOHEE (1825), MANUSCRIPT TOTAL OF NORTH CAROLINA (1835), AND COMPUTER TOTALS OF NORTH CAROLINA								
	I Meigs Census of Overhill Towns 1809		II Aquohee District (1825)		III MS Census of N.C. 1835		IV Computer Totals of N.C.	
	1	2	1	2	1	2	1	2
Families	608	(29.43%)	389	(28.0%)	638	(24.10%)	636	(24.10%)
Males	1,750		1,245	(17.34%)	1,850	(22.48%)		
Females	1,898		1,319	(18.95%)	1,794	(21.55%)		
Total	3,648	(29.43%)	2,564	(18.40%)	3,644	(22.02%)	3,599	(21.74%)
Slaves	5	(.85%)	19	(1.83%)	37	(2.32%)	32	(1.99%)
Intermarried Whites	72	(.60%)	4	(1.95%)	22	(10.94%)	20	(10.36%)
Cattle	2,115		1,799					
Horses	593		1,191					
Sheep	259		765					
Hogs	1,955		5,544					
Ploughs	40		446					
Looms	70		145					
Spinning Wheels	270		346					
Blacksmiths	4		5					

Note: The numbers in columns 1 represent the absolute figures in each named category. The percentages in parentheses in columns 2 are the percentages in each named category of the totals within the Cherokee Nation.

Source: see note 6.

TABLE 4-A

PERCENTAGES OF STATE POPULATIONS IN CATEGORIES OF RACE, SKILLS, AND LITERACY				
	GEORGIA	ALABAMA	TENNESSEE	NORTH CAROLINA
Farmers	21.8	22.2	21.8	22.0
Mechanics	1.3	.9	7.8	.3
Weavers	16.2	10.6	20.8	8.3
Spinners	24.8	17.6	32.3	19.1
English Readers	4.0	15.0	14.8	1.5
Cherokee Readers	14.9	19.4	18.1	14.7
Full bloods	81.0	61.3	56.8	88.9
Half bloods	5.9	14.9	21.0	2.5
Quarter bloods	7.5	13.5	14.5	6.2
Mixed Negro	.01	.3	1.2	.5
White Intermarriage	.7	2.2	2.9	.5
Mixed Spaniards	.5	.7	---	---
Mixed Catawbas	.01	3.3	.5	---

Note: Each figure represents percentage of total state population falling in named category.
Source: 1897 transcript.

TABLE 4-B

PER CAPITA WEALTH BY STATES (EXCLUDING SLAVES)						
	SLAVES	FARMS	ACRES IN CULTIVATION	CORN GROWN	WHEAT GROWN	CORN SOLD
N.C.	.0008	.193	1.918	21.78	.0180	1.634
Ga.	.0906	.191	2.159	30.79	.1372	7.570
Ala.	.2052	.189	5.031	61.56	.1664	11.640
Tenn.	.1796	.155	4.121	49.79	.3762	10.519

Source: 1835 Manuscript Census, except for slaves.
      Slaves are based on 1897 transcript adjusted for omissions.

TABLE 5

DISTRIBUTION OF FARM AND SLAVE-OWNERSHIP BY COMMUNITY TYPE*			
	ALL FAMILIES	MORE FULL BLOOD COMMUNITIES	LESS FULL BLOOD COMMUNITIES
Farms	94.2	95.1	93.2
Any Slaves Owned	7.4	2.4	13.5
1-2 Slaves Owned	2.5	1.0	4.4
3-4 Slaves Owned	1.4	.6	2.5
5-9 Slaves Owned	1.8	.5	3.5
10 or More Slaves Owned	1.5	.2	3.1

*Note: Each figure represents percent of families in each community type owning farms or slaves.
Source: 1897 transcript.

TABLE 6-A

DISTRIBUTION OF HOUSEHOLDS BY COMMUNITY TYPE AND STATE		
	PERCENTAGE OF TOTAL FAMILIES	
	LESS FULLBLOOD	MORE FULLBLOOD
TOTALS	45.8	54.1
Tennessee	12.8	3.1
Alabama	8.2	1.2
North Carolina	1.6	22.4
Georgia	23.2	27.4

Note: Each figure represents percentage of total families in each designated category.
Source: 1897 transcript.

TABLE 6-B

DISTRIBUTION OF HOUSEHOLDS OF EACH TYPE BY WEALTH, SKILLS, AND LITERACY		
CATEGORY	FAMILIES IN LESS FULL BLOOD COMMUNITIES	FAMILIES IN MORE FULL BLOOD COMMUNITIES
Owning Farms	93.2%	95.1%
Owning Slaves	13.5%	2.4%
Member with Any Skill	90.1%	87.7%
Spin or Weave	89.6%	87.2%
Weaver	71.1%	57.1%
Spinner	86.2%	83.4%
Mechanic	15.7%	7.8%
Reader of English or Cherokee	64.7%	53.9%
Reader of English	15.1%	2.0%
Reader of Cherokee	33.9%	47.7%
Reader of English and Cherokee	15.7%	4.2%

Source: 1897 transcript.
Note: Each figure represents percentage of each type in designated category.

TABLE 7-A

DISTRIBUTION OF HOUSEHOLDS BY FAMILY TYPE AND STATE			
	FULLBLOODS	MIXED BLOODS	NO FULLBLOODS
TOTALS	69.5%	12.6%	17.9%
Tennessee	10.9%	22.8%	31.2%
Alabama	7.0%	11.4%	16.3%
North Carolina	30.0%	12.0%	9.8%
Georgia	52.2%	53.8%	42.7%

Source: 1897 transcript.

TABLE 7-B

DISTRIBUTION OF HOUSEHOLDS OF EACH TYPE BY WEALTH, SKILLS, AND LITERACY			
	FULL BLOODS	MIXED BLOODS	NO FULL BLOODS
Owning Farms	90.7%	88.6%	75.4%
Owning Slaves	1.0%	10.8%	30.4%
Spinners	85.4%	91.3%	77.1%
Weavers	60.6%	78.7%	64.3%
Mechanics	11.0%	14.4%	10.8%
Readers of English or Cherokee	55.8%	59.5%	70.3%
Readers of Cherokee	52.7%	51.3%	38.8%
Readers of English	6.87%	22.8%	54.7%
Readers of English and Cherokee	5.0%	14.7%	23.4%

Note: Each figure represents percentage of family type in designated category.
Source: 1897 transcript.

TABLE 7-C

PEARSON CORRELATIONS OF RACIAL MIXTURE OF FAMILIES IN THE 129 COMMUNITIES WITH SLAVE OWNERSHIP, SKILLS, AND LITERACY*			
	ALL FULL BLOOD	MIXED BLOOD	NO FULL BLOOD
Percentage of families with at least one slave	−0.62 .001	.17 .022	.61 .001
Percentage of families with at least one member skilled	.16 .029	.24 .002	−0.30 .001
Percentage of families with at least one reader of Cherokee	.60 .001	−0.26 .001	−0.54 .001
Percentage of families with at least one reader of English	−0.59 .001	−0.03 .353	.67 .001
Percentage of families with at least one reader of both English and Cherokee	−0.48 .001	.35 .001	.37 .001

* The upper figure in each pair represents the correlation coefficient.
  The lower figure in each pair represents the level of significance.

TABLE 8

NAME	PLACE	MALES UNDER 18	MALES OVER 18	FEMALES UNDER 16	FEMALES OVER 16	TOTAL CHEROKEES	SLAVES, MALE	SLAVES, FEMALE	TOTAL SLAVES	WHITE INTERMAR.	FARMS	ACRES CULT.	HOUSES	BU. WHEAT GROWN	BU. CORN GROWN
THE CHEROKEE ELITE															
TENNESSEE															
John Brown	Hamilton Co. Lookout Mt.	2	2	1	1	6	9	3	12	1	1	79	8	--	2000
Alexr. Nave	Tenn. River	2	2	2	4	10	7	7	14	1	1	100	17	50	1400
James Brown	Coltewah	1	1	1	1	4	14	14	28	--	1	100	12	--	2000
Wm Williams	Coltewah Candy Creek	1	1	1	2	5	6	5	11	1	1	107	34	--	2700
Aisley Eldrige	McMinn Co. Candy Creek	2	--	5	12	8	8	13	21	21	1	150	12	--	1500
Wm Blythe Sr.	Hiwassee R. Tenn. R.	3	--	1	2	6	9	4	13	1	1	227	30	--	4000
Joseph Vann	Hamilton Co.	5	1	6	3	15	55	55	110	--	1	300	35	--	3200
James Vann	Hamilton Co. Long Savannah	2	1	1	--	4	5	9	14	1	1	100	20	--	2000
Sam'l Packs	McMinn Co. Candy Creek	7	--	1	3	11	7	5	12	1	1	100	10	20	1000
Jesse Mayfield	McMinn Co. Mouse Creek	2	--	3	1	6	8	7	15	1	1	200	24	10	3500
John Ross	McMinn Co. Red Clay	3	2	1	1	7	13	6	19	--	1	60	6	--	--
Lewis Ross	McMinn Co. Cha-ta-ta Creek	2	1	3	1	7	24	17	41	1	1	--	--	--	--
David McNair	McMinn Co. Cheaton Creek	4	1	2	1	8	11	10	21	1	1	243	40	100	3500
James Pettit	McMinn Co. Conesewaga Cr.	3	--	1	1	5	17	27	27	1	1	175	30	10	4500
ALABAMA															
George Lowrey	Wills Valley	--	1	--	1	2	7	13	20	--	1	150	10	--	200
Eliz. Pack	Jackson Co.	2	2	3	3	10	16	13	29	--	1	175	6	60	3000
Chas. Multon	Creek Path	--	1	--	--	1	4	10	14	--	1	70	2	--	1000
Sam'l Gunter	Creek Path	--	1	--	2	3	11	11	22	--	1	200	13	--	2400
Edw. Gunter	Creek Path	2	2	5	1	10	17	13	30	--	2	225	4	--	4000
John Gunter Jr.	Creek Path	2	1	1	2	6	14	16	30	--	3	325	35	--	4000
Alex. Gunter	Blount Co.	--	1	--	1	2	11	11	22	1	1	150	7	--	2000
Rch'd Ratliff Jr.	Turkeytown	3	1	3	1	8	6	7	13	--	1	50	5	--	600

TABLE 8

																	THE CHEROKEE ELITE	
BU. WHEAT SOLD	BU. CORN SOLD	FOR HOW MUCH	BU. CORN BOUGHT	FOR HOW MUCH	MILLS	FERRYBOATS	FARMERS	MECHANICS	ENGLISH READERS	CHEROKEE READERS	HALF BLOODS	QUADROONS	FULL BLOODS	MIXED NEGRO	WEAVERS	SPINNERS	RESERVEES	RESERVEE DESC.
--	1000	$580	20	$30.50	--	--	2	2	3	--	6	--	--	--	1	2	1	4
--	750	60	--	--	--	--	3	1	6	3	--	10	--	--	2	4	--	10
--	200	66	40	15	--	--	1	--	4	--	3	1	--	--	1	2	--	1
--	1400	700	--	--	--	--	1	1	2	1	2	2	--	--	2	2	--	--
--	--	--	--	--	--	--	--	--	2	--	7	--	1	--	1	3	--	8
--	1000	333	--	--	1	2	1	--	6	--	--	6	--	--	2	3	--	--
--	500	250	7200	324	1	1	1	--	5	--	--	15	--	--	3	5	--	--
--	120	9	--	--	--	--	1	--	2	--	--	4	--	--	1	1	--	--
--	100	33	100	25	--	--	1	1	8	--	--	11	--	--	3	3	1	11
--	800	320	92	30	--	--	1	--	4	--	--	6	--	--	1	1	--	6
--	--	--	700	33	--	2	2	--	5	1	6	--	1	--	2	2	2	5
--	--	--	--	--	1	3	1	6	--	--	--	7	--	--	--	--	1	5
--	500	250	--	--	--	2	1	7	1	--	8	--	--	--	1	2	--	--
--	4000	2000	700	240	--	--	1	--	2	--	--	5	--	--	1	1	--	--
--	500	500	--	--	--	--	1	--	1	1	2	--	--	--	--	--	2	--
--	200	100	--	--	--	2	--	6	2	1	7	2	--	--	1	2	3	5
--	--	--	--	--	--	--	1	--	--	--	1	--	--	--	--	--	--	--
--	--	--	--	--	--	--	1	--	1	2	3	--	--	--	1	1	--	--
--	--	--	--	--	--	2	2	--	--	10	--	3	--	--	--	4	1	9
--	200	100	--	--	--	--	1	--	3	1	2	3	1	--	2	1	--	1
--	400	20	--	--	--	--	1	--	2	1	1	--	--	--	--	1	--	--
--	--	--	--	--	--	--	1	--	3	1	8	--	--	--	--	1	--	

TABLE 9

	MEAN PER HOUSEHOLD AND RANGE PER HOUSEHOLD									
	NATION		FULLBLOODS		MIXED		NO FULLBLOODS		ELITE	
	MEAN	RANGE	MEAN	RANGE	MEAN	RANGE	MEAN	RANGE	MEAN	RANGE
Family size	6.27	1-28	6.22	3-27	7.39	2-28	5.51	1-16	6.2	1-15
Adults	3.21	1-21	3.21	1-13	3.76	1-21	2.75	1-14	3.39	1-8
Children	3.05	0-17	3.01	0-17	3.62	0-14	2.75	0-11	3.70	0-11
Full bloods	4.85	0-27	6.22	1-27	4.14	1-27	0.0	0.0	.19	0-3
Half bloods	.52	0-19	0.0	0.0	1.41	0-19	1.94	0-16	1.97	0-10
Quarter bloods	.55	0-15	0.0	0.0	1.08	0-11	2.15	0-14	4.29	0-15
Mixed Negro	.02	0-10	0.0	0.0	.09	0-6	.06	0-10	0.0	0.0
Slaves	.58	0-110	.02	0-7	.32	0-8	.92	0-9	24.51	10-110
Spinners	1.51	0-16	1.49	0-10	1.86	0-7	1.32	0-16	1.80	0-6
Weavers	.92	0-6	.88	0-6	1.22	0-5	.86	0-5	1.34	0-5
Mechanics	.13	0-6	.12	0-3	.17	0-3	.10	0-2	.39	0-6
Cherokee readers	.98	0-16	1.01	0-16	1.13	0-9	.80	0-8	.43	0-3
English readers	.38	0-11	.09	0-7	.47	0-9	1.22	0-11	3.53	0-8

PART II

Slavery

A NOTE
ON AFRICAN SOURCES
OF AMERICAN INDIAN
RACIAL MYTHS

Anyone who reads much in the folklore and mythology of Native Americans will come across myths about the original creation of mankind. These myths vary considerably over time, from region to region and from tribe to tribe, but most of them have two things in common: they seek to explain the origin of the different colors (hence races) of mankind and the origin of the different life-styles (or primary characteristics of culture) of the various races. Many whites who heard these creation myths believed that they were of very ancient origin among the Native Americans, and so apparently did many Native Americans. But it seems unlikely that those which speak of the creation of red, white, and black people could have preceded the discovery of America and the importation of black slaves. Because Europeans in Africa found similar myths among African people, it appears likely that many of the Native American creation myths owe their origin to contact between African slaves and Native Americans after 1620. African creation myths often served the same functions as the Native American creation myths described here, but in Africa the myths mention only two races at creation—black and white.

More needs to be done to draw together and compare all the variations of these creation myths. At the same time, scholars should find these myths useful in tracing the development of separatist movements among those Native Americans who opposed assimilation. Many believers in these myths were obviously convinced that the Great Spirit(s) created the different races and put them on different continents in order to keep them separate. Since each race, from its origin, was allegedly given a different way of life, separatists had a strong argument against acculturation. A theory of polygenesis, used by white racists in the nineteenth century to refuse equality to red and whites (and later browns and yellows), was thus used by Native Americans as a means of preserving ethnic integrity and self-respect. Yet inadvertently, this defensive use of the myths may have played into the hands of those who believed that "you can't change an Indian."

THE LONG DEBATE over the African origin of certain American Indian myths and folktales has recently been summarized by Alan Dundes in "African Tales Among the North American Indians," reprinted in *Mother Wit from the Laughing Barrel: Readings in the Interpretation of Afro-American Folklore* (Englewood Cliffs NJ, 1973). Despite the argument over the African or European origin of some Indian folktales, those making distinctions between red, white, and black men seem demonstrably African. While Stith Thompson's motif-index mentions some African sources for folk literature on the origin of races and colors (A 1614), it does not include African sources for the Indian story of the vocational choices offered to red, white, and black men by the Great Spirit at their creation. Perhaps the most frequently cited of these is the famous Seminole creation myth. First told to white Americans by the aged Seminole chief, Neamathla, in 1823 or 1824, he claimed that it was handed down to him from his forefathers. Thomas L. McKenney, who appears to have been the first to publish this myth in 1838, said it was a "commonly received notion among Indians from the earliest times of which we have any account."[1] Neamathla's story of the separate creations of the red, white, and black people by the Great Spirit and of the vocational choices that separated them had two purposes: first, it supported the desire of the Indians to sustain their own identity and way of life rather than adopt that of white Europeans; and second, it gave to the red man, as "a person of color," a status superior to that of the black man, a necessity forced upon the Indian by the slave status of black people in America and the efforts of white Europeans to place the Indian in the same caste.[2]

---

[1] Thomas L. McKenney and James Hall, *History of the Indian Tribes of North America* (Philadelphia, 1838) 2:38.

[2] For studies that refer to the Neamathla creation myth, see Alan Dundes, "Washington Irving's Version of the Seminole Origin of Races," *Ethnohistory* 9 (Summer 1962) 257-64; William C. Sturtevant, "Seminole Myths of the Origin of Races," *Ethnohistory* 10 (Winter 1963) 80-86; William McLoughlin, "Red Indians, Black Slavery, White Racism," *American Quarterly* 26 (October 1974) 367-85. There are other Indian creation myths dealing with racial differentiations in terms of color, but usually these do not in-

This two-edged myth seems to have been prevalent first among the Indians of the Southeastern United States. It is well known that the Seminoles had a particularly close relationship with black slaves who were either runaways from white masters or captured from the whites by the Indians.[3] The striking similarity between the Seminole myth and African creation myths prevalent on the Gold Coast in the seventeenth centuries clearly indicates African origins. The Gold Coast version (among the Ashanti and Fanti) is probably not the original one, hence the purpose of this note is to stimulate further research into this topic.

Naturally the African version of the myth does not include reference to the creation of the red man, but it serves a similar purpose, namely to prove that God created blacks at the same time as whites and decreed their separate destinies from the beginning of time. The Africans faced the burden of white-imposed colonialism, persecution, and slavery long before the American Indian and sought their own explanation for these differences in the mysterious designs of their Great Spirit. I present here, in inverse order, four versions of the same myth: first, the original version of the Neamathla myth in 1824;[4] second, the version printed by T. E. Bowdich in *Mission from Cape Coast Castle to Ashantee* in 1819; third, the version reported by J. H. Bernardin de St. Pierre in his *Etudes de la Nature* in 1784; and finally, the English version published in 1705 of Willem Bosman's account (printed first in Dutch in 1704), *A New and Accurate Description of the Coast of Guinea*. The similarities speak for themselves and demonstrate that the American Indians sought to establish their place in creation and in the multiracial society of the New World simply by adapting the explanation that the Africans had already established after they came in close contact with white Europeans.

---

clude the selection of vocation. Some of these concern the baking of original man in an oven (underdone creations coming out white, overdone, black, and Indians, just right). Some concern original man's washing (or the material from which he was made being washed) in clean, slightly dirty, or very dirty (muddy, black) water. There are probably African origins for some or all of these myths (usually attributed to the Seminole, Creek, or Cherokee). For some versions of the washing creation myth, see the Dundes article; for some versions of the baking myth, see Sturtevant's article and Melville J. Herskovits, *Man and His Works* (New York, 1948) 68-69.

[3]See Laurence Foster, *Negro-Indian Relationships in the Southeast* (Philadelphia, 1935) and Kenneth W. Porter, *The Negro on the American Frontier* (New York, 1971).

[4]Dundes, in the article cited above, refers to a version of the myth published in London in 1819 that I have not found; "Seminole Origin of Races," 263, n. 7.

In addition, since St. Pierre begins his account with a reference to it, I have added an African (Moorish) version of the interpretation of the "Curse of Canaan" or the "Curse of Ham" from Genesis 9:25. It indicates that even the white American, seeking to use the Old Testament to support his theory of racial superiority, was himself building upon a much older exegesis. While this exegesis did not originate with black Africans, it may well have originated in Africa. It certainly derives from the white enslavement of Africans. But again, its precise date and origin is still undetermined. It suggests another important point for anthropologists and ethnohistorians to keep in mind, namely that Christianity may well have come first to the American Indian from runaway African slaves. Furthermore, if these slaves presented it to the Indians in such terms as the "Curse of Canaan," it is easier to understand why the missionaries may have made so little headway when they reached the Indians with their sacred story of creation and racial differentiations.

I
CHIEF NEAMATHLA'S CREATION MYTH
AS TOLD TO
WILLIAM P. DUVAL IN 1823-1824[5]

Listen, father, and I will tell you how the Great Spirit made man, and how he gave to men of different colours the different employments that we find them engaged in . . . the Master of Life said, we will make man. Man was made, but when he stood up before his maker, he was *white*! The Great Spirit was sorry; he saw that the being he had made was pale and weak; he took pity on him, and therefore did not unmake him, but let him live. He tried again, for he was determined to make a perfect man, but in his endeavour to avoid making another white man, he went into the opposite extreme, and when the second being rose up, and stood before him, he was *black*! The Great Spirit liked the black man less than the white, and he shoved him aside to make room for another trial. Then it was that he made the *red man*; and the red man pleased him.

My father, listen—I have not told you all. In this way the Great Spirit made the white, the black, and the red man, when he put them upon the earth. Here they were—but they were very poor. They had no lodges nor horses, no tools to work with, no traps, nor any thing with which to kill

---

[5]McKenney and Hall, *Indian Tribes of North America*, 2:38-39.

game. All at once, these three men, looking up, saw three large boxes coming down from the sky. They descended very slowly, but at last reached the ground, while these three poor men stood and looked at them, not knowing what to do. Then the Great Spirit spoke and said, "White man, you are pale and weak, but I made you first, and will give you the first choice; go to the boxes, open them and look in, and choose which you will take for your portion." The white man opened the boxes, looked in, and said, "I will take this." It was filled with pens, and ink, and paper, and compasses, and such things as your people now use. The Great Spirit spoke again and said, "Black man, I made you next, but I do not like you. You may stand aside. The Red man is my favourite, he shall come forward and take the next choice; Red man, choose your portion of the things of this world." The red man stepped boldly up and chose a box filled with tomahawks, knives, war clubs, traps, and such things as are useful in war and hunting. The Great Spirit laughed when he saw how well his red son knew how to choose. Then he said to the negro, "You may have what is left, the third box is for you." That was filled with axes, and hoes, with buckets to carry water in, and long whips for driving oxen, which meant that the negro must work for both the red and white man, and it has been so ever since.

II
THOMAS E. BOWDICH'S
VERSION OF THE MYTH, 1819[6]

The Negro tradition of the book and the calabash, cited by St. Pierre, is familiar to every native of these parts, and seems the source of their religious opinions. Impressed that the blind avarice of their forefathers inclined all the favour of the supreme God to white men, they believe themselves to have been committed to the mediating care of subordinate deities, necessarily as inferior to the primary, as they are to Europeans.

---

[6]T. E. Bowdich, *Mission from Cape Coast Castle to Ashantee* (London, 1819); I have cited the 3d edition, London, 1966, 261-62. I wish to thank Joseph P. Reidy of Northern Illinois State University for calling this to my attention. Bowdich's version has frequently been quoted by later authors, often without giving him as the source. See John Beecham, *Ashantee and the Gold Coast* (London, 1841) 172-73 and George MacDonald, *The Gold Coast Past and Present* (London, 1898) 45-46.

As the Ashantee manner of relating this tradition differs a little from that of the Fantee, I will repeat it, on the authority of Odumata and other principal men. In the beginning of the world, God created three white and three black men, with the same number of women; he resolved, that they might not afterwards complain, to give them their choice of good and evil. A large box or calabash was set on the ground, with a piece of paper, sealed up, on one side of it. God gave the black man the first choice, who took the box, expecting it contained every thing, but, on opening it, there appeared only a piece of gold, a piece of iron, and several other metals, of which they did not know the use. The white men opening the paper, it told them every thing. God left the blacks in the bush, but conducted the whites to the water side (for this happened in Africa) communicated with them every night, and taught them to build a small ship which carried them to another country, whence they returned after a long period, with various merchandise to barter with blacks, who might have been the superior people.

III
J. H. BERNARDIN DE SAINT-PIERRE'S
VERSION OF THE MYTH, 1784[7]

On regarde, en général, les nègres comme l'espèce d'hommes la plus infortunée qu'il y ait au monde. En effet, il semble que quelque destinée les condamne à l'esclavage. On croit reconnaître en eux l'effet de cette ancienne malédiction: "Que Chanaan soit maudit! qu'il soit, à l'égard de ses frères, l'esclave des esclaves!" Ils la confirment eux-mêmes par leurs traditions. Selon le Hollandais Bosman, "les nègres de la Guinée disent que Dieu, ayant créé des noirs et des blancs, leur proposa deux dons,

---

[7]J. H. Bernardin de St. Pierre, *Etudes de la Nature* (Paris, 1784); I have cited the 1834 edition of his *Ouevres Completes*, ed. L. Aime-Martin, 3:328. For readers who have no French, here is my translation: "In general, the blacks are regarded as the most unfortunate members of the human race. Indeed, it appears that some fate has condemned them to slavery. We seem to recognize in them the effect of that ancient malediction: 'Cursed be Canaan! a servant of servants shall he be unto his brethren!' They confirm it themselves by their folklore. According to the Dutchman, Bosman, 'the blacks of Guinea say that God, having created black as well as white men, offered them two gifts of knowledge, either how to acquire gold or how to read and write; and as God gave the choice to the blacks, they chose gold and left to the whites the knowledge of letters— which God granted them. However, angered by their covetousness for gold, He resolved at the same time that the whites should have eternal dominion over them and that they should be obliged to serve them as slaves.' "

savoir, ou de posséder l'or, ou de savoir lire et écrire; et comme Dieu donna le choix aux noirs, ils choisirent l'or, et laissèrent aux blancs la connaissance des lettres: ce que Dieu leur accorda. Mais, qu'étant irrité de cette convoitise qu'ils avaient pour l'or, résolut en même temps que les blancs domineraient éternellement sur eux, et qu'ils seraient obligés de leur servir d'esclaves."

IV
WILLIAM BOSMAN'S
VERSION IN 1698 (1705)[8]

Almost all the Coast Negroes believe in one true God, to Whom they attribute the Creation of the World and all things in it. . . . They are not obliged to themselves nor the Tradition of their Ancestors for their Opinion, rude as it is, but to their daily Conversation with the Europeans who from time to time have continually endeavoured to implant this Notion in them . . . a great part of the Negroes believe that Man was made by Anansie, that is, a great Spider; the rest attribute the Creation of Man to God, which they assert to have happened in the following manner: They tell us that in the beginning God created Black as well as White Men; thereby not only hinting but endeavouring to prove that their Race was as soon in the World as ours; and to bestow a yet greater Honour on themselves they tell us that God, having created these two sorts of Men, offered two sorts of Gifts, viz. Gold and the Knowledge of Arts or Reading and Writing, giving the Blacks the first Election, who chose Gold and left the Knowledge of Letters to the White. God granted their Request, but being incensed at their Avarice, resolved that the Whites should for ever be their Masters and they be obliged to wait on them as their Slaves.

V
THOMAS E. BOWDICH
ON THE "CURSE OF HAM"
AS TOLD BY THE MOORS, 1819[9]

Amongst other observations, I recollect the Moors to have said that Moses spoke like God, that Abraham was the friend of God, that Jesus

---

[8]William Bosman, *A New and Accurate Description of the Coast of Guinea*, trans. from the Dutch (London, 1705) 146-47. The original version, printed in Utrecht in 1704, was based on Bosman's experiences in West Africa in the 1690s.

[9]Bowdich, *Cape Coast Castle to Ashantee*, 273.

was a spirit of God, but that Mahomet was the best beloved of God. . . .
I questioned them concerning the origin of nations; they told me, that
Japhet was the most active in covering the nakedness of his father, which
Ham discovered, and thence the subjection of black men the descendants of Ham, to Europeans the descendants of Japhet. Shem, from
whom they were themselves descended, they said, was neither so good
or bad as his brothers, and therefore his children enjoyed a medium of
endowment and favour.

COMMENT

These various myths share a belief in polygenesis because they derive
from a similar need to account for black slavery, which is not conducive
to the belief that God created all men as brothers or as the children of
one original mother. The African, by setting the creation in Africa and
the Indian by setting it in America (among his forefathers) demonstrate
the ethnocentrism inherent in all mythology. While the Moor, like the
Indian, is able to find an intermediate status for himself between the
dominant white and the enslaved black people, the Ashanti and Fanti
can only explain their position in terms of God's anger and an unfortunate aboriginal choice of their own. The fact that the Ashanti were skilled
metal workers (particularly in gold and iron) and the Indians were
skilled hunters and trappers, explains their vocational choices at the creation. However, nothing can satisfactorily explain the mysterious will of
God either in creating different races or in allowing whites to attain those
technological skills that he used to dominate other people. Further study
of African creation myths is obviously necessary before we can fully understand their significance in the world of white, black, and Amerindian
history.

RED INDIANS, BLACK SLAVERY,
AND WHITE RACISM:
INTERRACIAL TENSIONS
AMONG SLAVEHOLDING INDIANS

In certain respects the new interest in Native American history followed the renewed interest in black history. Americans are trying hard to face up to the fact that this is a multiracial society. We first faced this fact in the Revolutionary era, and lived up to some of its possibilities by abolishing slavery in all of the Northern states. The Southern states continued to debate the evils of slavery until 1831, but most such debates centered on how quickly the freedmen could be removed from the United States. The first American Indian policy had as its avowed goal the integration of Native Americans as citizens on terms of full equality. Henry Knox, Washington's secretary of war, estimated in 1789 that it would take about fifty years to "incorporate" all of the Indians east of the Mississippi. Ironically, just fifty years later, the removal policy was finally completed.

By a tragic compromise, the American Constitution was permitted to include the recognition of black slaves as human property. Because the Revolution was fought as much for the sacred right of property as for the inalienable rights of man, the conflict over racial equality in a multiracial society persisted until 1865 in terms of slavery and continues today in terms of civil rights. This conflict in America's fundamental values was given added complexity by the decision of the Southeastern Indian nations to adopt the institution of black slavery. After all, it was the basis of the agricultural system of their white neighbors, and it certainly helped to distinguish red men from black men—a distinction needed to prevent whites from lumping blacks and Indians as "people of color." Furthermore, once black slavery became institutionalized among the Southeastern tribes, the runaway slave could no longer find a haven there and the Indian nations were no longer a threat to slaveowners for this reason.

This essay explores some of the cultural confrontations that arose from slaveholding among the Native Americans. The most tragic consequence was the division among Native Americans themselves over this question and their fratricidal warfare during the Civil War. After 1865 some Southeastern tribes were forced, against their will, to accept freed blacks as equal citizens while others successfully opposed this. The oppressed are continually turned against each other by their oppressors.

MANY QUESTIONS HAVE BEEN RAISED about black-Indian relations in North America.[1] None of them has been really answered yet—or rather, there are contradictory answers so far. Some historians have argued that until whites interfered, the Indians were generally friendly toward blacks; others have argued that the Indians always considered black people as the allies of the whites and hence feared and disliked them; still others have said that the Indians learned to look upon black people the same way white people did and so considered them to be little more than another form of property, like horses and cattle. Some historians have said that various Indian tribes in North America were generally friendly toward runaway black slaves and provided a refuge for them. Others say that the Indians usually joined the white slave hunters in tracking down runaways and returning them to their masters for the rewards offered. Some historians have claimed Indians never killed, tortured, or scalped slaves in warfare; others have asserted there is evidence they did all three.

These contradictory answers to black-Indian relations (especially during the Colonial Period) result from the fact that there is far too little evidence upon which to draw any general conclusions. There are records, which show that Indians sometimes welcomed blacks into their tribes and sometimes did not; that sometimes blacks joined with Indians in making war on white communities; and that sometimes blacks joined

---

[1]The most extensive writing on this subject has been by Kenneth W. Porter in a long series of articles starting in 1932 in the *Journal of Negro History*. Many of these have recently been anthologized as *The Negro on the American Frontier* (New York: Arno Press and the New York Times, 1971). The only book devoted to this subject is Laurence Foster, *Negro-Indian Relationships in the Southeast* (Philadelphia: University of Pennsylvania, 1935). Foster was concerned primarily with the peculiar case of the Seminole Indians. The standard histories of the other Southeastern Indian nations—Creek, Cherokee, Choctaw, and Chickasaw—offer some scattered details and unsupported generalizations but no extensive treatment. Gary B. Nash has a short summary of "African-Indian Contact" in the colonial period in *Red, White and Black: The Peoples of Early America* (Englewood Cliffs NJ: Prentice-Hall, 1974) 290-97. See also Lerone Bennett, Jr., "The Road Not Taken: Colonies Turn Fateful Fork by Systematically Dividing the Races," *Ebony* 25 (August 1970) 71-77.

their white masters in fighting against the Indians. There is evidence that blacks were adopted into some tribes, intermarried among them, and became important chiefs and councillors. There is also evidence that other tribes simply made chattel of any black men they caught and treated them the same way white men did.

One reason for the conflicting evidence on black-Indian relations is that there were a great many different Indian nations in North America, and they did not all treat black men the same. Furthermore, Indians who were friendly to blacks at one period in their history often later became hostile toward them. For example, it is generally agreed that the Southeastern Indians at first welcomed runaway slaves because they had important skills that were helpful to the Indians: for example, they could speak English and thus serve as interpreters and negotiators with whites; they also knew how to repair guns and traps, to shoe horses, to improve agricultural methods, to spin and weave, to make butter, to build houses, barns, and wagons.[2] Yet by 1820 most of the Southeastern Indians were practicing the same kind of black slavery in their communities as the neighboring Southern white communities.

Among these slaveholding Indians we do not know to what extent black slaves had an easier life than among white slaveholders. Many slaves did run away from white masters because they thought they would have an easier life among the Indians. Moreover, many travelers' accounts and missionary reports in the nineteenth century state that Indian slaveholders did not work their black slaves as hard as white slaveholders did. Nevertheless, there are scattered accounts that tell of Indian slaveowners who whipped, maimed, hung, and burned slaves as late as the 1850s in the Indian Territory (now Oklahoma).[3] No one denies

---

[2]These and other generalizations can be found scattered through the various works on the Southern Indians by James Mooney, Charles Royce, Grant Foreman, Angie Debo, Grace Woodward, Marion Starkey et al. See also Charles M. Hudson, ed., *Red, White and Black* (Athens GA: Southern Anthropological Society, 1971); Leonard Bloom, "The Acculturation of the Eastern Cherokees," *North Carolina Historical Review* 19 (October 1942): 323-58; David Corkran, *The Cherokee Frontier* (Norman: University of Oklahoma, 1962); Henry T. Malone, *Cherokees of the Old South* (Athens: University of Georgia, 1951); John R. Swanton, *The Indians of the Southeastern United States* (Washington: Bureau of American Ethnology, 1946).

[3]For accounts of slave hangings and burnings in the Cherokee Nation in 1805, see John Howard Payne Papers, Newberry Library, Chicago, 2:45; for an account of hanging and burning among the Choctaws in 1859, see Charles K. Whipple, *The Relation of the A.B.C.F.M. to Slavery* (Boston: R. F. Wallcut, 1871) 202-203.

that most Southeastern Indians frequently engaged in buying, selling, and stealing slaves both from white slaveowners and from each other. Yet at the same time, there is ample evidence that the Seminole Indians in Florida were notably hospitable to runaway slaves. Even when blacks had Seminole masters, they were pretty much free to live by themselves and run their own black communities, paying only nominal annual tribute to their owners. During the great Seminole Wars of 1817-1819 and 1835-1842, many of the leading warriors, chiefs, and councillors were black men or men of mixed black and Indian ancestry. In fact, many accounts by United States Army commanders say that it was the black warriors who were the most skillful, determined, and brave; without their help, the Seminoles could never have held out so long against the American armies. At the same time, it is also evident that the Creeks, who joined with the United States troops to conquer the Seminoles, did so in order to obtain black slaves from them since the army commanders told the Creeks they could keep as slaves any blacks they captured.[4]

It is too soon to unravel all of these contradictions or to offer any simple sociological theories to explain them all. Until there are more detailed monographs of the various Indian nations and scholars know a lot more about their relationships to black people, there will be no answers to these complex questions. At the moment all one can say is that some Indian tribes had very good relationships with black people and some did not.

Without trying to offer any final answer as to why this was so, I do want to add something to what William S. Willis has written about black-Indian relations in his well-known article entitled, "Divide and Rule: Red, White and Black in the Southeast."[5] Willis has made it clear that one reason why some Indians were hostile toward black people was that white people purposefully tried to create fear and hostility between

---

[4]See Foster, *Negro-Indian Relationships*, and Edwin C. McReynolds, *The Seminoles* (Norman: University of Oklahoma, 1954).

[5]Willis's article originally appeared in the *Journal of Negro History* 48 (July 1963): 157-76. It has since been reprinted in several anthologies. Willis also indicates that white colonists may have given up enslaving Indians (or shipped Indian captives off to slavery in the West Indies) because they believed that Indian slaves might stir up black slaves to revolt or run away. Willis does not mention that after 1800 there is ample evidence that Indian nations, like the Creeks and Seminoles, often used their black slaves when fighting against white men or against each other.

them. As Willis says, the white colonial governors, settlers, and army commanders in the Carolinas in the eighteenth century deliberately spread frightening stories of Indian cruelty among their slaves, armed slaves to kill Indians, and paid Indians to capture and return runaway slaves. This was all a very conscious and calculated part of white policy in the years when the Indians and blacks in the Southeast outnumbered the white settlers and could, together, have wiped out the whites. But while this policy of divide and rule succeeded among the Creeks and Cherokees to some extent, it did not succeed among the Seminoles; they lived in Spanish Florida under a rather different social order.

Since the Seminoles were, according to all reports, more friendly toward blacks than any other Southern tribe, we obviously need to ask why. Was it the difference between the institution of slavery as practiced in Spanish and English colonies? Was it Spain's different cultural attitude toward racial miscegenation? Was it a less rigid or clearly established economy in Florida and hence lack of interest in recapturing runaway slaves (most of whom, incidentally, came to the Seminoles from Georgia and not from Spanish slaveowners)? Did the Seminoles as outcasts or "runaways" from the Creek nation in Georgia need the blacks to aid them against Creek raids (some of the blacks were runaway Creek slaves)? Were the Seminoles too weak to control the slaves; had they no economic use for them; did the terrain, soil, and climate make it difficult to utilize slave labor on farms or plantations?

It appears from the writing of Kenneth Porter and Laurence Foster that none of these factors was so important as the political necessities, especially after 1776. Florida was not well settled or defended by its European owners; Americans were eager to encroach upon it. Both Spain and England (when they controlled Florida between 1776 and 1783) used the Seminoles and their slaves as buffers against the expansionist tendencies of the Georgians. If, in pre-Revolutionary Carolina, white imperialists had consciously divided Indians against blacks for survival, so in Florida conscious white imperialist policy encouraged black and Indian fraternization and solidarity along the American border (even providing them with arms and forts) to fight against other whites. In both cases—Carolina and Georgia—red and black men were consciously used by white men to foster white goals.

After 1819, when the United States gained control of Florida, the Seminoles and their slaves fought shoulder to shoulder against American

Indian removal policies, which meant a return to former Georgian and Creek masters for black runaways or their descendants. Nevertheless, even if black slaves had a somewhat easier and freer life among the Seminoles, they were still slaves, not equals. We must consequently look for some other factors at work among the Indians besides calculated white policy—something that caused them to make a distinction between themselves and black people, something that was less deliberate, more unconscious, than the policies and actions Willis describes. This factor, very simply, was acquired racial prejudice or racism.

We know from Winthrop Jordan's study, among others, that Europeans had developed racial prejudices against Africans long before there were slaveholding British colonies in North America. The first time Indians ever saw black men, they appeared as the slaves of Spanish, French, or English masters. Consequently, without any conscious policy of divide and rule, the white man showed the Indian by his actions that he considered darker people inferior to white-skinned people. It did not take the Indians long to discover that white Europeans were as ready to enslave red people as black.

Of course, most North American Indians had practiced a variety of slavery for centuries before white men arrived. It was not the institution of slavery itself that was new or startling (though the European forms of it were very different in their characteristics). What was new was the racist quality of it—the assumption that slavery was not simply the result of being captured by an enemy but rather was assumed to be the lot of all darker peoples when they came into contact with whites. What I am suggesting is that after the white man arrived in North America, each Indian tribe suddenly faced a new problem in dealing with enemies. And this problem (which needs more study) was due not to the Indians' inferior firepower against white warriors but to their darker skin, a symbol to the European of inferior intellect and ability.

In British North America this was not at first a serious problem because the British tried to treat the Indians as independent nations whose chiefs were to be courted as allies against the Spanish or French. Hence the British pretended to treat the Indian chiefs with some respect, to give them presents, to make treaties with them, to bring influential chiefs to England to meet the king and have their portraits painted by Sir Joshua Reynolds and other court painters (and sometimes to give them a black slave or two as a royal present).[6] At first, perhaps, the respect was real since it stemmed from fear; later it stemmed primarily from economic motives. Seldom were heathen savages accepted as social equals. The English in particular were contemptuous of them, treating them as lackeys for the fur trade and despising the French and Spanish who took intermarriage and Indian land rights seriously. Smaller tribes on the East Coast, the first to recognize this, were destroyed and their people enslaved when they tried to drive the English out. Larger tribes on the interior managed (often by playing their own game of divide and survive among the rival empires) to maintain their self-respect and their independence of action, at least up to the time of the American Revolution. But by siding with the British in 1776, all the Indians east of the Mississippi went down to final defeat. They lost their independence when the white Americans won theirs. Some of the Indian nations, like the Creeks and Seminoles in the Southeast and the Delawares and Shawnees in the Old Northwest, managed to wage destructive wars against the Americans from time to time thereafter, but even these tribes knew that they would never again have total freedom. They were simply fighting to avoid total extermination.

The policy the new American nation adopted to deal with the defeated Indians after 1790 was based upon the view that the Indians would give up their old way of life and adapt themselves to the ways of the white man.[7] Because American intellectuals like Knox, Washington, and Jefferson still held the romantic view of the noble savage, they believed that the Indian was potentially, at least, the equal of the white man. The Indian's problem was not that he was innately inferior, but that he was still a savage. He needed only to be civilized and Christianized to become capable of full citizenship and equality in the American Republic. The Indian policy of the age of Washington and Jefferson was directed toward the ultimate amalgamation, incorporation, or integration of the Indians into white America as equals—a form of extinction, no doubt, as Ber-

---

[6]See Malone, *Cherokees of the Old South*, 60-83.

[7]For early federal Indian policy, see George D. Harmon, *Sixty Years of Indian Affairs, 1789-1850* (Chapel Hill: University of North Carolina, 1941); Francis P. Prucha, *American Indian Policy, 1790-1834* (Cambridge: Harvard University Press, 1964); and Bernard W. Sheehan, *Seeds of Extinction* (Chapel Hill: University of North Carolina, 1973).

nard Sheehan has demonstrated, but on the surface a benevolent policy, at least in theory.[8]

But there were two fatal flaws in this policy: first, most Indians opposed it, and second, white frontier Americans opposed it. Frontier whites did not hold the same view of the Indian that Eastern intellectuals did. Far from seeing the Indian as a noble savage and potential equal, they saw him as a degraded savage and an encumbrance on coveted land. From 1790 to 1838 there was a fierce struggle in America between the Eastern elite and the Western frontiersmen over what the proper policy toward the Indian should be. The frontier people wanted to exterminate them or drive them out while the Easterners wanted to civilize them. No one asked the Indian what he wanted.

What the Indians wanted was clear enough. They wanted to be left alone to live out their lives in their own way on what little land was left to them in the East. Unfortunately, so little land remained to them that they could no longer live by hunting or even by a combination of hunting, fishing, and small-scale communal farming. Realizing that they would now have to adopt an agrarian way of life to survive, the Indians accepted from the federal government the plows, hoes, spinning wheels, looms, and other forms of technical assistance that Washington and Jefferson sent to them as part of the federal policy for economic acculturation. The Indians also accepted, though somewhat less willingly, the white missionaries who wanted to bring them Christianity. They accepted them because they came with promises to build schools—to teach them reading, writing, and arithmetic so that they could better cope with government officials and surrounding whites. Many missionary establishments also included model farms where Indian school children were taught how to become farmers or farmers' wives at the same time that they were taught the academic skills they needed to do business with frontier neighbors. But when the missionaries insisted on trying to convert them to Christianity—that is, to change Indian beliefs, values, and views of human nature and the supernatural—then the Indians drew back.

---

[8]One may argue that American federal Indian policy was motivated by fear as well as by unconscious envy. I think Prucha and Sheehan are mistaken in their emphasis on its essential benevolence. In practice the policy was certainly based primarily upon selfishness, greed, and contempt among frontier politicians and voters, to whom federal policy makers were usually willing to yield.

A famous confrontation took place in 1805 between the Seneca chief, Red Jacket, and a Presbyterian missionary named Cram in New York State.[9] The Reverend Cram told a council of the Six Nations of Iroquois that he had come to bring them civilization and Christianity. He said there was one true way of religion, one true book of revelation, and one true God whom he had come to tell them about. After he had finished speaking, Red Jacket stood up to answer him:

> Brother, you say there is but one way to worship and serve the Great Spirit. If there is but one Religion, why do you white people differ so much about it? Why not all agree, as you can all view the book? Brother, we do not understand these things. We are told your Religion was given to your forefathers and has been handed down from father to son. We also have a Religion that was given to us, and we worship accordingly. It teaches us to be thankful for all the favors we receive, to love each other and be united. We never quarrel about religion.

Then Red Jacket went on to make a very significant point about red and white people and how they differed:

> The Great Spirit has made us all, but he has made a difference between his red and white children. He has given us different complexions and different customs. To you he has discovered the arts; to us they have been kept out of sight. We know these things are so, and since he has made us different in other respects, why may we not conclude that he has given us a different Religion according to our understanding[?] The Great Spirit does right. He knows what is best for his children.

Red Jacket's people were few and weak and wished only to be left alone. But farther west, near the Great Lakes, the Shawnees were still powerful and still hoped, with British aid from Canada, to force white Americans back east of the Appalachians. They consequently took a somewhat less conciliatory view of Indian-white relations. In 1807 a chief named The Trout delivered a speech to the Shawnees and their allies in which he told them what the Great Spirit had said to him in a dream or vision. In essence, God told him to reject the American policy of assimilation:

> My Children [the Great Spirit said], you are to have very little intercourse with

---

[9]National Archives Microfilm, microcopy 221, "Letters Received by the Secretary of War, Main Series, 1801-1871," roll 7, frames 2314-2318. See also Anthony F. C. Wallace, *The Death and Rebirth of the Seneca* (New York: Random House, 1969) for a first-rate study of Indian acculturation and Christianization.

the whites. They are not your Father, as you call [their President], but your brethren. . . . I am the Father of the English, of the French, of the Spaniards and of
the Indians. I created the first man, who was the common Father of all those people as well as yourselves. . . . But the Americans I did not make. They are not my
Children. But the children of the Evil Spirit. They grew from the scum of the
great Water when it was troubled by the Evil Spirit. And the froth was driven into
the woods by a strong east wind. They are numerous, but I hate them. They are
unjust. They have taken away your lands which were not made for them.[10]

A few years after this speech, the Shawnees joined with the British under
the great chief, Tecumseh, and tried to drive the Americans out of their
homeland. In that war they were joined by many other tribes between
the Appalachians and the Mississippi, from the Great Lakes to the Gulf
of Mexico. It was a war for both political and cultural survival. These
Indians were willing to take from the white man what was useful, but
they did not want to be assimilated, to lose their own values and religion,
to become swallowed up and incorporated in the westward march of the
Euro-American.

The important point here is that in this struggle to maintain their
own identity, the Indians came to some understanding in their own
minds about the differences between the various races of mankind that
the Great Spirit had (or had not) created. There were many ways to do
this. If they were few and weak, the Indians could conclude, as Red
Jacket did, that the Great Spirit had made Indians and Europeans of different colors because He meant them each to live in their own separate
ways; they were not to oppress, destroy, or intermingle because, though
they were different, they were all equal in God's eyes. If they were a
strong people, they might assume that their God was different from and
superior to the white man's God; in fact, like The Trout, they might conclude that the white Americans were the children of the Devil, the Evil
Spirit. The problem was complicated by the fact that there were three
races, not two, in America. And this implied not separate but equal, nor
inferior and superior, but some kind of hierarchy, especially since black
men seemed doomed to slavery.

In the northern part of the United States where the Seneca and Shawnee lived, there were so few black people that multiracialism was not a

---

[10]National Archives Microfilm, microcopy 222, "Letters Received by the Secretary
of War, Unregistered Series, 1789-1861," roll 2, frames 0859-0861.

significant problem, especially since slavery was forbidden in the Northwest Territory and abolished north of the Mason-Dixon line. But in the Southern part of the United States, where the Cotton Kingdom was spreading westward onto the land of the Creeks, Cherokees, Choctaws, and Chickasaws, it was not only a significant but a growing problem. This multiracial issue was complicated by the growing tendency of white Southerners to insist that black slavery was a blessing rather than a curse. Moreover, as the Southern Indians struggled to adapt themselves to agriculture, the form of agriculture they were inclined to imitate (and encouraged to imitate) was the Southern plantation system. Matters ultimately reached the point where a federal Indian agent said in an official report that the best and fastest way to civilize the Indians would be to give each Indian family a couple of black slaves.[11] Political patronage being what it was, and the American Democratic party being so successful in antebellum years, it is not surprising that most of the federal agents appointed to live among the Southern Indians and direct the government's acculturation policy were Southern-born slaveholders who did their best to set their wards a good example by establishing their own slave plantations within the grounds of the federal agency in each tribe.

In addition, many of the missionaries who came to bring Christianity to the Southern Indians were themselves slaveholding Methodists and Baptists. But at the same time, these Southern missionaries were in competition with better-financed and more completely staffed mission agencies established by Northern religious associations. These Northern missionaries assumed that the Northern way of life (specifically the New England way) was the way ordered by God for all Americans (if not for all the world).[12] These Northern-based missionaries discovered with consternation that the Southern Indians were making the great mistake of adopting a plan of civilization that included the wicked sin of slave-

---

[11]The statement made by George M. Butler, Cherokee Indian agent, in his annual report to the secretary of war, 1859, reads: "I believe if every family of the wild roving tribes were to own a negro man and woman who would teach them to cultivate the soil . . . it would tend more to civilize them than any other plan that could be adopted."

[12]See Robert F. Berkhofer, *Salvation and the Savage* (University of Kentucky, 1965) and Robert T. Lewit, "Indian Missions and Antislavery Sentiments: A Conflict of Evangelical and Humanitarian Ideals," *Mississippi Valley Historical Review* 50 (1963-1964): 39-55. Indian missions begaⁱ ⁱn earnest shortly after 1800, sparked by the evangelistic zeal of the Second Great Awakening.

holding. Thus even those Indians who were willing to listen to missionary teaching were confused by conflicting programs for their improvement, as if the myriad sectarian divisions among Christians were not confusing enough.

To take only one example out of many in which Northern missionaries and Southern Indians came into conflict, we may cite the case of the Reverend Lee Compere. Compere was employed by the Boston-based foreign mission board directed by the Baptists.[13] In 1826 he established a mission station among the Creeks in Alabama. Within two years he had built up a small church consisting of the members of his own family, two or three old Creek women, and a large group of black slaves owned by the Creeks. Black slaves were often the first and most devoted converts of Christian missionaries because they understood English better than their Indian masters and because they found certain aspects of Christianity important to them in their effort to discover their own place in God's scheme of things.

The Reverend Compere also tried to maintain a small school, but he discovered that the Creek slaveowners did not like to have him teaching or preaching to their black slaves. Some of these Creek chiefs (or "Kings") forbade their slaves to come to the mission station. On 18 May 1828, Compere wrote home to Boston a sad fact:

> Persecution has reared its hideous head, and not only threatened but bound and whipped and tortured some poor creatures who had been in the habit of worshipping the God of Heaven with us. . . . Yesterday . . . my poor family . . . as they were assembled for worship in their usual way in my absence, with a few coloured persons, a band of savage monsters rushed in upon them, seized the poor black people, bound them with cords & belts and such other things as were convenient to them; they were then led out one by one to a post in the yard and beat[en] unmercifully, on which post the blood yet remains as a witness against them.

When he returned, Compere questioned those Indians who were involved in the beating of his black church members. He received two explanations: first, "that two of the Principal Chiefs were the most obstinate opposers" of his missionary work and second, "that they said if they allowed the black people the liberty [of attending Christian wor-

---

[13]Compere's letters are among the archives of the Baptist Board of Foreign Missions, American Baptist Historical Society, Rochester, New York.

ship] that the Indians would go and hear preaching and then the Kings of the Towns would lose their authority." Indeed, some Creeks might become Christians, and, considering their old chiefs pagans or heathen, refuse to respect them anymore.

Compere then asked why this had suddenly occurred after he had been there two years. He was told that the incident "originated in phrensy, bordering on despair. . . . All the white men that came into their country said they were their friends, that the Government called them their children, and yet they had been promised many things which had not been done for them, and therefore the Indians did not believe that white people were, any of them, their friends, that it was not worth their while to think about worshipping God for . . . they would be destroyed anyhow." Here the Creeks were referring to the government's new plan to remove them from their homeland and have them continue their acculturation west of the Mississippi. Soon after this Compere gave up his mission work among the Creeks as an impossible task. Before he left, though, he made an interesting comment on the whole situation. He concluded that the government's policy of trying to civilize and Christianize the Indians so that they could be integrated into the white population as citizens was futile in the Southern states:

> . . . were they amalgamated with the white population . . . notwithstanding all their present improvement [in civilization], their situation would be an unfortunate one, for their descendants could not expect to enjoy those facilities for improvement which would be so essential to their benefit [like schools, churches, political suffrage]. They would be viewed [by whites] as a coloured population and that of itself would create a perpetual barrier to their [integration].

Compere was correct. It was all very well for the Eastern intellectuals to talk about the noble savage and what a good citizen he would make once he was educated and converted to Christianity; however, the white frontier South had no intention whatever of allowing such a program to succeed. Civilizing the Indians would never change the frontiersman's attitude toward them. They were not only heathen savages ("You can't change an Indian"), they were also of a different and darker race. The governor of Georgia had made this perfectly plain four years before Compere wrote to his missionary board about it. Governor George M. Troup sent a letter to the secretary of war in 1824 in which he told him frankly what he thought of the federal policy of integration:

[As for Indian] incorporation and amalgamation with our [white] society [in Georgia] . . . the answer is that if such a scheme were practicable at all, the utmost rights and privileges which public opinion would concede to the Indians would fix them in a middle station between the negro and the white man, and that as long as they survived this degradation, without the possibility of attaining the elevation of the latter, they would gradually sink to the condition of the former—a point of degeneracy below which they could not fall. . . .[14]

The secretary of war at this time was John C. Calhoun, often considered the major architect of the new federal Indian policy of removal. Historians have not yet faced the importance of increasing racism in the development of this major shift in policy.

The doctrine of white supremacy was well known to the Indians long before Governor Troup explained it so frankly to the secretary of war. Consequently it is not surprising that some Indians evolved a different theory of the creation of man from those of Red Jacket and The Trout to take into account the multiracial situation they faced. One Indian shaman or medicine man explained it to a missionary in these words:

. . . in the beginning the Great Spirit created three men and placed them in a state of trial, forbidding them to eat of the fruit of a certain tree. But in the absence of their creator, they made an examination and concluded that the fruit was good. Accordingly, they took, each of them, an apple. But one of them put his into his pocket untested. Another did the same after eating a piece of his. The third devoured his entire.

When the Great Spirit came back, he perceived that the apples were gone and became displeased. "Did I not tell you," says he, "not to eat of that fruit?" Whereupon the [first] one took his apple from his pocket [untouched]. Unto him the Great Spirit said, "I give you the bible and knowledge of letters to guide you in the troubles you will fall into." Then the other took out his [apple] partly eaten. For his disobedience the Great Spirit changed the color of his skin and gave him His law in his *heart* only. The third, because of his having devoured the whole of his [apple] was blacked all over and left without moral obligation.[15]

---

[14]Walter Lowrie, ed., *American State Papers: Indian Affairs* (Washington: Gales and Seaton, 1834) 2: 475-76. Troup's statement was nothing new to the Cherokees and other Southern tribes. For years the courts of Georgia and Tennessee (and the territorial courts in Alabama and Mississippi) had treated Indians like blacks in refusing to accept their testimony as evidence.

[15]Francis L. Barker to the Reverend Solomon Peck, 12 January 1850, Northern Baptist Board of Missions. Barker was a missionary to the remnant of the Shawnees in Kansas, some of whom appear to have owned slaves. A very interesting variation on this syncretic creation myth was first printed in 1819 and attributed to the Seminoles. Two articles discussing this Seminole myth deserve attention: Alan Dundes, "Washington

Clearly the Indians had heard missionaries explain the Christian version of creation and the fall of man in the Garden of Eden. But in this syncretic version, the emphasis is not upon Original Sin; no Devil or Indian Eve appears. The snake in this Edenic garden is racism, and the biblical story has been adapted to deal less with sin than with the complexities of a multiracial world. God, if not the author of Original Sin, is the author here of an ineradicable hierarchy of races.

Having been conquered by superior European numbers, firepower, technology, and cunning, the Indian was ready to admit that the white man had certain advantages that stemmed from his knowledge of how to read and write. But in order to save himself from total degradation, the Indian gave himself a position in the human hierarchy above that of the black slave. The Great Spirit, while changing his people from white to red and denying them the knowledge of reading and writing, nevertheless wrote the divine law in their hearts.[16] Only the black man was reduced to the spiritual blankness of animals. This was what the institution of black slavery, the example of white racism, and the teachings of Christianity had done for the acculturation of the Indian by 1850.

It is tragic that this theory of innate racial differences was forced upon American society by the prejudices of white Europeans and ironic that the only way the Amerindian could discover to keep himself from annihilation was to develop a theory of multiple creation or polygenesis. The theory of polygenesis was utilized by whites in pre-Civil War America to justify white supremacy and black slavery. The abolitionists insisted that God had made only one race of man, that all of the human species were descended from Adam and Eve, and that because God "made of one blood all nations," no man of any color had the right to enslave another man of a different complexion. Southern proslavery Christians insisted that, at least since the Deluge, God had cursed the children of Ham to slavery and turned them black. But pseudo-scientific racists, North and South, argued that the various races had been created sepa-

---

Irving's Version of the Seminole Origin of Races," *Ethnohistory* 9 (Fall 1962): 257-64, and W. Sturtevant, "Seminole Myths of the Origin of Races," *Ethnohistory* 10 (Winter 1963): 80-86. I have discovered another version of this myth, which is included as an appendix to this essay for the light it sheds on the issue under consideration.

[16]It is possible that these Indians had heard Mormon missionaries preach about God's curse on the Lamanites.

rately; they might even be different species. In any case, archaeological evidence proved that black people had been slaves to the Caucasians since the beginning of recorded history.[17]

Caught in an impossible dilemma not of his making, the Indian ended up on the side of the white Southern racist who was *his* enemy as well as the black man's. In order to understand what this meant for the multiracial society of the Southeastern United States, we need only look at the development of black slavery among the Cherokee Indians (generally conceded to have become the "most civilized" of all the Indian nations). The Cherokees were located chiefly in the northwestern part of Georgia and the southeastern corner of Tennessee. Numbering twelve to fifteen thousand, they were among the largest of the Southern tribes. They were also the most eager and skillful in adapting to the white man's ways. Though they lost much of their original land after 1777 in various treaties, they generally struck shrewd bargains for it and became the richest Indian nation in the United States. They also took the greatest advantage of the federal government's gifts of technical assistance in order to shift from a hunting to a subsistence farming economy.[18] Natu-

---

[17]See William Stanton, *The Leopard's Spots* (Chicago: University of Chicago, 1960). The federal agent to the Cherokees, Return J. Meigs, reported in 1805, before slavery was deeply entrenched among them, that they already had clear-cut notions about the separate creation of whites and Indians: "Many of the Cherokees think that they are not derived from the same stock as the whites, that they are favorites of the great spirit and that he never intended they should live the laborious lives of the whites." National Archives Microfilm, microcopy 208, "Records of the Cherokee Indian Agency in Tennessee, 1801-1835," 13 February 1805. Meigs, being a good Jeffersonian, believed in monogenesis. But the Indians' feelings were shared by the white frontiersmen for different reasons. A New England missionary to the Cherokees reported in 1818: "The sentiment very generally prevails among the white people near the southern tribes (and perhaps some farther to the north) that the Indian is by nature radically different from all other men and that this difference presents an insurmountable barrier to his civilization." Cited in the Brainerd Journal, 24 June 1818, MS in the Papers of the American Board of Commissioners for Foreign Missions, Houghton Library, Harvard University, Cambridge MA.

[18]The Cherokees, like most Southern tribes, had never been nomadic hunters, and as fur traders they had given only minimal attention to farming during the Colonial Era. After 1800 Indian men or black slaves replaced Indian women as the primary figures in farming. As Winthrop Jordan points out, the Indian dared not allow his women to work in the fields as soon as he sought "civilization" and equality, for in the South the only women who worked in the fields were black slaves (at least among the more respectable whites). W. D. Jordan, *The White Man's Burden* (New York: Oxford, 1974) 49-50, 66.

rally, the agricultural system that they adopted was the Southern slaveholding plantation system. As one of their leading chiefs wrote in 1826,

> Cotton is generally raised for domestic consumption and a few have grown it for market and have realized very good profits. . . . The African slaves are generally mostly held by half breeds and full Indians of distinguished talents. In this class the principal value of property is retained and their farms are conducted in the same style with the southern white farmers of equal ability . . . Cherokees on the Tennessee River have already commenced to trade in cotton and grow the article in large plantations, and they have realized very handsome profits. All those who have it in their power are making preparations to grow it for a market, and it will soon be the staple commodity of traffic for the Nation.[19]

Obviously, then, the progress of Cherokee civilization (and Christianization, since their second principal chief, Charles Hicks, became a Christian in 1813) went hand in hand with the increase of black slaves among them. In 1809 there were more than 12,000 Cherokees in the nation and they owned 583 slaves. Sixteen years later, in 1825, there were 14,000 Cherokees and they owned 1,277 black slaves (some wealthy chiefs owned as many as sixty or seventy). By 1835 there were 15,000 Cherokees and 1,592 slaves. And by the time of the Civil War, after the Cherokees had been forced out of Georgia and Tennessee and into Oklahoma, there were 17,000 Cherokees and 4,000 black slaves.[20] It is not surprising that when the war came, the slaveholding Indians joined the Confederacy against the Union.

It is generally argued that the Cherokees treated their slaves very leniently.[21] Travelers, missionaries, federal agents and, of course, Cherokee slavemasters testified to this. At the same time, it is possible to find more than isolated examples of Cherokee cruelty to their slaves, and a careful search might reveal that the treatment of slaves varied as much among red masters as among white. What is more, it can be shown very

---

[19]John Ridge to Albert Gallatin in the John Howard Payne Papers, 8:103. However, the majority of the Cherokees at this time were still subsistence and not commercial farmers.

[20]For this and other details of slavery among the Cherokees, see Michael Roethler, "Negro Slavery Among the Cherokee Indians, 1540-1866" (Ph.D. thesis, Fordham University, 1964) esp. 120, 147, 157, 161.

[21]See especially ibid., the preface, and 131.

easily that the status of black slaves and black freedmen among the Cherokees declined steadily over the years. Accepting the standards of neighboring white civilization, the Cherokees gradually adopted all the worst features of Southern black codes (including the mounted, armed patrols to enforce them). Here is a record of this Indian slaveholding nation between 1819 and 1860 as seen in its written laws (and it differs little from that of the neighboring Southern Indian nations comprised of Choctaws, Creeks, and Chickasaws):[22]

1819 no contract or bargain entered into with any slave or slaves without the approbation of their masters shall be binding. . . .

1820 no one may purchase any item or property from a slave without permission from his owner

1820 no slave shall be allowed to sell or buy spirituous liquor

1824 there shall be no intermarriage between any Cherokee and any negro or between any white and any negro in the Cherokee Nation

1827 according to the constitution adopted for the Cherokee Nation, "no person who is of negro or mulatto parentage either by the father or mother's side shall be eligible to hold any office of profit, honor, or trust under this government" nor could such a person vote

1841 no slave shall be allowed to carry firearms, knives, dirks, or other dangerous weapons

1842 any free negro or slave aiding another slave to run away shall receive 100 lashes and be removed from the Cherokee Nation

1848 anyone teaching a negro to read or write shall be banished from the Cherokee Nation

1855 no public school teacher "suspected of entertaining

---

[22]These laws, discussed in Roethler's thesis, are also available in *Cherokee Laws* (Tahlequah, Cherokee Nation: Cherokee Advocate Office, 1852), from which I have compiled this list.

sentiments favorable to abolitionism" shall be allowed
in the Nation

1859 all free blacks in the Nation shall be required to leave
(this bill, though passed by both houses of the Cherokee legislature, was vetoed by the chief)

It is not surprising that under the increasing severity of the Cherokee
slave system there should have been several slave rebellions—in 1841,
1842, 1850—in which large numbers of blacks organized to escape to
Mexico.[23] It became increasingly difficult for Northern antislavery missionaries to operate effectively in such a climate even when they remained silent on the issue. The Boston-based American Board of
Commissioners for Foreign Missions, which had for forty years maintained the most extensive mission stations among the Cherokees, closed
down its operations in 1859 and Southern proslavery Presbyterians took
over their work.

Without making excuses for the Cherokees, it has to be recognized
that they faced a difficult situation, especially during the years before
1838 when they were struggling desperately to retain their homeland in
Georgia and Tennessee. This struggle was at its height when the words
of William Lloyd Garrison and the actions of Nat Turner provoked the
white South to frantic hysteria in defense of slavery as a divinely ordained institution. The Cherokees could not hope to remain in the heart
of the Deep South and at the same time advocate abolition or racial
equality. The South would not accept passive silence on the issue; only
participation in and forthright defense of slavery were evidence of sympathy toward the Southern way of life.

The farthest any Cherokee ever went toward opposing the slave system was to sympathize with the African Colonization Society. Here is a
statement written by a Christianized Cherokee, David Brown, to a friend
in New England in 1835:

You perceive [from my description of our nation] that there are some African
slaves among us. They have been, from time to time, brought in and sold by
white men. They are, however, generally well treated, and they much prefer living in the nation to a residence in the United States. There is hardly any inter-

[23]Slave rebellions are mentioned briefly in Roethler, "Negro Slavery Among the
Cherokee," 184-85, but we have no details.

mixture of Cherokee and African blood. The presumption is that the Cherokees will, at no distant day, cooperate with the humane efforts of those who are liberating and sending this prescribed race to the land of their fathers.[24]

This was a very tepid antislavery outlook, to say the least. The institution was blamed wholly on the white men who introduced it and not on the red men who perpetuated it among them. It was the "prescribed race" that was the problem rather than slavery itself. The extent to which antiblack racism entered into Cherokee thinking is apparent in Brown's obvious pride that there is very little "intermixture of Cherokee and African blood." There is little evidence that the Cherokees supported the Colonization Society or any other antislavery activity. Brown, whose own family owned slaves, may simply have been making a tactful remark for consumption in the North, where he knew there was increasing embarrassment over the existence of slavery among the Cherokees.

The Cherokee Nation, like the South itself, paid a heavy price for its use and defense of the peculiar institution.[25] During the Civil War the Cherokee territory in northeastern Oklahoma became a no-man's land between the Union armies in Kansas and the Confederate armies in Arkansas and Texas. The Cherokee chief, John Ross, at first signed a treaty with the Confederacy in 1861 and then in 1863 repudiated it to support the Union. Many Cherokees, however, remained sympathetic to the Confederacy and a fratricidal struggle went on within the nation for the duration. A Cherokee chief, Stand Watie, is credited with being the last Confederate general to surrender.[26]

The Cherokees are proud of the fact that they officially freed all their slaves three years before the American nation ended slavery. But while John Ross and his Union chiefs declared the slaves free in February 1863, most of them belonged to masters who were still part of the Confederacy and had to fight their way to freedom. After the Civil War, over Ross's strong objections, the freedmen were admitted by treaty to full citizenship in the Cherokee Nation (other Southern tribes resisted this

---

[24]David Brown's letter is printed in Thomas L. McKenney, *Memoirs* (New York: Paine and Burgess, 1846) 39.

[25]See Annie Heloise Abel's exhaustive three-volume study, *The American Indians as Slaveholders ad Secessionists* (Cleveland: Arthur H. Clark, 1915).

[26]For Stand Watie's life and letters, see E. E. Dale and G. L. Litton, *Cherokee Cavaliers* (Norman: University of Oklahoma, 1939).

successfully). Thereafter many of them settled in black communities in Oklahoma where they maintained a separate existence both from their former Indian masters and from the white man.

After the Cherokee government was abolished and Oklahoma became a state in 1908, these black communities tried to maintain political control over their local governments in towns like Boley and Van Zandt in Okfuskee County. However, Oklahoma was a Southern-oriented state, and these black communities were first gerrymandered and then counted out at elections. In 1910 a grandfather clause in the state's constitution disenfranchised all blacks. Four years later many of these former Indian slaves (or their descendants) in Oklahoma became so discouraged with their lot that they followed Chief Alfred C. Sam in a forlorn effort to return to Africa. That is another story, though.[27]

Although many books have been written about the Indians in the old Southeast, few of them deal at any length with the multiracial aspects of their history. If they mention them at all, attention is paid chiefly to the whites who intermarried and their mixed-blood descendants, who were usually the most prominent figures in Southern Indian politics and economics. A large chapter has yet to be written about America as a multiracial nation—red, white, and black—and how the white man, unable to accept his own myth of equality, forced inequality on others.

---

[27]See William E. Bittle and Gilbert Geis, *The Longest Way Home* (Detroit: Wayne State University, 1964).

APPENDIX

[Note: The following syncretic myth, attributed to Nea-Mathla, chief of the Seminoles in 1825, was printed under the title "Indian Legends" in *The Indian Advocate*, October 1847, 6. Photostatic copies of this newspaper are available at the Oklahoma Historical Library, Oklahoma City, Oklahoma.]

Father [said Nea-Mathla to the superintendent of Indian Affairs], it is not my wish to have my children made white men of. When the Great Spirit made man he made him as he is and under three marks. He assigned to each a color at the creation [and he assigned] the duties of each, and it was never intended that they should mingle.

Father, this was the way in which the Great Spirit made man. He stood upon a high place. Then taking into his hand some dust, he mixed it and then blew upon it, sending it from his hand in front of him—when there stood up before him *a white man*!

The Great Spirit was sorry. He saw what he had made was not what he aimed at. The man was white. He looked feeble and sickly. When the Great Spirit, looking at him, said, "White man, I have given you life. You are not what I want. I could send you where you came from, but no—I will not take away your life. Stand aside."

The Great Spirit mixed up the dust again, and drying it, blew upon it again—and there stood before him *a black man*! The Great Spirit was grieved. He saw now this man was black and ugly, so he bade him stand aside.

When, mixing up the dust again, he blew upon it—and there stood before him A RED MAN! The Great Spirit smiled. At this moment he looked up and saw an opening in the heavens and through it descended slowly three boxes. They came down at last and rested on the ground. When the Great Spirit spoke, saying "I have given life to you all. The red man alone is my favorite, but you shall all live. You must, however, fulfill each of you, the duties that are suited to you. These three boxes contain the tools you are to use in getting what is necessary to support you."

So saying, he called to him the white man. "White man," said the Great Spirit, "you are not my favorite, but I made you first. Open these boxes and look, and choose which you will take. They contain the implements you are all three to use through life."

The white man opened the boxes, looked in and said, "*I'll take this*." It was full of pens and ink and paper and all the things you white people use. He looked at the black men saying, "I made you next, but I cannot allow you to have the second choice."

Then turning to the red man he smiled and spoke saying, "Come, my favorite, and make a choice." The red man looked into the two remaining boxes and said, "I'll take this." That was full of beaver traps, bows and arrows and all the kinds of things the Indians use. Then the Great Spirit said to the negro, "You take this," and that [box] was full of hoes and axes—plainly showing that the black man was made to labor for both the white and red man.

Father, thus did the Great Spirit make man and in this way did he provide the instruments for him to labor with. It is not his will that our red children shall use the articles that came down in the box which the white man chose any more than it is proper for the white man to take the implements that were prepared by the Great Spirit for the use of his red children.

PICTORIAL
ARCHIVES

James Vann's tavern, built at Diamond Hill, Cherokee Nation, in 1803-1804 and now located at New Echota, Georgia. (Courtesy of Georgia Department of Archives and History)

James Vann's home at Diamond Hill, Cherokee Nation, near Spring Place, Georgia, constructed in 1803-1804. (Courtesy of Georgia Department of Archives and History)

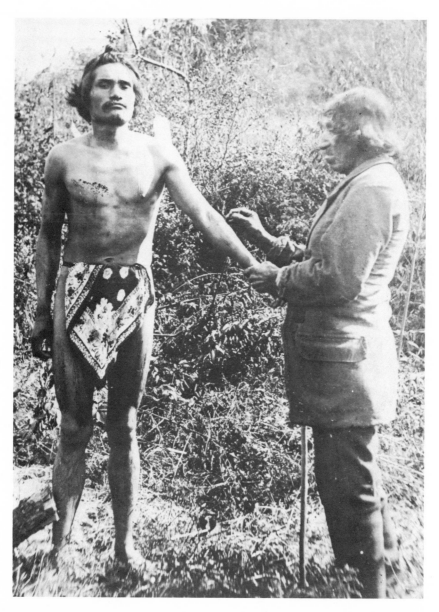

A Cherokee being "scratched" for the Cherokee Ball Play (an early form of lacrosse). (Courtesy of State of Tenn e, Tourism Development Division, C3-319 Cordell Hull Bldg., Nashville TN 37219)

The Reverend Cyrus Byington, missionary to the Choctaws (Courtesy of Oklahoma Historical Society)

The Reverend Evan Jones, missionary to the slaveholding Baptist Indians (Courtesy of Oklahoma Historical Society)

The Reverend John B. Jones, son of Evan Jones (Courtesy of Oklahoma Historical Society)

Chief John Ross, ca. 1863 (Courtesy of Gilcrease Institute, Tulsa, Oklahoma)

The John Ross House, Rossville, Georgia (Courtesy of State of Tennessee, Tourism Development Division, C3-319 Cordell Hull Bldg., Nashville TN 37219)

John Ross's home at Park Hill, Cherokee Nation (Courtesy of Gilcrease Institute, Tulsa, Oklahoma)

Cherokee Male Seminary (Courtesy of Gilcrease Institute, Tulsa, Oklahoma)

The Reverend Oswald Woodford, instructor at the Male Seminary (From the collection of Virginia Duffy McLoughlin)

Cherokee Female Seminary (From the collection of Virginia Duffy McLoughlin)

Pauline Avery (center), later the wife of Oswald Woodford, and two students at the Cherokee Female Seminary, Park Hill, 1855. Miss Avery was then principal of the Female Seminary. Note the care these young women took about their appearance. (From the collection of Virginia Duffy McLoughlin)

The front page of the Cherokee Phoenix for 13 March 1828 publishes the text of laws passed by the Council of the Cherokee Nation in both English and the Cherokee syllabary. (Courtesy of American Antiquarian Society, Worcester MA 01609)

PRESBYTERIANS AND
SLAVEHOLDING INDIANS,
1838-1861

When the first missionaries came among the Southeastern tribes, there was not yet any dispute among denominations or within denominations over the institution of slavery. Hence there were no differences between missionaries from the South and missionaries from the North so far as denominational teachings about slavery. Michael Coleman has argued forcefully that among the missionaries there was no racism toward the Indian (and if his reasoning is correct, there should have been no racism toward the African). There may have been "ethnocentrism," he concedes, but not "racism." I am somewhat skeptical of that claim. Although theologically Coleman may have a point, there were distinct political ramifications for the Indian missionaries on this point. Any student of missionaries to the Southeastern Indians recognizes that, from their first arrival, those missionaries who came from the Northern states were upset over the existence of slavery among them. After 1830 this became a distinct embarrassment for Northern missionaries, for once slavery became a "sin," missionaries were obligated to eradicate it just as they would polygamy or infanticide among the Indians. Eventually, of course, major denominations split over this issue, as their Southern members came to see slavery as a blessing ordained by God and not a sin imposed by Satan.*

The Presbyterians were strongly situated both in the Northern and Southern states. However, the inherent conservatism of Presbyterian Calvinists, as upheld by the theologians at Princeton College and Theological School, led to a decided bias in favor of the Southerners' claim that slavery was a political and not a spiritual matter. Missionaries to the slaveholding Indians had three options: they could be mildly antislavery as the American Board of Commissioners for Foreign Missions was; they

---

*See Michael C. Coleman, "Not Race, but Grace: Presbyterian Missionaries and American Indians, 1837-1893," *Journal of American History* 67 (June 1980): 41-60.

could be clearly antislavery, as the American Baptist Union was after 1845; or they could try to be strictly neutral on the matter as the Presbyterian Board of Foreign Missions did. This essay attempts to evaluate the success of the policy of neutrality among the Presbyterian missionaries to the Choctaw Indians between 1831 and 1861. The evidence indicates that the missionaries could not, in fact, sustain such a stance. There was no tolerance for neutrality among slaveholders, and the Presbyterians chose to be proslavery in action although neutral in theory. After 1861 the Presbyterian missionaries to the Southeastern Indians openly sided with the Confederate States of America.

FOUNDED IN 1838 to provide a denominational foreign mission board for the Presbyterians (the Old School Presbyterians, that is), the Presbyterian Board of Foreign Missions had from the outset a very different outlook toward mission work among slaveholding Indians than did its closest rival, the American Board of Commissioners for Foreign Missions (which served the New School Presbyterians and the New England Congregationalists).[1] The difference increased until 1859 when the latter organization, unable to reconcile its antislavery conviction with the determined proslavery position of the Southern Indians, withdrew from that field. The Presbyterian Board (located in New York City) thereupon took under its patronage most of those A.B.C.F.M. missionaries who had been abandoned by their Boston-based board for refusing to expound and practice an antislavery position among the Choctaws, Cherokees, Chickasaws, Seminoles, and Creeks.

Some Presbyterians in the North opposed this decision, arguing that their denomination already had the reputation of being "emphatically *the Slave Church of America.*" To take in missionaries whom "the venerable American Board" had dropped for their desire to remain neutral about slavery could very well lead many Northern Presbyterians to leave the Church: "In this way some of our churches have bled freely already and much of the blood they have lost was of their best blood."[2] The image of

---

[1]For the role slavery played in the Presbyterian schism of 1837 and the reasons underlying the establishment of the Presbyterian Board of Foreign Missions, see Ernest T. Thompson, *Presbyterians in the South* (Richmond, 1963) vol. 1, chs. 24, 25, and 28.

[2]This petition (and most of the other documents cited below) is in the archives of the P.B.F.M. at the Presbyterian Historical Society in Philadelphia (hereinafter PHS). Indian MS, box 10, vol. 1, 39.

the bleeding body was prophetic, for the Presbyterian denomination was dismembered in the following year. It was also indicative of the depth of the prevailing spiritual anguish over this issue.

Despite protests, the P.B.F.M. unanimously voted in 1859 to accept the Choctaw mission of the A.B.C.F.M. into its ranks. Until the Civil War put an end to Northern-based mission operations among the Southern Indians, the P.B.F.M. continued to add other missionaries as they were abandoned by the Boston board. The Presbyterian Board denied that slavery had anything to do with its decision to take in the A.B.C.F.M.'s abandoned missionaries. It simply decided that these dedicated, experienced missionaries (most of whom had joined the presbytery formed in the Indian Territory despite their Congregational origins) wanted to continue their work and deserved to continue. The board had had its own missionaries in the Indian Territory complementing the work of the A.B.C.F.M. since 1842. That the Indians in what is now the state of Oklahoma were slaveholders, many of them cotton planters, was considered immaterial to the salvation of their souls. One can read the *Annual Reports* of the P.B.F.M. from 1838 to 1862 without finding a single reference to slavery. The board evidently made a determined effort to avoid saying anything at all about this controversial question in its official publications. Yet its official correspondence reveals an almost constant concern with issues relating to slavery in the Indian Territory. There seemed to be no end to the crises it provoked, some petty, some ludicrous, and some tragic.

Between 1838 and 1862 the Presbyterian Church professed to be neutral on the question of slavery. Insisting that slavery was a civil or political matter and that it was accepted (and certainly not condemned) by Christ and the Apostles, leading theologians and ecclesiastical leaders of the denomination, North and South, refused to allow debates over slavery to influence their missionary work among the slaveholding Indians.[3] There were great advantages to this position: first of all, the Presbyterians avoided (until the war) the sectional division over slavery that split the Baptist and Methodist denominations in the 1840s. Second, it enabled its missionaries to the Southern Indians to receive support from church members North and South. Third, it avoided friction with the

---

[3]The theological defense of this position of benevolent neutrality is amply described in Thompson, *Presbyterians*, 1:384-91.

Indians themselves. Having adopted the white Southern way of life as the model for their own progress and civilization, the Southern Indians (often referred to as "The Five Civilized Tribes") were as antagonistic toward antislavery agitation after 1830 as any group of white slaveowners in Mississippi or South Carolina.

The P.B.F.M. did not place any political test upon its missionaries. It took pride in the fact that men and women from the North as well as the South served in its ranks, bringing the gospel, pure and simple, to the heathen. What is of interest to the historian is how the Northern-born missionaries adjusted to the situation in the Indian Territory. And of equal importance, what did the board do when some of its missionaries were accused of being proslavery or antislavery—or even abolitionist? How, in short, did the Presbyterian Church deal in practice with the policy of neutrality when it operated in slaveholding territory?

The missionary archives of the board from 1838 to 1861 reveal a wide variety of incidents that throw light on these questions. In coping with these, the missionaries seem to have had a strange concept of neutrality. Despite their profession of equal spiritual concern for both masters and slaves, the missionaries consistently demonstrated more concern for the feelings of the red man than the black.[4] While the choices were so excruciating that no historian can make facile judgments regarding them, the evidence seems to indicate that the board and its missionaries entered this difficult field of operations already predisposed toward the position of the slaveholders. If it did not investigate the political outlook of its missionaries before it employed them, it certainly made it clear after they got to Indian Territory that they must toe the line in either approving slavery or maintaining silence on the issue. Freedom of thought was perhaps tolerable, but not freedom of speech or action.

Where the Prudential Committee of the A.B.C.F.M. persistently, though quietly, tried to persuade its Indian missionaries to witness against slavery, the Presbyterian Board willingly accepted the complicity

---

[4]Membership statistics in Presbyterian mission churches in Indian Territory reveal a small number of black members. However, since (as noted below) slaveholding Indians feared the influence of mission work upon their slaves, the missionaries took pains to preach only to slaves whose masters gave them permission to listen. It appears that the slaves enjoyed Christian services and wanted to attend mission schools; many more would have come into mission stations had the missionaries encouraged them to do so with or without their masters' permission.

of its missionaries in the system. When, as happened on occasion, Presbyterian missionaries were criticized by Indians and Southern whites for not being sufficiently cordial toward slavery or were accused of being surreptitiously sympathetic to abolition, the board went out of its way to protest against such changes. The tone of the Presbyterian mission to the Southern Indians was always one of sympathetic understanding toward the slaveowners; its tone toward antislavery advocates was always one of hostile irritation. Northern-born Presbyterian missionaries who dared to express openly their antislavery views were not only considered inimical to the mission work but were frankly told that their position was unscriptural.

Of course, few dedicated antislavery missionaries ever applied to the P.B.F.M. for positions. They found more congenial colleagues in other societies, like the American Missionary Association, led by Lewis Tappan and Amos Phelps (which never sent any missionaries to the slaveholding Indians). It is ironic therefore that in its effort to defend the status quo in slavery, the Presbyterian Board ran into almost as much controversy in the Indian Territory as the A.B.C.F.M. with its avowed effort to alter the status quo.[5] With each passing year official neutrality became increasingly difficult. The board found itself increasingly on the defensive not so much against Northern antislavery advocates as against ardent Southern proslavery advocates—many of them American Indians.

The issue of slavery came up in numerous and complex forms in the Indian Territory. There is at least one instance in which a missionary, with the board's approbation, brought his personal slaves with him to the Choctaw Mission—a problem that the A.B.C.F.M., drawing its missionaries almost wholly from New England, never had to face.[6] There is also an instance in which a prospective missionary wife with apparent abolitionist sentiments was discouraged from coming by her fiancé and

---

[5]The controversy over slavery with the American Board is discussed in Robert T. Lewit, "Indian Mission and Anti-slavery Sentiment: A Conflict of Evangelical and Humanitarian Ideals," *MVHR* 50 (June 1963): 39-55. For the American Missionary Association, see Bertram Wyatt-Brown, *Lewis Tappan* (Cleveland, 1969) 292-314.

[6]See the letters of the Reverend Charlton Wilson (nephew of the Reverend J. Leighton Wilson, one of the corresponding secretaries of the P.B.F.M.) PHS, box 11, vol. 3, 17 (12 March 1855) and box 6, vol. 3, 205 (9 January 1860).

by the board until they were satisfied that her abolitionism was not really very radical.[7] But the more common problems arose after the missionaries reached their stations and began their work. Almost immediately they were faced with four decisions that had to be made: (1) In view of the great shortage of free labor, was it permissible to hire slaves from their masters to work at the missions? (2) If it would save money for the mission and perhaps enable a slave to earn his way to freedom, should the mission purchase a slave? (3) If an Indian slaveholder wished admission to the church, should he be allowed to do so without emancipating his slaves? (4) If there were laws passed by the Indian councils (or tribal legislatures) prohibiting the teaching of reading and writing to slaves, should the missionaries deny slaves or their children the right to enter their schools? To all of the questions the A.B.C.F.M. answered "No," while the Presbyterian Board answered "Yes."

In addition, there was the question of what should be done about a missionary who was too friendly with the slaves or a missionary who wished to marry a man with some African ancestry? What was to be done with missionaries who, after seeing slavery among Indians, began to protest against it? Should he or she be told to be quiet or be sent away as a potential troublemaker? And suppose a missionary was suspected of having abolitionist views by the Indians or was falsely accused of having such views? Should he be defended on principle or asked to retire for the good of the mission?

During the whole process of saving Indian souls in the antebellum years, the missionaries seemed to be walking on eggs. Highly sensitive to criticism and mistreatment by whites, the Indians often were ready to find faults where none existed. The Presbyterian missionaries found themselves constantly on the defensive despite their best efforts to remain neutral in word and deed. At times it seemed that only ardent espousal of slavery could quiet Indian suspicions: If a missionary did not oppose slavery, why didn't he own slaves? The Reverend William S. Robertson, one of the board's missionaries to the Creeks, wrote in 1856:

Council meets soon. It is said great things are to be done. . . . All the white men

---

[7]See Harold P. Faust, "The Presbyterian Missions to the American Indian, 1838-1893" (Ph.D. thesis, Temple University, 1943) 316-17. Faust's thesis, based on a thorough study of the P.B.F.M. archives, contains much material on this subject. See esp. 316-34.

who are suspected of being abolitionists are to be sent off they say, myself among the rest . . . I suppose if poor Dick had not died they could not have a shadow of a hook to hang their charges on. But now not being worth a single darkie I am suspected.[8]

I shall try briefly to give some examples of these various problems as they are revealed in the missionary correspondence. In the course of describing them, it will be pertinent to ask the following kinds of questions: What alternatives, if any, were available? How was the status of slavery among the Indians affected by the work of the missionaries? Did the board purposely cover up or remain silent on these issues in its official publications because it found them embarrassing or because it thought them unimportant? What, in practice, did it mean to say that the only scriptural means for improving the lot of the slaves was to convert their masters to Christianity?

The first mission that the Presbyterians undertook to the slaveholding Indians was among the Creeks, who had been driven from southern Georgia, Alabama, and Mississippi in the early 1830s.[9] The Reverend John Fleming, an A.B.C.F.M. missionary, had begun work among the Creeks in the Indian Territory in 1832, but in 1837 he was expelled by the Creek Council for alleged antislavery activity. Fleming denied the charge, but it did him no good. Not only was he banished from the Creek Nation, but for five years thereafter all missionaries were banned. In 1841 the Presbyterian Board sent Robert M. Loughridge, a native of South Carolina and a graduate of Princeton, to talk to the Creek chiefs about permission to open a mission school. The chiefs were wary. They told him they would permit a school but would not allow preaching around their nation. A contract was drawn up in 1842 and approved by the board, which included this as its first clause:

The [Presbyterian Missionary] Society promises on their part, 1st, That their Missionaries shall not interfere in any manner with the relation existing between

---

[8]Letter dated 24 October 1856 among the Worcester-Robertson Papers at the University of Tulsa, Tulsa, Oklahoma.

[9]See Robert M. Loughridge, "History of Presbyterian Mission Work Among the Creek Indians," MS at PHS, and Angie Debo, *The Road to Disappearance* (Norman, 1941) 116-21, and Grant Foreman, *Advancing the Frontier 1830-1860* (Norman, 1933) 141-43.

Master and Slave by learning them to read or exciting them in any manner to disobedience.[10]

By 1846 Loughridge had won the confidence of the Creeks and was permitted thereafter to preach anywhere in their nation. Black slaves were also admitted, like their slaveholding masters, to the mission church he formed at Kowetah. But Loughridge never defied the clause about teaching slaves to read and write. The only slaves, old or young, who were admitted to his mission school (or church) were those who had the express permission of their masters.

Loughridge also appears to have been the first of the Presbyterian missionaries to purchase a slave in the Indian Territory. He did so in 1850 after moving from the Kowetah Station to Tullahassee, sixteen miles eastward, where the P.B.F.M. had established a boarding school among the Creeks. While Loughridge did not seek the board's permission to buy the slave, apparently he had no doubt that it would approve.

> . . . in the kitchen and house work we have an Indian woman hired and a black woman. They are I suppose the best help we could get in the nation. The black woman has lived with us a great deal and is a member of our Church. I have not yet informed you that we had taken the responsibility of *purchasing* this woman. I had hired her for the year and, depending upon her help, we had concluded to commence the school and make all arrangements for so doing. About a week before our school was to commence, her master determined to take her out of the country and sell her. We did not know what to do. We had no time to consult the Board. The [Creek] people and the Gov[ernment] too were expecting us to make a beginning in the school, and we felt it almost impossible to commence if we failed to secure her help.
>
> She felt very badly about leaving the country and appealed to us to buy her if it was possible; she is a member of our church—the first fruit of my labors there, and we felt bad to see her thus torn away. Under all the circumstances, we felt it to be our duty to buy her and accordingly did so. We paid ($400) four hundred dollars. The draft to Wm. Drew for this amount was for this purpose. We felt that we ourselves would bear this expense if the Board would not justify the measure. If the Lord spares her life her wages would soon pay that amount. We formerly had to pay $6 per month for her.[11]

The board paid the four hundred dollars to William Drew, but unfor-

---

[10]PHS, box 9, vol. 1, 391-93.

[11]PHS, box 12, vol. 2, 12. For slaves purchased by Presbyterian missionaries at other stations, see Faust, "Presbyterian Missions," 318.

tunately Celia did not live to earn her way to freedom. On 16 April 1855, Loughridge wrote to the board describing "the very sudden death of Cealia, our cook." She died of "apoplectic convulsions" and everyone at the mission mourned her passing.[12] There is no evidence that Loughridge broadcast this action or informed the Indians in the nation that Celia was working her way toward freedom. Since Presbyterian missionaries were careful not to upset the Indians about the question of slavery, good deeds like this (if it may be considered such) went unnoticed. So far as Indian and white neighbors could see, the missionaries were just slaveowners like everyone else who could afford it. Of course, another reason for silence was that many Northern people would not have taken well to the idea that Indian missionaries were buying their own church members to slave in missionary kitchens. One may argue that as an individual case this was an act of Christian kindness given the circumstances, but an endless series of such purchases might add up to a different conclusion.

In 1850 the Reverend James Ross Ramsay of Maryland, a graduate of Jefferson College and Princeton Theological Seminary, came to join Loughridge in the Creek Nation. In one of his first letters back to the mission office in New York he told Walter Lowrie, corresponding secretary of the P.B.F.M., "I am using a negro man, a slave named Robert Foster, for interpreter and he promises to do well; [he is] also a member of our church, a young, healthy man and one of natural talent. I have come to the determination of asking the Board thro you whether they will not give me their consent to buy him in order that he may work out his time and at length become a free man." Ramsay then listed the reasons why he thought this was important:

1. The mission needs the constant services of such a man on the farm. Robert is a very trusty fellow and handy; can turn his hand to almost any kind of work either in the house or out of doors.

2. The Board would not be likely to lose any thing by this transaction so far as present appearance is concerned. Robert enjoys the best of health and is a very able bodied man, so that there is every prospect of him living

---

[12]PHS, box 6, vol. 1, 18.

> to work out his freedom; at the rate I am now paying
> his master, he would be likely to work out his time in
> five or six years. He is very fond of living at the Mis-
> sion and prefers working here to any other place.
>
> 3.   It would be a very charitable and benevolent act to re-
>   deem our brother from slavery and it seems to be al-
>   most a duty in this case seeing there would be so little
>   sacrifice to the board in effecting it. He is a member of
>   our church and makes a good interpreter, and it is not
>   easy always to get an Interpreter when we want him
>   and while under the control of his present master who
>   is a heathen [i.e., Indian] we are very uncertain about
>   getting his services for any great length of time. He
>   may be taken away and exposed to the greatest trials
>   and temptations.
>
> Considering all these things, I desire you to ask the
> Board whether they will consent to our purchasing
> Robert Foster provided I can get him for the sum of six
> hundred or seven hundred dollars, or less, if I can.[13]

Here then, a year after the purchase of Celia, another Presbyterian
church member is to be purchased. In this case he would do two jobs—
one utilizing his "natural talent" and one his muscle power. The "transaction" is presented as a combination of utility, benevolence, and shrewd
investment. It would appear that Ramsay felt religious duty toward a
Christian brother was not sufficient motivation to the board.

The proposal fell through, but eight years later Ramsay, now laboring among the Seminoles at the Oak Ridge Mission Station, again made
the same request:

> Mr. Lowrie (Walter) will remember that when I labored at Kowetah I made an
> application to the Board to buy our Interpreter, Robert Foster, a slave belonging
> to a Creek named A. Foster. Mr. Lowrie gave me authority to buy him if I could
> get him for $600 or 700, but his master would not at that time listen to any offer.
> Recently, however, he has expressed a willingness to sell Robert and set his price;
> [he asks] too much, but considering the offer our Chief Jumper [Chief of the Sem-
> inoles] has made, [it] might be paid without discommoding us very much. I am
> going to try. . . . His master agrees to take $1200; perhaps he may be prevailed

---

[13]PHS, box 12, vol. 2, 42.

upon to take 1000. Robert has been Interpreting for us all the time with but little interruption for the last eleven years . . . we have constantly been annoyed with the probability that some day, without any previous warning, his master would take him away.[14]

Then Ramsay added another point to clinch the argument in favor of buying Foster—denominational rivalry. "Recently Mr. Buckner, the Baptist preacher whose constant and untiring effort is to baffle and hinder us in our work has been trying to persuade Foster [the slave's master] to take him [the Interpreter] away from us and hire him to the Baptists and then compel him against his own will to interpret for them and against us." Foster's purchase not only became a matter of denominational competition but of conscience. Could the board allow a Presbyterian church member to misinterpret the gospel to the heathen, and so be compelled to tell ignorant Indians that God commended baptism by total immersion only to adult believers?

Still, one wonders what would have happened if the case were reversed and the interpreter had been a Baptist, or had, after his purchase by the Presbyterians, wished to become a Baptist? How would Ramsay have reacted then?

Ramsay also relayed the information that Chief John Jumper, a member of the Presbyterian mission church and the owner of many slaves, was willing to loan the mission eight hundred dollars, interest-free, for the purchase. "I have taken it," Ramsay wrote, "on the condition that my brethren, the other missionaries, will assume their share of the responsibility. The responsibility I refer to is that in the case of his death [Robert Foster's] before redeeming all [to Jumper], others shall bear part of

---

[14]PHS, box 6, vol. 1, 231. One suspects, from the following remarks of Ramsay, that Robert Foster was a more effective interpreter—at least to his fellow slaves—before he entered the restrained service of the Presbyterians: "Our Interpreter at present is an African. He speaks the Seminole language with great fluency and mostly is warm and energetic [as a speaker]. He is also a member of the Presbyterian Church. But still he is an African. I mean an African of this country. And he will have African ways and will try to lead our people in the same way. And they most willingly follow him as all the Creeks do the Negroes among them in such things as having frequent fasts followed by feasts, great camp meetings, observing Christmas, which they call 'Big Sunday' with a great feast and sitting up all Christmas night singing and shouting and praying. Such things I think can be carried too far and will ultimately be subversive of our rule and church Government altogether. The Interpreter, who heaps up this great pile of rubbish on religion is almost adored while he who preach faithfully warns his people will be considered, to say the least, severe." PHS, box 6, vol. 1, 143.

the responsibility of making up the balance with me." Ironically, Chief Jumper was to leave the Presbyterian church and join the Baptists a year later, but by then the transaction had been completed. On 19 January 1860, Ramsay wrote jubilantly to the board:

> I now have the satisfaction of informing you that we have accomplished it. And although we place ourselves under considerable [financial] risk in case of Robin's death [Robert seems also to have been called Robin] or inability to repay what has been paid for him, still I cannot but think that we were providentially directed to it just at the right time. Our opponents, the Baptists, would have had him and would not have stopped at any price. As it is now, I hope we shall not hereafter be disturbed on that point, as he now belongs to me.[15]

Thus did policy mix with charity and divine providence rescue the chosen. Ramsay noted that he had "conferred with the brethern about it," but he meant the missionary brethren, not the church members. They had "all concluded that the welfare of the church demanded it though we would be running a great risk."

Chief Jumper received the genuine thanks of the missionaries, but while he "asks no percent" on his loan, "yet he expects all to be repaid." Jumper's magnanimity lay in the loss of his interest: "The Interest on the $800 which he lent would in 5 years amount to 1200 at 6 per cent, the common interest out here. Thus if no accident should happen [to Robert Foster], and he should live, Jumper would give $400 towards it. The sum which we had to pay Foster was $1200 against next Christmas." In their minds the missionaries felt the same way as Jumper—that they were both making a financial sacrifice to aid in mission work and were beating out their rivals, the Baptists. Robert Foster undoubtedly was grateful for the opportunity to earn his freedom. The wages that the board would have paid to his former master now went to Ramsay, to be kept against the date when the final payment was to be paid.[16] Whatever

---

[15]PHS, box 6, vol. 3, 138.

[16]Idem. Ramsay went on in this letter to explain the providential timing of the transaction, pointing out that "John Read, who had been interpreting for Bemo [the Baptist minister in the region] has fallen into drunkenness and left the neighborhood . . . I have heard that he says if he had known that Read was gone he would have gone and offered Foster $400 per year for Robin. . . . The transaction is very gratifying to all our people as well as to R. himself . . . R. will have $1000 to pay without interest which by industry and economy he can do in five years and then obtain his freedom." After that, hopefully, he "will most likely continue with us" for wages.

pleasure Robert Foster may have felt at that moment turned to ashes a few months later when he found himself in a terrible dilemma regarding his loyalty to his new master and his loyalty to his cousin, a runaway slave.

Hiring or purchasing individual slaves with special tasks or skills was only one aspect of the slave-labor system used at Presbyterian missions. Field hands and unskilled labor gangs were also employed and kept more or less in permanent residence at some, if not all, of the stations. For example, take the plans drawn up in 1851 by the board's architect for the female boarding school in the Chickasaw Nation. When the Chickasaws were removed from northern Mississippi to the Indian Territory in the 1830s, they had been forced to merge with the Choctaws and had become subject to their dominance. They did not like this, however, and in 1849 they arranged to purchase a piece of the Choctaws' territory for themselves and set up their own tribal government. The Bureau of Indian Affairs agreed to help them pay for the establishment of a missionary school in his new area and the Presbyterians were asked to undertake it.[17] The board thereupon hired James S. Allen, who had considerable experience as a builder and contractor, to go to the Chickasaw country and erect the buildings for the school. It eventually became known as Wapenucka Female Seminary and was one of the more successful Presbyterian schools in the Indian Territory during the 1850s.

However, examination of Allen's long and detailed correspondence with the board regarding the erection of the buildings indicates that from the outset he relied upon slave labor for the unskilled work of ground-clearing and construction. Moreover, Allen fully expected that the mission would need to have separate slave quarters behind the school buildings for permanent use. On the plans he drew up and sent to the board on 1 October 1851, he drew in a small building labeled "slave room";[18] and on 1 June 1852, he estimated the costs for building "the black houses."[19] How much of the expenses for slave labor were paid by the Bureau of Indian Affairs and how much by the board is not spelled

---

[17]See *Annual Report* of the P.B.F.M. (New York, 1849) 7 and *Annual Report* (New York, 1850) 7.

[18]PHS, box 6, vol. 2, 37.

[19]PHS, box 6, vol. 2, 45.

out. But clearly the school utilized slaves to do the field labor connected with the mission farm as well as the menial tasks of the school like chopping wood, washing, and carrying water.

A similar arrangement prevailed at Spencer Academy in the Choctaw Nation. Founded in 1842 and endowed by the Choctaws, who appointed trustees to supervise it, the school opened under Presbyterian direction in 1844. Its one hundred students received part of their training each day in husbandry—working on the model farm and shops over which the Presbyterians appointed a lay missionary assistant. The man appointed to take charge of this work in the 1850s was Nathaniel Wiggins, who was described as "steward and farmer" for the school. It was Wiggins's duty to manage the slaves who worked at the station. But his labors in this respect did not meet the standards of the school's superintendent, the Reverend James Frothingham. In a letter to the junior corresponding secretary of the board, the Reverend J. Leighton Wilson, 21 January 1859, Frothingham spelled out his objections to Wiggins and in so doing revealed a great deal about the position of slave labor at the school.

Wiggins, Frothingham said, "is very much disliked by all of the residents at Spencer." Not only did he "possess no missionary spirit" but he was "a mere laboring man." Wiggins's "influence by word and example is bad." The following charges were made against him:

1st He exceeds the limits of his office as Steward and withholds from others here the things of which he has charge. In the garden he thus acts overbearing. . . . In the store and grocery he also controls in an ungenerous manner. . . .

2nd His example as a religious man is very bad. He has for some months been in the habit of leaving the Dining room immediately after Breakfast and Supper, the time for morning and evening worship, in order to attend to his stock or to other work. . . . This is a bad example for the boys and still worse for the servants who are hardly compelled to attend worship at any time and who shelter themselves under the shadow of a missionary's example. . . .

3rd He talks continually to every body about Mr. Evans's family, especially his "laziness and not working." . . .

> This conversation among the blacks had led to trouble;
> they being constantly told of Mr. E's faults will not
> treat him respectfully. . . .

> 4th He has no control over the servants, is familiar with
> them, and loses their respect. Last summer, twice, he
> went out on fishing parties of the Chickasaws and ne-
> groes, blacking his face and holding such intimacy
> with them as no Missionary has ever done before. Our
> own servants were among the party.[20]

For this overfamiliarity with servants (i.e., slaves) Frothingham requested that Wiggins and his wife "may be recalled." Missionaries were
expected to treat slaves the same way other slave masters did, that is, to
keep them in their places. Mr. Wiggins's fault seemed to be that he
treated them as equals. We are not told how many of these servants were
members of the mission church whom he might conceivably have considered Christian brethren. But obviously that would have made no difference. The worldly position of slaves and their spiritual state were two
totally different realms. That was the example the mission set for the Indian boys at the school, and how could it do otherwise? The parents of
most of the students, as slaveholders, expected the missionaries to uphold the caste lines upon which the system was based. Wiggins's behavior was a threat to the mission because it was a threat to the institution
of slavery.

The social segregation imposed on the missionaries by the existence
of slavery was further illustrated by the traumatic situation that arose
when one of the young mission assistants announced that she was going
to marry a man with African blood in his veins. Miss Jane Garrison of
Greenfield, Missouri, had been appointed as a missionary assistant at
Tullahassee Mission among the Creeks in 1857. She served faithfully as
a teacher at the school and fell in love with one of the former pupils of

---

[20]PHS, box 10, vol. 2, 264. The Reverend Samuel A. Worcester, the noted
A.B.C.F.M. missionary to the Cherokees, fell into the same mistake as Wiggins in 1855
and was accused of promoting abolitionism "by admitting negroes into his family circle
as companions, thus breaking down distinctions between the owner & the Slave, which
has a pernicious influence upon the slave portion of the community where he resides."
See letter of George M. Butler, U.S. agent to the Cherokees, to George W. Manypenny,
commissioner of Indian Affairs, 22 June 1855, in the "Letters Received" files of the Bureau of Indian Affairs, National Archives, Washington DC.

the school, Sandford Perryman. Perryman was a member of a wealthy Creek family that owned many slaves. But in the past the Creeks, like other Southern Indians, had occasionally intermarried with slaves, and one of Perryman's grandparents had been black. He thought of himself as an Indian; but as Indians progressed up the path toward white civilization, many of them adopted the white attitude that anyone with even a drop of black blood was to be classed as a black. After 1830 all the Southern Indian tribes prohibited intermarriage between Indians and blacks. Normally this did not concern the missionaries, but when a white girl from the mission station became involved in this delicate problem of caste, the missionaries were caught in a difficult situation. Fortunately, there seemed a way out. Robert Loughridge, the superintendent at Tullahassee, explained it to J. Leighton Wilson in a letter dated 1 August 1860:

> There has been considerable excitement lately among the whites and half breeds [i.e., Indians of mixed Indian and white ancestry] around here by the fact that Miss Garrison was about to be married to a young man, one of our former pupils, who is one-fourth African. Her time [at our station] was out, but she declined returning home, intending to be married about this time. But I succeeded in getting her off home.[21]

Unfortunately Miss Garrison had a mind of her own. She went home and then came right back again to proceed with her marriage. On 12 November 1860, Loughridge wrote again to the board:

> Herewith I send you Miss Garrison's final voucher. She returned immediately to the Nation and was married to young Perryman to whom she was engaged. I have not seen her since her return. The objection to the marriage, especially by the whites in the Country, is that he is 1/4 African and shows it very much. She is living with him about 65 miles distant up the Ark[ansas] River. But the excitement has pretty well died away.[22]

In any case, with the payment of the last voucher, the board had wiped its hands of the affair. And neither Loughridge nor any of Miss Garrison's former colleagues at the mission had dignified the marriage with their presence. It had been a close call, though. When the Civil War came, Sandford Perryman enlisted in the Confederate Army for a year,

---

[21]PHS, box 6, vol. 3, 15.

[22]PHS, box 6, vol. 3, 18.

and then in 1862 he and his wife fled to the North, losing $50,000 in farm equipment, stock, and slaves. Robert Loughridge fled south to Texas, after urging the Creeks to join the Confederacy.[23]

But the excitement over Miss Garrison was mild compared to the tortuous complications involving the Reverend Edward Eells and Misses Hollingsworth, Mathers, and Denny. Eells had been sent by the board to take charge of Koonsha Female Seminary among the Choctaws in 1855. Not long after his arrival he was caught flirting with one of the missionary teachers, a Miss Hollingsworth: "I believe I wrote you about Mr. Eells putting his arms around Miss Hollingsworth and kissing her on the stairs of the Seminary," the Reverend Alexander Reid wrote to the corresponding secretary of the board on 7 March 1856. "I accused him of this, but he denied it." Reid concluded that Eells was unfit "to be at the head of our important female seminary." The embarrassment was not caused because Reid was a prude nor because Miss Hollingsworth said she had no interest in Mr. Eells and he had forced his attention upon her. Eells was already married; his pregnant wife was at the mission with him.[24]

Eells was a slippery fellow, however. He not only denied that he had ever kissed Miss Hollingsworth, but counterattacked by accusing two of the mission teachers who had attacked his character of being abolitionists—Miss Esther Mathers and Miss M. E. Denny. Furthermore, he told the Choctaw Indians that he was being persecuted by these abolitionists and others at the mission because he was opposed to their position on slavery. It was a stupid accusation, of course; who could suspect the Presbyterian Board of harboring abolitionists? But the times were hysterical and the Choctaws showed extreme sensitivity on this issue. However sound the Presbyterian Board and missions as a whole might have been about slavery, there was always the possibility that some of the missionaries, especially those with Northern upbringing, were not so sound on the subject. And there were missionaries of other boards around, like those of the A.B.C.F.M., who were known to be under pressure to persuade the Indians to give up that sinful institution.

---

[23]See Perryman's letter of 11 February 1863, PHS, box 6, vol. 3, 115 and biographical sketch in John B. Meserve, "The Perrymans," *Chronicles of Oklahoma* 15 (1937): 166-84.

[24]PHS, box 10, vol. 2, 24.

Eells was clever enough to accuse the other missionaries at the Good Water Station of joining in the plot to ruin him for their own nefarious—abolitionist—purposes:

> When the teachers at Good Water learned that I ascribed Miss Mathers' ill will against me to my opposition to her Abolition sentiments, they too became open enemies and used no small pains to injure me, besides laying upon us—in the very spirit of Abolitionism—a ceaseless course of slights and insults. Two of them made visitations among my Choctaw people for the purpose of setting them against me, but without success. I am credibly informed that every Choctaw that knows me is my friend.[25]

In other words, the Choctaws knew him well enough to realize that he was no abolitionist. "That those ladies are abolitionists," he wrote to Walter Lowrie on 18 February 1856, "we know from their repeated admission, and also from a note Miss Denny addressed to me in Nov. last wherein she complains that she and her associates have been greatly pained at my remarks upon the subject, and declares that she believes slavery to be a sin, &c. &c. Myself and wife are fully of the opinion that our servants [slaves] are tampered with. It is certain that they became exceedingly insolent to us and correspondingly free and intimate with at least Miss Denny."[26]

Here indeed was an imbroglio! How was the board from 1500 miles away to unravel this tangle of charges and countercharges? But Eells overplayed his hand. He turned upon the board itself: "Had you told me beforehand that I was liable to be surrounded with teachers of Abolition sentiments, I should have known how either to refuse so disagreeable a situation or to avoid the subject altogether." Claiming to be concerned only for the good name of the board, he went on to say that he had tried to refrain from all discussion of the the topic since "I knew that it was important for our Board to maintain its good reputation in the nation upon that point, that you had pledged us at Washington to Col. [Peter] Pitchlynn [President of the Choctaw Trustees of Education] as sound, and I had sometimes inquiries from prominent men how we stood and expressly as to the teachers as well as myself." Eells was at the time in Lamar, Texas, preparing to return to the East.

---

[25]PHS, box 10, vol. 2, 14.

[26]Idem.

This whole episode, which began over a kiss on the back stairs, had rapidly expanded into a major problem for the mission. Three of the missionaries at Good Water had written to the board on 31 January 1856, urging Eells's removal because of growing Choctaw animosity:

> We fear much for the school if he does remain, for he has already prejudiced many of the Choctaws against us and the board by telling them he has been dismissed and persecuted on account of his views respecting slavery! Of course the Choctaws (being very sensitive on that point) sympathize with Mr. Eells as an *injured* and *wronged* man, and feel that the rest of us are opposed to slavery and I suppose dangerous teachers for children of slaveholders . . . Mr. Eells has it in his power to do much harm, and we do not doubt he will exert it to the utmost.[27]

Eells left without doing the great damage that was feared, at least so far as anyone could tell. But he had indeed touched both the Choctaws and the Presbyterian Board at their most delicate point.

How far some of the Presbyterian missionaries would go to defend the status quo was revealed in a minor aspect of the Eells case. Long before he had become involved in the scandal at Good Water and was still in good graces of the board, Eells had written to it about one of the missionary teachers who accompanied him and his wife on the trip west. He was obliged, he said, to report her "shocking abolition sentiments" expressed to him "on board the S. Boat from Cincinnati." "She said she hated slavery worse than sin, and that if she were convinced the Bible sanctioned slavery, she would have no regard for the Bible, or words to the import."[28] In these circumstances Eells felt obliged to disabuse her at once of such heresy. "I showed . . . what the Bible says of Abolitionists in I Timothy 6:3-5." This chapter deals with "the duty of servants" (presumably slaves) and "corrupt teachers." The Apostle exhorted servants to honor their masters and "if any man teach otherwise and consent not to wholesome words . . . He is proud, knowing nothing . . . from such withdrew thyself." It was a favorite text of slaveowners against abolitionists. If the woman felt as Eells says, she evidently held her tongue, for there is no record of further action against her.

---

[27]PHS, box 10, vol. 2, 10.

[28]Faust, "Presbyterian Missions," 317. Faust lists this letter as box 10, vol. 1, 1014, but having been unable to locate that letter in the archives, I have quoted Faust. Faust "withheld" Eells's name out of delicacy, but there is no doubt that in the context Eells is the person concerned. The young lady was probably Esther Mathers.

One final episode, the most critical of all for the Presbyterian Board, may be cited to round out the picture—the one involving the conflict of loyalties forced upon J. Ross Ramsay's black interpreter, Robert (or Robin) Foster, in the summer of 1859. It involved the mission in the case of a runaway slave, the worst of all possible crimes short of slave insurrection itself. The slave, owned by a Creek of mixed Indian and white ancestry, was named Luke. He was one of many in the summer of 1859 who tried to run away from the Creek or Cherokee Nations to find freedom in Mexico. "There is considerable excitement now among the Creeks," wrote Robert Loughridge on 6 August 1860, from Tullahassee, "about a great number of runaway Negroes in the Country. One of whom killed a white man lately who was endeavoring to capture him. A Mexican was taken lately who was said to be the pilot for the negroes on their way to Mexico. The people met yesterday a few miles distant to hang the Mexican, but I understand they concluded to turn him over to the U. States authority. The Cherokees also are much excited about abolitionism."[29]

Luke escaped his pursuers and with his wife gradually made his way secretly from the Creek Nation southwest toward Mexico. Early in September he and his wife arrived at Oak Ridge Mission in the Seminole Nation where J. Ross Ramsay was located. Luke, being related to Robert Foster, went to him for help. All he wanted Foster to do was to help him persuade Ramsay to write a pass permitting Luke and his wife to go through the Seminole Country to Fort Cobb or Fort Arbuckle further southwest (toward Mexico). Under normal circumstances this would have been no problem. Missionaries often wrote passes for slaves who had been given permission by their masters to go to the forts or missions to find work. Indian masters were not always able to write English. Luke, however, preferred to say simply that he had received oral permission from his master but had somehow forgotten to obtain written permission. He now found that necessary and did not want to return all the way back to the Creek Nation to get it. All Robert had to do was to vouch for Luke and say he knew him to be an honest man.

Yet of course that made Robert an accessory to the escape. Even if Robert did not know that Luke had shot a white man who tried to capture him, he must have known that any aid he and Ramsay gave to Luke

---

[29]PHS, box 6, vol. 3, 14.

and his wife would be a serious breach of trust as well as of the law. Where did his loyalty lie? With the man who had purchased him to help him to freedom or with his relative and fellow slave?[30] This is the way Ramsay a month later described what happened:

> It is well known in that region [where Ramsay lived] especially among the Seminoles, that I have been in the habit of writing passes for their slaves when they are about starting to the garrisons to hunt work. They have been so accustomed to this that their slaves often come and get passes without any written order from their owners. (This plan, however, I now find to my sorrow is not a wise one.) But this is the way in which I was betrayed into [my] present difficulty which I suppose my enemies [the Baptists] are making themselves very busy in swelling into a mountain.
>
> The negro in question was named Luke. He was a stranger to me though I knew his brother, who is a noted preacher in the Baptist Church. Luke and a woman he called his wife and who is a half sister of a little negro girl who is our nurse, came to the house of my interpreter, Robert [Robin] who is his cousin, purporting to be simply on a visit and stayed with him some days. While there he came to me in company with Robert and informed me that he was on his way to the fort with the consent of his owner seeking work—told me the name of his owner (in which I have since heard that he lied) and asked me to write him a paper to enable him to obtain work either at Fort Arbuckle or Fort Cobb, as he had forgotten to obtain one before leaving home, and it is a fact that no negroes are allowed to stay about the Forts unless they have a pass. The request was granted on the authority of Robert who knew him well, though I believe he was totally ignorant as well as myself of his real character and intentions at that time. I wrote a pass similar to others that I had written about as follows.:
>
> This is to certify that the bearer is the property of _____ and with his consent is seeking work in the vicinity of Fort Arbuckle or Fort Cobb.[31]

With the pass in his possession, Luke moved southwestward again toward Fort Cobb about 100 miles from Oak Ridge. But here his pursuers caught up with him as he lay hidden in a hayfield. "While riding from the hayfield behind the officer to the garrison he had taken a large knife from his pocket and cut his own throat and soon after his arrival at the Fort expired." The pass was found in his pocket "and on inquiry being made as to who had written it, his wife told [them] it was I. His

---

[30]Robert claimed later that he had no idea that Luke and his wife were running away, or at least so he told Ramsay. Given the circumstances, there was hardly anything else he could say. Somehow I have my doubts.

[31]PHS, box 6, vol. 3, 150.

wife and the pass were sent back to Moty Kenard, principal chief of the Creeks. The woman had been whipped and I understood that a demand was going to be made to have Robert whipped also for signing his name to the pass, and they were very angry at me. I immediately wrote a letter to Moty Kenard disclaiming any intention to aid the negro and stating my total ignorance of his character either as a criminal or runaway, also endeavoring to exculpate Robert and forbidding them to punish him as he was my property."[32]

But this was not the impression that Loughridge got about the incident. Loughridge later told Lowrie that Ramsay had written to Chief Kenard "that he was deceived by his interpreter in regard to the boy, &c."[33] When the slave was captured Ramsey fortunately was already on his way out of the Indian Territory to make a brief visit home to Pennsylvania on personal business. He learned about the capture of Luke at North Fork in Indian Territory on his way east and wrote a hasty note to Kenard asserting his innocence. But he did not wait for an answer. Loughridge meanwhile rode over to the Creek Council house to look into the matter. "I found there was a good deal of feeling against Mr. R." he wrote on 12 October 1869, "and all I could say seemed to do but little in quieting it. One [Indian], the most excited, said it did not matter much now if Mr. R. *stayed away*." The Creeks were so wrought up that Loughridge told the board, "I don't know that it will be safe for him to return."[34]

The Reverend John Lilley, who had replaced Loughridge as superintendent of Kowetah Station among the Creeks, wrote to the board on 3 November 1860, protesting the unfairness of the accusations occasioned by Ramsay's mistake. Many people "cry out abolition and call us all abolitionists and threaten Mr. Ramsay with violence, *Even to Tar and Feather Him* and endeavor to get the Indians excited to violently drive us out of the country without even a hearing. This is base as it is false. We never meddle with their Slaves or their laws in regard to them. There are some half breeds and whites who would like to drive us and Presbyterianism out of the country. . . . Our persons, Mission premises, Mission

---

[32]Idem.

[33]PHS, box 6, vol. 3, 17 (dated 12 October 1860).

[34]Idem.

property is all in danger. . . . Perhaps a line from the Secretary of War to the Agent [here] would lead that Officer to give us at least the protection his authority affords in time of danger."[35]

Ramsay, having reached Slate Hill, York County, Pennsylvania, wrote letter after letter to his colleagues in Indian Territory and to the board trying to find out when it would be safe to return to his post. But for months the reports were contradictory, some saying that the excitement had died down and that it was probably safe to come back, others arguing that it was still a ticklish situation and that perhaps Ramsay should wait a bit longer. The board delayed a decision until finally, before any action was taken, Fort Sumter was fired upon and the Civil War was on. Shortly thereafter most of the Indians among the Five Civilized Tribes declared their alliance with the Confederacy and the Reverend J. Leighton Wilson left the New York Mission Office of the board to join his fellow South Carolinians in their secession both from the North and the Northern Presbyterians. The runaway slave affair was perhaps a fitting climax to the difficulties the Presbyterian missionaries had with the slaveholding Indians.

J. Leighton Wilson, in a letter to Cyrus Byington, the Presbyterian missionary to the Choctaws in 1861, blamed the war on the abolitionists.[36] Cyrus Kingsbury, Byington's older colleague among the Choctaws, blamed Lincoln: "What could have induced the Lincoln Administration," he wrote after Fort Sumter fell, "so suddenly to change its policy and to plunge the country into such a horrible war? How easily all matters might have been settled if there had been a mind for it?"[37] If Kingsbury meant that it would have been an easy matter for the federal government not to have meddled in the issue of slavery, that was an odd point of view for someone who had seen how difficult it was for the Presbyterians (who had no obligation to hold the nation together) to follow such a policy in the Indian Territory.

---

[35]PHS, box 6, vol. 3, 152. Lilley visted North Fork "and tried to get the names of the gentlemen who was going to Tar and feather" Ramsay, "but they were not to be found; the whites blamed the Indians and the Indians blamed the whites. They had it reported that [Ramsay] sneaked through North Forks at night to escape being caught." PHS, box 6, vol. 3, 154.

[36]PHS, box 10, vol. 1, 275.

[37]PHS, box 10, vol. 1, 274 (dated 7 May 1861).

The Presbyterian Foreign Mission Board, though dedicated to avoiding controversy over slavery and convinced of the folly of trying to mix spiritual salvation with social reform, had been totally unable to avoid involvement in this issue from its first entrance into slaveholding territory as a mission field. What did these Presbyterian missionaries really want the country to do about slavery? Did they really believe that people could ignore it, forget about it, leave it up to God to solve in his own good time?

The Reverend James Thornwell of South Carolina, generally accepted then and since as the most persuasive spokesman for the Presbyterian point of view on slavery in the 1850s, said that slavery was "determined by the Providence of God" and as such men must not interfere with it. However, he wrote in 1851,

> We do not ask . . . [our brethren] to patronize Slaves; we do not wish to change their own institutions; we only ask them to treat us as the Apostles treated the slaveholders of their day, and to leave to us the liberty, which we accord to them, of conducting our affairs according to our own convictions of truth and duty. [38]

This, he said, was a "reasonable demand." It was not quite the position that the Presbyterian Board took in the Indian Territory. The policy of the board there seems to have been, "When in Rome, do as the Romans." Assuming that the Presbyterians were never sincerely committed to altering the institution of slavery; concluding that "neutrality" was just a convenient name for acquiescence in the system; and without doubting that they were nevertheless eager to do all they could to make the system as benevolent as possible, the historian is still bound to ask whether they could have done anything about it if they had wanted to? Or was their position the only sensible, pragmatic, possible one if there were to be missionaries to the Southern Indians at all?

Admittedly the odds were heavily stacked against altering the institution with any rapidity among the Indians, even though it had only become a fundamental part of their way of life within the preceding generation. The Indian economy was becoming more dependent upon slaves with every step they took toward civilization and every year made eradication of that system that much more difficult. Moreover, the racial tensions between red men and white placed unbearable pressure upon

---

[38]Thompson, *Presbyterians*, 1:536, 538.

the Indian to dissociate himself from black people lest he be relegated to the same caste. Although Indians were not citizens and their territory was a foreign mission field, the missionaries were hardly free agents in a free environment.

The most persuasive defense of the Presbyterian position was that the American Board, which had tried to bring pressure upon its missionaries to persuade the Indians to abandon slavery, had failed. The American Board closed out its missions to the Southern Indians in 1859 and 1860 precisely because its missionaries believed they could not cooperate with that policy—set in Boston under pressure from Northern antislavery proponents; to do so, they were convinced, would do more harm than good to the advancement of Christianity.

There was one mission board, however, that did adopt a different policy in the Indian Territory with some success, the American Baptist Missionary Union. Based in Boston as the foreign mission board of the Northern Baptists (after the Baptist schism of 1845), the A.B.M.U. instructed its missionaries in the Indian nation to make slaveholding a bar of communion in 1852. The Reverend Evan Jones, superintendent of the Baptist Mission to the Cherokees for thirty years and his son, John B. Jones, who had grown up among the Cherokee, were not eager to raise trouble for themselves. Nonetheless, they were both committed antislavery men and they executed, as politely and quietly as possible, the decision of their board. Not only did they refuse after that date to admit slaveholding Cherokee to their communion, they firmly expelled from their mission churches several Christian Indians who declined to emancipate their slaves.

These Indians complained to the federal agent, George M. Butler, that the Baptists were meddling in Indian civil affairs. Butler wrote to Washington on two separate occasions calling the Joneses dangerous abolitionists and demanding their expulsion. But the commissioners of Indian Affairs took no action. The Joneses rode out the storm. In fact, they went even further. As the secession sentiment grew stronger among the Cherokees they helped to organize a secret society that was dedicated to maintaining the Union. It is true that John B. Jones was finally expelled from the Cherokee Nation in 1860 for openly espousing antislavery views. But he was expelled by order of the government agent, not by action of the Cherokee Council, though there were individual Cherokee slaveholders who threatened him and his father with "the fist and the cowhide" for their abolitionism. In 1861 Evan Jones was also forced to leave the nation because of growing Confederate sympathies among the Cherokees that outweighed the pro-Union minority he had tried to organize. George M. Butler took his stand with the Confederacy after 1861, but Chief John Ross of the Cherokees, though the owner of more than 100 slaves, was for the Union and always remained a close friend and supporter of the Joneses. Even more significant, the mission churches of the Baptists contained in 1860 five times as many Indian members as those of the Presbyterians (including those founded by the American Board).[39]

The choice of the Presbyterian Board was not the only one possible. Providence allowed a wider latitude for human action than the Presbyterians acknowledged. After the war everyone agreed with that. Slavery was abolished when Americans were willing to pay the price.

---

[39]For the work of the Joneses in the Cherokee Nation, see the MSS of Carolyn Foreman, "The Reverend Evan Jones" and "John B. Jones" at the Oklahoma Historical Society, Oklahoma City; *The American Baptist Missionary Magazine* (Boston) 39 (1859): 274; 40 (1860): 138-39, 271; 41 (1861): 200; 42 (1862): 212-13; *The Watchman and Reflector* (Boston), 11 October 1860; letters of George M. Butler to the commissioner of Indian Affairs, 22 June 1855 and 30 June 1858 in "Letters Received, Bureau of Indian Affairs," National Archives; and Annie H. Abel, *The American Indian as Slaveholder and Secessionist* (Cleveland, 1915) 47, n. 56, 292, 293, and passim.

THE CHEROKEE PREACHER
AND THE BAPTIST SCHISM
OF 1844-1845

This is really a footnote to Baptist history. I was struck by the irony that a Baptist Indian preacher may in some sense have been the starting point of the great schism over slavery that split the mighty Baptist denomination in 1844-1845. As it turned out, the Reverend Jesse Bushyhead died before his name could become famous in terms of that schism. The questions raised by the antislavery Baptists about his owning slaves thus became moot just as the crisis peaked. In any case, it would only have been accidental that he rather than a white slaveholding Baptist preacher produced the test case that led to denominational division in 1844-1845.

Still, it was interesting to see how cautiously the Baptist leaders in the North and in the Baptist Foreign Mission Board skirted around this matter when it was first raised. Part of the problem stemmed from the fact that the Baptist mission among the Cherokees had from the start been led by a Northern Baptist from Philadelphia. The Reverend Evan Jones, the leading figure in the Baptist mission to the Cherokees, was born in Wales and reached manhood in England. He came to the United States in 1821 with a decided antislavery bias, and it was with some difficulty that he kept this bias under control in the interest of Christianizing the Cherokees. Like his Presbyterian colleagues, he tried for two decades to separate the issue of slavery from the mission of soul-winning, but in the end, he could no more accomplish that division than they. In 1845 he was saved from considerable embarrassment by the timely (it must be said) death of his good friend, Jesse Bushyhead. After the schism, with the founding of the Southern Baptist denomination, he was to find that his problem over slaveholding Baptist Cherokees became worse rather than better. (This aspect of the Baptist dilemma over slaveholding among the Cherokees is discussed in part III, ch. 5.)

CONSIDERABLE ATTENTION HAS BEEN GIVEN by historians of religion to the great Baptist schism of 1844-1845, but comparatively little attention has been paid to the Cherokee Baptist preacher, the Reverend Jesse Bushyhead, who may have precipitated it. For a year or more Bushyhead's name was familiar to thousands of Baptists all over the nation; but by the end of the nineteenth century when A. H. Newman wrote his authoritative history of the denomination, he misidentified him as "John" Bushyhead, a mistake that almost all subsequent Baptist historians have perpetuated.[1] When Bushyhead became the first ordained Cherokee Baptist in 1833, he was hailed as a hero of the denomination, bringing Christianity to a pagan people in their own tongue. In subsequent years Bushyhead's fame rose as he was elevated to high position in his nation. In 1842 he came to New York City to address an admiring throng of Baptists gathered for the annual meeting of the Baptist Board of Foreign Missions (B. B. F. M.).[2] Then, suddenly, in 1844, he became the center of the controversy that rent the nation's largest denomination in two. Some antislavery Baptists had discovered that Jesse Bushyhead was the owner of black slaves.

Because he was in the pay of the B.B.F.M. as an assistant missionary, this information shocked Baptists all over the North. For years the Baptist Foreign Mission Board had been unwittingly supporting a missionary who was inculcating slavery principles among the heathen when he was supposed to be uplifting and Christianizing them. To the Baptists of the slaveholding states, Bushyhead became a symbol of the right of slaveholders to be appointed as missionaries. To the antislavery Baptists in the North, he became a symbol of the denomination's participation in a heinous sin. To the Executive Committee of the B.B.F.M., he became an acute embarrassment.

According to A. H. Newman, writing in 1894, "Sometime after the [Triennial] Convention of 1844, the Board of Foreign Missions was said to have produced the resignation of John [Jesse] Bushyhead, a highly re-

---

[1]A. H. Newman, *A History of the Baptist Churches in the United States* (New York, 1894) 445.

[2]*Baptist Memorial and Monthly Chronicle* 5 (16 May 1842): 155.

spected Indian Baptist preacher on the ground that he was a slave-holder."[3] The antislavery Baptists considered this a righteous action, cleansing the denomination of a corrupt agent. The proslavery Baptists considered it an uncharitable and basely political action to disrupt the denomination and cast unwarranted aspersions upon almost half of the Baptists in the country. "The impression commonly prevailed in the South thenceforth," Newman continued, "that slaveholders would be rigorously excluded from appointment as missionaries, agents or officers of the Board." Robert G. Torbet, seventy years later, wrote in his scholarly history of the denomination that the forced resignation of Bushyhead led the Alabama Baptist Convention, in November 1844, to send "a letter embodying what is known as the Alabama Resolutions to the Board of Managers of the Triennial Convention insisting that the Foreign Mission Agency, which they supported, give slaveholders and non-slaveholders the same privileges."[4] When the board said, in response to these resolutions, that it "could not appoint" any slaveholder as a missionary, it precipitated the withdrawal of most Southern Baptists associations from the convention and the creation of the Southern Baptist Convention in 1845. Robert A. Baker, the historian of the Southern Baptists, has, as Newman and Torbet did, traced the schism at least in part to the effort of the Foreign Mission Board "to secure the resignation of a beloved slaveholding missionary to the Indians in order to conciliate the abolitionists."[5]

The purpose of this article is to provide a footnote to Baptist history that says it didn't happen just this way. Jesse Bushyhead was never forced to resign, and he probably did not own any slaves. It is time to resurrect Jesse Bushyhead from obscurity and to clear him from any responsibility in the great schism of 1844-1845. In the same effort we may rescue the B.B.F.M. from the imputation that it made Bushyhead a sacrificial scapegoat in the vain hope of avoiding the schism. The schism would have come, and did come, without Bushyhead. But where there is smoke, there may be fire, and the matter bears investigation.

---

[3]Newman, *History*, 445.

[4]Robert G. Torbet, *A History of the Baptists*, rev. ed. (Valley Forge, 1963) 291.

[5]Robert A. Baker, *Relations Between Northern and Southern Baptists*, 2nd ed. (Fort Worth, 1948) 76. Baker rightly notes that this was based on "rumors."

First, there is the question of mistaken identity: a diligent search of all the available records in the Baptist Foreign Missions Archives indicates that there never was a Cherokee Baptist preacher named "John" Bushyhead. An equally diligent search of the census roles and genealogical records of the Cherokee Nation reveals no Cherokee of that name in 1844.[6] The records do show that there was a Cherokee missionary named Jesse Bushyhead and that he was an eminent figure in his nation. Jesse Bushyhead first appears in the records of the B.B.F.M. in a letter from the superintendent of the Baptist Mission to the Cherokee, the Reverend Evan Jones, on 7 September 1832.[7] At that time Jones spoke highly of Bushyhead's work as a Baptist convert and exhorter among his people. Three months later, Jones recommended him for an appointment as an assistant missionary in the pay of the board. The board accepted Jones's recommendation. In April 1833, Bushyhead was ordained, and thereafter for eleven years he worked closely with Jones not only as pastor of his own church at Amohee, but in spreading the gospel, saving souls, and founding new churches. In addition, he assisted Jones in translating the Bible and religious tracts into the Sequoyan syllabary in which the Cherokee wrote their language. Bushyhead was generally acknowledged to be one of the most effective bilingual writers and speakers in his nation.

The records did not show that the board inquired—or that Evan Jones inquired—as to whether Jesse Bushyhead owned any slaves at the time of his appointment or ordination. It was not considered an issue of importance. William Lloyd Garrison had then barely raised the banner of abolitionism, and the various denominations were still blissfully ignorant of the problems that lay in store on this question. It was, of course, well known that the Cherokee Indians had adopted the institution of slavery. Living in the South, they followed the agricultural system of the South when they had to give up the fur trade as their principal means of support. The Cherokee had owned black slaves at least since

---

[6]I am indebted to William Brackney and Dean Kirkwood for help in researching the Baptist missionary archives at the American Baptist Historical Society and at Valley Forge; I am indebted to Rella Looney and Martha Blaine for help in researching the Cherokee census rolls and genealogies at the Oklahoma Historical Society.

[7]Evan Jones to Solomon Peck, 7 September 1832, Records of the American Baptist Mission Union, "Indian Missions," American Baptist Historical Society, Rochester, New York; hereinafter cited as "Indian Mission Papers," ABHS.

the Revolutionary era, and as they became increasingly agricultural, they increased their accumulation of slaves.[8] According to the first Cherokee census, taken in 1809, some 12,395 Cherokee owned a total of 583 black slaves; by the census of 1824-1825, there were 1,277 black slaves in the nation; and by 1835, there were 1,592.[9]

Through a conspiracy of silence, the various missionary agencies that sent ministers to "civilize and Christianize" the Cherokee did their best to avoid calling attention to this matter. The institution was not exactly hidden; it simply was not talked about. Hence whether Jesse Bushyhead owned slaves would not have been a question that anyone wanted to raise in 1832. In these early years of missionary effort, with stiff rivalry among the Baptists, Presbygationalists, Presbyterians, Methodists, and Moravians, the addition of a talented chief like Jesse Bushyhead to labor for the Baptist cause was more important than his possible participation in slavery. Certainly at that time no missionary agency made slavery or antislavery a part of its preaching and no Cherokee convert was denied membership in any mission church because he owned slaves. In fact, most missionaries found it useful to employ slave labor and some missionaries bought slaves to assist in the laborious work of constructing and maintaining a mission.

The next questions to be answered are who first brought up the question of Bushyhead's being a slaveowner and when? It was not the proslavery Baptists in the South, but the antislavery Baptists in the North. The villains (or heroes, depending upon one's perspective) were the men associated with the founding of the American Baptist Free Mission Society (F.M.S.). John R. McKivigan has recently brought back to light the history of this organization (originally named the American and Foreign Baptist Mission Society).[10] Its organizers started by holding an antislavery convention of Baptists in New York City in 1840. After the failure of the Triennial Convention to meet their demands for a positive

---

[8]See Rudi Halliburton, Jr., *Red Over Black: Black Slavery Among the Cherokee Indians* (Westport CT, 1977) and Theda Perdue, *Slavery and the Evolution of Cherokee Society, 1540-1866* (Knoxville, 1979).

[9]See W. G. McLoughlin and Walter H. Conser, Jr., "The Cherokees in Transition," *Journal of American History* 64 (December 1977): 678-703.

[10]John R. McKivigan, "The American Baptist Free Mission Society," *Foundations* 21 (October-December 1978): 340-55.

stand against slavery in 1841, they formed, in 1843, an abolitionist mission society as an alternative to the B.B.F.M. Antislavery Baptists who wanted to be certain that their money for missionary work did not go to support anyone who was in favor of slavery (or who failed to oppose it) could send their donations to the F.M.S. instead of the B.B.F.M. The preamble to the F.M.S. constitution pledged it to be "distinctly and thoroughly separated from all connection with the known avails of Slavery in the support of any of its benevolent purposes."[11]

In January 1844, the F.M.S. issued the first number of a monthly newspaper, the *Free Missionary*. Edited by K. Arvine in Boston, this magazine launched a campaign to force the B.B.F.M., and the Baptist Home Mission Society as well, to take a firm stand against slavery regardless of the risk of dividing the denomination. Officially the Triennial Convention, which appointed the managers of the home and foreign mission boards, had adopted in 1841 a position of "neutrality" on the slavery question (the so-called "Baltimore Resolutions"). One means by which the Free Missionary Society tried to expose what it considered the hypocrisy of "neutrality" was to demonstrate that the board was employing slaveholders as missionaries. Presumably many antislavery Baptists would be shocked to learn that this was happening; they would demand an explanation and perhaps they would withhold their donations. This would force the board either to acknowledge its approbation of appointing slaveholders as missionaries or else force it to give up the practice.

Among the first of several slaveholding missionaries currently employed by the board whom the *Free Missionary* publicized in its pages was "Mr. Bushyhead, a Missionary among the Cherokees. He lives in a fine dwelling, has a plantation and several wretched human beings under his irresponsible power."[12] Where the editor obtained this informa-

---

[11]This constitution is quoted in full in the *Free Mission Record* (New York, 1857) 6.

[12]Quoted in A. T. Foss and Edward Mathews, *Facts for Baptist Churches* (Utica NY, 1850) 102. This book is a prime repository for many of the documents in the controversy. For references in it to Bushyhead, see 102-105. For other references to Bushyhead, see *Free Missionary* 1 (June 1844): 27 and 1 (December 1844): 82-84. It should also be noted that when the federal government took a census of every Cherokee family in 1835, Jesse Bushyhead's family was listed as containing ten mixed-blood Cherokees and four slaves. Exactly which members of the family owned these slaves was not noted. A typescript copy of the census is at the Gilcrease Museum, Tulsa, Oklahoma.

tion, he did not say. But suddenly Jesse Bushyhead became the central figure in a great national drama.

Many Baptists knew of Jesse Bushyhead, for his effective missionary work had been featured regularly in reports of the Cherokee mission published in the *Baptist Missionary Magazine* for a dozen years. Many of the leading Baptists had seen, heard, and met Bushyhead in New York City in 1842 when he told the annual meeting of the B.B.F.M. that "the Baptists are now the prevailing denomination" in the Cherokee Nation and that "knowledge of the Gospel has extended pretty much over the Cherokee country and there are Christians in almost every part."[13] He had made a very favorable impression upon all who heard him.

Those who knew something of his life knew that he was of mixed ancestry, having descended from a marriage between John Stuart, a British Indian agent, and a Cherokee. Jesse Bushyhead (whose Cherokee name was rendered Tas-the-ghe-tee-hee or Dta-ske-gi-di-hi) was born shortly after the turn of the century in the Great Smoky Mountains between North Carolina and Tennessee. His parents were well enough off to send him to school in Tennessee. There he became interested in Christianity and returned to his hometown of Amohee to preach his new faith among his friends. Through study of the Bible, he concluded that he should be baptized by immersion. The ordinance was administered in 1830 by a Baptist itinerant preacher from Tennessee. Largely through Bushyhead's efforts, nineteen Cherokee were converted; a Baptist church was formed at Amohee, and he was licensed to preach in it.[14]

Evan Jones, who was then superintendent of the B.B.F.M. mission in Valley Towns, North Carolina, was so impressed with Bushyhead's piety, zeal, and oratorical ability that he enlisted him in the missionary cause soon after he met him. The salary provided by the B.B.F.M. enabled Bushyhead to devote most of his time to preaching, although he continued to serve his people in various political capacities. In 1834 he was chosen by the Cherokee Council to be a justice in the Cherokee Su-

---

[13]*Baptist Memorial and Monthly Chronicle* 5 (16 May 1842): 155.

[14]For biographical data on Bushyhead and Evan Jones, see Walter N. Wyteh, *Poor Lo: Early Indian Missions* (Philadelphia, 1896) 47-48; James W. Moffitt, "Early Baptist Missionary Work Among the Cherokees," East Tennessee Historical Society *Publications* 12 (1940): 25-26.

preme Court, and on more than one occasion was a delegate for his nation on important negotiations.

Evan Jones, born in Brecknockshire, Wales, in 1788, had come to America early in 1821 with his wife and family. Settling near Philadelphia, he joined an early group of volunteers for mission work among the Cherokee and went to Valley Towns with the pastor of his church, the Reverend Thomas Roberts, in September 1821.[15] Roberts left the mission in 1824; Jones was ordained pastor of the mission church in 1825 and became superintendent at the same time, a position he retained until 1866. Jones was always antislavery in principle, but he had given the matter little attention prior to 1844. To him the chief work of a missionary was to spread the gospel and rescue the heathen from hellfire. He had never preached against slavery as a missionary and had little call to face up to the horrors of the institution because he worked chiefly among the full-blood Cherokee who owned few slaves. In 1838-1839, Jones and Bushyhead were appointed by the principal chief, John Ross, to head contingents from the Cherokee Nation on the 800-mile "Trail of Tears" to northeastern Oklahoma. Here the Baptist mission was reconstituted and the two men continued their work. In 1844 he and Bushyhead, 1,500 miles from Boston where the B.B.F.M. was located, were only barely aware of the storm that was brewing over the slavery issue back East.

When the Triennial Convention met in 1844, it once again failed to take a clear-cut stand for or against slavery. The *Free Missionary* magazine redoubled its efforts to bring the matter of slaveholding missionaries before the public. In its issue of August 1844, the magazine suggested that the Executive Committee of the B.B.F.M. was secretly trying to purge Bushyhead in order to avoid any embarrassment over the question. Read carefully, the item in the *Free Missionary* does not say that the board had forced Bushyhead to resign; it merely suggests that the board had instituted such action. Later reports claiming that the board did force his resignation probably stemmed from a misreading of this article. After referring to Bushyhead's slaveholding, the article said,

It is believed by some persons in Boston, who lend searching gaze upon the

---

[15]For biographical data on Jones, see William Cathcart, *Baptist Encyclopedia* (Philadelphia, 1881) 612, and E. C. Routh, "Early Missionaries Among the Cherokees," *Chronicles of Oklahoma* 15 (December 1937): 449-65. The author is currently preparing a full-length biography of Evan Jones.

doings of the old Board, that they are going to play the same game with the South that was played with the North at Baltimore in 1841. . . . Eld. [Robert] Pattison [Corresponding Secretary of the B.B.F.M.], we understand, has never presented this subject before the Board; at least, they have taken no action upon it, notwithstanding the publicity of Bushyhead's character and conduct. But Eld. Pattison has written a letter to him on the subject—a *private letter*! Now it is firmly believed by some who know more about these things than we do, that the Elder and his coadjutors intend, by their *personal* advice, to persuade Mr. Bushyhead to give up his connection with the Board without their passing any vote on the subject . . . and at the same time so manage the matter that the South can get no charge to fasten upon the Board.[16]

In short, the F.M.S. accused the B.B.F.M. of trying to sweep the issue under the carpet. The editor surmised, correctly, that "the South will not be satisfied with such double dealing," and neither would the abolitionists in the denomination. "Like the South, we say to the Board: Be frank and honest; be either for us or against us . . . how long before you will see it is vain to endeavor to keep up the marriage compact between two such eternal antagonisms as Liberty and Slavery!"[17]

A careful study of the B.B.F.M. archives shows no record of a letter from Pattison to Bushyhead at this time or at any other time. It would have been strange had he so written. All communications concerning the mission were addressed to the superintendent; it would have been extraordinary for the board to write directly to one of the assistant missionaries on a matter of such importance. There is a record that Pattison did write to Evan Jones about the matter; in fact, he wrote two letters. He did not, as was usual, record either of them in the file of "Domestic Letters Sent." We know of them only because Jones later mentioned having received two letters on that subject. Since Jones's answer to these two letters is the best and only contemporary evidence we have of the board's reaction to the news that Bushyhead owned slaves, it seems useful to put the whole letter on record. It reveals that Jesse Bushyhead both was and was not a slaveholder, depending on how one defined the term. However, he certainly was not the Simon Legree the abolitionists had tried to make him.

---

[16]Quoted in Foss and Mathews, *Facts*, 102-103.

[17]Commenting on this article in their book in 1850, Foss and Mathews stated as fact what Arvine in 1844 only inferred: "We see how it was that a letter came to be addressed to Bushyhead." *Facts*, 103.

Cherokee, Creek Nation
August 26, 1844

My Dear and honored Brother,

I received your favor of June 17th by Bro. Cogswell in the midst of the distress and mourning on account of the death of our beloved brother Bushyhead, which prevented my answering it immediately. Yours of July 11 has now come to hand, and to your inquiry, I reply that Mrs. Bushyhead had a Black woman inherited from her father, who, according to the laws of the Nation, belonged to her exclusively: the property of the wife not being liable for the debts nor subject to the disposal of the husband. This woman has for several years been released from all claims on her labor, though provided for as before with board and clothing. The only daughter of this woman whose labor would be profitable is married to a free man and has been allowed to go with her husband to a grazing country 80 or 90 miles distant. Bro. B. furnished them with stock to keep on shares, so as to commence business for themselves. And from my knowledge of Bro. Bushyhead's sentiment on the Slavery question, I have no doubt the younger ones would be disposed of in a similar way when opportunity should offer.

About the years 1840, or 41, Bro. B. purchased a Black man with his wife and child (*by his own desires for the purpose of affording him an opportunity to become free*). The man is a Baptist Preacher. As soon as he came home, Bro. B. told him he must not consider himself any more as a slave but act faithfully as a free man. He furnished him with a horse to ride to his preaching places on sabbath days. This is the black man I have once or twice had occasion to allude to, having been called on several times to baptize hopeful converts, the evident fruit of the blessing of God on this man's labors.

With regard to this transaction, I am fully satisfied that our dear departed brother was actuated by the same generous and benevolent motives which pervaded and governed his conduct in all relations in life and in the disposition of all his time and talent.

I remain, Dear and Honored Brothers, Yours very Sincerely,
Evan Jones[18]

The correspondence between Jones and Pattison in 1844 was never revealed to the public or even hinted at. It indicates, however, that Pattison was quietly investigating the allegations and might well have tried to solve the problem informally just as the abolitionists suspected.

---

[18]Jones to Peck, 26 August 1844, "Indian Mission Papers," ABHS.

Bushyhead's death on 17 July 1844 seemed to end the problem so far as Pattison and the Foreign Mission Board were concerned. Fate had intervened to help bury the matter in an orgy of tributes to the departed. Without adverting to his having been denounced as a slaveholder, the board saw to it that notices of Bushyhead's sterling character and worthy career were brought to the attention of all Baptists through the pages of the *Watchman Reflector*, the official organ of the denomination, published in Boston. Pattison sent to the *Watchman* a letter written to the board by Hervey Upham, who was employed at the Cherokee Mission as a printer. Written 5 August 1844, the letter was not intended for publication, but it proved opportune for allaying the controversy. It contained a general account of the progress of the Cherokee Mission and referred to the success of the first issue of *The Cherokee Messenger* (a Baptist magazine that was the first periodical published in Oklahoma), for which Jesse Bushyhead had just completed the translation of the book of Genesis prior to his death. The Cherokee, Upham reported, "are very much pleased" to have such a Christian paper published in their own language in their nation.

> Mr. Jones has probably written to you an account of bro. Bushyhead's death. It will be a great [loss] to us—a loss which will be almost impossible for us to bear up under, but we know that all things are in the hands of our Heavenly Father and that he orders all things aright. It may be that God has taken him away from evil to come. He has been, you well know, Chief Justice of the Nation for some time and being a man of undaunted courage, it had devolved on him to try and condemn men of the most abandoned character when no other judge in the Nation would have dared to perform the duty. This trait in his character has raised him up a great many enemies among that portion of the nation who are opposed to law and civilization. A number of attempts had been made to take his life but were prevented apparently by the hand of God. On one occation [*sic*] a band of men formed themselves into three parties to proceed to as many different places to murder those who were obnoxious to them, but it so happened that after burning one house and murdering the inmates, some misunderstanding arose which prevented them from carrying out their plans. Within a few weeks past we have heard of a similar attempt being made, but they were again foiled. So that perhaps God has taken away bro. B. and permitted him to die peaceably in the bosom of his family to save him from a more violent death.[19]

---

[19]Upham's original letter to the board, 5 August 1844, is in "Indian Mission Papers," ABHS; it appeared in the *Watchman-Reflector*, 25 October 1844.

A second letter by Upham concerning Bushyhead was published in the *Watchman-Reflector* on 10 January 1845. This was addressed directly to the editor, probably at Pattison's suggestion. Here Upham referred to Bushyhead's work as founder and president of the National Temperance Society of the Cherokee. A few days before his death from "prairie fever," Bushyhead had appeared at a large temperance meeting at the council grounds "under a burning sun with sweat pouring from his face, eloquently pleading with them to refrain from the intoxicating cup and persuading them to sign their names to the temperance pledge." Upham included in this letter an obituary printed in the official newspaper of the Cherokee Nation published at Tahlequah, *The Cherokee Advocate*:

> The subject of this notice was a man of great distinction among his tribe. He was in his acquirements a self-made man. He obtained in his youth a very limited education, which he improved to enable him to be a good English speaker as well as an able orator in Cherokee. He was a correct interpreter and translator and at his demise was extensively engaged in translating English into Cherokee [for the Baptist mission]. He has occupied many public stations which he discharged with fidelity and for the good of his people. His name will live as long as his tribe, while his exulting spirit has joined the righteous in Heaven.[20]

By printing these two letters (which, in effect, transformed the dead Bushyhead from a sinner into a saint), the B.B.F.M. hoped to put a quietus upon the clamor of the abolitionists.

But, as everyone now knows, their effort failed. The impression still prevailed, because the board had done nothing to dispel it, that Bushyhead had been forced to resign from his ministry because he owned slaves.[21] Southern proslavery Baptists now became as determined as the Northern abolitionists to clarify the issue. At a meeting held in Marion, Alabama, on 25 November 1844, the Alabama Baptist Convention passed a series of resolutions designed to compel the Foreign Mission Board to make its position explicit. The Reverend Jeremiah Jeter of Virginia told the board that the impetus behind those resolutions came from

---

[20]*Watchman-Reflector*, 10 January 1845.

[21]The fact that Bushyhead was dead did not, of course, mollify the abolitionists: "And now, how does his death affect the matter? Was the Christian fellowship of the Convention for slaveholders involved in his appointment and support, made null and void by the mere fact of his death? Certainly not. It lived when he died and ever will live until the Convention or its Board express sorrow for having had a slaveholding missionary and declare they never will appoint another." *Free Missionary* 1 (December 1844): 84.

the belief that "Eld. Pattison had written, or caused to be written, a letter for the express purpose of inducing the loved and useful Missionary, Bushyhead, to resign because he was a slaveholder."[22] The Alabama Resolutions were an abstract statement of the right of slaveholders to be appointed as missionaries; they threatened secession from the denomination if these rights were abridged.

> 1.*Resolved*, By the Convention of the Baptist Denomination in the State of Alabama, that when one party to a voluntary compact between Christian brethren is not willing to acknowledge the entire social equality with the other, as to all the privileges and benefits of the union, nor even to refrain from impeachment and annoyance, united efforts between such parties, even in the sacred cause of Christian benevolence, cease to be agreeable, useful or proper.
>
> 2.*Resolved*, That our duty requires us, at this crisis, to demand from the proper authorities in all those bodies to whose funds we have contributed, or with whom we have in any way been connected, the distinct, explicit avowal that slaveholders are eligible, and entitled, equally with non-slaveholders, to all the privileges and immunities of their several unions; and especially to receive any agency, mission, or other appointments which may fall within the scope of their operations or duties.[23]

Additional resolves stated that this was to be forwarded to the mission board of the Triennial Convention requesting an answer and "that the Treasurer of this body be, and he is hereby instructed, not to pay any money intended to be applied without the limits of this State" to the Triennial mission boards until they received a satisfactory response from "our non-slaveholding brethren" in Boston.

The Alabama Resolutions came before the B.B.F.M. on 17 December 1844, and the board responded first, "that in the thirty years in which the Board has existed, no slaveholder, to our knowledge, has applied to be a missionary" (indicating their belief that Jesse Bushyhead had not, technically, been a slaveholder). Then, rather unwisely, the

---

[22]Quoted in Foss and Mathews, *Facts*, 103-104. Jeter made these remarks in April 1845, when the Alabama Resolutions and the response to them were being discussed at the annual meeting of the Foreign Mission Board. Robert A. Baker, who has read the diaries and letters of the Reverend Basil Manly, Sr. (who probably drew up the Alabama Resolutions) informs me that he has found no mention of Bushyhead by Manly. Personal letter to the author, 4 July 1980. I am indebted to Dr. Baker for his helpful comments on this manuscript.

[23]The Resolves are printed in full in the *Baptist Missionary Magazine* 25 (August 1845): 220-21.

board answered the hypothetical questions of the Alabama Convention: "If, however, any one should offer himself as a missionary, having slaves, and should insist on retaining them as his property, we could not appoint him. One thing is certain, we can never be a party to any arrangement which would imply approbation of slavery."

Meanwhile, the Free Mission Society had identified three other foreign missionaries appointed by the B.B.F.M. who were tainted by slavery, none of whom were acknowledged in this reply. According to an article in the *Free Missionary*, one of these was "Mr. Roberts, one of their missionaries in China [who] was formerly a slaveholder" who had disposed of his slaves, but "we have seen no indications of his being penitent for holding men in bondage—nor tokens of his being anything but a slaveholder still, setting aside the mere external relation." The second was "Mr. Stevens, who, at the time of his appointment [to Burma] was a justifier of human chattelship on Bible principles—an heir to slaves." The third was "Mr. Binney, who was sent to Burmah last fall [and] was a Northern man with Southern principles. He was bitterly opposed to abolition and pleaded for American slavery as sanctioned by divine revelation."[24] The abolitionists obviously took a broad view of the term *slaveholder* and a narrow view of the amount of leeway to be given to the board in making its appointments.

However, none of these cases involving foreign missionaries was pressed by the Southern or Northern Baptists. The issue of slaveholding missionaries finally came to a head in the Home Mission Board, where the Georgia Baptists brought a test case in the fall of 1844. The Georgia Baptist Convention received an application for support by its local home missionary society from James E. Reeve. Reeve was a slaveholder and neither he nor the Georgia Convention made any bones about it. In fact, they purposely baited the Home Mission Board of the Triennial Convention by turning Reeve's application over to them, claiming they did not have sufficient funds to support Reeve. On 7 October 1844, the board rejected him, saying "we deem ourselves not at liberty to entertain the application" because Reeve had breached the board's rule of neu-

---

[24]*Free Missionary* 1 (December 1844): 84. Arvine called these men "slaveholders in spirit," if not in fact. For evidence of other slaveholders who had been approved by the B.B.F.M. as missionaries to China and Siam, see William W. Barnes, *The Southern Baptist Convention*, 1845-1953 (Nashville, 1954) 23.

trality on the issue. "When an application is made for the appointment of a slaveholder or an Abolitionist *as such*, the official obligation of the Board to act ceases."[25] In short, Reeve's slaveholding being irrelevant, he should never have mentioned it. The effort to avoid this issue had finally arrived at such tortured logic.

By the end of 1844 it was evident that the Triennial Convention could no longer speak for, or represent, all the nation's Baptists. Its Foreign and Home Mission Boards had both fallen under the control of Northerners whose position of neutrality displeased both Northern abolitionists and Southern proslavery advocates. Although moderates, such as Francis Wayland in the North and Richard Fuller in the South, still held a commanding influence, they concluded in April 1845 that it was wiser for the denomination to agree to divide its benevolent activities, permitting those in the South to support home and foreign missions on their own terms while leaving those in the North to do the same. In May 1845, at a convention in Augusta, Georgia, the Southern Baptists formed the Southern Baptist Convention and created their own home and foreign mission boards. In November 1845, the old Triennial Boards reconstituted themselves and changed the name of the Foreign and Home Mission Boards to the American Baptist Missionary Union.

Probably it is a small matter to lay to rest such minor mistakes as I have addressed here. At best, this essay can be no more than a small footnote in that mighty struggle within the Baptist denomination (and all other denominations at that time) to draw a clear line between religion and politics when, in fact, no such line can ever be drawn. Still, it is worth something, as Americans face at last the reality that we are a multiracial nation, to do justice to Jesse Bushyhead. He deserves to be remembered for what he did, not for what he did not do.

---

[25]See Foss and Mathews, *Facts*, 124-26 and Baker, *Relations*, 2nd ed., 76-80, for the reactions of abolitionists and Southern Baptists to this decision.

THE CHOCTAW SLAVE BURNING: A CRISIS IN INDIAN MISSIONS, 1859-1861

The kind of dilemma a missionary could face by living among slaveholding Indians was nowhere more dramatically evident than among the Choctaws. Cyrus Byington was one of the most dedicated and sincere missionaries ever to serve any Native American tribe. His concern for the welfare of the Choctaws is beyond doubt, and his services rendered to them, particularly in devising a means of writing the Choctaw langage in Roman letters and then in insisting that it be taught to every child, was of incalculable advantage to them. The Choctaws admired and respected Byington and yet, in the end, they placed him in an impossible position.

Byington, however, blamed the antislavery wing of his own denomination for his predicament. As a missionary of the American Board of Commissioners for Foreign Missions, he was subject to the control of New Englanders. While the American Board was ostensibly interdenominational (including Presbyterians and Dutch Reformed ministers), it was in fact dominated by Congregationalists. Among the Indians, the American Board's missionaries generally called themselves Presbyterians, but underneath many of them were basically New England Congregationalists, and as such, antislavery in outlook. Byington himself was opposed to the institution of slavery, but he, like most missionaries to the slaveholding Indians, decided that this was a matter to be settled by politicians and not by missionaries.

Over the years the American Board in Boston placed increasing pressure upon its missionaries in Indian Territory to work for the abolition of slavery there. It expected them to preach against slavery and to exclude slaveholding Indians from membership in mission churches. The grim incident at the center of this essay merely dramatizes a pervasive problem. Byington just happened to be the missionary upon whom the dilemma fell with especial ferocity.

WHAT SHOULD A CHRISTIAN CHURCH DO if one of its members burns another at the stake? Is it a mitigating circumstance if the woman burned is a slave and the woman who ordered her burned believed that the victim persuaded another slave to murder her [the victim's] husband? Does it matter if the confessed murderer was tortured and then, after implicating the woman burned, jumped into a river and drowned himself? Is it significant that the slave who was burned continued to assert her innocence until her death? And that she was the mother of eight children? Does it matter that the mistress and her slave were both members of a missionary church among the slaveholding Choctaws living in Indian Territory in 1859? Are the missionaries blameworthy if they continue the mistress in good standing in their mission church and make no effort to inform their mission board in Boston of the affair? What is the public to think about missions to slaveholding Indians when one of the missionaries surreptitiously reveals the whole story to the press a year after the event?

The murder of Richard Harkins, a prominent Choctaw leader of mixed white and Indian ancestry, on 28 December 1858, raised these and other controversial issues in the year 1859. The murder occurred ten miles from Stockbridge Mission Station, founded in Indian Territory in 1836 by the American Board of Commissioners for Foreign Missions in Boston. Harkins and his wife were members of the mission church led by the Reverend Cyrus Byington, one of the oldest and most respected of the board's Indian missionaries. The mission boards of the Congregationalists and the Presbyterians found the incident a major embarrassment when it was finally revealed. The abolitionists found in it further proof that mission work which failed to denounce slavery among the Indians was bound to fail. Since the American Board of Commissioners abandoned its mission to the Choctaws and other slaveholding Indians in 1859, many assumed that this incident was the cause. The fact that the Presbyterian Board of Foreign Missions in New York accepted Byington and the other A.B.C.F.M. missionaries at once into its patronage and made no effort to reassess its own missions to the slaveholding Indians confirmed the popular view that Presbyterianism was "the Slave Church of America." The Presbyterians had managed to avoid the schisms that had divided the Methodists and Baptists into Northern and Southern (antislavery and proslavery) branches in 1844 by insisting that slavery was a purely civil or political question outside the moral and spiritual sphere of the Christian church.

To people in the South, the incident merely revealed once again the danger and folly of involving the church in political or social questions. Proslavery Christians, while deploring the slave-burning itself, commended the missionaries for refusing to divert their efforts to Christianize the Indians by meddling in social and political institutions. They saw no reason why Byington should expel Mrs. Harkins from his church. One member of the Choctaw mission sent a scornful letter to a Northern newspaper stating that

> the action of Northern men of a certain class in respect to the Choctaw Mission, often reminds me of a flock of turkey buzzards. . . . [They] look with cool indifference upon the [Indian] members we have educated, the general good that has been effected through our labor. But show them a dead negro who has been put to death by a set of men who fear neither God, man, or the devil any further than suits their convenience, and they are all down on us at once.[1]

Both as an example of the problem of the Christian attitude toward slavery and missions in 1859 and as a challenge to the commonly held view that black slaves were better off with Indian rather than white masters, this incident deserves closer examination.[2]

The first documentary evidence we have of this wretched affair is in a letter to the Reverend J. Leighton Wilson, one of the corresponding secretaries of the Presbyterian Board of Foreign Missions. Dated 12 January 1860, more than a year after the event, it came from the Reverend Alexander Reid, superintendent of Spencer Academy, a Choctaw school

---

[1]Quoted in Charles K. Whipple, *The Relation of the American Board of Commissioners for Foreign Missions to Slavery* (Boston, 1861) 245.

[2]The best studies of slavery among the Southern Indians (usually called the Five Civilized Tribes) are by Kenneth Porter, "Relations Between Negroes and Indians," *Journal of Negro History* 17 (1932): 287-367 and 18 (1933): 282-321; Martin Roethler, "Negro Slavery Among the Cherokee Indians, 1540-1866" (Ph.D. thesis, Fordham, 1964); Annie Heloise Abel, *The American Indian as Slaveholder and Secessionist* (Cleveland, 1915); Theda Perdue, *Slavery and the Evolution of Cherokee Society* (Knoxville: University of

in the Indian Territory operated by the P.B.F.M.[3] Reid was not writing about the slave-burning, but about the imminent dismissal of the Reverend Jason D. Chamberlain, steward of Stockbridge (Iyanubbi) Female Seminary in the Choctaw Nation, a neighboring A.B.C.F.M. institution. Since all missionary schools were ultimately controlled by the Choctaw Council and its educational trustees, it appeared to be the Choctaws who were anxious for Chamberlain's dismissal. "Mr. C. has always been considered . . . a vile Abolitionist," said Reid; hence the Choctaw "Trustees and people have become very much prejudiced against him and are not willing that he should keep the school after the first of May next." But Chamberlain did not want to be removed. He hinted that if pressed, he would reveal a dreadful secret to the world. Reid said, "The man is certainly deranged in his mind . . . he seems possessed with the notion that God is calling on him to make some Awful disclosure respecting the Mission which will convulse and horrify the whole Christian world. The result of his disclosure he thinks will be the destruction of the Choctaws." Reid then hazarded a guess as to what this secret might be—a secret hidden from the outside world but one well enough known to everyone in the Choctaw Nation:

> The Awful Secret which he threatened to make public I think must be this: About a year ago a black man killed his master without any provocation. The Master was a worthy man and a member of Mr. Byington's church. Afterwards the man made confession and accused one of the black women of having instigated him to do the deed. Having made this confession and discovered the body of his master, he got away from those in charge of him, jumpt into Little River, and drowned himself. Lucy, the instigator of the murder, was taken by the enraged relatives and burned. The poor woman was also a member of Mr. Byington's church and protested to the last her innocence.[4]

Tennessee Press, 1979); Rudi Halliburton, *Red Over Black* (Westport CT, 1977).

[3]I have found no discussion of this incident in any of the standard histories of the Choctaws (such as those by Angie Debo, Grant Foreman, W. David Baird, or Henry B. Cushman), nor in any of the studies of missionary work among the Five Civilized Tribes, such as Robert K. Berkhofer, Jr., *Salvation and the Savage* (University of Kentucky, 1965); Robert T. Lewit, "Indian Missions and Antislavery Sentiment," *Mississippi Valley Historical Review* 50 (1963): 39-55; or Harold P. Faust, "The Presbyterian Mission to the American Indian, 1838-1893" (Ph.D. thesis, Temple University, 1943). Nor is it mentioned in the works of Porter, Roethler, and Abel cited above.

[4]This, and most of the other letters cited below, are in the archives of the Presbyterian Historical Society, Philadelphia (hereinafter PHS), Record Group 31, Presbyterian Board of Foreign Missions. For Reid's letter, see PHS, box 10, vol. 1, 57. The other principal documentary sources are the archives of the American Board of Commissioners for

Reid went on to note that the murdered man, Richard Harkins, was the brother of George W. Harkins, one of the important chiefs of the Choctaw Nation and that his wife, Lavina, was the daughter of Colonel Peter P. Pitchlynn, another influential Choctaw leader.[5] Reid concluded, "But the mission and the church here are no more responsible for it than the Pres.[byterian] Church is for the John Brown affair."[6] Reid failed to mention that the murderer's confession had been wrung from him by torture and that his wife was tortured before she was burned.

When Chamberlain was fired in May 1860, he did reveal his awful secret. He wrote an account of the slave-burning to Professor Samuel C. Bartlett of Chicago Theological Seminary.[7] On 22 October 1860, Bartlett wrote a letter of inquiry to the Reverend Selah B. Treat, secretary of the A.B.C.F.M., and another to the Reverend Walter Lowrie, secretary of the P.B.F.M., which had accepted responsibility for Stockbridge and other A.B.C.F.M. missions among the Choctaws after their support from the A.B.C.F.M. was discontinued in July 1859.[8] Treat wrote back on 27 October 1860, disclaiming all knowledge of the affair and stating only that Chamberlain had hinted at some disclosure on 7 December 1859 and again on 2 May 1860, but he had never specified what it was. Treat insisted that the decision of the A.B.C.F.M. to discontinue its mission to the Choctaws in 1859 had nothing whatever to do with "the burning of slaves in the Choctaw Nation."[9] Since the Choctaw missions had now ceased to be under the control of the A.B.C.F.M., Treat told Bart-

---

Foreign Missions at Houghton Library, Harvard, and the Cyrus Byington Family Letters at the Thomas Gilcrease Institute (hereinafter TGI), Tulsa, Oklahoma.

[5]See also W. David Baird, *Peter Pitchlynn: Chief of the Choctaws* (Norman, 1972) 88.

[6]For a similar letter explaining Chamberlain's imminent dismissal in terms of his abolitionism, see James Frothingham to J. L. Wilson, 25 April 1859, PHS, box 10, vol. 2, 282. Frothingham's letter, however, says nothing about "the awful secret."

[7]Why Chamberlain chose to reveal his secret to Bartlett rather than to the officials of the A.B.C.F.M. in Boston, I have not discovered. Probably he believed they would ignore it.

[8]Bartlett's letters and the responses of Lowrie and Treat discussed below are quoted in Whipple, *Relation*, 204-205.

[9]The reasons given by the A.B.C.F.M. for dropping the Choctaw missionaries were vague: "The termination of their connection will greatly relieve the Board of the serious and painful embarrassments to which it has been subject." Cited in Whipple, *Relation*, 212. Antislavery people, like Whipple, quite naturally inferred that this vague terminology was covering up the slave-burning and "other discreditable fruits of slavery among the Choctaws." Ibid., 210.

lett that he saw no way in which the board could be held responsible or take an ex post facto action.

The Reverend Walter Lowrie responded to Bartlett's inquiry on 30 October 1860. The only information he had on the subject was contained in the letter of Alexander Reid cited above. He quoted parts of it without mentioning his source. Lowrie felt that the affair was no concern of the Presbyterian Board, however, for it had occurred before the Presbyterians admitted Byington and the other A.B.C.F.M. missionaries as members of its mission to the Choctaws.

Angered by the refusal of either board to assume any responsibility for investigating the matter or assessing the blame, Bartlett then wrote to Cyrus Byington. Byington had been preaching and teaching among the Choctaws since 1820 when they still lived on their ancestral lands in Mississippi. He remained with them during their march over "the Trail of Tears" from Mississippi to Indian Territory (now southeastern Oklahoma) in 1832-1833. And he had helped them reestablish their educational system there. A man of great dedication, industry, and personal integrity, Byington enjoyed the highest esteem among the Choctaws, and several of the leading Choctaw families in the area of Stockbridge had joined his mission church. He and his distinguished colleague, Cyrus Kingsbury, had steadfastly refused to be moved by the efforts of abolitionists urging them to preach against slavery in the Indian nation. Born and educated in New England, neither of them could be described as proslavery. Yet they knew that to attack it would only arouse the antagonism of the Choctaws, lead to their expulsion from the nation (like Chamberlain's), and induce the Indians to allow only Southern missionaries—if any—to preach to them. Believing that their primary duty was to convert the heathen to Christianity, Byington and Kingsbury also had steadily resisted the growing pressure from the antislavery elements in the A.B.C.F.M. to refuse to admit slaveholders to their churches and to expel those who were already members.

Byington did not send a reply to Bartlett until 14 January 1861, which was after Bartlett had become tired of waiting for it and published his correspondence with Treat and Lowrie in the *Independent* on 26 December 1860. *The Independent*, though staunchly supportive of the A.B.C.F.M. and its efforts to avoid being drawn into the abolition excitement, nevertheless editorialized over the "horrid revelation." While calling upon the public to suspend final judgment until further information was received, the editor concluded that "the whole transaction is a fearful comment upon the bloody code of slavery and the brutalizing influence of the system wherever it exists."

> The public will ask with astonishment, has such a crime been connived at, or even ignored by a Christian church, and by the missionary teachers of the nation? Has no testimony been uttered against it?—no inquiry been instituted?—no discipline inflicted upon the accomplices of the crime, if such were in the church? These questions must be answered. Mr. Byington cannot long remain silent.[10]

Byington did, however, remain silent. In his letter to Bartlett on 14 January, he merely said that he had written to Walter Lowrie about it and that it was now up to Lowrie either to publish his letter or, "if he thinks best, to do nothing with it."[11] But Byington did say, "Were you to come here and learn on the grounds from others how that painful scene transpired, you might see that in some things you could improve the statements you have made to the world about Brethren here whom you have not seen and before you had heard them speak." He also asked Bartlett to reveal who had informed him of the matter.

The letter that Byington wrote to Lowrie is the most detailed account we have of the affair and the only one that describes the action taken by the church to which the murdered man, his wife, the slave Lucy, and some of the lynch mob belonged. Bartlett had stated in his letter to the *Independent* that "this transaction took place within ten miles" of Byington's station and that "church members were not clear of participation in the crime." The editor of the *Independent* had implied that Byington "and other missionaries had designedly withheld the fact from the Boards to which they are or were responsible." Byington's letter of 12 January did not reach Lowrie until 14 February 1861. Meanwhile the *Independent* had received and published "additional authentic evidence

---

[10]Quoted in Whipple, *Relation*, 202-203. In his letters published in the *Independent* on 6 December, Bartlett had also pointed out that Lucy was "the mother of eight children," and that prior to being burned alive she had been tortured by hanging; yet she was "persisting in her innocence, though three times hung up to extort confession of guilt." Despite her cruel mistreatment, she died "with words of prayer and praise upon her lips!" Bartlett said he had been told that "the dead body of a slave [Prince] was also burned; he having been put to the torture and having committed suicide to escape the doom that awaited him." Ibid., 203, 206. It is interesting that neither Byington nor any other missionary ever referred to the tortures.

[11]A copy of this letter in Byington's hand is at PHS, box 10, vol. 1, 56.

touching the burning of the slave-woman in the Choctaw nation." This evidence, from "a person who was in the Choctaw nation at the time," revealed the shocking news that "soon after this crime was perpetrated, a 'big meeting' of the mission church was held for the communion, but no notice was taken of this horrible transaction." It appeared that Mrs. Harkins, and possibly other church members, had partaken of communion; if so, the church was guilty of condoning her act. The editor declared, "If Mr. Byington was guilty of silence and inaction toward such a crime, he is unworthy of any countenance from the Christian community."[12]

The letter giving Byington's side of the story and his defense of the mission and its church in Stockbridge deserves to be quoted in full:

Hon. Walter Lowrie, Esq.

Dear Sir,

The *Independent* of Dec. 6th was handed to me this week that I might read the articles which reflect injuriously on our mission, and the copy of your letter to Mr. Bartlett. There is in the paper a request that I make a communication to the public. What I write I prefer for many reasons to submit first to your judgment.

My information about the Murder of Mr. Harkins I obtained from others. Now it may not be full and correct. There was a deep and strong excitement of feeling at the time. There were no known witnesses of the murder and of the placing of the body in the river. The most important statements were made by Prince, the murderer of his master. The murder was committed in the day time near Mr. H's house on Tuesday the 28th of Dec. 1858 in an adjoining County where we have never had a Missionary Station.

For some days it was believed that Mr. Harkins was drowned in the Little River while attempting to ford it on horseback. The tracks of his horse were seen at the ford and the horse was found in the woods with the saddle on him. These circumstances brought many persons to the place. The body was looked for in vain until Saturday, January 1. Prince was then strongly suspected of having killed his master. He soon confessed that he had done so and that his master's body was carried off and put into the river a mile distant and fastened there with a rope to a large stone. The relatives and friends of Mr. H. took Prince to the spot and found the body.

---

[12]Quoted in Whipple, *Relation*, 206.

This was on Sabbath morning. Prince leaped into the river and was drowned. He had previously confessed that after he killed his master he rode his horse into the river at the ford and afterwards let him go. He also accused Lucy of instigating him to kill their master. The rope used in tying the body to a stone was Lucy's. But she asserted her innocence to the last. Mr. H's body was taken to the house. Prince's body was found. The feeling and the transactions that followed at the burning you may imagine. I make not [no?] attempt to describe these. Many persons had come to the place even from a distance.

The only member of my church then in church fellowship present and who was free, was the widow of the murdered man. Her feelings were greatly moved as you may well suppose.*

My duty to her as her pastor was a solemn one. I visited her often, read the Bible to her and prayed with her and her family. In March 1859 at my suggestion, she freely went before the session and requested the Ruling Elders to make such inquiries as they chose. She submitted herself to them, as a church member. Her appearance and answers were satisfactory to them. Her christian character has been good for years, and is so at this time. But yesterday she told me she had maintained family worship since her husband's death.

We hope the Lord has helped us in our trials. And this result being so early obtained and so well known here, I wrote no account of it to anyone.

The reason for my writing you now is to meet the call in the *Independent* of Dec. 6. The pieces in this paper have need of revision in the judgment of good men in our mission who know much more about the facts as they occurred than strangers at a distance.

I am sorry to trouble you with these statements. But I write to you and not to the *Independent* and am a member of a mission under your patronage and am willing that you should dispose of this letter just as you think best. May the Lord deliver us from all our danger.

Ever Yours with respect and affection,
Cyrus Byington

P.S. If you compare my statement with that you sent to Mr. Bartlett, you will soon see how far they confirm each other. My brethren express great satisfaction with your letter.

*As Mrs. Harkins appeared before our Session the first time it met in her vicinity and gave the Ruling Elders satisfactory evidence of her christian character, I do not deem it proper to give details of what she said and did while under the excitement occasioned by the murder of her husband and by her belief that her own maid servant had instigated another servant to destroy him.[13]

Byington said nothing about the torture of Prince and Lucy nor about any other members of his church who might have participated in "the transaction" (a strangely businesslike term). He did not indicate whether Mrs. Harkins had ordered or merely acquiesced in the burning.[14] And he offered no real justification for having failed to report the whole affair to his superiors in the A.B.C.F.M. or to his later patrons in the P.B.F.M. until after Chamberlain and Bartlett had revealed the whole sordid story.

Lowrie decided not to publish Byington's letter. On 26 March 1861, he received a letter from Byington's married daughter, Mrs. Lucy Dana, who was living in Belpré, Ohio. She felt that the accounts of the affair published thus far had "cast a blemish on my Father's name" and she urged Lowrie to release her father's letter because she felt it would clear his character. "May we not hope to see some statement from you which may restore my Father's good name?"[15] Lowrie replied on 30 March that there was so little difference between her father's letter and the one he had sent to Bartlett (quoting Alexander Reid) "that we thought it was not necessary to publish it. . . . From the published statement we do not see how any candid mind can doubt that no possible blame could attach to your father in these painful and distressing circumstances."[16] However, Lowrie concluded, if Mrs. Dana had more information she wished to publish, she should feel free to do so.

Apparently she did, for on 3 May 1861, two anonymous letters appeared in the *Congregationalist* providing further information. The first came from a lady who claimed to have been for five years "an assistant in mission labors" in the Indian Territory. She had written to a male friend at the Choctaw Mission, she said, and his reply "proves what I

---

[13]PHS, box 10, vol. 1, 56. Byington used the term "servant" to describe slaves not only because this was common in the South, but because it enabled him to apply scriptural references to "servants and masters" to slavery.

[14]There is a letter in the Byington Papers at the Gilcrease Institute stating that Mrs. Harkins "instigated the crime." But another statement reads, "The heathen relatives" of Mrs. Harkins "seized the woman." This and the details of the torture remain unclear. See Byington Letters, TGI, dated 30 March 1861, 13 April 1861, and 29 July 1861.

[15]PHS, box 10, vol. 1, 267.

[16]Ibid., 268.

had supposed." That was "that the whole affair was conducted by a *lawless mob* with whom the national [i.e., Choctaw] authorities, even, dare not interfere. How then should our mission brethren meddle with them?"[17] (Of course, no one had suggested that the missionaries should meddle with the mob as a whole—but only with those who were members of the mission church and therefore subject to its spiritual oversight.)

This anonymous former missionary went on to say that she detested slavery as much as Professor Bartlett; nevertheless, "Have a care, my friends, that in your zeal against slavery you lay no stumbling-stones in the pathway of those who amid trials and self-denials that some Christians know little of, have toiled on for years to give the Gospel to those who had it not." The letter which she received in answer to her inquiries then followed. It was also anonymous. But in many ways it was more revealing than Byington's letter to Lowrie, especially regarding the attitude of the Choctaws toward slavery and toward the mob that had for three or four days tortured the two slaves on the Harkins' plantation:

Choctaw Nation,
March, 1861

Miss _____ ;

In regard to the inquiry respecting the burning of the slave woman, I have only to say that Dr. Lowrie's letter to Rev. S. C. Bartlett contains the substance of the facts in the case. The public meeting [the mob] was composed only of the relatives, the Harkinses and Pitchlyns, "Captain Whiskey" presiding, as usual on such occasions. They constituted judge, jury, and executioners, and conducted things in precisely their own way. The only free member of the church, in good standing, who was present and took any part in the transactions was Mrs. Harkins, wife of the murdered man. There was one other free member of the church present, but he was *not* in good standing [presumably he was under church censure for some sinful action], and it is not known that he took any part, except as a spectator.

Now, what would Mr. Bartlett have us do in a case of this kind? Shall we discipline those members who took a part in the affair? That has *already been done.* Mrs. Harkins voluntarily gave herself up to the discipline of the church, made all the confession which the most fastidious

---

[17]This letter and the one accompanying it are quoted in Whipple, *Relation,* 244-47.

could desire, was restored to fellowship, and now leads a consistent Christian life. What more could be done in the way of discipline?

Would Mr. B. have the church, or any member of it, institute a *legal* process against the parties? Such a measure, in this country, and in [the] case of the *families in question*, would be simply ridiculous. Some of those very persons have since been tried for the murder of a *free white* citizen of the nation, and acquitted.[18]

Would Mr. Bartlett have the church, its pastor, or any of its members from the pulpit or the stump, bear a public witness against the sin of such proceedings? That would have been about as wise as to preach a sermon against the supremacy of the Pope beneath the walls of the Vatican.

This is a land of liberty! The broad stripes and bright stars wave over us yet, or did then, at least, and we are still under protection of that government which guarantees to us freedom of speech and freedom of opinion, but actually there is no more freedom of opinion here than there is in Spain. On any thing pertaining to slavery we have to conduct ourselves just as we would under the most despotic government in the world.

Would Professor Bartlett have us publish to the world the matter? We can see no good that would arise from such a course, nor any necessity for us to take it while there are so many men in the North ready and willing to save us the trouble.

The action of Northern men, of a certain class, in respect to the Choctaw Mission, often reminds me of a flock of turkey buzzards. You know with what indifference they flap their lazy wings over the most beautiful landscape. The purling stream, the waving trees, the blooming flowers, have no attraction for them. But show them a dead carcass, and they pounce upon it at once. So certain Northern men can see nothing of the *good* that has been effected here by the Mission. They take an extra grip on their purse strings and look with cool indifference upon the members we have educated, the general good that has been effected through our labor.

But show them a dead negro who has been put to death by a set of men who fear neither God, man, nor the devil, any further than suits their own convenience, and they are all down upon us at once.

I can only speak as an individual, but I think I hazard nothing in saying the Mission would be *exceedingly obliged if some one* of that class, Mr. Bartlett for example, would *come down here* and tell us precisely what we ought to do and *show us* precisely *how to do it.*

Yours truly,

---

[18]This is a reference to the murder of Hugh C. Flack in the Choctaw Nation on 5 December 1860. The accused were David Loring and Clay Harkins, all related to Mrs. Richard Harkins. For information on this incident, see microfilm series M-234 in the

Bartlett naturally responded to this challenge and on 17 May 1861 the *Congregationalist* published his rebuttal. "I think the Church is entitled to a better account, in a more responsible shape" than two anonymous letters, he wrote. The tone of the communication is far from satisfactory. A murdered church member is only a "dead negro"! A Christian brother, asking a simple explanation of the murder, is a "turkey buzzard" pouncing on "a dead carcass"![19] The explanations of the circumstances were also "defective," said Bartlett. They stated that only one free member in good standing was present, but what did the church do about the free member who was not in good standing? Mrs. Harkins was said to have made a confession and then to have been restored to church fellowship? "When was it—before or after the call for information? Was any notice taken of the case before the next communion? Did Mrs. H. then partake with the church? Who took the initiative, the church or Mrs. H.? . . . What was the discipline? Was Mrs. H. debarred from the communion? —and how long? Is a simple 'confession' all that is necessary to restore to church fellowship *a person who has taken part in a murder*? Is the murder of Christian slaves by 'Christian' masters too trivial or too common an affair in the Choctaw nation to require even a passing allusion in communicating information from the mission to the Board that employs them?"

The last published word in the affair came in August 1861, from Charles K. Whipple, an ardent Boston abolitionist who attacked the A.B.C.F.M. for its equivocal stand on slavery.[20] Whipple's 241-page analysis of the A.B.C.F.M.'s position on slavery was entitled *The Relation of the American Board of Commissioners for Foreign Missions to Slavery*; while Southerners (and many at the Choctaw Mission) had found the A.B.C.F.M. much too antislavery in its outlook, Whipple found it much too unwilling to take a public stand against slavery. He devoted

---

National Archives records of Indian Affairs, reel #176, frames 0154-0160 and 0192-0195. Unfortunately, the Bureau of Indian Affairs appears to have taken no interest in the burning of the slave.

[19]Quoted in Whipple, *Relation*, 246-47.

[20]Whipple, a graduate of Amherst, treasurer of Garrison's Nonresistance Society of Boston, and editorial assistant of *The Liberator* is cited often in the pages of Carleton Mabee's *Black Freedom* (New York, 1970).

several pages and an appendix in his book to the case of the burned slave. His conclusion fairly states the abolitionists' view:

The Prudential Committee, to whom the Board entrusted the management of its affairs, allowed their missionary servants to live among the slaveholding Choctaws for more than forty years, pretending to preach the Gospel to them, yet not opposing slavery; they allowed them to honor that infamous system by admitting slaveholders as the first members of their churches; they allowed them, when this course was called in question by Christians in New England, to make excuses for slaveholding; to declare it not only justifiable but sometimes indispensable; to maintain, when specifications of gross wickedness, inherent in it, were brought up—the buying and selling of men and women as property and the separation by such sales of husbands and wives, parents and children—that they would make no rule forbidding those things to church members; and to acquiesce in the wicked custom prevailing among those slaveholders of preventing their victims from learning to read the Bible!

The Prudential committee had evidence, from time to time, through all those forty years, that the custom of buying and selling human beings as property and of holding and using them as such, tends to the commission of frightful excesses of cruelty against these unfortunate victims, often on mere suspicion of fault and sometimes when that suspicion is entirely groundless. They knew that fugitive slaves were hunted with bloodhounds; that slaves, resisting even cruel and unreasonable punishment, were killed sometimes quickly, by a pistol shot, sometimes slowly by the scourge; and that there were many well-authenticated instances of those poor unfortunates having been *burned alive!* Having let the practice go on which is accustomed to lead to these excesses of wickedness, is their advocate [the *Independent*] entitled, in the very act of condemning the last and worst one, to declare *them* GUILTLESS of it? Having allowed and argued for their systematic teaching of the alphabet through a course of forty years, is their advocate authorized to declare, when the letter Z is reached, that the utterance of that letter is a horrible crime and to declare in the same breath that the teachers have "no responsibility whatever" for its utterance by the pupils?[21]

The *Independent* had exonerated the Prudential Committee and the A.B.C.F.M. of all blame on 31 January 1861, when it discovered that Byington was no longer in any way attached to the A.B.C.F.M. but had transferred his work to the patronage of the Presbyterian Board. Whipple and his Garrisonian friends were, in 1861, beating a dead horse in regard to the Indian missions of the A.B.C.F.M. By closing down its mission stations among the Southern Indians, the A.B.C.F.M. had, in effect, conceded that Whipple was right; there was no longer any pos-

---

[21]Whipple, *Relation*, 207-208.

sibility of persuading the missionaries to take action against slavery. The board had been trying, quietly, to do this since at least 1848—instructing its missionaries among the Choctaws, Cherokees, Creeks, Seminoles, and Chickasaws to allow no slaveholders in their churches and to employ no slaves in mission work.[22] The missionaries had refused, however.

At first these refusals to comply with the board's requests were based upon arguments of expediency: to refuse to allow slaveholders in mission churches would antagonize the Indians and turn them against the gospel; to abandon slave labor would force the missionaries to spend all their time doing menial tasks (building, cooking, washing) because free labor was unavailable at any price; to purchase slaves to work at the missions enabled the slaves to earn enough money to buy their freedom.[23] "Our objection," said the Choctaw missionaries to the board's request in 1856, "to giv[ing] the Indians correct views on his subject," is based upon the conviction that it is not "a part of our duty as missionaries to interfere with the civil relation between master and slave." Did missionaries to Siam, Turkey, Burma, and the Sandwich Islands try to "correct the civil disorder" in those countries or try "to bring the system of wrong and oppression prevailing there to an end"? And if they had, "would it not in all probability have been fatal to their work?"[24] It may be noted, however, that these same missionaries felt perfectly free to tell the Indians in the strongest terms that they disapproved of, and found sinful, their practices of polygamy, witchcraft, infanticide, intemperance, and the continuance of their "heathen" rites of religion, medicine, and sports (especially on the Sabbath).

At the same time, the Indian missionaries developed a series of scriptural arguments in regard to slavery that were not essentially dissimilar from those of proslavery ministers in the South. These took the line that neither the Old nor the New Testament specifically condemned the institution and hence, as ministers of the Gospel and nothing but the Gos-

---

[22]See Lewit, "Indian Missions and Anti-Slavery Sentiment," and the archives of the A.B.C.F.M. at Houghton Library, Harvard.

[23]Byington wrote to his wife on 6 November 1856, "We have helped 12 slaves to freedom" by letting them work to pay off their purchase price to the mission. Byington Letters, TGI, vol. 1, 607.

[24]See copy of letter from Cyrus Kingsbury to D. N. Adams, 30 April 1850, PHS, box 10, vol. 1, 375.

pel, they would not go "beyond Scripture" on this subject. "The simple question with us is," wrote Byington and Kingsbury to Treat in 1858, "shall we treat it as did the inspired Apostles? or shall we treat it on the principles with which human wisdom, as appears to us, has exalted above revelation?"[25]

> We assure you that we are not insensible to the evils connected with slavery. In our opinion their only antidote is the gospel. As ministers of Christ we regard it as our duty and privilege to preach the gospel to masters and servants according to the example and instructions of Christ and his apostles and to act according to our own best judgment in the reception of members to our churches in their instruction, and in the exercise of discipline.[26]

In 1859, as matters neared a final showdown between the board in Boston and the missionaries among the slaveholding Indians, the Choctaw missionaries issued "A Brief Statement in regard to the relation of the Choctaw Mission of the A.B.C.F.M. to slavery—prepared by a committee of the missionaries." Byington was among its signers, if not its drafters.

> The course of the mission in regard to slavery was from the beginning substantially as follows: When any, whether masters or servants or belonging to neither of these classes, gave evidence of a saving change, they were received into the fellowship of the churches. Instruction was given in the mutual duties of masters and servant as laid down in the Scriptures. Slaves were also purchased from time to time in accordance with their own wishes with a view to their working out their own freedom. In this way a number were liberated. Slave labour was also employed as the missionaries had need of it. This course they believed, and still believe, was in accordance with the example and instructions of Christ and his apostles and the wisdom of it has been confirmed by all their experience.[27]

Caught between the rising antislavery tide in New England and the intransigence of its missionaries, the A.B.C.F.M. had little choice but to put an end to its mission work among the Southern Indians. But the Presbyterians, still closely united with their members in the South and dominated by conservative theologians in the North, were more ready to accept the position on slavery that the missionaries put forth. The Pres-

---

[25]PHS, box 10, vol. 2, 359.

[26]Ibid., 349.

[27]Ibid., 360.

byterian Board of Foreign Missions had missionaries of its own among the slaveholding Indians. Its missionaries had established increasingly close ties with the missionaries of the A.B.C.F.M. ever since 1848 and sympathy with them was strong. Almost all Presbyterians in the field heartily endorsed the unanimous decisions of their Foreign Mission Board to take the A.B.C.F.M. missionaries under its patronage and enable them to continue their work among the slaveholding Indians.[28] But the action was not taken without protest: there were some Presbyterians in the North who considered it a mistake. While the negotiations for the transfer of the missions and their staffs were still under way, five Presbyterian pastors in Ohio sent a petition to Walter Lowrie, which they asked him to present for the consideration of their Board of Foreign Missions:

> Through the press we have learned that the American Board of Foreign Missions have [*sic*] cast off its mission among the Southwest Indians on account of their connection with slavery and that our Board is thinking of adopting it. This gives us much uneasiness. Wishing to avoid *if possible* all the public agitation of the matter, we have concluded quietly to lay before the Board itself our objections to this adoption.
>
> We will not raise the question of the *lawfulness* of the measure. This would bring up with it other questions which we do not wish at present to discuss. We only raise the question of expediency. We deem it inexpedient to adopt this discarded mission, 1st Because our Board is straitened for funds to support the missions already under its care. 2nd In every part of the heathen world fields far more extensive and at least as promising are accessible to us whitened for the harvest. 3rd The field occupied by that particular mission has been so long cultivated that it now requires comparatively little attention. 4th That attention can be given it without any direct agency of our Board. . . . 5th At the present crisis our Board cannot adopt a mission cast off by so venerable a body as the American Board on account of its connections with slavery without doing much injury in many of our churches.
>
> On this point permit us to speak plainly. The Associate Reformed Church, the Baptist, the Methodist, the Methodist Protestant and the N[ew] S[chool] Presbyterian [churches] have all divided North and South on the question of slavery. Some of these churches and others besides them becoming larger and more influential every year have made slaveholding a term of communion. It is very manifest from the action of the lower conferences that the Methodist General Conference will take this stand at its next meeting. In a little while our church

---

[28]For the reasons offered by the board in defense of its action, see *Annual Report*, Presbyterian Board of Foreign Missions (New York, 1860) 26-27.

will be the only prominent church in the Free States at all mixed up with slavery. In view of these things, our church is already regarded by thousands out of her communion and by very many in her communion, as emphatically *the Slave Church of America*.[29]

In short, the adoption of the Choctaw missionaries was seen not as an effort to sustain the preaching of the Gospel to the Indians, but an effort to sustain a proslavery position within the Presbyterian church. The petitioners went on to point out that already "many of our ministers and many of our members . . . have withdrawn from us and have gone into other organizations" because of this. "Our churches have bled freely already and much of the blood they have lost was their best blood." The conviction among Christians that slavery was a sin was "intense and is becoming more so every year." If the venerable American Board could no longer stand the "odium" of the Indian missions, neither could the Presbyterians. The petition concluded by begging the board to reject the proposed adoption of the A.B.C.F.M. missions. But this plea went unheeded. The result, in the eyes of many Northerners, was to condone the position of the Choctaw mission in regard to the slave-burning.

It remains only to ask whether the missionaries and their boards had any alternative. Were Byington, Kingsbury and Worcester[30] correct in asserting that the choice was not between neutrality and antislavery in Indian mission work but between neutrality and no missionary work at all? Or, perhaps worse, between neutral missionaries from the North (who in their hearts at least were antislavery) and proslavery missionaries from the South (who would preach that the Bible endorsed slavery and God willed it).

Since all of the Southern Indian tribes practiced slavery and all of them eventually allied themselves with the Confederacy, it would seem that it was no more possible for a missionary to have opposed that institution in the Indian nation than in any state of the South. The Indians, seeking desperately to maintain a social status above that of the blacks, had rapidly developed the same attitude toward them as their white neighbors in the South. Whatever advantages runaway slaves may have found among these Indians in the colonial era; however benign slavery

---

[29]PHS, box 10, vol. 1, 329.

[30]For the position of the Reverend Samuel Worcester on slavery among the Cherokees, see Althea Bass, *Cherokee Messenger* (Norman, 1936) 233-39, 340-41.

had been among them then; and no matter how many blacks intermarried or were adopted into the Southern tribes prior to 1800, the process of "civilization" that took place after that date totally altered their position. As the Southern Indians adopted the white man's way of life, they adopted his attitude toward slavery and black people. Intermarriage with blacks became illegal; blacks were denied any position of honor or trust in the Indian nations; slave codes were drawn up defining their status in precisely the same terms as in the slave states.[31] By the 1850s the Southern Indian nations were even passing laws expelling free slaves from their borders and prohibiting missionaries from teaching any slave to read or write. That was the way Southern whites defined the status of blacks in a Christian civilization and the Indians felt obliged to live up to that practice. Their economy too was based on slavery once they gave up hunting for husbandry. For missionaries to challenge the institution of slavery was not only to challenge the divine and Southern concept of social order, but the whole progression by the heathen savage from barbarism to civilization.[32]

It is true that missions to the Indians came under the heading of "foreign" mission activity. After all, the Indians were treated as separate nations making war and peace with the United States; they maintained their own tribal governments; they spoke a foreign language; and they had an alien cultural tradition. Missionaries like Byington and Kingsbury had used this analogy to defend their unwillingness to interfere with the civil or cultural institution of slavery. And it is true that in Turkey, Burma, China, and elsewhere missionaries who did interfere in civil affairs were expelled. In the Indian nations United States government agents had exercised the same right against missionaries who annoyed the Indians or hindered relations between them and the government. Missionaries were in Indian Territory on sufferance, not by right.

There were missionaries, however, who managed to maintain an antislavery position among the Southern Indians. The Baptists, Evan Jones and his son, John B. Jones, went so far as to expel slaveholding Cherokees from their mission church in 1853. There were protests against this, and in 1855 the government agent threatened them with ex-

---

[31]See Perdue, *Slavery*, and Halliburton, *Red Over Black*.

[32]For the racial prejudice inherent in the American effort to "civilize" the Indians, see Roy Harvey Pearce, *Savagism and Civilization* (Baltimore, 1953).

pulsion. But they managed to ride out the storm. In fact, in 1859 they organized an antislavery Indian society known as the Ketoowah Society, which was designed to counter the pro-Southern secession element among the slaveholding Cherokees. Yet as the crisis of the Civil War approached, the Joneses' position became untenable. John B. Jones was expelled by the government agent (a pro-Southern man) in 1860 and his father followed in 1861.[33] Still, their efforts indicate that there was perhaps more leeway than men like Byington and Kingsbury acknowledged, at least prior to 1859. After that date not only was an antislavery position impossible, but so was neutrality. The missionaries either had to preach that Christian civilization permitted slavery or get out of the Indian Territory.[34] These Indians had taken their stand with the South's definition of a civilized, Christian society.

---

[33]For the Joneses, see Abel, *American Indian as Slaveholder*, 47, 93, 135, 199, 217, 218, 236, 240, 293.

[34]It is hardly surprising that even though the Choctaws allied themselves with and fought for the Confederacy, Byington and Kingsbury continued to live among them, preaching and teaching, throughout the war years. Byington died in 1869 and Kingsbury in 1871.

PART III

Missionaries

THE MYSTERY BEHIND PARSON BLACKBURN'S WHISKEY, 1809-1810

Slavery was not the only issue that complicated missionary activities among the Southeastern Indians. Here, as everywhere, missionaries could not help mixing Christianization with issues of secular behavior and acculturation. The Reverend Gideon Blackburn was an ardent civilizer and from the outset of his mission among the Cherokees in 1803, he did his best to lead them from "savage" to "civilized" habits, laws, and institutions. He boasted that he had persuaded the Cherokees to pass their first written laws in 1808, and he frankly meddled in every aspect of their affairs, from teaching table manners to their children in his schools, to "improving" the nation's political and economic development. Ostensibly he came to teach the Cherokees how to read, write, and do arithmetic; but he wanted the government to help pay for his schools and in return for its help, he felt obliged to advance its policies. Blackburn was something of an ecclesiastical entrepreneur. Without that temperament he would never have taken on the task of raising money to support Indian education by his own efforts.

In the days before the temperance movement had become an evangelical crusade, Blackburn ran a whiskey distillery in Maryville, Tennessee. He sold corn whiskey to his parishioners there and to anyone else who would buy it. He did not, however, think that Indians could hold their liquor and firmly opposed selling liquor to them. It was therefore unfortunate that in his effort to improve his standing with the secretary of war, he devised what he thought was a clever means to disguise an exploring expedition for a water route from Maryville to Fort St. Stephen on the Tombigbee, a project suggested to him by the secretary: he would ship some of his whiskey down the rivers under the nominal management of a Cherokee. Blackburn never got to prove his point and ended his career among the Cherokees in disgrace. He was a prime example of the danger a missionary courted when he meddled in politics even for the sake of spreading the Gospel.

RECENTLY, WHILE PERUSING THE FEDERAL ARCHIVES for information on missionary life among the Cherokee, I kept coming across references to "Parson Blackburn's whiskey." So many were there, I concluded that the event must have had some important significance. So I collected all of them I could find in order to piece the story together. Obviously the event had something to do with the Reverend Gideon Blackburn, the eminent Presbyterian who in 1803 started the first Presbyterian mission among the Cherokee. And when I discovered, in Walter B. Posey's *The Presbyterian Church in the Old Southwest*, a reference to the fact that Gideon Blackburn was the proprietor of a whiskey distillery in Maryville, Tennessee, I realized that the subject was of some interest. Of course, in pre-prohibition days there was nothing odd about a parson's selling whiskey, especially on the frontier. But as the evidence piled up, I caught a faint whiff of brimstone nonetheless. However common it was for parsons to distill and sell whiskey among the white people of the frontier, it was against federal law to sell it among the red people. Yet here was Parson Blackburn's name coming up again and again in the Indian archives.

When I got all the material together, I discovered another surprising fact. The incident involving Parson Blackburn's whiskey coincided precisely with the demise of the first Presbyterian mission among the Cherokee. Not wishing to jump to conclusions, I then read all the accounts I could find about that mission. There was, I discovered, considerable discrepancy in the various official explanations for its demise. Some accounts attributed the demise to the lack of generous support from the Presbyterian Assembly; some to the lack of local Presbyterian support; some to Gideon Blackburn's family and personal problems; some to his ill health. But clearly there was some mystery about it. The federal government had given financial support to Blackburn's efforts and his extremely active subsequent career showed no signs at all of ill health. But none of the accounts of the mission contained any reference to the incident so prominent in the Indian archives.

I concluded, on this basis, that the record of this famous mission was incomplete. In order to make it complete, I have here assembled the most important documents on the incident. I do not consider what follows to be an earth-shaking essay; nor is it a "definitive" account. There are, I fear, still some missing parts to the puzzle. My effort here is simply to provide the documents in the Indian archives, with a few comments of my own—mostly to tie the documents together and put them in context. Perhaps with the help of these notes and documents, some future historian or archivist will find the missing pieces and give us a final answer to the mystery of Parson Blackburn's whiskey and the demise of the first Presbyterian mission among the Cherokee.

Although much has been written about the Presbyterian mission schools founded by the Reverend Gideon Blackburn among the Cherokee in 1804-1805, there has always been some mystery about their demise in 1809-1810. By all accounts they were extremely successful, much moreso than the small mission school established at Spring Place among the Cherokee by the Moravians in these same years. Blackburn claimed to have taught more than 300 Cherokees to read and write English within a few years. Yet "strangely enough," wrote Walter B. Posey, "the blush of enthusiasm paled, and Blackburn decided by 1810 that the final strain and general debilitation of health necessitated his leaving the mission work."[1] Dorothy Bass, the most recent writer on this mission, concluded: "It is difficult to know why Gideon Blackburn abandoned his educational enterprise, or even exactly when that happened."[2] V. M. Queener, the first to discuss Blackburn's work in a scholarly way, maintained that Blackburn gave up his mission work "because of continued impaired health and the growing needs of his family."[3] But if the schools were so successful, why didn't the Presbyterians find someone else to continue them? And why is it so difficult to pinpoint precisely when they did cease to function?

A careful study of some of the primary sources in federal archives and Moravian mission records offers an explanation. Parson Blackburn was alleged to have engaged in the illegal whiskey trade among the Indians. He did so clandestinely using others to front for him, but he was

---

[1]Walter B. Posey, *The Presbyterian Church in the Old Southwest, 1778-1838* (Richmond VA: John Knox Press, 1952) 63-64.

[2]Dorothy C. Bass, "Gideon Blackburn's Mission to the Cherokees," *Journal of Presbyterian History* 52:3 (Fall 1974): 219.

[3]V. M. Queener, "Gideon Blackburn," East Tennessee Historical Society *Publications*, no. 6 (1934): 23.

found out in 1809 and his missionary work ended in general disrepute. So, at least, the general rumors of the time indicate. Seeing that this was an embarrassment to all, particularly to the federal Indian agent who had supported Blackburn's mission, as well as to the federal government (which had provided funds for it) and to the Presbyterian Church and others from whom he had obtained financial support, the matter was hushed up. In fact, it could be argued, there was a conscious effort made by Blackburn and his friends to whitewash the whole business and to lay the blame upon the Creek chiefs who had exposed it.

The records are more than ample on the incident itself. It occurred in April 1809, when the Creeks seized two boats filled with whiskey on the border of their territory. The boats had stopped at Turkey Town where the Cherokee chief, Pathkiller, lived and where the traders temporarily stored their cargo in Pathkiller's house. Among the white men engaged in this enterprise was Samuel Blackburn, Gideon Blackburn's brother. Gideon Blackburn himself was present in Turkey Town (sometimes known as Little Turkey's Town, Sennecca, or Esenaca) and later made a deposition on behalf of his brother's claims against the Creeks for sending one hundred warriors into the Cherokee Nation to seize the cargo and the boats. According to Samuel Blackburn and his partners, they had unloaded the cargo simply to await permission from the Creeks to sail on down the river to Mobile, where they planned to dispose of the whiskey, powder, and lead. According to Big Warrior, chief of the Creek, the cargo was left with Pathkiller (whom he called Path Maker) "and the path maker is to sell the goods for the benefit of the owner."[4]

Since, by law, it was illegal for any white person to sell alcoholic beverages to the Indians within their territory, Big Warrior felt justified in seizing this illegal cargo. In this he was supported by the federal agent among the Creek, Colonel Benjamin Hawkins. It was the difference of opinion between Colonel Return J. Meigs, agent among the Cherokee, and Hawkins that led to the voluminous correspondence on the subject of reimbursement to the traders. Samuel Blackburn and his partners not only enlisted Meigs on their side but also Governor Willie Blount of Tennessee, Enoch Parsons, the attorney general for eastern Tennessee, and Pleasant M. Miller, congressman from east Tennessee. In the mass of

---

[4]Records of the Bureau of Indian Affairs, M-271, "Letters Received by the Office of the Secretary of War Relating to Indian Affairs, 1800-1823," roll 1, frame 0629.

testimony that resulted, Gideon Blackburn's name appears repeatedly, not only as a witness, but as the man who gave security for the enterprise and therefore was responsible to pay for the lost cargo. The project started in Maryville, Tennessee, where Blackburn lived. The Maryville merchants, John Nichol and John Montgomery, who supplied the 2,226 gallons (or 65 casks) of whiskey and other supplies for the trip, made a deposition on 23 December 1809. In it they said that James McIntosh, the mixed-blood Cherokee who was legally responsible for the goods, "proposed to give as security [having no money himself] his father [a white man named John McIntosh or Quotaqueskey] and the Reverend Gideon Blackburn and for which we now hold their notes."[5] Furthermore, it is well known that Parson Blackburn himself ran a distillery in Maryville. As Walter Posey noted, there was nothing questionable about his trade on the frontier: "Distilling and selling was a respectable home industry, conducted by laymen and sometimes by clergymen. Gideon Blackburn was at one time a large-scale dealer in liquor."[6] Blackburn's connection with the venture was certainly known. John Sevier, who was governor of Tennessee from 1803 to 1809, "noted in his diary," writes Posey, "that some Creek Indians about 1807 'seized upon & took away Parson Blackburn's whiskey.' "[7] Sevier, writing long after the date, clearly referred to the incident that occurred in Turkey Town in April 1809.

Perhaps more important, the Indians generally believed that Blackburn was part of this enterprise and convinced the Moravian missionaries of it. Three months after the incident, on 23 July 1809, the Reverend John Gambold of the Spring Place mission gave the following report of it in a letter to his brethren in Salem, North Carolina:

> Even in this land, where in truth very little Gospel light has appeared, the opponents [of Christian truth] have received a reason for slander. In fact, Mr. Blackburn undertook a journey through this land, principally to reconnoiter the waterways here as far as the Bay of Mobile, for which a conversation with the Secretary of War with him is supposed to have been the inducement. For this purpose he entered into a sort of company with one of his own brothers and two or three others; they built several boats and purchased a large quantity of whisky in

---

[5]Records of the Secretary of War, M-221, "Letters Received, Main Series, 1801-1870," roll 34, frame 5370.

[6]Posey, *The Presbyterian Church*, 99.

[7]Idem.

order to trade with that on their journey and thus they traveled down the Connesaga River. At the border between the Cherokees and the Creeks they were stopped by Chief Pathkiller. This man, who is now in the position which was formerly held by Little Turkey [principal chief], and whose main responsibility it is to see that the treaties with the U.S. and the other neighboring Indians are observed exactly and the peace of the land which rests on them, had received word from Col. Meigs that these people had underhandedly obtained the pass on which they were traveling from his son [Meigs's son] during his absence, and that he could in no way grant his protection to an undertaking which is so against the laws. To be sure, they had prepared themselves a little for such an eventuality by taking along a half-breed Indian who claimed that the freight was his property, only nobody believed him. Now they appealed to Col. Hawkins for a pass, but as can be easily understood, they received none. Then they wanted to try to sell the whisky right on the spot, but could obtain no license for that as it was an undertaking which went contrary to all the Indian treaties. Pathkiller was indeed kindly inclined towards Mr. Blackburn as a man who had done much for the Indians and deserved consideration, and did all he could to help him, but the Creeks, on the contrary, on whose border the brandy was, did not show themselves kindly disposed and confiscated the whole boat as contraband and with that, the reconnoitering trip and the traffic involved in it, and other far-reaching projects, came to an end for this time. Now the whole matter would not cause so much commotion and would even be quickly forgotten if Blackburn, a man well-known far and wide, described as having great gifts and also known among other things for the blessed preaching of the Gospel, had not been at the head of this undertaking, but just because of that the disgrace of this venture falls in large part on religion. In that connection, I remember that James Vann [a Cherokee chief] told me already two years ago: "Blackburn is not so disinterested as he wishes to appear; he is a secret Speculator." His schools in this land seem to be decreasing greatly and now that his credibility has gone down very much, he may find it difficult to keep them going in any way. But enough of this sad story.[8]

Gambold received the story secondhand and there were errors in the version he heard as to the parts Path Killer and Meigs played and the request to Hawkins for a pass. Both Path Killer and Meigs had supported the venture. Samuel Blackburn and his friends, instead of asking Hawkins for a pass, forged Hawkins's name on a pass they wrote themselves, as they later admitted. The most intriguing part of Gambold's version of the incident is whether Gideon Blackburn, or any of his collaborators, was acting in collaboration with the secretary of war to open up a new

---

[8]John Gambold to Charles G. Reichel, 23 July 1809. Moravian Archives, Winston-Salem, North Carolina. The original is in German; this translation and the others that follow were obtained through the help of the archivist, Miss Mary Creech.

water route to Mobile through Indian Territory. If this is so, Blackburn may be innocent of the charge of selling whiskey, only to be implicated in a more far-reaching effort to subvert the Indians whom his mission was supposed to help.

Before pursuing this, the Moravian letters are useful, and undoubtedly more accurate, in another respect. They provide the most precise evidence available for the dates when Blackburn's two mission schools (conducted not by him but by persons hired by him) finally closed. In a letter dated 8 January 1810, John Gambold reported that "day before yesterday a Mr. Foreman, a white man who settled here already some 40 years ago, told us that Mr. Blackburn's school at the Tellico Blockhouse has gone to pieces." On 3 May 1810, he added in another letter:

> In regard to Mr. Blackburn's school troubles, I must try to prevent a misunderstanding or hold it back. That school of which Mr. Black [one of Blackburn's teachers] was formerly in charge on the Highwassee and which was last kept in the former Blockhouse at Fort Tellico, to be sure, according to reports about it, has gone to pieces; whether forever, time alone will tell. On the other hand, the other school, which was first on the Chicamaga, and for a long time has been on the other side of the Tennessee below the new Garrison on James Brown's plantation, where Joe Vann goes to school now, is still in existence; at least, I have learned nothing to the contrary.[9]

From these reports it seems safe to say that the original school, started in 1804, closed at the end of 1809, and the second school (started at South Sale Creek in 1806) closed in the early summer of 1810.

In fairness to Gideon Blackburn, it is necessary to give his side of the story. This can best be done by quoting a long letter—in effect, a legal brief—written by Governor Willie Blount (who succeeded Sevier) to the secretary of war on 1 March 1811. Blount, seeking recompense from the Creeks for the goods they confiscated, not only exonerated the traders from any blame but insisted that the Creeks must be punished for interfering with this "honorable and laudable enterprize." His line of argument lends credence to the view that the venture was concocted for the purpose of undermining the sovereignty of the Indian nations. He argued that no passport or permission was needed by any American who chose to travel through Indian land on navigable waterways. By "natural

---

[9]John Gambold to Christian Benzien, 8 January 1810 and 3 May 1810, Moravian Archives.

right" and "the law of Nations," citizens of the United States could freely "navigate streams communicating with the Ocean in a foreign Territory where these streams take their rise within the limits of the United States." (Mobile was, of course, still in Spanish West Florida, but Blount was also claiming the right of white Americans to traverse freely through any Indian territory without the permission of the chiefs of the tribes who owned the territory through which navigable rivers passed.) Beneath the surface of this apparently trivial incident lies a more complex question: Were Gideon Blackburn and his brother Samuel, Quotaqueskey and his son James McIntosh, Pathkiller and the eighteen Cherokee chiefs who supported the venture cat's-paws in a plan engineered from Washington, or were they willing agents of the government, eager to profit from the opening of new trade routes through Indian Territory? Blount's letter throws some light on this:

> *Knoxville*
> *March 1st 1811*

Dear Sir,

It appears from papers in my possession, a copy of which I understand is with you, that certain citizens of this State residing in Blount County, entered into an agreement with James McIntosh, a half-breed of the Cherokee Nation, to enterprize in a trade with Mobile; and that they formed a copartnership, and purchased a certain quantity of Articles for that trade to the amount of $2,463.98 $^3/_4$, consisting of 2,226 gallons of Whiskey, and sundry other articles, amounting to the aforesaid sum and this purchase was made in February, 1809. The understanding of the contract and agreement by the parties was that James McIntosh was to take the whole management of the property whilst passing thro' the Nation; that it should be considered as his; that he should give bond and security for the aforesaid amount; that said [Robert] Houston and [Samuel] Blackburn were to assist as hands in navigating the Boats down the Coosa to Mobile; that the cargo was to be disposed of at Mobile; and that the nett profits should be equally divided between said Houston, Blackburn and McIntosh after the cost of the whole should be discharged. They were not to trade with the Cherokees or Creeks. This enterprize was approved by the Highwassee Chiefs [Cherokees]. McIntosh, with the aforesaid property, descended the Coosa river to Turkey Town in the Cherokee Nation with two Boats laden with said property which he stored with a Chief of the Cherokees residing there; and whilst using his best endeavors to obtain the consent of the Creeks pass thro' their Nation with it, they, the Creeks, upward of one hundred in number, came and forcibly took the property, the boats and everything belonging to them, and carried all off into the Creek Nation; for which they have as yet made no satisfaction either in whole or in part. The better to be enabled to pursue after this property whereby to save it from destruction, a paper purporting to be a passport from Col. Hawkins was fabricated; which a party of the Creeks forcibly took and carried to Col. Hawkins. 40 Towns of the Cherokees have, in Council on this subject, disapproved the conduct of the Creeks. The sufferers estimate their loss at the hands of the Creeks at $5,948.12 $^1/_2$. McIntosh has been qualified [given a deposition under oath] that the Creeks robbed him of the aforesaid property at Turkey Town in the Cherokee Nation. The Reverend Gideon Blackburn has made oath that he saw part of the property stored at Turkey Town before he left there. S. Blackburn and R. Houston have made oath that the property was consigned to James McIntosh, that they saw the Creeks take it by force; that they heard McIntosh demand it of them as his property, alledging that they must pay for it. Messrs. Nicol and Montgomery have been deposed that they sold much of the aforesaid property to S. Blackburn and R. Houston & that they understood it was to be sent down the Coosa river to Mobile. Isaac White swears that the Boats were owned by S. Blackburn, R. Houston and J. McIntosh; that he went with them to Turkey Town; that McIntosh bartered some small quantities of Whiskey for provisions, and to pay hands for aiding up Highwassee [River] etc. Accompanying these papers are sundry letters of correspondence between the Cherokees and Creeks which have relation to the foregoing business; and the copy of one from Col. Hawkins to Alexander Cornalls and the Big Warrior of the Creek Nation which to me is a curiosity as coming from an Agent of the United States respecting property owned by white people passing from one place to another within the jurisdiction of the United States, and particularly thro' the Nation where he is an agent by appointment.

According to my way of thinking, the people of the United States have a natural right to claim the navigation of rivers passing thro' the Territory of the United States, and this right is sanctioned by the general principles of the law of Nations—nay, they have a natural right to navigate streams communicating with the Ocean in a foreign Territory where these streams take their rise within the limits of the United States, & in support of this opinion I beg leave to refer you to the documents and correspondence between our government and Spain as appears from the records in the office of the Secretary of State of the United States in 1801 & 1802, when the President endeavored to obtain for the citizens of the United States residing in Tombigby and Alabama Rivers, the free navigation of the Mobile river to its confluence with the ocean before it was known that Spain had ceded Louisiana to France. Since the United States purchased that country from France, the navigation of Mobile has been claimed by the United States as included in that purchase. See the instructions to our minister at Madrid to claim the free navigation of the Mobile under the law of Nature and to represent to his Catholic Majesty the propriety and necessity of giving orders to his officers not to interrupt the free communication with our territories thro' the waters of the Mobile. See there also the proceedings of the Governor of Orleans Territory and of other officers of the United States on the free navigation of that river, and I believe that a committee of the House of Representatives of the United States, perhaps in 1810, reported a resolution expressive of this opinion, that the United States was authorized by the law of Nations to claim and to exercise the right of navigating that stream, and others similarly situated. These people then certainly had the right to navigate the waters leading into the Mobile in February, 1809, which was many years after the purchase of Louisiana, and a right to proceed down all the tributary streams unmolested, and of course, the Creeks are bound to pay for the property they have forcibly taken from citizens of the United States and from a Cherokee Indian within the limits of the United States and within the limits of the Cherokee Nation as a place too of safe deposit in said Nation from all people except indeed from robbers; pursuing a lawful trade; engaged in an honorable and laudable enterprize; & conducting themselves with more than ordinary propriety and strictness when compared to many others; manifesting a serious desire to promote harmony and disposed to open a trade and communication thro' a channel so anxiously desired by the general government, and by the people of this Country in general. The right of the people of the United States to navigate our waters is unquestionable; by the 9th Article of the Treaty of Hopewell between the United States and the Cherokees, the United States have undertaken to manage the concerns of that Nation, for their benefit, and for the benefit of the United States jointly. The interference of the government in behalf of those injured citizens is solicited and expected. To account for the delay in representing this misconduct of the Creeks to government, I am authorized to say that it has been occasioned inconsiderable part by the expectation entertained by those who has sustained the loss, that the Agent of the United States resident in the Creek Nation would thoroughly examine the case and make report in full thereon with his opinion to the department of War; which expectation in them was raised by his positive promise to them that he would do so without delay, and that he would send them a copy of said report and opinion; which they believe he has not done; and their reason for believing so it that he has never informed them that he had made a report, altho' frequently solicited for an answer. . . .[10]

---

[10]Willie Blount to Secretary of War William Eustis, 1 March 1811, M-221, roll 34, frames 2097-2098. In a follow-up letter of 18 March 1813, Blount said of the Creeks, "They should be compelled not only to refund it [the confiscated cargo] or to pay the value but should moreover be made to suffer punishment for their outrage." M-221, roll 50, frame 4793.

This letter by Blount, written almost two years after the incident at Turkey Town, lays the burden for it upon Benjamin Hawkins. It alleges that the owners of the whiskey had no intention of selling it among the Indians and explains that James McIntosh of the Cherokee Nation was given sole management of the property out of concern for the letter of the law. Although Blount states in a general way that one purpose of the expedition was to "open a trade and communication thro' a channel so anxiously desired by the general government," he makes no mention of the fact that several of the persons concerned in the affair had written letters specifically stating that the articles were being sent down the rivers "at the request of the President."[11]

It was this allegation that troubled Hawkins, for he felt certain that if the president had indeed requested such an expedition, he would have notified both Meigs and Hawkins and told them to so inform the Cherokee and Creek chiefs. When the Creeks first spied the boats coming down the river toward their border, they wrote immediately to Hawkins for information about them. In their letter of 11 April 1809, they enclosed the "fabricated" passport signed with Hawkins's name and said they were holding up the boats until he could come and clarify the situation. Hawkins's reply from the Creek Agency, which was one hundred miles from the scene of the confrontation, was written on 20 April 1809:

> I have just received your favor of the 11th by a man from Cowattah, and have paid him two dollars; if your date is right it has been long on the path. I send Mr. Limbaugh, an assistant agent, up to you without loss of time, who will attend the Chiefs and write for them and do anything they require of him.
>
> I have read the papers sent by Mr. Curnall [interpreter and scribe for the chiefs]. The one signed with my name is forgery. I have never heard any thing of this Boat or the object of the owners, but what you send me. As they have forged a pass in my name, I have no doubt that David McNair [who wrote on their be-

---

[11]For example, whether duped or not, the eighteen Cherokee chiefs who provided James McIntosh, Samuel Blackburn, and their partners with a letter of goodwill at the outset of their journey, on 12 March 1809, said they were carrying goods "which our father the president wants to send to his white children at Fort St. Stephens." M-221, roll 39, frame 5366. Meigs said later that "what they say about the wish of the President is undoubtedly without authority," but he did not say that it was inaccurate. M-221, roll 39, frame 5355.

half] tells a falsehood when he says that Boat is out with "Articles at the request of the President."

If the President should have occasion to use your paths or water courses, he will let you know it by the public Agents. He keeps me with you for the purpose of communicating his wishes to you and to aid you in all your concerns.

I wish there may be a very friendly intercourse between us and our white neighbours; we are safe in our lands and if we can restrain our young men and keep them within the bounds of good neighbourhood we have nothing to fear. The new President, Mr. Madison, has come into office with a disposition perfectly fatherly towards us; he will aid us in our plan of civilization.

If your Chiefs are determined the Boat shall not pass down the river, order her back, and give time for the owners to get back. . . .[12]

Hawkins then wrote to the secretary of war to inform him of the situation and perhaps to find out whether he had missed some vital communication: "A runner has just arrived from the Chiefs of the upper [Creek] towns to inform me that they have ordered a boat built in the Cherokee nation for the navigation of the Coosau and Allabama rivers and loaded for Fort Stephens, to be stoped [*sic*]. The persons on board, five white men and a half breed Cherokee, asserted that they were going with supplies at the request of the President for Fort St. Stephens and that they had a pass from me. The Indians report the cargo is 50 odd Casks of rum, some powder and lead, and having got possession of the papers, sent them to me, and the pass with my signature is a forgery."[13] If the secretary of war had authorized this expedition at the request of the president or on his own authority, there had certainly been a failure of communication. There is no record of any such authorization and Hawkins apparently received no reply to his message.

After Christian Limbaugh reached the scene, the Creeks investigated with him and on 1 May reported their decision through Big Warrior Hawkins (as translated by Limbaugh):

You have often warned us of [to] never suffer such things to come among us, and it was agreed between you and the Chiefs of our nation to put a stop to speculators, and now they have come among us without leave or license. I must now inform you what I have heard concerning this Boat. A white man is the owner of it

---

[12]Benjamin Hawkins to the Big Warrior, 20 April 1809, quoted in Blount's letter, cited in n. 10 above.

[13]Benjamin Hawkins to Secretary of War John Smith, 23 April 1809. M-221, roll 23, frame 7582.

and brought it down Coosay river [to] the Little Turkey's town (Sennecca) and then he left it with the Path maker, a Cherokee chief, and the articles that is in it, and the path maker is to sell the goods for the benefit of the owner. I have taken this resolution, and it is nothing but right, that we shall take the goods and divide it among us. And I shall do it.[14]

On the same day, Big Warrior also wrote to Pathkiller and told him what he had decided, berating the Cherokee chiefs for letting white traders and speculators invade the Indian lands with forged documents: "Now I must blame you more than the whites, that you let them into your land. Now I shall caution you of never hearing [of] any more such doings. The small parcel of land and the few rivers we have in our Country is for us to live upon. It is our whole dependence."[15] He went on to tell Pathkiller that if there were any other goods in his possession given to him by these white traders, he expected "you will take have [half] to your Nation and send the other half to me." Meanwhile, he intended to distribute what he had seized among his own chiefs.

The Cherokee chiefs responded on 27 May, "It is very true that our beloved man [Pathkiller] knowed that you would not allow the water path to be travelled and that on [that] account he stopt them and they took his advice not to go any farther. We thought [hoped?] you would not stop them as they were going among their own people to trade and it is necessary that friends should take their own affairs when any thing happens and the Friendship remain."[16] What this seemed to say was that so far as the Cherokee were concerned, they did not want to spoil their friendship with the Creeks; it was the Creeks' decision and they could manage their affairs as they saw fit.

The matter thus ended up in the laps of Hawkins and Meigs to untangle. Meigs, at the request of Gideon Blackburn, looked over a large group of affidavits that Blackburn and McIntosh had obtained from those concerned and decided on 5 February 1810 to support these claims against "the Robbery of the Creeks." He told Blackburn that he should not feel "diffident" about pressing for repayment by the Creeks and

---

[14]Big Warrior to Benjamin Hawkins, 1 May 1809, M-271, roll 1, frame 0629. In seizing the cargo Big Warrior clearly did not follow Hawkins's advice, though Hawkins later defended his action as justified.

[15]Big Warrior to the Cherokee chiefs, 1 May 1809, M-271, roll 1, frame 0620.

[16]The Ridge and other chiefs to Big Warrior, 27 May 1809, M-271, roll 1, frame 0624.

asked him to look over the report he was forwarding to Hawkins.[17] In this report he said that "in March last the Reverend Gideon Blackburn stated to me that such an enterprize was in contemplation disclaiming any Idea of trading with the Indians." He then went on to argue that frontier needs and the intent of nature clearly supported the venture: "As the population of this Country was rapidly advancing also that of the Tombigby country and both laying under great disadvantages as respects commerce, I could not but wish success to an innocent enterprize calculated to bring into use the canals which nature has prepared evidently for the purpose of commercial intercourse, and knowing that the Cherokees woud [sic] favor an object of this kind, I had no hesitation on giving a passport to descend the waters leading through the Cherokee Country so far as their southern boundary." (He did not note that the passport the traders received was not signed by him but by his son, Timothy, in his absence.) He did admit that the traders had "committed an error" in forging Hawkins's name to a pass granting access to the Creek country; but he took their word for it that they did this only to prevent those who entered the Creek country in boats from being abused by the Creeks while they negotiated for passage through the nation.[18] Meigs tried to argue that "by their [the Creeks'] conduct in seizing the property it appears to be an act of violence committed by them on the rights of the Cherokees as well as the rights of the [trading] party." (Yet it is interesting that the Cherokee never pressed any claim against the Creeks or asked for any punishment of the warriors who entered Pathkiller's house and took the whiskey.)

Hawkins read Meigs's report but was not convinced by his arguments nor by the affidavits of the traders. He went over the whole matter with the Creek chiefs and on 31 December 1810 forwarded all the documents, together with his "reversal of Col. Meigs' decision," to the secretary of war. The decision of the Creeks to seize the merchandise, he concluded, was "a correct one." His letter explaining why he disagreed with Meigs and Blount constitutes the last official word on the incident.

---

[17]Return J. Meigs to Gideon Blackburn, 25 February 1810, M-221, roll 39, frame 5352.

[18]Return J. Meigs's report to Benjamin Hawkins, 25 February 1810, M-221, roll 39, frames 5353-5560.

Creek Agency
31 December 1810

The undersigned, agent for Indian affairs, makes the following remarks and report on the statement and claim of James McIntosh, a half breed Cherokee, and others, for a seizure of Whiskey and other articles of merchandize at the Little Turkeys town in April, 1809, and condemned by the Creek Chiefs 1st May following.

The statement and claim is numbered 1 to 13 accompanyed by a letter from Col. Meigs, agent for the Cherokees, dated February 1810. To which is added four numbers 14, 15, 16, 17 being original documents appertaining to the subject.

It is manifest from the documents that the merchandize was not accompanyed with a license or passport obtained from legal authority; that marked N. 4 of Timothy Meigs, Clerke of Col. Meigs, if he had authority, was only to Benjamin Blackburn, John P. Houston, Isaac White and Robert Houston [McIntosh's name is not mentioned in Meigs's document] to go down the Alabama river. Col. Meigs, in his letter of 25 September, 1810, admits a knowledge of the enterprise communicated to him by the Reverend Gideon Blackburn in March 1809 and says he had no hesitation in giving a passport to descend the waters leading thro' the Cherokee Country as far as their southern border. If the No. 4 is this passport, I do not know how property of this description of the cargo seized could come into the Cherokee Country, to pass the same legally, without License and with such a passport.

The parties concerned seem to think other passports necessary as well as a false destination of the Cargo. In No. 3, forged for the 18 Cherokee Chiefs, it states, "some supplies which our father, the President, wants to send to his white children at Fort St. Stephens" [not Mobile]. In the note on N. 2 "that the articles were sent by the request of the President." In N. 14, "Mr McIntosh was instructed by the President to carry supplies to Fort St. Stephens." It is obvious the forged pass, N. 14, which James McIntosh says "We wrote a kind of pass as if from Hawkins" is not of his hand writing or of any of his party but must have been a deliberate act of older date. If the transaction was really innocent, why obtain false papers to cover the enterprise, when Col. Meigs, the agent, had no hesitation in giving a passport to descend the waters thro' the Cherokee agency? If he had given a description of the enterprise, and particularly of the property, there is no doubt but the passport would have been respected, so far as to cover the property back, if the Creeks had refused its passing down the Coosau. And as there appears to have been full time, why did not the party concerned apprise the Creeks, or their agent for Indians affairs there, of it, to obtain their consent or at least that precautionary measures might have been taken by him to secure the property and protect its return?

2ndly In N. 9, Isaac White [a member of the boat's crew] says Mr. McIntosh *bartered* some small quantity of provisions for some hands to assist up the Hiwassa, and for hauling the loads across from Wookoah to Conasauga. The difference between bartering and offering for sale is not material when merchandize is found without License or support in the Indian Country.

3rdly It appears this transaction took place early in the spring of 1809. The merchandize condemned in May of that year by the Creeks, and [yet] the first complaint is the 22 January of this year to Col. Meigs as the agent to the Cherokees, and on the 24 April, twelve months after the seizure of the merchandize, to Col. Hawkins as agent for the Creeks. Why this delay as there is a mail weekly to the Creek agency? If there was no occasion for disguise and the enterprise laudable, why not apply without delay for redress?

4thly The plea of Mr. [Enoch] Parsons, the Attorney General of East Tennessee N. 16 might be applicable if the whole procedure was according to Law and within the municipal regulations of some one of the United States, but the carrier in this instance, as well as his assistants, who appear to be partly concerned, was carrying a quantity of merchandize into Indian country without a License or passport and bartering some of it against a positive statute of the United States.

5thly Col. Meigs in his letter of the 25th February 1810 gives it as his opinion that the Creeks who took the property have committed themselves and ought to return the property or pay for it. It appears to him to be an act of Violence on their part against the rights of the party. He charges them with forceably seizing, taking and carrying away the property; and he brands this conduct with the epithets base, illiberal and unjust. All opinions on an *ex parte* are liable to be erroneous and no more than this. The Creek Chiefs who do the Executive business of the Nation, on hearing of the boat and its object, appealed to the agent for Indian affairs, N. 17, to come himself or send someone in his place to know if he gave the order, as was alleged, for the boat to pass, saying if he did, "we are to blame for stoping it." N. 10 is from the Executive chiefs and expresses an anxious concern for the situation of the boat and party under examination, promises safety and protection; N. 11 is the answer to N. 17; N. 15, the condemnation for coming without leave or License and with a forged pass, and N. 12 the notification of the chiefs to the Path Killer who lives in Esenacca and had charge of the goods condemned.

The Creeks are to a certain extent an Independent people and treated as such by the United States; they claim and have long claimed the jurisdiction of Coosau river. The Cherokees have long admitted that the lands of Esenaca (Little Turkey's Town) were borrowed from the Creeks. The authority exercised by them is between them and the Cherokees and not at issue for this examination. Lastly, the foregoing remarks, being the result of a careful examination of all the documents accompanying the case, I am of opinion [that] the decision of the agent of the Cherokees is erroneous, that the Creeks and Cherokees, or either of them, had a right to seize and condemn the merchandize in question to their own proper use, and that the condemnation by the Creeks is valide and conclusive.

Benjamin Hawkins
agent for I. A.[19]

Here the case rests. Perhaps the fact that the traders had in fact "bartered" or sold whiskey (as they admitted) undermined their case. Perhaps the explicit references to requests by the president would have been an embarrassment if made public. In any case, the secretary of war did nothing about the matter. On 25 December 1810, Enoch Parsons wrote a letter to President James Madison about the matter, which he left with Pleasant M. Miller, a congressman from eastern Tennessee, on 1 January 1811. Parsons said he had been retained as agent for the traders and had visited Hawkins and written to him but could not get him to assess the sum requested for payment against the Creek annuities.[20] Congressman Miller forwarded Parson's letter and documents to the secretary of war; nothing happened. On 18 March 1813, Governor Willie Blount sent another long letter to the secretary of war noting that "the owners never have received compensation" for their losses and demanding action.[21]

However, the Creek civil war intervened and ultimately General Andrew Jackson settled in battle all the issues that the more devious methods of those associated with Parson Blackburn's trading expedition had failed to settle, at least so far as opening up trade routes to Mobile were concerned.

---

[19]Benjamin Hawkins to the secretary of war, 21 December 1810, M-271, roll 1, frames 2097-2098.

[20]It is interesting that the bills of lading provided for the goods contain the prices paid for them and the prices the Creeks were being charged for confiscating them: 65 barrels of whiskey bought at 4/6 per gallon was charged at 12/ per gallon; 535 pounds of powder, purchased at 4/6 per pound was charged to the Creeks at 12/ per pound; two boats bought for $50 each were charged at $100 each. The total of the original lading was $2,463.98 3/4 and the total assessed against the Creeks was $5,948.12 1/2. Apparently this represents the profit that the traders expected to make on their cargo had they reached Mobile. M-221, roll 39, frames 5344-5346 and 5358-5359.

[21]Willie Blount to the secretary of war, 18 March 1813, M-221, roll 50, frame 4793.

The evidence of the incident at Turkey Town, taken as a whole, seems to exonerate Gideon Blackburn from the charge of trying to sell whiskey to the Indians in contravention of the Intercourse Act. However, it does not do much to strengthen his credibility. He seems clearly to have been implicated in a carefully designed effort to test Indian sovereignty over navigable waters within their borders. One of the most revealing items in the documentation appears in the deposition by Samuel Blackburn and Robert Houston made on 20 January 1810. They swore "that they had no design of going down the Coosee river with boats when they first made their purchase of whiskey from the Merchants of Maryville [in February, 1809] but intended to carry it down the Mississippi River. That in consequence of the information from Quotaqusky [John McIntosh, father of James McIntosh] and the Ridge [a prominent Cherokee chief] on their return from Congress and the contract made in favor of James McIntosh, they changed their resolution to the route of the Coosee."[22] They asserted that they had no intention of selling whiskey to the Indians at any time.

This implies that The Ridge and Quotaqueskey (and Gideon Blackburn as well, if the Moravians' information was correct) had been in Washington discussing with the secretary of war the problem of opening up the Coosa River and others between Tennessee and the Gulf.[23] The sticking point was the refusal of the Creeks to allow such a trade and the belief of their agent that they had the right to prevent it. James McIntosh, the son of a white father who had been accepted into the Cherokee Nation by virtue of his marriage to a Cherokee, was the key to the plan. "In January, 1809," he said in his deposition, "as my Father returned from the Federal City, he entered into a contract for Whiskey, powder, lead, etc. as you can see by the Bill accompanying, with Samuel Blackburn and Robert Houston. The design of the contract was that I should take the whole management of the property while passing through the nations of Indians, that it should be considered as my own, that I gave my Bond,

---

[22]M-221, roll 39, 5369. Both The Ridge and Quotaqueskey were well-to-do Cherokees, owners of slaves who cultivated large fields and were very enterprising in trade.

[23]The Ridge and Quotaqueskey were in Washington to arrange a treaty concerning the Cherokee Nation; while there, such a conference might well have occurred. Blackburn went often to Washington to seek aid for his mission schools.

secured by my Father for the amount of the aforementioned Bill. . . ."[24] (It is conjecture why he neglected to mention, if he knew it, that the Reverend Gideon Blackburn also gave his note to secure the bill. But if the Moravian account is correct, Blackburn may have initiated the whole project, for as a missionary he had the freedom to reconnoiter the riverways and the enterprise to push it once he concluded that a short portage from the Wokoah, or Amoi, River to the Connesaga made the river route feasible.)

It is significant that the Creeks almost immediately detected the hand of John D. Chisholm in the venture. Writing to Hawkins on 1 May 1809, they specifically said Chisholm was behind it and that in their opinion he was responsible for forging the pass. He was, they said, a dangerous man who should be put out of the Cherokee Nation; but because he was white, the Indians did not want to take this upon themselves.[25] Chisholm was the confederate of the recently assassinated Cherokee chief, Doublehead.

There were good reasons why the Cherokee Nation never pressed the matter of reparations for the Creeks' trespass. This became clear after the Creek War when Jackson, in the treaty of 1814, forced the Creek to cede a wide swath of land from Tennessee to the Gulf. Included in that cession was Turkey Town and other land surrounding it, which Jackson said belonged to the Creek. The Cherokee, protesting this, said that originally the land had been Creek; however, during the American Revolution the Creek Nation had permitted them to settle on it (whether permanently or as a loan was unclear). Obviously had the Cherokee raised the issue of a Creek trespass in April 1809, that would simply have brought this complication into the open.

That the federal government was interested in opening up a trade route from Tennessee to the Gulf in 1809, we know from many documents, starting in 1810, instructing the agents to the Cherokee and the

---

[24]M-221, roll 39, frame 5360. Being an Indian, McIntosh could not be prosecuted for selling whiskey to Indians en route because the law only prohibited non-Indians from selling to Indians. Thus the venture was thought to be protected against just such an eventuality as occurred. Whether the whiskey was to be traded with Creeks or Choctaws prior to arriving at Mobile remains a moot point. It would certainly have been ill-advised in calling attention to a venture that had other designs.

[25]Big Warrior to Benjamin Hawkins, 1 May 1809, M-271, roll 1, frame 0629.

Creek to sound out these nations on their willingness to grant rights of navigation and rights to a turnpike through their land to Mobile. It is therefore not beyond conjecture that what ended in formal negotiations may have begun in a clandestine (and less costly) probe into Indian Territory. Because high profits were involved, the Blackburn brothers, like any enterprising frontier merchants, were willing to risk some capital on it. They knew they could count on full support from political leaders in Tennessee, such as Blount, Sevier, and Parsons.

Hawkins made the most telling indictment of the episode, and of the assumed innocence of those hoisted by their own petard afterward, when he asked, "If the transaction was really innocent, why obtain false papers to cover the enterprise?" Here, and not in illicit whiskey trading, lies the ruined credibility of Parson Blackburn. Even those who supported the venture thought Blackburn was fully implicated. In July 1815, when John Sevier was engaged as a commissioner drawing the lines of Jackson's treaty with the Creek, he sent on to the secretary of war a statement by the Creeks in which they said, "From what you say about the whiskey, you must have thought it was taken on our land; it was."[26] Realizing that federal officers had short memories, he added a footnote to this remark, saying: "The whiskee taken from Parson Blackburn in Turkeytown thirty miles above Fort Strother. The town is settled by Cherokees in which resides the Pathkiller, headman of the Nation. The whiskee was taken by Creeks between six and eight years since, alledging it was within their territory, which the Cherokees did not contest [at that time]."

Gideon Blackburn and the Presbyterian missionaries were not the only ones suspected of "speculating" and secretly conniving against the Indians at that time. The Moravian mission records reveal that they faced the same charges. Part of the criticism of Blackburn was obviously based upon antimission sentiment, which began to grow stronger among the Cherokee after 1809.

It is ironic that many years later, in 1834, Gideon Blackburn joined the temperance movement in America and began preaching sermons attacking the evils of the liquor traffic.[27]

---

[26]The Creeks' chiefs to John Sevier, 21 July 1815, M-221, roll 66, frame 9561.

[27]Posey, *The Presbyterian Church*, 99.

CHEROKEE ANTIMISSION SENTIMENT, 1823-1824

So much has been written about the speedy success of Cherokee acculturation that historians have neglected to note the resistance displayed toward it. Not all Cherokees were pleased at the intensive efforts of their leaders and the missionaries to force them to adopt the white man's beliefs and moral standards. This incident in 1824 was probably only one of many that led to the movement known as "White Path's Rebellion" in 1827. It is of interest because it documents specifically the variety of causes why the headmen or chiefs of the town of Etowah (sometimes called Hightower) wanted their chiefs to help them expel a missionary of the American Board of Commissioners for Foreign Missions.

Etowah was one of the most traditionalist areas in the Cherokee Nation, along with being the largest town in the nation. Neither the chiefs nor the people in this area spoke much English; the person who acted as scribe for the appeal to the second principal chief was a mixed-blood trader named Walter Adair. The letter expressed widespread resentment in that region and was signed by eight chiefs. These same chiefs had originally requested that a missionary be sent to their town to start a school and that a blacksmith accompany him. The chiefs were not totally averse to acculturation, but they soon found that they had got more than they bargained for. The missionary split the town into two hostile parties—the pagan and the Christian. Violence broke out and the slaves seemed about to rebel.

The second principal chief, Charles Hicks, was a convert to Christianity. We owe the documentation for this incident to his decision to send to his mission pastor, the Moravian John Gambold, the reply that he gave to the Etowah chiefs. The incident is made more significant by the growth of antimission sentiment in 1824-1827; it reveals how many different ways "Christianization" could tear apart the cultural fabric of Cherokee town life.

MOST ACCOUNTS OF THE CHEROKEE INDIANS during the early nineteenth century say little about antimission sentiment. Partly this is because the best-known Cherokee leaders, fighting desperately against federal removal policies, did not want to alienate white American public opinion. Furthermore, they found among New England missionaries after 1817 a vital source of support in this fight, as the work of Jeremiah Evarts and the Reverend Samuel A. Worcester indicates. Many Cherokee welcomed the mission schools to teach their children and increase their technical skills. Mixed-blood chiefs, in particular, believed that rapid acculturation (or deculturation) would prove that "savages" could be "civilized" and thus the Cherokee would be allowed to remain upon the lands of their forefathers. Persistent missionary activity after 1800 succeeded in converting some influential chiefs to Christianity. In addition, many Cherokee of mixed white and Indian ancestry were nominally Christians. By virtue of their more rapid acculturation, these "progressives" tended to become better farmers and traders, to assume positions of leadership (vis à vis whites) and to become what might be termed a "red bourgeoisie" among the Cherokee. Some of them became slaveowners and cotton planters.

But while this progressive element has received the bulk of attention from ethnohistorians, there was an equally strong element among the Cherokee who opposed, at least in part, the acculturation process. James Mooney noted one aspect of this resistance when he described the Ghost Dance movement among the Cherokee in 1811-1812 (Mooney 1896: 676-77). Mooney attributed the movement primarily to the influence of Tecumseh and the Prophet and the general confusion over the role the Cherokee should play in their confederacy. Other historians have referred briefly to a movement in 1826-1827 known as "White Path's Rebellion" (Mooney 1900: 113-14, 237-38; Malone 1956: 87). Robert Berkhofer follows the traditional explanation of this movement when he describes it as opposition "from the fullbloods, who led an abortive attempt against the progressive halfbreeds" to resist increasing centralization of the government under a written constitution modeled on that of the United States (Berkhofer 1965: 138). No effort has been made to relate Cherokee opposition to missionary activity to the 1827 rebellion against political centralization because of lack of evidence.

Recently, however, I discovered in the missionary records of the Moravians an exchange of letters between some local chiefs and the principal chiefs of the Cherokees in 1824 that indicate there was strong antimission sentiment in the 1820s. Letters among the archives of the American Board of Commissioners for Foreign Missions corroborate this and link it to White Path's movement. To understand this, it is necessary to explain the relationships among various kinds of intratribal factionalism associated with acculturation, political centralization, and missionary efforts.

Robert Berkhofer's chapter, "Christians versus Pagans," in *Salvation and the Savage* (1965: 125-51) is the most important effort to date to delineate such relationships. Referring to the Cherokee, Berkhofer argues that the missionaries to that tribe arrived on the scene (in 1817) during such an advanced stage of acculturation and tribal division that they "were thrown into already existing factions rather than creating them." (1965: 138). The factions he cites are those favoring removal to the West and those opposing it. But the letters cited below indicate that the missionaries who came in 1817 did, in fact, create factions. Moreover, after 1819 most of the proremoval Cherokee went to the West to settle on land provided in treaties, leaving the antiremoval faction unchallenged in the East (at least until after 1832). Furthermore, Berkhofer should have pointed out that there existed a strong pro-Christian or promission sentiment among the Cherokee well before 1817 as a result of the Moravian mission, founded in 1801; the Presbyterian schools of the Reverend Gideon Blackburn (1803-1810); and the nominal Christian adherence of many influential Cherokee of mixed white and Indian ancestry. I do not find any evidence to support Berkhofer's claim that among the Cherokee "Indian church members switched religious affiliation according to politics" (1965: 138), at least not between the years 1817 and 1832.

The dispute described in the Etowah letters (cited in the appendix at the end of this essay) appears on the surface to be simply a question of antimission sentiment—a conflict between Christian converts in a mission church and the traditionalists. But beneath the surface lies the more far-ranging issue of Cherokee political autonomy and survival in their homeland, an area of 20,000 square miles in 1824 inhabited by 13,000 Cherokees and 1,300 black slaves owned by the Cherokee. From the year

1807 (if not from the date of the Louisiana Purchase), the Cherokee had faced white demands for total removal. They had lost a thousand of their people by voluntary emigration to the West in 1809-1810; they lost another 3,000 or more in subsequent years, most of them in the years 1817-1819. In their effort to combat this, they had taken two important steps after 1810: they had gradually consolidated political power in the hands of a national council and executive committee, and they had used every possible means to develop their economic skills and self-sufficiency.

Welcoming missionaries of the various Protestant denominations was an important element in this conscious policy of economic acculturation. Having accepted the necessity of becoming farmers and of trading with their white neighbors, the Cherokee needed to read and write English, to master basic arithmetic, to learn the arts of husbandry and domestic manufactures. In the absence of government-sponsored schools, the free schools provided by missionary agencies provided these skills. Since missionary schools were primarily designed from the Protestant viewpoint to convert the Indians to Christianity, the Cherokee faced the problem of increasing friction between such converts and those who disdained conversion. Precisely such a situation occurred in the Cherokee town of Etowah (or Enhalla) in 1823-1824.

Yet despite Berkhofer's implications, neither the local chiefs who advocated the recall of the American Board's missionaries and school teachers from their town in 1824, nor the two principal chiefs of the nation to whom they appealed for help, Pathkiller and Charles R. Hicks, were in disagreement over the removal policy. Nor was there apparent disagreement at that time over the increasing centralization of political power in the nation. The Etowah chiefs, though traditionalists, recognized the importance of tribal unity and strength vis à vis white pressures for removal. They supported Hicks as second principal chief (though he was a Christian convert) to manage their dealings with the whites because he was devoted to maintaining the tribe's political autonomy, local self-government, and the lands of their fathers. They also supported Pathkiller as principal chief, a traditionalist and full blood who neither spoke nor wrote English, in order to sustain the views of those in the nation—the large majority—who wished to accept only so much acculturation and so much political centralization as was needed for economic self-sufficiency and national unity.

The subtle undercurrents in this correspondence reached their climax three years later when a chief named White Path of Ellijay led a protest among those who felt that political centralization and acculturation were proceeding too fast and too far. Mooney describes White Path as "an influential full-blood and councilor" who "headed a rebellion against the new code of laws, with all that implied. . . . From the townhouse of Ellijay he preached the rejection of the new constitution, the discarding of Christianity and the white man's ways, and a return to the old tribal law and custom. . . ." But he concludes, "It was now too late, however, to reverse the wheel of progress, and under the rule of such men as Hicks and Ross, the conservative opposition gradually melted away." (Mooney 1900: 113) A journal kept by an American Board missionary in 1827, William Chamberlain, notes at the height of this nonviolent rebelling that White Path's party was considered "the heathen party" by the missionaries (A.B.C.F.M. Papers, Chamberlain's MS Journal, 3 May 1827). The Etowah incident in 1824 and White Path's opposition to the Cherokee constitution in 1826-1827 were two phases of the same sequence. While the missionaries tried to remain politically neutral, they were invariably caught up in the conflict. Ethnohistorians need to define more clearly this relationship, particularly for large, advanced tribes scattered over wide areas with sophisticated mixed-blood leaders.

The Etowah chiefs in Georgia had not realized, when they asked the American Board mission center at Brainerd (Chickamauga, Tennessee, forty miles to the north) to send them a school teacher and a blacksmith, that they were about to produce a factionalism they could not control. They merely wanted to improve their people's skills. When the factionalism caused trouble, they wrote to the principal chiefs (Pathkiller and Hicks) to ask for the withdrawal of the mission. In doing so, they faced the reality of growing centralization, for removal of the missionaries rested with the National Council, not with the local chiefs. Control over town affairs in this respect had been whittled away without the town chiefs fully realizing what it meant for them. Moreover, it now became evident that while Pathkiller and Hicks were united in opposing removal and supporting the political independence of the Cherokees against the whites, they were not united in regard to the role of missionaries, the rate of acculturation, or the extent of political centralization. Pathkiller, though eloquent and influential in internal Cherokee affairs, had allowed

Hicks to control the external affairs with the whites. Relationships with missionaries constituted external affairs. Hicks did not wish to alienate people whose services were so valuable and whose influence he needed with the federal government and the white public at large. The absence of any expression from Pathkiller in the Etowah incident is unfortunate. He probably sympathized with the local chiefs, however, as he later did with White Path.

Both Pathkiller and Charles Hicks died early in 1827. At the same time the imminent election of General Andrew Jackson to the presidency of the United States made the threat of Cherokee removal stronger than ever. Consequently Cherokees of both factions concluded in July 1827 that unity against removal was the critical issue. A violent antimission outbreak would have cost the Cherokee essential white support against Jackson. They ratified their new constitution in October 1827, and in 1828 elected as principal chief a man who had only one-eighth Cherokee blood but who was fiercely determined to oppose Jackson's removal. John Ross, the new principal chief, managed to defuse White Path's Rebellion so adroitly and so quietly that almost no record of it remains. When the constitution was implemented, White Path, after a short time, yielded to the necessity for tribal unity and agreed to serve in the upper house of the new bicameral legislature. For the next ten years, 1828-1838, John Ross, aided by White Path, led a stubborn effort to resist Jackson's removal policy. In that fight he received the active support of the missionaries, particularly those of the American Board, at least until 1832.

To place the Etowah incident in context, it is necessary to know that in response to the request for a school by the chiefs of Etowah, the American Board in 1823 sent the Reverend Isaac Proctor and an assistant there (Walker 1931: 51-52, 69). The missionaries called the town Hightower (a mispronunciation of Etowah). Proctor evidently made some converts very quickly and formed a mission church in the town. The converts from this church, not Proctor directly, caused the friction that led eight local chiefs to write to Charles Hicks in Fortville, Tennessee, in May 1824, asking him to tell the American Board to remove Proctor's school and church. As the chiefs explained to Hicks (partly in writing and partly through oral messages delivered by the messenger who brought their letter), there were four basic problems arising from the new mission station: first, the young Indian scholars at the mission school did not like

Proctor's teaching methods and complained against him (probably for his use of corporal punishment); second, the chiefs claimed that Proctor and his assistant were trying to prevent the new converts from "our common custom of meeting in our townhouse"; third, the new converts appear to have goaded some of the traditionalists by singing provocative hymns and implying that the Christian ritual of communion was too strong medicine for non-Christians to witness; and fourth, some of the Cherokees' black slaves seemed to have caught the antimission spirit and refused to work for their masters once these masters became Christians (perhaps from the assumption that a converted Indian master did not deserve respect and would not receive support from local Indian authorities).

The eight chiefs who wrote to Hicks were important men whose names appear on various documents and treaties. But they did not comprise all of the local chiefs. One important Etowah chief, John Beamer, did not sign the complaint because he himself had become a convert. It is important to note in view of Berkhofer's comments that this correspondence makes no reference to removal factions. All parties involved—local chiefs, principal chiefs, missionaries, converts, and traditionalists—were agreed in opposing removal.

The reply of Hicks to the complaints of the Etowah chiefs provides the key to the incident. He dismissed the complaints of the Cherokee students against their school teacher as typical children who disliked the tedious process of sitting in classrooms. Hicks dismissed the complaint that Richard Rowe's slaves would not obey him after his conversion because, as a slaveowner himself, he thought Rowe was to blame for not whipping ("correcting") his servants into obedience. (Hicks provided suitable Christian doctrines to distinguish the spiritual equality of slaves' souls before God from their duty in this world to obey their masters. There is no evidence that the missionaries, though from New England, advocated any antislavery views among the Cherokees.) He jettisoned the complaint that Christian converts were using hymns that threatened death to the heathen by noting that this meant simply spiritual death or separation from God in the next world. Finally, he rejected the complaint that the missionaries were interfering with local political authority in keeping converts from attending meetings at the town councilhouse on two grounds: a Christian minister might legitimately tell his congregation not to participate in "allnight dances and drinking," and beyond this, "I am confident that the society [i.e., the mission church] to which they have joined do not forbid our people to Exercise their public authority which any of them may be vested with" (see appendix).

These two last points are important. Cherokee culture, like most Indian cultures, intricately related religious ceremonies and political authority. To be a participant in one required participation in the other. One could not be a member of the town council, helping to make its decisions, if one did not also share in the values imbedded in the ceremonies, rituals, dances, and singing that were fundamental to membership in the culture. For Hicks to argue that a Cherokee converted to Christianity might legitimately exclude himself from Cherokee religious ceremonies without in any way failing to exercise "publick authority" either as a chief (in the case of John Beamer) or as an ordinary member of the tribe (by giving his voice in council debates and decisions) was simply to reveal how far he himself had moved from his own cultural values toward those of white American Protestants. When Hicks argued, in effect, that the church and the state (religious and political authority) were separate spheres of human activity, he was upholding religious liberty as a matter of private conscience; like Roger Williams among the Puritans, this displayed a fundamental chasm between Hicks's cultural views and those of the majority of the community in which he participated. The fact that Hicks sent apologetic copies of this correspondence to his spiritual adviser among the Moravians (because he and his family were members of the Moravian mission church at Springplace, Georgia) indicates the extent to which he himself was deculturated.

We have no other details concerning the incident at Etowah except that we know from the records of the American Board that Isaac Proctor did not leave there until 1826, and then he was succeeded by another of the board's missionaries. In August 1824, Hicks told another missionary of the board that "there is now a very powerful opposition to the Missions among the chiefs," and he listed Pathkiller as one of these opponents. (A.B.C.F.M. Papers, Chamberlain's MS Journal, 11 August 1824) Some years later, in May 1828, the board missionary who had succeeded Proctor in 1826, Daniel S. Butrick, wrote from Etowah that the school there had to be closed because only five children attended; he noted that the mission church had nine Cherokee members, several of whom "the year past were at one time very much disaffected on account of the sermons I preached on conjuring, rain-making, etc" (A.B.C.F.M.

Papers, Butrick's MS Journal, 8 May 1828). More evidence may someday be found linking antimission factionalism to White Path's Rebellion. The Etowah mission was finally closed in 1831 by the actions of the state of Georgia.

Berkhofer's description of the Senecas in the 1820s applies equally to the Cherokees: "After 1819, the difference between Pagan and Christian no longer revolved about the acceptance of white ways so much as the speed and degree of adoption." (Berkhofer 1865: 137) Charles Hicks favored the speedy adoption of white ways by the Cherokees both politically and religiously. The Etowah chiefs favored slow development of education and a minimum amount of centralization—just enough to provide unity against white pressures. As political pressure from the state and federal governments mounted under Jackson's rising star in the 1820s, the "progressive" mixed-blood chief (usually the most sympathetic to Christianization) accelerated the movement toward political centralization. This pace reached a peak in 1827 with the proposal for adoption of a written constitution, which included an article guaranteeing "the free exercise of religious worship" and "liberty of conscience." This pushed the traditionalists, under White Path, into the short-lived, but deeply felt, rebellion that linked the antimission sentiment revealed in the Etowah letters of 1824 to a general protest against overly rapid acculturation. Had it not been for the crisis over removal muting this protest, the Cherokees might have become as divided as the Senecas between a pagan and a Christian faction.

REFERENCES

A.B.C.F.M. Papers

Archives of the American Board of Commissioners of Foreign Missions, Houghton Library, Harvard University, Cambridge, Massachusetts.

Berkhofer, Robert K.

1965   *Salvation and the Savage.* Lexington: University of Kentucky Press.

Malone, Henry T.

1956   *Cherokees of the Old South.* Athens: University of Georgia Press.

Mooney, James

1896   *The Ghost Dance Religion.* Washington: Bureau of American Ethnology, 14th Annual Report, part 2.

1900   *Myths of the Cherokees.* Washington: Bureau of American Ethnology, 19th Annual Report, part 1.

Moravian Archives

Archives of the Moravian "Cherokee Mission Papers," Winston-Salem, North Carolina.

Walker, Robert S.

1931   *Torchlights to the Cherokees.* New York: MacMillan Company.

APPENDIX

[The following letters are located in the Moravian Archives, Winston-Salem, North Carolina, "Cherokee Mission Papers," Box M 482 (1820-1827).]

(1) Charles R. Hicks, second principal chief, to the Reverend Johan R. Schmidt, from Fortville, Cherokee Nation, 5 June 1824.

I send you the foregoing copy of the letter from the Etowah Chiefs or headmen to gather [with] the [oral] statement of the express[man] and the replies made to each subject [by me]; it is no doubt some of these verbal statements may not be correctly answered, beside[s] he informed me about other things which is not here entered, and I have since received a communication from Mr. I[saac] Proctor at Etowah which informs me that the Converts had denied [*sic*] in attending to their [the non-converts'] frolicks and whisky drinking which had in part raised this complaint against them; altho' I have refered [offered] to have the subject discussed at Extra Council, but I doubt whether it will have [a] hearing on this subject. [The remainder of this letter concerns Hicks's daughter's desire to have her child baptized by the Moravians at Spring Place Mission.]

(2) Chulioa and the other local Cherokee chiefs at Etowah to Charles R. Hicks and Path Killer, 26 May 1824. (Since these chiefs could not write English, it was written for them by a mixed-blood Cherokee named Walter Adair.) The messenger who brought the letter added oral comments from the chiefs.

We, the Chiefs of this place, En,hal,la [Etowah], who met here in order to discuss on several subject[s] relative to our local affairs, we have for some time beeng [been] [in] Darkness with respect of the indulgence given to the Missionary Teacher [Isaac Proctor] here at this place; the black smith we have pitched here on the High[est] recommendation has not realized the Expectation in us entertained of him; in [the] first place, he is [not] such [a good] workman as he ought to be; in [the] next place, he is Extravagant to charge for his work. As for the [missionary] teachers, they are complained of very much by the young people [who] are under their care for Edducation; they are trying to doe away [with] our common custom of meeting in our townhouse; other strange rules the[y] are adopting which appears to us ought not to be suffered; it is our wish that the missionaries here should be moved back to Chicama[u]ga to the [religious] society [the American Board] they belong [to].

Chulioa   X
Shoeboots   X

Cannutohu X
Esannoo X
oo le na wai X
Caul la hu X
Ca che ta nue X
Nau ta ta gut X

[written by Walter Adair]

(3) Charles R. Hicks to Chulioa and the other Etowah chief, 28 May 1824.

I have nothing to say against the missionary that have [*sic*] beeng [been] established at Etowah as it was with their [the chiefs] own free consent, and as the Path Killer has been named in their letter it was proper he should [advise] on it, and have the subject discussed in our next council altho' the complaint appears to have risen in consequence of some of our people having joined the [religious] society there by reason of which they would not attend allnight dances and drinking with them; the religion of which they had embraced forbids them to be at such places; and I am confident that the society to which they have joined do not forbid our people to Exercise their publick authority which any of them may be vested with; as to the complaints of the Scholars about their Teachers, similar ones have long ago been raised at other missionary schools but when examined into the subject it has beeng [been] found to be groundless, and no doubt this is the case with those at Et,a,wah—Scholars who [are] giting tired of their tuition.

The expressman [messenger] then stated verbally that the converts were continually singing—"you will die, you will die"—in reply stated that I expected this hymn was translated out of their Hymn book or it abounded with numbers of such Hymns, but that the unbeliever and believer were both subject [according to Christian teachings] to suffer in the flesh by reason of the first man [Adam, who] had committed a crime by his disobedience to the commands of his creator from which [the] hymn means death to the soul of the unbeliever in the next life by been [being] banished from the presence of god, and the soul of the believer will be received at the god [good?] place above because he has believed in the word of the son of god.

He [the messenger] stated also that Richard Rowe's negroes will not obey him since he has joined the church and [he] himself had to turn in to ploughing his fields [because the slaves would not]. I stated to him [the messenger], if any of my black people were disobedient to my orders I would assuredly correct them for it because the Gospell requires Servants to be faithful to their masters and are told the[y] have the same privileges given them as their masters to believe on god to obtained [obtain?] sallevation for their souls; and he also stated that the converts had beeng [been] saying that next Sunday the[y] were [to] pertake of the red physic [i.e., communion wine] which would make the Heathen faint if present; he [the messenger] was told [by me] it was an ordainance of the Son of god [who] had required his believers [to] celebrate in remembrance of his death when he [was] about to suffer for the sins of men, but [I] did not know [? believe] it would make one faint in being present when the believer participated of it, etc. etc. [Here ends the copy of the letter that Hicks sent to the Etowah chiefs. He evidently transcribed the copy for Schmidt in order to show his lack of sympathy with antimission sentiment in the tribe.]

THE METHODISTS AND THE REMOVAL QUESTION, 1831-1832

Just as it is a serious mistake to speak about "the Indians" as though they were all more or less alike, so it is a mistake to speak of "the missionaries." One problem all missionaries faced was that their mission boards did not seem to understand the need the missionaries in the field felt to demonstrate their sympathy for the Indians when the government treated them unjustly. How could a missionary claim to be helping the Indians when he took no interest in their political oppression? Could saving souls be separated from social justice?

History has made heroes of two members of the American Board of Commissioners for Foreign Missions who stood up against the injustice the state of Georgia showed the Cherokees: the Reverend Samuel A. Worcester and Dr. Elizur Butler. But as this essay shows, Worcester and Butler may have been goaded into action over the removal question by the action of the young Methodist circuit riders in the Cherokee Nation. Furthermore, Worcester and Butler had the full support of their board in Boston for their political activism; the Methodist missionaries, whose board was the Tennessee Methodist Conference, found no support at all from their board. Tennessee, after all, was Andrew Jackson's home state; when Methodist missionaries dared to denounce Jackson's Indian policy, they immediately aroused the anger of their coreligionists in that state. The matter was fought out, however, on the high ground of the missionary's duty to save souls and not meddle in politics.

ON 31 MAY 1831, the Reverend James Jenkins Trott, a Methodist missionary to the Cherokees, was arrested in the Cherokee Nation by the Georgia Guard and forced to march 110 miles to prison at Camp Gilmer.

Released after four days, he was required to post a five-hundred-dollar bond and ordered to keep out of the part of the nation that was within the territorial limits of the state of Georgia. He refused to obey the order. Married to a Cherokee who lived near his mission station at New Echota, he went to visit his wife and two children in July. On 6 July, he was again arrested and forced to march 110 miles back to prison. With him this time were two Presbyterian missionaries, the Reverend Samuel A. Worcester and Dr. Elizur Butler. Two of Trott's friends, the Reverend Dickson C. McLeod and the Reverend Martin Wells, who were also Methodist circuit riders within the Cherokee Nation, heard of his arrest. They saddled up and rode after him. When they caught up with the prisoners along the road, the officer in charge, Colonel C. H. Nelson, ordered them curtly to "Flank off!" When McLeod made some disparaging remarks about the treatment of the missionaries, Nelson ordered him off his horse, arrested him, and made him march with the prisoners. Wells, who was left holding McLeod's horse, was also ordered with oaths to flank off. When he refused, "Col. Nelson cut a stick and making up to Mr. Wells gave him a severe blow on the head."[1]

The trip to prison took four days. At night the prisoners were sometimes chained to each other to keep them from running away. Upon their arrival at the "filthy" jail, a guard shoved Trott through the door shouting, "Damn you, go in there and from there to hell." Because McLeod lived in the Tennessee area of the Cherokee Nation, he was released after two days. Two months later the other three missionaries were sentenced to four years at hard labor. Their crime was failure to obtain a permit from the governor to reside and preach in the Cherokee Nation—a permit they could obtain only after taking an oath of allegiance to the state.[2]

The story of the arrest and imprisonment of the missionaries to the Cherokees is well known, but it is always told in terms of the Presbyterians, Worcester and Butler. There is some justice to this, for it was they who, with the help of their mission board in Boston, brought the test case before the United States Supreme Court that resulted in John Mar-

---

[1]Various accounts of the incident written by Trott, McLeod, and Worcester can be found in the Methodist *Christian Advocate and Journal and Zion's Herald*, 29 July 1831 and 12 August 1831; the *Cherokee Phoenix*, 2 July, 9 July, 16 July, 30 July 1831 and 3 September 1831.

[2]This law is quoted, with the required oath, in Edmund Schwarze, *History of the Moravian Missions among Southern Indian Tribes of the United States* (Bethlehem, 1923) 194.

shall's famous decision (which Andrew Jackson refused to execute). Still, some explanation is needed for the failure, even by most Methodist historians, to give much attention to the Reverend J. J. Trott and his friends.[3] In certain respects they deserve more credit than Worcester and Butler. The two Presbyterians acted out of their own private conscience; the majority of their Presbyterian colleagues in the Cherokee Nation opposed their stand.[4] The Methodist missionaries, however, stood together, and three months before the Presbyterians spoke out, they issued a unanimous declaration opposing the removal of the Cherokee Indians. Worcester and Butler acted only after receiving full assurance from their mission board that they would be granted its wholehearted support. Trott and McLeod acted knowing full well that they would receive no support whatever from their superiors in Tennessee.

It is a classic example of the situation H. Richard Niebuhr described in *The Social Sources of Denominationalism*: the perspective taken by the missionary boards regarding Georgia's effort to harass the missionaries to the Cherokees was dictated less by transcendent Christian values than by mundane, political, regional, and racial values.[5] The Presbyterians

---

[3]The standard works dealing with the Methodist Indian missions are Nathan Bangs, *An Authentic History of the Missions under the Care of the Missionary Society of the Methodist Episcopal Church* (New York, 1832); Enoch Mudge, *History of the American Missions to the Heathen* (Worcester, 1840); Isabelle G. John, *Handbook of Methodist Missions* (Nashville, 1893); Anson West, *History of Methodism in Alabama* (Nashville, 1893); Marion E. Lazenby, *History of Methodism in Alabama and West Florida* (n.p., 1960); Mary T. Peacock, *The Circuit Riders and Those Who Followed* (Chattanooga, 1957); Walter B. Posey, *The Development of Methodism in the Old Southwest, 1783-1824* (Tuscaloosa, 1933); Wade C. Barclay, *History of Methodist Missions, 1769-1844*, 2 vols. (New York, 1950); George F. Mellen, "Early Methodists and Cherokees," *Methodist Review* 66 (Nashville, 1917): 476-89. None of these provides a full discussion of the Methodists' stand on Indian removal, and Barclay is the only one to mention the effort of the Methodist missionaries to protest against removal.

[4]Although they were Congregationalists, these missionaries of the A.B.C.F.M. were called Presbyterians in the Cherokee Nation. For discussions of the internal divisions among the Presbyterian missionaries regarding the proper posture on the removal question, see W. G. McLoughlin, "Civil Disobedience and Evangelism among the Missionaries to the Cherokees, 1829-1839," *Journal of Presbyterian History* 51 (Summer 1973): 116-39, and Edwin A. Miles, "After John Marshall's Decision: *Worcester v. Georgia* and the Nullification Crisis," *Journal of Southern History* 39 (November 1973): 519-44.

[5]Niebuhr has a chapter on "Sectionalism and Denominationalism," but does not mention the Indian removal question. H. R. Niebuhr, *The Social Sources of Denominationalism* (New York, 1929).

were responsible to a board in Boston, most of whose members had no love for Southerners, for frontier oppressors of the Cherokees, or for supporters of Andrew Jackson. The Methodist missionaries were responsible to a missionary society under the Tennessee Conference of the Methodist Episcopal Church. The members of that conference were ardent Jacksonians, Southerners, and frontiersmen; the donations for their religious activities came largely from people who thought the Indians should remove across the Mississippi and let white settlers plant cotton on the rich black soil where they lived. Not all of them favored removal by force, but as Christians they did not believe the Methodist Episcopal Church should become involved in what struck them as a political and not a moral controversy. In this respect Cherokee removal prefigured the schism that split the Methodists (and the Baptists) into Northern and Southern denominations over the abolition of slavery.

One of the key articles in the Methodist Discipline, Article 6, was perfectly clear on the separation between religion and politics:

> As far as it respects civil affairs, we believe it is the duty of Christians, and especially all Christian ministers, to be subject to the supreme authority of the country where they may reside, and to use all laudable means to enjoin obedience to the powers that be. . . .[6]

The difficulties experienced by Trott, McLeod, and the other Methodist missionaries who sided with the Cherokees resulted from their conviction that silence was not a "laudable means" to take in this case. They persisted in making a transcendent moral issue out of what most Methodists in that region of the country chose to describe in strictly political terms.[7] The Methodists in the South would use Article 6 against their Northern brethren in 1844, when they decided to split off because abolitionists insisted upon questioning the legitimacy of slavery under the Constitution. But in 1861 the article was to give the Southern Methodists difficulty when the South decided to renounce its allegiance to the "Black Republicans" elected with Abraham Lincoln.

---

[6]Quoted in John M. McFerrin, *History of Methodism in Tennessee* (Nashville, 1879) 373-74.

[7]As noted below, some Methodists in the North took a different view; this found expression in the pages of the *Advocate*, written and published in New York City.

In a sense the decision of the Tennessee Conference not to support the protest of their missionaries in the Cherokee Nation against removal prejudged the fundamental question at stake. That question, which the United States Supreme Court finally decided in March 1832, was the extent to which the Cherokee Nation was a foreign nation. The Presbyterian and Baptist mission boards placed missions to the American Indians under their Foreign Mission Boards. After all, the Cherokee spoke a different language, they had a different culture, they governed themselves by their own political system, and they dealt with the United States of America only through treaties. According to the final clause of Article 6 of the Methodist Discipline, the missionaries might be said to have owed allegiance to the Cherokee government rather than to the state of Georgia: "And, therefore, it is expected that all our preachers and people who may be under any foreign government, will behave themselves as peaceable and orderly subjects."

Even if the Methodists of the Tennessee Conference were correct in assuming that the Cherokee were not really a "foreign" nation, they still prejudged the issue concerning the sovereignty of Georgia and the sovereignty of the federal government in this situation. The Presbyterians assumed loyalty to "the powers that be" in Congress under the treaty power of the Constitution; the Methodists assumed their missionaries should be loyal to the states' rights theory by which Georgia abrogated the treaties with the Cherokee and, in effect, nullified the Trade and Intercourse with the Indians Act passed by Congress. Georgia's unilateral assertion of its jurisdiction over the land of the Cherokee would seem to have been the revolutionary act, not the protest of the missionaries against it.

It might be argued that for both denominations the overriding desire was to sustain their missionary activities by giving no political offense. As it turned out, neither the Presbyterians nor the Methodists succeeded in convincing the Cherokee that they were loyal to the best interests of the Indians. The Tennessee Conference, by pulling the rug out from under its missionaries, steadily lost ground among the Cherokee. The Presbyterians, after reaching the very brink of success in 1832, pulled back at the last minute, refusing to put Jackson to the final test for fear of fomenting secession and civil war.[8] In the end, they put pa-

---

[8]See Miles, "After John Marshall's Decision."

triotic loyalty above moral justice (as the Cherokee saw it) and they too lost out. The missionaries who gained the most by this crisis were the Baptists, who worked wholeheartedly with the Cherokee against the removal effort. The Baptist missionaries, however, had the good fortune of being located for the most part in the North Carolina area of the Cherokee Nation as well as having a mission board in Boston that fully sympathized with their stand.[9] In this essay, however, there is space only to consider the clash between the Methodist circuit riders and their mission agency.[10]

The Methodists got a late start among the Cherokee. They were first invited into the nation in 1822 by a mixed blood named Richard Riley, who asked a circuit rider in Alabama to come across the Tennessee River and preach at his home.[11] This preacher, Richard Neely (or Neeley), decided that his brethren had been neglecting the Cherokee and persuaded the Tennessee Conference to include regular circuits through the Cherokee nation starting in 1824.[12] By this time the Moravians had been preaching in the nation for twenty-three years, the Presbyterians (of the American Board of Commissioners for Foreign Missions) for eight years, the Baptists (of the American Baptist Foreign Mission Society) for six. Nevertheless, the Methodists made rapid headway, particularly in the Alabama region of the nation. They had a very different style and approach from the other denominations. Their enthusiastic "love feasts," quarterly meetings, and camp meetings proved extremely popular; their willingness to admit Cherokee to their religious societies (or classes) without a great deal of doctrinal knowledge seemed more democratic; they were more willing to grant official status as interpreters, exhorters, licensed preachers, and circuit riders to Cherokees who were

---

[9]For the Baptists, see Solomon Peck, *History of American Missions to the Heathen* (Worcester, 1840).

[10]For a full-scale study of the missionaries and removal, including the Presbyterian, Baptist, and Moravian missions as well as that of the Methodists, see William G. McLoughlin, *Cherokees and Missionaries* (New Haven: Yale University Press, 1984).

[11]For Riley's role in the inauguration of Methodist missions, see *The Methodist Magazine* 7 (1824): 192-95 and 11 (1828): 256-58.

[12]In 1823 the Tennessee Conference sent Andrew Jackson Crawford to conduct a school near Riley's home and while he preached in the vicinity no formal circuits were established that year.

bilingual and even to some who spoke only Cherokee (opening up places for a native ministry that the other denominations were slow to sanction). In addition, the Methodists preached an Arminian rather than a Calvinistic theology, emphasizing the ability of the sinner to act for himself in obtaining his salvation rather than waiting passively for God to act first upon him. There was an egalitarian and participatory spirit in Methodist evangelism that contrasted sharply with the formalism and paternalistic elitism of the other missions. In addition, the young, uneducated, dedicated Methodist circuit riders (most of them in their early twenties) were enthusiastic and friendly. Poorly paid, their self-sacrifice was evident, and as they made their rounds they ate and slept in the homes of the Cherokee (whereas the other missionaries lived in well-constructed mission compounds). Two of the first missionaries, Richard Neely and James J. Trott, married Cherokees and began to raise families in the nation. By Cherokee custom, to marry into the tribe was to be adopted as a member of the tribe.

Trott started his work among the Cherokees in 1825. Born in North Carolina in 1800, he had moved to West Tennessee in 1815 and joined the Methodists in 1821. A year later he felt a call to preach and in 1823 "joined the travelling connexion" as an assistant circuit rider. The Tennessee Conference assigned him to the Wills Valley circuit in the Cherokee Nation in 1827. In 1828 he married Sallie Adair, a mixed-blood Cherokee of some education; they had a son, Benjamin, and a daughter, Mary. Also born in North Carolina (in 1802), Neely moved to Rutherford County, Tennessee, as a child, was converted in 1819, and became a licensed Methodist preacher in 1821. He married a mixed blood named McNair, but the strenuous life of a circuit rider was too much for him and he died of tuberculosis in February 1828. Dickson C. McLeod, born in North Carolina in 1802 and admitted "on trial" as a Methodist preacher in 1823, was first assigned to the Cherokee Nation on the Salakowa circuit in 1828; he left the Cherokee Nation in 1832 and died in 1840.

The reports of the circuit riders to the Indian Missionary Society of the Tennessee Conference each year reveal an astonishing success story among the Cherokee. Starting with thirty-three converts the first year when Neely preached at Richard Riley's, the denomination grew to 283 in 1825, 400 in 1827, and 1,028 in 1830. Roughly half of these were in the Alabama section of the nation where the other denominations had the fewest missions. In 1830 the two Moravian mission stations in the Georgia area of the nation reported only forty-five Cherokee members; the Baptist mission in North Carolina reported ninety; and the Presbyterians (who were strongest in Eastern Tennessee and Georgia) reported 167.[13] Obviously the Methodist style of Christianity had an appeal that far outdistanced that of their rivals.

The missionaries of other denominations expressed some sharp criticisms of Methodist theology and methods in their private correspondence, charging them with being superficial in their doctrinal preaching and willing to count anyone as a convert who expressed any interest in the Gospel. "Their manner of receiving members is directly calculated to lead souls to hell," said one Presbyterian missionary; "no more than one out of twenty of their members was a real christian."[14] The coming of the Methodists should be viewed as "a calamity to this people." The Methodist preachers were ridiculed as uneducated and their religious meetings as overly emotional and excessively concerned with numerical results. The Reverend Henry G. Clauder of the Moravian mission spoke of "ignorant Methodists who maintain absolute Christian perfection as possible"; and he deplored "the curious custom prevalent in Methodist meetings of jumping and tumbling about like persons bereft of sense."[15] A Presbyterian said after attending a Methodist prayer meeting, it was "a scene of utter confusion, as you may well suppose, when perhaps 30 Cherokees were all praying aloud at the same time."[16] Their missionaries were also accused of "sheep stealing," that is taking converts from other mission stations.

A Baptist missionary went to visit a group of Cherokees who had received his preaching and expressed interest in becoming Baptists only to find that "the Methodists were here a few days ago and took seventeen

---

[13]See *Phoenix*, 1 January 1831.

[14]Isaac Proctor to Jeremiah Evarts, 10 July 1828, Papers of the American Board of Commissioners for Foreign Missions, Houghton Library, Harvard University (hereinafter A.B.C.F.M. Papers).

[15]Diary of Henry G. Clauder, 12 December 1828, 7 March 1829, Moravian Archives, Bethlehem, Pennsylvania.

[16]David Green to Jeremiah Evarts, 28 July 1828, A.B.C.F.M. Papers.

of the inquirers into their Society."[17] Methodist mission schools were considered shallow and useless because they lasted only six months in any one location and were taught by circuit riders more interested in saving souls than in teaching. Itinerating schools, wrote the editor of the *Cherokee Phoenix* (himself a dedicated Presbyterian convert), "will but poorly qualify" a Cherokee to teach others: "It is not from schools of this nature that an ignorant child will derive great permanent benefit."[18] But unlike the Presbyterians, the Methodists firmly believed that Christianization must precede civilization. Hence for them, elaborate school systems with trained and educated teachers were of secondary importance. Thomas L. Douglass, in a report as chairman of the Missionary Committee of the Tennessee Conference, said in 1824:

> Indeed, your committee are of opinion that a great parade about Missionary establishments and the expenditure of many thousands of dollars to give the heathen science and occupation, without religion, is of but little advantage to them. For after all their acquirements they are still savages, unless their hearts be changed by the grace of God and the power of the gospel. . . .[19]

But once a Cherokee was converted, the Methodists held, his savage spirit was transformed disappeared and he could easily be led into civilized ways by his own motivation to improve himself.

Much of the criticism of the Methodists by other missionaries seems to have stemmed from jealousy of their success. One Presbyterian expressed admiration for their egalitarianism and criticized the snobbery of his own denomination, which preferred to concentrate its effort upon the more acculturated Cherokee of mixed blood: "If we will not condescend to the poorest class of Cherokees . . . they will either go to the Baptist or methodist meetings where they can find someone who does not feel above them."[20]

The tremendous success of the Methodist missionaries in "christianizing and civilizing" the Cherokee clashed with the rising demand by the frontier whites for the removal of all Indians to some place west of the

---

[17]Evan Jones's Journal, 16 May 1830, American Baptist Foreign Mission Society Papers, Baptist Historical Society, Rochester, New York.

[18]Elias Boudinot, *Phoenix*, 12 November 1828.

[19]*The Methodist Magazine* 7 (1824): 194.

[20]Daniel Butrick's Journal, 4 November 1828, A.B.C.F.M. Papers.

Mississippi River. Southern whites were particularly anxious to get rid of the five large tribes, which were blocking their effort to expand "the Cotton Kingdom." The federal government did its best to negotiate removal treaties with the Cherokee, Creek, Choctaw, Chickasaw, and Seminole throughout the 1820s, but the Indians were uncooperative. They did not want to leave their ancestral lands; they were doing their best to become farmers, herders, traders, and artisans. Ever since their first treaties with George Washington, they had been promised that they could remain where they where and eventually be incorporated into the Republic as equals. The government had provided them with plows, spinning wheels, axes, looms, and other technical assistance to help their transformation from a fur-trading to an agricultural economy. Since 1819 the government had provided money for mission schools to teach their children reading, writing, arithmetic, and vocational skills, like blacksmithing. In 1827 the Cherokee had adopted a constitution modeled on that of the United States. They had a republican form of government with biennially elected representatives to a bicameral legislature and elected chiefs. They had a written code of laws administered by a highly efficient mounted police and a series of local and circuit courts under a Supreme Court. In 1821 Sequoyah had invented a syllabary in which they could write their own language and since 1828 they had their own bilingual newspaper. As the missionaries of four denominations could testify, they were rapidly increasing in the number of converts to Christianity.

The election of Andrew Jackson in 1828 seemed to change the whole arrangement. Jackson had frequently said that it was foolish to make treaties with savages. As a Tennessee planter and long-time Indian fighter, he was convinced that Indians were not, and probably never would be, able to meet the standards required for equal citizenship. He was more than willing to help the Western frontiersmen find some way to force the Indians off their land. His plan was to give them land in the West in exchange for the land they would give up in the East. This proposal was not original with Jackson. Jefferson, Madison, Monroe, and Adams had all offered this alternative to the Indians. Jackson was the first to insist that the federal government would not take "no" for an answer. The people of Georgia decided to implement Jackson's plan by asserting that the sovereign states had, under the Constitution, the right to assume jurisdiction over all the land within their borders at any time—regardless of treaties with the Indians.

The first step in this new Indian policy began shortly after Jackson was elected. In December 1828, the Georgia legislature passed a series of laws assuming possession of all Indian land within its border, abolishing all Cherokee tribal government, and reducing the Indians to second-class citizens by denying their right to testify in court against a white man.[21] These laws were to go into effect on 1 June 1830. Georgians assumed that by that time Jackson would have clearly explained to the Cherokee that if they did not exchange their land in Georgia for land in Oklahoma, then he could do nothing to stop the Georgians from expropriating their land and giving it to their own white citizens. This would leave the Cherokee only those few barren acres to live on that no whites wanted.

Georgia's actions placed the missionaries in a dilemma. Should they support the Cherokee in resisting or should they acquiesce in the new policy? The four denominations had invested a considerable amount of time, money, and effort into building schools and mission churches within the Cherokee Nation. Their missionaries told the mission boards that the Cherokee were making astounding progress toward civilization and Christianization. Indeed, the Cherokee by 1828 had attained the reputation as "the most civilized tribe in America." Still, the American doctrine of separation of church and state seemed to imply that saving souls and not meddling in politics was the chief task of religion. So long as the government did not interfere with the right to preach the Gospel, the missionary was, it seemed, obliged to accept whatever policy the majority chose to enact, and the majority had clearly elected Jackson to remove the Indians.

However, white Christians were citizens. They had the right to speak freely as well as to vote, and many of them had opposed Jackson and his policy from the beginning. Many Methodists had opposed Indian removal when John Quincy Adams advocated it. A long editorial in the Methodist *Christian Advocate and Journal And Zion's Herald* (the quasiofficial organ of the denomination) in December 1828, took issue with a statement by Adams's secretary of war, Peter B. Porter, in which he not

---

[21]See Ulrich B. Phillips, *Georgia and State Rights* (Washington, 1902; Macon GA: Mercer University Press, 1983) 66-86.

only advocated Indian removal but blamed the missionaries and the well-to-do mixed-blood Indians as the prime obstacles against it. In a report to Congress, Porter alleged that most Indians would be favorable to removal, but the missionaries had a vested interest in opposing it. "Missionaries and teachers with their families," Porter told Congress, "having acquired principally by the aid of this [federal civilization] fund, very comfortable establishments, are unwilling to be deprived of them by the removal of the Indians." They had become "agents" who were "operating, more secretly to be sure" than the "half-educated" Indian opponents of removal, "but not with less zeal and effect, to prevent such emigration."[22]

The Methodists felt particularly indignant about this allegation. They had expended little money on missionary establishments and had never taken any money from the government's "civilization fund" to support their schools. All of their budgets went toward paying itinerants; such schools as they taught in were built by the labor of their converts. "If comfortable establishments were the only inducements presented to these self-denying men to persuade them to remain in their present stations," wrote the *Advocate's* editor, "we venture to predict that they would soon abandon them 'to the moles and the bats.' " Methodist missionaries worked in conditions of great deprivation to bring the Gospel to the heathen; "in the prosecution of their benevolent designs [they] are reduced to all the privations and hardships peculiar to half civilized society, and are obliged from their scanty allowance to unite the most rigorous economy with the most patient industry."

> Nay, such is the strong attachment of these devoted missionaries to the eternal interests of those Indians that should the event come to pass, now so much deprecated by some and wished for by others, that they must be removed beyond the Mississippi, rather than abandon them to their own deplorable fate, they would remove with them, identify their interests with the interests of the Indians, share in their privations and suffering, with a view to exalt them ultimately to all the blessings of Christianity and civilization.[23]

What the Methodist editor objected to was the effort "to *compel* them" to sell their country and "remove into the remote forests," and to compel

---

[22]Porter's report is printed in the *Phoenix*, 7 January 1829.

[23]*Advocate*, 19 December 1828.

this "either by direct coercion or by the intrigues which too often disgrace state policy, or by that cupidity which so frequently characterizes mercantile and speculating operations." Against this "we would protest with all the energies which a just regard to original right can inspire, with all the force which may be derived from a sense of their indubitable rights, as the free and original lords of the soul—with all the argument which can be based on the faith of the most solemn treaties" and by the Golden Rule of Christianity: "DO TO OTHERS AS YE WOULD THEY SHOULD DO UNTO YOU."

On 8 January 1830, a year later, the *Advocate* published a memorial adopted at a meeting of citizens in New York City on 9 December 1829, and then sent to Congress to oppose the removal bill. The effort of the Georgians to assert sovereignty over Cherokee territory, these citizens asserted, was "entirely mistaken, it is subversive of the plainest principles of justice" and would make force the first and only arbiter between separate communities." The decision of Jackson to support this states' rights position was simply "reducing independent tribes to a state of vassalage . . . with a particular view to driving them into exile or insuring their speedy extinction. Such a usurpation of power exerted by the strong over the weak" was an "enormous injustice" and "a great public calamity." No individual state can "lawfully get possession of Indian territory lying within its chartered limits except by means of the treaty making power of the United States." The petitioners requested Congress to "interpose" between Jackson and the Indians to "save the Cherokees from such injustice and oppression."[24]

As regular readers of (and frequent contributors to) the *Advocate*, the Methodist missionaries to the Cherokee no doubt felt compelled to add their own firsthand testimony against compulsory removal. Who knew better than they the progress the Cherokee were making and how strongly they were attached to the land of their forefathers? On 25 September 1830, eight of the ten Methodist missionaries assigned that year to work among the Cherokee assembled at the Chattooga campground in the nation to express their feelings on the topic of the day. Their ultimate goal was to arouse the Methodist Church to add its Christian witness on behalf of justice for the Cherokee. The Reverend Francis Owen, superintendent of the mission among the Cherokee, was chosen chair-

---

[24]Ibid., 8 January 1830.

man; the Reverend Dickson C. McLeod of the Wills Valley circuit was chosen secretary. Participants in the discussion were the Reverend Greenberry Garrett of Selacoa circuit; Jacob Ellinger of Coosewattee circuit; Joseph Miller of Chattooga circuit; William M. McFerrin of the Agency station; Nicholas D. Scales of Lookout Mountain circuit; James J. Trott of the Mount Wesley and Asbury station. Probably also present were most of the Cherokee assistants, interpreters, and exhorters: Jack Spear, John Fletcher Boot, Young Wolf, Edward Graves, Turtle Fields, Joseph Blackbird, and William McIntosh. Two missionaries were not present, Robert Rogers of the Valley Town Circuit and G. M. Rogers of Connesauga circuit. The following resolutions were "unanimously adopted" by those present:

> *Resolved*: That it is the sincere opinion of the meeting that the present oppressed condition of our brethren, the Cherokees, and the future prosperity of the missionary cause among them do most importunately solicit from the Tennessee Annual Conference a public and official expression of sentiment on the subject of their grievances.
>
> *Resolved*: That the present missionaries in the Cherokee nation and belonging to the Methodist Episcopal Church give, as soon as practicable, a public detail of the civil, moral and religious condition of this nation and embody their several accounts in one condensed general report.
>
> *Resolved*: That all the missionaries in their detailed accounts unequivocally testify that the Cherokee nation is firmly resolved not to remove from their present home unless forced so to do either by power or oppression.
>
> *Resolved*: That it is the unanimous opinion of this board of missionaries that a removal of the Cherokees to the west of the Mississippi would, in all probability, be ruinous to the best interests of the nation.
>
> *Resolved*: That whereas it has been stated to the public that the missionaries in this nation are associated with, and under the controlling influence of the principal men of the nation, merely in order the more effectually to extend our missionary operations here, we do hereby most solemnly and unhesitatingly deny the charge. It is unanimously resolved by this missionary convention, that the present aggrieved condition of the Cherokee in this nation calls for the sympathy and religious interposition of the Christian community in these United States, together with all the true and faithful friends of humanity and justice.
>
> *Resolved*: That the secretary of this meeting forward the above resolutions to the editor of the *Cherokee Phoenix* and to the editors of the *Christian Advocate* and *Journal* for publication.[25]

---

[25]Ibid., 29 October 1830; *Phoenix*, 1 October 1830.

The list of resolutions was signed by all the white missionaries present. The *Advocate* printed it on 29 October without comment, but the editor of the *Cherokee Phoenix*, Elias Boudinot, used the occasion to urge the other missionary denominations to similar actions:

> The time has come when it is the duty of every friend of justice and humanity to speak out and express his opinion and raise his voice in favor of oppressed innocence. Why should not missionaries, the true friends of the Indians, who toil day and night for their spiritual good, be permitted to exercise the sacred right of freemen, *liberty of speech* and *freedom of opinion*? Must their mouths be muzzled because they are embassadors of religion?

Boudinot was aware that some missionaries were reluctant to speak out in support of the Cherokee for fear that they would be accused of meddling in politics.

Some of the Methodists, however, were so exercised about the matter that they could not refrain from injecting it into their sermons. Dr. Elizur Butler, a Presbyterian missionary, attended a camp meeting (probably at Chattooga) the same month in which these resolutions were adopted and could hardly believe his ears:

> I was tolerably well pleased with the fore-part of the meeting. Near the close of the discourse the speaker imagined a council held in hell which extended to some of the state legislatures and also included the President of the U.S.: all for the purpose of rob[b]ing the Cherokees of their country and breaking them up as a Nation. He also imagined a council held by Christians, by holy angels, and finally by the Father, Son, and Holy Ghost, for the purpose of saving the Cherokees; and he predicted the Salvation of the Nation. This much affected the minds of some, even produced groaning and tears.[26]

The willingness of the Methodists to preach so directly and colorfully to the Cherokee on matters of direct personal interest was, of course, part of their great attraction.

Apparently the work of the Methodists and the comment of Boudinot had their effect. On 28 December 1830, the Presbyterian missionary, Samuel A. Worcester, called a meeting of all the missionaries in the nation to meet at his home in New Echota, the nation's capital, to discuss passing a set of resolutions on the question. After some debate, the res-

---

[26]Elizur Butler to Jeremiah Evarts, 22 September 1830, A.B.C.F.M. Papers. Butler did not identify the speaker, but it was later attributed to James J. Trott by Colonel J. W. A. Sanford; see *Phoenix*, 29 October 1831.

olutions were adopted and signed by nine members of the American Board of Commissioners for Foreign Missions, two members of the United Brethren (or Moravian) Mission, and the superintendent of the Baptist Mission. These resolutions were essentially a reiteration of the Methodist resolves. The third of the five resolutions stated

> that we view the removal of this people to the West of the Mississippi as an event to be most earnestly deprecated; threatening greatly to retard, if not totally to arrest their progress in religion, civilization, learning and the useful arts, to involve them in great distress, and to bring upon them a complication of evils for which the prospect before them would offer no compensation.

The fourth resolution, however, went beyond the Methodist pronouncement by specific reference to the Georgia laws:

> That the establishment of the jurisdiction of Georgia and other states over the Cherokee people, against their will, would be an immense and irreparable injury.

The resolves did not specifically state that Georgia's action was unconstitutional, simply unconscionable.

Following the resolutions was a long description of the remarkable progress the Cherokee had made toward acculturation and an estimate of the numbers who had embraced Christianity in each of the four denominations at work in the nation. The twelve signers concluded by noting that while none of them had publicly advised the Cherokee to oppose removal, they had freely expressed their private views against it when asked:[27] "If the free expression of such an opinion be a crime, to the charge of that crime we plead guilty. If we withheld our opinion when called for, we could not hold up our heads as preachers of righteousness among a people who would universally regard us as abettors of iniquity."[28] In short, the missionaries felt trapped. If they spoke out against removal, they would be accused by whites of meddling in politics. If

---

[27]Henry Clauder, one of the Moravian signers, reported, "Mr. McLeod of the Methodist Church and some others were also present but did not unite with us." Diary, 29 December 1830, Moravian Archives. It was probably because of this statement that McLeod and the other Methodists present did not sign the New Echota resolutions, for they had publicly (in their sermons) exhorted the Cherokee to oppose removal.

[28]The New Echota resolutions were printed in an "Extra" edition of the *Phoenix*, 1 January 1831.

they did not at least let the Cherokees know where they stood, they would lose all respect and influence among them.

The people of Georgia were well aware that the missionaries had expressed such views and that their moral support gave the Cherokee added courage to resist. Furthermore, the missionaries carried great weight with the churchgoing public at large. Consequently, even before these resolves were adopted (and perhaps more in reaction against the resolves of the Methodists in September), the legislature of Georgia passed a law on 22 December 1830, requiring all whites living within the Cherokee nation to swear an oath of allegiance to the state of Georgia prior to 1 March 1831 and to obtain a license from the governor if they wished to remain within the nation. Those who failed to do so would be required to leave the state. Any who refused to leave could be sentenced to four years or more at hard labor in the state penitentiary.[29] The law was clearly aimed at the missionaries, though it also enabled the state to take action against whites who had married Cherokees and were now siding with them against Georgia.

Meanwhile the Chattooga resolves adopted by the Methodist missionaries had come before the Tennessee Conference for consideration. The conference met in Franklin, Tennessee, on 12 November, but the result was a bitter disappointment. After "an animated debate," the conference not only refused to endorse the resolves but also severely criticized the missionaries for daring to publish them before the conference could respond to them:

> *Resolved*: That whatever may be our private views and sentiments as men and free citizens relative to the sufferings and privations of the aboriginal nations of our country or of any particular section of the United States, or of the policy adopted and pursued by the State authority or General Government, yet, as a body of Christian ministers, we do not feel at liberty, nor are we disposed, to depart from the principles uniformly maintained by the members and ministers of our Church in carefully refraining from all such interference with political affairs.
>
> *Resolved*: That however we may appreciate the purity of motive and intention by which our missionary brethren were actuated, yet we regret that they should have committed themselves and us so far as to render it impossible for us to omit with propriety to notice their proceedings in this public manner.
>
> *Resolved*: That while we have confidence in the wisdom and integrity of our rulers, we sincerely sympathize with our Cherokee brethren in their present afflic-

---

[29]Schwarze, *Moravian Missions*, 194.

tions and assure them of our unabating zeal for the conversion and salvation of their souls.[30]

This repudiation of the missionaries by the Conference led the Cherokee to see the Methodists in Boudinot's words, as "abettors of iniquity."[31] The *Cherokee Phoenix* printed the conference resolves with the following comments: "We sincerely regret that so respectable a body as the Tennessee Conference should call the *Indian question* merely a *political question*. It is exactly the way enemies of the Indians blind the people. . . . Perhaps nothing has a greater tendency to prejudice the cause of the Indians." The editor believed, as did most who read the resolves, that "the Missionaries are censured for expressing their honest opinion." Further, he contended that the conference members, "in approbating the present policy in regard to the Indians (for such is the inference drawn from their 3d resolution), have as much interfered with *political affairs* as their Missionaries." Not to act in such a crisis was in itself an action.[32]

In January 1831, the missionaries of all denominations received notice from the governor of Georgia that they were expected to comply with the oath law by 1 March or face the consequences. The Baptists had no missionaries residing in Georgia, but the Presbyterians and Moravians immediately wrote to their mission boards for instructions. Clauder reported that "the instructions received from his Society [in Salem, North Carolina] were to the effect he should remove from the Cherokee country at once if he could not pursue his missionary labors peaceably."[33] The

---

[30]*Phoenix*, 8 January 1831.

[31]This impression was greatly strengthened by the activities of Dr. Alexander Talley, the prominent Methodist missionary to the Choctaw Nation who was an ardent advocate of the nation's removal. In 1831 Talley played a leading role in writing a treaty that effected their removal and many of the Choctaw petitioned for his removal from their nation. Angie Debo, *The Rise and Fall of the Choctaw Republic* (Norman, 1934) 52, 63, 64.

[32]*Phoenix*, 8 January 1831. The action of the conference may have helped to convince the Georgians that the churches would not oppose their effort to put a quietus on missionary opposition to removal. When Trott was arrested, Colonel J. W. A. Sanford of the Georgia Guard referred to him as a preacher "who had been discountenanced by his own Conference for his officious and overzealous interference in Indian politics." *Phoenix*, 29 October 1831. However, the conference did not have any idea how rough the Georgians would be on their missionaries, so it is not accurate to suggest that they willfully threw them to the wolves.

[33]Schwarze, *Moravian Missionaries*, 196.

American Board decided that each of its missionaries would have to follow his own conscience, but it promised its full support to any of them who chose to disobey Georgia and bring a test case before the United States Supreme Court.[34] The Methodist missionaries received no instructions; yet Dickson C. McLeod reported on 12 February 1831, on the frustrating state of religious affairs and the position the missionaries would be compelled to take: "The disagreeable excitement and almost utter confusion produced by the operation of the laws of that state [Georgia], in opposition to those of the nation, are wholly indescribable . . . all white men in this part of the nation are placed in very unpleasant and precarious circumstances." The Methodists had four missionaries residing in Georgia or itinerating regularly within it: McLeod, Trott, Nicholas Scales, and John W. Hanna.

> Having every reason to believe that our taking the oath prescribed by the Georgia legislature would be attended with ruinous consequences to the missionary cause here, and being ourselves conscientiously opposed to the measure, we shall be compelled to move our residence from this disputed ground in order to avoid the fearful penalty of the law. These things will doubtless operate very much against our success.[35]

As it turned out, Trott refused to change his residence (probably because his wife was ill), and the others felt that if they resided outside the state, they would still be able to itinerate in peace. McLeod said in this report that he and his colleagues were determined to do all they could "for the spiritual benefit of these disheartened and injured people. Never will we give over our united efforts for the salvation of the Cherokees until we are called off by proper authorities or driven away by the propelling edicts of a republican state." It sounded as though McLeod expected to be called off by his superiors.

As soon as the 1 March deadline passed, Governor George R. Gilmer ordered the arrest of all white men who had not complied with the law. The first group of missionaries rounded up on 12 March included Samuel Worcester, Isaac Proctor, and John Thompson, all of the American Board. Treated roughly by a newly constituted group of civil law enforcement officers known as the Georgia Guard, they were taken before

---

[34]See McLoughlin, "Civil Disobedience," and Miles, "After John Marshall."

[35]*Advocate*, 11 March 1831.

the Superior Court of Gwinnett County where Judge Augustin S. Clayton released them on the ground that missionaries were "agents of the government" because their missions were supported in part by government funds. On 7 May Dr. Elizur Butler was arrested, but he was released temporarily because of sickness in his family. Meanwhile Governor Gilmer had written to Jackson's secretary of war, John Eaton, to see whether, in the view of the government, missionaries were in fact federal agents. Eaton assured him that they were not and relieved Worcester of his postmastership to make it easier for Gilmer to arrest him. On 16 May Gilmer wrote to all the American Board ministers, telling them what Eaton had said and giving them ten days to sign the oath or leave the state. At this point all the board's missionaries in Georgia, except Worcester and Butler, took up residence elsewhere in the nation. The Methodist missionaries received no ten-day notice and three of them—Trott, McLeod, and Wells—continued to itinerate within Georgia.

The arrest of the missionaries in March had stirred up widespread censure of the Georgians from outside that state. The Methodist *Advocate* joined dozens of other religious and secular newspapers in denouncing the action. An editorial on 20 May called the action "most singular and [it] cannot fail to call out a burst of disapprobation"; in fact, "a more outrageous act could not have been looked for" among the "Turks and Arabs." According to the *Advocate*, "As this oath was designed only for those who resided on the Cherokee lands [in Georgia] the missionaries of the Methodist Episcopal Church have avoided its obligations and penalties by removing their families out of the Cherokee district" in that state, though continuing to ride their circuits within it.[36] But the *Advocate* was mistaken: Trott had not moved his family, and on 31 May he was arrested by the Georgia Guard while visiting them. Forced to march 110 miles (mostly on foot) to the prison, he spent four days on the road and eight more before he was arraigned. "I was chained four nights in succession and compelled to lie on the floor." Then he was released on bail of $500, told to leave Georgia, and ordered to return in September for trial in the Superior Court. The colonel of the Guard who arrested him, J. W. A. Sanford, "stated to me that he did not suppose the missionaries would be allowed to itinerate and preach in the territory of

---

[36]Ibid., 20 May 1831.

Georgia [even] provided they were to remove their residence, for it was the determined policy of the state to expel from her charter [limits] all white persons who refuse to obey her laws and pursue a course detrimental to her interest." If there had ever been any doubt of the antimissionary purpose of the law, Trott announced, "It is now clear as noon day that they [the legislators] designed to destroy missions in that part of the nation which they so confidently claim."[37]

On 22 June the Georgia Guard took over the Presbyterian Mission at Etowah (Hightower) and arrested the Reverend John Thompson, who came to protest against this trespass on mission property. After marching him to Camp Gilmer, they lectured him on his insubordination to Georgia's laws and then released him.[38]

On 6 July Trott was arrested again for making a visit to his home. The next day the Guard picked up Worcester and Butler for the second time. They also arrested John Wheeler, employed to help print the *Cherokee Phoenix*. In this general roundup seven white men married to Cherokees were arrested for failure to take the oath. They were all forced to walk to Camp Gilmer and sometimes chained up at night. At one time Butler was forced to walk with a chain around his neck and the other end fastened around the horse's neck of one of the mounted guards. It was on this occasion that McLeod and Wells went to Trott's aid and McLeod was arrested for not flanking off. After his arrest, he said, "I was told that if I opened my mouth I should be run through with a bayonet."[39] Being very devout men, the missionaries found it sacrilegious that they were made to march on the Sabbath; and the profanity of the guards they considered a form of intentional mental "torture."

McLeod was released from Camp Gilmer after two days, and no further charges were brought against him. The rest were let out on bail and told to return for their trial at Lawrenceville, Georgia, on 15 September.

---

[37]Ibid., 29 July 1831 and *Phoenix*, 2 July 1831. Colonel Sanford also told Trott "that the Cherokees were going backward and that they were incapable of understanding the Christian Religion and that if God wished them to become religious he would make them so without so much concern on the part of missionaries." Ibid.

[38]Robert S. Walker, *Torchlights to the Cherokees* (New York, 1931) 261-62. On 31 May, Henry Clauder had been arrested, but he was released when he promised to leave the state. Schwarze, *Moravian Missions*, 196.

[39]*Advocate*, 12 August 1831; *Phoenix*, 3 September 1831.

Citizens and newspapers around the country were shocked. "Why was Mr. Trott, the Methodist minister put in chains?" asked the Methodist *Advocate*. "The conduct of the authorities of the state of Georgia toward the missionaries stationed among the Cherokee Indians . . . is a barbarous outrage. . . . Has it come to this? Is a missionary, peaceably pursuing his calling, for no other crime alledged than a refusal from conscientious motives to take an oath of allegiance to a particular state, to be suddenly apprehended, bound in chains, and incarcerated in prison? . . . Are these inquisitorial transactions to be tolerated in a Christian land?"[40] A letter from McLeod printed in the *Advocate* on 12 August added new details:

> I am prepared to prove that in the present hostile measures of the state towards the missionaries in this nation and other white citizens, policy prevails over law. Col. Nelson told me that their orders from the Governor were to let the missionaries feel the heaviest weight of the law and that they did not intend to show them any mercy.[41]

Stirred by this mistreatment of their missionaries, the Methodists, through the Reverend John Howard of Georgia, sent a letter to Governor Gilmer demanding an explanation. Gilmer asserted that McLeod's statements "are wholly destitute of truth" and placed the blame entirely upon the missionaries for refusing to obey the law. Three hundred white men had obeyed it, Gilmer noted; only a handful had not. "The missionaries alone publicly denied the power of the state to extend its jurisdiction over them and expressed their design to disregard the law." The governor regretted, of course, any excesses committed by an individual guard who may have been overzealous because he was "so much excited by the improper conduct of these men," but unfortunately the missionaries "were in the constant habit of speaking in the most opprobrious terms of our government." They were, he was convinced, dupes of political operators: "The missionaries have not been compelled to desert their religious labor by any conduct of the authorities of the government, but by their improper connection with political parties and refusal to obey the laws."[42]

---

[40]*Advocate*, 8 July 1831, 29 July 1831. *Phoenix*, 20 August 1831.

[41]*Advocate*, 12 August 1831.

[42]*Advocate*, 30 September 1831; *Phoenix*, 29 October 1831.

The trial on 15-16 September went as expected. The lawyers for the missionaries (hired by the American Board) tried to show that the law under which they were arrested was unconstitutional because the Cherokee were under the protection of federal treaties and the state had no jurisdiction over their country. Judge Clayton said he thought the law perfectly constitutional. The jury took fifteen minutes to agree with him.[43] Trott explained his position in the following terms:

> *Believing* that the law was *unconstitutional* and *knowing* that it was passed for the purpose of stripping the Cherokees of religious and educational privileges, by driving the Missionaries from the field of their labors, in order to force the Nation into a treaty with the United States, I could not conscientiously take such oath. I was compelled to do this, leave my field of labor, without any instructions to that effect, or continue at my post of honor in the Lord, and leave the event with Him; and, in the name of the Lord, I preferred the latter alternative.[44]

In his decision sentencing all eleven defendants to four years at hard labor, Judge Clayton took notice of the pleas of Trott, Worcester, and Butler that they had had to rely upon their private conscience in refusing to obey the law. If, he said, anyone could treat such a serious matter with "a smile," he might be inclined to "ask if this be not the doctrine of *Nullification*?" In any case, he was sure such views could only lead to "anarchy." At best their conduct sprang from "misguided zeal" designed to arouse public sympathy by sheer "fanaticism."[45]

The convicted men were then marched to the penitentiary at Milledgeville, Georgia. On 22 September they were all asked by the prison inspectors whether, if pardoned, "they will now give assurance that they will not again violate the laws of the State."[46] All except Worcester and Butler agreed to these terms and were pardoned. Trott was accused by some of admitting his guilt by signing the oath and accepting the pardon: "This is a slander, and has not the shadow of truth in it," he answered. "I was not only willing to be imprisoned four years, but by the help of my Lord and Master, to suffer death even, rather than take such

---

[43]*Phoenix*, 15 October 1831.

[44]J. Edward Moseley, *Disciples of Christ in Georgia* (St. Louis, 1954) 127.

[45]*Phoenix*, 15 October 1831.

[46]Ibid., 22 October 1831.

an oath."[47] The pardon was granted simply by his agreement not to return to the state of Georgia.

Several days after his release, Trott's Cherokee wife died and a few weeks later, in October 1831, he underwent a new religious experience. He had read the works of Alexander Campbell in prison and six weeks after the trial he left the Methodist denomination to join the Campbellites (later known as the Disciples of Christ). He wrote a moving letter to Campbell on 1 December 1831, describing his conversion as well as his continued commitment to the Cherokee. "The Cherokees are an interesting people and with them (God willing) whatever their destiny may be, I expect to live and die. My heart's desire and prayer to God is that the primitive gospel may be introduced, prevail, and triumph among this oppressed people."[48] By "primitive gospel," Trott meant the nondenominational, nonritualistic, noncreedal form of Christianity Campbell taught. Trott was weary of denominationalism. Soon after this, he remarried—again to a Cherokee—and began preaching "the primitive gospel" among the Cherokee. But the turmoil over removal made it difficult and he made only a few converts to the new religion.[49]

During this period the Methodist mission effort among the Cherokee went into rapid decline. By 1834 the denomination had lost more than half the converts it had made by 1830. With the total at only 508, the Tennessee Conference decided to close its missionary effort. The explanation given at any time (and by Methodist historians ever since), for this decision and the decline that precipitated it, was best expressed by Anson West:

> From the close of 1830 the membership steadily declined and the field contracted, not because the Indians were less interested in the gospel than formerly, not because the membership apostatized, not because the Missionaries engaged

---

[47]Moseley, *Disciples*, 128.

[48]*Millennial Harbinger* 3 (February 1832): 85.

[49]Trott did not at first go west with the Cherokee, but remained in the South as an itinerant Campbellite preacher. In 1856, however, he moved into the Cherokee Nation again, purchased land for a mission, and made seventy-five converts to the Disciples before he was forced out by the fighting during the Civil War. He returned to the nation in 1866 but became ill and went to Nashville, where he died in 1868. Moseley, *Disciples*, 123-31.

in the work were not efficient and faithful, but because many emigrated to the Cherokee possessions west of the Mississippi River.[50]

But this explanation is not adequate. Grant Foreman, the most thorough scholar of Cherokee removal, concluded that "only about 2,000 of the eastern Cherokee had removed by May 23, 1838."[51] When a census was taken by the federal government in 1835, there were still 16,542 Cherokee (plus 1,592 black slaves) in the eastern part of The Cherokee nation, and that was an increase of almost 3,000 since the census of 1825. What is more important, the other three denominations continued their work and the number of their converts continued to increase until the time of removal in the fall of 1838. The growth of the Baptists was particularly heavy in the years after 1830.[52]

It seems obvious that some other cause is needed to explain the failure of the Methodist mission to the Cherokee after 1830. The evidence points pretty clearly to the failure of the leaders of Southern Methodism to support the stand of their missionaries in the field. Or, to put it another way, the Methodists were willing to lend their tacit support to the removal program. They did not totally desert the Cherokee. After 1834 missionaries from the Holston Conference continued to itinerate in the nation. One of these, the Reverend David B. Cumming, marched with the Cherokee along the "Trail of Tears" in 1838-1839 (at that time, there were still 480 Methodists in the nation).[53] But the Methodists in the Ten-

---

[50]West, *Methodism*, 398. It is worth noting that on 22 December 1832, Georgia repealed its law requiring an oath of allegiance; hence white missionaries were free thereafter to preach in the Georgia part of the nation. Evidently few were aware of this, however.

[51]Grant Foreman, *Indian Removal* (Norman, 1932) 286.

[52]For the census figures, see W. G. McLoughlin and W. H. Conser, Jr., "The Cherokees in Transition," *The Journal of American History* 64 (December 1977): 678-703. Between 1831 and 1838 the Moravians increased from forty-five to 132 church members; the Presbyterians remained static at 167; and the Baptists increased from ninety to more than 500.

[53]See Barclay, *Methodist Missions*, 131-34. Barclay comes closest among all the historians of Methodist missions to explaining the decline when he says "widespread demoralization set in" after 1830. However, he seems to use that term to refer to Cherokee political demoralization. I would argue that there was a more general demoralization, which included (especially after the Presbyterians seemed to acquiesce in removal in 1833) a loss of faith—particularly faith in the white man's professions of benevolence, humanity, and Christian concern. The strong growth of the Baptists after 1830 seems to me to stem from their continued effort to identify Christian brotherhood with active support of social justice for the Cherokee.

nessee Conference wanted to believe that removal of the Cherokee was probably in their best interest. In any case, they chose to act as though it was not an issue about which they could or should do anything. What they did do was to assign some of their missionaries to the Arkansas Conference in the hope that they could serve the Cherokee emigrants when they got to their new land.

Much as the Cherokee were attracted to the Methodist version of Christianity, Methodism failed them on the critical issues of dignity and patriotism. After 1830, to be a Methodist was to be a traitor to the Cherokee Nation. Cherokee nationalism was a more potent force than Cherokee Methodism. It was not so simple as the Methodists thought to separate what was Caesar's from what was God's. They found that out again in 1844 and in 1861, and missionaries of all denominations are still finding it unanswerable today.

CIVIL DISOBEDIENCE
AND SOCIAL ACTION
AMONG THE MISSIONARIES
TO THE CHEROKEES, 1829-1839

The celebrated example of the New England missionaries who brought a test case to the Supreme Court to help the Cherokees fight against removal has been told many times, but somehow the division among the ranks of the American Board's missionaries over this heroic action by their two colleagues has been allowed to drop from sight. The action that made Samuel Worcester and Elizur Butler heroes to the Cherokees and to thousands of churchgoers, naturally made villains of those of their colleagues who declined to join with them, or so at least the Reverend Daniel S. Butrick felt. In an effort to justify his refusal to go to prison to test the constitutionality of Georgia's oath law, Butrick wrote a careful analysis of the true role of the missionary. His argument is as pertinent to missionaries today as it was then. Should a missionary teach his congregations to rebel against political oppression or instruct them to obey the powers that be? How can a missionary help his people to distinguish between what is God's and what is Caesar's? What example should he set in his own political behavior?

Part of the problem in this case was whether the missionaries to the Cherokees (who were part of a foreign mission board) were really working in a foreign nation or were under the Constitution of the United States. Indian nations were considered part of the foreign mission field because the Indians spoke another language, had a different culture, and dealt with the United States by treaties. But the whole point of the case Worcester and Butler brought was the extent to which the Indian nations were independent of state authority by virtue of the Constitutional clause that declared treaties to be "the supreme law of the land." President Andrew Jackson said Georgia's power was supreme. Butrick therefore chose to obey Georgia as the power ordained of God in that situation. Not until the United States fought a bloody civil war was the question of states' rights finally resolved.

Butrick ultimately found more support among his colleagues than Worcester and Butler did, and to many his defense of the missionary's neutrality in politics is still convincing.

> Man, who made me a judge or
> divider over you?
>
> Luke 12:14

IN THE YEARS 1829 TO 1833, the United States was faced with a double-edged political crisis, which included one of the first efforts among Christian ministers to resort to conscientious civil disobedience. One side of this crisis was the nullification procedure instituted in South Carolina and abetted by John C. Calhoun, then vice-president of the United States. The other side was "the Indian Question" centering on the policy of removing all Indians west of the Mississippi (a policy Calhoun had strongly supported as secretary of war from 1817 to 1825). Though Calhoun played no direct part in the affair of the Christian missionaries, his stand on both issues hovered in the background throughout. The missionaries argued among themselves as to whether in taking sides with the Indians they might not be fueling national discord, which could lead to civil war.

The other significant figure, whose part was much more direct in this aspect of the crisis, was Andrew Jackson, whom Calhoun hoped to succeed as president. Jackson strongly supported removal of the Indians to the West, but he equally strongly opposed the doctrine of nullification. He was also shrewd enough to say, when the crisis was over, that the "next pretext" for raising the issue of secession "will be the Negro or slavery question." The missionaries who precipitated the crisis over Indian removal did not see that slavery was also one of the sleeping dogs in the Indian question. Though William Lloyd Garrison was to raise his unquenchable voice in the midst of this crisis, it was not until a decade later that Americans began to realize how deeply embedded slavery was both in nullification and in removal. Ostensibly the state of Georgia wanted the Indians' land only to provide farms for their expanding population, while South Carolina was concerned only with the tariff and the cost of manufactures to an agrarian economy. Little was made of the fact that this agrarian economy was based on slavery and that the Cherokees, whom the missionaries were dedicated to civilizing, were giving up the life of hunters for the life of slaveowning cotton planters.

However, I am concerned in this essay only with the behavior of the missionaries to the Cherokees in this portentous decade. While John C. Calhoun and the nullifiers opposed the tariff laws in legalistic terms and their sound and fury ended without resistance to government, the missionaries spoke and acted as revolutionaries. Refusing to obey the law of Georgia that required them to support the removal policy, the missionaries placed Christian consciences against "the powers that be" and went to jail for their beliefs. Whether the power of Georgia in this case was rightfully asserted over the Indians was, of course, the crux of the issue. But whether a Christian minister should, as the saying now goes, "lay his body on the line" to test the legitimacy of political power was—and still is—a hotly debated religious issue. Fifteen years before Thoreau spent his night in jail and published his secular defense of civil disobedience, a handful of Presbyterian and Congregational ministers in the Cherokee Nation (within the boundaries of Georgia) passionately argued out the same problem on biblical grounds. That debate deserves reconsideration today.

While the main outline of the story is familiar, it will help the reader to understand the debate better if I hastily summarize the chronology of events that punctuated the arguments pro and con among the missionaries of the American Board of Commissioners for Foreign Missions.

On 8 December 1829, Andrew Jackson delivered his first message to Congress as president and in it he made clear his determination to enforce the removal of all Indians to the west of the Mississippi; eleven days later the legislature of Georgia passed a series of laws declaring that all the territory within the state's boundaries occupied by the Cherokees was under the sovereignty of the people of Georgia. Moreover, the Cherokees must abandon their right to govern themselves and accept the sovereignty of the state government as of 1 June 1830. During that year the missionaries to the Cherokees so effectively bolstered their opposition to the state's effort that on 22 December 1830, the Georgia legislature passed a law to force the missionaries (and all other white men among the Cherokees) to acknowledge the sovereignty of Georgia over the Indians' land and to obtain a license to preach. Otherwise, they would be asked to remove themselves from the state by 1 March 1831. On 29 December 1830, the Reverend Samuel A. Worcester called together twelve missionaries to the Cherokees who signed a set of eight resolutions deploring the actions of the Georgia legislature; then, after consulting the Prudential Committee of the American Board in Boston, the five missionaries of that body who resided in Georgia decided to test the validity of the law requiring them to take an oath of loyalty to the state of Georgia. The Methodists and United Brethren missionaries were advised by their missionary agencies to withdraw from the state (the Baptists were already on record as favoring removal of the Indians to the West). On 12-17 March 1831, three of the American Board's missionaries were arrested and tried before Judge Augustin S. Clayton in the Superior Court of the state. Clayton declared that the missionaries were "in some sense agents of the United States" and released them.

Governor Georgia Gilmer thereupon obtained assurances from Secretary of War John Eaton that the federal government did not consider these missionaries in any sense its agents, and on 16 May 1831, he advised the missionaries that they had ten days to comply with the law or depart. At this point three missionaries of the American Board came to a disagreement with their two colleagues and with the majority of the Prudential Committee. The Reverend Daniel S. Butrick of the Hightower Mission Station, speaking for John Thompson and Isaac Proctor, said they could no longer see any justification for refusing to obey the law; at the same time the Reverend Samuel A. Worcester of New Echota Mission, speaking for himself and Dr. Elizur Butler of Haweis Station, said they were prepared to suffer imprisonment rather than obey the law.[1] The Prudential Committee, though expressing its opinions by majority vote, told each missionary that he must make his own decision in the matter.[2] The three led by Butrick thereupon moved out of Georgia to

---

[1]In 1830 the American Board had eight mission stations with thirty-seven missionaries, assistant missionaries, farmers, teachers, mechanics, and wives at work among the Eastern Cherokee. But only four of these eight stations (New Echota, Hightower, Haweis, and Carmel) were within the boundaries of Georgia and only five of the missionaries and assistant missionaries were involved in the decision over civil disobedience. There were other white men arrested and tried for failure to take the oath or depart, but they did not plead Christian conscience. Details of the crisis may be followed in the pages of the *Missionary Herald* (published by the American Board in Boston) for the years 1829-1839.

[2]See the *Missionary Herald* 29 (March 1833): 110.

mission stations in Tennessee and North Carolina, from which they continued to minister to their Cherokee churches as itinerants.

Worcester and Butler remained at their posts until they were arrested by the Georgia Militia on 7 July 1831 and taken to Camp Gilmer in chains for refusing to comply with the law. Their trial was set for 16 September and they were released on bond until that time. At this trial the jury found them and nine other white men (including the Reverend James J. Trott, who was married to a Cherokee) guilty; the judge sentenced them to four years at hard labor in Milledgeville Penitentiary. Upon reaching the prison, they were offered a pardon by the governor if they would admit their guilt, sign the oath, and agree to abide by the law. All except Trott, Worcester, and Butler accepted the offer. (Trott however, agreed to leave Georgia and was released.)

With the backing of the American Board, Worcester and Butler employed William Wirt, former attorney general of the United States, to appeal their case to the United States Supreme Court. On 3 March 1832, John Marshall declared the law of Georgia unconstitutional and confirmed the rights of the Cherokees under the treaty-making power of the federal government. His mandate for the release of the missionaries was delivered to the state court on 17 March, but the court refused to accept it. On 28 November, the missionaries took the next step and informed the governor (now Wilson Lumpkin) of their intention to file a motion with the Supreme Court to have the mandate enforced. That next month the state of Georgia repealed the law under which the missionaries had been arrested and offered a pardon to the them if they would withdraw their motion. The Prudential Committee advised them to do so; and on 8 January 1833, they told the governor they had instructed their attorney to withdraw the motion, thereby avoiding a final confrontation between national and state power. On 14 January they were released from prison and returned to their missionary stations. Despite John Marshall's decision, Andrew Jackson refused to dispute Georgia's assertion of sovereignty over the Cherokees and their land. Within two years, the mission buildings of Worcester and Butler had been taken over by the state and occupied by citizens of Georgia and the missionaries were evicted. In April 1835, Samuel Worcester moved to the Western part of the Cherokee Nation (in what is now northeastern Oklahoma). Butler and the other missionaries remained in the East until the fall of 1838 when the United States Army, at bayonet point, forced the Cherokees to leave their ancestral lands and walk 800 miles over what became known as "The Trial of Tears." Butler and Butrick walked the trail with their missionary congregations.

While much has been written to explain the position of Worcester and Butler, who became popular heroes of the Whigs and the Northern supporters of missions, little has been said of the counterarguments of Butrick and the majority.[3] Without in any way derogating the courage and self-sacrifice of the minority, it seems to me that the other side deserves a hearing. Looking back now, we can see that both parties in the dispute spoke less for the Indians than for their own position as white, Anglo-Saxon Protestants. Both saw themselves as divinely commissioned to Christianize, civilize, and Americanize the "wild savages of the forest." And while they spoke of the red men as brethren and fellow human beings, there was never any doubt that the Indians had far to go before they became the equals of the white. The best thing that Worcester and his eleven colleagues could think to say on behalf of the Cherokees in their manifesto of 1829 was that under the tutelage of the missionaries, some of them had "risen to a level with the white people of the United States." Jeremiah Evarts, a founder of the American Board and one of the most eloquent opponents of Indian removal, saw nothing patronizing in saying to Worcester when he was arrested:

By standing firm in this case, & being willing to suffer for righteousness sake, you will do much to encourage the Cherokees. Courage is the thing they want, i.e., long continued courage or fortitude . . . I have often said, "White men, in a high state of civilization, are alone competent, & expect deliverance by the slow progress of law. Such men have been the Hampdens, the Sydneys, & Baxters &

---

[3]The principal reason why Butrick's arguments have been neglected is that the American Board, to whom he wrote them, preferred not to air the split in its ranks, pretending throughout that its missionaries were unanimous in support of Worcester's position (as they had seemed to be in 1829). Moreover, Butrick, though he published some of his views in contemporary religious journals, was no more eager to enter the controversy against Worcester than against the state of Georgia; he wanted to ignore it, in fact. Nevertheless, when John Howard Payne was gathering information for his never-written history of the Cherokees in the 1840s, Butrick was willing to recapitulate and supplement his position for him. I have therefore drawn both upon the archives of the A.B.C.F.M. at Houghton Library, Harvard University and the Payne Papers, Newberry Library, Chicago.

Bunyans of every age." . . . Now God is likely to bring this trial upon white men
of a select character, who went out for a holy purpose. . . .[4]

Both liberals and conservatives who manipulated the Indians ("for their
own good") succeeded only in making their lives worse. It was the conservative, Daniel Butrick, who quoted Jesus to the Cherokees when they
looked askance at his stand: "Man, who made me a judge or a divider
over you?" Though Butrick, in my opinion, took the weaker side on the
issue of 1829-1833, his position enabled him to take a stronger stand than
Worcester and the American Board in the later stage of the removal crisis
from 1834 to 1839.

In the years 1829 to 1833 the missionary arguments over the Cherokee situation can be divided into three categories: theological and moral
(relying chiefly upon scriptural interpretation); legal or constitutional
(relying chiefly upon interpretation of the United States Constitution);
and expedient (relying chiefly upon interpretation of the United States
Constitution); and expedient (relying upon past or future relationships
with the Indians, the government, the public, and the supporters of
missions).

The arguments of Worcester and the American Board being better
known, they may be summarized first.[5] To begin with the legal and constitutional arguments: Every citizen must recognize that under the Constitution, the treaty-making powers of the president and the Senate are
the supreme law of the land; the treaties with the Cherokees had sustained their right to self-government (within certain limits) and their
right to ownership of the lands upon which they resided under these
treaties. Hence the laws passed by the state of Georgia in 1829 laying
claim to the Cherokees' land within its borders and extinguishing the
rights of the Cherokees to manage their own affairs must be unconstitutional, null, and void. Furthermore, the missionaries were in the
Cherokee Nation by express agreement both of the federal government
(through the Bureau of Indian Affairs) and the Cherokee people

---

[4]For Worcester's manifesto, see the *Cherokee Phoenix* (New Echota) 1 January 1831
(microfilm at the American Antiquarian Society, Worcester, Massachusetts). Evarts is
quoted in Althea Bass, *Cherokee Messenger* (Norman, 1936) 140.

[5]The most succinct and complete statement by Worcester and Butler of their position
appeared after the event in the *Missionary Herald* 29 (May 1833): 183-85.

(through their elected National Council or legislature), and Georgia had no right to expel them or set any limits on their self-government. The attempt to make the missionaries take an oath to uphold the sovereignty of Georgia if they wished to reside in Indian Territory was also unconstitutional because the missionaries were all citizens of other states (notably Massachusetts and Vermont) and under the Constitution every state was bound to respect the rights and immunities of citizens of other states.[6] And finally, there is an argument that Worcester did not at first use, but Judge Clayton handed it to him when the case was first brought to trial: missionaries were agents of the federal government and, as such, not subject to the law passed by Georgia.[7]

Worcester's arguments from expediency were first that the Cherokees expected, needed, and deserved the support of the missionaries in behalf of their efforts to retain their rights. To deny whatever help they could give would not only weaken the Cherokee position, but would lead the Cherokees to lose faith in them as men and as missionaries ostensibly working for their good: "We felt, therefore, that Christian philanthropy demanded a temporary sacrifice of our personal liberty in order to obtain a decision [of the Supreme Court] of so much importance to thousands

---

[6]The American Board put this argument another way. Even admitting the right of the state of Georgia to jurisdiction over the land of the Cherokee, the missionaries "still have a right to remain, if the constitution of the United States is to be regarded, which provides that 'the citizens of each state shall be entitled to all the privileges and immunities of citizens in the several states.' Of these privileges and immunities, the simplest and most obvious is the right of residence, they cannot constitutionally be deprived. . . ." *Missionary Herald* 27 (August 1831): 251. Worcester argued that he was already a citizen of Peacham, Vermont, and he had no desire or need to repudiate that. He also said of the oath of loyalty to the state of Georgia, "An oath to demean ourselves uprightly *as citizens*, would be an acknowledgment under oath that we *were* such—a virtual declaration upon oath of what we did not believe to be true, and therefore *perjury*." Ibid., 29 (May 1833): 183.

[7]In a letter to the board, 13 April 1831, Worcester expressed his surprise at Clayton's arguments: "We supposed, indeed, that we were *authorized* by Government but that we should be denominated *agents*, we did not suppose." Nevertheless, he urged the board immediately to put J. F. Wheeler, the printer who had handled most of Worcester's Scripture translations, on its payroll, for Wheeler resided at New Echota and had been arrested along with Worcester. Wheeler was not released in May 1831, because he was not an "agent," being simply a paid employee of the Cherokee Nation, for whom he printed the *Cherokee Phoenix*. When printing Scripture translations, he was apparently paid by the board for each job.

of our fellow men."[8] Second, the cause of missions in general would suffer if those who had paid to support mission work found the missionaries so supine as to abandon their work at the advent of difficulty. Third, though the board stressed this more strongly than he, considerable missionary property was at stake and would be lost to Georgia if the claims of that state were not refuted.[9] In addition to the importance of sustaining the missionary enterprise, Worcester also argued that he had certain duties as a citizen to sustain: he must uphold the cause of justice to a helpless minority; he must uphold the supremacy of the Constitution against the illegal action of the state of Georgia; and he must not, in the current crisis over nullification and secession, lend support to those who would destroy the Union by placing states' rights above national sovereignty: "We did not see that our character as missionaries exonerated us from the obligation, or divested us of the rights of American citizens."[10]

It is significant that when Worcester was languishing in the Milledgeville Penitentiary in Georgia, he inveighed against the deplorable apathy of the public in general toward the grave injustice taking place, and he called upon the board to arouse both the ministry and citizenry to their responsibility.

> Have not ministers and private citizens felt so much that politics belonged not to them as to withold their votes when they ought to have been given? I am not, and would not be a politician, but . . . It does appear to me that the Cherokees would hardly endure another four years of the reign of the present administration and indeed that our whole country is hastening to ruin. . . .[11]

Worcester summarized the moral and theological goals of his civil disobedience as "to save our country from the guilt of covenant-breaking

---

[8]*Missionary Herald* 29 (May 1833): 184.

[9]See ibid., 27 (May 1831): 165: "Abandoning their stations, it seemed to them, would be attended with a considerable sacrifice of property."

[10]Ibid., 29 (May 1833): 184. Though not brought to trial on the issue, Worcester was generally accused, like all the missionaries, of having encouraged the Cherokees to oppose the state of Georgia; to this charge he argued that like any citizen, he had the right to freedom of opinion and expression under the Constitution (though he denied ever exhorting the Indians to resist).

[11]Letter to David Greene dated 26 June 1831, in the archives of the A.B.C.F.M., Houghton Library.

and oppression and robbery."[12] He later expanded this to say, "Whether this should be done [civil disobedience] was not a question of mere political expediency, but of clear moral obligation—a question of right or wrong—of keeping or violating the commands of God, of obtaining, as a nation, Divine favor or incurring Divine vengeance."[13] The covenant breaking was of two kinds: first, the national covenant of the government (through its treaties) with the Cherokees and, second, the missionary covenant (both collectively by the American Board and individually by each missionary) to preach the Gospel to them, to save their souls, to educate their children, to improve their moral condition (and concomitantly, to advance their progress from savagery to civilization). Worcester nowhere that I have seen quoted Scripture in defense of his action, but relied (as the antislavery reformers generally did) upon the general biblical principles of brotherly love and fair dealing for his theological authority to resist unjust laws.[14] He thought that the Prudential Committee of the American Board relied too much on legalistic and expedient arguments; and after reading its statement defending the willingness of Butler and himself to go to jail, he wrote, "I should have been glad if that preamble had distinctly stated the moral reasons which induced us to stay [in jail] as well as the justifying grounds in a legal point of view." "I understand," he wrote in this same letter, "that the *New York Observer* denominates us martyrs in the cause of *liberty*. If we are not suffering for the sake of *righteousness*, let us yield the conflict."[15]

Although Worcester had initially managed a show of unanimity among all of the missionaries on behalf of the Cherokees in the manifesto issued on 29 December 1830, he was early aware that several of them were not at all persuaded by his arguments. Daniel S. Butrick told John Howard Payne some years after that he and others felt they had been manipulated into putting their names to that statement. Among other things, it viewed "the removal of this people to the West of the Missis-

---

[12]Ibid.

[13]*Missionary Herald* 29 (May 1833): 184.

[14]He does refer indirectly to "the command of our Redeemer to preach the gospel to every nation," but not to any specific text counseling civil disobedience or even obedience to God rather than men, though of course this is implicit.

[15]Letter to David Greene, 14 November 1831, archives, A.B.C.F.M.

sippi as an event to be most earnestly deprecated" and deemed it "an immense and irreparable injury" to see "the establishment of the jurisdiction of Georgia and other states over the Cherokee people." Worcester so managed the manifesto, Butrick said, that "we must sign the Document prepared or be censured as unfriendly to the Cherokees, whereas in my opinion the Cherokees should never have been taught to expect political aid from missionaries."[16]

Worcester told the board as early as 28 January 1831, that after conversing with Butrick and Proctor, he realized unanimity would not prevail. And in May he wrote, "I regret this breach in our ranks, but I hope that if they are, as I believe, mistaken, the rest of us may have grace to maintain our ground."[17] By the rest of us, he meant Butler and the majority of the board.

Butrick conceived of the role of the missionary primarily in a spiritual and educational capacity, and this accounted for the essential difference between his position (supported by Proctor and Thompson) and that of Worcester and Butler. He could see no way in which a missionary might take a stand on political issues without jeopardizing his spiritual position, no matter how vital to the Cherokees such issues might appear. Once he descended from the purely spiritual level into the quagmire of mundane problems, the missionary was without any sure guide. Far better to abstain from all such controversy than to take sides and risk not only mistaken social judgments but a confusion of the church and the world—the things that were God's and those that were Caesar's. The manifesto of 1829, he said, "placed missionaries in a daring attitude and brought upon them much odium which they might otherwise have avoided."[18] They were ministers of God, not "Cherokee patriots."

Butrick's conservative theological position represented what came to be called later in that decade "the Old School" among Presbyterians—churchmen for whom social and moral arguments carried weight only insofar as they were scripturally based. While this led him to take a nar-

---

[16]Butrick to John Howard Payne, 12 January 1841, Payne Papers, 9:1, Newberry Library. While I have cited throughout the typescript transcription of Butrick's correspondence with Payne, this transcript contains a number of errors that I have corrected from the originals, which are also at the Newberry Library.

[17]Worcester to Greene, 25 May 1831, archives, A.B.C.F.M.

[18]Butrick to Payne, 12 January 1841, Payne Papers, 9:1.

row and unsympathetic stance on this particular issue—since his refusal to act in effect condoned the status quo and the view that "might made right"—in later controversies concerning the Cherokees it enabled him to speak more boldly and forcefully than some of his former opponents. The abiding and insoluble dilemma was between those Christians who tried to avoid the complexities of judging relative cultural issues because they saw how limited the vision of any human group must be, and those who argued that despite the obvious risks, it was the duty of Christian conscience to apply, to the best of one's ability, the absolute judgments of scriptural truth to pressing social issues. Otherwise how is God's kingdom to come on earth?

Since Butrick's position was guided primarily by theological assumptions, it is best to begin its delineation at that point. In defending his views, he referred to the works of two then well-known English theologians as well as to John Locke. He seems to have had before him the annotated Bible edited by Thomas Scott (1747-1821) as well as Scott's five-volume *Commentary on the Holy Bible*; he may also have had in his library Scott's *An Impartial Statement of the Scripture Doctrine in Respect of Civil Government and the Duties of Subjects* (London, 1792). Of David Bogue (1750-1825) he cites his two volumes of theological lectures and refers to his *Objections Against a Mission to the Heathen Stated and Considered* (Cambridge, 1811).

When the crisis began early in 1831, Butrick said that he, Proctor, and Thompson at first accepted the view of the majority of the Prudential Committee of the American Board, which claimed the missionaries should "remain at our stations" because "we were in the [Cherokee] nation by permission and under the protection of the U. States government."[19] But when the secretary of war told the governor of Georgia that the missionaries were in no sense agents of the government and thereby acknowledged that sovereignty of Georgia over the Indian Territory, Butrick and his friends made a decision. "As missionaries to the heathen, we cannot feel that we are called upon to enter further into this controversy. And when we think of suffering in this cause, we cannot say, 'The love of Christ constrains us.' It has appeared to me more like suffering

---

[19]Ibid., 9:2.

in a *political* contest from motives of worldly policy than in the spirit of Christian meekness."[20]

The president of the United States had granted the missionaries the right to enter the nation and it had always been assumed that he had the right to remove any who were in his opinion a hindrance to the Indians or to the government's relations with them. "But the President says that this authority, with which we have supposed him invested, belongs to the several states within whose chartered limits we reside; and the state of Georgia exercises the same in accordance with the President's views. The state authorities, therefore, in my opinion, become the existing authorities of the 'powers that be'. . . . It is not for us to enquire into the justice of this change of power or the right of rulers to govern." Butrick here cited "Locke and Dr. Scott" in reference to Romans, chapter 13:

> Whether we take powers here, in the abstract, for political authority, or in the concrete for the persons actually exercising political power & jurisdiction, the sense will be the same. How men come by a rightful title to this power, or who has this title, the apostle is wholly silent and says nothing of. To have meddled with that would have been to decide of civil rights, contrary to the design and business of the gospel and the example of our saviour, who refused meddling in such cases with this decisive question, "Who made me a judge or a divider over you?"[21]

In short, Butrick did not see it as part of his province to challenge the jurisdiction of Georgia by civil disobedience (thereby forcing the United States Supreme Court to to make a judgment as to who held rightful title

---

[20]Letter to David Greene, 25 April 1831, quoted in ibid., 9:6.

[21]Letter to Greene, 12 May 1831, quoted in ibid., 9:8. Unfortunately Butrick nowhere lists the title, edition, or page of the works by Scott, Locke, and Bogue that he is citing, so it is difficult to trace these quotations. In some cases it appears to be Scott or Bogue who is citing Locke and not Butrick himself. He may well have had in mind the following statement by Locke in the first *Letter Concerning Toleration* (1689) in which Locke answers the hypothetical question regarding disobedience to a tyrannical magistrate: "The private judgment of any person concerning a law enacted in political matters, for the public good, does not take away the obligation of that law, nor deserve a dispensation." In other places Butrick seems to refer to Locke's comments on Romans 13 in *The Reasonableness of Christianity* (1695).

to power over the Indians and their land).[22] This might be all right for a citizen to do, but it was not proper for a missionary. Here he might have quoted David Bogue, to whom he refers elsewhere in his argument:

> The sole business of a missionary is to promote the religion of Jesus. Whatever may be the duties of a settled pastor in his own country, where he is not only a minister of the Gospel but likewise a subject, a citizen, and a member of the community (all which relations lay certain obligations upon him and call for a corresponding conduct), it is certain that a missionary who is an alien in a foreign land has nothing to do with civil affairs and his only business is to propagate religion.[23]

Why didn't Butrick consider himself acting as a citizen in his homeland? First, because Indian territory *was foreign* mission territory (after all, the Indians spoke a foreign language, had a heathen culture, and made war upon and treaties with the United States); second, he was not a settled pastor over a community of citizens (he was merely the temporary pastor of the mission church at Hightower, and Indians did not have the vote); and third, Butrick took a very high view of his calling which, he said, made him "dead to this world."

> . . . some may be ready to say that as citizens of the United States we are bound to bear our part in the political struggle of the day and do all in our power to put down those rulers who do not act according to our views of justice. . . . [But] As a missionary to the heathen, I feel that I have a right to be dead to the

---

[22]Butrick later in the same letter quotes Scott again, but in such a way as to virtually contradict Locke's theory of the right of the people to judge when a ruler has broken his compact: "If then, the most learned and intelligent men find many difficulties and differ widely in their opinions respecting this subject, how shall the bulk of the people decide it." This is one of the few points in the controversy in which Worcester directly, though not by name, referred to Butrick's position. He first distinguished between opposing illegal authority and "rightfully constituted authority," and then pointed out that in 1831 there were two contending authorities and hence he was required to make a choice: "Supposing that the Cherokee government was of rightful authority [rather than the state of Georgia], an oath inconsistent with the recognition of that authority would have been a violation of the injunction to regard the powers that be. We are the more particular on this point because, by a *petito principii*, the requirements of scripture to which we refer, have often been urged as demanding of us that allegiance to the state of Georgia which the oath would have recognized. Scripture could not require us to recognize at the same time two conflicting authorities." *Missionary Herald* 29 (May 1833): 183.

[23]David Bogue, *Objections Against a Mission to the Heathen Stated and Considered* (Cambridge, 1811) 11.

political world. That I have no call from the example of our Blessed Redeemer or his apostles to engage in political controversies or to speak evil of dignitaries.[24]

Citing Scott's *Commentary* on Romans 13, he noted that Jesus had to put up with Pontius Pilate and the apostles with Nero, and "I do not suppose that any rulers at the present day are worse than Nero."[25]

Worcester, however, argued that as missionaries it was their duty to save the souls, raise the morals, and improve the social standards of the Cherokees; could Butrick deny that Andrew Jackson (perhaps not quite so bad as Nero) and the governor of Georgia (perhaps not quite so wicked as Pilate) were interfering with these legitimate efforts? Would not breaking faith with the Indians, ignoring treaty obligations, dispossessing them of their homeland, removing them by force to the arid plains of the Far West amount to their destruction and with it the destruction of all the missionaries' work? Butrick faced this issue. Perhaps the civil authorities were engaging in unrighteous actions, but that was not up to the missionaries to correct; it was up to God: "The President, the Congress and the Supreme Court of the U. States are all accountable to God, as also the governors and officers of each state. They are appointed by his Providence and vested with authority from God. If they abuse that authority, he will punish them."[26] And beyond that, how did Worcester know what Providence had in store for the Cherokees?

Suppose by suffering we could procure for the Cherokees the continued possession of this country, who knows but that very possession might prove their ruin,

---

[24]Letter to Greene, 12 May 1831, quoted in Payne Papers, 9:12.

[25]I do not know what edition Butrick had, but this quotation can be found in Thomas Scott, *A Commentary on the Holy Bible*, 5 vols. (Philadelphia, 1858) 5:61.

[26]It is interesting that in January 1833, when Worcester and Butler decided to withdraw their motion to compel Georgia to enforce Marshall's mandate, they abandoned any effort to force Jackson to his duty: "We had much reason to believe that the President would not interfere." *Missionary Herald* 29 (May 1833): 185. But if this was their object, Worcester and Butler knew Jackson's intransigent position long before that. In fact, even before Worcester was arrested in July 1831, he wrote to the board, "I do not indeed see how that court [the United States Supreme Court] can well decide against me, but I think it very likely, if in my favor, to be an inefficacious decision of 'the mere question of right' which will not take me out of prison, unless there be a new administration of the Executive Government. I apprehend there is danger of my having to suffer the full penalty of the unrighteous law; but still it appears to me that the effort ought to be made, though it end in defeat." Letter to Greene, 31 May 1831, A.B.C.F.M. archives.

and ban them from the Kingdom of heaven? Their gold mines might prove a greater snare than all the dangers of the west. . . . Who knows but these very afflictions are designed to take them to a far distant region and render them a light to all the nations west of the Rocky Mountains.[27]

Time was to prove that Worcester had more foresight than Butrick as to this. He had rightly said in the manifesto of 1829, "Hard is the task of that philanthropist who would attempt to elevate, or even to sustain, the character of a broken-hearted people."

To Worcester's claim that he and Butler had to engage in civil disobedience because of their duty to God, Butrick replied, "In my opinion we are bound to obey [the laws of Georgia] if obedience implies no direct disobedience to God." He then cited Lecture 23 of Dr. Bogue: "It is only when christians are commended to do things contrary to the law of God that they are to refuse obedience."[28] Butrick, let it be said, was never in favor of signing the oath required by the Georgia law. He did not feel obliged to obey that aspect of the law because there was another alternative that allowed him to maintain his allegiance both to his native state of Massachusetts and also to his calling as a missionary. He could, and did, remove to the American Board's mission at Candy's Creek, in the state of Tennessee, and from there he itinerated into Indian Territory in Georgia to minister to his mission church.

The question now arises, Does the law of Georgia require anything unlawful? anything which we cannot perform without violating some command of God, or neglecting some duty positively enjoined? In my opinion it does not. It relates simply to our place of residence. It does not interfere with our traveling through the nation and labouring as faithfully as St. Paul in every part of the country.

To this he later added a footnote, which read: "Thus the event proved. During the two years of our residence at Candy's Creek I visited Carmel

---

[27]Letter to Greene, 25 April 1831, Payne Papers, 9:7. Gold was discovered by a black slave in the Dahlonega region of the Cherokee Nation within the boundary of Georgia in 1828. Providence could hardly have weighted the stakes more heavily against the Indians.

[28]Letter to Greene, 12 May 1831, quoted in Payne Papers, 9:9.

statedly, & other churches in Georgia as often as I pleased."[29] Of course, after Georgia repealed her oath law (due to Worcester's challenge—also Providential?), all the missionaries had freedom to circulate in the nation.

Worcester later acknowledged the weight of Butrick's argument on this point: "It is said, indeed, that we were not forbidden to preach the gospel in disputed territory. True—but every one must perceive that the prohibition of the residence of missionaries within a given territory is a great RESTRAINT upon the preaching the gospel there."[30] And he thought restraint of gospel preaching an infringement of missionary rights.

This is probably the hinge of the disagreement between Worcester and Butrick. Worcester was ready and willing to look behind the law to its motivation and purpose, Butrick preferred to avoid these subtleties. Worcester insisted that "the law not only *did* operate, but it was *designed* to operate as an interruption to missionary labors."[31] Butrick merely took the law as it was and tried to find a way to do the Lord's work despite it. He was not concerned with the intent of the law but only with its effect; and so far as he could see, it did not affect his work materially. Perhaps that was because Butrick saw his principle work as preaching the Gospel and saving souls, while Worcester was primarily a scholar, interested in educating minds and making translations into the Cherokee

---

[29]Let it be said for Butrick's colleague and supporter, John Thompson of Carmel Station, that after he removed himself from Georgia in order to comply with the law regarding residency, he—like Butrick and Proctor—felt he had a perfect right to visit his mission church. Consequently when he was arrested in June 1831, and told by Colonel Nelson of the Georgia Guard that he had no right to itinerate, he refused to yield: "Here is the ground on which I am willing to meet him. And I am determined to disregard all prohibitions so far as this point is concerned . . . the opposition which I here meet is persecution against the church." *Missionary Herald* 27 (September 1831): 282-83. But Thompson was released and so was not compelled to suffer for righteousness' sake. Still, it is important to note that there was a clear line upon which these missionaries were prepared to take a stand and go to jail for conscience' sake.

[30]Ibid., 29 (May 1833): 184.

[31]Ibid. Worcester also pointed out that the law was designed to interrupt, if not stop, the regular instruction of the Cherokees in mission schools, the translation of the Bible and other works into Cherokee (for which translators were needed), and the use of the Cherokee printing press in New Echota.

syllabary not only of Scripture but of other useful moral and philosophical works.

Worcester unquestionably was correct about the intent of the law. The nub of Georgia's quarrel with the federal government was that in 1802, when Georgia had reluctantly ceded its western lands to the government, Congress had agreed to extinguish the title of the Cherokees to all land within the boundaries of Georgia as rapidly as possible. Yet thirty years later, little had been done in this direction. In fact, so far as the Georgians were concerned the government had been working in just the opposite direction.

> The authorities of the state [said Worcester] had charged it upon the Government of the United States, as a violation of the compact with Georgia [in 1802], that they had caused the Cherokees to be instructed, because their progress in knowledge and in civilization had the effect to attach them to their home and render them unwilling to part with those lands which the United States were conditionally bound to purchase for the use of the state. The authorities of the state were therefore opposed to the instruction of the Indians within her chartered limits, and wished to expel the missionaries because they communicated instruction. We did not consider the desire of the state to obtain the lands of the Cherokees as a sufficient reason why they should be left to perish [spiritually] through ignorance [of the Gospel], and believing that the laws of our country were on our side, we were disposed to contend for the right of continuing among them our labors for their temporal, and especially their eternal welfare.[32]

"Temporal welfare" was precisely what Butrick did not think missionaries should pursue. First save the Indians' souls and then their temporal lives would improve. Whether that improvement would advance more rapidly in Georgia or in Oklahoma, what mortal could guess?

As for the arguments of Worcester and the American Board based upon expediency, Butrick made short shrift of them: Will it improve our standing with the Indians to demonstrate that we are hypocrites, he asked. When the missionaries came into their country, they swore that they would not engage in any political activities or interfere in any aspect of tribal life. When the Cherokees asked Butrick why he did not act on their behalf, he told them that "it was no more our duty to enter the list of combattants to defend their political rights, than it would be in case of war, to enter their ranks and fight their battles—that if a dispute

---

[32]Ibid. This was precisely what Judge Clayton had in mind when he spoke of the missionaries as in some sense government agents.

should arise between them and the Creeks, and if we supposed the Creeks were greatly abused, and therefore should attempt to defend their cause, would not the Cherokees at once say that we were acting out of character, and enquire, who made us judges and dividers over them?"[33] If they took sides now, and Providence later proved them wrong, how then would the missionaries defend themselves from Cherokee criticism? A Cherokee patriot today might, as the world turns, be a Cherokee traitor tomorrow.

As for hurting the cause of missions by refusing to take a stand against the state of Georgia, this was clearly a nearsighted position. One had only to talk to the frontier people, Butrick said, to know that nothing could be worse for the mission movement than for the missionaries to take political action in defense of the Indians: "The people in Georgia, many of them, at best consider us worldly, designing men having our temporal interests interwoven with that of the Cherokees."[34] If missions were supported only by the people of New England or the Northeast, this might be an argument; however, the movement appealed for support throughout the country. Did it aid the cause of missions to seem to support the position of Henry Clay, Daniel Webster, and the Whig party when the country was overwhelmingly for Jackson? In any case, it was the merest vanity to seek the approbation of the world for one's actions. Missionaries should be above acting merely to attain the gratitude of the Cherokees or the praise of society. The harder the course, the more righteous it just might be.

If one wanted to get down to this level of argument, however, Butrick shrewdly noted that by attacking the government at this critical time, the missionaries could hardly expect much support and trust from the government in the future. Here he proved more prescient than Worcester and the board, for from 1830 onward the Democrats, especially the Southerners, saw to it that they controlled all aspects of Indian affairs in Washington; by the 1840s the Northern missionaries found themselves totally incapable of sustaining a stand against slavery in the Indian Territory without risking the expulsion of all their missionaries. Virtually

---

[33]Extract from Butrick's Journal dated 13 June 1831; quoted in Payne Papers, 9:15.

[34]Ibid., 9:16.

all Indian commissioners, superintendents and agents were Southerners or frontier Westerners.

It is now possible to address the portentous connection between the nullification crisis of 1828-1833 and the whole Indian question. Jackson was a hero to many Northerners for his bold defense of the Union against Calhoun and the South Carolina nullifiers. Jackson and Daniel Webster at least saw eye-to-eye on that. Yet how did it help Jackson in this crisis to drive a wedge between him and those Southern states most likely to side with South Carolina (Georgia, Alabama, Mississippi, North Carolina—all of which were anxious to remove the Indians within their bounds)? Any argument from expediency called upon the Unionists to help Jackson unite these other states against South Carolina if the country was to avoid a clash of arms.

Worcester himself finally acknowledged the strength of this argument as the nullification crisis reached its climax in the winter of 1833. Justifying himself for accepting the governor's pardon without pushing the final appeal to federal power, he said, "The political aspect of our country was in other respects such [that in January 1833] . . . it were better to suffer unjustly than to seek redress at the hazard of civil war."[35]

Butrick was even consistent to the point of refusing to hazard an opinion as to whether the Indians might be better off if they voluntarily removed themselves from the harassments of grasping Eastern frontiersmen and removed to the isolation of the Far West. Here, so Calhoun swore, "Force . . . should it be necessary, must be used to prevent the whites from crossing the boundary line" of Indian territory.[36] Butrick did not know whether the government could make good on this. "I think I have never desired to sway the minds of the people in their national affairs. I have never desired to prevent their going West nor to send them there. . . . As we do not wish to prevent the Cherokees from emigrating, so on the other hand, we do not wish to urge their removal lest they should say, as some do already, that one object in [our] coming here was to get them away."[37]

---

[35]*Missionary Herald* 29 (May 1833): 185.

[36]Quoted in Margaret L. Coit, *John C. Calhoun* (Boston, 1950) 131.

[37]Copy of a letter to John Ridge and Elias Boudinot, 25 November 1836, in Payne Papers, 9:36-38.

So much for the debate over Christian civil disobedience among the Cherokee missionaries—its justification, motives, and goals in the years 1829 to 1833. Today Worcester's arguments, as well as his stand, seem the more convincing as well as the more admirable, though Butrick scored several telling points. It would be unfair to leave the discussion here, though. For while Worcester, in popular estimation, won the first round in the great debate, he abdicated the ground after 1835. His decision to move west at a time when the Cherokees, under Chief John Ross, were making their last and most desperate effort to hold the line against Jackson (hoping that a change of administration in 1836 would bring Clay, Webster, Frelinghuysen, and their Whig friends to power) seemed to many Cherokees rank desertion; it irreparably damaged the respect that his earlier sacrifice had earned. Indeed, Worcester acknowledged by his going that their cause was hopeless even before the Cherokee faction that signed the fateful Treaty of New Echota did. His departure may even have hastened this schism, which proved the final undoing of the Cherokees.

It is all the more striking, therefore, to note the course of Daniel Butrick in the years 1834 to 1839. Without reversing his principles one iota, at least so far as he was concerned, he emerged in this period as a supporter of the Cherokees almost equal to Worcester and Evan Jones, the Baptist missionary in Valley Towns, North Carolina, who succeeded Worcester as the missionary champion of resistance to removal.[38]

In December 1835, Andrew Jackson, through the agency of the Reverend John F. Schermerhorn (whom the Cherokees named "The Devil's Horn"), took advantage of a schismatic faction among the Cherokees to obtain a removal treaty. The treaty, signed by a mere handful of the leading men, was rejected out-of-hand by the principal chief and the overwhelming majority of the nation. Nevertheless, Jackson got the Senate to ratify it and the army to put it into effect. Worcester made no public comment; Butrick not only commented, he acted.

First, he denounced the treaty and all who had a part in it; second, he persuaded the members of his missionary church to censure those brethren in the church who had participated in it; third, he persuaded

---

[38]Evan Jones so greatly abetted John Ross in these years that he was finally expelled from the Cherokee Nation by the United States Army. There is no biography of Jones, but I hope soon to remedy that deficiency.

the church publicly to disavow fellowship with J. F. Schermerhorn as a Christian minister; and finally, he took the American Board to task for allowing itself to benefit financially from the infamous treaty at the expense of the Cherokee. His justification for these actions was a lesson in simplicity itself: The treaty faction had failed to obey the powers that be. They had acted in knowing violation of tribal law, ceding away the land collectively owned by the nation in a treaty that neither the chief nor the National Council had approved.

"Though I have been blamed by some of my missionary brethren for censuring those members of our church who signed the New Echota Treaty as being guilty of moral evil," Butrick wrote in 1841, "yet, unless ignorant of my own heart, I have not censured the signing of that treaty from any political or party motives, but for the same reason that I would censure any other course of conduct which seemed directly opposed to the dictates of [divine] inspiration."[39] The leaders of the treaty faction were John Ridge and Elias Boudinot, who agreed with Worcester in 1835, that the cause was hopeless and that for the good of the nation a treaty should be signed while it was possible to get the best terms from the government. Butrick knew these men personally, and members of their family were members of his mission church. He wrote to them soon after word of the treaty got out, and told them "that in all communities holding land in common, it was of vital importance that it should not be at the disposition of any one or two individuals, but of a majority, or persons authorized by a majority," which the treaty faction was not. "And that under any common circumstances they could not expect forgiveness in thus acting for the nation."[40]

As Butrick explained to John Howard Payne, who may have wondered how he could reconcile this defense of majority rule with his former apolitical stand, "though I might not be a politician, yet I might be a peacemaker." In his letter to Boudinot, he said,

> Now though I have disclaimed all interference with political affairs, yet I have considered it my duty to strengthen the hands of the chiefs, not merely because they were deserving it personally, but also because it was my duty to God. . . . Now you will see at once that your proceedings at New Echota were directly at variance with my sentiments. . . .

---

[39]Letter to John Howard Payne, 19 January 1841, Payne Papers, 9:24.

[40]Ibid., 9:25.

He insisted that Boudinot and the others concerned in the betrayal of the tribe confess their crime and ask forgiveness. When they did not, he drafted the following resolution of excommunication, which was adopted by his church:

> Resolved, that it will not be our duty to unite in Christian fellowship with any members of Presbyterian or Methodist churches who voted for the New Echota Treaty, or signed it, or assisted as a committee in executing it, inasmuch as they acted by usurped authority, in opposition to the known will of the national chiefs, and the great council of the Cherokee people, thus disposing of property not their own, and placing the life of the whole nation at the mercy of speculators . . . exposing the whole population who would not acknowledge the justice of such usurpation to be taken by armed soldiers, dragged with all the insult and suffering of prisoners of war, from house and home, and everything of an earthly nature but the clothes they might have on—hurried at the point of the bayonet to forts and then to filthy and polluted boats or goaded on by land to faint and die by the way.[41]

The Prophets scarcely spoke with more righteous indignation. It is hardly surprising that shortly after the Cherokee arrived in the West, three of the leaders of the treaty faction (including Ridge and Boudinot) were assassinated by anguished Cherokee, and the rest of the faction were in danger of losing their lives as well.

As for the Reverend Schermerhorn—a Judas if ever there was one—Butrick minced no words about him and his treaty, which he referred to as that "screwing, grinding, torturing instrument" Schermerhorn had badgered out of the despairing faction as agent for the government. "Mr. Schermerhorn was a minister who professed much friendship to the mission cause and visited all the stations; the [Cherokee] people generally will not readily believe that the missionaries were ignorant of his intentions." So a resolution was presented and adopted by Butrick's Indian church that said,

> Resolved, that in our opinion, the Rev. J. F. Schermerhorn has forfeited the confidence of the church of Christ, 1st, by his abusive conduct towards the principal chief and council of the nation; 2nd, by taking advantage of our national distress to induce a few individuals of our people to violate a law, the penalty of which he doubtless knew was death in every Indian tribe; 3rd, by acting in direct opposition to the injunction of the President of the United States who positively for-

---

[41]Butrick was at this time pastor of the Brainerd Mission Church; its resolutions, adopted 31 October 1838, are contained in his Journal under that date; ibid., 9:93-94.

bade his making a treaty with a small minority [but who nevertheless approved it]; and 4th, by making a treaty so destructive in its nature . . . [that] almost the entire infantile population, as well as many, if not most, of the aged and infirm, have already been swept away by that mercyless treaty.

Nor did he spare his own missionary board for its willingness to benefit financially from that same treaty. Schermerhorn, it appeared, in an effort to win the mission boards of the various denominations to his side, had browbeaten those who signed the treaty into granting payment to the mission boards for all improvements they had made during their years in the eastern part of the Cherokee Nation. It was bad enough that Boudinot and Ridge could not be persuaded by Butrick's arguments to ask the government to alter this clause and to pay the mission boards out of a separate appropriation (rather than compel the Cherokee to take it out of the five million dollars that was ostensibly granted them in payment for their land), but for the mission boards not only to accept it but to instruct Butrick and others not to make a public issue out of it was shocking.

In fact, one of the first missionaries of the American Board to come into the nation, the Reverend Ard Hoyt, had repeatedly assured the Cherokees "that we never should call on them for land, or anything else as pay for what we were doing." He had even given them an official statement to that effect, which their chief still had. How would it now look for the missionaries to take advantage of that treaty and permit the government to deduct from the price paid for their homeland twenty thousand dollars or more, to be added to the coffers of the American Board? If the board took that money, the Indians "will honestly class us among other white men who have manifested duplicity—such double dealing as to forfeit forever their confidence."[42] The corresponding secretary told Butrick that he had a "wholly distorted view" of the situation, and that it was perfectly just for the board to expect the government to pay for the improvements that had been made through the donations of mission supporters. But Butrick pointed out that "Mr. Schermerhorn stated positively, last fall, that the Cherokees had received the benefit of mission improvements and therefore *they should* pay for them." The Cherokees knew perfectly well that the government would not pay it for them but

---

[42]This and the following quotations from Butrick's letters to David Greene are contained in letters written between 24 June and 26 November 1836; ibid., 9:41-48.

would deduct that money from the price offered for their land, "and doubtless most of them blame us as the cause of this."

In another letter on the subject to the board, on 26 November 1836, Butrick wrote: "It may be well for the Prud. Committee to know that mission improvements were valued at nearly, or quite as much again, as they were worth. . . . Whether the Indians think of this, I know not, as it is dangerous making enquiries, yet I presume they do, and will ever remember it."

There is no indication that the board was ever persuaded by Butrick to decline the money it was technically entitled to under the treaty. But he had done what he could and what his conscience told him he should. That was all Worcester had done. Who can say now which of the two men was more faithful to his missionary calling or stood up more courageously for the Cherokee? Both continued to work among the Cherokee in the West for many years after, but both died before the nation was torn to pieces in the Civil War—a war in which most of the treaty faction sided with the South and most of its opponents, led by John Ross, Evan Jones, and his son, John Butrick Jones, sided with the Union.

What impact did the civil disobedience of the Cherokee missionaries have upon the public at large? Pious churchgoers in Georgia, according to Worcester, looked upon the imprisoned missionaries as "deluded good men."[43] Democratic politicians saw them as soft-headed dupes of the Whigs out to defeat Jackson. New England missionary supporters hailed them as Christian martyrs. The great mass of the public—especially west of the Appalachians—if they thought about it at all, probably wondered why anyone would go to jail for an Indian. Some, like the Reverend Isaac McCoy, considered them absolutely wrongheaded for not recognizing that removal was the best and only way to sustain and civilize the Indians.[44]

But there were those who were troubled by the spectacle for more complex reasons:

---

[43]Letter to David Greene, 8 November 1831, archives of the A.B.C.F.M.

[44]McCoy, one of the earliest Baptist missionaries to the Indians, is credited with having influenced John C. Calhoun to adopt the policy of removal as secretary of war as well as persuading his own denomination to petition Congress in support of that policy. For his position on the question, see Isaac McCoy, *History of Baptist Indian Missions* (Washington, 1840) and *Remarks on the Practicability of Indian Reform* (New York, 1829).

These transactions present a new scene in the history of the United States. . . . Heretofore, when they [Americans] have seen men seized, tried, convicted and imprisoned, they have seen them to be the intemperate and profane, the fraudulent, riotous, and frequenters of the haunts of dissipation and crime; they have seen them taken for their deeds of dishonesty and outrage. . . . Now they witness a new scene. They behold men of highly civilized minds, men of irreproachable moral and religious character, citizens pursuing lawful occupations in a peaceable manner, charged with no crime but that of being found occupying their own houses and lands, where they had gone with the express approbation of the government of the United States; Christian ministers, entirely unimpeached, who would be admitted to every pulpit of their own denomination throughout the United States—such men our citizens now see dragged from their schools, their pulpits, and their ministrations at the Lord's table, chained one to another, like felons of the first order and hurried before a criminal court and to prison. . . .

Our citizens have been accustomed to see offenders against the laws arrested by civil officers, acting in obedience to the warrant of a civil magistrate, but now they see armed soldiers, without any civil precept, scouring the country, arresting whom they please, detaining them as long as they please, and releasing them when and where they please. . . .

Such scenes as these are strange and unexpected in this country.[45]

The citizens of the United States of America had emerged from their childhood as a revolutionary people. They had withstood the doubts and scorns of monarchical Europe toward their democratic republican principles, secure in the faith that they were right. But now, turning westward in the course of expanding the empire, it became apparent that nationalism was not to be so holy or romantic a venture as it had seemed in 1776. Hitherto *they* had been the recipients of injury and injustice; now they were injuring the rights of others.

Foreign visitors to the United States in the Age of Jackson were surprised at the touchy self-esteem of the Americans. Mingled with justifiable pride there was now a sense of guilt. The civil disobedience of the Cherokee missionaries, it seems to me, raised for the first time in many American minds some question as to whether national self-interest, the power to manipulate others, and the progress of mankind were really one and the same. Indian removal was the nation's first bitter taste of the arrogance of power.

---

[45]*Missionary Herald* 27 (September 1831): 283-84.

REVEREND EVAN JONES
AND THE
SLAVEHOLDING BAPTIST INDIANS,
1845-1861

Historians often imply that what happened in the past was "inevitable." The Civil War is often spoken of in these terms and so is the division of the Baptist and Methodist denominations over the slavery question. What makes history worth studying, however, is that there were always other options open at the time. Why a people or a nation took one option rather than another is the essence of historical scholarship.

Given the apparently insurmountable obstacles toward emancipation of slaves in the Cotton Kingdom, it is not surprising that most missionaries to the Southeastern Indians believed there was nothing they could do (or ought to do) to change that situation. Even those who fervently disliked slavery felt their hands were tied. The Southeastern Indians were firmly committed to the institution of slavery after 1789. For a missionary to question it was to risk being expelled from their nation. All of the federal agents among the Southeastern tribes after 1825 were from the South and most of them, if not slaveholders, were strong advocates of slavery. Some of them even stated that the advance of slavery among the Indians was the most important aspect of their improvement and civilization. They certainly did not see any conflict between slavery and the Christianization of the Indians, as Northern abolitionists did.

After the Northern and Southern Baptists split in 1845, the Cherokee mission of the Baptists remained under the auspices of the Northern mission board located in Boston. Though the board was averse to abolition, it was strongly opposed to slavery. It therefore asked the unthinkable of its missionaries to the Cherokees: "Why cannot you preach anti-slavery and rid our mission churches of that sin by expelling any Indian members who persist in owning slaves?" Faced with that query—nay, command—the Reverend Evan Jones had to ask whether he could do the impossible without ending his usefulness and destroying his mission. One may argue that because of certain peculiar circumstances, his solution to this question was not so difficult as it would have been for other missionaries. Nonetheless, most people thought his effort to do what his board ordered was flying in the face of reality. Because he succeeded, historians must either believe in miracles or deny the inevitability of history.

RECENT STUDIES OF SLAVEHOLDING among the Cherokee Indians have noted the difficulties it posed for missionaries who held antislavery principles.[1] Robert T. Lewit, in a pioneering article on this subject in 1963, examined the manner in which the Boston-based American Board of Commissioners for Foreign Missions (A.B.C.F.M.) struggled with this question. In the end, Lewit reported, the board was unable to resolve it. The A.B.C.F.M. closed its Cherokee mission in 1859 and transferred its Choctaw mission to the care of the proslavery foreign mission board of the Presbyterian Church.[2] The Baptist Board of Foreign Missions (B.B.F.M.), also based in Boston, followed a very different course with its Cherokee mission. The Baptist denomination had split into Northern and Southern branches in 1845 because the Northern-dominated mission board refused to appoint slaveholders as missionaries. The schism did not entirely resolve the problem of the Northern Baptists' connection with slavery, for the Cherokee mission still remained under their care and the Cherokees were firmly committed to the institution of black slavery. In 1845, when the Cherokee population was roughly 15,000, about seven percent of its 2,600 families owned slaves, who numbered nearly 1,500. Slaves had been used for half a century for much the same purposes as those owned by Southern white planters. In fact, one cause of the schism between Northern and Southern Baptists in that year had been the alleged ownership of slaves by one

---

[1]See Rudi Halliburton, Jr., *Red Over Black: Slavery Among the Cherokee Indians* (Westport CT: Greenwood Press, 1977); Theda Perdue, *Slavery and the Evolution of Cherokee Society, 1540-1866* (Knoxville: University of Tennessee Press, 1979); W. G. McLoughlin, "The Choctaw Slaveburning: A Crisis in Mission Work Among the Indians," *Journal of the West* 12 (January 1974): 113-37; W. G. McLoughlin, "Indian Slaveholders and Presbyterian Missionaries, 1837-1861," *Church History* 42 (December 1973): 535-51; Michael Coleman, "Not Race but Grace: Presbyterian Missionaries and American Indians, 1837-1893," *Journal of American History* 67 (June 1980): 41-60.

[2]Robert T. Lewit, "Indian Missions and Antislavery Sentiments: A Conflict of Evangelical and Humanitarian Ideals," *Mississippi Valley Historical Review* 50 (1963-1964): 39-55.

of the native Baptist preachers among the Cherokee, the Reverend Jesse Bushyhead.[3]

I propose to examine the way in which the Baptist Board of Foreign Missions faced this complex problem after 1845 as the antislavery movement came to dominate American politics and religion. Of all the mission societies among the slaveholding Indian nations in what is now Oklahoma (then Indian Territory), only that sponsored by the Northern Baptists expelled slaveholders from their mission churches and steadfastly maintained a Christian witness against slavery in the Indian Territory. In this struggle their missionaries suffered considerable harassment and were in imminent danger of mob action by irate Cherokee slaveholders. The federal agents to the Cherokee, invariably Southerners who owned slaves and encouraged slavery among the Cherokee, did their best to intimidate the Baptist missionaries for their "abolition" principles. Because the Cherokee Council was dominated by slaveholders, it too raised questions of Baptist interference in the political affairs of the nation. While the Baptist missionaries, led by the Reverend Evan Jones (later in conjunction with his son, the Reverend John B. Jones) were at first reluctant to obey the board's order to expel slaveholders from their churches, eventually they became ardent antislavery activists and encouraged the formation of an antislavery organization in the Cherokee Nation.

Like the A.B.C.F.M, the B.B.F.M, was caught between the need to appease the abolitionist faction in its denomination and its fear of antagonizing the Cherokee. The Cherokee Council had the right to expel from the nation any missionaries who interfered in the Indians' internal affairs. The members of the B.B.F.M. in Boston, though basically antislavery in their statements, were not radical abolitionists. Fear of jeopardizing a highly successful missionary enterprise (begun in 1817 and then reaching new heights of success) led them to act quietly and informally to purge the mission of all connection with slavery. The American Baptist Free Mission Society, a group of ardent abolitionist Baptists who formed their own antislavery missionary organization in

---

[3]For the allegation, see *Free Missionary Magazine* 1 (June 1844): 27. Bushyhead died before the allegation could be proved.

1842 because they believed the B.B.F.M. was palliating the sin of slavery, continually accused the B.B.F.M. of lethargy on this issue.[4]

The B.B.F.M. could easily have dodged the whole problem by turning its Cherokee mission over to the Southern Baptist mission board or to the American Baptist Free Mission Society. But it chose to wrestle with the problem itself. In 1844 the board had considered turning its Cherokee mission over to the American Indian Missionary Association (A.I.M.A) founded by the Reverend Isaac McCoy in 1842. McCoy was a Baptist missionary who had been employed by the B.B.F.M in the 1820s among the Pottawatomi.[5] He became the foremost clerical advocate of Indian removal in 1827 and even persuaded the Baptist Board to support that policy in a petition to Congress that year. However, Evan Jones, who had started work as a missionary among the Cherokee in 1821, opposed McCoy's position and in 1829 persuaded the board to reverse its stand and oppose removal of the Southern Indian nations.[6]

After removal of the Indians, McCoy had founded the A.I.M.A. because he believed that Indian missions deserved more attention than they were receiving from most foreign mission boards. The A.I.M.A. was designed to be interdenominational and to concern itself only with American Indians. When the B.B.F.M. became aware of the likelihood of a schism between Northern and Southern Baptists, it sent a letter to the Cherokee missionaries asking whether they would prefer to come under the auspices of the A.I.M.A. Evan Jones and his colleagues declined the option: "I have consulted all the brethren and sisters connected with the mission," Jones wrote on 27 September 1844, "on the subject of a transfer to the Indian Missionary Association, and the unanimous decision is that . . . we prefer to remain under the patronage of the Board at Boston."[7]

---

[4]For the constant attacks by the abolitionist Baptists on the B.B.F.M., see A. T. Foss and E. Mathews, *Facts for Baptist Churches* (Utica: published by the American Baptist Free Mission Society, 1850).

[5]For McCoy's career, see Georga A. Schultz, *An Indian Canaan: Isaac McCoy and the Vision of an Indian State* (Norman: University of Oklahoma Press, 1972).

[6]See *Baptist Missionary Magazine* 10 (December 1830): 362-63. Jones believed that removal of the Cherokee would destroy all the progress they had made in civilization and Christianization and that it was an abridgment of their treaty rights.

[7]This letter from Jones to Peck and all letters cited below from the Cherokee missionaries of the B.B.F.M. to the board are filed under the names of the senders (chronologically) among the Records of the American Baptist Missionary Union, "Indian

Jones favored this not because of private animosity toward McCoy but because the A.I.M.A., despite its interdenominational pretensions, was in fact dominated by Southern, proslavery Baptists from the outset. Jones realized that if his mission came under its auspices, he and his colleagues would soon be embroiled in disputes over their antislavery views. They would have to acquiesce in slavery or face replacement by proslavery missionaries. While Jones and his colleagues were far from ardent abolitionists, they were even farther from being in favor of slavery. To them it was a regrettable evil. To its credit, the Boston board did not press the matter, even though it recognized that so long as it maintained a Cherokee mission, it would be open to charges by the abolitionists of conniving with slavery in that nation. Over the next eight years, the B.B.F.M. undertook what it considered a moderate but determined effort to bear Christian witness against slavery by eliminating Cherokee slaveholders from its mission churches.

The first step in this long and delicate process was a letter written to Evan Jones by the Reverend Solomon Peck, one of the corresponding secretaries of the B.B.F.M., on 22 November 1848. Peck sought to obtain from Jones the facts regarding the extent to which the Baptist mission churches in the Cherokee Nation were implicated in slaveholding.[8] In 1848 the Baptist mission included fourteen meetinghouses scattered over a two-hundred mile circuit and served 1,100 members and many more congregants.[9] In addition to the mission church led by Jones in the town of Cherokee (sometimes called Breadtown or Baptist Mission), there were four other organized churches (some with several branches) led by four ordained native preachers and one licensed native exhorter.[10]

Missions" at the American Baptist Historical Society, Rochester, New York. They are hereinafter cited as Indian Mission Papers, A.B.H.S.

[8] A copy of this letter from Peck is among the Jones letters in Indian Mission Papers, A.B.H.S.

[9] Jones gave this figure in his answer to Peck. It should be noted that the Baptists considered as members only adults who had been baptized by immersion after a conversion experience. Many other Cherokees attended Baptist services, but had not experienced conversion.

[10] The five mission churches were located at Cherokee, Delaware Town, Taquohee, Dseyohee, and Flint. The Delaware Town church had branches at Honey Creek and White Water; the Flint church had branches at Skin Bayou, Grand River, and Spring Creek. The ordained native preachers were John Wickliffe, Oganaya, Tanenole, and Lewis Downing. The licensed preacher was Dsulaskey. See Jones's letter of 25 March 1848, Indian Mission Papers, A.B.H.S.

In 1842 the Reverend Jesse Bushyhead had told the annual convention of the board that "the Baptists are now the prevailing denomination" in the Cherokee Nation and "knowledge of the gospel has extended pretty much over the Cherokee country and there are Christians in almost every part."[11] The Baptists had always worked primarily among the full-blood Cherokee, most of whom were poor and less acculturated than the slaveholding element in the nation. Some of the wealthy Cherokee owned ten or twelve black slaves; a few owned more than fifty. But among the full bloods, few owned any. The majority of slaveholding Cherokee who were Christians belonged to the Methodist mission churches and the churches of the American Board; a few belonged to the Moravian mission church. (Later, in the 1850s, the Southern Baptists began to compete with the Northern Baptists, making some converts among the slaveholding Cherokee but few among the full bloods.)[12] Jones's response to Peck's inquiries on 24 February 1849, indicated that out of 1,100 converts, only five owned slaves. Furthermore, Jones attempted to show that these slaveowners treated their slaves mildly and had generally inherited rather than purchased them:

> One brother has a male slave inherited from his parents, brought up in the family, treatment very kind, food and clothing comfortable and sufficient. He [the slave] is a member of the church. Strong feelings of confidence and attachment exist between them. The owner considers slavery a great evil and would rejoice in its removal on any plan which would secure the permanent welfare of the slaves.[13]

A female Cherokee owned "a family of slaves," the mother of whom "was bequeathed to her by her father." "The mother has been set at liberty for several years. She and her daughters are members of the church. They are all treated kindly. Labor quite moderate. Their religious privileges the same as those of the family."

---

[11]*Baptist Memorial and Monthly Chronicle* 5 (16 May 1842): 155.

[12]Available statistics on Christian Cherokee slaveholders are sparse, but in 1848 a census among the A.B.C.F.M. converts showed twenty-four slaveholders owning twenty-three slaves among 237 church members; in 1855, 750 Southern Methodist converts owned a total of 140 slaves. Halliburton, *Red Over Black*, 97, 101.

[13]Jones to Peck, 24 February 1849, Indian Mission Papers, A.B.H.S.

Peck had also asked whether any of the missionaries owned slaves or employed slave labor. Jones said that no white missionary and no native minister owned slaves, but that "slave labor has been employed to a small extent" because of the shortage of labor. This occurred "only in cases of absolute necessity in which other help could not be obtained, and always on condition of the person being employed being willing to render the needed service." Furthermore, "When slaves have been employed by missionaries, they have been treated as if they were free and their condition for the time has been decidedly bettered, and when taken away they have generally left with regret."

Jones was constrained to note, in answer to another inquiry from Peck, that "no public instruction distinct from the ordinary Gospel precepts is given" on "the righteousness or evil or sin of slavery." "The sentiments communicated in ordinary and private intercourse are that the system of slavery is essentially evil in its nature and in its influence on the persons and interests affected by it," but the missionaries did not feel free to preach against slavery from the pulpit because slavery was legal in the nation. "The tendency, however, of the influence exerted by this Mission has been in decided opposition to slavery and favorable to its extinction. We believe the hopes and anticipations of intelligent and pious Cherokees look forward to the extinction of slavery." (Jones probably referred here only to Baptist converts.) He noted that about fifty slaves were members of the Baptist mission churches, but their owners were not.

The most critical question the board posed was, "Are slaveholders giving evidence of piety received into church membership on the same terms and as freely as non-slaveholders?" Here Jones had to admit that neither he nor any other Baptist missionary or native preacher would prevent a slaveholder from joining a mission church if he were otherwise piously converted. "The march of public sentiment in the Cherokee Nation on the subject of slavery is not sufficiently advanced to justify the adoption of any measure on the subject in reference to church membership."

The letter was signed by the white male missionaries in the pay of the board, Evan Jones, Willard P. Upham (the schoolmaster), and Hervey Upham (the printer). In sum, the letter showed these important facts: the Baptist missionaries and most of their Cherokee converts were opposed to slavery in principle but sometimes employed slave labor; few

Baptist converts and no missionaries owned slaves; there was no effort to preach against slavery or to prohibit slaveholders from becoming church members.

The board in Boston was not satisfied with this state of affairs. Jones had undoubtedly hoped the board would drop the whole matter because the connection of the Baptist mission with slavery was so slight, but the board took the opposite view. Because the connection was minimal, the board had believed it could easily be eliminated entirely. Thus began a four-year struggle, quietly but firmly maintained by the board and with equal quiet postponed by the missionaries. Sometimes, in fact, Jones's prolonged silences in regard to this matter were deafening. He simply did not want to be pushed into actions that might damage a Christianizing effort to which he had devoted thirty years, although he fully sympathized with the board's position.

On 17 April 1849, Peck responded to Jones's factual account of the problem. The board, he said, was pleased to find the mission so slightly involved in slavery. It now wished to pursue the matter further. "I wish also to inquire," Peck wrote, "whether it is possible in any way to disconnect yourselves from slavery altogether?" This he thought might be done "by those [members] now owning slaves giving them their freedom or else withdrawing to some other religious denomination." Also, he wondered whether Jones and his colleagues might agree to "hereafter receiving to membership no slaveholders?" He noted further that some abolitionists were interested in knowing whether "the present slaveholding members receive[d] their property before or subsequent to entering church relations," for it was not well to have members so ill-informed on this great sin that they would become slaveowners *after* they became Christians.[14]

Notably, the board did not specifically order Jones to take any action; it simply inquired whether he thought it possible to take action. Neither side wished to assume full responsibility or to act hastily. Because of the congregational autonomy of Baptist churches, the board might well have

---

[14]Copies of the letters from the corresponding secretaries of the Executive Board to the missionaries were recorded in letterbooks as they were written. This letter from Peck to Jones, 17 April 1849, can be found in the Records of the Baptist Board of Foreign Missions, "Domestic Letters," 7:94-95, located at the Board of International Ministries, Valley Forge, Pennsylvania. Hereinafter letters sent are referred to as "Domestic Letters," B.B.F.M., Valley Forge.

feared that it lacked the power to order a church to take action. (It could, however, cut off mission funds if that became necessary.)

Jones was not eager to take the responsibility for instituting any of these actions. Even if the Baptist converts were willing to accept them, the slaveholding Cherokee in general and the federal agent would not, and whites in the adjoining states of Arkansas and Texas would object if they learned about it. Furthermore, it would be difficult to impose this ex post facto test of membership without raising questions as to its fairness. Some slaveowners might argue that the request to free their slaves was a financial hardship, however much they might be sympathetic; others might simply see it as interference with their property rights. The alternative—dismissing them to another denomination—was an affront to those who had chosen the Baptist persuasion and been taught to believe it was the truest form of Christianity. Jones hesitated to answer, and on 30 November 1849, Peck complained that the board had been waiting seven months for his reply: "The subject, you are aware, is one of deep interest," and the board wished some information before its next meeting.[15]

Jones seems to have been feeling his way toward an answer by consulting privately with the native Baptist ministers and talking to various trusted associates in the nation. Another two months passed, and on 1 February 1850, Peck wrote to Willard P. Upham to ask why Jones had not answered the board's inquiries. Peck asked whether Upham himself would explain to the board "the sentiments and influence of the missionaries and native assistants as bearing upon the extinction of slavery among the Cherokees?"[16] But before Upham received this letter, Jones had written to explain the delay. The problem was that some of the slaveowners lived at great distances from the mission—as much as one hundred miles—and he had not had time to consult with them. He had at last talked to a distant widow who owned three slaves—"one man, raised in the family, one woman, brought into the family ten years ago in the lifetime of her deceased husband, and a small child." These slaves "are treated with all kindness and with regard to labor, they are not

---

[15]Peck to Jones, 30 November 1849, "Domestic Letters," B.B.F.M., 7:132, Valley Forge.

[16]Peck to Upham, 1 February 1850, ibid., 7:150.

pressed at all harder than the mistress herself." They all attended religious meetings together.

When he had finally managed to visit another distant "sister who was supposed to own slaves, I was rejoiced to learn that she had, from principle, declined to accept any of the slave property of her late husband." This meant that out of 1,100 Baptist converts, only four were slaveholders. He was also happy to reply to the question of whether people became slaveholders before or after joining the church: in every case, those asked had been slaveowners before entering the church. No Cherokee had bought or accepted a slave by inheritance since becoming a Baptist.

After explaining these facts, Jones expressed his reluctance to act upon the board's request to work toward total severance of the mission from slavery without direct orders. "I shall be very glad to be aided by the mature judgment of our brethren who are more thoroughly acquainted with it"—meaning that he wished the board to bear the burden for implementing the action. He offered some hope that further delay and private conversation might solve the problem with the four offenders. "One of our members had thoughts of withdrawing from the church until some settled plan of proceeding shall be determined on" so as to avoid giving embarrassment to the board. Perhaps "others might follow the example. They are all desirous to avoid being stumbling blocks or occasions of offence to those kind friends [in New England] who have sent the precious Gospel to them." He was happy to report that "our native assistants and preachers unanimously lament the existence of this evil" and would do all they could to quietly witness against it. To them, as to him, it was hard to see why they should be subject to such pressure when, of all denominations, the Baptists among the Cherokee were the least sympathetic and least connected with slavery:

> My own sphere of labor, however, and that of our native brethren, lie chiefly among that class [full bloods and poor] who speak the Cherokee language and who constitute the great body of the population, and among whom there is not much difficulty to be apprehended on the subject of slavery.[17]

---

[17]Jones to Peck, 15 February 1850, Indian Mission Papers, A.B.H.S. Between seventy-five and eighty percent of the Cherokees were full bloods. See W. G. McLoughlin and Walter Conser, "The Cherokees in Transition," *Journal of American History* 64 (December 1977): 688.

In response to the letter Peck had addressed to Upham, the Baptist missionaries sent a joint answer on 15 March 1850, saying that they and the native preachers "are decidedly and steadfastly opposed to slavery and the direct tendency of their influence is to extend their own sentiments and views. We have no apology to make for slavery nor a single argument to urge in its defence, and our sincere desire and earnest prayer is that it may be speedily brought to an end."[18]

The board decided that it must assume the responsibility for giving the order so that its missionaries would be able to argue that *they* had not initiated antislavery activity in the nation. The Executive Committee of the board reported at the annual meeting in Buffalo in May 1850, "The Committee are of the opinion that things are in a fair train to lead to the utter extinction of this evil in the Cherokee churches." To assure that goal, "The Committee desire to give the mission their full and hearty cooperation in respect to the result aimed at, viz. a complete separation of the churches from every form of slavery.[19] To make it clear to Jones and his colleagues that the approval of the committee's report by the full board was tantamount to an order to proceed with the business, Edward Bright (another of the corresponding secretaries) wrote on 22 August 1850:

> Neither the Board nor the Committee have any desire to exercise disciplinary power over the Cherokee churches. . . . Nevertheless, the Board claim[s] the right of saying where and under what circumstances the means entrusted to their stewardship shall be expended; and it is the deliberate conviction of the Board that such means ought not to be expended for the support of churches which persist in fellowshipping so great an evil as American Slavery.[20]

Because the Baptist churches in the Cherokee Nation were not self-supporting, the threat of losing B.B.F.M. funds was too serious to be ignored. Bright went on to express confidence that the missionaries would faithfully carry out the orders in the most expedient and expeditious manner: "The Committee do not deem it necessary to do more at the

---

[18]Jones et al. to Peck, 15 March 1850, Indian Mission Papers, A.B.H.S.

[19]American Baptist Mission Union, *Annual Report* 36 (May 1850): 98.

[20]Bright to Jones, 22 August 1850. Inadvertently this letter was not copied, as it should have been, into the letterbook of "Domestic Letters," but it was copied into the letterbook of "Overseas Letters," 4:336-37, B.B.F.M., Valley Forge.

present time than to express the earnest hope that all scriptural means may be used to 'provide for the entire removal of the evil at the earliest possible day' from all the churches under the care of the Mission."

Jones could at this point have read the board's letter to each of the Cherokee mission churches and left the matter to the will of the majority in each church. But he feared that such debates would not only cause controversy within the churches, but also might attract the attention of slaveholders and the federal agent. It would place a great burden on the native ministers. Consequently, he took it upon himself to carry out the order. He went to each of the four slaveowning members and explained the situation to them privately. Then he urged them to act in a faithful Christian way to end the sin of slavery.

"They received the communication in a very good spirit," he said of the first three slaveholders whom he visited. "But they could see no way by which they could disentangle themselves from their connection with their slaves at the present time, but said they would by no means suffer *their* connection with the churches to deprive their people, who are not so entangled, of the blessings of the Gospel of Christ." They promised to withdraw their membership very soon. He also talked with the native ministers and "they agreed entirely in the sentiments of the resolution and were quite willing to do all in their power to carry it into effect." They also agreed "to prevent the reception into the churches of any more persons owning slaves."[21]

But the Cherokees moved slowly, and fourteen months went by before the board heard from Jones again. On 23 October 1851, he apologized for not writing, saying that he had been very ill. He was happy to report, however, that "one individual has already withdrawn from the churches; two more I presume will do so on Saturday or sabbath next. The fourth I have not yet had an opportunity to converse with." He explained that it was important to move slowly and quietly. "We have aimed to act in this matter in the fear of God, affecting neither secrecy nor publicity."[22]

The board was not pleased. It did not like having to report that another year had gone by and still their churches had not terminated their

---

[21]Jones to the board, 23 October 1851, Indian Mission Papers, A.B.H.S.

[22]Jones to the board, 23 October 1851, ibid.

connection with slavery. "Your previous letter of October 23, respecting slavery was of an excellent bearing so far as it goes," but the board wished him to bring the matter to an end "as early as practicable."[23] Jones was not to be rushed. He was not finding it easy to move the Cherokee, even though they agreed in principle with the order he had to carry out. Ultimately he had to resort to rather high-handed pressure in order to get two of the slaveholders to agree to leave the church. One of these, John Foster, later described the painful process:

> Rev. Evan Jones informed me that I must withdraw from the church. I said to him that I did not wish to withdraw. He informed me that I could not remain a member of the church unless I would set my slaves free. I proposed to leave the matter to the church to which I belonged. He said I must go to the Secretary of the Church and get a letter of withdrawal or dismission. I spoke to the Secretary who said he did not wish to give it. Mr. Jones said he must give it to me. Mr. Jones wrote the letter and the Secretary signed it and handed it to me.[24]

Another member, the widow of Jesse Bushyhead, said that Jones "informed me that he wished me to withdraw from the church as no one could remain a member and own slaves. I accordingly withdrew."[25]

Later it turned out that both John Foster and Mrs. Bushyhead (as well as Mrs. William Musgrove, a third slaveholder) felt very much offended at being forced to leave their churches. Their vexation was to be used against Jones by those Cherokee who disliked his antislavery position. On 2 March 1852, Jones wrote happily to the board that his long effort had finally succeeded: "I hasten to avail myself of the unfeigned pleasure and satisfaction of announcing to you the important fact that Slaveholding has been separated from all our Churches." He was gratified that "this great difficulty has been removed without [so far as he was then aware] exciting any hostile feelings in the churches or any alarm in the country. I trust our Dear Brethren will unite with us in thanksgiving for our deliverance from so great an evil."[26] He could not resist chiding

---

[23]Peck to Jones, 23 January 1852, "Domestic Letters," B.B.F.M. 7:181, Valley Forge.

[24]National Archives Microfilm, Record Group 75: Records of the Bureau of Indian Affairs, M-234: Letters Received by the Office of Indian Affairs, 1824-1880, roll 97, frame 0074. This microfilm is hereinafter referred to as M-234. Foster's affidavit is dated 4 June 1855.

[25]M-234, roll 97, frame 0075, affidavit of Mrs. Elizabeth Bushyhead.

[26]Jones to Peck, 2 March 1852, Indian Mission Papers, A.B.H.S.

the abolitionists for pressing him and the denomination so hard. He also did not wish to have them making any great demonstrations over it. This might reach the Cherokee and arouse the opposition of proslavery elements and their white neighbors in Arkansas and Texas: "I trust also that our more ardent friends will not make any vainglorious parade about it, for I assure you, there is no glory due to any one but God whose wise and gracious providence has brought this whole thing to pass."

The board itself could not keep from boasting. At the annual meeting in July 1852, it announced the happy event to the public and in its annual report, published later that year, it italicized the heading relating to its Indian missions: "*Slaveholding Separated from the Mission Churches.*"[27] Though the boast might cause some embarrassment to its missionaries in the field, the board felt that it was a matter of considerable pride. No other missionary board among the five slaveholding Indian nations was able to carry out this principle, and only the A.B.C.F.M. was even interested in trying. Probably years of feeling inferior to the Congregationalists of New England made the Baptists in that region exult in their success while their rivals in Boston were suffering acutely from their inability to carry out the same policy.

The pleasure of the board and the optimism of Jones were to be short-lived. The slavery issue was stimulating increased vehemence in the Cherokee Nation, as it was everywhere in the United States. Some of the Cherokees who had been forced to withdraw from the Baptist churches complained to their friends. They believed they had been branded as sinners and punished by expulsion for actions that were perfectly legal and proper. Some of the more zealous proslavery Cherokee complained to the federal agent. Word also got around that the A.B.C.F.M. was trying to force the same policy upon its mission churches in the nation. The agent was warned that these two Boston-based mission boards were interfering in Cherokee affairs. The federal agent, George M. Butler, was himself a proslavery Southerner who had brought his own slaves into the Cherokee Nation when he took office. He firmly believed that abolitionism was a dangerous movement and that missionaries had no right whatever to promulgate such views under

---

[27]American Baptist Missionary Union, *Annual Report* (July 1852): 297-98.

cover of their religious or educational activities.[28] He wrote to the commissioner of Indian Affairs, George W. Manypenny, informing him that both Evan Jones and Samuel Worcester (the superintendent of the A.B.C.F.M. mission) were dangerous men who should be removed from the nation. His letter, written in June 1855, explained precisely why he believed Jones and Worcester "had interfered with the Institution of Slavery in the Cherokee Nation." Worcester, he wrote, was "tinctured with Abolition sentiments" because "he refuses to employ Slave labor" at the mission "unless the slave shall receive wages." Also, "by admitting negroes into his family circle as companions," Worcester was "breaking down the distinction between the owner and the Slave." Finally, Worcester was, according to reports he had heard, "inculcating Anti Slavery sentiments from the pulpit."[29]

The charges against Jones included affidavits from three of Jones's church members stating that Jones had required them to withdraw from the Baptist church against their wills simply because they owned slaves. Butler maintained that "Mr. Jones is only the instrument in the hands of the Baptist Board" in Boston, which was ultimately responsible for his actions, just as Worcester's board in Boston lay behind his abolition sentiments. Butler also asserted that "the subject of Slavery is a question that should be left entirely with the Cherokee people to settle, and it should be the duty of every Philanthropist to keep down agitation of the slavery question in this country, which cannot be done if religious Bodies draw a line of distinction between a slave owner and a non-slaveowner." So far as Butler was concerned, "the Boards under which they [Worcester and Jones] operate were attempting to accomplish a political object under the garb of Missionary Labor." In his opinion, the commissioner should request those boards "to withdraw those Instructions" about expelling slaveowners from mission churches "and leave the Subject of Slavery to be settled by the Cherokee People."

Commissioner Manypenny did not find the actions of Worcester or Jones so heinous as Butler did. No action was taken on the complaint. The Cherokee Council then proceeded to act on its own (no doubt at the insistence of the same persons who had complained to Butler). In Oc-

---

[28]See his annual report for 1854, cited in Morris L. Wardell, *A Political History of the Cherokee Nation, 1838-1907* (Norman: University of Oklahoma Press, 1938) 119-20.

[29]Butler to Manypenny, 22 June 1855, M-234, roll 97, frame 0080.

tober 1855, the council passed a bill stating that "the Cherokee People are and have been for many years a Slaveholding People" and that slavery was a recognized institution under its laws and constitution. "Whereas some of the Missionary Churches now situated in this nation have expelled some of our Cherokee citizens from the participation of Church privileges because they refused to emancipate their slaves, and others have been threatened with expulsion," the council requested the principal chief, John Ross, to write to "the different Boards of Missions . . . upon the institution of Slavery as a Church Principle" and report their answers. Furthermore, this bill made it "unlawful for any missionary to council or advise any Slave in any way whatever to the detriment of his owner" and required the proper authorities in every district of the nation "to report all missionaries so offending to the [federal] Agent who is hereby requested to place them beyond the limits of our nation." The bill was passed while John Ross was out of the nation, but upon his return he vetoed it, and the council failed to pass it over his veto.[30]

Three years later the fear of abolition sentiments among the missionaries revived with even greater strength. This time it did not abate until the A.B.C.F.M. was forced to close its mission and the Baptist Board suffered the expulsion from the nation of its most ardent antislavery missionary, the Reverend John B. Jones, son of Evan Jones.[31] In June 1858, George Butler once again wrote to the commissioner of Indian Affairs (now Charles E. Mix) about the problem. The mission boards "at a distance are governing the actions of, and acting in concert with, certain parties here whose sole object is the abolition of slavery in this nation." This was producing "political strife and discord" that might "prove fatal to the peace and happiness of the Cherokees."[32] Butler's fears were confirmed by a letter he received from William P. Adair in August 1858.

---

[30]Butler to Mix, 12 October 1855, M-234, roll 98, frame 0795. The upper house of the Cherokee Council, controlled by the mixed bloods, had passed the bill over Ross's veto by a two-thirds vote; but the lower house, controlled by the full bloods, had sustained the veto. Halliburton, *Red Over Black*, 100. Ross, though himself a large slaveholder, feared that the bill would alienate the missionaries whom he felt had done much good in the nation; he also feared that it might add to the tensions between the mixed bloods and the full bloods, especially those full bloods who were admirers of Evan Jones.

[31]For biographical information on Evan and John B. Jones, see E. C. Routh, "Early Missionaries to the Cherokees," *Chronicles of Oklahoma* 15 (December 1937): 449-65.

[32]Butler to Mix, 30 June 1858, M-234, roll 98, frame 0774.

Adair was one of the leading figures in the Cherokee Nation, a well-educated mixed blood and slaveholder who combined management of a large plantation with a legal career and membership in the upper house of the council. His letter contained a complaint against Evan Jones for harboring a slave and refusing to give her up to her legal owner.

The details of the case were complex. The slave was an elderly woman named Peggy who had emancipation papers from her mistress, Mrs. Lucinda Polone. Mrs. Polone was a Cherokee mixed blood who had received Peggy as part of the estate of her mother some years before. She had freed Peggy, but in doing so she forgot that her mother had given her only half-ownership; Peggy was willed jointly to Lucinda and her younger brother, Rider Butler. Rider was still a minor and Adair had been retained as legal counsel by Rider's guardian. Peggy had fled to Jones and given him her emancipation papers to hold so that Adair could not legally sell her in order to obtain Rider Butler's interest in her. Exasperated by Jones's behavior, Adair wrote to the federal agent explaining that Jones had refused to hand over "the free papers" to him as the law required. Jones took the view that the papers belonged to Peggy and he would yield them to no one but her. This refusal held up the legal settlement of the estate. "Now all these things prove clearly to my mind," Adair wrote, "that Mr. E. Jones is interfering with the private property of Cherokee Citizens; that he is interfering with Slavery" and "that he is upholding abolition principles and doctrines." Jones "may 'gull' a few of the ignorant class" by his religious guise, "but I think the more enlightened parties would rejoice at his removal." George Butler forwarded Adair's letter to the commissioner with the request that he be given the power to expel Jones from the Cherokee Nation.[33]

Butler also sent Mix a letter that Jones had written to him on 3 September 1858, after he had accused Jones of fomenting abolition and demanded that he exonerate himself or face expulsion. Jones responded that if he had acted improperly, then formal charges should be brought against him and he should be informed of the law he had broken. To him the issue was not abolitionism but rather religious liberty. "You are no doubt aware of the fact," he told Butler, "that the Denomination to which I belong, though peaceable and law abiding people, have in all ages as-

---

[33]Adair's letter of 21 August 1858 is included with Butler's letter to Mix, 12 October 1858, M-234, roll 98, frame 0781.

serted with conscientious earnestness their right to enjoyment [of] unmolested freedom in religious matters." So far as he was concerned, his actions in the Cherokee Nation had been taken as a minister of God in the performance of his duties as a missionary. Therefore, "I must with all due respect claim the right to immunity from the exercise of censorship over our teaching and preaching by any officers of government. And I must say that I regard such extra-judicial and unwarranted summons from an officer of the United States as a grievance and an invasion of my most sacred rights."[34] Believing that he, and all missionaries, were protected by the First Amendment, Jones pitted the American Constitution against the Cherokee Constitution.

Jones had also answered Adair's letter demanding Peggy's "free papers," and Butler enclosed this letter in his complaint to the commissioner. Jones said that he had inquired into the will of Lucinda Polone's mother and discovered that she had left two slaves jointly to Lucinda and her brother. The family clearly understood that Lucinda was to have Peggy and her brother was to have a young male slave named Randall. Peggy was over sixty-five and had raised Lucinda from infancy. In Jones's opinion, Adair had intimidated Lucinda into rescinding the emancipation of Peggy by threatening to attach other property of hers in order to pay Rider Butler's claim against the estate. Jones was obviously trying to strengthen Lucinda's resolve in order to save Peggy's freedom. He considered Adair's actions unjustifiable and unconscionable.[35]

Butler, in summing up his charges against Jones in a letter to the commissioner on 12 October 1858, mentioned for the first time the actions of Jones's son. John B. Jones had graduated from Rochester Theological Seminary in 1855; after ordination he was appointed by the B.B.F.M. to assist his father among the Cherokee. Young Jones was even more ardent in the antislavery cause than his father. Butler told Mix that the two Joneses were both "instruments of the Baptist Board of Missions that are at Boston, Mass." and both were "attempting to degrade slaveholders and place the institution of slavery upon the same level as mur-

---

[34]Jones's letter of 3 September 1858 to Butler is included with Butler's letter to Mix, 12 October 1858, roll 98, frame 0789.

[35]Jones's answer to Adair on 24 July 1858 is included with Butler's letter to Mix, 12 October 1858, M-234, roll 98, frame 0798.

der, etc." This they did by refusing to admit slaveholders to membership
in their churches and by preaching abolition from their pulpits. Evan
Jones's refusal to turn over Peggy's free papers to "Mr. Adair, a prominent Cherokee" was clearly an interference with Cherokee law. In a concluding paragraph he added, "Mr. Worcester and all of his denomination
stationed as preachers are believed to be Abolitionists" and therefore
"immediate action upon this subject" was necessary or their activities
"must lead to bloodshed."[36]

Once again the commissioner of Indian Affairs refused to involve the
War Department in such a complex and explosive issue. Butler, frustrated and angry, included in his annual report that year a strong statement that was forwarded to Congress and the president: "There are a few
Black Republicans who are particular fondlings of the abolition missionaries that have been and still are making themselves officious upon the
subject of slavery."[37] If the commissioner would not respond to private
complaints, Butler hoped this public report would stir up action.

The matter did reach the public early in 1859, but not through
Congressional action. News of the "abolitionists among the Cherokees"
was printed first in the proslavery newspapers in the adjoining state of
Arkansas. One of these, the Fort Smith *Times*, located in Van Buren,
singled out Evan Jones as "an abolitionist and a very dangerous man"
who was "meddling with the affairs of the Cherokees and teaching them
abolition principles."[38]

Tension increased in the nation at large in 1859, the year of John
Brown's raid on Harper's Ferry. The Cherokee Nation was located directly south of "Bleeding Kansas" on the border between North and
South. Moreover, the Cherokee themselves were bitterly divided on the
issue and abolition became a subject of acute political controversy within
their nation. The proslavery element (consisting primarily of the educated mixed bloods) organized in 1859 a secret society known as the
Knights of the Golden Circle in order to coordinate their activities. To
counter this group, the antislavery element (consisting primarily of the
less acculturated full bloods) decided to organize their own secret soci-

---

[36]Butler to Mix, 12 October 1858, M-234, frame 0779.

[37]Quoted in Wardell, *Political History*, 120.

[38]Quoted in Annie H. Abel, *The American Indian as Slaveholder and Secessionist*
(Cleveland, 1915) 47, n. 56.

ety. Because the Baptists were particularly active among the full bloods, Evan and John Jones assisted in the formation of the group, known as the Keetoowah Society.[39]

Because the society's membership and activities were secret, little is known of its origin—other than that it occurred in the spring of 1859 and that the Joneses were closely associated with it. Most historians believe that John B. Jones and a Cherokee named Bud Gritts wrote the original constitution.[40] Ostensibly the society sought to preserve some of the ancient ceremonies and rituals of the Cherokee and could thus be seen as a reaction of the full bloods against acculturation. However, it was not anti-Christian; its meetings opened and closed with prayer, and the Baptists missionaries participated in its activities. The Keetoowah Society thus combined the old ways and the new in an important syncretic movement that attracted those who had clung to the older traditions, who had resisted the assimilationist policies of the mixed bloods, and who yet found certain aspects of Christianity helpful in their lives. It was also a rallying point for the opponents of slavery within the nation. A closer study of this movement will undoubtedly show that the Keetoowah organization reflected a distinct class antagonism, for the full bloods were the poorer element in the nation and resented the dominance of the wealthy, acculturated, mixed-blood slaveholders.

Rumors about the Keetoowah Society were soon being discussed in the Arkansas newspapers. It was described as a dangerous and "a secret organization . . . among the full blood Indians alone" that "is growing and extending daily." The Fort Smith *Times* reported that "they hold meetings in the thickets and in every secret place to initiate members," and "the mixed-bloods are becoming alarmed" at the machinations of "this secret cabal."

The Joneses are said to be the leaders in the work and what these things are tend-

---

[39]Perdue, *Slavery*, 123, 129-31; Halliburton, *Red Over Black*, 118-20; Wardell, *Political History*, 121-22, 130; Abel, *Indian as Slaveholder*, 292-94. Because both the Keetoowah Society and the Knights of the Golden Circle were secret, it is difficult to tell which was formed first. Evan Jones refers to a secret proslavery society in the Cherokee Nation as early as May 1855, so it seems likely that the Knights preceded the Keetoowah. There is a letter to Jones from John Ross referring to this proslavery "lodge" in the Jones file, 5 May 1855, Indian Mission Papers, A.B.H.S.

[40]See Emmet Starr, *History of the Cherokee Indians* (Oklahoma City: Warden Co., 1921) 479-80.

ing to, no one can predict. We fear that something horrible is to be enacted on the frontier, and that this secret work will not stop among the Cherokees, but will extend to other tribes.[41]

The commissioner of Indian Affairs wrote to the superintendent of Indian Affairs, Elias Rector (an Arkansan and cousin of the pro-Southern Henry Rector, who was elected governor of Arkansas in 1860), on 4 June 1860, stating, "It is believed that the ultimate object of this organization is to interfere with the institutions of that people.[42] The Cherokee agent was instructed to make a thorough investigation of the Keetoowah Society. He was to find out "who are the counselors of this secret organization" and to "proceed at once to break it up." The secretary of war would "place such force . . . as may be necessary at the disposal of the agent for this purpose."[43]

As animosity mounted between the proslavery and antislavery factions, threats were made against the Joneses. John B. Jones reported these to the board on 17 November 1859.

> On account of our position on the slavery question, we also have to contend with strong opposition from many of the politicians both in the Cherokee Nation and the State of Arkansas. The border papers vilify us and stigmatize us as abolitionists, and some of the slaveholders threaten us with the fist and the cowhide and expulsion from the Cherokee country. One man, who is now a member of the upper house of the National Council, has said that they would have us out of the Nation if they had to resort to a mob to accomplish their purpose.[44]

Jones held the federal agent partly responsible for this. "The agent of the United States government actually issued an order to take my person and effects and remove them out of the Nation." The agent, evidently acting without orders from Washington, had instructed the Cherokee sheriff of the district in which the mission was located to seize and eject Jones. The sheriff came to the mission to do this, but "was deterred from executing the order," Jones reported, "by fear of the common people and of the operation of the United States' law." The Joneses believed that the agent had no right to expel them for preaching the Gospel and refused to obey

---

[41]Quoted in Abel, *Indian as Slaveholder*, 293.

[42]Ibid., 292.

[43]Ibid.

[44]John B. Jones to the board, 17 November 1859, Indian Mission Papers, A.B.H.S.

the sheriff's order to leave the nation. The full bloods had massed around the mission to prevent the sheriff from carrying out the order.

John Jones also told the board in this same letter that "a bill was introduced into the Council now in session imitating the laws recently passed by some of the Southern States, expelling all the free negroes from the Cherokee soil." The council believed that freed slaves would gravitate toward the full bloods and perhaps encourage slaves to run away from their masters and seek refuge in the regions where the full bloods were dominant. (This bill, too, was vetoed by John Ross.) Jones concluded his letter, "We have taken our position on Christ's law: 'All things whatsoever ye would that men should do to you, do ye unto them.' " This was the basic religious premise of abolitionist Christians in their attack upon the sin of slavery.

John Jones's letter was published in the *Baptist Missionary Magazine* in May 1860, and quickly found its way into the hands of the federal agent—(at this time Robert J. Cowart, a slaveholder from Georgia). For Cowart, this was evidence enough to evict Jones: He had admitted in print that he preached and supported abolitionism. On 17 September 1860, Cowart wrote to Jones giving him two weeks to pack up and remove himself from the nation.[45] For some reason Cowart decided not to act against Evan Jones at the same time, but it seemed clear that he soon would. John Jones decided that he had better go and departed for Kansas on 25 September 1860.[46] His father remained and continued the work at the mission, including his support of the Keetoowah Society.

Meanwhile Samuel Worcester had died and the American Board, finding it an embarrassment to explain why it still permitted slaveholders in its mission churches and still allowed its missionaries to hire slave

---

[45]A copy of Cowart's letter to John B. Jones is among Jones's letters to the board, 7 September 1860, Indian Mission Papers, A.B.H.S. Cowart stated that 500 citizens of the Cherokee Nation had petitioned him to remove Jones on the basis of a reprint of his letter of 17 November 1859, in *The Arkansan* of 14 July 1860.

[46]On the day he left, Jones sent a letter to Cowart stating that he was going under protest, for he had broken no law. A copy of this letter of 25 September 1860 is among the John B. Jones letters, Indian Mission Papers, A.B.H.S. Jones said his real fear was that white, proslavery vigilantes would cross into the Cherokee Nation and lynch him if he remained. The Baptist mission was only a few miles from the Arkansas border. After a short stay in Kansas, Jones removed to Alton, Illinois, hoping in vain that with Lincoln's election he would be restored to his post.

labor, concluded to close its mission in the Cherokee Nation. The B.B.F.M. now maintained the only antislavery mission in the nation.

Cowart's investigation of the Keetoowah Society proved fruitless. "I firmly believe," he wrote the commissioner, "that they are gotten up with a view to aid in conveying those abolition plans of operation into a successful termination," but he could find no concrete evidence of its membership or officers in order to act against it.[47]

When the Baptists in New England learned of the expulsion of John B. Jones, they published an angry editorial in their chief newspaper, *The Watchman and Reflector*. They insisted that their missionaries to the Cherokee

> have never been anti-slavery propagandists. They have attempted no general crusade against the institution of slavery as it exists in the Cherokee Nation and in the Southern States. All they have attempted is to weed their churches of its pestilent presence and to leaven their own people with views of its unchristian principles and blighting practices.[48]

They noted also that "intimations have been given to Mr. [Evan] Jones, the elder, and Mr. [Willard] Upham that similar rescripts will soon be issued to them," and they would be forced to leave. "We would like to know by what right an agent of the United States government overrides the nationality of the Cherokees . . . under what article . . . peaceable citizens and worthy ministers of the Gospel, pursuing their high and beneficent work in a strictly legal way, are interrupted in that work, rudely separated from their trusting flocks, driven from their homes?" They answered their own question the whole action was simply one more "outrage on freedom and Christianity by the slave power" that now threatened the safety of the Republic. Their readers must now see "the dark power at whose instigation this new outrage has been perpetrated, and the supple and unscrupulous officials who have lent themselves to its behests." There could be only one conclusion: "There is in this country today, an irrepressible conflict between civilization and barbarism, freedom and slavery."

Six months later the Civil War began with the firing upon Fort Sumter. Evan Jones remained at his post for another two months while John

---

[47]Quoted in Abel, *Indian as Slaveholder*, 293-94.

[48]*Baptist Watchman and Reflector* (Boston) 11 October 1860.

Ross tried desperately to keep his nation neutral. The Confederate States of America sent envoys who pressed him hard to ally with them. One by one the other Indian nations in Indian Territory joined the Confederacy. Finally, the absence of any Union troops to lend support if he refused, plus the urgent demands of the proslavery faction in the council, led Ross to agree to a treaty with the Confederacy in August 1861.

Evan Jones, who had left the nation in June, was surprised at Ross's action but recognized his problems. Jones had closed the mission because the proslavery forces were eager for a fight and the Baptist mission was bound to be one of the first sites for such action.[49] For the duration of the war, he lived in Lawrence, Kansas. John Ross, on the arrival of Union troops in June 1862, renounced his treaty with the Confederacy, but this merely split the nation. The war took hundreds of lives over the next three years as Cherokee fought against Cherokee. The Union victory in 1865 meant that the Joneses could return with honor and respect to reopen their mission and try to reconcile the two factions. Their witness against slavery had been difficult, but they had demonstrated that it was not impossible.

---

[49]There are no extant letters from Evan Jones explaining his reason for leaving the nation in June, but once Texas and Arkansas had joined the Confederacy, he doubtless feared the same kind of vigilante action that his son had feared.

"A MODEL OF PROPRIETY AND SUCCESS": OSWALD WOODFORD AND THE CHEROKEE MALE SEMINARY, 1851-1856

Coauthor
VIRGINIA DUFFY McLOUGHLIN

To everyone's astonishment the Cherokees, within fifteen years after their calamitous march along "The Trail of Tears," had erected in the West an efficient form of constitutional government, had established a thriving farming and herding economy, and had built a nationwide public school system. In 1851 they capped this renascence by building two elegant institutions of higher learning. They then sent recruiters to Yale, Mt. Holyoke, and Andover Seminary to hire teachers for these seminaries (or academies). It is difficult to believe that they had no trouble finding Yale men and Mt. Holyoke women willing to travel 1,500 miles to take these jobs in Indian Territory. Perhaps most astonishing of all, these highly educated and very proper Christian ladies and gentlemen from New England's finest institutions of learning found themselves perfectly at home in the parlors of their well-to-do employers in the Cherokee Nation. The Cherokees who led the nation in the 1850s were eminently respectable and cultivated people. They also paid better salaries than most Eastern schools of the same caliber.

When my wife, Virginia McLoughlin, inherited a group of letters written by her mother's uncle, Oswald Woodford, that touched upon the role of these seminaries in Cherokee life during the 1850s, we decided to look more closely into their history. Oswald Woodford was one of the Yale graduates who taught at the Cherokee Male Seminary during its early years. He believed that he was helping to raise the Cherokee people to the ultimate level of respectability by advancing their best students to the point where they could apply to attend Yale or Mt. Holyoke. By so doing, the Cherokee would prove beyond doubt the capacity of their people—and of all red people—to compete with whites at the highest levels of educational achievement.

However, both Woodford and the Cherokee leaders who hired him were blind to the fact that the education of "the talented tenth" in the Cherokee Nation led to as much resentment as pride among the Cherokee people. In the end, the male and female seminaries only deepened the division between the mixed-blood Cherokee elite who sent their children to the seminaries and the great mass of full-blood citizens whose children seldom finished grade school. One can learn much about Cherokee life in the 1850s by reading E. Franklin Frazier's Black Bourgeoisie *and by considering Booker T. Washington's critique of W. E. B. DuBois's theory of "the talented tenth" as the key to black equality in America.*

THERE HAVE ALWAYS BEEN TWO BASIC VIEWS among the Indians with regard to handling the white man. The first held that whites would not treat the Indians with equal respect until they demonstrated that they could do everything the white man could do and do it just as well. The second held that it was neither possible nor desirable to overcome the white man's prejudice by imitating his ways; the Indians might adapt from the whites what was useful to them, but their integrity and self-respect must ultimately rest upon maintaining their own cultural heritage and ethnic identity.

The Cherokee were no exception to this division. Generally speaking, the leadership of the nation rested with those who took the first position, while the rank-and-file majority held the second. With some exceptions, it can also be said that those of mixed Indian-white ancestry supported the first position while those of full-blood ancestry supported the second. As the Cherokee Nation became more acculturated, those of mixed ancestry developed the white man's avidity for the accumulation of property, education, and material comfort. They settled on the most productive land, bought the most slaves, reaped the greatest profits from their industry; or, if they entered into trade, they dealt most profitably with white and red. They sent their children to school, kept them there longer, and expected them to marry others who had achieved the same levels of wealth and education. Eventually, this fundamental difference over how to relate to the dominant white culture produced significant differences in wealth, social class, ethnic identity, and educational skills within the Cherokee Nation.

Furthermore, this ideological difference created social and political animosity. Each side assumed that the other was acting detrimentally toward the nation's welfare. This animosity became evident among the

Cherokee in the 1850s, when the nation was enjoying a halcyon period of stability and prosperity. The internal division, however, was masked by the Cherokees' firm unity on any political issue involving the nation vis à vis the federal government; when the nation's rights were at stake, the Cherokees firmly united behind their leaders. The decision to establish a male and a female seminary for the brightest graduates of the Cherokee grammar school system institutionalized the growing class division within the nation. (The term *seminary* then was equivalent to the term *academy*, *Latin school*, or *Classical high school*; it did not imply ministerial training, but rather preparation for college by learning Latin and Greek, which were prerequisites for college entrance.) The recently discovered letters of Oswald Langdon Woodford, one of the first teachers at the Cherokee Male Seminary, and its third principal, provide some insight into this aspect of Cherokee history.[1] Woodford and those who supported the seminaries unquestionably believed that they were uplifting and advancing the Cherokee people, giving them more respectability and hastening the time when the white man would treat the Indian as an equal. In hindsight, their efforts seem only to have added to the burden of being a Cherokee in a white man's country.

Oswald Woodford arrived in the Cherokee Nation in January 1851. He had left his home in Avon, Connecticut, three weeks earlier in order to become a teacher in the Cherokee Male Seminary near Park Hill. In 1851 the Cherokee had pretty much recovered from the terrible ordeal of removal and the Trail of Tears. That experience in 1838-1839 had been devastating—almost as devastating as the years of guerrilla warfare from 1777 to 1794, during which they had fought desperately to keep the invading Europeans from surrounding their land in Tennessee, Alabama, Georgia, and North Carolina. Just as they had risen from the ashes of that defeat to become by 1825 a nation of farmers and to earn the title of "the most civilized tribe in America," so after 1839 they had worked hard to reconstruct their social order and to establish a stable, prosperous Cherokee Nation in the northeast corner of what is now Oklahoma.[2]

---

[1] The Oswald Langdon Woodford letters were part of the family letters inherited by Virginia Duffy McLoughlin, coauthor of this article. Oswald Woodford was her maternal grandmother's brother. The Woodford Papers are in the possession of the authors.

[2] Morris J. Wardell, *A Political History of the Cherokee Nation, 1838-1907* (Norman: University of Oklahoma Press, 1938); Grant Foreman, *The Five Civilized Tribes* (Norman: University of Oklahoma Press, 1963); Gary E. Moulton, *John Ross, Cherokee Chief* (Athens: University of Georgia Press, 1978).

Although the treaty of New Echota in 1835, under cover of which they were forcibly removed from their homeland, was a fraud, signed by only a handful of their chiefs, it had required the United States government to reimburse them for the cultivated fields and farm buildings they had been forced to leave. With that money, they had made a remarkable recovery in the western foothills of the Ozark Mountains. The Cherokee Nation was now bounded by the state of Arkansas on the east, the Arkansas River on the south, and the Nebraska/Kansas Territory to the north. The easiest way to get there from the East was by steamboat up the Arkansas River to Fort Gibson. As Woodford discovered, however, the water was too low during many months of the year even for the shallow draft of the paddle-wheeled riverboats to get that far up the river.

Woodford was a senior at Yale in the spring of 1850 when two respectable Cherokees arrived on the campus recruiting teachers for their new seminary, which was to open in the spring of 1851. He found their offer attractive in two ways. First, they provided a very good salary of $600 a year, plus room and board; and second, he was a dedicated young Christian looking for an opportunity to be of service to humanity. Moreover, like most young men in the East, he was eager to see the West. Only two years before, while he was a sophomore, the United States had conquered Mexico and obtained a vast new empire that finally extended the nation's boundary to the West Coast. A year after that, fabulous veins of gold had been found in California, a sign to many Protestant patriots that God had somehow hidden this El Dorado from the Spanish and Mexican Catholics and permitted its discovery only when a Protestant nation owned the land. In 1849 Woodford had written a long article for the *Yale Literary Magazine* entitled "California Ho!" in which he had expounded this thesis.

> Scarcely had the thunder of battle died away upon the ear, and the citizen soldiery resumed their peaceful avocations, when the whole nation was thrown, with electric suddenness, into a state of unheard of excitement. A humble individual, while strolling beside a stream that came dashing down the mountains where he had been a thousand times before, observing as usual on its pebbly bottom, small flaky substances glittering in the sun, feels for the first time a curiosity to examine the beautiful spangles more closely. . . . The secret of the grand discovery struggles forth from those remote wilds . . . and CALIFORNIA GOLD in huge characters, with appropriate "marks of wonder and astonishment" stare in the reader's face from every page of every public journal. . . . I have not space, nor is it necessary, to speak of . . . the impulse thus given to the spread of civilization

and Christianity, in a word, of the long stride the world has taken in this event towards the latter day glory. . . . In all these events then, we cannot fail to see the striking clearness of the hand of Deity.[3]

Woodford became part of this divine "impulse" a year later when he accepted an equally unforeseeable opportunity to go west and participate in "the spread of civilization and Christianity" among the Cherokee.

Woodford, born in 1827, was a dyed-in-the-wool Connecticut Yankee of the most pious, moral, and earnest type. His ancestors were among the earliest Puritan settlers in Hartford, and though not of the wealthy elite, they were of the religious elect. His father, Zerah Woodford, was a farmer in Avon, not far from Hartford, and the family had sacrificed much to send the frail and scholarly Oswald to Yale. In one of his letters home from college, Woodford imagined his toiling family ("I suppose father and Edgar and Brainerd are sweating and steaming over the scythe and cradle under these burning suns.") while he sat in his cool college room poring over his Latin and Greek grammar.[4] Woodford was a diligent, serious, introspective young man with a deep concern for his own soul and the souls of all mankind. In his junior year he underwent a dramatic religious conversion that deepened his commitment to lead a life of Christian service. His ambition was to be a minister. However, his family could not afford to send him to divinity school, and the opportunity to teach in the Cherokee Nation, where he might save sufficient money for this, seemed designed by God.

Woodford was not the only teacher whom the two Cherokees, William P. Ross and David Vann, recruited during their trip to New England in the spring of 1850. The Cherokee legislature had voted in 1846 to build two seminaries, one for men and one for women. When the buildings neared completion, Ross and Vann were sent to recruit not only at Yale, Andover Theological School, and Newton Theological Institution, but also at Mount Holyoke Female Seminary.[5] The Cherokee legislature wanted two male teachers, two women teachers, and two

---

[3]Oswald Langdon Woodford, "California, Ho!" *Yale Literary Magazine* 14:7 (June 1849): 317-18.

[4]O. L. Woodford to his parents, Zerah and Minerva Potter Woodford, 12 July 1849, Woodford Papers.

[5]Mrs. William P. Ross, *The Life and Times of Hon. William P. Ross, of the Cherokee Nation* (Fort Smith AR: Weldon & Williams Printers, 1893) 192.

principals; but while they offered very good salaries, their recruiters had some difficulty finding New Englanders who would teach in their nation. Not that New Englanders were not eager to help the Indians to become Christianized and civilized, but the Cherokees, like all of the Southeastern Indians, had adopted the institution of black slavery. By 1851 New Englanders generally (and the churchgoing community in particular) were increasingly opposed to that peculiar Southern institution. The Cherokee recruiters "were nearly defeated in their object" of finding teachers in New England, according to one report, "on account of anti-slavery sentiments" at the schools they visited.[6] Oswald Woodford, however, was not of the radical abolitionist persuasion. Though he disliked slavery and hoped some peaceful way would eventually be found to put an end to it, he deplored those fanatical types around William Lloyd Garrison and Theodore Weld who insisted on "total, immediate, uncompensated emancipation" without regard to any of the difficulties this would involve.

Woodford's attitude toward this problem is manifest in a letter he wrote home after he had stopped at the home of his Uncle Sidney in Mantua, Ohio, on his way to the Cherokee Nation. Northern Ohio was a hotbed of abolitionist sentiment in 1851, due largely to the work of Theodore Weld and his associates. Woodford noted that "Uncle Sidney and his wife were living by themselves in a wing of the house, her invalid sister, Miss Wheeler, being connected with the family, as also a *black man*—perhaps a run-away slave, for Uncle Sidney and his wife are out & out, from top to bottom, ultra, and, I must say, in my opinion, fanatical abolitionists."[7] Woodford clearly suspected that he was staying at one of the stations in the Underground Railroad and that the black man, evidently posing as a servant (which his uncle clearly could not have afforded), was really on his way to Canada. Being a discreet young man, and loyal to his family, Woodford had no intention of doing anything about this illegal behavior by his aunt and uncle; nevertheless, he was

---

[6]Elizur Butler to Reverend S. B. Treat, 13 February 1851. Papers of the American Board of Commissioners of Foreign Missions at Houghton Library, Harvard University, Cambridge, Massachusetts; hereinafter referred to as A.B.C.F.M., letter #183, ABC 18.3.1, vol. 11.

[7]O. L. Woodford to his parents, Zerah and Minerva Potter Woodford, 7 January 1851, Woodford Papers.

clearly shocked by it and he knew that his parents in Avon, Connecticut, would be shocked as well. He was prepared to live with slavery among the Cherokee and had no stomach for the illegal abolition activity among his relatives.

After leaving his uncle, Woodford took passage on the steamboat *Daniel Webster* from Cincinnati, down the Ohio to the Mississippi, and then down the Mississippi to the mouth of the Arkansas, where he boarded another and smaller steamer to take him up the Arkansas. The boat had to stop seventy-five miles short of its goal because of low water, and Woodford went the rest of the way on horseback. A few months after his arrival, he learned that merciful Providence had presided over his journey: "The Steamboat Webster on which we came from Cincinnati to the mouth of the Arkansas, has since been destroyed by fire, and many lives lost. How good was God in preserving me from all harm."[8]

Woodford's destination in the Cherokee Nation was the small, park-like community of Park Hill, about five miles south of the capital at Tahlequah. At Park Hill he met the dedicated chief, John Ross, and his white, Quaker wife.[9] They lived in a magnificent mansion surrounded by cultivated fields and orchards; Ross and his family were served by forty black slaves. Living nearby in neat, two-story clapboard homes were the most successful and influential members of the nation. Like Ross, they were of mixed ancestry and were slaveowners. They dressed as whites, educated their children to have the same outlook as whites, and prided themselves upon setting an example for their people of what industry and piety could do to raise the Indian from savagery to civilization. Most of them were farmers and ranchers; but some, like William P. Ross and Major George Murrell, owned merchandising stores in Tahlequah.

The two new seminaries were built near Park Hill because this was also the center of missionary activity, where Methodists and Presbyterians (really Congregationalists) had established churches. The people of the community lived a sedate, middle-class Victorian life.[10] Wood-

---

[8]O. L. Woodford to his sister, Henrietta Woodford, 10 June 1851, Woodford Papers.

[9]See Moulton, *John Ross, Cherokee Chief*, 139-46.

[10]See Carolyn Thomas Foreman, *Park Hill* (Muskogee OK: The Star Printery, Inc., 1948).

ford's letters home speak highly of the culture and refinement of these Cherokee leaders. Their homes, he said, contained elegant furniture, chinaware, rugs, pianos, and clocks; they were similar in every way to the homes in Avon, Connecticut. The Cherokee read the same secular and religious newspapers that he read at home, kept a Bible on their parlor table, attended church regularly, and entertained each other in the evenings with social parties at which talented Cherokee daughters and sons played the flute, violin, or piano and sang plaintive songs about romantic love, motherhood, and homes far away. A Yale graduate and member of Skull and Bones found himself perfectly at home among these respectable, cultivated Christian people. Among the well-educated New England missionaries who also lived in Park Hill, he found congenial companions for pious conversation. The doctor who cured his toothaches and prescribed for his headaches was a recent graduate of Bowdoin Medical School, the son of a missionary to the Cherokees. He became Woodford's closest friend. Later, Woodford's Yale roommate was to join the community as a teacher at the Male Seminary.

When he arrived in January 1851, Woodford discovered that the completion of the seminaries had been delayed because the low water in the Arkansas River had prevented delivery of the furnishings. The buildings (located three miles apart) were among the most magnificent in the region, equal to any public high schools in Arkansas or Missouri and finer than most. They were each built to house one hundred students. "Each was 100 by 160 feet in dimensions, two storeys above a basement, and with a two-storey portico of Greek columns around three sides."[11] Each also contained classrooms and a refectory. They were said to have cost the nation at least $35,000 each and probably more. Each was erected on the top of a small hill where they could be seen for miles around. They formed the acropolis of the Cherokee Nation (of which Park Hill was the Athens). As one visitor wrote,

> After having traveled through a dreary and thinly inhabited country, you catch a glimpse at a distance of two or three miles, of two splendid buildings, looming over the broad expanses of a magnificent prairie; and then, remembering that you are in Indian country, the effect is most striking.[12]

---

[11]Althea Bass, *Cherokee Messenger* (Norman: University of Oklahoma Press, 1936) 12-14.

[12]*Missionary Herald* 48 (October 1852).

The buildings were constructed, said this visitor, General Waddy Thompson, "in the most perfect architectural taste and style." This was just the effect that Chief Ross and the Cherokee elite wanted the seminaries to have. They were built to symbolize the crowning achievement of a once pagan and savage people. Education was the key to success, status, and respect among the whites; therefore, the Cherokee were determined to prove that they were capable of assimilating and appreciating all that white culture had to offer. Having twice risen, phoenixlike, from the ashes of defeat at the white man's hands, they were more determined than ever to win his respect. Here on the prairie, they had made "the desert bloom like the rose." (This was the favorite biblical text of Chief Ross, who named his magnificent mansion "Rose Cottage" and who lined the winding carriage road leading to his home with rosebushes.) Woodford was suitably impressed. No college graduate from New England could have asked for better pay, better employment, or better social life than he found at Park Hill. It was a far cry from the experience of those missionaries who in this same decade went to live among the Sioux, Arapahos, Cheyennes, and Apaches—Indians who still lived in teepees, shot buffalo, and rode bareback to attack wagon trains on their way to California or Oregon. Furthermore, Woodford's surroundings were also a far cry from those of the first missionaries who came to live among the Cherokee fifty years earlier when Cherokee men too were hunters rather than farmers and when their cornfields were tilled by Cherokee women rather than by black slaves.

Upon his arrival Woodford was courteously taken into Chief Ross's home, and he lived there for five months until his rooms at the seminary were properly furnished. "Rose Cottage" was built to accommodate many guests; so his presence was not inconvenient. Ross, now sixty-one, and his young wife, twenty-four, had two young children, Ann and John, and were pleasant, friendly hosts. Woodford wrote home of his fondness for their children. Annie was six: "Her hair is not quite black, but very dark—she has large, bright dark eyes, very light complexion, as light as any white girl, not looking much like a little Indian girl as she is—though after all, she has very little Indian blood as her mother is white and her father is almost a white man."[13] After he moved to the seminary, he wrote home to his young sister, Henrietta, of his life at Rose Cottage.

---

[13]O. L. Woodford to his sister, Henrietta Woodford, 10 June 1851, Woodford Papers.

I used to have some high glees with them while there [with Annie and Johnnie]. We used to get into that elegant parlor that I have described in some of my letters and play hide-and-coop and run-and-chase among the sofas, chairs, pianos, tables &c. and when I got tired, Annie and Johnnie, for they were never tired, would pretend to gather flowers from the Brussels carpet which looked like a bed of brilliant roses, and bring them to me.[14]

Woodford's first task at the seminary was to screen the applicants for the school, almost all of whom were graduates of the Cherokee public school system. The Cherokee legislature had created a system of grammar schools in 1841 and tried to model it on that which Horace Mann was building in Massachusetts in these same years. Twenty-one grammar schools were built throughout the nation and were staffed by teachers (many of them whites at first).[15] The superintendent of the schools, chosen and paid for by the Cherokee government, insisted that the schools be conducted only in English. The grammar school curriculum included the same subjects as those in New England grammar schools, and the Cherokee children were taught from the same spelling, history, geography, and arithmetic textbooks as those used in Massachusetts, where the superintendent purchased the books. This meant that the children learned the same ethical values and religious morality as did white children in Hartford, New Haven, Worcester, or Boston. The schools were also permeated with a Christian influence. Approximately 3,000 of the 20,000 Cherokees were Christians in 1855, and most of those living in Park Hill or Tahlequah attended mission churches. The Reverend Samuel A. Worcester's Congregational church at Park Hill had 200 Cherokee members.

William Potter Ross, nephew of Chief John Ross, had served as editor of the *Cherokee Advocate* from 1844 to 1848. It was published weekly in Tahlequah. He then became a lawyer and a merchant in Tahlequah. In 1851 he was a member of the Board of Directors of the Cherokee Seminaries. He said in later years that Chief John Ross shared the fears of benevolent whites about the future of the Indian in nineteenth-century

---

[14]Ibid.

[15]See Appendix IV. For descriptions of the public school system, see William P. Ross, "Public Education among the Cherokee Indians," *The American Journal of Education and College Review* 1:1 (August 1855): 120-22; and Abraham Eleazar Knepler, "The Education of the Cherokee Indians," (Ph.D. thesis, Yale University, 1939).

America: He "knew that the aborigines of this continent were disappearing as the morning mists before the superior education, enterprise, and activity by which they were surrounded, and that the only hope for their preservation from fraud, corruption, and extermination was to be found in the dissemination of knowledge among them and in their adoption of habits and industry and the precepts of the Christian religion. Hence he was the early advocate of a well-defined form of government, the promoter of the arts of domestic life, and the friend of education and the early missionaries among the Cherokee people."[16] John Ross had met the New England missionaries of the American Board of Commissioners of Foreign Missions in 1817, when they first came to the nation. He was impressed by their educational methods, their seriousness of purpose, their self-discipline, and their high standards. Although he had chosen to join the Methodist denomination in 1829, he felt that the Methodists did not have the same respect for education that the New England Congregationalists had. For the Cherokee seminaries, therefore, he sought Congregationalist teachers. (The law establishing the seminaries specifically said that the teachers must be Christians.) Ross tried to model the Female Seminary after Mount Holyoke Female Seminary in South Hadley, Massachusetts.[17] New England Congregationalism was still heavily tinged with the Calvinist ethic, and Oswald Woodford was a typical representative of its heritage and outlook.

While the graduates for admission to the seminaries were on the whole the better graduates from the Cherokee public school system, Woodford found them somewhat below his high standards. He administered to each of them a rigid test in reading, writing, geography, and arithmetic. The curriculum at the seminaries would be rigorous; and because room, board, tuition, and books were free, the principal and teachers did not want to admit students who would not finish the course. Twenty-five were to be admitted in successive years until each of the four grades was filled.

Woodford soon discovered that even the best graduates of the Cherokee grammar schools could not meet the standards he and the principal, the Reverend Thomas Van Horne, wished to set. The public school

---

[16]Ross, *Life and Times of Hon. William P. Ross*, 256.

[17]See Althea Bass, *A Cherokee Daughter of Mount Holyoke* (Muscatine IA: Prairie Press, 1937) 14.

system took in any student who wanted to attend; by law they were taught in English. Full-blood students who spoke no English consequently made much slower progress than those who were of mixed ancestry, where English was spoken in their homes. (This was a problem that public schools in New England and elsewhere in the United States handled equally badly; the children of non-English-speaking European immigrants were required to work twice as hard to get their education and melt into the prevailing culture.) After looking at the tests of the applicants, Woodford and the other teachers realized that they had to set lower admission standards than they had hoped:

> A "good examination" in reading, spelling, geography, arithmetic, and grammar was the legal requisite of admission, though to fill up the number allowed, it was found necessary to give the word "good" considerable latitude.[18]

He found that most of those who gained admission were of mixed ancestry and from well-to-do families. But the myth of a classless society, with equal opportunity for any hardworking individual to pull himself or herself up by the bootstraps, prevailed among the Cherokees as among white Americans.

In one way, however, the Cherokees were more progressive than the whites. They paid the women teachers at the Female Seminary the same wages as the male teachers at the Male Seminary. Woodford and his male friends were not at all pleased to find that their services were considered no more important than those of mere females. William P. Ross thought this was humorous.

> We pay our male and female teachers in connection with the seminaries, the same salaries; an arrangement to which the gentlemen object, but to which I believe the ladies have never interposed any objection. We think their services at least as important to us as the services of the other sex, and if the men agree to work for a stipulated sum, they should not find fault if we pay the ladies quite as much.[19]

Woodford's first year at the male seminary passed pleasantly. He enjoyed the social life, made friends easily, and indulged in his hobbies of quail hunting and gathering specimens of wild flowers. In September

---

[18]Report of O. L. Woodford, 19 September 1852, 32nd Congress, 2d Session, House Executive Document 1 (Serial 673) (Washington: Robert Armstrong, printer, 1852) 409-10.

[19]William P. Ross, "Public Education," 121.

1852, he wrote a report for the Bureau of Indian Affairs that indicates the various trials and tribulations as well as the successes of the schools. It is worth quoting at some length, for it provides considerable insight into the the educational standards and the curriculum that were established. It also points out the division that existed by color, education, and wealth between the Cherokee bourgeoisie at Park Hill and the average Cherokee farmers in the rest of the nation. The full bloods at this time constituted two-thirds or more of the Cherokee population; yet as Woodford notes, the students at the seminary were almost wholly of "the white race."

Sir: In compliance with your request, I furnish you below with a few facts relative to the Cherokee Male Seminary.

It was the intention of the Board of Directors that the school should commence about the first of October, 1850, and teachers were engaged accordingly; but, owing to the unfinished state of the buildings, and the difficulty of getting the necessary furniture, the commencement was delayed many months. Finally, on the 6th of May last, the public exercises of opening took place. These were of exceeding interest, and were attended by a large concourse of people.

The term closed on the 6th of August, having continued only thirteen weeks, contrary to the letter of the law, which requires each term to be twenty weeks in length. The unseasonableness of commencement and the inexpediency and danger of protracting the term through the hot and unhealthy months, were the causes of the abridgment. Of course, as this was the first session of a new institution—and a short one at that—we could hardly expect to do more than get a fair start. However, such a spirit has been manifested, and such progress made on the part of the pupils, as gives the teachers, and all acquainted with the facts, much gratification and ground for encouragement.

Twenty-five regular boarding pupils were admitted according to the law, and two or three day-scholars have been in attendance most of the term. These have applied themselves with exemplary diligence and faithfulness to their studies; and all, even the lowest, were found, on examination of the instructors' records, to have maintained through the term a standing of more than medium scholarship. To awaken the faculty of thought, and excite a habit of independent investigation, and to arouse an intellectual enthusiasm, has been, and will continue to be, the especial effort of the instructors; and the peculiar nature of the Indian, as well as the defects in elementary instruction among the Cherokees, has made such an effort the more imperatively necessary.

What, precisely, Woodford meant by "the peculiar nature of the Indian" is not clear. He probably shared the prevalent view of white men that most Indians were by nature intellectually lazy, if not dull-witted (or "stupid"). His next remarks in this report are even more puzzling. To speak of "minds that have grown old in stupidity or dissipation" certainly does not apply to the students he was teaching. To describe the students as properly belonging "to the white race" was to imply that white ancestry was more important than cultural identity. Yet his statement that some of "those most thoroughly Indian" in ancestry were among "our best scholars" contradicted the first part of this sentence.

> To do this for minds that have grown old in stupidity or dissipation, is always a hard task; but I am of opinion that no company of young men of any race would prove, under similar circumstances, more susceptible of intellectual excitement than these have done. Most, to be sure, more properly belong to the white race; though a few are entirely or chiefly Indian, and in all traces of Indian blood may be discovered. Some of our best scholars are those most thoroughly Indian. In age they are from fourteen to twenty-one—sixteen predominating. . . .

That the seminary made no concession to the alleged "stupidity" of "the Indian" was evident in the curriculum, which was the same as that in any New England academy:

> At the close of the term, however, the first class had nearly completed Greenleaf's National Arithmetic, Davies' Algebra, (though some knew not so much as the meaning of algebra before), Green's Analysis of the English Language, and could read well in Latin. One student of Greek made excellent progress, and a small class in French (extra) did very well. The second class, though moving much slower, seemed to have acquired a thorough insight into the rudiments of geography, arithmetic, and grammar, reading, and spelling from McEllicott's Analytical Manual; composition and elocution were attended to by all, and good progress made, particularly in reading. The greatest desideratum still is a more thorough awakening of a scholarly enthusiasm.
>
> Lessons in instrumental music on the violin, flute, and clarionet, were given to some fifteen students by a skillful teacher, and the music of his pupils at the public examination was highly commended.
>
> The students have organized a literary society, styled the Sequoyan Institute (from the celebrated inventor of the Cherokee alphabet, George Guess, whose Indian name was Sequoya), in which weekly debates are held, with other literary exercises. They have made provision, by a tax and initiation fee, for a Society library, to be under their own control.

Globes representing the earth and heavens, Bliss's outline maps, Dr. Cutter's physiological charts, and several large maps of different parts of the earth's surface, besides a good variety of reference books are here for our use; and it is expected that a philosophical [scientific] apparatus, to cost $1,000, will ere long be added. The institution is also provided with a library, consisting of religious, historical, biographical, scientific, and literary works, furnished mostly by the benevolence of publishers, and other friends of the seminary. It is still small, but we hope further donations will be made.

Woodford closed his report on a note of optimism and noted that the seminary did not neglect the religious instruction of its students.

A sermon is usually preached to the students every Sabbath, and an hour is spent besides in the study of the Holy Scriptures.

On the whole, the present prospects of the seminary seem to be eminently encouraging.

Yours, very respectfully,
O. L. *Woodford, Assistant Instructor*[20]

Woodford's reference to the Sequoyan Institute deserves mention because it reflects a common trend in American educational institutions at this time. As Frederick Rudolph has pointed out, few academies or colleges provided more than rote learning in these years, and none offered extracurricular activities.[21] To enrich their academic lives, students themselves began to develop extracurricular groups after 1850—debating societies, literary clubs, fraternities. School authorities frowned on these because they were outside their control. Woodford had tried to form such a literary society at Williston Seminary when he was preparing for Yale in 1845, but the authorities refused to countenance it, and it was disbanded. He found no objection raised to such an organization in the Cherokee Nation. In fact, the Cherokee Nation provided funds for the Sequoyan Institute to publish a newspaper (*The Sequoyah Memorial*) several times a year, in which the students could display their talents. The few issues that have survived indicate that it was a typical high school publication, filled with romantic poetry, earnest moral exhortation, and sentimental stories. Under its banner head *The Sequoyah Me-*

---

[20]Report of O. L. Woodford, 19 September 1852, House Executive Document 1.

[21]Frederick Rudolph, *The American College and University* (New York: Alfred A. Knopf, 1962) 136-55.

morial carried the motto, "Truth, Justice, Freedom of Speech and Cherokee Improvement." In one issue the student-written articles covered such subjects as "Laziness, the Road to Misery," "The Happiness of Obeying the School Rules," the dangers of "Intemperance," "The Disadvantages of Yielding to Temptation." The only articles differentiating this paper from any other high school paper in the United States were those dealing specifically with the Cherokees; one of these, entitled "A Glance at the Past and Present Condition of the Cherokees," contrasted the refinement and progress of their nation from its savage past to its civilized present.[22] In one issue the students printed an article on "The Schools":

> There are twenty-one public schools that are supported by the Nation, besides several mission schools and private schools; then there are two seminaries supported at the public expense. So every young Cherokee, if he has a mind to, may obtain a good common school education with but very little expense. Many of them are reaping the advantages thus held out to them. The brightest prospects of an educated and generous people are the result. The bow and arrow have been laid aside—the day of bowie knives and pistols is fast passing away. The wilderness is becoming the situation for cultivated farms. This reform is fast completing, and should our country remain on the stage of nations until her sons and daughters shall be competent to manage the future destinies of our nation, we may yet reach the summit of civilization and refinement. . . .[23]

That the seminary students felt themselves superior to those members of their tribe who still indulged in traditional ceremonies and pastimes like the Cherokee Ball Play (a form of lacrosse) is evident in an article deprecating such heathen behavior, but blaming its continuance in part on unrefined whites from surrounding white communities.

> Some persons are apt to be seen in any place where they are not gaining ground in the way of obtaining honor, but the most of our people are not posted up in learning and so they will have to be excused, not knowing better or not caring, one of the two. But if our white brothers would set us an example, we might become more enlightened. The white men that come to this nation love the dishonorable sports as well as the unenlightened people of this nation.[24]

---

[22]*The Sequoyah Memorial* (Tahlequah, Cherokee Nation) 31 July 1856. This issue is at the Oklahoma Historical Society.

[23]Quoted in Althea Bass, *A Cherokee Daughter of Mount Holyoke*, 21.

[24]*The Sequoyah Memorial*, 31 July 1856.

The students at the Female Seminary also published a literary magazine called *Cherokee Rose Buds*, dedicated to similar moral striving. Under its masthead the editors wrote that the magazine was "Devoted to the Good, the Beautiful, the Fine."[25]

After striving for a year and half to uplift the Cherokee, Woodford had saved enough money to pay for his ministerial education. He wrote home to his parents, in May 1852, that he could not make up his mind about which theological school to attend because "friends advise variously"; but "I incline toward Andover."[26] He said he would start for Connecticut in August. He also noted that things had gone well at the seminary that year. The main problems concerned student discipline. Young Cherokee men between fourteen and twenty-one (the average age was sixteen) often became frustrated by the tedium of rote recitation and of memorizing the elements of "moral and mental philosophy" as the white man understood them. Woodford believed, however, that discipline and good order were essential; student pranks, immoral habits, and acts of rebellion could not be tolerated. He rejoiced that strict discipline had prevailed.

> In the school, matters have put on a better face. . . . It is far from being what we might wish it, but things are quite tolerable. Three have this term insured their suspension, probably four; and this indeed, or rather the consequence of it, afford our chief cause of joy. With tobacco we have commenced a summary course, expelling on the third offense, and two or three have reached the limit of black marks and have been suspended for general bad conduct. The dross seems now nearly removed and greater subordination, industry and happiness seem to be beginning. I am more and more convinced that with proper management, the school might be made a model of propriety and success.[27]

At the closing exercises of the seminaries after their first year of operation, an elaborate celebration was held at which, according to the report in the *Cherokee Advocate*, the crowd was comprised of the nation's elite:

---

[25]Scattered issues of *Cherokee Rose Buds* are located at the Oklahoma Historical Society, Oklahoma City, Oklahoma, and the Gilcrease Institute, Tulsa, Oklahoma.

[26]O. L. Woodford to his parents, Zerah and Minerva Potter Woodford, 26 May 1852, Woodford Papers.

[27]Ibid.

"We have seldom seen so many together, distinguished alike for virtue, morality, Christianity, industry and intelligence."[28]

To make the school "a model of propriety and success" was precisely what the Cherokee leaders wished, and even before Woodford had completed his theological training at Andover, he received an invitation to return and assume the post of principal in the Male Seminary. The original principal, the Reverend Thomas Van Horne, had left and so had his successor, F.S. Lyon. This time the Cherokee Board of Directors agreed to pay Woodford's travel expenses. "I shall write [to them]," he told his parents, "for two hundred dollars to use in my outfit and for the journey."[29] He graduated from Andover in January 1855, and was ordained in February; the next month he made the long journey by train, stagecoach, and riverboat back to the Cherokee Nation.

The Cherokee leaders were delighted to have him back, and he entered immediately into the usual round of social events at Park Hill, dining with the chief, attending soirees at the Murrell house, visiting with the various missionaries from New England who lived there (particularly the Reverend Samuel A. Worcester) and horseback riding with Dr. Daniel Dwight Hitchcock, his particular friend. As principal of the Male Seminary, he worked closely with Miss Pauline Avery, the principal of the Female Seminary. Avery was a graduate of Mount Holyoke (in 1850), and their friendship quickly turned into a romance.[30]

However, the school continued to be plagued with disciplinary problems. In June 1855, Woodford wrote to his sister, Henrietta, in Avon:

> Since last I wrote we have had some stir here in expelling several from the school. Last Thursday morning two were cut off for throwing stones into Mr. Grant's window and one for having reached the limit of black marks which is 75. Last Monday morning another was cut off for the cause last mentioned. He had 47 marks when this term began. It created an excitement for a while but the school has been very quiet and orderly

---

[28]*Cherokee Advocate*, 21 February 1852, microfilm published by the American Antiquarian Society, Worcester, Massachusetts.

[29]O. L. Woodford to his sister, Henrietta Woodford, 9 January 1855, Woodford Papers.

[30]For Avery, see Althea Bass, *A Cherokee Daughter of Mount Holyoke*, 18-20.

since. It is necessary once in a while to get rid of some of the worst. We are doing well now.[31]

It did not seem to bother Woodford that the need for such drastic disciplinary measures had cut the original entering class from twenty-five to five, and that subsequent classes were also seriously depleted. Scarcely twenty per cent of those who entered the seminary completed the four years and graduated. This was not enough to serve the school's main purpose, which was to train teachers for the twenty-one Cherokee grammar schools. The public school board still had to employ whites to teach in some of its grammar schools.

If the seminaries were to prepare the brightest Cherokee youth for college, here too they failed, for there is no record of any graduate's matriculating at any of the colleges in the United States during these early years. It began to appear as though the schools were an expensive symbol of Cherokee respectability with little practical advantage to the nation as a whole. Some opposition to the schools had been voiced as early as 1852, but it was ignored.[32]

The official newspaper of the nation, the *Cherokee Advocate*, printed in full a long address Woodford gave to the Cherokee Educational Association on the subject of "School Discipline." The address revealed much about Woodford's prim views of student-teacher relationships.

> All valuable discipline must have for its basis respect and regard for the teacher implanted in the heart of the pupil. . . . If this course of affectionate firmness and thoroughness is pursued from the outset, the beautiful fruits of order and industry will soon be apparent. . . . And this is the true idea of a good school, in which authority shall be so perfect as apparently to have no existence—submission so complete as to be a matter of course and of pleasure, and mutual interest and affection the great bond uniting teacher and pupils, and insuring their mutual happiness and success.[33]

---

[31]O. L. Woodford to his sister, Henrietta Woodford, 27 June 1855, Woodford Papers.

[32]Elizur Butler to S. B. Treat, 21 July 1852, A.B.C.F.M., letter #192, ABC 18.3.1., vol. 11. The essence of the opposition at this time was that the money could be better spent on other things.

[33]*Cherokee Advocate*, 24 February 1852. Woodford's talk to the Cherokee Educational Association entitled "School Discipline," delivered probably in January 1852, was published in three installments of the *Cherokee Advocate*, 17 February 1852; 24 February 1852; and 4 March 1852.

Woodford's interest in submission and order did not lead him to resort to many of the meaner sorts of discipline commonly practiced by schoolteachers at that time. In fact, he deprecated

> frequent punishments which are degrading even to the smallest child. I mean such as pulling the hair, boxing the ears, snapping the head violently with the finger, wringing the nose, and even tickling, which I remember to have had practiced upon myself.

He refused to allow the practice where "the offending one is made to stand in the middle of the room while all the scholars point their fingers at him" or to require "bending over and holding a nail on the floor, standing on tiptoe and reach up to a certain point, holding the tongs or a book at arm's length, until these positions become absolutely insupportable torture" or to confine offenders to dark closets or coal bins. Woodford did not abandon the use of "the rod" when occasion warranted, but the most common form of punishment at the seminary was the withdrawal of privileges and the amassing of "black marks" on the offender's record. Woodford's Calvinist theology led him to ridicule the new psychology of the Phrenologists, which implied that human nature could be molded toward goodness by moral training. "To us who believe that there is a Holy God in Heaven, that the nature of man is thoroughly corrupt, that his will is opposed to virtue and goodness," there could be no possibility of education without submission to authority. The corrupt will of the child "must be subdued before there is hope of virtue." Firm and constant discipline was the best way to subdue the willfulness of unruly students. The rod should be administered, he said, "not in anger but with affectionate firmness." This view of human nature, of God, and of child training was not one that fit the traditional ways and beliefs of the Cherokees. Traditional Cherokees disliked corporal punishment.

None of Woodford's letters make mention of the existence of slavery among the Cherokees nor even allude to the mounting crisis between the free and the slave states that was filling the pages of the newspapers and the rhetoric of the politicians. He voted the Whig ticket, like most conservative Yankees, and was more concerned with efforts to repeal "the Maine Law" than with the rise of the Republican party.[34] He noted with

---

[34]See O. L. Woodford to his sister, Henrietta Woodford, 21 April 1855, Woodford Papers.

pleasure the spread of temperance among the Cherokees through the efforts of the Reverend Samuel Worcester's temperance pledge and "Cold Water Army." He reported happily that "the majority of the boys [at the seminary] signed the pledge."[35] He was equally concerned with the attendance at weekly prayer meetings. The seminaries were clearly designed to inculcate evangelical Christianity among the students, and their purpose was as much to turn out "Christian ladies and gentlemen" as to turn out educated citizens. Woodford preached to the students and faculty at compulsory religious services every Sunday.

In August 1855, Woodford sent a report to the Bureau of Indian Affairs on the condition of the Male Seminary:

> I have to state that the number of pupils with which the last session closed is 46, including three resident graduates. . . . In February last a class of five was regularly graduated at the institution, being the remains of the class with which the seminary opened in 1851, and the first that has completed the four years' course. In March last, the beginning of our academical year, a new class of 23 was admitted. There are now of under graduates in the first [senior] class 5, in the second class 6, in the third class 11, and in the fourth class 21. The classes have been thinned out more or less every term by expulsion and voluntary withdrawals from the institution.[36]

The three resident graduates were trying to master Virgil's *Aeneid* in Latin and Xenophon's *Anabasis* in Greek. He proudly reported that "during the past year the institution has been in charge of three teachers, all graduates of eastern colleges." He did not mention that the overwhelming majority of students were of mixed white-Indian ancestry.

By 1855 it had become obvious to most Cherokees that the seminaries were serving the needs of a small elite and not of the nation as a whole. The benefit to the nation of the exorbitant expense of the schools was out of all proportion to the gain. The Cherokee Nation had always contained a division between the full bloods and those of mixed ancestry. Not that the full bloods were ardent traditionalists; many, in fact, had embraced Christianity and accepted the need for acculturation to the extent of becoming farmers, living in cabins of hewn logs, and dressing in white man's clothing. Nevertheless, the full bloods had generally lived in the

---

[35] Ibid.

[36] Report of O. L. Woodford, 11 August 1855, 34th Congress, 1st Session, House Executive Document 1 (Serial 840) (Washington: Cornelius Wendell, printer, 1856) 452.

more remote parts of the nation (in the Great Smoky Mountains when the nation was in the East and later in the Ozark hills forty or fifty miles east of Park Hill). Because of their poverty full bloods did not own black slaves; most of them lived on rocky soil not conducive to large-scale cash-crop farming or herding. They spoke Cherokee (as few mixed bloods did) and on regular occasions practiced their old dances and religious ceremonies (which none of the mixed bloods at Park Hill did). In fact, to many at Park Hill, the "backward" full bloods were a source of embarrassment. Mixed bloods married mixed bloods; full bloods married full bloods. Mixed bloods looked to the white man for approval and self-respect; full bloods cared little for white opinion. This did not mean that full bloods opposed their mixed-blood chiefs or did not want their children to learn how to read and write and do arithmetic in English; however, the manner in which the mixed-blood elite offered schooling was clearly not compatible with the needs or outlook of the full bloods.

Controversy over what form higher education should take among the Cherokees had begun as early as 1823 when Charles Hicks, the second principal chief, advocated the establishment of "a National Academy" in New Echota. The Reverend Ard Hoyt, missionary of the American Board, reported on 14 August 1823, that it was "not yet determined whether it shall be of a higher order or to admit those who have received no education. . . . I understand Mr. Ross is for the former and Mr. Hicks, the latter."[37] Hoyt implied that Ross favored the kind of classical academy or high school such as that established at Park Hill twenty-eight years later, while Hicks favored a vocational high school. It is interesting that after a generation this division over what kind of secondary school education the nation should support was still raging.

In 1856 this problem came to a head. W. A. Duncan, the Cherokee superintendent of public schools, issued a report attacking the educational philosophy underlying the Male and Female Seminaries. The schools would, he said, produce a group of esthetes, intellectuals, and finishing-school ladies who performed no useful function in exchange for the four years of higher education that the tribe had given them out of its own treasury. "All cannot live here without manual labor. Each cannot be a professor, lawyer, doctor, preacher, school-master. The

---

[37]Ard Hoyt to Jeremiah Evarts, 14 August 1823, A.B.C.F.M., letter #104, ABC 18.3.1., vol. 3.

means, opportunities and occasions are wanting for so many. All could not find such employment at home [i.e., in the nation] and to seek it elsewhere would be to take one step towards the overthrow of the nation. For in that case it is clear that the ulterior result of our expenditures and labors would be to educate children for other countries [i.e., to improve the whites' communities in the surrounding states]."[38] In short, Duncan argued that the nation ought to spend more money on training in practical trades—blacksmiths, mechanics, harness-makers, veterinarians, agronomists, tanners, and so forth. What good did it do the Cherokee people to have a handful of scholars who could read and write in Latin or Greek? The nation needed more vocational training in practical subjects and less classical training in dead languages.

Duncan's report did not touch upon the class division that the schools (grammar and high schools both) were fostering in the nation, but a letter written by one of the students at the Female Seminary makes this point. It appeared in an early issue of *Cherokee Rose Buds*; and while it is clearly a plea for the full bloods to endorse the educational system, it also reveals how racial and social tensions were accentuated by the educational system the nation had adopted. The letter is signed "Na-li" and was entitled "An Address to the Females of the Cherokee Nation."

> It is sometimes said that our Seminaries were made only for the rich and those who were not full Cherokees, but it is a mistake. I thought I would address a few lines to the other class in the Nation. My beloved parents were full Cherokees. They belonged to the common class, and yet they loved their children as well as the rich; but they had never attended school, and therefore did not know the value of learning and probably would never have made provision for me to attend school. But those beloved parents have been called from this world and left me a lonely orphan. . . . At the time of my mother's death, a kind missionary teacher came and took me under her care. Under the influence and teaching of the missionaries, I was prepared to enter this institution.
>
> I should not have said so much about myself, but I feel that a great many of the full Cherokees can have the benefit of the Seminary as well as I. . . . I feel it is no disgrace to be a full Cherokee. My dark complexion does not prevent me from acquiring knowledge and of being useful hereafter. . . . Once more I urge you to attend some *Public School*; be studious and persevering and then after a

---

[38]Report of W. A. Duncan, 25 September 1856, 34th Congress, 3d Session, House Executive Document 1 (Serial 893) (Washington: Cornelius Wendell, printer, 1857) 692.

while you will probably be well prepared to enter our institution. If you should not succeed the first time, "try, try again."[39]

Na-li had touched a very tender wound of the Cherokee people. There was none of what we would call racial prejudice against those of "dark complexion," but there was certainly social prejudice stemming from the feeling that these full-blood Cherokees refused to "try, try again"—failed to overcome the disadvantage of neither speaking nor understanding the language in which the public schools were taught. Woodford and those who worked with him at Park Hill believed firmly in self-reliance and lifting oneself by one's own bootstraps through hard work and perseverance. Consequently, they felt the same way toward the "backward" or "lazy" full bloods that Yankees in Boston felt toward non-English-speaking European immigrants. Such persons seemed to lack the will and incentive to better themselves; little allowance was given for the far greater hurdles they had to leap just to get a start up the ladder toward learning and respectability.

The eminent Cherokee scholar, Jack F. Kilpatrick, who edited in 1964 the historical sketch of Lucy Hoyt (a member of the first graduating class from the Female Seminary and a classmate of Na-li), remarked in his introduction to this historical sketch that her "verbiage is replete with the young ladies' finishing school posturing. The spirit of Scott and Tennyson pervades her pages . . . what is intriguing [about her autobiography] is the fact that a scant few miles from her desk her tribesmen were 'going to water' [an ancient Cherokee purification ritual] with the same frequency, the same earnestness, and for the same purposes as they did in prehistoric times. Neither they nor Wahnenauhi [Lucy's Cherokee name] could enter, nor did they want to enter, into the respective worlds of each other, yet they were indissolubly bound together by the only ties that Cherokees ever understood, or still understand—a fierce loyalty to common ancestry."[40] Despite this fierce loyalty, the Cherokee people were to find themselves engaged in fratricidal warfare after 1861 in which most of the upper-class, mixed-blood residents of Park Hill took one

---

[39]*Cherokee Rose Buds*, 2 August 1852; this issue is at the Gilcrease Institute, Tulsa, Oklahoma.

[40]Jack F. Kilpatrick, ed., "The Wahnenauhi Manuscript," Smithsonian Institution, Bureau of Ethnology, Bulletin 196, *Anthropological Papers* (Washington, 1966) 182.

side and most of the "dark complexioned," poor Cherokees in the back-woods areas assumed the other.

In 1856 the Cherokee legislature discovered that they could no longer afford the cost of maintaining the two seminaries. Attempts to sell a large area of land (called "The Neutral Land"), belonging to the Cherokee Nation, but located in Kansas, had failed. The Cherokees did not feel the United States government offered them a fair price. Until that sale could be effected, the legislature ordered that the seminaries be closed. Chief Ross expressed the hope that this would only be temporary, though he indicated that when they reopened, he thought the parents of students should be prepared to pay room and board in the future to lower the drain on the treasury.[41] Such a system would have further contributed to making the seminaries a finishing school for the sons and daughters of the mixed-blood and well-to-do Cherokees who lived in or near Park Hill.

Oswald Woodford was evidently not particularly shocked or hurt by the decision to close the seminaries. He and Pauline Avery had decided to get married. They would, of course, do so back home in the East [they were married in Buffalo]. They probably would have resigned anyway at the end of the school year in 1856. Perhaps their resignation contributed to the decision to close the schools. It never occurred to either of them that their work among the Cherokees had been anything but beneficial to the nation. Chief Ross and the mixed bloods and missionaries certainly thought it had. How else could the Cherokees obtain the respect of the white man except by proving their people as capable of education, refinement, and Christian behavior as whites? They had wanted the Male and Female Seminaries to be models of "propriety and success," and by the best light of their day, they succeeded.

As a postscript, it may be noted that Woodford found after 1856 that he could no longer ignore the slavery question. The Kansas-Nebraska Act in 1854 had aroused intense antagonism between the North and the South. Emigrants from both sections poured into what had formerly been mostly Indian territory in the effort to insure that Kansas would have a constitution that adhered to their respective regional positions on

---

[41]Address of Chief John Ross to the Cherokee National Committee and Council, 35th Congress, 1st Session, House Executive Document 2 (Serial 942) (Washington: James B. Steedman, printer, 1858) 507.

slavery. Woodford was a regular reader of Henry Ward Beecher's weekly Congregational paper, *The Independent*. He knew that Beecher had said that a Sharpe's rifle was of more use to a Northern emigrant to Kansas than a Bible in this fight to keep Kansas from becoming a slave state. Woodford's brother Edgar had started for Kansas in 1856 with a group of Connecticut people who had named themselves "The Beecher Bible and Rifle Colony."[42] When Woodford and his fiancée, Pauline Avery, returned to Connecticut, they discovered that the Kansas Emigrant Aid Society was doing all it could to encourage Yankees to emigrate. After their marriage Woodford and his wife could not resist another chance to serve God and humanity. Woodford accepted a position in the Congregational Home Missionary Society and founded the first Congregational church in Grasshopper Falls, Kansas, in 1858. As pastor he received $200 less a year than he had made as principal of the Cherokee Male Seminary.[43] When the Civil War broke out in 1861, Oswald Woodford was too ill to enlist, but his brother Edgar did. In that war Edgar fought against those slaveowning, well-to-do Cherokees whom Oswald Woodford had served at Park Hill. With him in the Union army were most of the full bloods who had not felt welcome in the school system of the Cherokee Nation.

[42]Alberta Pantle, comp. and ed., "The Connecticut Kansas Colony—Letters of Charles B. Lines to the New Haven (Conn.) *Daily Palladium*," *Kansas Historical Quarterly* 22 (1956): 1-50, 138-88.

[43]See Virginia McLoughlin, ed., "Establishing a Church on the Kansas Frontier: The Letters of the Rev. O. L. Woodford and His Sister Henrietta, 1857-1859," *Kansas Historical Quarterly* 37:2 (Summer 1971): 153-91.

APPENDIX

Oil Spring
[Cherokee Nation]
September 7th 1847

To James McKissick Esqr.
Agent for Cherokees

Dr. Sir,

According to your request I herewith submit to you a brief report of the condition of the Public Schools, in the Cherokee Nation, accompanied with an exhibit of the several Schools, showing the number of pupils &c.

The National Council has provided for by law, the establishment of Twenty one common Public Schools, having two Sessions of five months each in the year; all of which have been in successful operation, closing their annual sessions, in the last week of July; and resuming their operations for the ensuing year on the 1st Inst.

The schools are distributed in the several Districts of the nation, according to their population as follows: to Saline two; Delaware four; Going Snake four; Flint four; Tahlequah two; Illinois two; Skin Bayou two; Canadian one, making the twenty one Schools.

The amount appropriated annually out of the general School fund, for the pay of teachers is Seven thousand dollars; each of whom receives a Salary of $333.33 1/2 for the two sessions taught in the year.

The Orphan children attend the common Schools for tuition, but their board & clothing are provided for, by an annual appropriation out of the Orphan fund of $3,600.00 One hundred & twenty one Orphans are distributed among the twenty [one] Schools, each of whom are allowed thirty dollars a year for his support. Orphans, under the present arrangement, are allowed the benefits of the Orphans fund until they arrive to the age of eighteen.

There is also another appropriation made annually out of the School fund, for the purchase of Books, which depends upon circumstances, but probably not exceeding two hundred dollars on an average.

The Schools this year, exhibit a greater number of pupils in total, than in any former year, though the average attendance in some of the schools is not as great as formerly, this deficiency has been caused in a great measure by sickness. Our schools having been visited the past year, by the mumps, hooping cough and Scarlet fever.

I am gratified to state that our schools are in a very prosperous condition. While they have augmented in number, the increase of interest both in parents and children, has also been quite apparent. Many of the pupils have made great proficiency, in the several branches which we taught, as will be seen in the exhibit of the schools. Music is taught in some of the schools, though not reported as one of the regular branches.

It would be proper to state that a commendable interest in the cause of education, is evinced by the Cherokee people, who now more fully appreciate its advantages to the rising generation.

The teachers are required to keep a correct record of the attendance of each scholar, so that the average attendance is ascertained with certainty.

With these few remarks, accompanied with an exhibit of the schools, I hope will give the desired information, with satisfaction.

Respectfully submitted,

With due respect
Your very Obt. Servt.
James M. Payne
Supt. Public Schools
Cher. Nation

NUMBER OF SCHOOLS	BY WHOM TAUGHT	OF BLOOD	RESIDENCE	RELIGIOUS DENOM.
LIST OF TEACHERS IN THE PUBLIC SCHOOLS OF THE CHEROKEE NATION IN 1847				
The following numbers to the schools are arranged according to the accompanying table				
1	John S. Crump	White	Not known	-----
2	Elizabeth Parks#	White	Bapt. M.S.C.N.	Baptist
3	Joseph Barker	White	Arks. State	-----
4	Charles Pulsifer	White	Mass. State	Presbyterian
5	James P. Laymance	White	Mo. State	-----
6	Eunice C. Chamberlain	Cherokee	Cher. Nation	Presbyterian
7	Willard P. Upham	White	Mass. " [State]	Baptist
8	Ignatius A. Few#	White	Cher. citizen by marriage	-----
9	Samuel Jones	White	Bapt. M.S.C.N.	Baptist
10	Samuel Newton	White	Arks. State	Presbyterian
11	Benj. F. Adams#	White	Arks. State	-----
12	J. S. Bartlett	White	Arks. State	Methodist
13	James M. Bell	Cherokee	Cher. Nation	-----
14	R. Lafayette Coleman	White	Missouri	-----
15	D. J. Bell	Cherokee	Cher. Nation	-----
16	Henry D. Reese#	Cherokee	Cher. Nation	Methodist
17	George W. Morris	White	Arkansas	Methodist
18	J. C. R. Orr	White	Dwight M. C. N.	-----
19	Daniel D. Hitchcock	White	Dwight M. C. N.	Presbyterian
20	John G. Gunter#	Cherokee	Cher. Nation	-----
21	I. C. McMaster	White	Ohio	Presbyterian
Those marked # are not teaching in the present sessions.				

[This list accompanied the letter of James M. Payne to James McKissick on the preceding page.]

INDEX

MP *The Cherokee Ghost Dance*

Designed by Margaret Jordan Brown

Composition by MUP Composition Department

Production specifications:
    text paper—60 lb. Warren's Olde Style
    endpapers—Legendry Scarlet
    cover—(on .088 boards) Holliston Crown Linen 13407
    dust jacket—Legendry Scarlet 80 lb. Prints black

Printing (offset lithography) by Omnipress of Macon, Inc., Macon, Georgia

Binding by John H. Dekker and Sons, Inc., Grand Rapids, Michigan

THE LIBRARY
ST. MARY'S COLLEGE OF MARYLAND
ST. MARY'S CITY, MARYLAND 20686